Different from the Others

DIFFERENT FROM THE OTHERS

German and Dutch Discourses of Queer Femininity and Female Desire, 1918–1940

Cyd Sturgess

berghahn
NEW YORK · OXFORD
www.berghahnbooks.com

First published in 2023 by
Berghahn Books
www.berghahnbooks.com

© 2023 Cyd Sturgess

All rights reserved. Except for the quotation of short passages
for the purposes of criticism and review, no part of this book
may be reproduced in any form or by any means, electronic or
mechanical, including photocopying, recording, or any information
storage and retrieval system now known or to be invented,
without written permission of the publisher.

Library of Congress Cataloging-in-Publication Data
Names: Sturgess, Cyd, author.
Title: Different from the others : german and dutch discourses of queer femininity and female desire, 1918-1940 / Cyd Sturgess.
Description: 1st Edition. | New York, NY : Berghahn Books, 2023. | Includes bibliographical references and index.
Identifiers: LCCN 2022029146 (print) | LCCN 2022029147 (ebook) | ISBN 9781800730939 (hardback) | ISBN 9781800730946 (ebook)
Subjects: LCSH: Lesbianism--Germany--History--20th century. | Lesbianism--Netherlands--History--20th century. | Lesbians in mass media--Germany--History--20th century. | Lesbians in mass media--Netherlands--History--20th century. | Sexual excitement.
Classification: LCC HQ75.6.G3 S88 2023 (print) | LCC HQ75.6.G3 (ebook) | DDC 306.76/630943--dc23/eng/20220922
LC record available at https://lccn.loc.gov/2022029146
LC ebook record available at https://lccn.loc.gov/2022029147

British Library Cataloguing in Publication Data
A catalogue record for this book is available from the British Library

ISBN 978-1-80073-093-9 hardback
ISBN 978-1-80073-094-6 ebook

https://doi.org/10.3167/9781800730939

To all those who are 'Different from the Others'

Contents

List of Illustrations — viii

Acknowledgements — x

List of Abbreviations — xiii

Introduction — 1

Part I. Sociomedical Discourses — 33

Chapter 1. Sex and the Cities: Mapping Queer Feminine Desires — 35

Chapter 2. Sexual Science: The Queer Feminine Mystique — 82

Part II. Community Discourses — 125

Chapter 3. Fashioning Femininities in *The Girlfriend* (1924–33) and *Women's Love* (1926–32) — 139

Chapter 4. Marys and Mollys: Identifying Queer Feminine Desires on the Dutch Press Landscape — 184

Part III. Literary Discourses — 231

Chapter 5. A Mother's Love: Eva Raedt-de Canter's *Boarding School* (1930) and Christa Winsloe's *The Girl Manuela* (1933) — 243

Chapter 6. When Object Becomes Subject: Feminine Protagonists in Anna Elisabet Weirauch's *The Scorpion* Trilogy (1919–31) and Josine Reuling's *Back to the Island* (1937) — 286

Conclusion — 331

Bibliography — 339

Index — 357

Illustrations

Figure 3.1. 'A Poem Dedicated to the Work of Magnus Hirschfeld', *Women's Love*, 1928. Spinnboden Archive, used with permission.   149

Figure 3.2. 'Katharina II of Russia', *The Girlfriend*, 1927. Spinnboden Archive, used with permission.   152

Figure 3.3. 'The Personal Perfume', *Women's Love*, 1931. Spinnboden Archive, used with permission.   160

Figure 3.4. 'Fashionable Masculine Transvestites', *The Girlfriend*, 1929. Spinnboden Archive, used with permission.   163

Figure 3.5. 'The Queen: Memories of a Transvestite', 'The World of Transvestites', *The Girlfriend*, 1930. Spinnboden Archive, used with permission.   166

Figure 3.6. 'Clothing and Transvestism', *Women's Love*, 1927. Spinnboden Archive, used with permission.   169

Figure 4.1. 'The Eternally Feminine and Air-Raid Protection', *Beatrice*, 1939. IISG, used with permission.   193

Figure 4.2. 'The Girls in Boulder Blue', *Beatrice*, 1939. IISG, used with permission.   194

Figure 4.3. An example of a popular cover style for *The Young Woman*, 1932. IISG, used with permission.   197

Figure 4.4. 'Bobbed Hair', *The Young Woman*, 1926. IISG, used with permission   201

Figure 4.5. Title page of *We*, 1932. IHLIA, used with permission.   205

Figure 4.6. 'To the Editors', *We*, 1932. IHLIA, used with permission.   207

Figure 4.7. Cover Image for *The Right to Live*, 1940. IHLIA, used with permission. 215

Figure 4.8. Book Review for Benno Stokvis' *The Homosexuals* in *The Right to Live*, 1940. IHLIA, used with permission. 219

Acknowledgements

It has become almost cliché to confess that projects of such proportions are never the result of an individual undertaking. Yet, despite its distinct lack of originality, it is certainly a sentiment that rings true in the case of this monograph. There is little doubt that this would have been a rather different book had it not been for the support of a large – and ever-growing – number of people and organizations. First, I would like to thank the Wolfson Foundation and the Leverhulme Trust for their financial support, without which this project would not have been possible. Second, my gratitude must go to my academic mentors, Caroline Bland and Henriëtte Louwerse, who have been endlessly generous with their time and energy during the span of this project. It was Caroline's undergraduate course on fin-de-siècle maternalism that motivated me to make my first forays into queering the maternal. Since then, it has been her unfailingly kind and considered feedback that has helped to guide this study into what it has become today – although any errors must be claimed as entirely of my own making. Henriëtte's sometimes less-than-gentle nudges over the years have enabled me to leave behind several spheres of comfort in order to gain some vital experiences as a researcher and teacher, as well as to create space for some valuable moments of introspection. For their expertise and guidance, for their unerring enthusiasm for this project and for their enduring support and friendship, I cannot thank either of them enough.

While I have had the benefit of working closely with colleagues at my own institution, the kindness of academics and activists that I have collaborated with over the years has known no bounds. Here, I must first express my thanks to Adrian Bingham for his comments and feedback during the formative stages of this project, as well as Liesbeth Minnaard, who provided me with some supportive suggestions as I began my study into this 'silent conspiracy'. I must also thank Henk de Berg and Heike Bauer for their advice and careful readings in the final stages of my research. Crossing geographical borders, the dedicated team at the Spinnboden Archiv in Berlin, and in particular Cordula Jurczyk and Sabine Balke, deserve special thanks for spending their summer hours with me in the archive and giving some much-appreciated clarification on smudged pieces of *Fraktur*. The team at the IHLIA Archive in Amsterdam, and Thea Sibbel specifically, also deserve a particular mention for providing me with extended access to research material, as well as answering my endless queries with patience and good humour. I would further like to extend my gratitude to Judith Schuyf, Gert Hekma and Doris Hermanns for inviting me into their homes and sharing the fruits of their labour – and their personal archives – with me. Our conversations were thought-provoking and affirming, and my own research has been greatly assisted by the invaluable work that they have already undertaken to make visible the lives and experiences of queers of the past. Furthermore, the Women in German Studies organization has offered me a crucial academic network of supportive sisters for nearly a decade. More broadly, this community has provided a regular sounding board for many of the ideas I explore in this book, and my fellow committee members have proffered several welcome and well-timed words of wisdom as I have rounded off this project. I would also like to thank all the reviewers of this book for their insightful suggestions on early chapters, as well as the editing team at Berghahn Books for their professionalism and patience.

Indebted as I am to the numerous scholars and activists I have worked with throughout this project, during the writing of it there have been moments in which only an encouraging word from a good friend has sufficed. As fortune would have it, I find myself very wealthy in such circles. From late-night phone calls to surprise care packages, from offers of places to stay for archival trips to volunteering rooms in which I could live indeterminably, those closest to me have so often left me humbled by their kindness. Nina, Joanna, Liz, Sarah, Kirsty and Deb – the *meninas* – you are all stars. Your positivity and humour shone so much light into our grey office and I count myself exceptionally lucky to have been put 'in constellation' with such exciting academics and wonderful friends. Jenny, your straight-talking and swagger have always been an inspiration to me, and this is not even to speak of your audacious drag acts. Long may Dave reign. Joost, for your exquisite baked goods, 1980s earworms and *pun*ishingly bad wordplay, I thank you heartily – your humour often made difficult days more bearable. To Lottie, Megan and Andrew, thank you for reminding me that there is life – and much laughter – outside the academic bubble. Those coffee breaks and bagel bites provided real moments of respite. Of course, I could not fail to mention Laura, Jen, Anna D., Andy, Samuel and Olivia. I could not have stayed sane without your friendship. Even though we have often been scattered across the globe, your support and care has never faltered. You have welcomed me into your homes, have sent supportive voice notes and cards, and have shown so much care over the years – it has meant far more than you will know.

Finally, alongside the chosen family that has been supporting me from the fringes, there have been those who have witnessed more enduringly the highs and lows of attempting to carve out a career in academic research. To this end, I would like to thank my parents and my sister for their persistent belief in me and their fierce encouragement. You have always been infinitely prouder of what I have achieved than I have been able to be, and I would not have made it to this point were it not for your pride. To Bella (and Nova), I have so much to be thankful to you for – too much to mention here. You encouraged my ideas before I could even put pen to paper to write the proposal for this project. You inspired me to think creatively about my research and to connect my historical writing to present-day queer communities. In other words, you motivated me to *think big*. For that I will always be grateful. Finally, *finally*: I would like to thank Anna; a reader who is as sharp as they are passionate and generous. You have played a key role in keeping me – and this project – on track in recent years and this book has become all the richer by way of your critical observations and subtle suggestions. As I have become, too, through your encouragement, kindness and care. Thank you.

Note on Translations

Unless stated otherwise, all translations provided are my own.

Abbreviations

The full name of an organisation will be provided on first reference in each chapter. Later references will appear abbreviated as indicated below.

BfM	League for Human Rights (Bund für Menschenrecht)
DFV	German Friendship Association (Deutscher Freundschaftsverband)
GdE	Community of the Special (Gemeinschaft der Eigenen)
NWHK	Dutch Scientific Humanitarian Committee (Nederlandsch Wetenschappelijk Humanitair Komitee)
WhK	Scientific Humanitarian Committee (Wissenschaftlich-humanitäres Komitee)

INTRODUCTION

A class of women ... in which homosexuality while fairly distinct, is only slightly marked, is formed by the women to whom the actively inverted woman is most attracted ... On the whole, they are women who are not very robust and well-developed, physically or nervously, and who are not well adopted for child-bearing, but who still possess many excellent qualities, and they are always womanly. One may perhaps say that they are the pick of the women whom the average man would pass by. No doubt this is often the reason why they are open to homosexual advances.
—Havelock Ellis, *Studies in the Psychology of Sex: Sexual Inversion*, 1908

Femininity! A patriarchal hype if there ever was one – a phony ideal created by men, not by Lesbians.
—Linda Strega, 'The Big Sell-out, Lesbian Femininity', 1985

Research for this study of queer femininities began with rather a different purpose in mind. Inspired by a recently completed project on female masculinities in German and Dutch interwar literature, I turned my attention to some largely overlooked exchanges between queer women across the German and Dutch border in the period between the two World Wars. A brief note from a self-defined Dutch 'transvestite' located in a supplement of the queer German magazine *The Girlfriend* (*Die Freundin*, 1924–33), the traces of the romantic/erotic relationship that brought together Dada artist Hannah Höch and Dutch author Til Brugman, and the decision of German author Christa Winsloe to publish her novel *The Girl Manuela*

(*Das Mädchen Manuela*, 1933) in Amsterdam after the National Socialists assumed power led me to conclude that there must have been a productive social network of women exchanging sexual knowledges (and desires) across German and Dutch borders during this time. Following Foucault's oft-cited contention that sexuality came to be considered the 'truth of our being' at the end of the nineteenth century, I embarked on a project that conceived of identity as central to the experience of desire, asking how cross-cultural exchanges might have shaped sexual practices in the interwar era and to what extent the medico-political project of sexual codification taking place in Germany from the late nineteenth century onwards had influenced the ways in which queer women conceived of their desires in the Netherlands and beyond. Furthermore, I wondered how modern gender politics had disrupted existing conceptions of sexual desire, as well as the social imaginary of such intimacies, in two cultural contexts that had encountered two vastly different experiences of the so-called Great War.

With the aim of weaving together a richer tapestry of historical gendered enactments and exchanges by queer women in the first half of the twentieth century, I began a comparative project that took Berlin and Amsterdam as the key sociopolitical sites for investigation. The placement of Berlin as a site of erotic alterity has become an almost self-evident fact in histories about sexual practices and identities written since the 1980s. Certainly, in the years of relative economic stability between the two World Wars, queer life became a palpable part of the urban German landscape as never before. Bars and clubs catering to the tastes of queer audiences sprang up in Berlin in unprecedented numbers, literary and cinematic production brought nonheterosexual desires to a broader and increasingly sexually cognisant audience, and a medicosocial movement founded in the German capital in the late nineteenth century began more fervently to lobby for the political rights and social acceptance of same-sex loving persons. Yet, while the visibility of queer desires in Berlin during the interwar period – and concomitantly the German archive – is perhaps a convincing enough motive for positioning this city as central to a study concerning discourses of queer identity and desire, the case for considering Amsterdam as a springboard for such investigations is far less readily apparent. Indeed, in spite of the existence of a few suggestively Sapphic images of cigar-smoking, motorcycle-riding women in the Dutch archive, the masculine tones that provided the overture to sociopolitical discussions of female sexual alterity in Germany appeared to have failed to capture the Dutch cultural imagination to the same degree.[1] Conspicuously absent from fin-de-siècle debates concerning sexual morality in the Netherlands, and rendered invisible in the writings of the queer male activists rallying against the Dutch law that restricted same-sex desires, evidence of the ways in which queer women in the Netherlands organized their lives and loves before the middle of the twentieth century remains frustratingly fragmentary. It is certainly for good reason that historian Judith Schuyf's extensive monograph on lesbian desire in the Netherlands refers to the topic as 'A Silent Conspiracy'.[2] In an earlier article, Schuyf touches on the significance of sexological discourses of gendered inversion to the formation of queer identities in Germany – identities that were shaped by the idea of an inborn reversal of gender traits. Following this theory, the female with same-sex desires was conceived of as a figure with a 'masculine soul, heaving in the female bosom'.[3] The link between a congenital reversal of gendered characteristics and the desire for one's own sex meant that female same-sex desire was conceptualized in countries influenced by German sexological discourses primarily through a framework of visible masculinity and/or culturally specific gender deviance. Doctrines of somatic inversion were slow to take root in Dutch society, however, which suggests the existence of alternative sociocultural frameworks for the cultivation of queer identities and desires:

> In Germany, lesbian women were conscious of an identity *as a lesbian*, and the form this identity took was the trademark of the German gay rights movement, Hirschfeld's Wissenschaftlich Humanitäres Kommittee [sic] (WhK), the 'Third Sex' … In The Netherlands [sic] lesbian women were, primarily, *women*. Thus, in the feminist magazines the discussion was about femininity.[4]

As Schuyf's above contention suggests, markers of masculinity in female-bodied subjects in the Netherlands during the interwar period were not yet primarily coded as a sign of sexual nonconformity. As such, transposing the focus of German sexological writings on gender inversion onto a Dutch historical context would mean to ignore the evidence that points to alternative queer modalities. Indeed, by discounting such alternatives in the search of something that aligned more readily with the dominant European discourses of sexuality and desire from the first half of the twentieth century, my original project risked falling into the trap 'of translating the unsaid into something we think we already know'.[5] Motivated primarily by what Julian Carter identifies as a 'desire for the recognition of the present in the past', my initial point of departure therefore sought to conceptualize historical practices of female same-sex desire through a single sexological lens.[6] Rather than foregrounding the signifiers of modern-day queerness in examinations of the past, an approach that Laura Doan already skilfully critiqued in her groundbreaking work *Disturbing Practices* (2013), this book attempts to explore instead how we might 'pose questions rather than provide answers about sexual identities we already know'.[7] By decentralizing the sexological invert from the study of queer female desires, I seek to find out what a focus on the construction of queer femininity might reveal about the myriad ways in which same-sex desire has been experienced and constructed by women in the past.

As I will argue throughout this book, the widespread acceptance of the masculine woman as the symbol of twentieth-century female queerness par excellence has led to an obscuring of queer feminine desires as a legitimate subject of historical study. Consequently, femininity has been undervalued in the examination of queer female subjectivities and neglected as a site of academic interest, even while explorations of queer (male) masculinities have flourished and thrived.[8] As the so-called invisible gendered performance, femininity has historically been viewed through normativizing frameworks, even within queer studies, which has almost entirely disguised the critical potential of femininity in research into the sexual past. Less readily legible as queer in the archives, the sexual difference of feminine women often becomes visible only through the gender deviancy of their partners, those whose marked masculinity is invariably linked – as either cause or consequence – to an immutable desire for their own sex. At once everywhere and nowhere, the queer feminine woman thus confronts historians with a contradiction in terms. Nonetheless, the persistence and ubiquity of feminine-gendered expressions in queer communities during the early twentieth century and beyond means that it would be remiss to ignore the possibility that female queerness has been historically coded and understood in ways that were not exclusively masculine. To put it even more strongly: while femininity may, in several respects, obfuscate the project of locating experiences of female queerness in the past, by creating space for the discussion of femininity in the present, we can make infinite the gendered embodiments that might be considered queer and, as such, included in historical studies of same-sex desires. Indeed, it is crucial that we begin to move away from a history of love and lust between women that is consolidated singularly, as Sarah Cefai has observed, 'around the image of the butch'.[9] Only in this way might we fully appreciate the nuanced ways in which female same-sex desires have been constructed in historically specific periods. To this end, this study will explore the productive potential of revaluing gender 'conformity' with the aim of redressing the imbalance in research on female femininities in historical studies of queer genders and sexualities. By focusing specifically on queer female-bodied femininities – read through a range of German and Dutch sociocultural, sexological and literary texts published since 1880 – this project seeks not only to make queer feminine women visible as subjects of historical study within their own right, but also to contribute to the growing discussion surrounding the plurality of queer female experience through history. However, to take femininity as the central lens through which to examine erotic and romantic desires between women also means to engage with femininity as an ideology that has long since been contested by queers and feminists alike. While the culturally bound debates relating to historical enactments of femininity will be discussed in Part I of this book, the complexities and contradictions inherent in the social imperative to reject 'bad' forms of femininity, one that has arguably served to preserve the vacuum in research about queer feminine desires to which I have just alluded, must first be acknowledged in order to appreciate the importance of this subject matter in the first instance and the need for its historical contextualization in the second. As the central tenets that form the critical study of femininity have largely resulted from a body of work emerging from North America, the following section will look specifically at those frameworks before applying the theoretical fruits of queer and feminist studies to the cultural contexts outlined above.

'Good' and 'Bad' Femininities

Against the backdrop of cultural conservatism that characterized vast areas of the United States in the second half of the twentieth century, Betty Friedan published a powerful critique of patriarchal forms of femininity. Friedan's *The Feminine Mystique* (1963) speaks of the growing discontent many housewives were experiencing in the United States in their return to domesticity in the aftermath of the Second World War, capturing the spirit of a cultural moment. Presenting idealized forms of femininity in American society as a cultural practice that was fundamental to women's oppression, Friedan claims that femininity had dominated women's lives for centuries and had served to confine women 'to the home [and] to keep us from developing and using our full personhood in society'.[10] Cemented through capitalist enterprises such as 'women's magazines, the movies, the television commercials … the mass media and the textbooks of psychology and sociology' – discursive forms that will be analysed in this book – Friedan suggests that the thrall of the feminine mystique had become so absolute by the 1960s that 'the highest value and the only commitment' for women in North America had become 'the fulfillment of their own femininity'.[11] The 'mystique' of the feminine, Friedan observes, was part of a blueprint that had been laid out guilefully for centuries. As part of a much broader social system, the pressures of femininity worked to instil a sense of shame in women who did not find completion in the domestic roles of wife and mother. However, in the wake of the civil rights movements emerging in the 1950s and 1960s, growing numbers of American women started to articulate their discontent with familial life and to question, along with Friedan, whether their commitment to the ideals of femininity had indeed served to prevent them from becoming 'fully human'.[12]

While Friedan's study rails against the damaging potentials of those forms of femininity used to entrap women within domesticity and to prevent them from reaching their 'full potential' as human beings, it certainly does not call for a rejection of femininity outright. Rather, it posits a revaluation of what she considers a culturally devalued way of being: 'the great mistake of Western culture, through most of its history, has been the undervaluation of ... femininity. It says femininity is so mysterious and intuitive and close to the creation and origin of life that man-made science may never be able to understand it'.[13] Alongside a revision of traditional femininities, Friedan further suggests a development of 'mutant' forms of femininity in which the objectives of the marital union can be combined with the desires of women to fulfil their own creative ambitions. Casting aside an idealized form of femininity that weds women to the homestead, Friedan instead lays out her own ideal in which women's creative impulses can be combined with more traditional feminine pursuits. In order to achieve this unification, Friedan argues that a woman 'must think of herself as a human being first ... and make a life plan in terms of her own abilities, a commitment of her own to society, with which her commitments as wife and mother can be integrated'.[14] Within Friedan's framework, 'bad' femininities, then, are those that define female achievement only in terms of domestic success. However, 'good' femininities offer a radical futurity for those who dare to envision a life *alongside* domesticity: 'Who knows what women can be when they are finally free to become themselves? Who knows what women's intelligence will contribute when it can be nourished without denying love?'[15] In presenting seemingly limitless possibilities for the future of (feminine) women's social, political and sexual experiences, Friedan's suggestion of mutant femininities arguably offers an early insurrection in the queering of gender norms. Yet, her framework fundamentally denies women one desire in its vision of a new feminist future: that for their own sex.

Speaking as the President of the National Organization for Women (NOW) at the First Congress to Unite Women in 1969, Friedan drew firm lines between the emerging women's rights movement, and with it her vision for the future of femininity, and the 'mannish' and 'man-hating' lesbians who undermined the potential of such an organization to achieve sociopolitical change.[16] Denouncing lesbians as a 'lavender menace', Friedan's slight sparked a wave of lesbian-feminist critiques of gender roles – and, specifically, femininity – in the late 1960s and early 1970s. In the writings that followed on the subject, queer feminists were seen to chew the meat provided to them by Friedan's formative work, while leaving the bones of its heteronormativity ostensibly behind them, eschewing the traditional butch-femme identities that had previously been so highly valued within North American and Western European lesbian subcultures after the Second World War.[17] In their place, the concept of the woman-identified woman began to gain traction, which offered a more androgynous paradigm with which to resist the purportedly heterosexual practices of penetrative sex and binary desire. Adopting this designation, the separatist group Radicalesbians sought to repurpose the core argument of *The Feminine Mystique* along queer lines.[18] Agreeing with Friedan's earlier contention that 'being 'feminine' and being a whole person are irreconcilable', the Radicalesbians' manifesto 'The Woman-Identified Woman' (1970) takes Friedan's critiques even further to link the core tenets of idealized forms of femininity to notions of slavery and race. Considering femininity to be something that is conferred upon women by men, the group defines the label as 'a slave status which makes us legitimate in the eyes of the society in which we live'.[19] In this way, the Radicalesbians considered femininity to 'dehumanize' women, positioning them in a 'supportive/serving caste in relation to the master caste of men'.[20] While the group drew heavily on Friedan's theorizing, the Radicalesbians ultimately rejected the notion of mutant femininities, claiming that it was futile to try to bend the limits of a patriarchal performance to one's own will.[21] Instead, they encouraged queer women to reject the practices associated with femininity altogether in order 'to achieve maximum autonomy in human expression'.[22] During this project for erotic emancipation, it was not only femininity that was cast aside. Indeed, as Biddy Martin observes, lesbian separatists found 'male identification in virtually any expression of gendered style whether femme or butch'.[23] For this reason, any gender presentation that fell within male-identified systems or engaged in the notion of a 'false consciousness' was to be rejected. Within such a logic, not only was the stylistic presentation of queer feminine women to be disavowed – and, with it, their supposed support of a system that upheld masculine privilege and power – but 'thinking, acting, or looking like a man', as Esther Newton writes, was also considered to 'contradict lesbian feminism's first principle'.[24]

During the early 1980s, activists and scholars such as Joan Nestle and Madeline Davis began to rebel against the devaluing of 'butch' and 'fem(me)' identities in their pro-sex, pro-femme writings. In a series of fierce debates that later became categorized as the 'sex wars', it soon became evident that femininity remained a key site of contention for many (queer and lesbian) feminists, who still believed the practice to be a form of patriarchal collusion. Amidst topics such as the supposed sexual subordination of women within BDSM subcultures and the harmful effects of pornography on women, activists and scholars such as Andrea Dworkin and Adrienne Rich criticized the 'damaging' revival of feminine gendered expressions. Butch-femme relationships were once again cast as 'het' facsimiles and any kind of power inequality between lesbian women, whether through a division of domestic labour or during erotic play, was denounced as 'weakening of lesbian politics', with femininity itself being labelled the ultimate 'self-betrayal'.[25] Writing of the butch oppression experienced by masculine-of-centre lesbians, self-defined 'fem' Linda Strega claimed that queer feminine women were sabotaging the fight for lesbian emancipation by adopting 'het values and het identification'.[26] According to Strega, identifying as a 'fem' was to align oneself with the 'enemy', the greatest act of betrayal one could commit against the lesbian community and those visible butch figures within it. During the sex wars, then, the practice of femininity by queer women was rejected by several prominent radical lesbian-feminists as a display of 'allegiance and orientation towards male values and desires', which evidenced a lack of commitment to the fight for emancipation and functioned as a betrayal of one's Sapphic sisters.[27] However, following the fierce defence of queer femininity by Joan Nestle, Madeline Davis and Amber Hollibaugh in the 1990s, a distinctive form of femme pride began to emerge. In Nestle's collection *The Persistent Desire: A Femme-Butch Reader* (1992), for example, feminine garb and gestures are not reviled as the accessories of the butch betrayer but are instead used to create an intellectual space in which queer femininity can be read almost exclusively as a subversive act. Indeed, in a retrospective look at the creation of the collection itself, Davis claims that in utilizing heteropatriarchal gender norms to new effect, femmes might even be considered the 'queerest of the queers'.[28] Echoing this sentiment, Mykel Johnson challenges the image of the apolitical femme that had plagued the lesbian movement from the 1970s by noting the distinctions in the ways in which homofemininities and heterofemininities are performed: 'femme dykes, as well as butch dykes, fuck with gender. [They] are not passing as straight women. Lesbian femme is not the same as "feminine" ... A femme dyke is not trying to be discreet'.[29] In keeping with Butler's troubling of gender, Johnson argues that performing femininity as a queer woman is about upsetting normative images by disrupting the assumed relationship between the *performer* and the *observer*: 'Even if she is "beautiful" by ... male standards, a femme dyke may do something to disrupt the image, intentionally break the rules. And she breaks the cardinal rule: her audience is female, not male.'[30] In this troubling of the relationship between gendered performer and observer, both Davis and Johnson take pains to create queer femme subjectivities that are *distinct* from heterosexual forms of femininity, an observation that, as we will see in Chapter 6, was already being made by the interwar authors Anna Elisabet Weirauch and Josine Reuling. Indeed, in a climate in which heterosexual femininities were considered anathema to homosexual liberation, femmes were at constant risk of their gendered performances being considered 'a capitulation, a swamp, something maternal, ensnared and ensnaring' rather than a radical or subversive act. This was especially true if a femme's performance of femininity, as Biddy Martin suggests, was 'not camped up or disavowed'.[31]

The impulse to distinguish between 'het' and queer forms of femininity gained greater significance in the face of the emergence of what Danae Clark terms 'commodity lesbianism' in the mid-1990s.[32] During this time, the carefully carved lines between heterosexual and queer femininities increasingly began to blur, especially as those femme embodiments that had been held up as radical were co-opted into mainstream culture as quick-fire concepts in order to market music, magazines, films and fashion. Although the commodification of queerness was of course itself not a new construct, the dawning of a 'decade in love with lesbianism', as Ann Ciasullo characterizes it, served to create a paradoxical sexual landscape in which 'designer dykes' and 'lipstick lesbians' were both everywhere and nowhere.[33] In this contradictory cultural climate, lesbian lives were garnering more interest within mainstream media outlets than ever before, but the 'luscious lesbians' being depicted were, as Clark observes, considered increasingly to be 'indistinguishable from straight women'.[34] During the 1990s, Ciasullo describes the growth of a 'sanitized' version of lesbianism across media outlets – an image that served to create, in turn, what Rosanne Kennedy acknowledges as 'an absent presence' of lesbian desire.[35] In this way, as Nestle concedes, it became all too 'easy' for queer communities 'to lose curiosity about what made [femmes] sexual heretics' in the first instance.[36] As a consequence, the label 'lipstick lesbian', as Lisa Walker notes, was soon adopted in queer communities as a slur to connote 'an apolitical creature ... a lesbian who doesn't want to be a dyke and doesn't want to be associated with dykes'.[37] Indeed, already by the end of the 1990s, the radical *femme*-ininity that had been put forth by Nestle and others was being dismissed as a naïve response to the powers of patriarchal commercialism and, as such, unconvincing as a political act.

Following more than a decade of commercialized queerness in the ironically termed 'gay nineties', the arrival of Showtime's *The L Word* (2004–9) created an unparalleled platform for displays of queer female femininity. In doing so, the series struck upon several enduring conceptual nerves within lesbian and queer communities. Abounding with glamorous, middle-class and mainly white cis women, *The L Word*, like many other mainstream television shows, based its female characters on several recognizable archetypes of femininity. However, with storylines circling around themes of promiscuity, bisexuality and motherhood, the series openly tackled many of the charges that had been levied against queer feminine women since the early twentieth century. Yet, the centrality of feminine women in the series and the notable absence of traditionally butch characters led many critics from the queer community to query the objectives of the directors, problematizing the validity of the performance of femininity for a queer audience:

> Even as [*The L Word*'s] characters wrestle with real-world lesbian issues, they do so garbed, coiffed, and made-up in the guise of feminine, heterosexual women – thereby not only defusing any potential threat or disruption of the heterosexual status quo, but also reifying the representation of all women as existing under the purview of the scopophilic male gaze.[38]

The suggestion that the queer feminine women in the show were 'made-up in the *guise* of feminine, heterosexual women' and that this supposed impersonation of heterofemininity failed to '[defuse] any potential threat or disruption of the heterosexual status quo' reinforces the anti-feminine sentiments that had persisted in queer communities since the 1970s. Furthermore, the focus on femininity being performed for the 'scopophilic male gaze' undermines Johnson's earlier contention that queer women might play out their femininities specifically for the pleasure of *other queer women*. Such dismissals of the subversive potential of the queer femininities that have been performed (literally and figuratively) onscreen have had important implications for what has been considered worthy of critical attention – academic or otherwise – in relation to this watershed series. It remains telling, for example, that the distinctions between central character Tina Kennard's embodiment of maternal femininity, Bette Porter's dominant *Powerfrau* aesthetic and Helena Peabody's high-class hyperfemininity have largely been ignored in favour of a blanket rejection of what has been considered a monolithic performance of femininity that serves only to make female same-sex desire palatable for nonqueer audiences. In this way, femininity is once again diffused as a legitimate queer gendered embodiment and read rather as an indication, as Walker suggests, of a feminine woman's 'desire to pass for straight and not of her desire for other women'.[39] Plagued by what Clare Hemmings has termed 'a specter of straightness', the alterity of femininity in the early 2000s continued to be rendered invisible by the apparent privilege of queer feminine women to pass as heterosexual.[40]

At the time of writing, debates on issues of femininity remain heated within many feminist, lesbian and queer circles. Even with the reboot of Showtime's series *The L Word* in 2019, which bears the alternate title *Generation Q*, there is still remarkably little that seems queer about femininity. Even while the femininity of its (now) older characters is described as 'soapy' and 'overblown' by the show's critics, these labels appear to carry little of the camp cachet that Martin had earlier suggested might turn the performance of femininity into a subversive act. Instead, it is the body hair of androgynous and butch characters that has been praised by viewers as 'relatable' and 'radical', while queer femininity continues to be considered as part of the 'time capsule that should have stayed buried'.[41] This is, of course, not to say that the growing visibility of butch and trans characters in the recent series presents an unwelcome change or that the – all too brief – acknowledgement of the colonizing actions of white queer people in Los Angeles does not mark the beginning of a crucial conversation about the effects of what Damaris Rose terms 'marginal gentrification' in North America. Rather, it reveals that the generosity that has recently been extended by viewers and critics to more reductive renderings of masculinity in the series is still yet to be afforded to its feminine characters, who continue to be the subject of ridicule and ire. Indeed, in spite of a welcome growth in recent years in scholarly interest on the subject of queer femininities, the refusal to read historical enactments of femininity as *equally* queer continues to preclude a valuable discussion of the critical potential of femininity within communities of women-who-desired-women in the past.[42] The continued marginalization of femininity within queer communities, as Sarah Cefai notes, therefore 'problematically re-privileges [lesbian] masculinity as *less* invested in heteropatriarchy, as a more liberated mode of desire and identity'.[43] This is largely evidenced in the criticisms and acclaim received most recently by the writers of *The L Word: Generation Q*. The view that queer femininity continues to serve damaging patriarchal ideals colours not only the ways in which activists and theorists conceive of gender and sexual politics in the present, but also the ways in which historians have narrated the events of the queer past. Indeed, more than thirty years after the publication of Nestle's *The Persistent Desire*, it still remains possible to conclude that queer women have historically been 'the victims of a double dismissal: in the past they did not appear culturally different enough from heterosexual women to be seen as breaking gender taboos, and today they do not appear feminist enough, even in their historical context, to merit attention or respect for being ground-breaking women'.[44] What Nestle already identified in the 1990s as a cultural dismissal of femininity continues, then, to shape historical studies on the subject of queer desire. Indeed, even a cursory search for the figure of the femme in the context of German and Dutch queer history writing forces us to acknowledge that both the lack of attention and the respect for femininity that Nestle identifies have led to vast gaps in accumulated knowledge about the relationships between gender, sexuality and desire in the past.

Locating the Femme in Histories of Sexuality

In adopting a comparative approach for this study, I was struck by several differences in the traditions and preoccupations of German and Dutch historians of sexuality. To a greater degree, German historical research since the 1970s has focused intensely on the construction of sexual subjectivities during the late nineteenth and early twentieth centuries, with specific attention being paid to the fin-de-siècle, the interwar and the Nazi eras.[45] While much early German history writing on the subject of same-sex desire appears to have been committed to what Doan has termed the 'recovery project' agenda, there has since developed an advancing number of publications that have engaged with queer methodological practices, as will be discussed shortly.[46] Conversely, Dutch scholars have not taken up queer frameworks nearly so proactively. Indeed, the analysis of historical female same-sex experiences from a queer perspective has remained quite untouched as the subject of comprehensive research in Dutch contexts at the time of writing. Furthermore, while histories of sexuality in German contexts have focused on the late nineteenth and early twentieth centuries, providing ample secondary source material to aid research into these periods, Dutch historical studies of same-sex desire have been concerned primarily with the period between the High Middle Ages and the eighteenth century.[47] Indeed, Anja van Kooten Niekerk and Sacha Wijmer's socioanthropological project *The Wrong Kind of Friendship: Lesbian Lives in the Years 1920–1960* (*Verkeerde vriendschap: lesbisch leven in de jaren 1920–1960*, 1985) and Judith Schuyf's cultural historical study *A Silent Conspiracy: Lesbian Women in the Netherlands 1920–1970* (*Een stilzwijgende samenzwering: lesbische vrouwen in Nederland 1920–1970*, 1994) remain the only two monographs to have been published that focus on female same-sex desire in the Netherlands in the early twentieth century. Additionally, while several significant contributions have been published on queer female desires in Dutch-language collections and journals, very few have been translated into English or made available to non-Dutch speakers. With this present volume then, I hope to present a broad historical account of Dutch discourses of queer female desire to an English-speaking audience in the first monograph on queer female desire in the Dutch interbellum to appear since the 1990s.

In terms of female same-sex desire in German contexts, the figure of the masculine woman has come to dominate the field of study. This is largely unsurprising, given the unprecedented social anxiety around the 'masculinization' of women during the interwar era, as has been demonstrated admirably in Katie Sutton's *The Masculine Woman in Weimar Germany* (2012). The preoccupation of contemporary German-speaking medicosocial discourses with the subject of gender deviance has resulted in an extensive collection of scientific and sociological documents, which are readily available for analysis both online and in archives. Heike Schader's *Virile Women, Vamps, and Wild Violets* (2004) further provides a wealth of information to readers in relation to the periodicals printed for queer women during the Weimar era. Outlining the various forms of masculinities and femininities depicted in the pages of these periodicals, Schader's study sheds light on the ways in which queer women gave new meaning to gender categories and blurred the lines between the binary designations of masculinity and femininity. However, while acknowledging the existence of queer femininities, Schader's research focus remains moored primarily to the concept of the masculine homosexual women. Furthermore, in terms of the production and structure of the magazines, Schader's study pays little attention to the types of discourses that are presented in the periodicals and how these themselves could be considered gendered genres. In exploring and comparing the nuances of literary writing and advertorials presented in these magazines, I aim to build on Schader's important discussions to focus on how what Hélène Cixous has coined *écriture feminine* has shaped the significances accorded to these magazines.

It is arguably Marti Lybeck's most recent exploration of the emergence of homosexual identities in Germany from 1890 to 1933 that has given most comprehensive attention to the struggles of negotiating femininity, gendered subjectivity and queer desire. *Desiring Emancipation* (2014) focuses specifically on the experiences of wealthy women from before the fin de siècle to the rise of National Socialism and addresses queer femininity at a time when the nonreproductive feminine subject was considered 'immoral, selfish, uncontrolled, fickle, vain, degenerate, and possibly evil'.[48] Lybeck's study provides significant insights into the fragility of class-bound gender formations by considering the ways in which bourgeois women transgressed notions of gender as desiring subjects. However, in its examination of periodicals, literature and records from women's clubs (*Frauenvereine*) during the 1920s, Lybeck's study nonetheless restricts itself to those women who 'saw themselves as a minority defined by congenital difference'.[49] Such women, Lybeck suggests, were able to shape a coherent social identity based on 'masculinity as the essence of the homosexual woman'.[50] By opening up this debate on class to explore more closely the nebulous relationship between femininity and homosexual desire, as well as those longings of aspirational white-collar workers depicted in magazines such as *The Girlfriend* (*Die Freundin*, 1924–33) and *Woman's Love* (*Frauenliebe*, 1926–32), my own study hopes to weave a further strand into the discussion stimulated by Lybeck's most recent contribution.

In terms of Dutch sociohistorical studies concerning queer women, Anja van Kooten Niekerk and Sacha Wijmer's sociological study *The Wrong Kind of Friendship* (1985) was stimulated by a range of sexological and psychoanalytical discourses that focus specifically on the image of the *manwijf* (mannish woman) between 1920 and 1960. Through a wide-ranging analysis, van Kooten Niekerk and Wijmer draw on – and corroborate – much of the work of Nestle and the pro-sex writers of their time by presenting the image of historical female same-sex relationships in the Netherlands that conformed to traditional masculine-feminine dichotomies, resulting in 'butch' or 'femme' relationships. Yet, from the corpus on which the study is based – an impressive body of interviews with twenty-one women born between 1904 and 1936 – the shifting nature of women's sexual and gendered performances suggests that gendered and erotic roles between women were far more fluid than this initial binary might suggest. Interviewee Greet van Halteren explains, for example, that queer women were known to oscillate between gendered roles depending on the presentation of their desired partner. If a woman attempted to attract a masculine partner, for example, she would adopt a feminine appearance, irrespective of her preferred gender role. The opposite would be true of those women who attempted to attract feminine partners. Speaking of her friend 'Adri', van Halteren hints at the dynamism that existed within the binary:

> To Greet's no small astonishment, Adri, one of her companions, fell in love with a 'real' masculine type, even more masculine that Adri was herself. This love resulted in Adri 'transforming' into a feminine woman '... I had never seen her like this, because before that point she had been a real boy. 'What *are* you?' I asked her. 'I've become a girl now', she said, 'because I have got such a nice girlfriend. Kid, I had to switch around again entirely'.[51]

Indeed, another interviewee, Hillie Seegers, termed herself a 'chameleon' in reference to her gender presentation, which depended on the role taken by her partner: 'in one relationship she was "feminine", in the other "masculine"'.[52] While these comments may appear to shore up the constellation of 'butch + femme', van Halteren's remarks suggest that this dyad was perpetually in flux, shifting depending on the mode of desire and the expectations within any given context. Indeed, after Adri's relationship with her 'real' masculine partner ended, she 'saw no reason to stay "femme"' and returned to her masculine forms of presentation.[53] Therefore, gender embodiment was clearly not a fixed phenomenon during this time: a feminine woman could 'become' a masculine woman, just as a masculine woman could don feminine apparel and enact traditionally feminine roles, or even a combination of the two. Indeed, as ambulance driver Trix S. also mentions in the study, 'that's one of the things I learned to discover later: that the very masculine-looking women, who play that role beautifully, almost always turned out to be the most feminine women out there, but in a very different direction, namely in the form of care, dealing with children et cetera'.[54] Thus, while the masculine woman could legitimately embody maternal qualities, the feminine-presenting woman could equally act as the sexual initiator, taking on the traditionally 'active' masculine role. Despite suggestions that *even* masculine women – the chief subjects of van Kooten Niekerk and Wijmer's study – engaged fluidly with their femininity, the sociologists do not engage with the critical potential of this gendered act in their work, or the significance of feminine gendered practices to the shaping of homosexual identities and communities in the Netherlands more broadly.

Building on this earlier sociological study, Schuyf's *A Silent Conspiracy* delves more deeply into the cultural and historical contexts that shaped women's social lives and desires in the Netherlands during the first half of the twentieth century. Without explicitly terming her practices as such, Schuyf deploys queer methods to close the gap between what she considers 'known' and 'unknown' qualities of lesbian desire. To craft a more nuanced narrative about what life may have been like for women-who-desired-women in the Netherlands, Schuyf analyses historical data about the experiences of unmarried female women during this time. While such an approach is undeniably important in furthering knowledge about 'what cannot be known', Schuyf's study stops short of engaging with the devaluation of the feminine within historiographical practices, or the consideration that this may be the reason why there is so little historical information about queer women during this period in the first instance, even in spite of the importance of femininity to many queer Dutch women. Furthermore, as the backdrop for the study, Schuyf charts the development of a sexual self-image as a lesbian that relies on the notion of a 'lesbian telos'. Here, the identity category 'lesbian' is situated as the uncontested culmination point of a woman's acknowledgement of her non-normative desires.[55] Although this framework is useful for those contexts in which lesbian is a known category, it remains unable to account for those women who, as this study will suggest, did not engage with the practice of sexual labelling, or, as Doan suggests, with women who 'had little sense of sexual selfhood or subjectivity' and who 'did not think to attach to themselves sexual labels or names'.[56]

Labels and Names

The processes of categorizing and labelling gendered acts and sexual desires have been steeped in political and personal debate for more than a century. For the purposes of this book, the term 'queer' will be deployed to describe the desires of women for their own sex, as a descriptor for the methodological practices undergirding this project and as an adjective that is 'unaligned with any specific identity category'.[57] Used in this way, I hope to avoid the projection of identitarian terms, such as 'homosexual', 'lesbian' or 'bisexual', onto subjects who may not have recognized such concepts or identified their desires in such ways. Although employing the term 'queer' is certainly not unproblematic, I use it as a referent to acknowledge the diverse manifestations of love between women without pinning down any of these enactments to a specific set of acts, expressions or identities. While Adrienne Rich's 'lesbian continuum' and Judith Roof's category 'lesbian-like' have been used in similar ways, and are able thus to define a wide scope of historical woman-woman relationships, these terms remain largely incongruous with the wider aims of this study, since they are still too closely linked to our present-day understandings of 'lesbianism'.[58] In spite of its anachronistic nature, 'queer' might be considered a more relevant descriptor for such a project because, in David Halperin's words, the term 'does not designate a class of already objectified pathologies or perversions … it describes a horizon of possibility whose precise extent and heterogenous scope cannot in principle be delimited in advance'.[59] In a similar way, the 'precise extent and scope' of what constitutes desire cannot be delineated in this study in advance with any single or fixed meaning. While this book is not the place to engage in philosophical debates pertaining to the multiple meanings and problematics of desire, a brief outline of what this rubric means to this project should hopefully make the parameters of the term within this context clearer. Employing the term broadly, I conceive of desire as an interweaving project of personal needs, longings and wishes for specific persons, objects and outcomes that are built both upon erotic impulses and socially constructed demands. The lack of fixidity with which the category queer desire is employed enables the term, as Corie Hammers states, to reveal 'as fiction this hetero-productive logic as it eludes/disrupts representation/meaning altogether'.[60] The term 'desire' is therefore not restricted to the longing for – or engagement in – certain romantic, erotic and sexual practices, but further includes aspirations to sexual selfhood, community building, and emancipation, acceptance and desires that may appear to be incongruous with today's personal-political project of queerness, such as desires for the heteronormative institutions of marriage and childrearing, for instance, or for the assimilation and acceptance into heterosocial structures, for erotic and romantic monogamy and for engaging in hierarchical, binary relationships. Indeed, to draw on Lee Edelman's conceptualizations, much like the category 'queer', desire fundamentally 'depends for its energy, for its continuing power to grip us, on the impossibility of knowing its boundaries, of knowing its coherence as a state'.[61]

In keeping with my approaches to queerness and desire, I seek to make visible through my discursive analysis the existence of multiple expressions of queer femininity and desire in German and Dutch writing from the fin de siècle through to the Nazi era – expressions that were coloured not only by sexual preference but also by markers of class, marital status, religion, race and national belonging. While the literary narratives explored in Chapters 5 and 6 depict almost exclusively feminine identities that belong to the sociocultural and educated elite, the periodicals considered in Chapters 3 and 4 include the voices and desires of the emerging white-collar classes and working women. The labels 'working-class', 'white-collar' and 'elite' had – and continue to have – diverse implications within the cultural contexts considered in this study. Although these terms will be fleshed out more fully in Chapter 1, the shifting nature of class categories is an important factor to bear in mind when building a sociohistorical narrative that draws on discourses from two distinct cultural contexts in the early twentieth century. In the most general Marxist sense, then, the terms 'bourgeois' and 'elite' are used in this book to refer to those who had the means to production as well as to those controlled the means of coercion, as well as those 'middle- and upper-class women who had the independence and the means to pursue their interests and desires'.[62] Particularly in terms of the German context, this category also includes those women who belonged to the realm of the *Bildungsbürgertum*, which comprised individuals who had achieved the required educational and cultural standard that enabled them to access the social circles of the bourgeoisie, even if they lacked the associated financial means of this group. However, with growing numbers of people being engaged as technical and clerical workers following the First World War, the 'homogenous social character' of what was known as the 'middle classes' had already been largely eroded in Germany by the 1920s.[63] Yet, even within this term, numerous distinctions could still be made. For example, the positions of sales girl and office personnel, as Helen Boak contends, were largely reserved for lower working-class girls, while administrative and bureaucratic roles, which demanded a higher level of education, were taken up by lower-middle and middle-class women who considered this kind of work less 'demeaning'.[64] The German proletariat, who, in the broadest sense, sold physical labour for economic gain is the most underrepresented in studies of queer history. Although working-class women appear only infrequently in the literary and medical discourses represented in this volume, I hope to offer significant glimpses of them in the study of magazines aimed at (queer) women in Chapters 3 and 4.

In the Netherlands, the upper-class structure of the late nineteenth century was modelled largely on the German *Bürgertum*. The *haute bourgeoisie*, as Evert Hofstee explains, consisted of those individuals with exceptional wealth – which was protected largely through 'inward' marriages between the nobility and other wealthy families – and those with honourable representative functions. The middle-class category in the Netherlands, if indeed it can be described as such, became much broader in the twentieth century and shows similar splinters to those described in the German situation. Ruptures were formed primarily between what Hofstee defines as the 'old middle class' and the 'new middle class'. The old middle class consisted of those families who worked in agriculture, commerce and industry, whose understanding of wealth 'in terms of property' can be considered a class-unifying factor. However, levels of education and wealth varied considerably within this category. Unlike the old guard, the 'new middle class' understood wealth in terms of material gain. There was little 'professional heredity' within families belonging to the new middle class, who worked in industries supported by technological advancement and increasing levels of education. The porous nature each of these so-called class distinctions is acknowledged by Hofstee, who grants that: 'It is possible that anyone [can belong] to the upper old middle class by profession, but that he [sic] is a nobleman by birth and a member of the upper new middle class by education.'[65] In terms of hard labour, distinctions were made in the Netherlands primarily between skilled and unskilled labourers, with the former receiving a 'monthly salary' and the latter receiving 'a weekly wage'. Yet, as will be outlined in Chapter 1, it is perhaps better not to employ rigid class categories when discussing subjects and citizens in the Netherlands. Indeed, as Peter van Rooden maintains, 'during the better part of the 20th century ... religion was probably a more important aspect of social identity than class or region'.[66] Certainly, the concept of pillarization – that is, the social segmentation of Dutch social, political and cultural life in accordance with political belief and/or religious denomination – played a much larger role in the structuring of Dutch society than class categories. For this reason, the discussion concerning Dutch discourses in this book will focus much less on class distinctions and will instead centralize the religious and political structuring of the 'pillars' in which these discourses emerged.

The discourses that shaped – and, in turn, were shaped by – the desires and femininities mentioned above in the early twentieth century have been rudimentarily distinguished in this book under the rubrics of *sociomedical*, *community* and *literary* discourses. Although the importance of visual culture to the creation of a queer aesthetic during this period cannot be overemphasized, the historical documents examined in this book are first and foremost textual.[67] Complementing the terminological fluidity I adopt in this study, I suggest that the discourses I examine should not be considered discrete categories, but genres that necessarily overlap and intersect. Undoubtedly, it is precisely these imbrications that are of most interest to this project. Thus, the term 'discourse' will be applied in this book in a broadly Foucauldian sense. In other words, I consider discourse to be a way of constituting knowledge about a specific subject – in this instance, knowledge about sexual pleasures and desires, as well as sexual and gendered subjects – and a process that is invariably linked to considerations of power and 'Truth'. The systems of meaning that are created through certain productions of knowledge ultimately gain the currency of 'Truth' and govern the ways in which our social worlds and social selves are organized (and controlled). Yet, as Foucault himself stated: 'Discourse transmits and produces power; it reinforces it, but also undermines and exposes it, renders it fragile and makes it possible to thwart.'[68] Thus, while this book cannot claim to offer a full representation of every existing textual discourse on femininity or queer desire in the interwar period, it expands on existing historical understandings of these experiences in two cultural contexts, by examining how specific expressions of these categories became possible under various regimes of power. In considering queer femininities to be sites of potential resistance to normalizing processes, gender is viewed in this volume in the most Butlerian sense – as a performative construct that becomes visible through a 'sequence of acts'.[69] The category femininity is therefore only ever deployed as shorthand for a more complex assemblage of gendered performances, as Amy Goodloe suggests, which themselves are 'situated in a web of multiple oppressions and identities'.[70] Despite the pitfalls that come with deploying the abovementioned labels and names, it must be acknowledged, as Gayle Rubin points out, that: 'Our categories are important. We cannot organize a social life, political movement, or our individual identities and desires without them. The fact that categories … never contain all the relevant "existing things" does not render them useless, only limited.'[71]

Queer Historiographical Methods

In almost forty years since the publication of van Kooten Niekerk and Wijmer's sociological study on lesbian lives in the Netherlands, approaches to writing histories of same-sex desire have undergone radical reconceptualizations, catalysed primarily by the critical interventions of queer theorists and scholars. While such early studies can be characterized by an effort to make *visible* lesbians of the past, later studies have called into question the categorizations that had hitherto seemed axiomatic. In what has since been dubbed the homosexual 'recovery agenda', literary scholars and historians such as Lillian Faderman and Brigitte Eriksson sought to uncover desires that had been hidden from mainstream historical accounts, and presented invaluable research on the diverse forms of love and friendship between women that they claimed had existed from the 'Renaissance to the present'.[72] While this teleological approach has clear disadvantages from a queer perspective, these early studies were crucial in the admission of same-sex desiring subjects into the master historical narratives from which they had been elided and, as Doan has argued, were instrumental 'in sustaining political identities and communities' at a time when historical legitimization was vital for homosexual emancipation.[73] Offering insights into the social organization of sex and desire in the past, the efforts of historians to project a universal image of lesbian experience across time and space has received considerable criticism, not least for the deployment of such narratives to achieve political ends, which traditionalists argue 'jeopardizes the historian's scholarly integrity'.[74] Not only have the scholarly integrity of recovery histories been subject to criticism, but so too have the methodological frameworks that underpin such approaches. While some opponents of minority histories have challenged the presumed existence of a universal lesbian narrative that passes over markers of race, gender and class, others have suggested that the ahistorical deployment of the category 'lesbian' neglects to account for the changing social and political implications that such classifications embody within specific historical moments.[75] Furthermore, the 'ideal of telos' that is presented in such histories through the construction of what Eve Sedgwick terms 'narratives of supersession' too easily 'conscripts past sexual arrangements to modern categories', as Valerie Traub has observed.[76] By constructing a history in which one 'model of same-sex relations is superseded by another, which may again be superseded by another', historians therefore risk 'reinforcing a dangerous consensus of knowingness about the genuinely *un*known'.[77]

One of the fundamental distinctions between queer historical approaches and 'ancestral' approaches, as Jack Halberstam contends, is that queer methods seek an 'application of what we do not know in the present to what we cannot know about the past'.[78] Based on what Sedgwick calls a 'denaturalisation of the present', Halberstam's own practice of 'perverse presentism' applies both a 'denaturalisation of the present but also an application of what we do not know in the present to what we cannot know about the past'.[79] To put this in more concrete terms and relating it back to Halberstam's own study of queer female masculinities, it is suggested that since the relationship between masculinity and lesbianism is not fully understood today, there is no way that one can claim with any certainty to *know* that a woman who presented in a masculine manner in fin-de-siècle Europe marked a type of 'proto-lesbian'. Instead, Halberstam suggests that by viewing subjects in the past through a lens of 'perverse presentism' historians might not only '[avoid] the trap of simply projecting contemporary understandings back in time', but also 'apply insights from the present to conundrums of the past'.[80] And, here, the converse almost certainly also applies. Thus, as an analytical tool and point of theoretical departure, queering as a historical method attempts to account for what Sedgwick describes as 'the open mesh of possibilities, gaps, overlaps, dissonances and resonances, lapses and excesses of meaning when the constituent elements of anyone's gender, of anyone's sexuality aren't made (or *can't be* made) to signify monolithically'.[81] Building on these ideas, Madhavi Menon's practice of 'unhistoricism', or 'homohistory', further engages with the struggle Sedgwick recognizes as inherent in the exploration of 'lapses and excesses of meaning' by insisting that 'neither past nor present is capable of a full and mutually exclusive definition'.[82] Rejecting what she terms 'the valorization of heterotemporality', which takes as its point of origin a supposedly known and stable 'present' in order to look back at the differences of the past, Menon instead favours the 'nonhetero, with all its connotations of sameness, similarity, proximity and anachronism'.[83] As can be seen from Menon's 'homohistory', Halberstam's 'perverse presentism' and Sedgwick's 'denaturalisation of the present', the methodological distinctions between queer and ancestral historiographical practices include a great deal of overlap. Certainly, the above survey should not be read as an attempt to dismiss the immeasurably valuable research that historians have undertaken under the banner of a 'recovery history' in favour of a newer and 'better' way of narrating the past. As Lisa Duggan already asserted in the powerful article 'The Discipline Problem' (1995), it is important that queer historians 'acknowledge their debt' to earlier modes of history writing, which have served to make queer historical practices possible.[84]

As the fields outlined above have developed and diversified, many scholars have taken up the call for a more hybrid approach to the historicizing of sexual subjects. In one attempt to build bridges between various methods of narrating sexual history, Carolyn Dinshaw's *Getting Medieval* (1999) points to a coalition between the premodern (roughly from the fifteenth century to the eighteenth century) and the modern (that is, the late eighteenth century onwards) by exploring how seemingly disparate 'entities past and present' can 'touch' across time.[85] The notion of 'touches', 'vibrations' and 'coalitions' that can develop between textual documents of the past and present is a useful way not only of conceptualizing historical shifts, but also for 'using ideas of the past, creating relations with the past, touching in this way the past in … efforts to build selves and communities now and into the future'.[86] Traub's chapter 'The Present Future of Lesbian Historiography' further tackles what Sedgwick termed 'narratives of supersession' and advocates a 'history that is attentive to the cyclical nature of certain recurrent sexual configurations'.[87] Sceptical of the idea that one historical form of organizing desires is displaced by another, Traub's 'cycles of salience' remain open to 'recurring patterns of identification, social statuses, behaviour, and meanings of women who erotically desired other women across large spans of time'.[88] Turning away altogether from the centralization of locating identitarian practices in the exploration of historical desires, Doan most recently proposed her model of 'queer critical history'. Like scholars such as Sedgwick and Traub before her, Doan's study highlights the dangers of seeking out sexual subjects of the past with the identitarian frameworks of the present. Drawing on both an ancestral impulse to chart the experiences of same-sex love between women across time and a Sedgwickian practice of 'denaturalising the present', Doan's model ultimately questions the efficacy of situating sexual identity as the premise for historical research into the sexual past. Suggesting instead that historians employ a practice of 'queerness-as-method' over the continual search for 'queerness-as-being', Doan's methodological approach recognizes the importance of the impulse to explore historical sexual desires, yet promotes a distancing from our contemporary sexual categories to describe what we cannot know. In terms of the practices of this book, the contention that queer femininities have been overlooked largely suggests that this project forms part of a recovery agenda. Moreover, as this study is motivated by the devaluing of the feminine from the historical past, I must concede further that this study might also be considered what Carla Freccero terms 'a political project for the present'.[89] Yet, while I duly acknowledge my debts to 'ancestral' approaches of narrating sexual history, the methodological approaches of this project remain unequivocally queer. By placing historical survey and archival research alongside literary and intertextual analysis, this study aims to provide multiple points of entry from which to examine historical desires that I consider to be often contradictory and always in flux. Furthermore, by reading queerly for the silences and omissions that have become characteristic of specifically feminine same-sex desires, this book hopes to remain open to 'the gaps, overlaps, dissonances and resonances' that may have informed the ways in which feminine women organized their desires for other women in the past.[90]

Setting the Parameters for Historical Research

As David Halperin has suggested, the concept of human sexuality is 'a distinctly modern production'.[91] However, exactly what characterizes the supposed caesura between the emergence of 'sexual modernity' and the 'premodern' sexual world has achieved little scholarly consensus. For some historians, such as Rictor Norton and Randolph Trumbach, the establishment of a network of molly houses in the eighteenth century can already be classed as evidence of the origins of a modern (homo)sexual subculture. For others, such as Faderman and Smith-Rosenberg, early nineteenth-century romantic friendships must still be considered 'premodern' sexual formations, given the distinctly 'modern' impulse to categorize sexual desires that took place in the second half of the nineteenth century. Yet others have argued that one must return to the 'lesbian-like' medieval woman-woman relationships visible in Judith Bennett's research to identify what Noreen Giffney, Michelle Sauer and Diane Watt term the 'lesbian premodern'.

Foucault's oft-cited contention that sexuality came to be considered the 'truth of our being' at the end of the nineteenth century has been taken up widely by scholars of sexuality, and continues to influence the way in which we conceive of our sociosexual lives. The centrality of German-language sexological discourses to this project of sexual codification has been noted in several recent studies, including Robert Deam Tobin's *Peripheral Desires: The German Discovery of Sex* (2015), which charts the emergence of new vocabulary and science of human sexuality within German-speaking Western Europe, and Robert Beachy's *Gay Berlin: Birthplace of a Modern Identity* (2014), which situates the German capital more specifically as the sexual homeland of modern identity politics. Yet, while many scholars have agreed with Foucault's thesis, there are those who propose revisions to the 'birthdate' of modern sexuality and contest the power Foucault accords to discourses of the male voices of sexual science. George Chauncey, for example, cautions scholars who assume that historical subjects uncritically internalized the discourses of sexual science, and observes that those who adopt the arguments of the latter give 'inordinate power to ideology as an autonomous social force ... oversimplify the complex dialectic between social conditions, ideology, and consciousness which produced gay identities, and ... belie the evidence of preexisting subcultures and identities'.[92] Susan Lanser also engages critically with Foucault's work, by examining 'modernity' through the lens of the Sapphic in *The Sexuality of History* (2014). Conceiving of modernity as 'the instantiation of the Sapphic within a logic of possibility', Lanser foregrounds female same-sex desire within the historiographic endeavour to document experiences of modernity.[93] Although Lanser's study of Sapphic modernity spans the longue durée between the late sixteenth century and the mid-nineteenth century, her inversion of Foucault's historical framework is still a useful way to engage with the emergence of female sexual identities and desires across cultural borders in the early twentieth century. In terms of the aims of this current project, what Lanser terms a 'Sapphic episteme' might be divided into the categories 'available as object' and 'present as sexual subject'.[94]

Through my examination of multiple textual discourses, it becomes possible to chart which knowledges enabled a logic of 'woman+woman' to emerge in my chosen social milieus, particularly in the sense of a self-defining sexual subject, which is clearly visible in Germany – both through the periodicals and literary discourses written for and by queer women – but not in the Netherlands. Indeed, as Jeffrey Weeks suggests, sexuality 'only exists through its social forms and social organization', which also means that discourses that facilitated the emergence of knowledges about queer desire 'for good and for ill' in Germany would be likely to have been received differently, and employed to different ends, in the Netherlands.[95]

In creating the timeline for this research project, too, it quickly became evident that attempting to demarcate strict temporal boundaries across cultural borders for the emergence of discourses about queer desires was at best impracticable and at worst paradoxical to the aims of this project. It is for this reason that I divided my timeline into two. First, in looking at the way in which queer feminine women became available 'as objects', I consider a range of discourses that emerged from 1864 to 1939 in order to account for the shifts in sexological thinking, as well as the divergences that existed between the development of German and Dutch sociomedical discourses. Second, in looking at queer feminine women as sociosexual subjects, I focus on texts published between 1919 and 1940, and therefore write mostly of the interwar period. Of course, this is not to say that women were not engaged in philosophical or literary considerations pertaining to their desires prior to 1919 – only that the changes in the gendered landscape after the First World War resulted in the development of a range of sexual subcultures within which such discourses proliferated as never before, making this period of particular relevance and interest to this project. The violent implications of the Nazi regime on the organization of female same-sex desires has had to be considered beyond the remit of this study, although the relationship between fascism and queer femininity would no doubt offer vital insights to the ways in which same-sex desires were configured in times of conflict, given the prominence and significance accorded to femininity during this time.

Although invested in the cultural contextualization of the logics that enabled women to attach labels and names to their queer longings, this study is not concerned with pinpointing *when* the logic 'woman+woman' became available in German and Dutch contexts. Rather, the underlying assumption throughout this book will be that such a logic might *not* have been available to women and that they may have experienced their desires in ways that are beyond our current understandings. However, given the intensified interest in categorizing desires at the end of the nineteenth century in Germany, Part I of this book will be concerned with plotting the ways in which queer feminine woman became available as *objects* of study. Yet, the chief focus of this volume will be on how queer feminine women became present as *subjects* through textual productions published by, for and about queer persons. To tackle the issues outlined in this introduction, this book has been structured into three main parts. Each part will contain an extended introduction that will contextualize the historical documents under analysis. Given that sexuality, as Jeffrey Weeks suggests, can largely be considered a 'fictional unity' that is 'a product of social and historical forces', Chapter 1 will plot the development of Amsterdam and Berlin into modern urban centres, and will chart the 'existential possibilities' that were available to feminine women in this period 'beyond the roles of wife and mother'.[96] This will include accounts of the queer subcultures that existed in Amsterdam and Berlin, as well as a textual mapping of sexual 'topographies' that developed in each city. In Chapter 2, the outline of sociocultural discourses of desire will be complemented by a summary of the emergence of a *scientia sexualis*. Here I will consider specifically the role that sexual science played in the discursive construction of knowledge about queer feminine desires. Looking more closely at the conflicting 'regimes of truth' that were produced in sexological studies, this discussion will lay the groundwork for Part II of this book, which narrows its focus to an examination of the sociocultural and medicolegal discourses that became visible in queer periodicals. In Part II, I will focus on the degree to which the social norms and sexological narratives discussed in Part I were contested and revised by those who actively partook in the existing sexual communities in Amsterdam and Berlin. By examining the ways in which queer femininities were depicted across community publications, Part II will contribute to a strand of queer scholarship that, as Joanne Hollows suggests, challenges 'the idea that the "feminine" is inherently worthless, trivial, and politically conservative'.[97] Looking at the magazines *The Girlfriend* and *Women's Love* in Chapter 3, the role that feminine woman played in sexological articles, literary contributions and social commentaries printed in the magazines will be discussed, as well as the role that femininity played in the politics and the fissures that divided Berlin's Sapphic subculture. Given the absence of queer periodicals for and by women in Dutch contexts, Chapter 4 will focus on two magazines that sat at the heart of Protestant and Catholic women's communities, *The Young Woman* (*De jonge vrouw* 1924–35) and *Beatrijs* (*Beatrice* 1939–67), as well as two short-lived magazines produced by queer men that emerged during the interwar era: *We* (*Wij*, 1932) and *The Right to Live* (*Levensrecht* 1940–47). Looking at the links between magazines and organizations that valued masculine principles and ideals, further suggestions will be made about what the absence of queerness and femininity from these community discourses might tell us about the construction of queer female desire in the Netherlands during this period.

In Part III, the ways in which queer femininity became visible in literary writing by German and Dutch women authors will be examined. Considering the queer feminine women in the position of both 'object' and 'subject', I argue that it is possible to assess the influence of sexological discourses on women's writing, while also appreciating the ways in which women writers challenged contemporary discourses about love between women by presenting their own conceptualizations and imaginings of queer femininity. Chapter 5 will therefore look at the role of the feminine 'object' in Eva Raedt-de Canter's *Boarding School* (*Internaat*, 1930) and Christa

Winsloe's *The Girl Manuela* (*Das Mädchen Manuela*, 1933), and will explore the significance of erotic maternal feminine figures in stories of adolescent queer female desires. As a counterpoint to the previous chapter's engagement with tomboy longings, Chapter 6 will offer an insight into novels that placed the feminine woman at the centre of the narrative framework. Focusing on the importance of creating hierarchies of 'acceptable' desire in these novels, this final chapter will investigate the queer feminine woman as a 'nonlesbian' subject. When concluding this volume, I will weigh up the shifts taking place across the texts examined in Part II and Part III to consider what such writings might reveal to present-day readers about the overlaps and distinctions between the discourses examined in this study across cultural borders and time.

Notes

1. Indeed, as I will mention later, a cultural image for female queerness only developed after the sexual revolution of the 1960s and 1970s, during which there was a revival of the 1920s aesthetic with musical films such as *Thoroughly Modern Millie* (1967) and *Cabaret* (1972), as well as renewed stage performances of earlier queer 'boarding school' novels such as *Olivia* (1949) and *The Girl Manuela* (1933).
2. Trans.: 'Een stilzwijgende samenzwering'. Judith Schuyf, *Een stilzwijgende samenzwering: Lesbische vrouwen in Nederland 1920–1970* (The Hague: IISG, 1994).
3. Trans.: 'die männliche Seele im weiblichen Busen'. Richard Krafft-Ebing, *Psychopathia Sexualis mit besonderer Berücksichtigung der konträren Sexualempfindung. Eine medizinisch-gerichtliche Studie* für Ärzte und Juristen (Stuttgart: Ferdinand Enke, 1907), p. 297.
4. Emphasis in original. Judith Schuyf, 'Lesbian Emancipation in the Netherlands', in A.X. Naerssen (ed.), *Gay Life in Dutch Society* (New York: Harrington Park Press, 1987), p. 21.
5. Laura Doan, *Disturbing Practices: History, Sexuality, and Women's Experience of Modern War*, (Chicago: University of Chicago Press, 2013), p. 160.
6. Julian Carter, 'On Mother-Love: History, Queer Theory and Nonlesbian Identity', *Journal of the History of Sexuality* 14(1–2) (2005), 107–38 (at p. 108).
7. Doan, *Disturbing Practices*, p. 90.
8. Not only does the journal *Men and Masculinities* have no *Women and Femininities* equivalent, but there has also been little interest in taking up the subject of queer femininities in the German or Dutch historical contexts. For more on historical masculinities, see, for example: Jack Halberstam, *Female Masculinity* (Durham, NC: Duke University Press, 1998); Sarah Colvin and Peter Davies (eds), *Masculinities in German Culture* (Rochester, NY: Camden House, 2008); Katie Sutton, *The Masculine Woman in Weimar Germany* (New York: Berghahn Books, 2011); Geertje Mak, *Mannelijke vrouwen: Over de grenzen van sekse in de negentiende eeuw* (Amsterdam: Boom, 1997).

9. Sarah Cefai, 'Navigating Silences, Disavowing Femininity and the Construction of Lesbian Identities' in *Geography and Gender Reconsidered: Women and Geography Study Group* (2004), 108–17 (at p. 112). Retrieved 23 May 2022 from https://gfgrg.co.uk/wp-content/uploads/2010/08/Cefai.pdf.
10. Betty Friedan, *The Feminine Mystique* (New York: W.W. Norton & Co., 1963), p. 22.
11. Ibid., pp. 15 and 70.
12. Ibid., p. 103.
13. Ibid., p. 70.
14. Ibid., p. 365.
15. Ibid., p. 395.
16. Making recourse to the 'myth of the mannish lesbian', Friedan effectively forecloses any possibility of lesbians or queer women being engaged in the project of femininity or feminism. See: Esther Newton, 'The Mythic Mannish Lesbian: Radclyffe Hall and the New Woman', *Signs* 9(4) (1984) 557–75.
17. See, for example, the foundational work of Elizabeth Lapovsky Kennedy and Madeline Davis, *Boots of Leather, Slippers of Gold: The History of a Lesbian Community* (New York: Routledge, 1993).
18. The Radicalesbians initially termed their group the 'Lavender Menace' as a clap back to Friedan's rebuke. They then changed the name to 'Lesbian Liberation', before finally settling on Radicalesbians. See: Linda Rapp, 'Radicalesbians'. Retrieved 7 April 2022 from http://www.glbtqarchive.com/ssh/radicalesbians_S.pdf.
19. Radicalesbians, 'The Woman-Identified Woman' (1970), p. 3. Retrieved 7 April 2022 from https://repository.duke.edu/dc/wlmpc/wlmms01011.
20. Ibid., p. 2.
21. This, as well as the notion of the inseparability of racism, sexism and homophobia, was later built on by Audre Lorde: 'For the master's tools will never dismantle the master's house. They may allow us to temporarily beat him at his own game, but they will never allow us to bring about genuine change.' See Audre Lorde, 'The Master's Tools Will Never Dismantle the Master's House', in Reina Lewis and Sara Mills (eds), *Feminist Postcolonial Theory: A Reader* (Edinburgh: Edinburgh University Press, 2003), p. 27.
22. Radicalesbians, 'The Woman-Identified Woman', p. 3.
23. Biddy Martin, *Femininity Played Straight: The Significance of Being a Lesbian* (New York: Routledge, 1996), p. 3.
24. Newton, 'The Mythic Mannish Lesbian', p. 557.
25. Linda Strega, 'The Big Sell-out: Lesbian Femininity', *Lesbian Ethics* 1(3) (1985), 73–84.
26. In 2017, Strega republished her article on a fellow activist's blog and included a highly problematic paragraph that suggests that parents force 'transgenderism' upon tomboy girls who 'resist femininity' rather than 'accept her as a young Butch or a Lesbian'. See https://bevjoradicallesbian.wordpress.com/2017/07/27/the-big-sell-out-lesbian-femininity-by-linda-strega (retrieved 7 April 2022)
27. Ibid.
28. Madeline Davis 'Epilogue, Nine Years Later', in Joan Nestle (ed.), *The Persistent Desire* (Boston: Alyson Publications, 1992), p. 270.
29. Mykel Johnson 'Butchy Femme', in Nestle (ed.), *The Persistent Desire*, p. 397.
30. Ibid., pp. 397–98.
31. Martin, *Femininity Played Straight*, p. 73.
32. Danae Clark, 'Commodity Lesbianism', in Corey K Creekmur and Alexander Doty (eds), *Out in Culture: Gay, Lesbian and Queer Essays on Popular Culture* (Durham, NC: Duke University Press, 1995), pp. 484–500.

33. Ann M. Ciasullo, 'Making Her (In)Visible: Cultural Representations of Lesbianism and the Lesbian Body in the 1990s', *Feminist Studies* 27(3) (2001), 577–608 (at p. 605).
34. Here, one need only think of the now-famous cover image for *Vanity Fair* in which hyperfeminine, scantily clad, 'straight' Cindy Crawford straddles queer, masculine-of-centre musician k.d. lang, as the former leans in to shave off lang's fake foam beard. Toying with the notion of queer femininity, Crawford is ostensibly heterosexual. However, Lang's performance of masculinity is considered undoubtedly queer. It is also interesting to note that this suggestion was not considered from the alternative perspective – that is, that heterosexual women were increasingly indistinguishable from *lesbian* women, as was the case during the moral and sexual panics during the interwar era. See Ciasullo, 'Making Her (In)Visible', p. 602.
35. Rosanne Kennedy, 'The Gorgeous Lesbian in LA Law: The Present Absence?', in Diane Hamer and Belinda Budge (eds), *The Good, the Bad, and the Gorgeous* (London: Pandora Press, 1994), p. 141.
36. Joan Nestle, 'The Femme Question' in Nestle (ed.), *The Persistent Desire*, p. 140.
37. Of course, as well as her more general desire for/interest in woman-ness. Lisa M. Walker, 'How to Recognize a Lesbian: The Cultural Politics of Looking like What You Are', *Signs* 18(4) (1993), 866–90 (at pp. 881–82).
38. Kim Akass and Janet McCabe suggest even more strongly that 'the fact that the series was renewed for a second season only days after its first episode premiered in January 2004 is partly attributable to the fact that it did *not* show the full diversity of the gay community'. See Kim Akass and Janet McCabe, *Reading 'The L Word': Outing Contemporary Television* (London: I.B. Taurus, 2006), p. 4; Susan J. Wolfe and Lee Ann Roripaugh, 'Feminine Beauty and the Male Gaze in The L-Word', *MP: An Online Feminist Journal* 1(4) (2006), 1–7 (at p. 5).
39. Walker, 'How to Recognize a Lesbian', pp. 881–82.
40. As Hemmings suggests, such privileges might include the queer feminine woman's unrestricted licence to traditional women's spaces, her ability to choose whether to disclose her sexual identity, and her embodiment of a gender and sexuality that is read and accepted as 'normal'. Yet, the perceived inequity between the ways in which the 'butch' and 'femme' women are valued in and by society has historically led to a dismissal of the issues faced by queer feminine women, such as sexual objectification, their exclusion from queer circles and their being held to the unrealistic societal standards that accompany enactments of 'normative' femininity. See Clare Hemmings, *Bisexual Spaces: A Geography of Sexuality and Gender* (New York: Routledge, 2007), p. 117.
41. Judy Berman, '*The L Word: Generation Q* Is a Valiant Effort. But the Show Is a Time Capsule That Should Have Stayed Buried' (2019). Retrieved 7 April 2022 from https://time.com/5744710/the-l-word-generation-q-review.
42. See, for example, Jennifer Burke (ed.), *Visible: A Femmethology* (Ypsilanti, MI: Homofactus Press, 2009); Hannah McCann, *Queering Femininity: Sexuality, Feminism and the Politics of Presentation* (New York: Routledge, 2017); Rhea Ashley Hoskin and Katerina Hirschfeld, 'Beyond Aesthetics: A Femme Manifesto', *Atlantis: Critical Studies in Gender Culture, and Social Justice* 39(1) (2018), 85–87; Amber Jamilla Musser, *Sensual Excess: Queer Femininity and Brown Jouissance* (New York: New York University Press, 2018).
43. Cefai, 'Navigating Silences', p. 113.
44. Nestle, 'The Femme Question', p. 140.
45. Scholars such as Manfred Herzer, Ralph Dose, James Steakley, Claudia Schoppmann, Ilse Kokula, Christiane Leidinger and Marti Lybeck, among others, have contributed

influential narratives to the historical discussion of same-sex desire in the German contexts.
46. Scott Spector et al. (eds), *After the History of Sexuality: German Genealogies with and Beyond Foucault* (New York: Berghahn Books, 2012) and Clayton J. Whisnant, *Queer Identities and Politics in Germany: A History* (New York: Harrington Park Press, 2016) being only two of the more recent studies that adopt a queer methodological approach.
47. See, for example: Dirk Jaap Noordam, *Riskante relaties: Vijf eeuwen homoseksualiteit in Nederland 1233–1733* (Hilversum: Verloren, 1995); Rudolf Dekker and Lotte van de Pol *Vrouwen in mannenkleren: de geschiedenis van een tegendraadse traditie Europa 1500–1800* (Amsterdam: Wereldbibliotheek, 1989); Theo van der Meer, *De wesentlijke sonde van sodomie en andere vuyligheeden. Sodomietenvervolgingen in Amsterdam 1730–1811* (Amsterdam: Tabula, 1984); Arend H. Huussen, 'Sodomy in the Dutch Republic during the 18th Century', *Eighteenth Century Life* 9 (1985), 169–78; Peter Altena and Myriam Everard (eds), *Onbreekbare burgerharten. De historie van Betje Wolff en Aagje Deken* (Nijmegen: Ventilate, 2004); Geertje Mak, *Mannelijke vrouwen: Over de grenzen van sekse in de negentiende eeuw* (Amsterdam: Boom, 1997).
48. Marti M. Lybeck, *Desiring Emancipation: New Women and Homosexuality in Germany 1890–1933* (Albany, NY: SUNY Press, 2014), p. 85.
49. Ibid., p. 156.
50. Ibid., p. 2.
51. Trans.: '… Ik had haar nooit zo gezien, want ze was echt een jongetje vóór die tijd. Wát ben jij? Vroeg ik haar. Ik ben nu een meisje geworden, zei ze, want ik heb zo'n leuke vriendin. Meid, ik moest weer helemaal omschakelen.' Anja van Kooten Niekerk and Sacha Wijmer, *Verkeerde Vriendschap: Lesbisch leven in de Jaren 1920–1960* (Amsterdam: Feministische Uitgeverij Sara, 1985), p. 141.
52. Trans: 'in de ene relatie was ze "vrouwelijk", in de andere "mannelijk"'. Ibid., p. 69.
53. Trans.: 'Nadat de relatie was afgelopen, zag Adri geen reden om "femme" te blijven en keerde zij terug naar haar oude vertrouwde mannelijke rol'. Ibid., p. 141.
54. Trans.: 'dat is een van de dingen die ik later heb leren ontdekken, da de erg mannelijk uitziende vrouwen, die dan ook nog prachtig die rol speelden, zich vrijwel altijd ontpopten als de meest vrouwelijke vrouwen die er waren, maar dan in een heel andere richting, namelijk in de vorm van verzorging, met kinderen omgaan enzovoort'. Ibid., p. 122.
55. By employing Barbara Ponse's theory of a 'gay trajectory' as a measurement of how women identified their desires in the past, Schuyf ultimately suggests that same-sex desires for women in the early twentieth century invariably resulted in a fixed sexual identity that was referred to using the category 'lesbian'. Schuyf, *Een stilzwijgende samenzwering*, p. 363.
56. Doan, *Disturbing Practices*, p. 144.
57. Ibid., p. 45.
58. Furthermore, as both the 'lesbian continuum' and the 'lesbian-like' romantic friendships have been deployed in ways that elide the erotic impulse between women, I do not consider them to be suitable categories for a study explicitly concerning desire and eroticism between women.
59. David Halperin, *Saint Foucault: Towards a Gay Hagiography* (New York: Oxford University Press, 1995), p. 62.
60. Corie Hammers, 'The Queer Logics of Sex/Desire and the "Missing" Discourse of Gender', *Sexualities* 18(7) (2015), 838–58.
61. Lee Edelman, 'Queer Theory Unstating Desire', *GLQ: A Journal of Lesbian and Gay Studies* 2(4) (1995), 343–46 (at p. 345).

62. Eric Weitz, *Weimar Germany: Promise and Tragedy* (Princeton: Princeton University Press, 2007), p. 307.
63. Maarten Prak, 'The Dutch Republic as a Bourgeois Society' *BMGN: Low Countries Historical Review* 2(3) (2010), 107–39.
64. Helen Boak, *Women in the Weimar Republic* (Manchester: Manchester University Press, 2015), p. 150.
65. Evert Willem Hofstee and Gerrit Andries Kooy, 'Class Structure in the Netherlands.' Transcript of a lecture given at the 50th Anniversary Meeting of the American Sociological Society in Washington DC, 2 September 1955. Retrieved 7 April 2022 from https://edepot.wur.nl/38393.
66. Peter van Rooden, 'Long-Term Religious Developments in the Netherlands 1750–2000', in Hugh McLeod and Werner Ustorf (eds), *The Decline of Christendom in Western Europe, 1750–2000* (Cambridge: Cambridge University Press, 2002), p. 12.
67. For a more comprehensive discussion of the role of queer visual culture in the construction of sexual identities during the interwar era, see: Richard Dyer, *Now You See It: Studies in Lesbian and Gay Film* (New York: Routledge, 1990); Alice A. Kuzniar, *The Queer German Cinema* (Stanford: Stanford University Press, 2000); Christoph Lorey and John L. Plews (eds), *Queering the Canon: Defying Sights in German Literature and Culture* (Columbia, SC: Camden House, 1998); Christopher Reed, *Art and Homosexuality: A History of Ideas* (Oxford: Oxford University Press, 2011); Claude Summers, *The Queer Encylopedia of the Visual Arts* (San Francisco: Cleis Press, 2004).
68. Michel Foucault, *The History of Sexuality. Volume I: An Introduction*, trans. Robert Hurley (London: Penguin, 1984), pp. 100–1.
69. See Judith Butler, *Gender Trouble* (New York: Routledge, 1990).
70. Amy Goodloe, 'Queer Theory: Another "Battle of the Sexes?"' Retrieved 7 April 2022 from http://amygoodloe.com/papers/lesbian-feminism-and-queer-theory-another-battle-of-the-sexes.
71. Gayle Rubin, 'Of Catamites and Kings: Reflections on Butch, Gender and Boundaries' in Nestle (ed.), *The Persistent Desire*, p. 480.
72. See, for example, Lillian Faderman, *Surpassing the Love of Men: Romantic Friendship and Love between Women from the Renaissance to the Present* (London: Women's Press, 1981); Lillian Faderman and Brigitte Eriksson (eds), *Lesbian-Feminism in Turn-of-the-Century Germany* (Tallahassee, FL: The Naiad Press, 1980).
73. Doan, *Disturbing Practices*, p. x.
74. However, such criticisms, as John Boswell identifies, overlook the undeniably political impulse of the original erasure of queer desire and other minority experiences from mainstream history writings, which itself cannot have stemmed from a purely scholarly interest in 'narrating history'. See John Boswell, 'Revolutions, Universals, and Sexual Categories', in Martin Duberman et al. (eds), *Hidden from History: Reclaiming the Gay and Lesbian Past* (New York: Meridian, 1989), pp. 17–37; Thomas Piontek, *Queering Gay and Lesbian Studies* (Urbana: University of Illinois Press, 2006), p. 7.
75. Halberstam, *Female Masculinity*, p. 54.
76. Valerie Traub, *Thinking Sex with the Early Moderns* (Philadelphia: University of Pennsylvania Press, 2016), p. 61.
77. Eve Kosofsky Sedgwick, *Epistemology of the Closet* (Berkeley: University of California Press, 2008), p. 45.
78. Halberstam, *Female Masculinity*, p. 53.
79. As outlined in *Epistemology of the Closet*, Sedgwick describes the process of a 'denaturalisation of the present' not only as an attempt to trouble the categories of

gender and sexuality that are often taken for granted, but also to 'render less destructively presumable homosexuality as we know it today' (at p. 48).
80. Halberstam, *Female Masculinity*, pp. 52–53.
81. Eve Kosofsky Sedgwick, *Tendencies* (London: Routledge, 1994), p. 8.
82. Madhavi Menon, *Unhistorical Shakespeare: Queer Theory in Shakespearean Literature and Film* (New York: Palgrave Macmillan, 2008), p. 3.
83. Jonathan Goldberg and Madhavi Menon, 'Queering History', *PMLA* 120(5) (2005), 1608–17 (at p. 1609).
84. Lisa Duggan, 'The Discipline Problem: Queer Theory Meets Gay and Lesbian History', *GLQ: A Journal of Lesbian and Gay Studies* 2(3) (1995), 179–91 (at p. 189).
85. Carolyn Dinshaw, *Getting Medieval: Sexualities and Communities, Pre- and Postmodern* (Durham, NC: Duke University Press, 1999), p. 12.
86. Ibid., p. 206.
87. Valerie Traub, 'The Present Future of Lesbian Historiography', in Noreen Giffney et al. (eds), *The Lesbian Premodern: The New Middle Ages* (New York: Palgrave Macmillan, 2011), p. 123.
88. Ibid., p. 125.
89. Carla Freccero, 'The Queer Time of the Lesbian Premodern', in Giffney et al. (eds), *The Lesbian Premodern*, p. 62.
90. Sedgwick, *Tendencies*, p. 8.
91. David Halperin, *How to Do the History of Homosexuality* (Chicago: University of Chicago Press, 2002), p. 29.
92. George Chauncey, 'From Sexual Inversion to Homosexuality: Medicine and the Changing Conceptualization of Female Deviance', *Salmagundi* 59 (1983), 114–46 (at p. 115).
93. Susan Lanser, *The Sexuality of History: Modernity and the Sapphic 1565–1830* (Chicago: University of Chicago Press, 2014), p. 28.
94. Ibid., pp. 18–21.
95. Jeffrey Weeks, *Sexuality*, 4th edn (New York: Routledge, 2017), p. 34.
96. Ibid., p. 11; Kirsten Leng, 'Permutations of the Third Sex: Sexology, Subjectivity, and Antimaternalist Feminism at the Turn of the Twentieth Century', *Signs: Journal of Women in Culture and Society* 40(1) (2014), 227–54 (at p. 228).
97. Joanne Hollows, *Feminism, Femininity and Popular Culture* (Manchester: Manchester University Press, 2000), p. 33.

Part I
SOCIOMEDICAL DISCOURSES

Chapter 1

SEX AND THE CITIES
Mapping Queer Feminine Desires

Everyone should go at least once to Berlin! ... But one cannot get about here without a guide. Perhaps here least of all. Theseus would have never dared venture into the Labyrinth without Ariadne's thread. And what was the Labyrinth in comparison to Berlin at night, in comparison to the metropolis of pleasure; equally confusing in its light and in its dark?!
—Curt Moreck, *Guide through Depraved Berlin*, 1931[1]

We are back in 1913 ... People are immensely respectable. No sign of crisis or war ... Towns too big of course, Amsterdam a swollen stone monster ... Not a beggar, not a slum. Even solid wealth ... A feeling that Holland is a perfectly self respecting rather hard featured but individual middle aged woman. Conventions of 1913. No women smoking or driving cars.
—Virginia Woolf, *The Diary of Virginia Woolf*, 1935

By the time that popular cultural writer Konrad Haemmerling (1888–1957) had published his *Guide through Depraved Berlin* under the pseudonym Curt Moreck in 1931, Berlin was already attracting vast numbers of sexual tourists from across the globe. For those keen to experience the freedoms of a city that catered seemingly to every taste and predilection, Haemmerling's trendy guidebook detailed an alluring array of dance halls, cabarets, massage parlours and saunas, and provided retellings of the sensational stories that made up the city's infamous erotic underbelly. With a rival to be found during the interbellum arguably only in Paris, the German capital quickly secured a reputation in Western Europe as a 'Metropolis of Pleasure'. Yet, while this moniker may call to mind images of unrestrained Dionysian landscapes, the phrase should prompt us further to consider the question of precisely whose pleasure the city was catering for and by whom such pleasures were defined – and controlled. Indeed, by the early 1920s, the visibility of the 'modern' German woman in the workplace, and on the streets, had become a source of great concern for many conservative social commentators who were struggling with changing gendered norms following the First World War. Moral alarmists were soon to suggest that an increased commercial interest in bob-haired flappers and feminine dandies would result in the germination of its (un)natural corollary: increased sexual deviance. Fanning the flames of this sexual panic, the suggestion of same-sex desire between women was also developing a certain cultural cachet within bohemian circles, and contemporaries were speaking of a 'lesbian wave' that was supposedly rolling over the city by the mid-1920s.[2] In fact, Berlin's Sapphic subculture caused such a stir that writer Ruth Margarete Roellig (1878–1969) published a guidebook entitled *Berlin's Lesbian Women* (*Berlins lesbische Frauen*, 1928), which provided a detailed mapping of the city's Sapphic spaces, pre-dating Haemmerling's own topographical renderings of Berlin's sexual sites by three years.

As a concentrated microcosm of the disastrous and painful results of the First World War, Berlin bore witness to some of the worst effects of the enduring political and economic instability of the Weimar era. Yet, arguably in response to this trauma, the city quickly rose as a hub of artistic and intellectual production, as well as a site for the establishment of sexual commerce and erotic subcultures. Across the border, in a country that had recently established a unique policy of 'political compromise', Amsterdam was another site characterized by social and political paradoxes following the war. While the capital seemed poised to lead the Netherlands into an outward-looking and international future in the first decades of the twentieth century, a marked political shift favouring the confessional parties served instead to make the city more insular and conservative in its politics. Comparatively backward in its morally conservative provinciality, Amsterdam, with its carefully constructed canal systems, mirrored remarkably few of the entertainment venues that were titillating tourists in Berlin. Rather than experiencing a period of liberation following the First World War, the desires of citizens of the Netherlands were structured, as Jet Bussemaker contends, by an 'increasingly severe sexual morality', which placed the home and the family firmly at the heart of Dutch social and political life, with a forceful rejection of any 'anti-social' elements.[3] By the late 1920s, the cleft between the ways in which the two cities were taking shape as sexual sites could not have been clearer. While Berlin boasted an estimated eighty bars, clubs and cafés in which women-loving-women were welcomed and approximately twelve social clubs that they could attend, same-sex desiring individuals in the Netherlands were found lamenting the lack of established queer networks in their cities.[4] As a contributor to the queer Dutch magazine *We* discussed in Chapter 4 claimed, Dutch contemporaries were often envious of the lives their German friends were leading, which they considered to be running 'so much more freely and smoothly ... than ours in our bleak country'.[5] Indeed, it was only following the loosening of the religious conservatism that lasted long into the postwar era that a period of what Elaine Showalter terms 'sexual anarchy' began to gain traction in the Netherlands. As Amsterdam café culture began to develop, there were increasing options to meet like-minded others in safe spaces. With more established meeting places existing by the 1960s, queer culture started to become a more visible part of public life for Dutch city-dwellers.[6]

Diametrically opposed as sexual cities only a century ago, Amsterdam and Berlin therefore present interesting sites of comparison for an analysis of queer feminine desires. While I will not be providing a history of queer urban development in this chapter, which has already been covered more comprehensively elsewhere, I will be offering an analysis of the political, social and economic forces in these two cities that made the creation of such spaces possible, or indeed impeded their creation, in the first instance.[7] Following a brief overview of the emergence of Berlin and Amsterdam as 'modern' municipalities, I will examine the limits of women's access to city spaces to add nuance to the narrative of the changes that took place within urban life in the face of modernity. Following this, I will offer a mapping of the sexual spaces available to queer women in Amsterdam and Berlin, and will compare the (support) networks that were available to them, considering in particular the significance accorded to femininity within such networks. Through the plotting of these spaces, I will not only highlight the sites that were of importance to queer women, but I will also chart the role that femininity played in women's access, or lack thereof, to such spaces. Finally, I will examine the ways in which pleasure was policed in Germany and the Netherlands, focusing specifically on the role of women in upholding or resisting these restrictions, and the relation of this struggle to contemporary expressions and understandings of femininity.

'A Child of War'

Prior to the establishment of the Weimar Republic, Berlin had been forced to grow quickly into its role as the heart of a recently unified German

Empire. Announced in 1871 as the capital of a new nation-state, the city experienced the onset of rapid economic and industrial growth, with workers from rural areas flocking to its urban centre in search of more lucrative forms of employment. This influx of labour, in conjunction with the earlier incorporation of the suburban districts of Wedding, Gesundbrunnen and Moabit into the city limits proper, saw Berlin soon achieve metropolitan status as a *Millionenstadt* at the turn of the twentieth century, with more citizens than ever before navigating its newly bustling streets. Such rapid population growth in the first decades of the twentieth century led to greater demand for housing, which resulted in the creation of what became known as 'rental barracks' (*Mietskaserne*) on the edges of the city. These so-called barracks housed 'the highest concentration of people per square meter in Europe', with the overcrowding of these tenements blamed for the rapid spread of diseases such as tuberculosis and typhoid, and the high density of working-class tenants linked to the violent political uprisings that shaped the cityscape in the aftermath of the First World War. Indeed, just over a decade before Haemmerling's guidebook was tempting tourists with its promotion of the vices and virtues of Berlin's entertainment venues, the German capital was one shaped by violence, political assassinations and unprecedented economic turmoil: 'a child of war, revolution and democracy'.[8]

While the first years of the Weimar era were distinguished by a struggle for economic survival and political instability, the Republic entered a period of relative economic prosperity following the Dawes Plan of 1924. With the aid of American financial streams, Berlin surfaced from its financial hardships as a 'laboratory of modernity' with technological innovation shaping its emergent consumer and leisure culture.[9] From moving assembly lines to advancements in office equipment, new life was sparked into German industry through processes of mechanization and mass production. As a consequence, much about urban life in Berlin during the mid-1920s rang with a tone of rationality, right down to the functionalist styles that became emblematic of Walter Gropius' (1883–1969) *Bauhaus* movement. Furthermore, as shopping boulevards became a more established part of the cityscape, the famous avenues on Kurfürstendamm and Tauentzienstraße bolstered a burgeoning consumer and leisure culture that brought thousands of new jobs to the city. With increasing numbers of young women taking on roles in offices and department stores, as will be discussed in the Part II, consumer culture undoubtedly exerted a discernible influence on the gendered fabric of the metropolis. Despite the heralding of an era of energetic technological innovation and the arrival of visible changes in the urban landscape following the war, access to the city continued to be regulated strictly along gendered lines. Women's experiences of public space and, accordingly, their abilities to experience pleasure within it were bound increasingly tightly to the growth of the 'discourse of violence' following the war, as well as the lived reality of violence on the streets, both political and sexual.[10]

Indeed, the brutality of the sexual acts depicted in the haunting images of Otto Dix (1891–1969) and the cinematic endeavours of Fritz Lang (1890–1976), for example, were stark reminders that city spaces remained highly contested gendered territories. The term 'sexual murder' (*Lustmord*) had already become firmly cemented in the German cultural imagination after eight women were murdered in sexually violent attacks in Bochum between 1878 and 1882. However, during the Weimar era, prolific sexual murderers such as Carl Grossmann and Fritz Haarmann, as well as the growing number of assaults that were being reported in offices and workspaces, meant that sexual violence – or, certainly, the threat thereof – had become an unavoidable part of the urban experience.[11] As Maria Tatar suggests, in the period following the First World War, the representation of mutilated female bodies in art and film was being employed as something of 'an aesthetic strategy for managing certain kinds of sexual, social, and political anxieties'.[12] Yet, as the cases of Grossmann and Haarmann suggest, this aesthetic strategy spoke equally of the very real threat that existed for women on the streets and inside the home. Indeed, as continues to be the case today more broadly, sexual violence in Berlin was not usually committed in fatal acts by unknown perpetrators, but often, as Renate Bridenthal rightly observes, by individuals known to the victim and existing as an accepted part of everyday life. In this way, as Tatar concludes, sexual violence against women in the city 'had a conspicuous presence, yet [was] also a closely guarded secret'.[13] Thus, while women in Berlin were experiencing greater freedoms and access to metropolitan space by the early 1920s (this will be discussed in more detail later on in this chapter), women's access to pleasure within the metropolis must be considered in the context of the violence, pessimism and anxiety that was shaping such urban contexts, with the female body, and its expressions of femininity, being considered as central to these social and political concerns.

A Conservative Modernity

The vision of Amsterdam in the mid-1920s offers us quite a different image than the bustling boulevards of Berlin in the years following the First World War. Industrialization had taken place comparatively late in the Dutch capital and the effects of urbanization revealed themselves only gradually. Indeed, as popular historical writer Geert Mak observes, 'if one were to be catapulted back into the Amsterdam of the middle of the nineteenth century, one would probably notice, first and foremost, a new experience of sound and silence'.[14] Following developments in transport links from 1870, the symphony of steam locomotives that Mak alludes to above grew alongside the Dutch economy, with Amsterdam experiencing something of a second Golden Age at the end of the nineteenth century, with colonial 'explorations' and global plunder affording many of the bulwarks of this economic prosperity. As a result of this increased affluence, the first real museums, art galleries and concert halls were built in the city centre, and the capital's suburbs soon became recognized as a 'bastion of bohemians'.[15] However, it was only during the final decades of the nineteenth century that national canal systems and harbours were expanded and improved with the controversial completion of the Central Station in 1889, which marked Amsterdam's position as a desirable (inter)national destination for travel and commerce. Following the establishment of new waterways within and, more importantly, to and from Amsterdam, a successful consumer culture emerged in the city.[16]

Mirroring the developments taking place across the German border, the growing demand for workers following industrialization led to the development of cheap housing for working families in the suburbs of Amsterdam. Unlike the German 'rental barracks', where poorer residents lived alongside the more affluent, the standard of living across these types of Dutch housing was invariably poor, with working families sometimes living together with others in damp and squalid cellar rooms.[17] Furthermore, in the first decades of the twentieth century, food shortages regularly resulted in riots in poorer areas. A potato shortage in Amsterdam during the First World War, for example, led to looting and social unrest in the city for several days. Following this, when a mutiny broke out among defensively mobilized Dutch soldiers posted in Amsterdam in 1918, the growing rebellious fervour culminated in what became known as the 'Red Week' (*de rode week*).[18] Around three thousand men, women and children joined the Socialist demonstrations, and violent clashes between demonstrators and police led to several civilian deaths. In contrast to Germany, this revolutionary mood soon petered out. This was due primarily to the upheaval caused by the 1918 election in which the Liberal stronghold was turned on its head. Following this election, the Liberal Union (Liberale Unie) fell out of favour, and the Social Democrats, Catholics and Protestants found themselves caught in a struggle for political power and forced to work together in fractious coalitions. These alliances, which were determined by a confessional majority, marked by the emergence of a politically and morally conservative agenda in the Netherlands – a vision of Dutch politics that remained largely unchanged until the late 1960s. Even with the expansion of the southern area of the city in 1917 pioneered by architect Hendrik Petrus Berlage (1856–1934) and the later development of West Amsterdam in 1925 by Cornelis van Eesteren (1897–1988), Amsterdam was yet to achieve the status of a 'modern metropolis' in the period immediately following the First World War. The seemingly paradoxical 'conservative modernity' that emerged during this time remained prevalent throughout the interwar era and was the result of the social and political pillarization (*verzuiling*) of Dutch society, which was already shaping the most fundamental aspects of daily life in the Netherlands. Indeed, as will become clear later on in this chapter, the vertical pluralism that structured Dutch society is essential to our understanding of the differences in the development of Amsterdam and Berlin as sexual sites. Moreover, as the processes of pillarization had specific gendered implications, as historian Mineke Bosch observes, it would be almost impossible to speak 'of a specifically Dutch trajectory of women's emancipation' or, indeed, any aspect of women's experiences of desire in the city during this period without reference to the matter of pillarization.[19]

Living Apart Together

Historian Ivo Schöffer claimed that during the first half of the twentieth century in the Netherlands, one 'only had to speak with another person for a single minute before one knew whether the other was a Christian, Catholic, Liberal or Socialist'.[20] Indeed, during a period of what Inge Bleijenbergh and Jet Bussemaker term 'institutionalized pillarization' in the Netherlands, political and religious segregation was entrenched at almost every level of social existence – from schools to trade unions, sports clubs to radio stations, and medical care to the purchase of meat and vegetables.[21] In terms of the class political differences that existed in Dutch society from the late nineteenth century – when pillarization first began to emerge as a sociopolitical phenomenon – the country could largely be divided into the following categories: the remaining nobility and political/economic elite; merchants and industrialists; white-collar workers; shopkeepers and independent craftspeople; day labourers and manual workers; and the unemployed. With respect to religious differences, Dutch society was split roughly into Roman Catholic communities, which were situated commonly in southern provinces such as Limburg and North Brabant, the Dutch Reformed and Orthodox Reformed communities, which could be found principally in the northern provinces, and a considerable minority of Dutch Jews in most large cities across the country.[22] While these political and religious groupings already existed in the late nineteenth century, the eruption of one of the longest domestic conflicts in Dutch history during this period, known as the 'School Struggle' (*de schoolstrijd*), resulted in the more formal establishment of what became recognized as pillarization.

Alongside what political scientist Arend Lijphart terms 'the franchise issue and the question of collective bargaining and the rights of labour', the 'School Struggle' was one of the great faultlines that divided Dutch society in the nineteenth century.[23] The struggle to achieve state funding for all schools, irrespective of religious denomination, in conjunction with the fight for (male) suffrage resulted in a bargaining stalemate between confessional and secular parties that was not resolved until the so-called 'Pacification' of 1917.[24] By the time a political agreement was reached, the political and religious subdivision of society had already become an inescapable feature of the Dutch sociocultural fabric. Indeed, as Bosch observes, when writing about the history of the Netherlands, pillarization must be considered the single 'most conspicuous factor of Dutch politics and society in the twentieth century'.[25] By the early 1920s, Catholic, Protestant, Social-Democratic and Liberal communities had carefully constructed their own social 'pillar' – or *zuil* – that enabled them to exist almost entirely independently from other political and religious groupings. While at a parliamentary level, political parties were forced to engage in a complex practice of compromise, consultation and coalition, the lived experiences of individuals 'on the street' rarely involved such interpillar exchanges. Yet, the close-quarters living arrangements in Amsterdam and the demographic diversity of the city complicates this image of pillarized life. Indeed, city-dwelling was characterized most often by the more polymorphous experience of 'district living' rather than the geographical religious divides mentioned above. Enhancing this urban heterogeneity were also those city communities that did not fit neatly into the Catholic, Protestant, Social-Democratic and Liberal pillars. Large Jewish communities could be found living in the areas around the Jodenbreestraat and the Oude Schans, for example, while Danish, Norwegian and Frisian sailors frequently lodged near the ports, and fairground communities resided intermittently by the Duvelshoek and along the Kalver Street. Yet, despite the existence of urban communities that were marked by their transience and refusal to be fixed within the pillared system, social segregation nonetheless remained a palpable part of Amsterdam life, irrespective of one's position within, or without, the existing pillars.

The specifically gendered ways in which the segmentation of society played out in the Netherlands, as Bussemaker keenly notes, must not be underestimated.[26] Indeed, many Dutch women in the early twentieth century, and particularly those who did not – or could not – work, were experiencing much more insular existences than Dutch men. With social lives centred primarily around the home – whether in paid or unpaid labour –

newspapers, radio stations and, later, television played an important role in keeping many Dutch women connected with developments taking place in the public sphere. Writing about the news sources available to young women during the interbellum, Anja van Kooten Niekerk and Sacha Wijmer corroborate Bussemaker's warning, as they observe that almost every source of information that entered the home was filtered through the political or religious mouthpieces of one's pillar: 'the Catholic educated girls were only allowed to tune into the KRO [Catholic Radio Broadcasting], while the Protestant girls were only allowed to listen to the NCRV [Dutch Christian Radio Association]'.[27] Even in the larger cities, the roles of many Dutch women were determined primarily by the political and religious orthodoxies of the pillar to which they belonged. The boundaries of this role could be made more, or less, inward-looking depending on the complex matrix of social and cultural factors that were bound up within one's pillar. For many Catholic women, social lives revolved around the domestic role as mother and homemaker. They were expected only to socialize only with Catholic neighbours and attend only Catholic gatherings.[28] For women within the Social-Democratic pillar, the pattern of daily life revolved heavily around the attendance of political meetings and rallies, the dissemination of party politics through pamphlets and magazines, and involvement with broader Socialist movements.

While the above description suggests that there was a 'typical' experience of life within a pillar, the ideological pluralism that existed in the Netherlands cannot be reduced so simply to homogeneous units, with crossovers emerging between religious and political leanings. For example, between Jewish workers who 'tended to identify themselves with the Socialists' or, indeed, those Catholics and Socialists who were brought together by the causes championed by the temperance movement.[29] However, even more than this, socioeconomic markers often transcended the vertical pillars of religious belief or political leaning – a distinguishing factor that became particularly apparent between the richer and poorer members of confessional communities, as acknowledged in Chapter 4. While matters of money shaped women's experiences *across* pillars, and pillars themselves were not homogeneous units, what is important to consider here is how the social segregation of Dutch society in the first half of the twentieth century narrowed the number of networks available to women in the Netherlands significantly, even in a comparatively modern urban space such as Amsterdam. While sexual violence, or the threat thereof, was certainly not absent from the urban life in the Netherlands, the dominant gendered threat perceived by social commentators of the time was that of modernity to domesticity, as will be discussed in more detail later in this volume. Moreover, access to urban space was shaped even more rigidly along the lines of religion and class than in Germany, which meant that for those women who did want to organize and meet like-minded others during this period, the offerings of contact available to them were essentially restricted to the confines of the pillar to which they belonged.[30] As we shall see, the workplace might be therefore considered a highly significant sphere for Dutch women-loving-women during the interbellum. In gainful employment, women had access to opportunities to extend familial and familiar networks through the obtainment of independent means, the creation of new connections with colleagues and, in some instances, the chance to live outside the family home.

The (Not So) Frivolous Flapper

Following the war, Germany experienced several gendered shifts across its metropolitan landscapes. Not only had the new Weimar Constitution granted men and women equal 'civil rights and obligations', but the tragic loss of life during the war also meant that women far outnumbered men in many urban spaces. According to figures published in 1924, almost two and a half million Germans had been killed during the First World War and, of the number of men who had died, over half were under the age of twenty-five.[31] When combined with the existence of an estimated 600,000 war widows, census figures indicate, as Richard Bessel notes, that a 'surplus' of women existed across all sectors of German society.[32] Yet, it was arguably within the inner-city office environment in which these demographic shifts were most profoundly felt. In his study *The Salaried Masses* (*Die Angestellten*, 1930), Siegfried Kracauer observes that approximately 3,500,000 salaried and waged employees were engaged in work across Germany by the end of the 1920s, of which 1,200,000 were women.[33] Kracauer's study concludes that the 'flooding' of women into salaried jobs in urban areas had been caused by three primary factors: the financial and societal effects of the war; the development of a broader understanding of what 'women's work' comprised; and the 'need of the new generation of women for economic independence'.[34] However, as Ute Frevert rightly points out, the figures Kracauer cites for female employees only included the number of women who entered into *gainful* employment after the war. Women had, of course, worked unpaid inside the home or as part of family businesses for centuries, and working-class women had always worked. Instead, the most interesting gendered changes, Frevert asserts, can be seen in the sectors to which women had been relocated during the war, such as engineering, chemical work and steel manufacturing.[35]

When the war came to an end, women were largely expected to leave the trade that they had recently entered. Indeed, new governmental guidelines were issued to employers in November 1918, which included advice on how best to deal with the dismissal of women workers during the demobilization process.[36] Although it was accepted that some women would have to remain in work, critics argued that they should remain only in functions that were suited to their 'nature', such as shop assistants in retail stores and other clerical roles. Yet, due to the continued shortage of male labour, the departure of women from the workplace during demobilization marked 'only a short-term downward trend'.[37] By the time of the 1925 census, it had been calculated that 1,700,000 more women were in full-time employment than had been in 1907. However, such growth must be considered in consonance with a population that had almost doubled in size over the same period. Indeed, the level of male employment across the same timeframe, as Renate Bridenthal and Claudia Koonz have demonstrated, shows similar increases to those found within female employment.[38] Therefore, the growth of the aggregate number of female workers should be considered as part of a more general upward trend in terms of employment figures following the war rather than a specific gendered development. Furthermore, white-collar work, which Kracauer suggested had seen floods of new female employees, had in fact the lowest total increase in female workers.[39] Nonetheless, white-collar work was still the fastest-growing industry across any sector in Germany and, according to the 1925 census, there were three times as many female stenographers, secretaries, clerks and typists following the war as there had been in 1907, with white-collar workers making up 30% of Berlin's total female workforce.[40] The ideal profile for such a female white-collar worker was to be found in the young, unmarried woman from a lower-middle class background, which lent itself to the supposition that femininity, defined by youth and beauty, was an essential characteristic of female success.

The image of the fashionable young urbanite, with her short skirts and even shorter haircut, was taken up enthusiastically in film and literature of the era. The commercial success of this image of the 'New Woman' meant that the figure became a popular, if highly problematized, symbol of modern German life. Employed as shorthand for a wide range of female types, the signifier 'New Woman', as Katie Sutton writes, was used to denote 'anything from rationalised worker to housewife, "new" mother to consumer, Olympic athlete to female *flâneur*'.[41] The image of a new 'boyish' type of woman in the workplace further created much anxiety around gendered roles and expectations, and, dually, created a space in which alternative models for female presentation could be explored and examined, revered or rejected. Indeed, as the boundaries of femininity were being reconfigured with women's entrance into the workplace, the cultural image of the 'New Woman', as Vibeke Rützou Petersen suggests, 'became the arena of an intricate play across the borders of both gender and class'.[42] On the subject of the modern working woman and her femininity, Konrad Haemmerling identifies in his guidebook an interesting process of symbiosis that occurred with women's entrance into office work and the development of what he terms a 'cosmetic uniform [for] the female sex'.[43] Indeed, the pressures that were placed on women's physical appearance by employers added, in many respects, further gendered layers to the conditions of women's access to city space by creating new, and increasingly unobtainable, feminine ideals. The beauty and age requirements for store assistants and office workers particularly impacted older female workers who 'were expected to dress more fashionably and appear more youthful' or risk losing their livelihoods.[44]

It was not only women's access to paid work that was limited, but also the accompanying financial dividends of their labour. Certainly, the image of the carefree female consumer that so captured the cultural imagination revealed little of the financial and social precarity experienced by many white-collar women workers during the Weimar era. Despite gender equality having been enshrined in law, women were earning on average 10% less than their male colleagues in similar positions and their monthly incomes were frequently 'below the subsistence minimum'.[45] Moreover, women received less formal training and had fewer opportunities to gain relevant experience in their field than their male colleagues, which resulted in them being paid less for their labour and receiving fewer prospects for promotion. In addition, as well as working long hours in the office, young women who still lived in the familial home were also expected to contribute their earnings to the family income and to assist with household responsibilities on their return from the office, which left them with little time, money or energy to enjoy the new leisure pursuits on offer to them in the city. As the low salaries of office work were rarely enough to ensure a woman's economic freedom from her family or partner, securing a job alone did not necessarily ensure financial, or social, independence for most women.[46] As well as low salaries and the additional burdens of domestic labour, the harsh reality of workplace harassment further belies the contemporary media image of the frivolous flapper. Indeed, reports of sexual harassment, as von Ankum has observed, increased exponentially as women entered office work during the Weimar era, a theme that was picked up by contemporary women writers such as Vicki Baum and Irmgard Keun.[47] Thus, while office work and other forms of gainful employment seemed to create opportunities for women to engage in the pleasures of the burgeoning leisure and consumer cultures, the limits of this access were shaped by women's paltry pay packets, poor career prospects and the persistent threat – or experience – of sexual harassment and violence. Furthermore, as the publications of Baum, Keun, Haemmerling and Kracauer suggest, access to this space was granted strictly on the ability to conform to increasingly idealized standards of femininity. The 'cosmetic uniform' worn by female shop assistants and office workers was a double-edged sword: while such performances of femininity granted women admission to spaces that had previously been denied them, this access was contingent upon their ability to maintain unobtainable standards, while simultaneously navigating the politics and experience of workplace harassment, sexism and ageism. As such, hidden behind the media image of Berlin's frivolous flapper was a much more complex reality of economic and domestic hardship that demarcated the limits of the 'New Woman's' access to, and experience of, pleasure within the city.

In comparison to other Western European countries, the image of the gainfully employed Dutch woman was still a rare sight in the Netherlands during this time. Dutch women had historically been 'depicted as being very good housewives' and, even in the first decade of the twentieth century, only 10% of married women were in paid employment.[48] By way of comparison, married women's labour participation during the same period in Germany, as Deborah Simonton observes, was around 45%.[49] Even after the First World War, which had demanded a re-evaluation of gender hierarchies in Germany, Dutch gender relations continued to be systematized through a strict dyad of 'breadwinners and care-givers'.[50] Indeed, the growing conservatism of family politics following the 1918 election served only to place further pressures on women to conform to the norms and expectations attached to idealized notions of (bourgeois) femininity. However, in spite of such gender conservatism, Amsterdam provided a hub of opportunity for unmarried female office workers in the interwar period. Indeed, the number of white-collar office clerks in the city increased from 400 in 1899 to around 37,000 by 1920.[51] Around this time, as Marjan Schwegman highlights, traces of the gendered changes that had taken place so visibly in Berlin could also be seen in the 'new femininity' that was slowly emerging within the Dutch cityscape. Not only were young women entering previously male-dominated workplaces, but women's fashions were also turning away from the prim styles of the prewar era to favour the iconic images of the Americanized 'Girl'. With these developments, Schwegman suggests, 'the modest, lady-like woman [changed] into a casual, boy-ish, somewhat forward personality' and, as in German print media, the image of the modern female office worker became an increasingly popular figure as the interwar era progressed.[52] This can be seen most clearly, perhaps, in Josine Reuling's novel *Interlude with Ernst* (*Intermezzo met Ernst*, 1934), which describes the life of a modern office worker and her struggle to find love while maintaining her career.

The issue at the heart of Reuling's novel was not a trivial one. In fact, refusing to marry, as Reuling's protagonist does, was often the only way in which women could remain in paid work. After 1918, the social agenda in the Netherlands was dominated by the confessional parties and their ideologies, which positioned motherhood as a woman's ultimate purpose in society.[53] After a consensus on the importance of women's role in the home was reached among confessionals in power, a new labour law was enacted in 1919 – the same year in which Dutch women gained the right to vote – that ultimately served to make women workers appear less attractive to employers than men. The inclusion of a clause that prohibited women from working on Sundays left many industries reluctant to take on women workers and, indeed, the Dutch Post Office already announced that it was making cuts to its female workforce in 1921.[54] Following this, a more direct gendered attack was made against women workers with the introduction of the Royal Decree in 1924, which enabled employers to dismiss female office workers under the age of forty-five if they were married, and, only a year later, some city councils were authorized to dismiss female teachers below the age of forty-five if it was likely that they were to get married.[55] Fuelled by the effects of growing unemployment during the Great Depression, the Dutch Rail Service also cut back aggressively on its female staff, stating that the organization had '*little* inclination to engage female staff, *no* inclination to allow female staff into higher ranks, but had not yet decided on the question of whether it would positively refuse all female employees'.[56] Following another prolonged period of recession and unemployment in the early 1930s, it became general practice in the Netherlands that women who were not in traditionally 'female' positions would be replaced by male workers. In the first half of the twentieth century, then, male breadwinnership, as Francisca de Haan asserts, was quite literally 'integrated into the salary scale', with most women being requested to resign from their positions after marriage.[57]

The distinction that was made between the male 'breadwinner' and female 'homemaker' in the Netherlands during the interwar period can be seen most explicitly perhaps in a memorandum to Catholic politician Carl Romme's (1896–1980) draft bill against married women's labour, which was published in 1937:

> According to the natural order, man should be the breadwinner for the family and the woman's task is the care of the family. In general, it would be an evil thing if the woman were to evade this task and search out a different terrain of work. The family is such a valuable element in society that, where possible, action should be taken against unhealthy family relations.[58]

Further to the strict governmental regulations that ensured that women conformed to their 'natural' roles as mothers and housewives, there was also the societal pressure on women to be modest in all aspects of their social and private lives. To avoid concerns about their decency, most working women would leave the familial home only after marriage, at which point they would also leave their salaried/waged position. Therefore, living alone in Amsterdam during the interwar era would have been a highly unusual choice for a woman not only because it was exceptionally difficult to secure fixed employment and a large enough salary to afford accommodation, but also because of the social stigma that was still associated with living as an independent woman.[59] Thus, while women had gained the right to vote in 1919 and were entering the world of work in much higher numbers than they had been before the First World War, much was being done in the Netherlands at an institutional level to prevent images of the economic independence of the modern woman from appearing desirable or achievable. Thus, while 'new' femininities were becoming visible in the office space, traditional conceptions that trapped femininity within the sphere of the domestic and maternal served to create the most established image of womanhood in the Dutch cultural imagination during the interwar period: the housewife. Having discussed the access women had to urban space in Amsterdam and Berlin more generally, I will turn now to the establishment of queer subcultures in these two cities, and the provisions placed on women's access to such sexual spaces more specifically.

'Bubis' and 'Mädis'

By the mid-1920s, Berlin's bar culture had established the German capital as a something of a mecca for same-sex loving individuals. With the introduction of more relaxed censorship laws, as will be mentioned in Chapter 3, a queer press was able to thrive as never before. Accordingly, events for queer audiences were advertised in the relevant media publications, which helped to ensure the successful development of queer spaces and subcultures. A growth in international tourism further supported such developments, especially as those with 'hard currency' could 'live like royalty' in the German capital during the years of hyperinflation.[60] Indeed, cultural historian Robert Beachy estimates that out of Berlin's almost four million inhabitants, there included a steady figure of approximately 280,000 tourists by the end of the 1930s.[61] After years of unforgiving hyperinflation and revolutionary fervour at the beginning of the Roaring Twenties, the relative economic and political stability that followed the Dawes Plan, as well as the growing social interest in 'sexual deviance', created an environment in which entertainment venues could attempt to turn queer cultural capital into hard financial gain. Accordingly, it was during the most stable and affluent periods of the Weimar Republic that its urban sexual subcultures truly flourished,[62] although, of course, gendered discrepancies existed in terms of access to space at the level of the queer cityscape too. Indeed, the differences in terms of the types of spaces that existed for men and for women on the queer scene were remarked upon both by Roellig and Haemmerling in their guidebooks. While Haemmerling comments on the aesthetic difference between locales for queer men and women, suggesting that spaces for queer women were 'simpler and more bourgeois, more for comfort and cosiness than for elegance, luxury, and pomp', Roellig saw the imparity as a reflection of the lower standing of women in the social sphere more generally: 'despite all tolerance, especially in sexual matters, a woman is for the time being … as socially ostracised as she ever was'.[63] However, in spite of these differences, Berlin's queer scene still had much to offer women in the mid-1920s.

As will be discussed more comprehensively in Chapter 3, Berlin's sexual subcultures comprised intricate systems of organizations, networks and clubs, with each their own social, political and sexual agenda. Events run at larger locales were often associated with the umbrella organizations that campaigned against Paragraph 175, the law that criminalized homosexual acts between men. Smaller groups would often frequent specific bars and cafés on certain evenings instead. This was not to say that smaller subgroups could not be affiliated with the larger movements. Members of the *Women's Club Monbijou* (*Damenklub Monbijou*), for example, would frequent the bar *The Magic Flute* (*Die Zauberflöte*) and were affiliated with the broader German Friendship Association (Deutscher Freundschaftsverband (DFV)). Those women who belonged to the *Violetta-Club* could instead be found at the club *Violetta*, which, after some hostile turf wars, functioned under the auspices of the League for Human Rights (Bund für Menschenrecht (BfM)). Furthermore, the *Club Monbijou of the West* (*Klub Monbijou des Westens*) – not to be confused with the *Women's Club Monbijou* – was located at the quiet intersection of the Wormser and Luther Streets and had over six hundred female members, who formed part of a 'strictly closed society' upheld through a door policy that was practised 'with polyphemic suspicion'.[64] The *Dorian Gray* on the Bülowstraße presented itself as one of the 'oldest and most renowned pubs in the worlds of women' and held regular 'Elite-days' on Friday evenings.[65] The *Dorian Gray* was not the only bar or club to be associated with queer literature. The *Taverne* was used as the clubhouse for the *Women's Club Scorpion* (*Damenklub Skorpion*), an organization that was said to have taken its name from the trilogy written by Anna Elisabet Weirauch (see Chapter 6).[66]

In her comprehensive study of Berlin's queer press, Heike Schader explores the emergence of subcultural 'types' in queer magazines during the interwar era and documents the prominent figures that appeared on Berlin's Sapphic circuit. Both the 'Ben Hur' and 'Don Juan' architype as well as the 'Gigolo' and 'Gentleman' could be easily identified in bars and clubs by their dapper tuxedos and sharp haircuts.[67] And, as gendered subcultural identities became more established, they began increasingly to influence the 'rules of the game' for many entertainment venues, with clubs becoming more explicit about the behavioural and sartorial standards that were expected from their patrons. A special feature of *The Magic Flute*, for example, was 'the very official distinction between "Bubis", the masculine women, and "Mädis", the feminine women'.[68] This gendered separation formed the basis of interaction between the two types, with 'Mädis' being given dance cards on arrival and 'Bubis' being expected to place their names upon them dutifully and respectfully. However, not all bars were designed to create a space in which 'Bubis' and 'Mädis' could mingle. Certain clubs were more exclusive in their clientele and catered only to specific subcultural types. Behind the locked doors of the *Tavern* (*Taverne*) – the favoured establishment of the *Women's Club Scorpion* – Roellig describes, for example, how guests were greeted at the door with a 'musty smell of beer and billows of smoke … and jarring jazz music'.[69] The 'closed society' of the *Tavern* created among them a masculine 'atmosphere of coarseness and autochthony', which often led, as Roellig notes, to brash displays of macho posturing: 'suddenly, from nowhere, a quarrel breaks out, voices yell, words fly … and it is certainly not uncommon that the dispute descends into a brawl'.[70] Other bars, such as the *Club Monbijou*, were coloured instead by the glamour of the hyperfeminine, providing a space in which 'the elite of the intellectual world of lesbian women, film stars, singers [and] actors' could meet and dance without being bothered.[71]

As well as clubs with closed-door policies and strict behavioural codes, there also existed various 'unaffiliated' venues that offered any paying customer a sample of Berlin's queer night life. *Eldorado* for instance, became known as a 'viewing spot' (*Schaulokal*); an establishment in which curious visitors would come to indulge their voyeuristic yearnings.[72] In his guidebook, Haemmerling reports that women who were 'normal through and through' would often frequent these bars on account of the 'unfamiliar' and 'appealing atmosphere' that they found within them and to be given the opportunity to 'flirt occasionally with the idea of a trip into abnormality'.[73] Haemmerling's observation that 'normal' – that is, *feminine* – women were flirting with perversion in these clubs echoes the contemporary claims of the 'lesbian wave' that was purportedly washing over the city. Furthermore, by suggesting that these trips 'into abnormality' were temporal – and situational – Haemmerling draws on sexological theories of his time to downplay the queer desires of feminine visitors, a position that will be explored further in Chapter 2. Interestingly, however, Haemmerling concludes that 'abnormal' women did not shy away from the curiosity of visiting voyeurs (*Sehleute*), but instead proudly displayed their sexual difference: 'One wears one's abnormality like a risqué nuance. One exhibits oneself with a vibrating pleasure for the perverse.'[74] However, in the popular and sensationalizing social commentaries that existed about these bars, the desires of feminine woman on the Sapphic circuit were invariably reduced either to erotic spectacles for curious heterosexual tourists or fleeting frissons of temporal pleasure.

Unsurprisingly, Haemmerling's assertion that queer women took pleasure in their objectification was refuted in magazines for women-loving-women, where instead discussions circled around the need for spaces in which queer women could be 'entirely themselves'. However, notwithstanding the need for safe spaces, the financial burden of catering to an exclusively female following often proved too great for many club owners, who were forced to open their events to (heterosexual) male patrons. Roellig's pithy remark that 'women are rarely substantial drinkers – and the landlord has to survive, too!' certainly echoes the earlier discussion in this chapter of the financial difficulties that many working women faced during this period.[75] With poorly paid jobs and financial responsibilities to their families, most women could not afford the luxury of attending regular evening events to support their local queer venues. In this way, feminine women's access to queer space was limited by many of the same factors that shaped their access to the city more generally: limited financial means and the threat of sexual objectification. Furthermore, while the gender presentation of queer feminine women may have granted them a certain cachet in celebrity bars like *Club Monbijou*, it appears to have presented a barrier to their entrance to others, like the *Tavern*, which catered only to masculine women. And, in mixed and 'open' clubs like *Eldorado*, the queer desires of feminine women were altogether defused by social commentators, who believed the female queerness they found 'on display' to be a temporal and situational vice that was committed by otherwise 'normal' women.

Baskets and Owls

Before the 1950s, there were very few recognized meeting places in Amsterdam for queer citizens and, almost certainly, there existed nothing like the range of bars or clubs outlined above in terms of scale or establishment. Instead, in *The Homosexuality of Men and Women* (*Die Homosexualität des Mannes und des Weibes*, 1914), Magnus Hirschfeld (1868–1935) alludes to the existence of various 'hotspots' in Amsterdam, such as the Kalver Street, where male sex workers could easily be found, or the cruising that was taking place at urinals in and around the city, which became spaces of significance for those seeking ephemeral erotic encounters.[76] Marie Jacobus Johannes

Exler, the author of the novel *Struggles of Life* (*Levensleed*, 1911), further described several rooms across the city that were rented out for private use by both male sex workers and long-term lovers alike. Turning to entertainment venues more broadly, the bars and cafés that were frequented by same-sex-desiring people in Amsterdam were by no means exclusively queer establishments during the first decades of the twentieth century. Public houses were subject to a range of stringent requirements and limitations, which made establishing a space exclusively for queer people an almost impossible endeavour. Not only did the owner of a bar need a licence to play music or to allow dancing – as was also the case in Berlin – but further permissions were also needed to employ female staff, for the sale of spirits and to extend opening hours until midnight.[77] Therefore, to afford the expenses of several permits, bars and cafés needed to attract as large an audience as possible and, equally, avoid any actions that could put them at risk of closure by the vice squad (*zedenpolitie*). For this reason, the emergence of a clandestine club and café culture for queer people in the Netherlands came with the development of a range of signs and signals to warn visitors of potentially risky situations, as well as to make bars and cafés themselves secure from forced closure. Those bars that could navigate the increasingly conservative moral climate while still catering to queer clients often had closed-door policies to check whether visitors were 'known' to the regulars. And after the term 'owls' (*uilen*) became a common way of referring to the vice squad, venues used this shared subcultural knowledge to implement extra measures to ensure the safety of their customers – and their permits. When a statue of an owl was placed in the window of a café or bar, for instance, the owner sent out a warning to their visitors that they were not only 'among friends'.[78]

Before a café culture began to emerge for women in Amsterdam during the 1950s, socializing in bars was an activity was primarily the preserve of men. As mentioned previously, unmarried women in the Netherlands had far fewer opportunities to gain economic independence and were expected either to live at home or as a servant in another house, with their cohabitants often being highly suspicious of any evening excursions that were made. Even by the late 1930s, when a more diverse range of locales had become established as queer meeting points, such as the *Hirsch Building* (*Hirschgebouw*) on the Leidseplein, the *Suisse* on the Kalver Street, and the *Red Lion* (*Rode Leeuw*) on the Damrak, women were rarely found to frequent these venues.[79] An exception to this rule was presented in the *Empire* bar, the oldest and most popular queer establishment in Amsterdam, which was run by retired sex worker Hermine Sophia Lauffer-van Exter – better known as Mie Lauffer – until 1932. Today, little more is known about Lauffer 'than that she smoked cigars'.[80] But as an established queer venue with a woman at the helm, this bar may have been more welcoming of female visitors, even though scant traces remain of the demographic make-up of its visiting clientele than the information published following a tip-off to the Amsterdam vice squad in 1932. When the *Empire* bar was raided, fifty-two customers and staff were arrested. Of those arrested, eighteen were women. According to the *Newspaper of the North* (*Nieuwsblad van het Noorden*), the individuals in question were arrested under suspicion of contravening the local drinking laws, but, following further investigations, other indiscretions had come to light that were considered to be 'contrary to public morals'.[81] Alongside Mie Lauffer, queer female proprietor Bet van Beeren (1902–67) owned the bar *The Little Basket* (*'t Mandje*), which opened in 1927. Van Beeren was surprisingly open about her queerness, at least on the subcultural circuit, and presented an entirely unconventional image for Dutch woman of this time. Known as the 'Queen of the Zeedijk', van Beeren purportedly rode a motorcycle, wore trousers (with a zip) and shirts, smoked cigarettes and drank gin by the bottle.[82] Host to a diverse crowd of sailors, travellers and sex workers, *The Little Basket* was an utterly singular establishment in Amsterdam during the interwar era. For this reason, it was often visited by the vice squad. However, in spite of this very real threat of closure, van Beeren is said to have hosted several parties throughout the year during which the usual rules of social etiquette were cast aside. The annual public celebration of the Queen's birthday and Carnaval, for example, offered a chance for van Beeren to allow patrons to bend the customs of social engagement. Dutch actor and writer Albert Mol (1917–2004) proclaimed of such annual events: 'it was an unbelievably good party, where people – irrespective of their gender – could dance with one another, which was quite a phenomenon in those days because that was not allowed anywhere, ever. [But] at Bet's bar it was allowed, it was possible, and nobody thought it strange.'[83]

It has been broadly suggested in histories of queer desire and culture that erotic relationships between women were not only cultivated in bars such as *The Little Basket* and the *Empire*, but also among networks of female sex workers.[84] As the lives of sex workers often leave little trace, and those that do remain present themselves too frequently in violent encounters with state regulators, it remains difficult to create comprehensive accounts of how such networks may have existed and thrived. However, by examining groups of working women in a broader sense, I hope to offer an insight into how employment opportunities were harnessed by queer women in the Netherlands as opportunities to meet like-minded others. Indeed, as some roles required travel or residential stays, work could grant women a degree of social freedom and interaction that was not available to them through any other means. Although women could still not be open about their desires at work, some spheres of employment – particularly those institutions that established homosocial environments – offered queer women an unparalleled opportunity to meet others who felt as they did. While sex work might not be comparable to some other forms of gainful employment, not least for reasons of criminalization, the danger to women's health and safety, and the social demonization of sex workers as 'vectors of disease', the very fact that sex work is 'first and foremost an income-generating activity' means that there might be considerable crossovers between the arguments I make about other industries and the lives of these underrepresented female workers.[85] Within the field of medical care, for example, young student nurses often lived together on hospital grounds and, once qualified, shared apartments or houses with other female hospital staff. In a series of interviews with women who had romantic and sexual relationships with other women between the 1920s and 1980s, Anja van Kooten Niekerk and Sacha Wijmer spoke with an ex-nurse who claimed that this close-knit homosocial setting presented a 'paradise' for queer women, who ostensibly 'had enormous choice' in such environments.[86] Transcripts from the interviews further suggest that during and after the Second World War, the Dutch armed forces formed another homosocial workplace setting in which queer relationships between women were able to flourish. As networks for women in the Netherlands were often created via familial contacts and confined to the local organizations affiliated to their pillar, work environments can be seen as spaces of queer opportunity. As well as nursing homes and army barracks, emancipation movements struggling for the political and social acceptance of homosexual people also offered women spaces in which to explore their desires and establish relationships with like-minded others in Amsterdam and Berlin.

Queer Activism in the City

In May 1897, medical doctor and sexologist Magnus Hirschfeld met with colleagues to discuss his plans to establish a scientific movement to defend the rights of homosexual citizens. Following his travels through Africa, the Americas and Asia, Hirschfeld established a medical practice in Charlottenburg in 1886 and, after receiving a suicide letter from one of his homosexual patients, he was compelled to found a movement to lobby for the equal rights of homosexual persons. The Scientific Humanitarian Committee (Wissenschaftlich-humanitär Komitee (WhK)) was strongly influential in disseminating material about queer desires and experiences, and their headquarters was a hive of queer activity, both scientific and social.[87] However, it was not until ten years after the establishment of the main organization that members of the board discussed the possibility of developing a separate women's subcommittee. During this meeting, the board concluded that they would contact female members to determine whether such a development would be valuable. Three years later, two women were elected on to the main committee as 'female chairmen': the author Toni Schwabe (1877–1951) and the police official Gertrud Topf (1881–1918).[88] By this time, the WhK had fully established itself as an outward-looking body of scientists, sex reformers and political activists, who sought to forge connections across national borders, with members located in Amsterdam, London, Rome, Vienna and Tianjin in northern China by 1910. Hirschfeld's commitment to developing international connections was cemented further with the foundation of the World League for Sexual Reform (Weltliga für Sexualreform) in 1928, which held conferences in Britain, Norway and Austria.

For the duration of its existence, the WhK appeared committed to working with women's organizations, representing the interests of both queer and 'normal' women alike.[89] In 1912, Helene Stöcker and members of the League of Human Rights joined the board of the WhK, followed by sexual reformer Johanna Elberskirchen in 1914. Stöcker was chiefly involved in the campaigns against Paragraph 175 (see below), but was also invited to give regular speeches at the committee gatherings on topics relating to women's rights and motherhood. The committee continued to invite a diverse range of female speakers to its assemblies to present papers, discuss literary works and talk about their personal experiences. The establishment of the *Yearbook for Intermediate Sexual Types* (*Jahrbuch für sexuelle Zwischenstufen*) in 1899 also gave women a space to have their research on the formations and experiences of queer desire between women published and promoted. Although primarily concerned with the abolition of Paragraph 175 and discussions of queer male desires, the *Yearbook* also took into serious consideration the specific experience of women-who-desired-women, as well as promoting broader discussions on women's legal rights and emancipation. Hirschfeld collaborated closely with Stöcker in relation to the abolition of the anti-abortion legislation Paragraph 218, for example, and Stöcker helped to inform committee members about women's sexual health and lives.[90] When Hirschfeld opened the doors of his Institute for the Study of Sexual Science (Institut für Sexualwissenschaft) to the public in 1919, researchers from across the world were invited to help build on the sexologist's ever-growing repository of sexological works. Located in a residence adjacent to Berlin's Tiergarten, the institute became a central hub for queer research. Not only did it create a space for public lectures and clinical trials, but it also became the living quarters of many researchers and patients, as well as the lodgings for a host of queer writers and artists.[91] As Berlin began to amass a growing reputation for sexual tolerance, no doubt aided by the launch of Hirschfeld's scientific institute, physician and psychotherapist Charlotte Wolff (1887–1986) recalls that visitors came to the German capital 'from all over the world ... to enjoy a freedom here that was denied to them in their home countries'.[92] These sentiments were echoed by the Dutch contributors to queer magazine *We*, mentioned at the beginning of this chapter and discussed in more detail in Chapter 4. Yet, while the committee and its publications served as something of a forum for women within the emerging scientific debates about female same-sex desires, the institute itself remained largely 'a male space'.[93] Although women were invited to present papers at the institute, and Stöcker worked actively with Hirschfeld on several campaigns, no women were formally employed by the organization.[94] Thus, while the WhK and the Institute for the Study of Sexual Science placed (queer) women's interests on their agenda, it remains debateable how many queer women felt that they had a place of their own within the organization and its buildings.

With membership crossing continents, it was not long before suborganizations began to appear at an international level. Indeed, Dutch lawyer and activist Jacob Anton Schorer (1866–1957) made his way to Berlin to study under Magnus Hirschfeld at the turn of the century, after matriculating from his law degree. Schorer worked closely with Hirschfeld and other leading names in the WhK for several years in Berlin.[95] Following what he considered to be the 'injustice and tyranny' of proposed Article 248bis (see below), Schorer returned to the Netherlands in 1910 determined to establish a Dutch faction of Hirschfeld's WhK. Undeterred by the earlier failed attempt by Lucien von Römer (1873–1965) to found a homosexual emancipation movement in the Netherlands in 1903, Schorer harnessed the impending threat of Article 248bis, which would effectively criminalize certain homosexual acts, to galvanize several other notable queer individuals to establish a group to advocate for the rights of what he termed 'Uranians'.[96] With a headquarters based at Schorer's apartment in The Hague, the Dutch Scientific Humanitarian Committee (Nederlandsch Wetenschappelijk Humanitair Komitee (NWHK)) consisted of the sexologists Arnold Aletrino (1858–1916) and Lucien von Römer, and the author Marie Jacobus Johannes Exler, mentioned earlier in this chapter. Although Aletrino and von Römer had already published widely on queer male desires, the organization was largely a one-man show, as Rob Tielman observes: 'Jacob Schorer *was* the NWHK, the NWHK *was* Jacob Schorer.'[97]

In many respects, the NWHK fulfilled similar functions to Hirschfeld's WhK, albeit on a more limited scale. In spite of its smaller scope for influence, Schorer's organization was able to disseminate thousands of copies of pro-homosexual pamphlets and brochures to eminent figures, students and sex researchers in the hope of convincing the public of the congenital, and therefore 'natural', origin of same-sex desires. The NWHK worked closely with the WhK in its early years, and adopted similar approaches and frameworks in its conceptualization of queer activism. The organization held regular committee meetings to which it invited guest speakers to deliver scientific papers; it also printed annual reports and newsletters for its members and created petitions to lobby against Article 248bis. The committee later became involved with the World League for Sexual Reform and made up a large part of the Dutch faction of the international umbrella organization. With a solid platform and international network, the NWHK was by far the largest communities for queer Dutch people until the 1960s. Yet, despite claiming to represent the interests of both male and female 'Uranians', there is no evidence of it allocating any functions on the committee to female members. Furthermore, little attention was paid to women's issues in the committee publications, even though the NWHK did commission the first Dutch publication to dedicate space to the experiences of queer women in the Netherlands, *The Homosexuals* (*De homosexueelen*, 1939). There is also little evidence of any existing links between the various feminist movements in the Netherlands and the NWHK, and, unlike the WhK, the movement for queer rights did not form part of broader social movements for sexual reform.[98]

Although the NWHK did not actively advocate the rights of queer women, who were also targeted by Article 248bis, the catalogue of Schorer's archive and library nonetheless demonstrates an interest by the lawyer in collecting information about queer female experiences. Schorer's archive contained studies such as P. Arduin's *The Women's Question and Sexual Intermediaries* (*Die Frauenfrage und die sexuellen Zwischenstufen*, 1900) and Edwin Bab's *The Women's Movement and Male Culture* (*Frauenbewegung und Freundesliebe*, 1901), as well as books written by women on the subject of queer desire, such as Elisabeth Dauthendy's *The Uranian Question and the Woman* (*Die urnische Frage und die Frau*, 1906) and Johanna Elberskirchen's *The Love of the Third Sex* (*Die Liebe des dritten Geschlechts*, 1904).[99] Although the NWHK focused its activism primarily on the persecution of male homosexuals under Article 248bis, when homosexuality is discussed in the NWHK's publications, it referred frequently to the same-sex desires of both men and women. Nonetheless, while Schorer maintained that women should not be excluded women from joining the committee, on account of homosexual tendencies being identifiable 'in women as well as men', it appears there was little done at an organizational level to promote or ensure their inclusion.[100]

Policing Same-Sex Desires

As is suggested in the outline of the development of queer urban sites and networks above, the options for establishing safe spaces for same-sex desiring individuals in Amsterdam and Berlin differed markedly. While Berlin formed an epicentre for erotic liberation with its burgeoning bar scene, an increasing number of sexual tourists and a long-established movement for homosexual emancipation, those seeking same-sex connections in Amsterdam had few recognized points where they could meet, and those that did exist were patronized primarily by queer men and were subject to frequent police raids and strict regulations. However, this should not suggest that the German vice squad (*Sittenpolizei*) took a less active position in the policing of queer desires in Berlin, but rather that the forces of law and order adopted a different strategy to control queer desires in the city. Indeed, from the late nineteenth century onwards, an exceptional degree of tolerance for queer bars and venues was exercised by vice squads in Berlin. In line with this attitude, the general approach adopted by authorities was to 'monitor' establishments rather than to prohibit them outright.[101] As Beachy outlines in his study on interwar urban sexuality, it can be said that police forces in Berlin adopted a policy of 'qualified toleration' as the capital's nightlife grew ever more notorious. Thus, instead of police forces being expected to investigate venues suspected of promoting immoral behaviours, they were instead deployed to ensure that 'homosexual fraternization' did not extend beyond 'certain limits'.[102] In this way, regulating forces could allow for the continuation of one of the city's most thriving tourist industries, while ensuring that the effects of Berlin's notoriety did not breach certain established moral codes. However, law enforcers in Amsterdam demonstrated little such tolerance. Introduced in 1926, the vice squad kept precise records on the movements and activities of queer individuals who transgressed Article 248bis, as well as other potential moral offenders, including sex workers and petty criminals.[103] Following a governmental drive to guard the population against what was perceived to be a growing urban 'immorality', the Dutch vice squad focused their attentions on public toilets, parks, bars and cafés – spaces already outlined above as significant queer sites – as well as on records of the general comings and goings of individual transgressors. In terms of the sizes of the cities and the number of bars, policing same-sex desire was certainly an easier task for the Amsterdam vice squad than for officers in Berlin, who were confronted with an ever-growing number of entertainment venues, of which it was difficult to maintain any kind of overview. However, perhaps the greatest divergence between the regulation of same-sex desires in these two cities can be found in the official laws introduced to regulate homosexual acts. While the German Paragraph 175 did not prohibit same-sex acts between women, the Dutch Article 248bis regulated same-sex acts between men, as well as those between women.

Paragraph 175

Following the Unification of 1871 in Germany, Paragraph 143 of the Prussian Penal Code, which outlawed acts of 'unnatural fornication' between men, was integrated into German law as Paragraph 175. Under this edict, same-sex acts between men were considered to be a criminal offence punishable with imprisonment. As a carbon copy of the earlier Prussian law, Paragraph 175 reads as follows: 'Unnatural fornication, whether between persons of the male sex or of humans with beasts, is punishable with imprisonment, with the further punishment of a prompt loss of civil rights.'[104] Considered commensurate to bestiality, penetrative same-sex acts between men were criminalized until 1933, when the law was redrafted to include a more comprehensive list of male-male intimacies. Although the edict did not recognize same-sex acts between women as a crime, 'unnatural' activities between women had also been historically punishable by death in several states across the German Empire. The cross-dressing soldier Catherina Margaretha Linck, for example, had been executed in Halberstadt in 1721 after she presented herself as male, married a young woman, and committed sexual acts with her new wife using a 'leather instrument'.[105] However, following the introduction of Paragraph 175, the German Penal Code appeared to no longer consider erotic acts between women to be a criminal offence. Although the omission of female same-sex desire in the law appears to constitute a shift in the way that same-sex pleasures were understood by lawmakers, this amendment should not be read as an indifference towards sex between women altogether. Instead, as Laurie Marhoefer contends, the amendment should be considered only as 'a different sort of state response to lesbian sex'.[106] Within this response, the central stumbling block encountered by lawmakers appears to have concerned the issue of precisely what constituted sex between women. While sexual offences 'against nature' and 'acts similar to sexual intercourse' between men were apparently more easily definable under categories of penetration, intercrural sex and frottage, legislators were unable to imagine how sex between women could be considered 'similar to sexual intercourse' when it did not involve, as Marhoefer acutely observes, the 'most freighted of political appendages, the penis'.[107] Since neither digital or oral stimulation nor the use of leather instruments constituted intercourse-like activities in the minds of lawmakers, sex between women '[remained] impervious to legal discourse', as Tracie Matysik writes, because it did not 'conform to existing and legitimate legal categories'.[108] Furthermore, as sex between women was often dismissed as 'temporal' – that is, a substitute sexual relationship until a heterosexual partnership could be formed – female same-sex desire was not considered to be a danger to the marital union in the way that the incurable deviance of homosexual men was considered to be.[109] Indeed, lawmakers argued that legislators would exacerbate the issue rather than help to combat against it by bringing women's attention to the act of lesbian love through its criminalization. Therefore, rather than outlawing sexual acts between women, the 'Law against Trash and Filth' (Schund- und Schmutzgesetz) was employed to prevent the dissemination of knowledge about queer desires through various levels of press censorship, and was enforced multiple times against the publications that existed for women in Berlin after 1924, as will be discussed in Chapter 3.[110] A further factor that coloured the debate around female same-sex acts was that intimacy between women was generally considered an essential part of a woman's 'feminine nature'. Unless women displayed visible signs of gendered and sexual deviance, law enforcers feared impinging upon the lives of 'innocent' women, an argument that was used by various feminists in their campaigns against the inclusion of women in Paragraph 175 (see below).

Although female same-sex acts were not criminalized when Paragraph 175 was introduced into the German Penal Code, this does not mean that the question of whether lesbian sex should be incorporated into the law was abandoned entirely. There were, in fact, repeated attempts to amend Paragraph 175 to include same-sex acts between women and, following a series of homosexual scandals in 1907, there was a renewed debate in the Reichstag in 1911 about expanding the law under a new legislative measure: Paragraph 250.[111] Advocates for the inclusion of women under the proposed law argued that if women wanted to enjoy rights equal to those of men, they must also accept equal punishment and responsibility for any sexual transgressions that they committed. The allusion to the campaign for women's emancipation marked a turning point in the discussion of female homosexuality within the women's movement, which had previously remained peripheral to the debate of suffrage and abortion. While queer activist Anna Rüling had already discussed the role of the women's movement in the homosexual question in her 1904 speech 'What Interest Does the Women's Movement Have in the Resolution of the Homosexual Question?', it was not until 1911 that the first explicit statement was made about the regulation of female homosexual acts by a key branch of the women's movement itself.[112] Helene Stöcker (1869–1943), arguably the best-known German campaigner for women's rights, published her thoughts on the proposed Paragraph 250 in the mouthpiece for the Association for the Protection of Mothers (Bund für Mutterschutz), *New Generation* (*Neue Generation*). In her article, Stöcker argued that the extension of Paragraph 175 to include women would be a 'grave error' (*ein schwerwiegender Mißgriff*). She dismissed the idea that an inequality would be abolished through the extension of the law and instead concluded that an inequality would be doubled.[113] Yet, while Stöcker worked closely with Magnus Hirschfeld and his Scientific Humanitarian Committee towards the abolition of the law against homosexuality, she was eager to emphasize that her radical Society for the Protection of Mothers and Sexual Reform (Bund für Mutterschutz und Sexualreform) – the organization that campaigned for the rights of unmarried mothers – represented the interests of 'normal love, the love between man and woman'.[114] Radical reformer Käthe Schirmacher (1865–1930) of the Alliance of Progressive Women's Associations (Verband fortschrittlicher Frauenvereine) supported Stöcker's key arguments, asserting that if the authorities were concerned with gender equality in laws against homosexual acts, they ought to begin by ensuring 'the relief from our burdens, our rights and not gags and punishments'.[115] Taking the subject of sex work as a central part of her rebuttal of the proposed law, Schirmacher controversially argued that as men had access to sex outside of marriage in brothels, for example, those men who still turned to their own sex for pleasure should rightfully be punished. It would be female sex workers who turned to each other out of disgust of men's immoral desires, Schirmacher contended, who would be worst hit by the proposed extension: 'Should these corpses be killed yet again, should sex between women also be punished? In that case, the prostitute does not have quiet even within her own four walls, the reach of arbitrariness devours even her last refuge.'[116] Anna Pappritz (1861–1939), chairperson of the Abolitionist movement, took umbrage at Schirmacher's suggestion of protecting sex workers from the extension of the law. In an issue of *The Abolitionist* (*Der Abolitionist*) from 1911, Pappritz rejected the idea that women-who-loved-women ought to be judged differently from men who engaged in same-sex acts, claiming that queer desire 'practiced by women' was 'equally as reprehensible, unsavoury, and loathsome as when committed by men'.[117] Although Pappritz agreed with Schirmacher and Stöcker's contention that queer women should not be forced into marriages with men, it was not out of sympathy, but rather informed by the eugenics-based belief that homosexual women may pass on a 'pathological disposition to [their] offspring'.[118]

The desire of most feminists to distance the women's movement from queer desire, as well as the scorn directed by Pappritz towards Sapphic love more generally, might be better understood in light of the link that had historically been established between same-sex desire and the women's movement by sex researchers and social commentators. Otto Weininger (1880–1903), for example, had aggressively put forward in his study *Sex and Character* (*Geschlecht und Charakter*, 1903) that the desire for emancipation was the result of the masculine qualities of same-sex desiring women. Feminine women, Weininger suggested, had 'nothing to do with the "Emancipation of Woman"'.[119] Other sex researchers, such as Iwan Bloch, contended that within organizations in which women's emancipation from men was the primary goal, it was logical that women would consider only intimate relationships with their own sex.[120] In what could be considered an attempt to contend these claims, some feminists approached the issue of the proposed Paragraph 250 from the perspective of gender essentialism. Focusing on 'the difficulty of distinguishing legally the *sexual* act from the *social* act', Liberal reformer Elsbeth Krukenberg (1867–1954), for example, opposed Paragraph 250 on the basis that it attacked the fundamental nature of women's existence:[121]

> What seems unnaturally 'feminine' in the man: remarkably warm, tender conduct between man and man, caresses, flattery, and the like, that is something entirely natural for women of all ages … Should the woman have to break with these habits in order not to raise suspicion?[122]

Krukenberg considered the proposed law to regulate homosexual acts between women to be an attack on a woman's *feminine* essence. Evoking a similar line of argument to the earlier work on queer desires by sexual radical Johanna Elberskirchen (1864–1943 (see Chapter 2), Krukenberg emphasizes that femininity – and, with it, the need/desire for homosocial intimacy – was part of a woman's essential nature and the basis on which the movement for emancipation had been developed.[123] The discussion around the regulation of same-sex desires continued apace throughout the first decades of the twentieth century. However, after a particularly fierce period of debate in 1929, a penal reform committee eventually voted to remove Paragraph 175 entirely from the Criminal Code, effectively decriminalizing homosexual acts. Although this was an achievement welcomed by activists, their joy was to be short-lived. While the reform committee abolished Paragraph 175, it summarily approved Paragraph 297, which outlawed 'sex between two men if one was under twenty-one and the other was not, if one party used a position of influence to pressure the other, or if one paid the other'.[124] Thus, while the new edict criminalized same-sex acts between men in even more elaborate terms than it had done previously, same-sex desire between women remained undefined and undefinable in the eyes of the law.

Article 248bis

Before the nineteenth century, it was general practice in the Netherlands, as Rictor Norton notes, that trials brought against men who committed sodomitical acts were hidden from public knowledge. And in the cases that concerned same-sex desire between women, a similar level of secrecy was employed to keep queer acts veiled from the general public. Indeed, in the separate trials of two women arrested and flogged for same-sex crimes in Leiden in the late seventeenth century, Norton describes how both parties were exiled and their cases were kept secret.[125] Following the introduction of the Criminal Code for the Kingdom of Holland in 1809, the punishments for two people of the same sex who committed 'unnatural fornication' remained in place, but the death sentence was removed from the law. This code only existed for two years and was replaced by the French Code Pénal in 1811, under which same-sex intimacy was no longer criminalized.[126] While same-sex acts were no longer punishable by law, we should not infer that this led to a greater social acceptance of same-sex desires. Indeed, in the years leading up to the turn of the twentieth century, the number of arrests made in conjunction with same-sex transgressions had risen from eight arrests and seven convictions between 1840 and 1849 to 187 arrests and 87 convictions between 1900 and 1909.[127]

By the time that Jacob Schorer returned to the Netherlands following his stay with Magnus Hirschfeld and his Scientific Humanitarian Committee, sociolegal understandings of intimate same-sex acts had progressed from something of a question of 'repulsive and nameless sin' to a 'psychological and medicolegal problem'.[128] As well as the emergence of a growing number of medical publications appearing in the Netherlands on the subject of homosexuality in the 1890s, queer desires had also become a popular subject of literary inquiry. Provocative novels such as Jacob Israël de Haan's *Lines from the Pipe* (*Pijpelijntjes*, 1904), Louis Couperus' *Mountain of Light* (*Berg van licht*, 1905) and Marie Jacobus Johannes Exler's *Struggles of Life* (*Levensleed*, 1909), taken alongside the increase in availability of cheap pornographic books and journals, led to a consensus within confessional circles that the public needed to be protected from 'a growing moral evil' (*een groeiend zedelijk kwaad*). As confessional parties further cemented their support bases at the turn of the twentieth century, local councils began to grow more convinced of the idea of a 'moral authority', which was later given form through the vice squad, which had the role of countering and controlling sexual behaviours.[129] By the first decade of the twentieth century, several attempts had already been made to expand the laws that categorized offences against morality to include same-sex acts. The Liberal Prime Minister Cort van der Linden unsuccessfully sought to pass a 'seduction law' in 1900, which he claimed would protect those under the age of twenty-one from the attempts of female sex workers to find trade, as well as from the promise of financial or material gain from older men attempting to seduce younger boys. A later effort by the Catholic Minister of Justice Anton Nelissen to pass a similar law in 1909 also failed.

Building on van der Linden's article against 'seduction', Nelissen further suggested the introduction of several other decrees against immorality, which included laws that prohibited 'pornography, propaganda for birth control aimed at minors, coupling (by which is meant a ban on brothels), abortion and gambling'.[130] Before Nelissen could see through his 'moral crusade', he fell ill and was succeeded by Edmond 'Robert' Hubert Regout (1863–1913). The fervour shown by the new Minister of Justice for the protection of youth against homosexuality soon resulted in Article 248bis becoming informally known as 'Regout's cuckoo egg'.[131]

Following eight days of fierce debate, fifty out of the eighty-seven members of the House of Representatives voted to accept Regout's proposed morality laws in 1911.[132] Thus, what had once been an 'unmentionable vice' in the eyes of the law now needed to be explicitly outlined in the Dutch Penal Code. Embedded among a number of laws introduced to prevent immoral behaviour and focused primarily on the protection of minors, Article 248bis reads as follows: 'The adult who commits fornication [*ontucht plegen*] with a minor of the same sex, whose minority status he [*sic*] knows or should reasonably suspect, shall be punished with a prison sentence of up to four years.'[133] In conjunction with the laws restricting homosexuality, many local authorities observed a cross-dressing ban (*travestieverbod*) for men and a trouser ban (*pantalonverbod*) for women, both of which were recognized in several major Dutch districts, including Amsterdam.[134] Thus, while originally conceived as a law to protect minors from being seduced by adults, Article 248bis effectively became a regulative measure against intimate acts between members of the same sex, especially when taken in conjunction with the other laws employed to uphold moral standards, as well as against any transgressions of gender conformity. Shaped by what Anna Tijsseling terms the 'Dracula thesis', adolescent sexuality was considered in the Netherlands to be a formative period in which innocent youth could be corrupted by sinful adults of either sex.[135] Thus, it was not only inequality in terms of the ages of consent for same-sex and opposite-sex intimate acts that was introduced with Article 248bis, but the idea that every same-sex-desiring person over the age of twenty-one was a potential criminal.[136] When looking at how the law specifically impacted on the behaviours and relationships of women, Judith Schuyf observes that in the sixty years in which Article 248bis was in force, forty-eight women were committed to trial in comparison to some 4,987 men.[137] Indeed, some women who were caught transgressing the law had not even been aware of its existence. Although one of the women interviewed by van Kooten Niekerk and Wijmer in their study of queer women living in the Netherlands between 1920 and 1960 recounted that she had heard about the law on account of her job as a court reporter, most of the other interviewees in the study remained 'ignorant' (*onwetend*) of the law for a long time and 'undertook risks as minors that they had not even been aware of'.[138] Yet, while statistically fewer women were apprehended for transgressing the law, for those women who did have encounters with Article 248bis, the experience proved invariably 'traumatic' (*traumatisch*). From the twenty-one interviews conducted by van Kooten Niekerk and Wijmer with queer women born between 1904 and 1936, two women were caught transgressing the law. Ton Oosterhout was followed by detectives from the vice squad as a minor in the 1950s and her name was placed on a blacklist for immoral behaviour. Recalling the interview, she mentions the intimate questions that were asked about the sexual nature of her relationship with her older female partner. For her, this contact with the vice squad was also her first encounter with the term 'lesbian': '"You have a lesbian relationship", that detective had said. I had absolutely no idea what that was.'[139] A decade later, Ien Duursma was also blacklisted for breaching the law. In this instance, as an adult. Duursma was picked up by the police from her houseboat and, like Oosterhout, questioned about her relationship: 'the [detective] asked me all kinds of things ... so intimate, especially about how you did it. Everything about your sexual life, unbelievable, right down to the finest details'.[140] Following the questioning, she was forbidden from seeing her younger partner until she turned twenty-one and both were sent to a psychiatrist for 'treatment'.

Of course, a person's proclivities and desires were regulated not only at a state level, but also within the local communities in which one operated. Given the vertical pluralism that structured society in the Netherlands, an individual's experience of their queerness would have likely differed markedly depending on the pillar to which they belonged. Unsurprisingly, perhaps, the Catholic pillar appears to have been most vocal in their denunciation of homosexual acts.[141] Resolutely rejecting the medical theories of congenital homosexuality that emerged at the end of the nineteenth century, the position of Catholic communities towards same-sex desire was based on the theology of free will between virtue and sin. Consequently, homosexual desire was considered a sin in Catholic doctrine *only* if it was acted upon.[142] As sexological literature became more widely available to a broadening reading public (see Chapter 2), the responses of both the Catholic and Protestant pillars became increasingly reactionary in the Netherlands. In 1937, the Catholic Father L. Bender produced the pamphlet *Pernicious Propaganda* (*Verderfelijke Propaganda*) in which he virulently attacked the activities of the Dutch homosexual emancipation movement. While the views of Protestant communities towards same-sex desires varied across denominations – ranging from homosexuality being considered a 'Catholic vice' to the denunciation of same-sex desires as the predestined fate of those who could not be saved – within Catholic communities, acting upon same-sex desires was unvaryingly sinful. One of the most openly vitriolic diatribes against queer people during this time is to be found in Ernest Michel's pamphlet 'Anti-homo, a Document against the Molluscs of Our Society' ('Anti-homo, een geschrift tegen de weekdieren onzer samenleving', 1929). Here, the Catholic poet and author drew on colonialist slurs in his damning indictment of male *and female* homosexual desires:

> You, Uranian rats; you, barren wreckers of marital unions; you, homosexual dogs; you, lesbian wretches; you, rotting innards of society, who flirt with Christ with such pleasure, but whom you have degraded to an Indian queer, to a sissy boy, to a personification of your own ghastly pleasures.[143]

While Michel's attack presents us with a particularly venomous commentary on same-sex desire, his views were not considered to differ greatly from other prominent Catholic figures, as Pieter Koenders has indicated.[144] Further to the creation of specifically anti-homosexual propaganda, religious organizations such as the League for Large Families (Bond voor Grote Gezinnen) and the Catholic Action for God (Actie voor God) were established in a bid to protect traditional family values through the dissemination of pamphlets and educative material in which they outlined their opposition to abortion, birth control and homosexuality. In terms of the Socialist and Liberal pillars, the sexual domain had instead long been considered a private issue that should not be controlled by the state, one's associated political organization or church. As such, these pillars can be conceived of as considerably more tolerant than their confessional counterparts. Indeed, Ton Oosterhout (who was mentioned above) grew up in a 'socialist environment' and met her first romantic partner 'through a [male] homosexual friend' of her mother's, who she describes as a 'bohemian-like woman'.[145] In practice, however, this low-level tolerance did not amount to much in terms of the political struggle for social recognition and emancipation within the Socialist Party, where the silencing of discussions that concerned same-sex desire, as Rob Tielman notes, was often 'rather the rule than the exception'.[146] In this way, the topic of homosexuality also remained unspeakable within most Socialist and Liberal milieus, even as queer desires appear to have been more widely accepted in some circles.

In a bid to combat the growing conservative rhetoric concerning the nature of same-sex love following the introduction of Article 248bis in 1911, Jacob Schorer published the pamphlet 'What Everyone Should Know about Uranisme' ('Wat iedereen behoort te weten omtrent uranisme', 1912), which included a petition for the repeal of the law. Amassing a total of 130 signatories, the petition featured the names of nineteen women. Four of these were active in the Dutch women's movement: Estella 'Stella' Hartshalt-Zeehandelaar (1874–1936), Maria Rutgers-Hoitsema (1847–1934), Annette Versluys-Poelman (1853–1914) and Titia van der Tuuk (1854–1939).[147] Unlike German feminists, for whom the threat of the proposed Paragraph 250 served as a catalyst to position themselves in the debate concerning the criminalization of queer female desire, the Dutch women's movement did not appear to engage at all with the regulation of female same-sex desire through the enactment of Article 248bis. Indeed, female same-sex desire was only rarely implied by the Dutch women's movement before 1940, as it was deemed irrelevant subject matter for a movement dedicated to achieving the emancipation of women through the enactment of more liberal laws relating to education, labour conditions and abortion rights. For the four feminists who signed the petition against the regulation of 'Uranisme', a term first employed by German lawyer and activist Karl Heinrich Ulrichs (1825–95), it remains likely that they considered the term only to refer to male same-sex desire. Certainly, for many Dutch feminists, as Myriam Everard writes, the active (and uncontrollable) sexual impulse was a matter that concerned only men.[148] Within this framework, there was little space to conceive of the existence – or merits – of an active female erotic drive. Campaigning against the standard of double morality, female reformers instead sought to bring men's excessive desires in line with women's more modest and morally appropriate romantic friendships and heterosexual yearnings. Given that Article 248bis presented a way of restricting libidinous male desire, it is not surprising, as Everard claims, that so few women signed Schorer's petition in the first instance – or, indeed, that the names of notable figures in the women's and sex reform movements, such as Aletta Jacobs (1854–1929) and Wilhelmina Drucker (1847–1925), remained absent from the list.[149] Based on the narratives that emerged from their series of interviews, van Kooten Niekerk and Wijmer were able to conclude that most women-who-desired-women who lived in the Netherlands in the first half of the twentieth century did not consider the women's emancipation movement as an organization in which their interests would be represented.[150] Indeed, of the nineteen women who signed Schorer's petition against Article 248bis, only Marie de Boer has been considered to have signed with a vested interest in defeating the law restricting homosexuality, on account of what Karen Hillege observes as her 'masculine demeanour', short hair, penchant for cigars and 'powerfully built frame'.[151] Aside from de Boer, and the four feminists who signed the petition, precisely what interests the other fourteen women had in blocking the proposal remain unknown.

Conclusions

Positioned in this chapter as nascent queer sites in the decades leading up to and beyond the First World War, Amsterdam and Berlin present us with altogether different images of urban sexual life. Following this overview, it is evident that a highly developed and successful queer subculture for women could proliferate in Berlin by the mid-1920s for several significant reasons. First, the economic boom after 1923 led to investments in consumer and leisure culture in the German capital that resulted in the establishment of a number of bars and entertainment venues that could cater specifically to networks of queer people, while reaping the financial benefits of those tourists who purportedly wanted to experience excursions 'into abnormality'. While Paragraph 175 criminalized homosexual acts between men, the vice squad in Berlin exercised a surprising degree of tolerance for the development of gay venues, given that it was difficult to exert control over the sheer number of establishments that were cropping up across the city. As well as the tolerance of regulating powers in this regard, love between women was also omitted from the purview of Paragraph 175 due the perceived 'definitional slipperiness' of Sapphic acts, as well as the fear that defining same-sex intimacies through law would serve to promote them to women who were supposedly ignorant of such kinds of knowledge. For these reasons, many of the bars and cafés that existed for women were paid little attention by the regulating powers so long as they did not contravene certain 'limits' on public decency. These venues were also bolstered by the existence of a successful queer press, which will be discussed in detail in Chapter 3. Organizations affiliated with such venues therefore had the advantage of a direct line of communication with their target audience. In this way, they could advertise their events, as well as lucrative offers, to ensure the survival of their local establishment. Undergirding each of these urban developments were the dramatic shifts that had taken place in the gendered landscape in the years following the First World War. Following the establishment of the Weimar Constitution, women achieved, on paper at least, the same fundamental rights as men, which included the right to voting power and to hold office. Moreover, stemming from a need for female workers to remain in paid work due to the loss of male life during the war, the growth in white-collar work saw more women with access to a disposable income, which offered a degree of financial independence. This meant that women were able to take a more active role in public life, both in the workplace as well as within the emergent consumer cultures, in which the print press and bar scene played a large part. Further to changes in the economic position of women, growing numbers of activist groups began to take up the question of the equal rights of queer people, leading to the creation of a visible support network for queer women in Berlin. The wider organizations that existed for men, such as the WhK – but also the BfM and the DFV – enabled women to facilitate their own networks more easily under the auspices of more established associations.

However, in the city of Amsterdam, experiences of urban sexuality continued to be structured by stringent codes of bourgeois morality after the First World War. Although the Netherlands had remained neutral during the conflict, the country did not remain untouched by the effects of war. There was economic and social unrest, although not to the same degree as in Germany, as well as more women entering the workplace due to the defensive mobilization of Dutch soldiers. Yet, already by the late 1920s, Dutch women were experiencing growing hostility on the job market due to the Great Depression, and many were forced to leave salaried and waged positions upon marriage, which pushed them back into the domestic (unpaid) sphere. In conjunction with this, the political and religious subdivision of society, which was coloured by the sociopolitical and morally conservative agenda of the confessional parties, served to entrench further the roles of 'breadwinner' and 'caregiver' in society – a gendered attitude that cut across social pillars. The cultural norms that moored a woman's femininity to the domestic sphere, stemming from a fear that the reputation of a 'respectable' woman might be damaged through associations of licentiousness or sex work, ultimately precluded many women from accessing the slowly emerging bar culture in the city. Furthermore, the introduction of the morality laws in 1911 saw an increased surveillance of immoral behaviours, a law that was extended to exercise control over the sexual intimacies of both same-sex desiring men *and* women. Moreover, the earlier mentioned transvestite law, which prevented crossdressing of any variety, arguably further impinged on women's abilities to create networks due to there being limits on the kinds of signals they were able to emit through sartorial codes and signifiers.[152] In addition to the lack of access to bar culture, the laws that saw queer desires between women criminalized, and the 'cross-dressing' ban, there was no queer press for women to speak of and there appears to have been very little engagement with queer female experience by the emancipation movement for queer rights in the Netherlands. While women were not excluded from the movement per se, Schorer and the NWHK did not develop their theoretical interest in the existence of 'Uranian' women into any kind of active involvement with women's issues. Consequently, members of the existing women's emancipation groups were reluctant to take up the notion of queer female desire and conceived of homosexuality, and active sexual desires more generally, to be associated exclusively with the male subject.

While the emergence and experience of Sapphic subcultures may have differed markedly in Berlin and Amsterdam, women's access to pleasure within these cities was informed by similar structural experiences. For example, although the popular media image of the frivolous flapper who frittered away her earnings on cheap entertainment and consumer goods soon became synonymous with the white-collar worker across Western Europe, it was undercut by the precarious reality of the modern woman's economic existence and the concomitant familial and domestic burdens placed upon her in both Germany and the Netherlands. Thus, while women were earning more than they had been previously in both countries, they often had little time to invest in the leisure pursuits that were on offer to them. Furthermore, in both Germany and the Netherlands, the 'new femininities' that were emerging on the urban landscape were experienced as a double-edged sword. While the 'cosmetic uniform' of femininity could ensure a woman's entry into the workplace, the security of her position was contingent upon maintaining increasingly unobtainable standards of beauty. And, while the performance of femininity gave women access to certain spaces – the workplace, for example – it still precluded their enjoyment of other social settings. In the Netherlands, maintaining a respectable position as a woman was predicated on the ability to comply to conservative bourgeois mandates of morality. This meant that the bar and café culture that was slowly emerging for queer people remained primarily the domain of the queer man. And, for queer feminine women in Berlin, bars such as the *Tavern* imposed strict closed-door policies that only allowed for masculine-presenting women. Even in bars in which queer feminine women were welcome, and even feted, their desires were invariably considered by social commentators as temporal or situational. Queer feminine women were thus always considered outsiders or sexual tourists; even within the bar culture that made up Berlin's socio-sexual fabric. The conflation of queer femininity with temporal desire that Haemmerling wrote about in his guidebook was undoubtedly determined by the growing influence of the medical discourses surfacing from the field of sexology. Indeed, the influence of this complex and highly diverse field of sexual research can be seen in much of the cultural production to emerge from Western Europe during this time. By taking stock of the sexological theories concerning queer feminine desire in the following chapter, I will examine the extent to which women appropriated and subverted such scientific discourses in their own communication channels and literary productions in Parts II and III of this volume.

Notes

1. Trans.: 'Jeder einmal in Berlin! Auch im nächtlichen ... Aber man kommt hier nicht ohne Führer aus. Hier vielleicht am allerwenigsten. Niemals hätte Theseus sich ohne Ariadnes Faden in das Labyrinth gewagt. Und was war das Labyrinth gegen das nächtliche Berlin, gegen die in ihrem Licht und in ihrem Dunkel gleicherweise verwirrende Metropole des Vergnügens?!' Curt Moreck, *Führer durch das 'lasterhafte' Berlin* (Leipzig: Verlag moderner Stadtführer, 1931), p. 10.
2. Heike Schader, *Virile, Vamps und wilde Veilchen: Sexualität, Begehren und Erotik in den Zeitschriften homosexueller Frauen im Berlin der 1920er Jahre* (Königstein: Ulrike Helmer, 2004), p. 28.
3. Jet Bussemaker, 'Gender and the Separation of Spheres in Twentieth Century Dutch Society: Pillarisation, Welfare State Formation and Individualisation', in Jet Bussemaker and Rian Voet eds), *Gender, Participation and Citizenship in the Netherlands* (Aldershot: Ashgate, 1998), p. 29.
4. This does not touch upon the periodicals that were aimed at queer women, which will be discussed in Chapters 3 and 4. See Schader, *Virile, Vamps und wilde Veilchen*, p. 252.
5. Trans.: 'zoovel vrijer en vlotter ... dan de onze in ons kille land'. L., 'Wij in den vreemde', *Wij*, 10 September 1932 (estimated), p. 7.
6. See Gert Hekma and Jan Willem Duyvendak, 'Gay Men and Lesbians in the Netherlands', in Nancy L. Fischer and Steven Seidman (eds), *Introducing the New Sexuality Studies*, 3rd edn. (New York: Routledge, 2016).
7. See, for example, Rory MacLean, *Berlin: Imagine a City* (Berlin: Weidenfeld & Nicolson, 2014); Brian Ladd, *The Ghosts of Berlin: Confronting German History in the Urban Landscape* (Chicago: University of Chicago Press, 1997); Anthony McElligott, *The German Urban Experience: Modernity and Crisis 1900–1945* (New York: Routledge, 2001); Willem Frijhoff et al. (eds), *Geschiedenis van Amsterdam: Hoofdstad in Aanbouw 1813–1900* (Amsterdam: SUN, 2006); Richter Roegholt, *Amsterdam na 1900* (The Hague: Sdu, 1993); Geert Mak, *Amsterdam: A Brief Life of the City*, trans. by Philipp Blom (London: Harvill Press, 1994).
8. Frances Mossop, *Mapping Berlin: Representations of Space in the Weimar Feuilleton* (Oxford: Peter Lang, 2015), p. 8; Stephen J. Lee, *The Weimar Republic* (New York: Routledge, 1998), p. 147.
9. Martina Hessler, '"Damned Always to Alter, But Never to Be": Berlin's Culture of Change around 1900', in *Urban Modernity: Cultural Innovation in the Second Industrial Revolution* ed. Levin et. al. (Cambridge, MA: MIT Press, 2010), p. 167.
10. Benjamin Ziemann suggests that violence against women can also be considered a form of political violence with 'politics here being defined as the conflict-ridden struggle about the relation between social order and male/female role models. The significance of the murder and rape of women is thus not limited to the immediate struggle between the people directly involved'. Benjamin Ziemann, 'Germany after the First World War: A Violent Society? Results and Implications of Recent Research on Weimar Germany', *Journal of Modern European History* 1(1) (2003), 80–95, at 94.
11. Otto Dix's postwar images, which often depicted scenes of brutal violence against women, as Maria Tatar has noted, attempted to deal with male anger at 'the female enemy on the domestic front'. With images of sexually available women blended with mutilated female bodies, Dix's imagery also engaged with the concerns with changing gender and sexual norms that characterized the Weimar era. Similarly, Fritz Lang's film *Metropolis* (1927) also took up the new challenges to the gendered status quo

as its central theme. See Maria Tatar, *Lustmord: Sexual Murder in Weimar Germany* (Princeton: Princeton University Press, 1995), pp. 68–69.
12. Tatar, *Lustmord*, p. 4.
13. Ibid.
14. Mak, *Amsterdam*, p. 190.
15. The first Golden Age in the Netherlands refers to the scientific innovations and cultural prosperity of the seventeenth century. Ibid.
16. Ibid., p. 221.
17. 'Introduction', in Corrie van Eijl et al. (eds), *Sociaal Nederland: Contouren van de twintigste eeuw* (Amsterdam: Aksant, 2001), p. 6.
18. Around 200,000 Dutch troops were mobilized during the First World War. See Maartje M. Abbenhuis, *The Art of Staying Neutral: The Netherlands in the First World War, 1914–1918* (Amsterdam: Amsterdam University Press, 2006), p. 217.
19. Mineke Bosch, 'Domesticity, Pillarization and Gender: Historical Explanations for the Divergent Pattern of Dutch Women's Economic Citizenship', *BMGN: The Low Countries Historical Review*, 125 (2010), 269–300 (at p. 285).
20. Trans.: 'slechts één minuut met iemand hoefde te spreken of men wist dat die ander christelijk, rooms, liberaal of socialist was'. Ivo Schöffer, *Veelvormig verleden: zeventien studies in de vaderlandse geschiedenis* (Amsterdam: Bataafsche Leeuw, 1987), p. 90.
21. Inge Bleijenbergh and Jet Bussemaker, 'The Women's Vote in the Netherlands: From the "Houseman's Vote"', in Blanca Rodríguez-Ruiz and Ruth Rubio-Marín (eds), *The Struggle for Female Suffrage in Europe: Voting to Become Citizens* (Leiden: Brill, 2012), p. 184.
22. Thanks are due here to Anna P.H. Geurts for some more nuanced insights into the character of class within the context of the project of pillarization.
23. Arend Lijphart, *The Politics of Accommodation: Pluralism and Democracy in the Netherlands* (Berkeley: University of California Press, 1975), p. 16.
24. During the Pacification, a political agreement was reached in which state funding was provided for religious schools and suffrage was granted to all men (and later to women in 1919). As Rudy B. Andeweg and Galen Irwin suggest, the 'Pacification' of 1917 is also an echo of the Pacification of Ghent in 1576, during which the Dutch provinces agreed to respect religious differences and stand united against the Spanish. See Rudy B. Andeweg and Galen A. Irwin, *Governance and Politics of the Netherlands*, 4th edn (Basingstoke: Palgrave Macmillan, 2014), p. 45.
25. Bosch, 'Domesticity', p. 283.
26. Bussemaker, 'Gender and the Separation of Spheres', p. 26.
27. Trans.: 'de katholieke opgevoede meisjes mochten alleen afstemmen op de KRO terwijl de protestantse meisjes alleen mochten luisteren naar de NCRV'. Anja van Kooten Niekerk and Sacha Wijmer, *Verkeerde vriendschap: Lesbisch leven in de jaren 1920–1960* (Amsterdam: Feministische uitgeverij Sara, 1985), p. 11.
28. The Dutch saying 'twee geloven op een kussen daar slaapt de duivel tussen' ('two faiths in one bed [lit. on one pillow] between them sleeps the devil') highlights the social taboo that surrounded what was termed at this time a 'mixed marriage'.
29. Ursula Langkau-Alex, '"Naturally, Many Things Were Strange But I Could Adapt": Women Emigrés in the Netherlands', in Sibylle Quack (ed.), *Between Sorrow and Strength: Women Refugees of the Nazi Period* (Cambridge: Cambridge University Press, 2002), p. 106.
30. Although the socializing of many women was limited to the confines of their pillar, the Catholic Women's Club (Katholiek Vrouwen Dispuut), the Dutch Organization of Housewives (Nederlandse Vereniging van Huisvrouwen), the Dutch Organization

of Female Farmers (Nederlandse Bond voor Boerinnen) and the Dutch Catholic Organization of Female Farmers (de Nederlandse Katholieke Boerinnenbond) represent only a small selection of a surprisingly diverse range of organizations that existed for women along the lines of class political background and religious faith. However, the supposedly apolitical Vrije Vrouwenvereniging (Free Women's Association) struggled to overcome the boundaries of cultural segmentation, despite its unprecedented attempt to unite women from all social backgrounds. For more on Dutch women's organizations, see Maria Grever and Berteke Waaldijk, *Transforming the Public Sphere: The Dutch National Exhibition of Women's Labour in 1898*, trans. by Mischa F.C. Hoyinck and Robert E. Chesal (Durham, NC: Duke University Press, 2004); Mineke Bosch, 'History and Historiography of First-Wave Feminism in the Netherlands 1860–1922', in Sylvia Paletschek and Bianka Pietrow-Ennker (eds), *Women's Emancipation Movements in the Nineteenth Century: A European Perspective* (Stanford: Stanford University Press, 2004).

31. See Karin Hausen, 'The German Nation's Obligation to the Heroes' Widows of World War One', in Margaret Randolph Higonnet et al. (eds), *Behind the Lines: Gender and the Two World Wars* (New Haven: Yale University Press, 1987), p. 128.
32. Richard Bessel, *Germany after the First World War* (Oxford: Clarendon Press, 1993), p. 225.
33. Siegfried Kracauer, *The Salaried Masses: Duty and Distraction in Weimar Germany*, trans. by Quintin Hoare (New York: Verso, 1998), p. 29.
34. Ibid., p. 30.
35. Ute Frevert, *Women in German History: From Bourgeois Emancipation to Sexual Liberation*, trans. by Stuart McKinnon-Evans (New York: Berg, 1993), p. 156.
36. Helen Boak, *Women in the Weimar Republic* (Manchester: Manchester University Press, 2013), p. 135.
37. Frevert, *Women in German History*, p. 176.
38. Renate Bridenthal and Claudia Koonz, 'Beyond Kinder, Küche, Kirche: Weimar Women in Politics and Work', in Renate Bridenthal et al. (eds), *When Biology Became Destiny Women in Weimar and Nazi Germany* (New York: Monthly Review Press, 1984), pp. 33–66.
39. Ibid.
40. Boak explains that the census was broken down into five occupational categories: independent workers, family helpers, white-collar workers and civil servants, manual workers, and domestic servants. There were also five employment sectors: agriculture, industry, trade and commerce, the civil service and the professions, and domestic service. Boak, *Women in the Weimar Republic*, p. 150.
41. Katie Sutton, *The Masculine Woman in Weimar Germany* (New York: Berghahn Books, 2013), p. 6.
42. Vibeke Rützou Petersen, *Women and Modernity in Weimar Germany: Reality and Its Representation in Popular Fiction* (New York: Berghahn Books, 2001), p. 80.
43. Trans.: 'ein kosmetisches Uniformstück des weiblichen Geschlechts'. Moreck, *Führer*, p. 52.
44. Mila Ganeva, *Women in Weimar Fashion: Discourses and Displays in German Culture 1918–1933* (Rochester: Camden House, 2008), p. 192.
45. Boak, *Women in the Weimar Republic*, p. 153.
46. Indeed, as Boak suggests, 'only when [a salary] provides [women] with the means to live independently of any other financial support can it be deemed emancipatory'. Ibid., p. 134.
47. Katharina von Ankum, 'Gendered Urban Spaces in Irmgard Keun's *Das kunstseidene Mädchen*', in Katharina von Ankum (eds), *Women in the Metropolis: Gender and*

Modernity in Weimar Culture (Berkeley: University of California Press, 1997), pp. 162–85.
48. Francisca de Haan, *Gender and Politics of Office Work: The Netherlands 1860–1940* (Amsterdam: Amsterdam University Press, 1998), p. 3.
49. Deborah Simonton, *A History of European Women's Work: 1700 to the Present* (New York: Routledge, 1998), p. 192.
50. Jet Bussemaker and Rian Voet, 'Introduction', in Jet Bussemaker and Rian Voet (eds), *Gender Participation and Citizenship in the Netherlands* (Aldershot: Ashgate, 1998), p. 6.
51. Ibid., p. 3.
52. In contrast to the debates around the masculinization of the modern woman in Berlin, it is interesting to note that in the case of the 'boy-ish' office worker in the Netherlands, discussions were framed in terms of a 'new femininity' as opposed to a perceived masculinization of women. See de Haan, *Gender and Politics*, p. 76.
53. Perhaps on account of the convenience of this arrangement, the Socialist and Liberal pillars rarely challenged this notion either. See Bussemaker, 'Gender and the Separation of Spheres', p. 22.
54. Ibid., p. 42.
55. As Leo Lucassen observes, the cuts at the rail service and the Post Office were only the tip of the iceberg for a more culturally widespread resistance to women's work. See Leo Lucassen, 'Sekse en nationaliteit als ordenend principe: De uitsluiting van vrouwen en vreemdelingen op de Nederlandse arbeidsmarkt (1900–1995)', in Corrie van de Eijl et al. (eds), *Sociaal Nederland: contouren van de twintigste eeuw* (Amsterdam: Aksant, 2001), p. 88.
56. De Haan, *Gender and Politics*, p. 99.
57. Ibid., p. 58
58. Cited in Jane Fenoulhet, *Making the Personal Political: Dutch Women Writers 1919–1970* (London: Legenda, 2007), p. 19.
59. Of course, some women lived with 'outside' family units as domestic servants or lady's maids, and others lived onsite at their jobs in hospitals or care homes; this is discussed briefly later on in this chapter.
60. Robert Beachy, *Gay Berlin: Birthplace of a Modern Identity* (New York: Vintage Books, 2014), p. 192.
61. Ibid., p. 196.
62. As the link between the rise of capitalism and the development of urban (homo)sexual subcultures has already been documented extensively elsewhere, it shall not be discussed in detail here. See, for example, John D'Emilio, 'Capitalism and Gay Identity', in Henry Abelove et al. (eds), *The Gay and Lesbian Studies Reader* (London: Routledge, 1993), pp. 467–76; Amy Gluckman and Betsy Reed, *Homo Economics: Capitalism, Community, and Lesbian and Gay Life* (New York: Routledge, 1999); Jeffrey Weeks, 'Capitalism and the Organization of Sex', in Gay Left Collective (eds), *Homosexuality: Power and Politics* (London: Allison & Busby, 1980), pp. 11–20; Justin Bengry, 'Courting the Pink Pound: *Men Only* and the Queer Consumer, 1935–1939', *History Workshop Journal* 68 (2009), 122–48.
63. Trans.: 'einfacher und bürgerlicher, mehr zur Behaglichkeit und Traulichkeit als zu Eleganz und Luxus und Pomp tendierend'; 'trotz aller Toleranz gerade in sexuellen Dingen, ist vorläufig eine Frau ... gesellschaftlich noch ebenso geächtet wie ehemals'. Ruth Margarete Roellig, *Berlins lesbische Frauen* in Adele Meyer, *Lila Nächte: Die Damenklubs der Zwanziger Jahre* (Cologne: Zitronenpresse, 1981), p. 30.
64. Trans.: 'streng geschlossene Gesellschaft'; 'mit polyphemischem Argwohn'. Moreck, *Führer*, p. 172.

65. Trans.: 'ältesten und bekanntesten Lokale der Frauenwelt'. Roellig, *Berlins lesbische Frauen*, p. 46.
66. However, in her guidebook to Berlin's Sapphic subcultures, Ruth Margarete Roellig remained undecided about the origins of the organization's name, claiming that 'scorpion' could just as well refer to a specific subcultural type as to Weirauch's novels: 'people born under this celestial sign, are considered to be tireless seekers of sensual pleasure, they only feel happy if they can fully live out their desire for love, just as their nature demands it'. Trans.: 'Denn Menschen, die unter diesem Himmelszeichen geboren sind, gelten als unermüdliche Sucher nach sinnlichen Genüssen, und fühlen sich nur glücklich wenn sie sich in ihrem Liebesdrange voll ausleben können, wie es ihre Natur verlangt.' As will become apparent in Chapter 6 in this volume, the supposed 'types' that gathered in the *Taverne* bar do not appear redolent of any of the characters that are presented (positively, at least) in Weirauch's works. Ibid., p. 57.
67. Schader, *Virile*, pp. 111–19.
68. Roellig, *Berlins lesbische Frauen*, p. 29.Trans.: 'Als Besonderheit des Klubs gilt die ganz offizielle Unterscheidung von "Bubis" den maskulinen und "Mädis" den femininen Frauen.' The name *Die Zauberflöte* could be an allusion to the German-Swiss poet and artist Else Lasker-Schüler, who adopted the alter-ego of Yusuf 'The Prince of Thebes' in an appeal to the Ancient Egyptian and Arab Near East cultures, and was often pictured playing a flute. For more on Lasker-Schüler, see Katrin Sieg, *Exiles, Eccentrics, Activists: Women in Contemporary German Theater* (Ann Arbor: University of Michigan Press, 1994).
69. Trans.: 'dumpfe Bierluft und Rauchschwaden … und eine grelle Jazzmusik'. Roellig, *Berlins lesbische Frauen*, p. 57.
70. Trans.: 'Atmosphäre von Derbheit und Urwüchsigkeit'; 'plötzlich, wie von ungefähr bricht ein Zank aus, Stimmen kreischen, Worte fliegen … – und es ist durchaus keine Seltenheit, daß der Streit bis zur Prügelei ausartet'. Ibid., p. 58.
71. Trans.: 'die Elite der intellektuellen Welt der lesbischen Frauen, Filmstars, Sängerinnen, [und] Schauspielerinnen'. Ibid., p. 71.
72. Ibid., p. 25.
73. Trans.: 'durch und durch normal und nur mit dem Gedanken an einen Ausflug ins Anormale gelegentlich kokettieren'; 'fremde und darum so reizvolle Atmosphäre'. Moreck, *Führer*, p. 157.
74. Ibid., p. 170.
75. Trans.: 'Frauen sind selten Trinkerinnen großen Stils – und der Wirt muß auch leben', Roellig, *Berlins lesbische Frauen*, p. 52. In a bid to make sure bars were as accessible as possible for women, many organizers attempted to keep the cost of entry as low as possible and some members-only bars threw 'student balls' (*Studentenbälle*) with lower-priced tickets, offering gifts to their patrons as well as attractive promotions on drinks and competitions. Jen Jack Gieseking's latest contribution *A Queer New York: Geographies of Lesbians, Dykes, and Queers* (New York: New York University Press, 2020) offers valuable present-day insights to the understanding of the difficulty of creating and maintaining queer female spaces, and the specific implications of gentrification, as well as the processes of economic decline, on such spaces.
76. Magnus Hirschfeld, *Die Homosexualität des Mannes und des Weibes* (Berlin: Louis Marcus, 1914), p. 910.
77. Gert Hekma, *De roze rand van donker Amsterdam* (Amsterdam: Van Gennep, 1992), p. 11.
78. The infamous Bet van Beeren, who will be discussed shortly, was said to have established this code. However, stories such as 'It's an Owl' ("t is een uil'), published in the queer

magazine *The Right to Live* in 1940, suggest that this code was in fact more nuanced than this and that some queer patrons used the code to identify other queer persons. In the story mentioned above, two men are depicted drinking in a café and fiercely debating whether a third man – situated across the café – is an 'owl'. When the magazine *The Right to Live* falls out of the suspect's briefcase, the riddle appears to be solved. Given that the man is accompanied by a close female companion, however, one of the original pair concludes that he must be a 'night owl', a play on words that refers to someone who is active at night. See Sjuul Deckwitz, 'Bet van Beeren', in Gert Hekma et al. (eds), *Goed verkeerd: een geschiedenis van homoseksuele mannen en lesbische vrouwen in Nederland* (Amsterdam: Meulenhoff, 1989), pp. 129–30; Hans van Beeck, ''t is een uil', *Levensrecht* (1) 1940, pp. 10–11.
79. Hekma et al. (eds), *De roze rand*, p. 17.
80. Trans.: 'weinig meer bekend is dan dat ze sigaren rookte'. Ibid., p. 19.
81. Trans.: 'kwam nogal een en ander aan het licht, ook dingen, welke in strijd waren met de openbare zeden'. 'Inval in een Amsterdamsche bar', *Nieuwsblad van het Noorden*, 17 September 1932.
82. Deckwitz, 'Bet van Beeren', p. 129.
83. Trans.: 'het was een ongelofelijk goed feest waarbij de mensen ongeacht hun sexe met elkaar mochten dansen en dat was in die tijd een soort fenomeen, want dat mocht nérgens, dat mocht nóoit (maar) bij Bet mócht het en kón het en niemand vond het vreemd'. Yvonne van den Heuij and Diana van Laar. 'Café 't Mandje', http://www.cafetmandje.amsterdam/geschiedenis (retrieved 18 April 2022).
84. See Hekma, *De roze rand van donker Amsterdam*; Judith Schuyf, *Een stilzwijgende samenzwering: Lesbische vrouwen in Nederland 1920–1970* (The Hague: IISG, 1994); Rob Tielman, *Homoseksualiteit in Nederland* (Amsterdam: Boom, 1982).
85. Global Network of Sex Work Projects, 'Policy Brief: Sex Work as Work'. Retrieved 18 April 2022 from https://www.nswp.org/sites/nswp.org/files/policy_brief_sex_work_as_work_nswp_-_2017.pdf.
86. Van Kooten Niekerk and Wijmer, *Verkeerde vriendschap*, p. 87.
87. Beachy, *Gay Berlin*, pp. 85–86.
88. 'Besprechung des Jahrbuchs', *Jahrbuch für sexuelle Zwischenstufen* 10 (1909), 441.
89. This contrasts particularly with Adolf Brand's anti-feminist Gemeinschaft der Eigenen (GdE). The GdE was a literary and cultural circle of homosexual men who separated themselves from Magnus Hirschfeld's WhK and his theory of the 'Third Sex' in 1903. The name of Brand's organization has inspired various translations into English. While the most popular translation appears to be the 'Community of the Special', the Gemeinschaft der Eigenen has also been translated as the 'Community of Self-Owners/the Self-Determined', and the 'Community of Free Spirits', foregrounding the separatist (and elitist) nature of its members. The term 'Eigen', in both the name of Brand's organization and his publication *Der Eigene* (*The Self-Owner*), was inspired by Max Stirner's philosophy that appeared in his seminal *Der Einzige und sein Eigentum* (*The Ego and Its Own*, 1844).
90. Kirsten Leng, 'Culture, Difference, and Sexual Progress in Turn-of-the-Century Europe: Cultural Othering and the German League for the Protection of Mothers and Sexual Reform, 1905–1914', *Journal of the History of Sexuality* 25(1) (2016), 62–82.
91. Beachy, *Gay Berlin*, pp. 160–63.
92. Trans.: 'von überall auf der Welt … um hier eine Freiheit zu genießen, die ihnen in ihren Heimatländern verwehrt würde'. Cited in Ute *Scheub, Verrückt nach Leben: Berliner Szenen in den zwanziger Jahren* (Reinbek: Rowohlt, *2000*), p. 133.

93. Bauer, *The Hirschfeld Archives: Violence, Death and Modern Queer Culture* (Philadelphia: Temple University Press, 2017), p. 79.
94. Ibid.
95. Rob Tielman, 'Schorer en het Nederlandsch Wetenschappelijk Humanitair Komitee (1911-1940)', in *Homojaarboek 1: Artikelen over emancipatie en homoseksualiteit* (Amsterdam: Van Gennep, 1981), p. 107.
96. Pieter Koenders, *Homoseksualiteit in bezet Nederland: Verzwegen hoofdstuk* ('s-Gravenhage: De Woelrat, 1983), p. 24.
97. Trans.: 'Schorer wás het NWHK, het NWHK wás Schorer.' Tielman, *Homoseksualiteit in Nederland*, p. 88.
98. In Germany, as James Steakley has argued, Hirschfeld's WhK might be considered as 'one of a panoply of efforts for reform which came to be known collectively as the *Lebensreformbewegung* [life reform movement]'James P. Steakley, *The Homosexual Emancipation Movement in Germany* (New York: Arno Press, 1975), p. 26.
99. Most of the publications listed in the catalogue were originally printed in German. Like Hirschfeld, Schorer was in the process of building a library and archive of sexological and emancipatory materials. Whereas Hirschfeld's Institute was destroyed in 1933 and the contents of his archive and library were burned or expropriated, Schorer pre-empted the Nazi attack on knowledge in the Netherlands and dissolved the NWHK, destroying the records. In spite of these pre-emptive moves, what remained of the NWHK library was confiscated by the Nazis and has been lost or destroyed. Since the 1980s, the IHLIA (Internationaal Homo/Lesbisch Informatiecentrum en Archief) has worked to piece together Schorer's collection from the catalogue of books that the activist compiled.
100. Trans.: 'bij vrouwen zoo goed als bij mannen'. Rob Tielman, 'Schorer', in *Homojaarboek 1*, p. 122.
101. As Robert Beachy describes, Commissioner Hüllessem adopted a policy of tolerance due to the 'impractical task of investigating dozens of small bars where homosexuals might congregate, a nearly impossible task in a large, sprawling city' (Beachy, *Gay Berlin*, p. 46). Furthermore, so long as homosexual activities did not cause a public disturbance, it was almost impossible for individuals to be charged under Paragraph 175. For a more comprehensive description of the policing of homosexuality in Berlin, see Beachy, *Gay Berlin*, particularly, pp. 42–84.
102. Ibid., p. 55.
103. The first city to introduce a 'vice squad' was Rotterdam in 1908, followed by The Hague in 1913 and Utrecht in 1918. See Schuyf, *Een Stilzwijgende samenzwering*, p. 112.
104. Trans.: 'Die widernatürliche Unzucht, welche zwischen Personen männlichen Geschlechts oder von Menschen mit Thieren verübt wird, ist mit Gefängnis von sechs Monaten bis zu vier Jahren, sowie mit zeitiger Untersagung der Ausübung der bürgerlichen Ehrenrechte zu bestrafen.' See 'Preußisches Strafgesetzbuch von 1851', http://www.koeblergerhard.de/Fontes/StrafgesetzbuchPreussen1851.pdf (retrieved 18 April 2022).
105. Although crimes of sodomy had become more closely associated with sexual acts between men by the early nineteenth century, sodomy was used as a broad referent to describe a diverse range of vices 'against nature' and was not reserved exclusively for the description of anal same-sex intercourse (between men). For more on the linguistic development of the terms 'sodomy' and 'sodomite', see Arthur Gilbert, 'Conceptions of Homosexuality and Sodomy in Western History', *Journal of Homosexuality* 6(1/2) (1981), 57–68; Gert Hekma 'A History of Sexology: Social and Historical Aspects of Sexuality', in Jan Bremmer (ed.), *From Sappho to De Sade: Moments in the History of Sexuality* (New York: Routledge, 1991). For more on the interesting biography of Linck specifically, see Brigitte Eriksson, 'A Lesbian Execution in Germany, 1721: The Trial Records', *Journal of Homosexuality* 6 (1980/81), 27–40.

106. Laurie Marhoefer, *Sex and the Weimar Republic: German Homosexual Emancipation and the Rise of the Nazis* (Toronto: University of Toronto Press, 2015), p. 71.
107. Trans.: 'beischlafsähnliche Handlungen'. Ibid.
108. Tracie Matysik, *Reforming the Moral Subject: Ethics and Sexuality in Central Europe, 1890–1930* (Ithaca, NY: Cornell University Press, 2008), p. 160.
109. Marhoefer, *Sex in the Weimar Republic*, p. 74.
110. Ibid., pp. 71–72.
111. The Eulenburg affair of 1906–9 was a domestic scandal that centred upon the German Emperor Wilhelm II and the 'allegedly abnormal and effeminate sexuality displayed by the Kaiser's circle of friends and advisers'. The daily press was outraged by the story, which brought queer desire firmly into the public domain. See Claudia Bruns, 'Masculinity, Sexuality, and the German Nation: The Eulenburg Scandals and Kaiser Wilhelm II in Political Cartoons', in Udo K. Hebel and Christoph Wagner (eds), *Pictorial Cultures and Political Iconographies: Approaches, Perspectives, Case Studies from Europe and America* (Berlin: Walter de Gruyter, 2011), p. 119.
112. See Anna Rüling, 'Welches Interesse hat die Frauenbewegung an der Lösung der homosexuellen Problems?', *Jahrbuch für sexuelle Zwischenstufen* 7 (1905), 131–51.
113. See Helene Stöcker, 'Die beabsichtigte Ausdehnung des §175 auf die Frau', in Ilse Kokula, *Weibliche Homosexualität um 1900 in zeitgenössische Dokumenten* (Munich: Frauenoffensive, 1981), pp. 267–78.
114. Trans.: 'die normale Liebe, die Liebe zwischen Mann und Frau'. Ibid., p. 267.
115. Trans.: 'unserer Entlastung, unseren Rechten, nicht bei unseren Knebelungen und Strafen'. Käthe Schirmacher, '§175 des deutschen Strafgesetzes', in Ilse Kokula, *Weibliche Homosexualität um 1900 in zeitgenössische Dokumenten* (Munich: Frauenoffensive, 1981), p. 257.
116. Trans.: 'Sollen diese Leichen nun noch einmal totgeschlagen, soll auch noch der Verkehr mit Frauen unter Strafe gestellt werden? Dann hat die Prostituierte ja nicht in den eignen vier Wänden Ruhe, und das Gebiet der Willkür verschlingt ihr letztes Refugium.' Ibid., p. 258.
117. Trans.: 'von Frauen ausgeübt, genau so verwerflich, widerwärtig und ekelhaft, als wenn es von Männern begangen wird'. Anna Pappritz, 'Zum §175', in Kokula, *Weibliche Homosexualität*, p. 260.
118. Trans.: 'ihre krankhafte Veranlagung auf ihre Nachkommenschaft'. The openly 'urnische' feminists Anna Rüling and Johanna Elberskirchen also shared this problematic view, claiming that the children of women-who-desired-women born through marriages to men 'make up a large percentage of the feeble-minded, the imbeciles, the epileptics, those with consumption and degenerates of all kinds'. Trans.: 'stellen einen großen Prozentsatz zu der Zahl der Schwachsinnigen, Blödsinnigen, Epileptischen, Brustkranken, Degenerierten aller Art'. Ibid., p. 262.
119. Trans.: 'mit der "Emanzipation des Weibes" nichts zu schaffen'. Otto Weininger, *Geschlecht und Charakter: Eine prinzipielle Untersuchung*, 10th edn (Vienna: Wilhelm Braumüller, 1910), p. 84.
120. Katharina Rowold, *The Educated Woman: Minds, Bodies, and Women's Higher Education in Britain, Germany, and Spain 1865–1914* (New York: Routledge, 2010), p. 131.
121. Matysik, *Reforming the Moral Subject*, p. 167, emphasis in original.
122. Trans.: 'was beim Mann unnatürlich "weiblich" anmutet: auffallend herzliches, zärtliches Benehmen zwischen Mann und Mann, Liebkosungen, Schmeichelworte u. dgl., das ist bei Frauen in allen Lebensaltern etwas durchaus Natürliches … Soll sich die Frau das alles, um nicht falschen Verdacht zu erregen, abgewöhnen müssen'. Such a statement, of course, does not refer to the existence of the visibly queer and masculine woman,

whom Krukenberg would have presumably considered 'unnatural'. Elsbeth Krukenberg, '§175', in Kokula, *Weibliche Homosexualität*, p. 256.
123. Ibid.
124. Marhoefer, *Sex and the Weimar Republic*, p. 120.
125. Rictor Norton, *Myth of the Modern Homosexual: Queer History and the Search for Cultural Unity* (London: Bloomsbury Academic, 2016), p. 138.
126. Schuyf, *Een Stilzwijgende samenzwering*, p. 102.
127. Gert Hekma, *Amsterdam: The Last Vestiges of the Sixties?* (Amsterdam: University of Amsterdam Press, 2000), p. 16.
128. Trans.: 'weerzinwekkende en naamloze zonde'; 'psychologisch en medisch-wettig probleem'. Van Kooten Niekerk and Wijmer, *Verkeerde vriendschap*, p. 24.
129. Frank van Vree, 'Media, Morality and Popular Culture: The Case of the Netherlands, 1870–1965', in Bob Moore and Henk van Nierop (eds), *Twentieth Century Mass Society in Britain and the Netherlands* (Oxford: Berg, 2006), p. 87.
130. Maarten Salden, 'Artikel 248 bis wetboek van strafrecht de geschiedenis van een strafbaarstelling', *Groniek Historisch Tijdschrift* 66 (1980), 33–48 (at p. 41).
131. H. J. van Heek, '"Het Koekoeksei van Regout" De parlementaire geschiedenis van artikel 248 bis', reprinted in Maurice van Lieshout, *Een groeiend zedelijk kwaad: documenten over de criminalisering en emancipatie van homoseksuelen 1910–1916* (Amsterdam: Het Spinhuis, 1992), pp. 12–33.
132. Anna Tijsseling, 'Schuldige Seks: homoseksuele zedendelicten rondom de Duitse bezettingstijd', unpublished doctoral thesis (Utrecht: University of Utrecht, 2009), p. 52.
133. The law was in force between 1911 and 1971, and read as follows: 'De meerderjarige, die met een minderjarige van hetzelfde geslacht, wiens minderjarigheid hij kent of redelijkerwijs moet vermoeden, ontucht pleegt, wordt gestraft met gevangenisstraf van ten hoogste vier jaar.' See Maartin Salden, 'Artikel 248 Bis wetboek van Strafrecht de geschiedenis van een strafbaarstelling', *Groniek Historisch Tijdschrift* 66 (1980), 38–48.
134. The trouser ban is a particularly striking point of comparison between the sexual and gendered control of bodies and their pleasures in Amsterdam and Berlin. While the trouser ban was not removed from the Amsterdam's local governmental laws until the late 1980s, in some exceptional cases, *Transvestitenscheine* were being granted in Berlin that permitted the holder to present as the gender they were not assigned at birth. Already in 1909, Magnus Hirschfeld had convinced local authorities in Berlin that his patient, Frau Katz, should be awarded a *Transvestitenschein* after she was detained on several occasions by authorities after they assumed that she was a man attempting to pass as a woman. For further information on the 'trouser ban', see Judith Schuyf and Marloes Schoonheim, 'Geschiedenis', in Mirjam Hemker and Linda Huijsmans (eds), *De lesbo- encyclopedie* (Amsterdam: Ambo-Anthos, 2009). For more discussion on *Transvestitenscheine*, see Beachy, *Gay Berlin*, pp. 171–72.
135. Tijsseling, 'Schuldige Seks', p. 52.
136. Tielman, *Homoseksualiteit in Nederland*, p. 118.
137. Schuyf, *Een Stilzwijgende samenzwering*, p. 117.
138. Van Kooten Niekerk and Wijmer, *Verkeerde vriendschap*, pp. 205–9.
139. Trans.: 'Je hebt een lesbische relatie, zei die rechercheur. Ik wist helemaal niet wat dat was.' Ibid., p. 206.
140. Trans.: 'die man heeft me alle mogelijke dingen gevraagd … zo intiem, vooral over hoe je het deed. Van alles over je seksuele leven, niet te geloven, tot in de finesses'. Ibid., p. 208.
141. Koenders, *Homoseksualiteit in bezet Nederland*, pp. 30–34.
142. Ibid.

143. Note especially the anti-East Indies prejudice in this quote: Dutch people who returned from the Indies, and particularly people who were born there (especially those of ethnically 'mixed' parentage), were said to have an overly sensual and effeminate nature. Trans.: 'Gij, uranische ratten; gij, onvruchtbare echtverbrekers; gij homosexueele honden; gij lesbische krengen; gij rottend vulsel van deze samenleving, die toch zoo graag coquetteert met Christus, maar dien gij gedegradeerd hebt thans tot een indisch homosexueeltje, tot een juffrouwachtig jongetje, tot de verpersoonlijking van uw eigen bleeke genietinkjes.' Ibid., p. 32.
144. Ibid., p. 33.
145. Trans.: 'bij een homoseksuele vriend'; 'een bohemien-achtige vrouw'. Van Kooten Niekerk and Wijmer, *Verkeerde vriendschap*, p. 205.
146. Trans.: 'eerder regel dan uitzondering'. Rob Tielman, *Homosexualiteit in Nederland* (Amsterdam: Boom Meppel, 1982), p. 69.
147. Myriam Everard, 'Vier feministen en het Nederlandsch Wetenschappelijk Humanitair Komitee. De historische verhouding tussen de Nederlandsche vrouwenbeweging en het lesbische', in Selma Sevenhuijsen et al. (eds), *Socialisties-Feministiese Teksten VIII* (Amsterdam: Sara, 1984), pp. 149–75.
148. Everard, 'Vier feministen', p. 149.
149. Ibid., pp. 165–66.
150. Van Kooten Niekerk and Wijmer, *Verkeerde vriendschap*, p. 14.
151. See Karen Hillege 'Eén van de acht: Marie de Boer. Over Helmondse ondertekenaars van de Schorer-petitie', in Michael Dallas et al. (eds), *Homojaarboek 3: Artikelen over emancipatie en homoseksualiteit* (Amsterdam: Van Gennep, 1985), p. 19.
152. The contemporary notion that a woman's rightful place was in the home means that only those women who attempted to escape the boundaries of gendered norms, such as Mie Lauffer, Bet van Beeren and Marie de Boer, have been documented in queer histories. It is also not insignificant that these women were working class, a category of women that has often been excluded from the parameters of idealized femininity.

Chapter 2

SEXUAL SCIENCE
The Queer Feminine Mystique

On 30 May 1864, a patient entered the Charité hospital in Berlin who would shape scientific discourses on female same-sex desire long into the twentieth century. Thirty-five-year-old 'Miss N.' had been admitted to the hospital's psychiatric ward after a prolonged series of manic episodes and was put under the care of German neurologist and psychiatrist Carl Friedrich Otto Westphal (1833–90). According to the medical testimony that Westphal had received on the patient's admittance, along with personal descriptions provided by the patient and their sister, Miss N. suffered from a 'raging urge to love women', which had driven the patient to obsessive onanism in their teenage years and behavioural disturbances throughout their adult life.[1] Based on his work with Miss N. and other patients on the psychiatric ward, Westphal published the article 'The Contrary Sexual Feeling' ('Die conträre Sexualempfindung') in 1869, in which he presented an analysis of Miss N. that would become paradigmatic for the ways in which female same-sex desires were conceptualized for more than a century to come. Deploying a methodology informed by the developing fields of criminology and psychiatry, Westphal's point of departure was undoubtedly indebted to the earlier works of lawyer and classicist Karl Heinrich Ulrichs (1825–95), considered by many historians to be the forefather of the modern homosexual rights movement. Between 1864 and 1879, Ulrichs produced a series of twelve pamphlets entitled *Studies on the Riddle of Man-Manly Love*, in which he laid out the first comprehensive and affirmative framework of same-sex desire in Western Europe. Deemed highly

controversial at the time of publication, Ulrichs argued that male homosexual desire was largely congenital and occurred as the result of a female 'spirit' (*anima*) existing within a male body. Although the nuances of female sexuality were paid scant attention in Ulrichs' initial studies, his proposal that same-sex desire was prompted by cross-gender identification nonetheless offered Westphal a workable frame of reference for his examination. Through his study of Miss N., the reader learns that the patient preferred boy's games and garments as a child, adopted an 'active' role during sexual acts, and that Miss N. considered themselves to be 'entirely as a man and would like to be a man'.[2] In the descriptions of the intimate acts that took place between Miss N. and a female cousin, the patient explains that although they were able to place their hand 'on the other girl's genitals', they did not ever allow themselves to be touched.[3] The sexual untouchability of Miss N. is seen to be central to Westphal's conceptualization of the patient's inborn masculinity, and thus his conclusions on congenital same-sex desire more generally. His physical examinations of Miss N. seek to confirm his hypothesis, as he claims that the hymen appeared fully intact and 'hardly [allowed] even the tip of the little finger to penetrate'.[4] Commenting little on the violence of such an examination, Westphal uses the 'evidence' of the intact hymen and of Miss N.'s feelings of masculinity to prove that the feelings of the patient were naturally resultant of their inborn cross-gender expression.

While Westphal conceives broadly of a link between the patient's same-sex desires and their innate masculine sensibility, his actual analysis complicates the image that he crudely sets out, and creates a paradigm of queer female desire that, in fact, shared much in terms of its basis with traditional depictions of femininity. Indeed, Miss N. is described not as a manly figure, but rather as a 'somewhat delicately built' individual who did not 'deviate from the female type' in disposition or appearance. The abovementioned intrusive examinations of Miss N.'s genitals were also unable to present Westphal with any evidence of the hypertrophy or atrophy that had previously been used as evidence of female sexual pathology in studies of criminal behaviour, leaving the psychiatrist with little physical 'proof' to authenticate his argument:

> The patient is ... of unprepossessing and insignificant appearance; physiognomy and habitus do not deviate from the female type ... Incidentally, there are no visible deformities in the external formation, particularly not in the genitals. The labia majora gape a little apart so that the labia minora are visible between the pubic column, the clitoris is of ordinary length.[5]

While presupposing the appearance of 'normal' genitals, Westphal evidently also has a ready image of what a deviant vulva might conceive. Yet, the figure of Miss N. does not correspond to such atypical representations. Indeed, while Westphal is sympathetic enough to take his patient's account of their masculinity into serious consideration, the psychiatrist's descriptions of Miss N.'s dissociative states, dizziness, amnesia and migraines were symptoms that would have more been readily associated during this time with the stereotypically 'feminine' malady *neurasthenia*.[6] The disconnect that existed between Miss N.'s conception of their own gender identity and Westphal's prescriptive descriptions of the patient's symptoms are insufficiently addressed in the study to draw further conclusions regarding the significance of Miss N's lived experience on Westphal's hypothesis. However, the fact that Miss N.'s delicately built body and typically feminine neurasthenic symptoms were of importance to the study suggests that psychic masculinity was initially conceived as not being *so* distinct from the realm of the passive and penetrable feminine that had come to be characteristic of normative 'modest' femininity by the late nineteenth century. Westphal's suggestion that Miss N. did not 'deviate from the female type' also laid the groundwork for many of the societal fears that came to be associated with homosexual desire, including the eugenic anxieties concerning the categorization of deviance – if queer women could not be outwardly identified as such, there remained an unspoken threat to the institution of marriage and, more worryingly, future progeny. This framework, in which *anyone* could be suspect of sexual deviance, lasted long into the twentieth century and, indeed, the 'invisible menace' resurfaced as a culturally widespread fear again during the 1960s and 1970s, as was discussed in the Introduction to this book. Yet, while Miss N. may not have deviated from the typical bourgeois female type in Westphal's article, the suggestion that his patient experienced masculine *feelings* in this initial study of same-sex desire trumps any stipulation for somatic gendered inversion and outward expressions of masculinity that would become characteristic of later sexological writing.

Given that cross-gender feeling was initially the only framework through which legitimate (that is, congenital) same-sex desires could exist, it is unsurprising that sexologists were ill-equipped to account for the queer desires of women who conceived of themselves as *women*. When the psychic contrary feeling was compounded by case studies of somatic cross-gendered identification in sexological writing at the end of the nineteenth century, the feminine woman was forced even further to the margins. Indeed, as Lisa Walker notes, the queer feminine woman in sexological writing has always been 'a contradiction in terms – a deductive impossibility'; a figure who frustrated the sex-gender systems based on complementarity by resisting the binary categorizations of nineteenth-century frameworks.[7] In later attempts to address the subject of femininity and to circumvent the problematics of a desire that did not fit the active–passive dichotomy, many sexologists and psychiatrists, who linked gender presentation to 'normative' functioning, sidestepped the problem of the feminine Sapphist by claiming that feminine desires were predominantly temporary and/or treatable. In most cases, a redirection of the sex impulse to an appropriate (male) object through marriage, and the subsequent production of offspring, was proposed as a 'cure' for such short-term deviancy. Yet, quite why the feminine queer woman presented such a definitional struggle for sexologists in history has been little explored, due to the bias towards the masculine element outlined earlier in this volume. For this reason, in this chapter I will consider more closely the marginalizing of the feminine subject in early theories of same-sex desire, as well as the question of when and how queer feminine women made their way onto the sexological stage as 'objects' of study.

Following a brief documentation of the emergence of sexology as a field of scientific research in Germany and the Netherlands, this chapter will chart the development of psychomedical discourses about queer feminine women across these two contexts. Focusing on the influence of German sexological thinking on the development of sexological theory across Western Europe, I will account for the popular growth of psychotherapy in the Netherlands, considering how these two fields shaped the discourses of desire in their respective homelands. After delineating broadly the boundaries of what Foucault termed the 'regulatory ideal' of sex and gender in terms of the German and Dutch contexts of the interwar era, I will examine how the discussion of 'normative' feminine desires in sexological writing served concomitantly to establish a seemingly inexhaustive spectrum of female behaviours that could be considered 'suspicious' and 'dangerous'. As will become clear, it is in the overlapping space of the normative/non-normative that it becomes possible to discern the key distinctions between German and Dutch conceptions of queer feminine desires between the two World Wars. While German sex researchers struggled in their attempts to classify the queer feminine woman as a discrete sexological 'category', a lack of interest by Dutch psychiatrists in individuals who conformed outwardly to gender norms, as well as a late engagement with sexological research in Dutch contexts more generally, meant that while queer feminine women remained at the fringes of sociomedical discourses in the Netherlands, they were always at the forefront of the minds of those who feared the consequences of the 'invisible menace'.

The Emergence of a *Scientia Sexualis*

The advent of a *scientia sexualis* in the nineteenth century, as Foucault has most famously claimed, informed an essential shift in the conceptualization of desire: sexual experiences were no longer thought of as invariably discrete acts, but became recognizable as a constituent part of a social identity.

Informed by an intensified interest in the individual during the late nineteenth century, gendered and sexual practices were considered a pathway to the 'Truth' about the human condition. Indeed, every conceivable social activity – from whistling to horseback riding – was investigated in exhaustive detail by physicians and psychologists across Western Europe and beyond who sought to discover more about the human sexual experience. Yet, while innumerable books, pamphlets and journal articles focusing on sex and desire began to appear towards the end of the nineteenth century, the body of research that emerged in this period cannot be considered by any means to represent a cohesive or unified field. The foundational frameworks of what would later become known as 'sexology' were built upon the theories of a range of researchers who worked across various disciplines. Not only did 'neurologists, alienists, public hygienists, medical forensics experts and even general practitioners' feed into the developing discourses about desire, but so too did writers, philosophers and social activists, who aimed to prevent or overturn those laws that regulated intimate same-sex acts.[8] By the interwar era, the term *Sexualwissenschaft* was serving as an umbrella concept that encompassed a range of methodological practices that, as well as the progressive reform movement of Magnus Hirschfeld and his Scientific Humanitarian Committee, also included the more radical theories of leftist psychoanalyst Wilhelm Reich (1897–1957), and the agendas of anti-Semitic masculinists such as Adolf Brand (1874–1945) and Hans Blüher (1888–1955).[9] This, of course, is not even to touch upon the highly racialized elements of sexology and eugenics as fields of study, or, indeed, the role that imperialism, as well as the orientalist and exoticizing tendencies of sexual researchers in German and Dutch colonies, played in the dissemination and creation of racially prejudiced and classist sexual knowledges. Thus, crossing not only disciplinary boundaries but also party lines, research on human sexuality in the early twentieth century was a profoundly politicized and problematic field that cannot be defined by any one methodological practice or unified by a singular scientific approach.[10]

Frequently attributed to Iwan Bloch's study *The Sexual Life of Our Times* (*Das Sexualleben unserer Zeit*, 1907), the use of the term *Sexualwissenschaft* to denote a domain of research was already in use in 1898, when Sigmund Freud (1856–1939) claimed in the *Vienna Clinical Review* that it was 'regrettable' that 'sexual science' was considered to be a frivolous field of research by many contemporary physicians.[11] However, it was only following Bloch's later publication that collective attempts were made across psychomedical disciplines to plot the parameters and future directions of this new scientific arena. As a practice that sought to scrutinize and categorize sexual behaviours, with the aim of distinguishing the normative from the non-normative erotic and gendered impulse, the results of sexological research were, in many respects, inevitably harnessed by governing powers to identify and regulate the socially undesirable. Described by Foucault in terms of 'biopower' and ''biopolitics', institutions such as prisons and asylums were surveilled by disciplining powers who sought to bring social bodies under control, so that they could be 'subjected, used, transformed and improved'. Biopolitical powers – seen in the normativizing discourses of sexological research, for example – further attempted 'to ensure, sustain and multiply life, to put this life in order', so that a society might be created that subscribes and conforms to reigning norms and ideologies.[12] However, to consider the field of sexology 'solely in terms of biopolitics, biopower, deviance, and pathology', as Kirsten Leng has most recently contended, would 'only allow us to tell part of the full story' of how sexological research developed into a field of study that shaped social norms and political landscapes.[13] Moreover, as Leng has rightly noted, the focus on the pathologizing tendencies of male sexologists in recent histories of sexuality has meant that the 'critical contributions' of women to scientific studies on sex have largely gone unnoticed.[14] While this chapter admittedly engages at length with the discourses that emerged through the writings of predominantly male German and Dutch researchers, this is not to reify further the voices of male 'experts'. Rather, I seek to engage critically with the indiscriminate indifference many of these sexologists showed to the subject of queer female desire, and to highlight the trivialization of a category of women who were often dismissed as being analogous to their queer male counterparts. In order to attempt to move away from the male-centeredness of the history of sexuality, this chapter will also include some of the vital contributions that were made to the sexological debate made by theorists and commentators such as Johanna Elberskirchen and Ina Boudier-Bakker in order to spotlight women's role not only in contributing new perspectives, or, indeed, supporting existing theories, but also in their attempts, at times, to topple them entirely.

In terms of the earliest male contributions to sexological writing, the launch of the *Journal for Sexual Science* (*Zeitschrift für Sexualwissenschaft*) by Magnus Hirschfeld in 1908 marked a milestone moment for the recognition of the field of sexual research. Following this, the appearance Albert Moll's *Handbook for Sexual Science* (*Handbuch für Sexualwissenschaft*) in 1912 and the establishment of the Society for Sexual Science (Gesellschaft für Sexualwissenschaft) in Berlin in 1913 point to a series of attempts to begin to codify the wide-ranging research interests in human sexual and gendered experience under the appellation of 'sexology'. Facilitated by the fact that German was the dominant language of scientific study during this period, as well as the reality that many of the early developments in the study of (homo)sexuality had been pioneered by researchers in German-speaking countries, Germany and Austria were undoubtedly at the forefront of the sexological campaign to make sense of the human – namely, male – sexual experience by the early twentieth century.[15] When Hirschfeld established the Institute for the Study of Sexual Science (Institut für Sexualwissenschaft) in 1919, Berlin was considered by most prominent researchers from across the globe to be the epicentre of European sexual research. This image was also reflected across the border in the Netherlands, where German publications on sexual matters were by far the most widely published and read by experts and laypersons alike. Although the term *homosexualiteit* had already appeared for the first time in 1892 in the *Dutch Journal of Medicine* (*Nederlandsch Tijdschrift voor de Geneeskunde*), it did not come into common parlance or gain significant traction in scientific research until at least the late 1920s.[16] Certainly, emic studies on same-sex desire appeared in Dutch contexts much later than in German-speaking countries. Thus, while Germany was leading the way for sexual research, then, it can be said, as Maurice van Lieshout observes, that the Netherlands 'made little contribution to the development of sexology as a disciplinary field' and did not play any significant role in the emergence of its theoretical or methodological approaches.[17] Despite a veritable explosion of scientific discourses on sexual behaviour in Western Europe at the end of the nineteenth century, the Netherlands must be considered therefore only a 'minor player' in this conversation, with much of the contemporary Dutch discourses of same-sex desire being shaped primarily by sexological works from German, French, and English-speaking countries. Yet, while the Netherlands did not play a central role in the emergence of the field of sexology, this should not suggest that Dutch researchers were not engaging with sexological theories on male subjects once the field had become established. At the turn of the twentieth century, physicians and psychiatrists such as Jacobus Schoondermark, Lucien von Römer, and Arnold Aletrino were all producing work on the subject of male homosexuality, drawing heavily on the research of Karl Heinrich Ulrichs and Richard von Krafft-Ebing.[18] However, before the publication of Jan Rutgers' *The Sexual Life in Its Biological Significance* (originally published in German as *Das Sexualleben in seiner biologischen Bedeutung*) in 1922, Dutch authors rarely engaged with the nuances of female (homo)sexuality, and it was not until the publication of Benno Stokvis' *The Homosexuals* (*De homosexueelen*) in 1939 that female same-sex desire became a central focus of a sexological collection published originally in Dutch.[19]

What might perhaps go some way towards accounting for the late engagement with sexological theories in the Netherlands is the widespread rejection by early Dutch sex researchers of the theory of gendered inversion. Instead, psychiatrists such as August Stärcke (1880–1954), Albert van Renterghem (1845–1939), Gerbrandus Jelgersma (1859–1942) and Jeanne Lampl-de Groot (1895–1987), among others, did much to familiarize Dutch researchers with psychoanalysis and, in particular, the ideas of Freud, whose theories found fertile ground on Dutch soil. Although the approaches of the aforementioned psychiatrists diverged in many respects, they were united 'in a shared rejection of the somatic style of medicine' and the approaches of the anatomical-physiological school of sexological thought.[20] With the opening of the Liébault Institute (Instituut Liébault) in Amsterdam in 1887, the first establishment for the study and practice of psychotherapy in Europe was founded.[21] The later International Conference on Psychiatry, Neurology, Psychology, and the Nursing of the Mentally Unwell (Internationaal Congres voor Psychiatrie, Neurologie, Psychologie, en Krankzinnigenverpleging), held in Amsterdam in 1907, established the Netherlands, and Amsterdam more specifically, as a centre for psychotherapeutic and psychoanalytical research. The religious strongholds in the Netherlands may also have encouraged a widespread acceptance of the practice of psychotherapy, which was considered by many to be a 'contemporary trend to restore the soul'.[22] Yet, while psychotherapy – and later psychoanalysis – was initially received more favourably in the Netherlands than the anatomical-physiological approaches of German-speaking sexologists, by the end of the 1930s both traditions had gained a foothold within Dutch society.

Given the dominance of German-speaking sexological studies across Europe, it would be almost impossible, as van Lieshout claims, to chart the development of Dutch psychosexual research without reference to the German tradition of the nineteenth century.[23] Indeed, even though psychosomatic theories were initially rejected by Dutch researchers, the two fields remained inextricably linked. Foundational theorist Karl Heinrich Ulrichs, for example, is said to have 'anticipated Freud in his assertion of the importance of dreams for sexology' with Freud frequently also referring back to the theories of Ulrichs in his own studies, as well as those of Albert Moll and Richard von Krafft-Ebing, especially in the former's work on innate bisexuality and polymorphous perversity. Thus, while discourses around female same-sex desire in the Netherlands appear to have been shaped primarily by psychotherapeutic and psychoanalytical methods until the late 1930s, and in Germany by a Cartesian dichotomy of body and mind/soul, these approaches were not mutually exclusive. Yet, given the remit of this volume, this chapter can only chart a basic map of what has already been outlined as a highly complex and contested field. To this end, I will examine the dominant discourses that engaged with the subject of queer female desire in four overlapping waves: first, the initial studies that posited queer desire as a *psychic* inversion; second, the studies that focused on *somatic* gendered inversion; third, those studies that addressed the contradictions and outliers of earlier scientific research; and, finally, the emergence of discourses of psychoanalytic research. As will become clear throughout this chapter, insofar as these waves demonstrate divergences within the field of sexological thought, they also establish how closely linked the various strands of sex research remained throughout the nineteenth and early twentieth centuries. However, in order to be able to examine more closely the image of the 'non-normative' feminine woman, it is key that we first situate the figure of the 'normative' woman in German and Dutch medicosocial discourses. Following this discussion, it will be possible to see how queer feminine woman were constituted as 'Other' by sexologists and psychiatrists, and why they remained on the margins of even those studies invested in the subject of female Otherness.

Ideal Women, Ideal Marriages

As the field of sexual science began to develop in the late nineteenth century, there grew concurrently a social and scientific imperative in the safeguarding of 'normative' desires. Predictably, women's bodies were situated at the centre of this struggle.[24] Informed by changing gender roles after the First World War (see Chapter 1) and the increased visibility of queer desires on the urban landscape by the mid-1920s, the boundaries of what Judith Butler terms the 'heterosexual matrix' were considered by social commentators to be under sexual siege.[25] These social and sexual shifts, as well as a more widespread movement towards viewing sex as pleasurable rather than functional, influenced physicians and educators such as Theodoor van de Velde (1873–1937) and Max Hodann (1894–1946), who felt compelled, in light of this newfound sexual progressivism, to make secure the most valued cultural institution of the hetero-patriarchal regime: marriage. Both van de Velde and Hodann published lucrative guides and handbooks in the Dutch and German language that were aimed dually at teaching husbands how better to understand the bodies and desires of their wives, and making sure marriage remained the sociopolitical bedrock of male-female relationships. As the supposed guarantor of the moral wellbeing of modern society, marriage not only had a prominent role to play in the medicosocial discourses that focused on heterosexual relations but equally those pertaining to the queer feminine woman, who was frequently seen as a normal woman who needed to be 'saved'.

After women obtained active suffrage rights in Germany and the Netherlands in 1919, a fresh wave of anti-feminist writings began to emerge in reaction to what was being considered a contravention of a normal woman's 'natural role'. *The Modern Woman and Her Failings* (*De moderne vrouw en haar tekort*, 1921) by Dutch author Ina Boudier-Bakker (1875–1966), for example, was one of many texts to employ arguments embroiled in discussions of 'innate femininity' to push back against the emergence of the modern woman. Published three years after the First World War, Boudier-Bakker's aptly titled *The Modern Woman* argued that office work had begun to undermine the important role of a woman as a wife, homemaker and mother. While Boudier-Bakker had 'no faith in the ability of men to provide renewal and leadership' after the wartime struggles, she was nonetheless convinced that the natural place of the 'normal' woman was to be found in the domestic sphere.[26] Like many other contemporary commentators, Boudier-Bakker suggests in her work that most women had been forced into the labour market due to the exceptional circumstances of the war and would only welcome a return to domesticity. Yet, domesticity is not aligned here with social passivity. Instead, Boudier-Bakker situates the Dutch housewife as a 'powerful figure who is confident that domestic work is of equal social importance to work outside the home'.[27] On the subject of the newly working woman, Boudier-Bakker maintained the idea of natural divide between the public and the private sphere, claiming that the soul of the office worker and stenographer '[grumbles] the entire day against this unnatural existence ... while her heart and desires draw her home'.[28] This desire to return to the domestic sphere, Boudier-Bakker argues, made many women less capable than men in the workplace. Employing a rhetoric long since used by anti-feminists to keep women out of education and the public sphere, she states that: 'Women's brains are generally only lucid when their *hearts* are in it.'[29] Yet, while Boudier-Bakker considers homemaking to be the 'natural' function for the 'normal' woman, she nonetheless acknowledges that women would unlikely find true fulfilment in these responsibilities. Indeed, the figure of the *un*happily married woman in Boudier-Bakker's work, whose only role is to care for her husband, children and homestead, comprised, as the author writes, 'many, perhaps most cases' of women in matrimony in the Netherlands.[30] Thus, while the spheres of domesticity and maternalism are positioned as 'naturally' suited to the feminine woman in Boudier-Bakker's work, so too is it natural to be unhappy with one's lot. It was the role of the normal woman, therefore, to learn find happiness in *un*happiness. As a symbol considered 'indispensable to the Social Order', the instutition of marriage, according to Boudier-Bakker, needed to be protected from the perceived cultural threat brought about by the gender shifts following the First World War. Engaging with this widespread social concern, Dutch and German sex reformers not only explored the problems of marriage in their writings but also attempted to reconceptualize the definitive symbol of social and sexual normality in their works to make the idea of marriage more popular, appealing, and in touch with the socio-scientific zeitgeist.

Commencing his bestselling trilogy with Balzac's words 'marriage is a science', Theodoor van de Velde (1873–1937) places his guidebook directly within the domain of sexological and literary discourses that were attempting to make the subject of sex more socially palatable after the turn of the twentieth century.[31] Van de Velde's *Ideal Marriage* (*Het volkomen huwelijk*, 1926) was aimed at 'medical professionals and ... married men' and is one of several attempts by reformers during this time to make scientific writing more accessible to a general reading public.[32] Beginning his study with the warning that he will 'state that which would otherwise remain unsaid', van de Velde's work adopts a supposedly more reassuring tone as he emphasizes that he will discuss 'only ... such emotions and sensations as lie within the limits of normal sexuality' and would omit 'morbid deflections, twisted and abnormal desires' in order to keep the portals to 'hell' firmly closed.[33] Much like Boudier-Bakker, the Dutch gynaecologist admits that marriage, at least within the Christian tradition, was often a failure. Yet, instead of resigning himself to this failure, van de Velde instead proposes a modern notion of companionate marriage, in which a woman was 'rehabilitated ... as an active, adult and equivalent sexual being'.[34] In spite of advocating a more progressive model, and indeed suggesting that the very future of marriage was dependent on this construct, van de Velde's work nonetheless continues to perpetuate a view of the marital union in which men are positioned as the '[natural] educators and initiators of their wives' and in which women are 'uninitiated' in sexual matters.[35] Indeed, while van de Velde promises to teach men more about the bodies and sensibilities of their wives, there is scant little time spent on exploring the nuances of 'normative' female sexuality – the physician glosses over the subject almost entirely, claiming that 'an exhaustive treatise on all aspects of adult female sexuality' would be 'superfluous for the medical practitioner' and 'too unwieldy and ... unintelligible for the layman'.[36] Thus, in spite of recognizing the need for new – active – forms of female desire, van de Velde anchors women's happiness in his study, like Boudier-Bakker, to the fulfilment of her own (passive) femininity.

Focussing exclusively on heterosexual sex acts in his first instalment, van de Velde tackles the spectre of the Sapphic only in his second publication *Sex Hostility in Marriage* (*De bestrijding van den echtelijken afkeer*, 1927). Here, he draws on the contemporary sexological research discussed later in this chapter to position femininity as the idealized gendered embodiment for all women, claiming that even the most 'fanatical' among the 'men-women' would readily admit 'that she would like to be ... exclusively feminine (or at one time wished to be) and would have been only too glad to have seen a "real" man enter her life'.[37] Thus, while suggesting that society was 'beyond' considering women as passive receptacles, van de Velde nevertheless creates an image of idealized femininity that is based on its constituent passivity, modesty and submissiveness, and argues that women – irrespective of their sexual object choice – desire to embody these ideals. In this way, normative desire in van de Velde's works, as Lisa Duggan writes, remains entirely contingent 'on gender differences ... interpreted within the context of male dominance'.[38]

The active/passive gender dichotomy that was characteristic of normative male and female sexuality in the Netherlands was also a distinctive part of the research being produced in German-speaking countries. As well as categorizing deviancy, sexologists at the fin de siècle had become increasingly committed to defining the definitional boundaries of 'normativity'. Within studies of female desire, this discussion was most often reduced to the Madonna/Whore dichotomy. In no other work of such significance was this division more acute than in Auguste Forel's *The Sexual Question* (*Die sexuelle Frage*, 1905), a text that incidentally continued to be tremendously popular in the Netherlands in the interwar period.[39] Positioned as 'a scientific, psychological, hygienic, and sociological study for educated persons', the Swiss neurologist's highly influential treatise concerned not only the nature of the male and female sex drive, sexual ethics and questions of sexual hygiene, but also extended its purview to nonreproductive sexual urges, sex work and other 'pathologies' (which are discussed later in this chapter).[40] Unlike van de Velde and Boudier-Bakker, for whom the ability to be content with a socially-learned (sexual) passivity was a key feminine characteristic, Forel's theory on what constituted normative female sexuality was grounded in the concept of a *biological* female chasteness. In fact, the neurologist suggested that sexual anaesthesia – that is, the lack of sexual feeling – was the defining feature of normal female sexual experience and that desire in women emerged only in 'the craving to play the role of the subjugated, defeated, and dominated sufferer'.[41] The libidinous woman, irrespective of her sexual object choice, was to be considered pathological.[42] Although Forel identifies the natural submissive traits of women as negative characteristics, he maintains that they are 'a major component of the normal [female] sex drive'.[43] The natural passivity of women in sexual intercourse, Forel contended, could be explained in part by the fact that 'voluptuous sensations' are awaked in women *during* the act of coitus. It was only through the habitual practice of heterosexual intercourse that a desire for sexual acts could be stimulated. Yet, Forel was quick to warn his (male) readers that even with regular 'practice', it was likely that many women would continue to find 'the act of copulation ... an uncomfortable, often disgusting or, at best, neutral event'.[44] Unlike the 'normal' men in his study, Forel suggested that 'normal' women were not driven by a yearning concentrated 'on the sexual organs or copulation', but rather by 'an unclear, general feeling, a yearning, for the founding of a family and the happiness of a mother'.[45] Thus, in order for a woman's desires to fall within the narrow range of the normative, they had to be directed exclusively towards the reproductive purpose and driven by a maternal drive rather than a longing for the erotic act itself. And, while the regular practice of sexual intercourse might increase desire in women, Forel cautioned that it could also have grave consequences. Indeed, the 'sensitivity and shame' that normal women possess might fade entirely if a woman experiences sexual sensations too frequently.[46] Influenced, at least in part, by Karl Möbius' *The Psychological Mental Weakness of Woman* (*Über den psychologischen Schwachsinn des Weibes*, 1900), Forel argues that a woman's 'lesser' mental faculties meant that they were more easily susceptible to 'excessive' and pathological desires, which dually tapped into many of the contemporary fears around female queerness. For Forel, then, 'normal' sexual desires ought to be 'completely absent' from the female subject until they had been 'awakened' by a male partner. However, once roused, female sexual desires were to be considered dangerous and in need of strict regulation. With normative femininity grounded in theories of sexual passivity and immaturity, and feminine desires considered dependent on the active male impulse to 'awaken' them, it is no surprise that the feminine woman who actively desired other women was little short of a mystery to many sexologists. But, with a closer examination of the approaches taken to the subject of female same-sex desire in the history of sexual science, I hope to offer a window into the complex and often contradictory understanding of queer female-bodied femininities that had emerged by the early twentieth century.

Queer Female Desire at the Margins: Early Theories of Same-Sex Desires

A vocal advocate for the emancipation of same-sex loving persons, Karl Heinrich Ulrichs offered the first positive and affirmative scientific framework for same-sex desire. Initially published under the pseudonym Numa Numantius, Ulrichs' series of twelve pamphlets on the 'riddle of man-manly love' were influenced by the works of forensic scientist Johann Ludwig Casper (1796–1864), who had been one of the first scientific experts to claim that same-sex desire was the result of a 'hermaphrodism of the soul'.[47] Using the term *Uranismus* to describe this phenomenon, and later 'third sex', Ulrichs further coined the categories *Urninge* and *Uranier* for men-who-loved-men and *Dioninge* and *Dionäer* for men-who-loved-women.[48] The entire framework behind Ulrichs' taxonomies was closely aligned with the broader interests of the natural sciences at this time, which were focused primarily, as Claudia Honegger notes, on 'determining more closely the connection between the bodily disposition and psychological capacity'.[49] Borrowing from literary and philosophical works, Ulrichs' early neologisms can be traced back to Plato's *Symposium*, in which the playwright Aristophanes presents the possibility of three sexes in a eulogy concerning the nature of love: 'The sexes were not two as they are now but originally three in number; there was man, woman, and the union of the two.'[50] Following this theory, Ulrichs suggests in his first publication *Vindex* (1864) that *Urninge* could be considered 'coordinated as a third sex from the sex of men and the sex of women'.[51]

Describing the phenomenon of homosexual desire as a psychic occurrence that develops in the early stages of embryonic growth, Ulrichs' writings challenged previous studies that had posited same-sex desire as the result of physical irregularities or excessive onanism.[52] With an understanding of anatomical bisexuality and sexual dualism at its core, Ulrichs positions psychic inversion as the aetiology of congenital queer desire. While he was initially dismissive of the idea of a 'fourth sex' – that is, women with a male spirit – Ulrichs nonetheless indicated his awareness of the phenomenon of 'female Uranismus' in his second publication, *Inclusa*. However, consigned to a single footnote in the lengthy study, the woman-loving-woman, as Mara Taylor notes, 'quite literally ... enters Ulrichs' texts in the margins'.[53] Transposing his original framework of male same-sex desire directly onto the female sex, Ulrichs points to the possible existence of a group of women with an inborn masculine element and therefore a desire *for* the feminine:

> The Third Sex may possibly actually correspond to a *fourth* sex, a sex of persons built like females with woman-womanly sexual desires, i.e. having the sexual direction of men ... Such women, however, appeared considerably less often than Urnings. A scientific investigation of their nature would be very desirable. The key to the riddle of their love would be formed from a congenital male element.[54]

Unlike earlier theories that posited homosexual desire as the result of genital hypertrophy/atrophy brought about through masturbation – as well as later studies that suggested a reversal of both somatic and psychic gender characteristics – Ulrichs' theory of psychic inversion positions the queer woman as *psychically* masculine but *physically* feminine. Yet, although Ulrichs suggests that a study on the nature of female same-sex desire would be 'very desirable', his observation that female queerness occurred considerably less frequently than male queerness leaves the woman-who-desired-women as a peripheral concern in this second publication and, as Heike Bauer observes, little more than 'a logical exercise'.[55]

However, by the time Ulrichs published his fourth pamphlet *Formatrix* in 1865, he had already revisited the limits of his three-gendered system and conceded to the 'chaos of varieties' that existed along the human sexual spectrum.[56] Following the success of his earlier publications, he had gained insider knowledge from a more diverse group of *Uranians* that had reached out to him through personal correspondences. With these more nuanced insights, he identified at least sixteen other types of sexual variations, including the *Uranodioning* man who was attracted both to men and women, the *Dioning* male who had feminine characteristics but was attracted to women, and as the *Urning* with a masculine, rather than a feminine, spirit. He also amended his earlier claim that same-sex desire between women occurred less frequently than that between men, explaining that he had since encountered many examples of women 'with a male love drive' and could conclude that 'the actual existence of the female [Uranism] seems equally as certain as that of male Uranism'.[57] Despite Ulrichs' revised supposition that queer women appear just as frequently as their male counterparts, his lack of personal knowledge about these women means that love between women remains 'unknowable' in his work.[58] While Ulrichs' early theories of queer women were exercises of logic, and only later informed by personal correspondences, Carl Westphal's study of queer subject Miss N. emerged directly from his observations of his subject at the psychiatric ward of the Charité hospital. Westphal's approach, which drew on biographical material and interviews with his patient, essentially reconceptualized approaches to sex research and its subjects, creating 'a new norm for sexology'.[59] Following the approaches adopted in Westphal's earlier case study, the first edition of one of the most significant compendium of sexual pathologies in the nineteenth century was published almost two decades later: Richard von Krafft-Ebing's study *Psychopathia Sexualis* (1886).

Somatic Signifiers: Questions of Queer Legitimacy at the Fin de Siècle

Introducing to the scientific world a lexicon that included terms such as 'sadism' and 'masochism', psychiatrist Krafft-Ebing's study *Psychopathia Sexualis* marked the first attempt by a sex researcher to create a comprehensive anthology of human sexual pathology.[60] The study, which ran to twelve editions before the psychiatrist's death, was a sexual sourcebook par excellence for late nineteenth-century researchers. Building on Westphal's methodological innovations, Krafft-Ebing worked closely with patients in the Feldhof mental asylum in Austria to co-produce fifty-one case histories for the first edition of his study.[61] Exploring a seemingly inexhaustible range of sexual behaviours, Krafft-Ebing's publications provided knowledge about a variety of sexual impulses that ranged from asexuality to hypersexuality, bestiality to necrophilia, and fetishism to flagellantism. Writing to Ulrichs in 1879, Krafft-Ebing acknowledged his debt to the earlier activist, claiming that the former's research on 'man-manly' love had been the driving force behind his own explorations on the subject of same-sex desire.[62] However, unlike Ulrichs, who was an advocate for seeing same-sex desire as a natural and congenital variant, Krafft-Ebing's focus on the pathological, as well as his distinctions between hereditary and acquired sexual impulses, ultimately created a new paradigm – one through which same-sex desires could be considered heritable, transmissible and dangerous to 'normal' individuals. Building on the studies mentioned earlier in this chapter, Krafft-Ebing distinguished between four stages of inborn inversion in his own refinement of the riddle of taxonomies Ulrichs articulated in his works. In the first stage of congenital inversion, 'Psychic Hermaphrodism', the sexual instinct was considered to be directed primarily towards the same sex, while weaker traces of the heterosexual impulse appeared episodically. The second stage, 'Homosexuality/Uranisme', was largely synonymous with Ulrichs' vision of the *Urning*, which referred to an individual with an exclusive desire for the same sex, but no signs of somatic inversion. The third stage, 'Virago/Effeminatio', described a figure whose sexual impulse was not only directed towards the same sex, but who also had a psychic disposition that resulted in 'spiritual' characteristics of the opposite sex. The final stage of inversion, 'Androgynie/Gyandrie', was employed to categorize those individuals in whom there was not only a psychic inversion of gender traits but also a somatic inversion of secondary sex characteristics.[63]

Despite moving towards a more nuanced framework of queer desire, Krafft-Ebing's *Psychopathia Sexualis* still fails to account adequately for the existence of queer female desires, which remain 'a muted discourse' in his works.[64] In a caveat that had already become representative of the study of female same-sex desire, Krafft-Ebing readily admits in one of his introductions that 'little is known about the manner in which the female Urnings satisfy their desires', but later concedes that while scientific evidence of its existence stood 'much more sparsely on offer', love between women had existed globally 'across time'.[65] Following both Ulrichs' and Westphal's formulations, same-sex desire in women was portrayed by Krafft-Ebing primarily as a psychic occurrence of gender inversion:

> The woman-loving-woman feels, in relation to the other [women], completely in the role of the man ... the genitals are normally developed, the sexual glands perform their functions properly, and the sexual type is completely differentiated. Feeling, thought, will, indeed, the entire character in general, correspond as a rule with the anomalous sexual instinct but not with the sex to which the individual belongs anatomically and physiologically.[66]

Although the sensibility, thoughts and aspirations of the female invert were typically masculine, the physiological presentation and psychological behaviours of women-who-desired-women are, again, emphatically stated *not* to have deviated typically from the female 'norm', i.e. the feminine woman.

However, much like the studies discussed previously, Krafft-Ebing focuses little on the woman who is marked by a femininity 'of the mind' and, interestingly, when she does become visible, her passivity and modesty remain the defining characteristics of her desire, distinguishing her little from the ideal 'normative' woman of the nineteenth and early twentieth century. Indeed, when discussing the sexual impulses of women characterized by the first stage of same-sex desire – 'psychic hermaphrodism' – Krafft-Ebing suggested that the erotic desires of womanly-women were often 'limited ... to mere kissing and embracing'.[67] The story of 'Mrs X.', for example, a twenty-six-year-old married woman with two children, is a typical case of Krafft-Ebing's psychic hermaphrodite. Suffering from neurasthenia, Mrs X. claims that she felt episodically attracted to men, but mostly to other women. Yet, when acting upon her desires for other women, she suggests that she could not imagine herself doing anything other than 'kissing, embracing, [or] caressing them'.[68] While the feminine woman with a feminine mind is considered to be sexually modest 'by nature' in Krafft-Ebing's work, in his second class of homosexual identification, 'Homosexuality/Uranisme' – a category that describes women who appear outwardly feminine but have a masculine 'mind' – all references to sexual modesty and passivity are removed, and replaced by the discussion of an active sexual drive, that is focused on genital sex. 'Miss X.', for example, was a twenty-two-year-old urbanite with a bourgeois background and described as a 'Beauté' who is 'idolised by the world of men'. However, in her case history, Miss X. claimed to have felt 'always as a man opposite the woman' and explained that when she engaged in sex with her partners, it was only ever she who assumed the 'active' role.[69] While Miss X deviates from the social norms that moored femininity to sexual modesty, she did not believe her desires to be 'unnatural [or] pathological'.[70] This was a view that was shared by Krafft-Ebing, who considered both Miss X and Mrs X to be examples of what he termed congenital perversion – their desires were inborn. However, alongside this category there existed a further group of same-sex desiring women in Krafft-Ebing's research, that presented a more dangerous form of deviance.[71]

The distinction that Krafft-Ebing makes in his study between what he terms a 'perversity' and a 'perversion' had far-reaching implications for future studies of female same-sex desires. While a perversion referred to a congenital impulse, a perversity could be considered instead a fleeting moment of sexual deviance carried out by an otherwise 'normal' individual.[72] In a publication in the *Yearbook for Sexual Intermediaries* in 1901, under the rubric 'New Studies in the Field of Homosexuality', Krafft-Ebing anticipates Forel in his discussion of the natural feminine propensity to commit perverse acts. While some feminine women were 'hyper-sexed' and could not be satisfied by men alone, Krafft-Ebing argued that the feminine sex drive was by nature more suggestable, which meant that feminine women could be seduced into Sapphic acts in homosocial settings, such as in prisons, boarding schools or convents. Wives of impotent men were also prone to this kind of temporal perversity, as were sex workers, whom Krafft-Ebing deemed particularly 'sensuous'. Over the twelve editions of *Psychopathia Sexualis*, Krafft-Ebing's position on queer feminine desires remains ambiguous. And, even in spite of his direct interactions with his subjects, the queer feminine woman still remains a marginal concern; less visible, less well researched and ultimately less 'knowable' than the queer male, or even the queer masculine woman. Yet, the distinctions Krafft-Ebing drew between 'perversities' and 'perversions' nonetheless shaped the future theories that did turn their gaze to the longings of feminine women. The unfixed desires of the peverse feminine woman in Krafft-Ebing's studies had other implications too. Indeed, if the perverted impulse of feminine women had not already become pathological through 'habitual practice', Krafft-Ebing influentially suggested that the sexual drives of the queer feminine woman might be corrected through 'the natural intercourse between woman and man'.[73] Not only did the line between 'normal and abnormal become blurred' through this statement, but the suggestion also created a theoretical space in which there was a distinct possibility that queer feminine women could be *cured* of their perversities.[74]

Intermediary Forms: Spectrums and Hierarchies of Queer Desire

Largely indebted to the research of Westphal and Krafft-Ebing, neurologist Albert Moll's *The Contrary Sexual Feeling* (*Die konträre Sexualempfindung*, 1891) adopted the taxonomical imperative of his predecessors' methodological approaches and focused it exclusively on the subject of same-sex desire.[75] Yet, unlike Krafft-Ebing's bifurcation of perversities and perversions, Moll's study suggests that the 'differentiation between the normal and abnormal appeared to be not so much qualitative and absolute but rather quantitative and gradual'.[76] Diverging away from the theory of degeneration, Moll moves instead towards a radical 'biogenetic concept of bisexuality', which controversially questions the self-evidence of the heterosexual impulse.[77] The innovative approaches that the neurologist adopted in his ethnographic practices also endowed his work with new critical perspectives. Instead of collecting his data from patients in psychiatric wards or criminals in prisons, as Westphal and Krafft-Ebing had done before him, Moll worked extensively with communities of same-sex desiring subjects in Berlin, which enabled him to get much closer to the subjects of his study and to engage with them largely on their own terms. His close collaboration with these communities further results in much ambiguity in his work; Moll did not shy away from the anomalies that did not fit into specific paradigms, but rather included them in an attempt to broaden understandings of the nuances of human sexual expression.[78] In his work on queer women, Moll, like others, is quick to recognize that his research on male homosexual desire far outweighed the consideration he had given to female same-sex feelings. The sexologist excuses his shorter study on queer women on account of the well-worn defence of there being a dearth of secondary sources. Furthermore, he suggests that the fact that queer acts between women were not subject to the law in Germany means that research on the nature of their desires was less 'pressing'. Moll concludes this caveat with a further dismissal on the need to study queerness in women as an individual phenomenon, stating that constructions of queer female and queer male desires were largely analogous. Following this list of methodological limitations, he quickly situates the contemporary queer woman within a truncated timeline of world historical contexts that skips frantically between Sappho's gynaecium in Lesbos to harems of the Orient and further includes references to queer women in the literary works of Diderot, Zola and Balzac. Finally narrowing his study to Berlin, Moll continues his description of the German capital in the same vein as his sweeping literary-historical overview and liberally proposes that evidence of same-sex desires in Germany could be seen not only among sex workers, but also barmaids, bohemian artists and bourgeois housewives.

On the dynamics of the romantic relationships that existed between queer women, Moll remains initially faithful to the dyadic notion of gender complementarity and claims that same-sex couples on the subcultural scene often corresponded to the roles of 'mother' and 'father'. In these relationships, he observes that the active masculine 'father' was often granted the freedom to stray romantically and sexually, while the feminine 'mother' is expected to remain loyal: 'just as in a normal marriage'.[79] In terms of erotic acts between women, he further agrees with the distinction between active and passive roles that had been outlined by his predecessors. With reference to his field research, Moll suggests that feminine women who adopted the role of the 'mother' often found the idea of assuming an active role in sexual relationships 'unpleasant and disgusting'.[80] However, unlike Forel, Moll does not suggest that queer feminine women find the act of receiving pleasure itself unpleasant, but only the *initiation* of the erotic act. Concomitantly, he contends that women who assumed the 'father' role claimed it would be impossible for them to find pleasure as a passive recipient of sexual pleasure. Yet, in a style that became typical of his research, Moll quickly turns on his initial claim of complementarity to conclude that 'in some cases the active and passive roles are by no means sharply separated'.[81] Presenting a third example of a couple who engaged in a mutual exchange of roles, Moll allows contradictions to shape his theory of the amorphous nature of queer female desire: 'At this point, X was pleasured by Y, who took on the active role in cunnilingus; shortly thereafter the roles were reversed and both continued in this way so that, soon one, and soon the other, was either active or passive.'[82] Concluding that 'much is still dark in this area and the information is often contradictory', Moll warns his contemporaries against making generalizations about the intricacies of queer female desire.[83]

In terms of the physical presentation of queer women, Moll's study initially engages with dominant theories of psychic inversion. Contending that the physiognomy of queer women was most often 'thoroughly normal' and not to be differentiated from nonqueer women, Moll concluded that, in terms a woman's desires for her own sex, masculinity was a definitive characteristic.[84] However, unlike the studies on same-sex desire that predated his own, in which femininity had remained a marginal concern, Moll adopts a surprisingly critical stance on the subject. In an attempt to account for the societal pressure to conform to gender typical roles, he posits that many queer feminine women might in fact be *hiding* their natural masculinity. Arguably pre-empting Joan Riviere's article 'Womanliness as a Masquerade' (1929), Moll considers the feminine presentation of many queer women to be artificial:

> Incidentally, the movements of Tribades only appear entirely masculine when they are free to let themselves go. If they believe they are being observed, or if they are not among themselves, where every discomfort [*gêne*] falls away, they seek to imitate the feminine artificially so as not to betray themselves.[85]

Despite femininity figuring in his work, then, and the paradigm of psychic inversion and binary complementarity being challenged through a presentation of more ambiguous images of queer desire, masculinity is ultimately considered to be the true expression of a woman's same-sex desires, while femininity is an artifice. As a pioneer in hypnosis and suggestion therapy, the sexologist further explored the ways in which feminine desires might be treatable. In much the same way as Krafft-Ebing, Moll argues that frequent platonic contact with the opposite sex and abstinence from same-sex pleasures might serve as the basis for the road to 'recovery'. For queer feminine women who were already married to men, the maternal instinct, Moll suggests, might eventually temper any same-sex inclinations:

> It is observable in [homosexual] women that, despite having homosexual tendencies, they sometimes also have maternal feelings. They long for offspring. I have known of several such marriages – even some threatening to end in divorce – in which the birth of a child has eventually resulted in a bearable union'.[86]

In Moll's account, the 'natural impulse' to conceive a child could help a queer feminine woman to sublimate her desires, at least enough to 'bear' marriage to a man. Through the transference of erotic love into the love of a mother for a child, as in Krafft-Ebing's work, queer feminine women could effectively be 'cured' of their sexual proclivities.[87] In this way, the queer feminine body in Moll's study remains implicated in what Butler has termed the 'problematic of reproduction'.[88] Moll, and other sexologists besides him, concluded that the erotic drives of queer feminine women could be channelled into the maternal instincts that were intrinsic to her feminine nature. However, complicating this portrayal, Moll acknowledges that sexual desires might not always be sublimated or 'transferred' successfully, mentioning, as a case in point, a married woman who had supposedly impregnated her girlfriend with her husband's semen so that she could raise a child with her female partner. Yet, while Moll considers many cases of female same-sex desire to be congenital, he did not exclude the theoretical possibility of finding a cure: 'I do not believe that curative treatment [for female same-sex desire] is so easy, however, for theoretical reasons, I do not think it is entirely out of the question, either.'[89]

Adopting a similar approach in his ethnographic fieldwork to Moll, including the latter's appreciation for the complexities and nuances of queer desire, Berlin-based sexologist Magnus Hirschfeld conducted thousands of case studies of queer people that he documented in an unparalleled body of work on homosexual experience. However, unlike Moll, Hirschfeld did not enter the community as an 'outsider', but rather was a key figure in the struggle for emancipation and equal rights. Working initially from the premise of Ulrichs' 'third sex', Hirschfeld is arguably most recognized for his theory of 'sexual intermediaries', which declared the existence of more than 43 million types of sexual and gendered variations.[90] Positioning his theory in contention with those that had shown little understanding of the 'nuances of sexual transitions', Hirschfeld asserted that the 'full man' (*Vollmann*) and 'full woman' (*Vollweib*) were 'imaginary entities'.[91] Fundamentally calling into question the sexual dimorphism that structured European society, he argued that there was 'no certain correlation between virility and masculinity and passivity and femininity'.[92] Acknowledging Moll's understanding of a 'congenital human bisexuality that evolved into monosexuality', Hirschfeld's point of departure suggested that every individual was originally bisexual (*zwitterhaft*) – that is, born with both masculine and feminine elements – and, furthermore, experienced a desire for both sexes.[93] Beginning with a note on the inconsistency in the ways in which queer women had been labelled in sexological studies, Hirschfeld initially argues for a level of uniformity concerning the terms 'Amor lesbicus', 'lesbian', 'Sapphic love' and 'Tribade'. While 'lesbian love' had historically been used as a catch-all phrase in some studies, in others it described women who engaged exclusively in oral sex with other women. Similarly, the terms 'fricatrice' and 'tribade' had been used both to refer to women who committed specific sexual acts, both terms etymologically linked to the verb 'to rub', as well as to those women-who-desired-women more generally.[94] Furthermore, the term *Lesbierinnen* had been used intermittently to allude equally to congenitally queer women and to those who engaged in same-sex acts only in homosocial environments. While Hirschfeld primarily attempts to use these terms with an appreciation for their specificity, he generally favoured the term 'homosexual woman' in his later studies, under which he identified two 'entirely analogous' groups:

> [In homosexual bars] we find a division of women who show something exquisitely virile in their clothing, hairstyle, carriage and movement, in their manner of talking, drinking, and smoking; many of them also have a deep, rough voice, a powerful, manly facial expression, narrow hips and a bone structure that reminds you more generally of the 'stronger' sex ... Alongside them there is a group of equal size ... who externally can hardly be distinguished from other women of their social sphere. They do their toilette and hair in the same fashion as the latter, hate neither corsets nor high heels, and are so thoroughly feminine in the expression of their feelings, taste, and thinking that no one would consider them homosexual. And yet they are just that in precisely the same way as their virile sisters.[95]

In a marked departure from previous studies, Hirschfeld describes not only a psychic inversion of gendered traits in the masculine queer woman, but also an inversion of secondary sex characteristics. Indeed, the 'deep, rough voice' and 'powerful, manly facial expression' of the masculine 'homosexual' woman stand in stark contrast to the 'somewhat delicately built' frame of Westphal's masculine patient 'Miss N.'. Yet, while congenital queer desires are linked to a masculine drive in Hirschfeld's work, he suggests that feminine women could be considered homosexual 'in precisely the same way' as their masculine counterparts.[96] Indeed, in line with his theory of sexual intermediaries, Hirschfeld argues that there existed a subgroup of queer women whose femininity was so thoroughly 'normal' that 'no one would take [them] for homosexual'. Yet, complicating this image further, Hirschfeld concludes, much like the British sexologist Havelock Ellis, that while the queer feminine woman was 'much more feminine than the virile homosexual woman', she could never be considered *as* feminine 'as a heterosexual woman'.[97] Diverging from Moll's suggestion that the queer feminine woman could sublimate her same-sex desires into motherly instincts, Hirschfeld also maintains that queer feminine women could become depressed to the point of suicide if they become pregnant precisely because 'they *lack* a maternal instinct' (emphasis my own).[98]

By implying that it was possible to distinguish between the feminine heterosexual and homosexual woman based on the latter's 'lesser' form of femininity, as well as her *lack* of maternal desire, Hirschfeld's research ultimately safeguards the cultural ideal of femininity as a property of the 'normal' heterosexual woman and, as such, continues to anchor homosexual desire to a degree of gender nonconformity. Despite maintaining that there existed an infinite number of sexual intermediary forms and expressions, then, Hirschfeld nonetheless remained bound by a dualistic notion of complementary sex-gender roles. Indeed, the more feminine a woman was, he argues, 'the less she deviates from the norm, the more she loves women who have masculine qualities, strong women with strength of mind, artists, authors'.[99] Thus, while femininity is positioned as a legitimate position for queer women in Hirschfeld's research, it emerges as such only in binary opposition to 'strong women with a strength of mind'. The tension between the theory of innumerable intermediary forms and the binarism that remained inherent in Hirschfeld's studies influenced the approaches adopted by homosexual rights campaigners across the world who found hope in the epithet: *per scientiam ad justitiam* (through science to justice).

The desire to achieve emancipation through scientific study was also reflected in the work of the Dutch Scientific Humanitarian Committee (NWHK), which commissioned and published *The Homosexuals* (*De homosexueelen*) in 1939. Collated by lawyer and activist Benno Stokvis, this publication formed part of a series entitled *Human Suffering* (*Menschenleed*) and was the first original study on same-sex desire to be published in Dutch that focused on the lived experiences of queer people. Of the thirty-nine autobiographies in the collection, nine comprised female narratives. Unlike the research that has been considered in this chapter thus far, there is no analysis of the narratives by a scientific 'expert'. In fact, aside from an introduction in which Stokvis advocates for the rights of queer people, there is no mediating 'authority' voice to be found. The autobiographies stand entirely on their own, divided only between 'male' and 'female' contributions.[100] Although originally intended for 'Doctors, Clergy, Judges, Lawyers [and] Police Officers', it is likely that *The Homosexuals* achieved much greater success among those who saw themselves reflected in this work than among the doctors and lawyers Stokvis aimed to educate.[101] In spite of this, as Judith Schuyf contends, Stokvis' anthology offers a rare insight into the 'image-forming' of the dominant Dutch culture and equally '[sheds] light on the mentality of the outside world' towards the subject of female same-sex desire.[102] Stokvis' commitment to including narratives of female 'homo-eroticism' in the collection, a terrain he declares in his introduction to be 'even harder to access still than the male, and thus even more neglected', also supplies an insight into the first explicit articulations of queer desire by female subjects in the Netherlands during the first half of the twentieth century.

Although the title of the publication suggests that those involved in the project self-reflexively defined their desires as 'homosexual', the way in which women engaged with their 'non-normative' preferences in the collection reveals that, even by the late 1930s, sexual preferences did not always result in sexual identities in Dutch contexts. Of the nine female autobiographies, for example, only a third use the term 'homosexual' in their narratives and, of these, only two accounts deploy the category with any sense of a community or identity. In the first, the reader is presented with an image of a community that remains ultimately unreachable for the author, who claims that: 'In truth, I have experienced little of true love. But enough to know and fully understand the fierce grief that is suffered among us "homosexuals".'[103] In the second contribution to deploy the term 'homosexual', the contributor laments the effects of a lack of understanding for same-sex desire in society: 'it is no wonder, then, that so many works of darkness can be found among us "homosexuals"!'.[104] In both autobiographical accounts, it remains telling that quotes placed around the word 'homosexual' appear to distance the contributor from a term that is used to categorize them from the outside, suggesting a reluctance to engage with the sexological theories attempting to define their desires. In the remaining autobiographies, where sexological terms are avoided, euphemisms are employed instead to explore the feelings of being an outsider. In autobiography XXVII, for example, the author attempts to describe the difficulty of navigating her feelings of otherness, making recourse to the concept of being 'different' from one's peers: 'As far back as I can remember, I always see myself as a recalcitrant and shy creature, "different from the others", sometimes proud of this "otherness", at other times deadly afraid of it.'[105] Although this feeling of otherness appears to be articulated by the women in Stokvis' collection less readily in terms of a 'homosexual' identity, their narratives are nevertheless redolent of the sexological frameworks of congenital inversion that corresponds to an innate sense of masculinity. In each of the nine narratives, it is possible to see explicit references to author's masculine 'predisposition' or 'nature', as well as an attempt to trace back the origins of their queer desires to their youth:

> Whenever I try to recall when the first signs of my 'otherness' revealed themselves, I must go back to my time as a child at primary school ... I was better friends with the boys; often I was allowed to participate in their wild games because I had 'such strong arms' and could fight and wrestle just as well as they could.[106]

While such statements call to mind sexological models, the continued use of euphemisms such as 'different' and 'like that' suggest that many Dutch women were still not defining their desires consciously in terms of an increasingly dominant socioscientific discourse. In fact, queer desires in Stokvis' collection – both female and male – continue to be structured along the binary lines of 'normative' and 'non-normative' rather than around a label that suggests a fixed social identity: 'Normal – abnormal – ... how often have those words gone through my head? ... Abnormal, the term that I hated most of all because of the foul taste it left in my mouth: unclean, despicable, dangerous.'[107] Thus, while the autobiographies in the collection are described as 'homosexual' by the editor Stokvis, the women in the collection appear to use the category with a marked degree of indifference. Thus, despite the similarities between these autobiographical accounts, in terms of the feelings of otherness and narratives of gendered difference that arise in the contributions, it seems unlikely that these resemblances indicate a sense of collective identity around a label or name. Rather, the collection appears far more likely to be indicative of the broader agenda of the NWHK in its attempt to find support for its claim that homosexuality was a congenital phenomenon that should not be restricted by Article 248bis.

Funded by the NWHK, the Dutch sister organization of Magnus Hirschfeld's WhK, Stokvis' *The Homosexuals* was influenced strongly by both the theory of inversion and the political aims of the organization to present the 'congenital' nature of gendered inverts as a way of lobbying for the decriminalization of homosexual acts. Indeed, Stokvis' collection was not only financially supported by the NWHK, but much of the material he received for his anthology also came from members of the organization itself. The women featured in Stokvis' collection therefore cannot be classed as representative of a random sample of individuals, but instead as women who had connections with the homosexual organization responsible for the publication and who were cognisant of the NWHK's discursive backbone. Although the framing of the material was carefully constructed in order to present a particular 'type' of homosexual desire to educate the masses – that is, inverted, congenital and therefore natural – it is clear that by the late 1930s, sexological theories of inversion were gaining traction in the Netherlands. Yet, even while the theories employed by both the German and the Dutch Scientific Humanitarian Committees were able to provide a framework of same-sex desire that could be politicized, not all proponents of the emancipation of queer people in Germany and the Netherlands had been in support of the theories of gender inversion. Indeed, some activists in the history of queer emancipation appeared to consider gender normativity, rather than gender deviance, to play the most vital role in the lobby for social acceptance.

Femininity as a (Queer) Woman's Right

Arguably one of the most outspoken activists and campaigners in the women's movement on the subject of female same-sex love, socialist feminist and openly homosexual Johanna Elberskirchen joined Hirschfeld and the Scientific Humanitarian Committee in 1914. As a proponent of 'free love' as a way of liberating women from the dominion of men, Elberskirchen, like Moll and Hirschfeld, was convinced by the concept of sexual intermediaries and forcefully rejected any notion of essential divide between women and men. In her early pamphlet *The Love of the Third Sex* (*Die Liebe des dritten Geschlechts*, 1904), Elberskirchen outlines her commitment to the theory of transitional forms:

> Everywhere in nature there exists transitional forms and variations in physical and chemical bodies, in plants, in animals ... and these transitions should be absent from man and woman? Each connection, every bridge? Man and woman should each comprise a single, strictly demarcated type! No, certainly not. A strict divorce between man and woman is out of the question.[108]

While the theory of transitional forms remains a key part of her analysis on same-sex desire, Elberskirchen nonetheless draws on her position as a woman to elevate herself as an unparalleled authority on the subject of female sexuality.[109] As well as promoting the theory of sexual intermediaries, Elberskirchen also supported the theory of the original bisexuality of men and women as proposed by Moll and Hirschfeld. Denying the existence of specifically gendered characteristics, she went further to claim that there existed no 'masculine' traits that could not be detected to some degree in women, and no 'feminine' characteristics that were entirely absent from men:

> After all, if we consider it more closely, we are all homosexuals – one more homosexual, the other less, in addition to our contrariness or heterosexual tendencies. Or, better said: we are all bisexual, all two-sexed, and, depending on our development, capable of feeling and loving as a two-sexed being.[110]

However, Elberskirchen does not situate her notion of two-sexedness (*Zweigeschlechtlichkeit*) within the wider social construction of gender complementarity and binary attraction, marking her out from her male contemporaries, who insisted on the feminine attraction to masculine natures. While Moll spoke of 'mothers' and 'fathers', and Hirschfeld implied that queer feminine women were attracted to masculine women 'of a strong mind', Elberskirchen argued that a woman's love for another woman demonstrated the only the most *feminine* of sentiments and, more strongly, that there was no space for the masculine element within such erotic configurations. In

What Has the Man Done to the Woman, the Child, and Himself? Revolution and the Emancipation of Women: A Break with the Man – a Guidepost to the Future! (1904), Elberskirchen dismisses the idea that queer desire in women was the result of a masculine drive and turns to the other inconsistencies that she considered had plagued previous writings about female same-sex desire.

Stressing the role of femininity in love between women, Elberskirchen opens her argument with her definition of homosexual desire: 'What is the nature of homosexuality, the love of one's own sex? The exclusion of the contrary sex, of course, that is, the male sex or, alternatively, the female.'[111] By 'excluding' the male element from their romantic relationships, Elberskirchen argues that women-loving-women actively reject the masculine: 'How can a woman's love for women embody characteristics of the "masculine"? The masculine element is excluded. One could better assume the opposite and say: in the love of a woman for other women, a trait of the feminine manifests itself.'[112] Turning her attention to the theories of queer desire between women that take gender complementarity as their basis, Elberskirchen is arguably the first social commentator and theorist to point to the elephant in the room, as she tackles the issue of the feminine woman who desires women:

> Thus, the interesting fact of two women loving one another is far from explained by saying that one represents the man, she feels masculine, and the other represents the women – female – and, therefore, normal! If one were to feel feminine, that is, normal, then one would be unable to love a woman and, therefore, *not* abnormal. Both are driven by their instincts to women, to their own sex. Both love in each other their own sex – the feminine. Not the masculine. Otherwise, a homosexual relationship would not be possible at all. Consequently, this is a matter of being pulled towards the feminine: from the feminine to the feminine.[113]

Radically, then, Elberskirchen rejects the notion of gender complementarity in her writings about desire between women and, in doing so, creates a space for femininity at the centre of her theorizing. The feminine woman in Elberskirchen's writing is not positioned as being so overly sensual that she has been seduced by the masculine element of a manly woman, and neither are her desires degenerate or excessive. Instead, the queer feminine woman in Elberskirchen's study is naturally attracted to the *womanliness* of her partner and not to the masculine nature of the congenital invert, as was being suggested widely in contemporary studies of the feminine woman's desire for her own sex. While going against the grain of writings about homosexuality of the time, Elberskirchen's contribution to the conversation surrounding female same-sex desire and the platform that she provided for the queer feminine woman was nonetheless still influenced strongly by contemporary social and moral codes.

Indeed, although Elberskirchen remains unapologetic about love between women in her work, her theory was above all concerned with a *spiritual* love, which places the erotic drive in an ambiguous light. In her writings, Elberskirchen remains locked between an instinctive sexual impulse that 'is as necessary as eating and drinking' and a higher spiritual connection that itself brings about the 'sexual hunger'.[114] Thus, the ideal expression of sexual passion in her writing was considered to be a consequence of a higher form of romantic friendship. The queer woman was positioned as a 'person of the "soul-love" … of the spiritualised love, a love that is stripped of everything that does not allow one to be fully conscious, of that which can be commonly associated with the physical love'.[115] In a departure from Hirscheld, who claimed that the feminine homosexual woman was *less* feminine than the heterosexual woman, Elberskirchen deployed the notion of spiritual love to position the queer feminine woman as *superior* even to the heterosexual woman, whose love for men stemmed purely from a base sexual love. Here, Elberskirchen inverts the normative/non-normative binary, classing heterosexual sex as a practice of 'excess' and, through its maltreatment of women, a form of female 'dehumanisation'.[116] Thus, like earlier studies on the ideal 'normal' woman's sexual passivity, the queer feminine woman in Elberskirchen's writing is characterized by her sexual modesty, not her erotic desire for other women. Interestingly, while Elberskirchen positions the queer feminine woman as *more* feminine than the heterosexual woman, she does not conceive of maternalism as constituent of this superior form of femininity. Remaining faithful to the eugenically inspired notion that same-sex desiring women would not be good mothers, she argues that procreation belonged to the, ironically more dehumanizing, forms of femininity associated with the heterosexual woman.

In a world dominated by the voice of male 'experts', Elberskirchen's theories present a challenge to previously assumed knowledge on the queer feminine subject. As an 'insider', as Leng observes, Elberskirchen was able 'to analytically and politically transcend the limitations of the man-made world' and accord a sense of legitimacy to her research through her position as an authority on female desire. Yet, in spite of this novel perspective, Elberskirchen's expertise remained caught within the parameters of a discourse that had been used systematically throughout the nineteenth century 'to prove women's physiological and intellectual inferiority to man, and thus to disqualify feminists' demands for women's greater inclusion in public life'.[117] In this way, despite highlighting key inconsistencies in previous research on queer women, Elberskirchen's limited legitimacy as a female sex researcher meant that her model of queer femininity was largely dismissed by her contemporaries. As a result, the 'third sex' model remained the primary framework through which to conceive of same-sex desires in the first half of the twentieth century. Nonetheless, Elberskirchen's theories still offer important insights into alternative models of desire in which queer feminine women were centralized and validated. And, with the establishment of psychotherapy and psychoanalysis in the early twentieth century, the dominance of the somatic models was called into question, with new significances accorded to the queer feminine and maternal.

Pseudo-homosexuals and Curable Queers

As the director of Zürich's Burghölzli Sanatorium, psychiatrist and neurologist Auguste Forel drew on a collection of patient histories gathered at his asylum to build evidence for his earlier-mentioned study *The Sexual Question*. The strict active–passive dualism that structured Forel's thinking about the subject of normal heterosexual impulses carried with it certain consequences for his theorizing about female same-sex desire. Given his belief in the fundamental differences in the way in which the sexual impulse manifested itself in men and women, as was discussed earlier in this chapter, Forel was one of few researchers who did not assume the self-evidence of a model of sexual inversion. While he writes at length on the 'pure' female invert who feels like a man, Forel was more concerned by the 'ill-defined pathological phenomenon' that was characteristic of female desire more generally, which he believed resulted from women's 'genetic predisposition for responsiveness to the advances of other women'.[118] While Forel concludes that queer desire in men was almost always the result of an abnormal hereditary sexual disposition – and gendered inversion – he suggests that women experienced sexual sensations that could be directed towards almost any object choice that stimulated their arousal:

> When an Urning woman wishes to seduce normal girls, she usually succeeds easily, as she is able to stir up in them an infatuated love ... Very gradually, through skilfully induced intensification, the female Urning often manages to evoke sensations of lust by kissing the nipples and the rubbing of the clitoris of her victim. The wonderful thing about it, however, is that the beloved usually, or at least very often, is not fully aware of the abnormality of the whole thing and remains, very easily, in an effusive state of love.[119]

Unless a subject's desires became pathological through the 'persistent practice' of Sapphic love, the 'innocent' feminine woman who indulged in 'Amor lesbicus' is considered in Forel's work to be a 'pseudo-homosexual'. The temporal nature of these feelings suggested that there was a distinct possibility that feminine women could be cured of their non-normative desires if they could be redirected towards a more suitable partner through marriage and fulfil their predestined roles as (re)productive members of society. In comparison to the fixed and immutable desires of the 'pure' masculine invert, the desires of feminine women only ever appear to be situational and temporal in Forel's work. As with Krafft-Ebing and Moll, Forel believed that through the practice of a healthy heterosexual partnership, normal instincts would return. This presentation of the seducing Sapphist clearly struck a chord with many conservative commentators in the Netherlands, where Forel's work continued to be popular during the interwar period. Given that the fear of seduction and contagion – the entire rationalization behind the introduction of Article 248bis – was well established here, his suggestion that the queer desires of 'normal' women were situational would no doubt have proffered hope of a 'cure' to what was considered a growing moral evil.

However, of all the so-called cures that became established in the field of psychiatry and psychotherapy in the twentieth century, none was more culturally recognized than the 'talking cure'. Ever since Westphal's study of Miss N., the 'voices of perverts', as Harry Oosterhuis terms them, had served to add legitimacy to sexological case studies. However, it was the Austrian neurologist and father of psychoanalysis Sigmund Freud who developed a model of desire in the late nineteenth century that, as Birgit Lang and Katie Sutton observe, essentially 'queered ... the case study genre that had formed the basis of sexological thinking on inversion up to that point'.[120] Already developing his theories of same-sex desire in *Three Essays on the Theory of Sexuality* (*Drei Abhandlungen zur Sexualtheorie*, 1905), Freud maintained a view that women – *and* men – were predisposed to psychic and somatic bisexuality. Within this framework, same-sex desire was considered a natural product of a more universal bisexuality and was viewed as an indication of an individual's 'arrested' sexual development – a result of environmental factors rather than inborn traits. Indeed, in his earliest writings on the subject of homosexual desire, Freud largely dismissed the theory that psychic and somatic 'hermaphrodism' were interrelated, although he conceded that in the case of female homosexuality, 'bodily and mental traits belonging to the opposite sex are apt to coincide'.[121]

Before Freud's article 'The Psychogenesis of a Case of Homosexuality in a Woman' ('Über die Psychogenese eines Falles von weiblicher Homosexualität', 1920), queer women appear to have been only a peripheral concern in his wider study of human sexuality.[122] Yet, by the time he published his article on eighteen-year-old Margarethe Csonka, Freud claims with great conviction that he is able to describe and categorize the phenomenon of same-sex love between women 'almost without gap and with entire certainty'.[123] In the study, Csonka is described as a young, beautiful and intelligent girl from a bourgeois family who had fallen in love with an older high-class sex worker, Baroness Leonie Puttkamer. When the patient's parents brought Csonka to Freud, the analyst considered her to be infatuated with Puttkamer. Angry that his daughter's choice of companion had brought shame on the family, Csonka's father attempted to dissuade her from seeking contact with the older woman, believing 'a quick marriage … should evoke the girl's natural instincts'.[124] When her father caught the couple walking arm in arm down the street, Csonka is said to have thrown herself onto a train track in a suicide attempt. She later recovered from her injuries.[125] In the physical descriptions of his queer female patient, Freud claims that he could not identify any 'striking deviation from the body type of a woman' and instead turns to experiences in the patient's childhood to trace the origins of her queer desires.[126] In perhaps the most interesting departure from previous studies, Freud conceived of his patient's maternal drive as the *origin* of her queer impulses rather than any innate sense of masculinity. Locating an incident in her adolescence in which Csonka became attached to a young boy, Freud discerns that she had been overwhelmed by 'a strong desire to be a mother and to have a child'.[127] Accounting for the redirection of his patient's libido from feelings of motherliness to a fixation on older women, Freud situates the pregnancy of the patient's mother as origin of her later queer feelings, concluding that her attachment to Baroness Puttkamer was the result of her seeking 'a replacement for the mother'.[128] Her maternal desire for a child, according to Freud, had developed into desire for a mother, as well as the desire for a 'mother-replacement'. Complicating matters further, Freud returned to his theory of universal bisexuality to observe that the Baroness' 'slender appearance … severe beauty and … harsh essence' was redolent of Csonka's brother and concluded that: 'The finally chosen object corresponded not only to [Csonka's] ideal for women but also to her ideal for men, combining the satisfaction of the homosexual desire with that of the heterosexual.'[129] In Freud's only study dedicated exclusively to the queer woman, same-sex desire is tied inextricably to his patient's natural maternal instincts, which are later transferred onto a mother-replacement. Indeed, instead of the maternal being employed to sublimate queer desire, or maternal instincts lacking in his queer subject, maternalism is presented by Freud as the *origin* of Csonka's same-sex longings. Moreover, Freud had little confidence that his queer female subject could transfer the object of her desire to a male object choice and did not argue that it was advisable for her to do so. Nonetheless, he suggested more broadly, like many of the sex researchers discussed in this chapter, that through a restricted object choice, 'normal' sexual feelings might develop in queer women.[130]

While 'expensive and lengthy' psychoanalytic analysis, as Harry Oosterhuis observes, remained the preserve of the elite for the first decades of the twentieth century, the introduction of a form of 'social psychiatry' in the 1930s, which was regarded by many as a science of the soul, led to psychoanalytic discourses gaining an unparalleled form of cultural traction in countries like Germany and the Netherlands.[131] Indeed, while the biological determinism that was promoted by theories of somatic inversion had been largely rejected in the Netherlands, the fact that the primary purview of psychoanalysis 'comprised education, marriage, family and sexuality' meant that the field was already 'closely intertwined' with many of the religious principles of Dutch society outlined in Chapter 1 meaning that it could therefore more readily be accepted as a scientific discourse with a social purpose.[132] Yet, as we have seen in Stokvis' collection of autobiographies, the somatic markers of queer desire that had long since been popular in German-speaking countries were clearly also influencing the field of Dutch sex research by the late 1930s, which served to complicate the narrative of female same-sex desire further still, bringing new perspectives to the by now well-worn analytic couch.

Conclusions

As has been described in this chapter, the images of queer feminine women that emerged within sexological and psychoanalytical writing in the late nineteenth and early twentieth centuries were often conflicting and based on little primary evidence. In a system in which 'normal' femininity had been defined by a lack of erotic and sexual feelings, the nineteenth-century feminine woman with queer longings was a marginal, if not inconceivable, figure, who frequently oscillated between the borders of 'normative' and 'non-normative' desires. Despite having received surprisingly little scholarly attention from historians of sexology, it is clear that femininity played a fundamental role in challenging normativizing theories of desire and sexual preference. Emerging as the enigmatic sexual object choice of the virile masculine woman, the feminine woman with queer desires became visible in early sexological studies as the presumed 'other' within a model of gender complementarity. Indeed, in the studies of Ulrichs and Westphal, congenital queer desire in women was only ever conceived as the result of a psychic masculine drive. And, although the idea of a feminine woman who desired women was imagined as a theoretical possibility in these studies, readers learned little of her lived realities. In Krafft-Ebing's panoply of perversions, which attempted to map more nuanced configurations of sexual preference, categorizations of desire began to move away from earlier models of psychic inversion. Indeed, the distinctions between 'perversity' and 'perversion' that emerged in his work had enduring consequences for the study of queer feminine women, whose desires became implicated in a theory of transitory sexual deviance that could be 'redirected' or 'cured'.

In an endeavour to build on Krafft-Ebing's increasingly innovative sexual topographies, sexologists in the late nineteenth century questioned the existence of 'true' forms of gendered and sexual expression. The fieldwork of Moll and Hirschfeld, for example, gave greater insights into the plurality of queer existence, privileging the voice of queer citizens in Berlin. For Moll, the queer feminine woman was an ambiguous figure, who sought to hide her true masculine nature. For Hirschfeld, there was no doubt that the feminine woman with fixed queer desires existed just as certainly as the masculine woman. Yet, within his infinite spectrum of sexual and gendered configurations, a queer feminine woman could never be *as* feminine as a 'normal' woman and therefore remained marked by a degree of gender deviance. Furthermore, the feminine woman appeared invariably to be drawn to the masculine element and therefore remained anchored to more reductive theories of binary attraction. While such biological discourses were taken up enthusiastically in Germany by conservative commentators and activists alike, albeit often to opposing ends, a 'rejection of the somatic style of medicine' in the Netherlands meant that sexological theories of female inversion did not find acceptance so quickly in the Dutch contexts. Instead, psychoanalytic studies presented a rather different picture of queer desire, in which female same-sex attraction was bound to maternal instincts and bisexual attraction, a theory we will see partially reflected in the literary discourses in Part III of this book.

Of the sexological theorists included in this volume, it was only Elberskirchen who centralized femininity in her analysis of queer female desire. And while same-sex love between women was discussed primarily in spiritual terms in her work, the fact that she suggested that queer feminine women were attracted to the *womanliness* of their partners challenged the active-passive dyad and theories of congenital masculine inversion that had hitherto dominated discussions on female same-sex desire. Even more radically, Elberskirchen posited that the queer feminine woman could be considered *more* feminine than even the idealized heterosexual women, given that she was able to exclude masculinity from her spiritual and social life altogether. It was not only the exclusion of the masculine element that gave Elberskirchen's ideas on queer femininity form, but also the rejection of erotic desire and a lack of maternal feelings. So, while the performance of femininity no longer precluded women from the discussion of same-sex desire by the early twentieth century, the queer feminine subject nonetheless remained caught up in the 'problematic of reproduction'. If she was not lacking in the normative maternal drive, the queer feminine woman was considered able to sublimate her queer desires into maternal instincts, allowing for the possibility of a supposed 'full return' to heterosexuality. Even in Freudian theories that situated the maternal as central to the experience of queer female desire, it was generally argued that the power of the maternal drive could help to reorient the desires of the 'pseudo-homosexual' woman. The figure of the feminine 'pseudo-homosexual' resulted in the fear that queer female desire was an ever-present threat – a dangerous consequence either of the oversexing of a woman through 'habitual coital practice' or the seduction of an innocent woman by a pathological invert. Quite how the conflicting discourses of seduction and spiritual friendship outlined in this chapter were taken up within communities of queer women in Germany and the Netherlands will form an important part of the discussion in the following chapters on the self-fashioning of queer identities in German and Dutch print press landscapes and the later analysis of literary texts produced by and for queer women.

Notes

1. Trans.: 'an einer Wuth Frauen zu lieben'. Carl Westphal, 'Die conträre Sexualempfindung, Symptom eines neuropathischen (psychopathischen) Zustandes', *Archiv für Psychiatrie und Nervenkrankheiten* 2(1) (1869), 73–108 (at p. 77).
2. Trans.: 'nichts vom weiblichen Typus Abweichendes'; 'überhaupt als Mann und möchte gern ein Mann sein'. Ibid., p. 77.
3. Trans.: 'machte sich dabei mit der Hand an den Geschlechtstheil des anderen Mädchens zu schaffen, liess sich selbst aber niemals berühren'. Ibid., p. 76.
4. Trans.: 'lässt kaum die Spitze des kleinen Fingers eindringen'. Ibid., p. 78.
5. Trans.: 'Die Patientin ist … von wenig einnehmendem, unbedeutendem Aeusseren; Physiognomie und Habitus haben nichts vom weiblichen Typus abweichendes … Im Übrigen zeigen sich keine Deformitäten der äusseren Bildung, namentlich auch nicht an den Geschlechtstheilen. Die grossen Schamlippen klaffen etwas auseinander, so daß die kleinen in der Schamspalte sichtbar sind, die Clitoris ist von gewöhnlicher Länge.' In defence of his genital examinations, Westphal stated: 'I expressly note that the patient underwent the examination without objection and even without the slightest trace of cynicism.' Trans: 'Ich bemerke ausdrücklich, dass sich Patientin der Untersuchung ohne Widerspruch aber auch ohne die geringste Spur eines Cynismus.' See ibid., pp. 77–78.
6. For more on neurasthenia, see David Schuster, *Neurasthenic Nation: America's Search for Health, Happiness, and Comfort 1869–1920* (New Brunswick, NJ: Rutgers University Press, 2011), p. 80.
7. Lisa Walker, *Looking Like What You Are: Sexual Style, Race, and Lesbian Identity* (New York: New York University Press, 2001), p. 4.
8. 'Introduction', in Vernon A. Rosario (ed.), *Science and Homosexualities* (New York: Routledge, 1997), p. 15.
9. Joachim S. Hohmann, *Sexualforschung und -aufklärung in der Weimarer Republik: Eine Übersicht in Materialien und Dokumenten* (Berlin: Foerster Verlag, 1985), p. 88. Furthermore, Laurie Marhoefer suggests, many early sexologists were influenced by the eugenics movement. This influence was irrespective of political leaning and even associations with more progressive political parties. Therefore, association with

a progressive political party did not necessarily result in a scientific position that could be deemed, certainly in the present day, as progressive: '[Eugenics] had broad popular support in Weimar-era Germany from the Right, the moderate middle, and the Left, but at the same time, the versions of eugenics backed by the various political players differed quite widely.' Laurie Marhoefer, *Sex and the Weimar Republic: German Homosexual Emancipation and the Rise of the Nazis* (Toronto: University of Toronto Press, 2015), p. 204.

10. While it is regrettable that this does not form a more central part of the remit of this volume, several important works have been published that focus specifically on this topic, with more focus in recent years on the problematic racializing tendencies of sexological work that has previously been considered progressive by queer activists and scholars. See, for example, Laurie Marhoefer, *Racism and the Making of Gay Rights* (Toronto: University of Toronto Press, 2022); Salvador Vidal-Ortiz et al. (eds), *Race and Sexuality* (Cambridge: Polity Press, 2018); Siobhan B. Somerville, *Queering the Color Line: Race and the Invention of Homosexuality in American Culture* (Durham, NC: Duke University Press, 2000).

11. 'Man erfährt dabei allerlei aus dem Sexualleben der Menschen, womit sich ein nützliches und lehrreiches Buch füllen ließe, lernt es auch nach jeder Richtung hin bedauern, daß die *Sexualwissenschaft* heutzutage noch als unehrlich gilt', cited in Volkmar Sigusch, *Geschichte der Sexualwissenschaft* (Frankfurt: Campus, 2008), p. 50.

12. Michel Foucault, *The History of Sexuality: Volume I*, trans. by Robert Hurley (London: Penguin, 1984), p. 138.

13. Kirsten Leng, *Sexual Politics and Feminist Science: Women Sexologists in Germany 1900–1933* (Ithaca, NY: Cornell University Press, 2018), p. 25.

14. Ibid.

15. Both Robert Deam Tobin's *Peripheral Desires* (Philadelphia: University of Pennsylvania Press, 2015) and Robert Beachy's *Gay Berlin* (New York: Knopf, 2014) situate Berlin as the birthplace of the modern homosexual identity and Germany more broadly as the country in which sex was 'discovered'.

16. Judith Schuyf, 'Lollepotterij. Geschiedenis van het "sapphisch vermaak" in Nederland tot 1940', in *Homojaarboek 1* (Amsterdam: Van Gennep, 1981), p. 31.

17. Maurice van Lieshout, 'Lustvijandig, wetenschappelijk voorzichtig en volhardend; de Nederlandse homobeweging in het begin van de 20e eeuw', *Groniek Historisch Tijdschrift* 66 (1980), 55–62.

18. Arnold Aletrino initially published under the pseudonym Karl Ihlfeld.

19. Given the status of German as the language of science during this time and the more liberal publishing climate that existed for sexological writing, many Dutch and British studies were printed initially in German and often only later in the author's native language. See also Havelock Ellis and J.A. Symonds, *Das konträre Geschlechtsgefühl*, trans. by Hans Kurella (Leipzig: Georg H. Wigand, 1896).

20. Ilse Bulhof, 'Psychoanalysis in the Netherlands', *Comparative Studies in Society and History*, 24(4) (1982), 572–88 (at p. 575).

21. Ibid.

22. Freud was not universally welcomed by psychiatrists and general practitioners in the Netherlands, and many found his focus on childhood sexual feelings to be unpalatable. Furthermore, as Ilse Bulhof notes, although some religious leaders in the Netherlands saw Freud as a welcome addition 'to traditional spiritual care and the training of preachers', a large number of 'Calvinist and Roman Catholic commentators denounced Freud because of his "materialistic" world view'. Trans.: 'op de traditionele zielzorg en de predikantenopleiding; de meerderheid van hervormde, gereformeerde

en rooms-katholieke commentatoren waarschuwde echter tegen Freud vanwege diens 'materialistische' wereldbeschouwing'. See Ilse Bulhof, *Freud en Nederland: de interpretatie en invloed van zijn ideeën* (Baarn: Ambo, 1983), pp. 273–79.
23. Van Lieshout, 'Lustvijandig', p. 55.
24. Kirsten Leng, 'Contesting the Laws of Life: Feminism, Sexual Science, and Sexual Governance in Germany and Britain c. 1880–1914', unpublished doctoral thesis (Ann Arbor, University of Michigan, 2011), p. 6.
25. In her work *Gender Trouble* (1990), Butler uses the term 'heterosexual matrix' to denote 'that grid of cultural intelligibility through which bodies, genders, and desires are naturalized ... to characterize a hegemonic discursive/epistemic model of gender intelligibility that assumes that for bodies to cohere and make sense there must be a stable sex expressed through a stable gender ... that is oppositionally and hierarchically defined through the compulsory practice of heterosexuality'. See Judith Butler, *Gender Trouble* (New York: Routledge, 1990), p. 208.
26. Jane Fenoulhet, 'Love, Marriage and Disappointment: Women's Lives in the Work of Ina Boudier-Bakker', *Dutch Crossing* 21(1) (1997) 52–68 (at p. 55).
27. Fenoulhet, *Making the Personal Political: Dutch Women Writers 1919–1970* (New York: Legenda, 2007), p. 65.
28. Trans.: 'hart heeft den ganschen dag gemord tegen het onnatuurlijk bestaan'; 'terwijl haar wenschen en verlangens naar huis trokken'. Ina Boudier Bakker, *De moderne vrouw en haar tekort* (Amsterdam: P.N. van Kampen en zoon, 1921), p. 35.
29. Trans.: 'Vrouwenhersenen in 't algemeen zijn alleen helder voor wat hun *hart* interesseert.' Ibid., p. 11. As Boudier-Bakker argues the failure of the modern marital union to fulfil the normative women's desires was evidenced by fewer women getting married in the Netherlands (and, indeed, Germany) after the war, and the increasing numbers of divorces that were taking place as men returned traumatized from the frontlines.
30. Theodoor van de Velde, *Ideal Marriage: Its Physiology and Technique*, 20th edn (London: William Heinemann Medical Books, 1947), p. 1.
31. The second instalment of Van de Velde's trilogy was *Sex Hostility in Marriage* (1931) and the final instalment was entitled *Fertility and Sterility in Marriage* (1931). Van de Velde's *Ideal Marriage* was a resounding success in Europe and was already in its forty-second impression in Germany by 1932. For more on van de Velde and his works, see Willem Melching, '"Het volkomen huwelijk" Opvattingen omtrent huwelijk en seksualiteit in het werk van Th. H. van de Velde', in Gert Hekma et al. (eds), *Grensgeschillen in de seks: Bijdragen tot een culturele geschiedenis van de seksualiteit* (Amsterdam: Atlanta, 1990).
32. See, for example, Marie Stopes, *Married Love: A New Contribution to the Solution of Sex Difficulties* (London: A.C. Fifield, 1918); and Max Hodann, *Geschlecht und Liebe in biologischer und gesellschaftlicher Beziehung* (Berlin: Universitas, 1932).
33. Trans.: 'Dit boek gaat vele dingen zeggen, die in den regel onuitgesproken blijven'; 'slechts die gevoelens en gewaarwordingen ... welke ten eenen male binnen de ... grenzen van het gezonde, normale, blijven'; 'De pathologie der liefde is een hel, waarvan de poort niet eens mag worden geopend'; 'Wij zullen trachten, met: alle kracht, die ons ten dienste staat, haar gesloten te houden'. Ibid., p. 21–23.
34. Trans.: 'als actief, volwaardig én gelijkgerechtigd geslachtelijk wezen gerehabiliteerd'. Van de Velde, *Ideal Marriage*, p. 197.
35. Although men are positioned as the educators of their wives, it is possible to see here that they are dually placed in the role of van de Velde's students.
36. Trans.: 'Het zou zelfs geen zin hebben, te dezer plaatse een volledige geslachtelijke physiologie der volwassene vrouw te schrijven. Zij zou veel te veel plaats innemen en

voor den leek grootendeels onbegrijpelijk zijn. Voor den arts is zij overbodig ...' Ibid., p. 50.
37. Lisa Duggan, 'The Social Enforcement of Heterosexuality and Lesbian Resistance in the 1920s', in Amy Swerdlow and Hanna Lessinger (eds), *Class, Race, and Sex: The Dynamics of Control* (Boston, MA: Barnard College Women's Center, 1983), p. 84.
38. Cited in Duggan, 'Social Enforcement', p. 85.
39. While there is a general dichotomous view of female sexuality in Forel's work, sexual desire is presented in his studies more generally, as Michael Trask points out, as being 'at once singular and 'variant', coherent and unstable, concentrated and diffuse' and contains multiple inconsistencies and contradictions'. See Michael Trask, *Cruising Modernism: Class and Sexuality in American Literature and Social Thought* (Ithaca, NY: Cornell University Press, 2003), p. 31.
40. Trans.: 'eine naturwissenschaftliche, psychologische, hygienische, und soziologische Studie für Gebildete'. Edward Ross Dickinson, *Sex, Freedom, and Power in Imperial Germany 1880–1914* (New York: Cambridge University Press, 2014), p. 251.
41. Trans.: 'die Sucht sich passiv zu geben, die Rolle der unterliegenden, bezwungenen, beherrschten Dulderin zu spielen'. Ibid., p. 99.
42. Auguste Forel, *Die sexuelle Frage: Eine naturwissenschaftliche, psychologische, hygienische und soziologische Studie* für *Gebildete*, 9th edn (Munich: E. Reinhardt, 1909), p. 252.
43. Trans.: 'ein Hauptbestandteil des normalen Sexualtriebes'. Ibid.
44. Trans.: 'der Begattungsakt ein unangenehmes, vielfach ekelhaftes, zum mindesten indifferentes Ereignis [ist]'. Ibid., p. 98.
45. Trans.: 'auf die Sexualorgane oder nach Begattung'; 'ein unklares, allgemeines Empfinden, eine Sehnsucht, nach Familiengründung und Mutterglück'. Ibid.
46. Trans.: 'Zart- und Schamgefühl'; 'Hier wirken das Routinenhafte, die Suggestibilität und die Willenskonsequenz der weiblichen Psychologie ... Dafür liefert die Prostitution traurige Belege'. Ibid., pp. 102–3.
47. A forensic scientist and criminologist, Casper asserted in his article 'Über Nothzucht und Päderastie und deren Ermittlung Seitens des Gerichtsarztes' (1852) that homosexual desire could be a congenital trait as opposed to an acquired one. See 'Introduction', in Hubert Kennedy and Harry Oosterhuis (eds), *Homosexuality and Male Bonding in Pre-Nazi Germany: The Youth Movement, the Gay Movement and Male Bonding before Hitler's Rise* (New York: Routledge, 2011), p. 12.
48. The terms 'Urningin' and 'Dioningin' were employed by Ulrichs to describe the *Urning*'s female counterpart, even though Ulrichs had made no contact with women who desired their own sex at this point.
49. Claudia Honegger, *Die Ordnung der Geschlechter. Die Wissenschaft vom Menschen und das Weib* (Frankfurt: Campus, 1991), p. 56.
50. Plato, *Symposium and Phaedrus* (New York: Cosimo, 2010), p. 15.
51. Trans.: 'dem Geschlecht der Männer und dem der Weiber als drittes Geschlecht coordiniert'. Carl Heinrich Ulrichs, *Vindex: Social-juristische Studien* über *mannmännliche Liebe* (Leipzig: Max Spohr, 1898), p. 25.
52. Eighteenth-century and early nineteenth-century studies that engaged with same-sex desire, such as the Swiss physician Samuel-Auguste Tissot's *L'onanisme* (1764) and Ambriose Tardieu's *La Pédérastie* (1857), posited both masturbation and inborn 'deformations' as the causes and origins of same-sex desires.
53. Taylor, Mara, 'Diagnosing Deviants: The Figure of the Lesbian in Sexological and Literary Discourses 1860–1931', unpublished doctoral thesis (Philadelphia: University of Pennsylvania, 2010), p. 73.

54. Trans.: 'Dem dritten Geschlechte kann möglicherweise thatsächlich ein *viertes* entsprechen, ein Geschlecht weiblich gebauter Individuen mit weibweiblicher Geschlechtsliebe, d.i. mit Geschlechtsliebe männlicher Richtung ... Derartige Weiber schienen indeß erheblich minder zahlreich vorzukommen, als Urninge. Eine wissenschaftliche Prüfung auch ihrer Natur möchte sehr wünschenswerth sein. Den Schlüssel zu dem Räthsel ihrer Liebe würde ein angeborenes männliches Element bilden' (emphasis in original). Numa Numantius, *Inclusa: Forschungen* über *das Räthsel der mannmännlichen Liebe* (Leipzig: Heinrich Matthes, 1864), p. 50.
55. Heike Bauer, 'Theorizing Female Inversion: Sexology, Discipline, and Gender at the Fin de Siecle', *Journal of the History of Sexuality* 18(1) (2009), 90.
56. Kennedy, *Ulrichs*, p. 72.
57. Trans.: 'mit männlichem Liebestrieb'; 'die thatsächliche Existenz des weiblichen vollkommen so verbürgt erscheint wie die des männlichen Uranismus'. Karl Heinrich Ulrichs, *Formatrix: Anthropologische Studien* über *urnische Liebe* (Leipzig: Heinrich Matthes, 1864), p. 59.
58. Taylor, 'Diagnosing Deviants', p. 41.
59. Ivan Crozier, 'Introduction: Havelock Ellis, John Addington Symonds and the Construction of *Sexual Inversion*', in *Sexual Inversion: A Critical Edition* (London: Palgrave Macmillan, 2008), p. 20.
60. The title of Krafft-Ebing's sourcebook, *Psychopathia sexualis*, had already been used in 1846 by Heinrich Kaan, whose work had viewed a variety of 'sinful' sexual acts as mental illnesses.
61. By the time of Krafft-Ebing's death, *Psychopathia Sexualis* had expanded to contain around 300 case studies.
62. Krafft-Ebing wrote: 'The study of your writings on male-male love interested me to a great extent ... From the day you sent me your writings – I believe it was 1866 – I turned my full attention to the phenomenon, which was just as puzzling to me, as it was interesting.' Trans.: 'Das Studium Ihrer Schriften über mannmännliche Liebe hat mich in hohem Masse interessiert ... Von dem Tage an, wo Sie mir – ich glaube es war 1866 – Ihre Schriften zusandten, habe ich meine volle Aufmerksamkeit der Erscheinung zugewendet, welche mir damals ebenso rätselhaft war, als interessant.' Cited in Ulrichs, *Vindex*, p. 7.
63. Although women in the 'Androgynie/Gyandrie' category bore markers of the opposite sex, Krafft-Ebing emphasized they should not be classified as intersex.
64. Harry Oosterhuis, *Stepchildren of Nature: Krafft-Ebing, Psychiatry, and the Making of Sexual Identity* (Chicago: University of Chicago Press, 2000), p. 244.
65. Trans.: 'Die Art der Befriedigung der weiblichen Urninge ist wenig gekannt'. Ibid., p. 63. '[V]iel spärlicher ... zu Gebot'; 'zu allen Zeiten'. Richard von Krafft-Ebing, *Psychopathia sexualis mit besonderer Berücksichtigung der konträren Sexualempfindung: eine medizinisch-gerichtliche Studie* für Ärtze *und Juristen*, 13th edn (Stuttgart: Ferdinand Enke, 1907), pp. 292–94.
66. Trans.: 'das weibliebende Weib fühlt sich dem anderen gegenüber in der Rolle des Mannes ... die Genitalien [sind] normal entwickelt, die Geschlechtsdrüsen funktioniren [*sic*] ganz entsprechend und der geschlechtliche Typus ist ein vollkommen differenzirter [*sic*]. Das Empfinden, Denken, Streben, überhaupt der Charakter entspricht jedoch in der Regel der eigenartigen Geschlechtsempfindung, nicht aber dem Geschlecht, welches das Individuum anatomisch und physiologisch repräsentiert'. Von Krafft-Ebing, *Psychopathia*, p. 57.
67. Trans.: 'beschränkt ... auf blosses Küssen und Umarmen'. Ibid., p. 257.
68. Trans.: 'sie zu küssen, zu umarmen, mit ihnen zu kosen'. Ibid.

69. Trans.: 'umschwärmt von der Herrenwelt'; 'immer als Mann dem Weibe gegenübe'. Here, 'active' refers to Miss X. carrying out the act on other women rather than allowing the act to be carried out on her person. We must assume that Krafft-Ebing considered the feminine partners of Miss X. to have been pathological or hypersexed women who desired more from a feminine partner than simply 'kisses and embraces'. Ibid., p. 263.
70. Trans.: 'unnatürlich [oder] krankhaft'. Ibid.
71. Given the environs in which Krafft-Ebing encountered his patients, these subjects constituted many of the cases of female inversion that he had presented in his work.
72. In fact, Krafft-Ebing regularly emphasized that intimate acts between persons of the same sex did not reveal a 'contrary sexuality' in and of themselves.
73. Trans.: 'natürlichen Verkehr zwischen Weib und Mann'. Krafft-Ebing, 'Neue Studien', p. 24.
74. Harry Oosterhuis, 'Sexual Modernity in the Works of Richard von Krafft-Ebing and Albert Moll', *Medical History*, 56(2) (2012) 133–55 (at p. 138).
75. Moll contributed a preface to the 16th and 17th editions of Krafft-Ebing's *Psychopathia Sexualis*.
76. Oosterhuis, 'Sexual Modernity', p. 144.
77. Steven Angelides, *A History of Bisexuality* (Chicago: University of Chicago Press, 2001), p. 42.
78. Ibid.
79. Trans.: 'ebenso wie in normaler Ehe'. Ibid., p. 525.
80. Trans.: 'unangenehm und ekelhaft'. Ibid., p. 544.
81. Trans.: 'in manchen Fällen die active und passive Rolle keineswegs scharf getrennt [sind]'. Ibid., p. 574.
82. Trans.: 'Hier würde die X von der Y, die activ war, durch Cunnilingus befriedigt; kurz darauf wurden die Rollen vertauscht, und beide lebten nun in dieser Weise weiter, sodass bald die eine, bald die andere activ bezw. passiv war.' Ibid.
83. Trans.: 'vieles ist sonst noch dunkel auf diesem Gebiete, und die Angaben sind oft einander widersprechend'. Ibid.
84. Trans.: 'durchaus normal'. Ibid., p. 547.
85. Trans.: 'Die Bewegungen der Tribaden erscheinen übrigens nur dann so vollständig männliche, wenn sie sich gehen lassen können. Wenn sie sich beobachtet glauben, oder wenn sie überhaupt nicht unter sich sind, wo jene Gêne wegfällt, sucht sie künstlich das Weibliche mehr nachzuahmen, um sich nicht zu verrathen.' Ibid., p. 255.
86. Trans.: 'Bei Frauen ist nämlich zu beobachten, dass sie mitunter trotz allen homosexuellen Empfindens Muttergefühle haben. Sie wünschen sich einen Sprössling, und es ist mir auch bekannt, dass in mehreren derartigen Ehen, bei denen sogar eine Scheidung drohte, es schliesslich [*sic*] zu einem erträglichen Zusammensein führte, wenn ein Kind geboren war'. Albert Moll, 'Die Behandlung der Homosexualität', *Jahrbuch sexuelle Zwischenstufen* 2 (1900) 1–29 (at p. 27).
87. This idea has significant implications for the understanding of the mother–daughter paradigm in queer literary production of this time (see Chapters 5 and 6).
88. As Butler explains: 'The classical association of femininity with materiality can be traced to a set of etymologies which link matter and *mater* and *matrix* (or the womb) and, hence, with a problematic of reproduction.' Judith Butler, *Bodies That Matter: On the Discursive Limits of 'Sex'* (New York: Routledge, 1993), p. 31.
89. Trans.: 'Für so leicht möglich halte ich die Heilung nicht, wenn ich sie auch schön aus theoretischen Gründen keineswegs für ausgeschlossen erachte.' Albert Moll, *Die konträre Sexualempfindung*, 3rd edn (Berlin: Fischer's Medicinische Buchhandlung, 1899), p. 266.

90. After four pages of calculations, Hirschfeld calculates a total figure of 43,046,721. See Magnus Hirschfeld, *Die Transvestiten: eine Untersuchung* über *den erotischen Verkleidungstrieb*, 2nd edn. (Leipzig: Ferdinand Spohr, 1925), pp. 287–90.
91. Trans.: 'Nuancen der Geschlechtsübergänge'; 'nur imaginäre Gebilde'. Magnus Hirschfeld, 'Ursachen und Wesen des Uranismus', *Jahrbuch* für *sexuelle Zwischenstufen* 5 (1903), 1–159 (at p. 127).
92. Trans.: 'keine absolute Übereinstimmung zwischen Virilität und Aktivität, Passivismus und Feminismus'. Magnus Hirschfeld, *Die Homosexualität des Mannes und des Weibes* (Berlin: Walter de Gruyter, 2001), p. 277.
93. Angelides, *A History of Bisexuality*, p. 42.
94. Hirschfeld was initially resistant to using the term *Homosexuelle*, which he considered to foreground only the sexual element, and continued to use Ulrichs' *Urning* and *drittes Geschlecht*. Hirschfeld claimed that Westphal's term *Konträrsexualismus* had been used 'almost exclusively by psychiatrists' ('fast ausschließlich von den Psychiatern') and it slowly fell out of favour. Eventually Hirschfeld also employed the term 'homosexual'. See Magnus Hirschfeld, *Die Homosexualität des Mannes und des Weibes* (Berlin: Louis Marcus, 1914), p. 22–23.
95. Trans.: 'hier findet sich eine Abteilung von Frauen, die in Tracht, Haarschmuck, Haltung und Bewegung, in der Art zu sprechen, zu trinken und zu rauchen etwas Viriles aufweisen; viele haben auch eine rauhe, tiefe Stimme, derbe männliche Gesichtszüge, schmale Hüften, wie überhaupt einen an das "stärkere Geschlecht2 erinnernden Knochenbau. Ihren Namen geben sie unter sich häufig eine virile Form. Daneben aber existiert eine nicht minder große Gruppe homosexueller Frauen, die sich äußerlich von anderen Frauen ihrer gesellschaftlichen Sphäre kaum unterscheiden; sie tragen Toilette und Frisuren nach derselben Mode wie diese, perhorreszieren weder Korsetts noch hohe Absätze, und erscheinen in ihren Gefühls-, Geschmacks- und Gedankenäußerungen so durchaus weiblich, daß sie niemand für homosexuell halten würde. Und doch sind sie es in genau so fixierter Weise, wie ihre virilen Schicksalsgenossinnen'. Here 'niemand' presumably means no *heterosexual* individual. Ibid., p. 272.
96. Ibid.
97. Trans.: 'niemand für homosexuell halten würde'; 'wesentlich femininer als die viril homosexuelle Frau'; 'wie ein heterosexuelles Weib ist'. Ibid., p. 109.
98. Trans.: 'überaus unglücklich'; 'es mangelt ihnen der mütterliche Instinkt'. Interestingly, maternal instincts are not altogether absent from Hirschfeld's work. Indeed, he maintains that for many queer feminine women, 'one of the most common dreams … is that they have conceived a child by the woman they love' ('einer der häufigsten Träume … ist, daß sie von einem geliebten Weibe ein Kind empfangen haben'). The maternal instinct, therefore, only appears as a result of the drive of a woman towards a love-object which, in this case, is another woman. Magnus Hirschfeld, *Der urnische Mensch* (Leipzig: Max Spohr, 1903), pp. 86–87.
99. Trans.: 'je weniger sie von der Norm abweicht, umsomehr liebt sie Frauen, die männliches an sich haben, kräftige geistesstarke Weiber, Künstlerinnen, Schriftstellerinnen'. Ibid., p. 276.
100. Birgit Lang and Katie Sutton have stressed the constructed nature of case studies through the ways in which sexologists selected material: 'that would best illustrate their theories, sometimes editing patients' statements before publication, and using a number of strategies to underline discursively the authenticity of their case materials, such as publishing these in the first person, and setting them off from the surrounding text by font size, margins and other textual markers'. See Birgit Lang and Katie Sutton,

'The Queer Cases of Psychoanalysis: Rethinking the Scientific Study of Homosexuality, 1890s–1920s', *German History* 34(3) (2016), 419–44 (at p. 434).
101. Trans.: 'Artsen, Geestelijken, Rechters, Advocaten [en] Politie-ambtenaren.' Maurice van Lieshout, 'De homosexueelen 1939: Mijnheer is zeker óók zoo?', *Sek* 11 (1981), 12–16.
102. Trans.: 'De beeldvorming van potten uit de medische bronnen is de beeldvorming vanuit de heersende cultuur. Ze werpt een licht op de mentaliteit van de buitenwereld.' Judith Schuyf, 'Lollepotterij', p. 21.
103. Trans.: 'Ik heb nog weinig [liefde] werkelijk belééfd. Maar genoeg om ten volle te kènnen en te begrijpen het felle leed dat onder ons, homosexueelen, geleden wordt'. Benno Stokvis, *De homosexueelen* (Lochem: De Tijdstroom, 1939), p. 163.
104. Trans.: 'geen wonder, dat er zooveel werken der duisternis onder ons, homosexueelen, gevonden worden!'. Ibid., p. 146.
105. Trans.: 'Hoe ver ik ook terug ga in mijn herinnering, altijd zie ik mezelf als een recalcitrant en schuw wezen, "anders dan de anderen", nu eens trots op dit "anders-zijn" dan weer dodelijk bevreesd ervoor'. Ibid., p. 146.
106. Trans.: 'Wanneer ik tracht mij te herinneren wanneer de eerste verschijnselen van mijn anders-zijn zich openbaarden, moet ik teruggaan tot den tijd dat ik als kind de lagere school bezocht … Met de jongens was ik betere vrienden; vaak mocht ik meedoen met hun wilde spelletjes omdat ik "zoo sterk in m'n armen was" en evengoed vechten en worstelen kon als zij.' Ibid., p. 156.
107. Trans.: 'Normaal – àbnormaal – … hoe dikwijls zijn die twee woorden door mijn hoofd gegaan? … "abnormaal", het begrip, dat ik het meest van alles haatte om den walgelijken bijsmaak, dien het voor mij had: onrein, verachtelijk, gevaarlijk.' Ibid., p. 146.
108. Trans.: 'Überall in der Natur giebt es Übergangsformen und Übergänge – bei den physikalischen und chemischen Körpern, bei den Pflanzen, den Tieren, den Individualitäten … Und dieser Übergänge sollte zwischen Mann und Weib fehlen? Jede Verbindung, jede Brücke? Mann und Weib sollten jeder für sich alleinstehender, streng abgegrenzter Typus sein! Nein, gewiß nicht. Eine strenge Scheidung zwischen Mann und Weib ist ausgeschlossen.' Johanna Elberskirchen, *Die Liebe des dritten Geschlechts: Homosexualität, eine bisexuelle Varietät keine Entartung – keine Schuld* (Leipzig: Max Spohr, 1904), p. 9.
109. Elberskirchen considered much of the research of dominant male theorists to be less scientifically objective than her own and more self-serving. See, for example, Johanna Elberskirchen, 'Offener Brief an Fräulein Dr. phil. Ella Mensch', *Frauen Rundschau* 5(12) (1904), 382.
110. Trans.: 'schließlich sind wir doch Alle, genau betrachtet, Homosexuale – der eine mehr, der andere weniger, homosexual neben unserer Conträr- oder Heterosexualität. Also richtiger: Wir sind Alle Bisexuelle, Alle Zweigeschlechtliche und je nach Entwicklung fähig, zweigeschlechtlich zu empfinden und zu lieben'. Ibid., p. 19.
111. Trans.: 'Was ist das Wesen der Homosexualität, der Liebe zum eigenen Geschlecht? Natürlich die Ausschließung das konträren Geschlechts, des männlichen bezw. des weiblichen.' Johanna Elberskirchen, *Was hat der Mann aus Weib, Kind und sich gemacht? Revolution und Erlösung des Weibes; eine Abrechnung mit dem Mann – ein Wegweiser in die Zukunft!* (Berlin: Magazin, 1904), p. 1.
112. Trans.: 'Wie kann nun die Liebe der Frau zur Frau einen Zug zum "Männlichen" haben? Das Männliche wird doch ausgeschlossen. Man könnte doch eher das Gegenteil behaupten und sagen: in der Liebe der Frau zur Frau manifestiere sich ein Zug zum Weiblichen!' Ibid.

113. Trans.: 'Wenn also zwei Frauen einander lieben, so ist diese interessante Tatsache noch lange nicht dadurch erklärt, daß man sagt, die eine repräsentiert quasi den Mann, sie empfindet männliche, die andere die Frau repräsentierend, weiblich, also – normal! Empfände die eine weiblich, also normal, dann könnte sie doch nicht eine Frau lieben, also doch nicht abnorm ... Beide treibt der Instinkt zur Frau, zum eigenen Geschlecht. Beide lieben im anderen das eigene Geschlecht – das weibliche. Nicht das männliche. Sonst wäre doch ein homosexuelles Verhältnis überhaupt nicht möglich. Folglich: Es handelt sich hier um einen Zug zum Weiblichen – vom Weiblichen zum Weiblichen'. Ibid., pp. 2–4.
114. Johanna Elberskirchen, *Geschlechtsleben und Geschlechtsenthaltsamkeit des Weibes* (Munich: Seitz & Schauer, 1905), p. 3.
115. Trans.: 'der Mensch der Seelen-Liebe, der Mensch der vergeistigten Liebe, einer Liebe die Alles abstreift, die nicht aufwachen läßt, das was Gemeines an körperlicher Liebe haften kann'. Elberskirchen, *Die Liebe des dritten Geschlechts*, p. 27.
116. Elberskirchen, *Was hat der Mann aus Weib*, p. 24.
117. Leng, 'Contesting the "Laws of Life"', p. x.
118. Rupp, *Sapphistries: A Global History of Love between Women* (New York: New York University Press, 2009), p. 147.
119. Trans.: 'wenn nämlich ein urningisches Weib normale Mädchen verführen will, gelingt ihr dies gewöhnlich leicht dadurch, dass sie dieselben zu einer schwärmerischen Liebe aufreizt ... Ganz allmählig, durch geschickt herbeigeführte Steigerung bringt es oft der weibliche Urning dazu, bei seinem Opfer Wollustempfindungen durch Küssen der Brustwarzen und durch Reibung der Klitoris hervorzurufen. Das Wunderbare dabei ist aber, dass die Geliebte sich in der Regel oder wenigstens sehr oft der Abnormität der ganzen Sache nicht recht bewusst wird und sehr leicht schwärmerisch verliebt bleibt'. Forel, *Die sexuelle Frage*, p. 288.
120. Working from the assumption that the patient's statement is never a straightforward utterance of 'truth' but can only provide the first clues to underlying unconscious processes and desires, Freudian analysts viewed the patient's initial 'confession' as a construct that worked to stabilize their personality at the starting point of analysis rather than as the final word on their condition. Lang and Sutton, 'The Queer Cases of Psychoanalysis', p. 420.
121. Sigmund Freud, *Sexuality and the Psychology of Love* (New York: Touchstone, 1997), p. 130.
122. In one of Freud's most famous analytic 'failures', he overlooked the desires of his patient 'Dora' (1900) for another woman. See Laura Doan and Jane Garrity (eds), *Sapphic Modernities: Sexuality, Women and National Culture* (New York: Palgrave Macmillan, 2006).
123. Trans.: 'fast lückenlos und mit voller Sicherheit'. Sigmund Freud, 'Über die Psychogenese eines Falles von weiblicher Homosexualität', *Internationale Zeitschrift* für Psychoanalyse 6 (1920), 1–24 (at p. 1). Remaining anonymous in Freud's study, the patient was given the pseudonym Sidonie Csillag in 2004 by the biographers detailing her life story. Her birth name was Margarethe Csonka (1900–99). See Ines Rieder and Diana Voigt, *Sidonie Csillag: La 'joven homosexual' de Freud* (Buenos Aires: El Cuenco de Plata, 2004).
124. Trans.: 'eine rasche Verheiratung ... die natürlichen Instinkte des Mädchens wachrufen [sollte]'. Ibid., p. 3.
125. In the biography written in 2004, Csonka is said to recall quite a different series of events from those that Freud describes in his study. According to Csonka, she did not know that her father saw her on the day she jumped onto the train tracks. She claims that she had attempted suicide because her lover had broken off their relationship.

126. Trans.: 'auffällige Abweichung vom körperlichen Typus des Weibes'. Ibid., p. 8.
127. Trans.: 'von einem starken Wunsche selbst Mutter zu sein und ein Kind zu haben'. Ibid., p. 9.
128. Trans.: 'ein Ersatz für die Mutter'. Ibid.
129. Trans.: 'schlanke Erscheinung ...strenge Schönheit und ... rauhe Wesen'; 'Das endlich gewählte Objekt entsprach also nicht nur ihrem Frauen-, sondern auch ihrem Männerideal, es vereinigte die Befriedigung der homosexuellen Wunschrichtung mit jener der heterosexuellen'. Ibid., p. 10.
130. While Freud considered these women to have a 'weak homosexual fixation', Forel had previously spoken about a 'weak hereditary disposition'.
131. Harry Oosterhuis, 'Insanity and Other Discomforts: A Century of Outpatient Psychiatry and Mental Health Care in the Netherlands 1900–2000', in Marijke Gijswijt-Hofstra et al. (eds), *Psychiatric Cultures Compared: Psychiatry and Mental Health Care in the Twentieth Century: Comparisons and Approaches* (Amsterdam: Amsterdam University Press, 2005), p. 76.
132. Ibid., pp. 77–78.

Part II

COMMUNITY DISCOURSES

What is Truth? For the multitude, that which it continually reads and hears ... The other, the public truth of the moment, which alone matters for effects and successes in the fact-world, is today a product of the press. What the press wills, is true. Its commanders evoke, transform, transpose truths. Three weeks of work by the press and the truth has been acknowledged by the world over.[1]
—Oswald Spengler, *Der Untergang des Abendlandes*, 1922

Introduction

In Oswald Spengler's chronicle of the ostensible decline of Western culture, the German philosopher and historian sketches a damning portrait of the early twentieth-century European press circuit. Depicting daily newspapers in his work as sirens who seduced the general public with a supposed 'truth of the moment', Spengler's study presents an arresting image of interbellum mass media as a tool 'which forces itself through the front doors of millions daily [and] spellbinds the intellect from morning until night'.[2] The unprecedented increase in both regional papers and consumer-oriented newspapers after the First World War was considered by Spengler to be a fundamental threat to the critical faculties of Western European citizens and he prophesized that a diurnal overload of news items would soon make it impossible for 'the masses' to discern between fact and fiction.

Spengler's above assertion makes clear assumptions about the class and educational backgrounds of the readers of daily papers, and effectively renders them powerless against the systems of supposed truths promoted by the press. Nonetheless, his proposal that print media had the power to create socially accepted 'knowledges' presents an interesting point of departure for the examination of what I refer to as 'minority magazines' during the interbellum, particularly when one considers the creation and dissemination of discourses about queer identities and desires. In keeping with the overarching aims of this volume, I will focus in the following two chapters on the discursive construction of queer feminine desires and identities in weekly and monthly periodicals specifically aimed at (queer) women in Berlin and Amsterdam. Although it is not possible to determine the extent to which such discourses influenced the sexual practices and identity formations of female readers – and, indeed, this is not the purpose of this study – the exploration of how the periodicals purchased by queer women acknowledged and, at times, resisted medicosocial discourses of identity and desire offers an essential 'community' counterpoint to the first two chapters of this book. Furthermore, such an analysis underlines the depth and diversity of sexual knowledges that were available to and, moreover, shaped by queer women in these two cities, while pointing out the very real differences in the social constructions of femininity and queer desire in these two cultural contexts.

In Berlin there existed at least six magazines for queer women in various formats by the mid-1920s. Appearing sporadically at weekly, fortnightly and sometimes monthly intervals, due to censorship laws and production issues, one cannot suggest that queer magazines were able to exert the same level of influence over public opinion as Spengler feared the increasingly popular daily newspapers might. Indeed, while these periodicals often asserted a pedagogic function through their aim to educate the 'masses' on the matter of homosexuality, their primary objective remained to serve the needs of increasingly visible and mobilized queer communities. Still, the power that a regular queer press could exercise over public (and private) perceptions of sexual identities and desires should not be underestimated. By revisiting Spengler's analysis, it becomes possible to conceive of queer periodicals as Foucauldian 'counterdiscourses' to medicolegal discussions about same-sex desire; publications that had the power to create their own 'truths' and 'knowledges' about queer female experiences.[3] Furthermore, quite unlike the central news organs and political mouthpieces that Spengler considered to be 'characteristically anonymous', queer publications were instead edited and written by well-known figures on the 'scene', and poems and literary supplements were submitted by readers and guest authors, which created periodicals written both for and by the queer community.[4] Unlike daily newspapers, then, minority magazines can be considered sites for the active and dynamic self-fashioning of specifically queer citizens, in which both writer and reader were engaged in the project of creating community-based 'truths' about their own lived experiences. Although the German periodicals at the centre of the analysis operate at times within the confines of the sociomedical discourses discussed in Part I, at other times, these publications present a radical departure from dyadic sex-gender configurations and offer far more nuanced images of women's romantic, sexual and social desires. It is in the melting pot of sexological, literary and political articles that informed these magazines that it becomes possible to locate the subcultural counterpoint to the sociocultural opinions and sexological theories that have already been described thus far. After exploring the interplay between these discourses in the publications that emerged for queer women in Berlin, I will compare this veritable explosion of queer print media with the dearth of such media in Amsterdam in order to ask what the absence of queer newspapers for women might suggest more broadly about queer female identities in the Dutch context during this time. Although the pitfalls of such an imbalance in primary materials remain almost unavoidable, a transnational evaluation of community-based print media can only serve to enhance our understanding of the ways in which women's historical desires and identities have been socially and culturally bound. Furthermore, such insights can develop our knowledge of how queer communities may have transferred their knowledges and practices across geographical borders.

In Chapter 3, I will focus largely on the periodicals produced by two competing emancipation movements for homosexual citizens in Germany: the League for Human Rights (BfM) and the German Friendship Association (DFV). On account of the absence of periodicals specifically for queer women in Amsterdam between 1918 and 1940, Chapter 4 will focus instead on the so-called 'cult of motherhood' that framed women's magazines more generally across the four primary pillars of Dutch society between 1918 and 1939, before spotlighting two magazines that were written and produced by queer men in this period: *We* (*Wij*, 1932) and *The Right to Live* (*Levensrecht*, 1940 and 1946–47). Although I remain conscious of the limitations of drawing conclusions based on such a narrow sample of queer material, positioning them alongside women's magazines highlights several points relating to the significance of motherhood to Dutch constructions of femininity, while emphasizing the gatekeeping structures of homosexual organizations in the Netherlands. In addition, this analysis will begin to explore the historical moment in which queerness came to be a more central part of women's social identities in Dutch society and of what such expressions of desire constituted. However, before making such considerations, it is important to explore some of the distinctions between the development of the German and Dutch press landscapes prior to the interwar period in order to address key points on the production, and availability, of queer print media to women in these contexts.

Berlin

The claim of Oswald Spengler that the interwar press functioned as 'an army with carefully organized branches and arms, with journalists as officers, and readers as soldiers' may appear somewhat histrionic considering the carefully executed manipulation of the print press and its critical role in Hitler's consolidation of power after 1933.[5] Nonetheless, Spengler's portrayal of the political and intellectual onslaught of an emergent mass media in the Weimar era is not an unfounded one. As Bernhard Fulda describes in his study of the Weimar newspaper circuit, the Roaring Twenties in Germany must be considered as 'undoubtedly the decade of the press'.[6] Indeed, by the time Spengler had published the second volume of *The Decline of the West* in 1922, Berlin had become established as 'the most important newspaper city of the world'.[7] Over two thousand periodicals appeared in the capital's news kiosks and bookstores each month and approximately 30% of the total number of periodicals sold across the country annually were purchased in Berlin.[8] While German newspapers in the nineteenth century could predominantly be characterized as 'small, distinctively elitist, political enterprises with a limited public', Fulda notes that rapid industrialization and developments in printing at the end of the nineteenth century resulted in a surge in consumer-oriented and tabloid press in larger cities.[9]

The emergence of commercial regional papers from the 1880s, as well as the popular boulevard press and over-the-counter newspapers at the fin de siècle, meant that daily newspapers entered the public realm at a rate never previously experienced. With many newspapers having earlier been reliant on monthly subscriptions, newer 'sensational' papers were sold in single copies at kiosks and by street vendors in various spots around the city. As a method of circulation initially employed by the leading publishing house Ullstein, at least forty companies had a stake in this new on-street approach to news distribution by the early 1920s.[10] The change in the distribution of newspapers from subscription to on-street sales gave many publications a chance of rapidly developing a large audience. As Gideon Reuveni notes of the change in Berlin's press landscape in the 1920s, 'unlike subscription-based distribution, which was generally intended for a defined group of readers, every day street sellers approached an undefined public with the goal of selling as many copies of newspapers as possible'.[11] Yet it was not only the development of increasingly sensational headlines that helped publications attract more readers, but also a better understanding of the needs and desires of their target audiences. In a bid to reach specific groups, many publishers developed localized and community-focused publications. These so-called 'district newspapers' were particularly popular in Berlin, with some of the largest boroughs in the city selling up to 27,000 copies of their local paper each day.[12]

As new markets were being discovered, women's hitherto marginal position as a procurer of periodicals also began to shift. During the early nineteenth century, women's magazines had been intermittently banned for breaching laws on women's political organization and participation. In the 1850s, a press law had been introduced that prohibited female editors from working in Saxony and Prussia, which meant that in some regions it had been almost impossible for women to establish long-lasting publications before the 1890s.[13] Following the sharp social and economic changes for women following the First World War, established broadsheets started to target female readers as a specific class of consumer who was considered to play a more central role in the media market by the mid-1920s. Ironically, with women's growing economic power – on account of their entering the workplace in larger numbers – came the idea that this audience would have more time to dedicate to reading magazines and purchasing consumer items. And, by the end of the 1930s, as Adrian Bingham notes, changes in women's social and economic positions in Britain and France meant that 'the female audience had moved from the margins to the centre of editorial calculations' and in Germany, too, popular newspapers 'could no longer afford to ignore or alienate female readers'.[14] Rapid industrialization and developments in printing techniques gave rise to a steady increase in daily and monthly newspapers that were available to purchase at kiosks and from vendors across the country. Furthermore, by the early twentieth century, shifting gender paradigms meant that women had become a more visible part of the urban landscape and their interests had to be taken more seriously by publishers. Quick to pick up on consumer trends, most major daily newspapers started to include supplements and serial stories for women and, soon enough, fashion journals and illustrated magazines targeted specifically at female readers began to appear in the city. Periodicals such as *Elegant World* (*Elegante Welt*, 1912–43) and *The Lady* (*Die Dame*, 1912–43) were aimed at female readers within the affluent beau monde. Journals such as *The Woman* (*Die Frau*, 1893–1944) and *The Woman without a Man* (*Die Frau ohne Mann*, 1921–25) offered discussions on important sociopolitical topics that were marketed at working-class and white-collar women.

Alongside the unprecedented increase in periodicals for women and the popularity of community-based magazines after the First World War, Berlin's ever-expanding queer nightlife, as discussed in Chapter 1, and the relaxing of censorship laws after the foundation of the Weimar Republic provided more freedom within the press circuit to meet the reading needs of emerging queer communities. Although many of these early magazines were intended predominantly for male readers, several periodicals appeared in Berlin between 1924 and 1933 that catered to the tastes of queer women. Acknowledged by Florence Tamagne as the 'definitive reference point for lesbians of the 1920s', these periodicals were the first regular publications to address the concerns and interests of queer women and were available from newspaper kiosks throughout Berlin and across Germany and Europe via subscription.[15] With quickly established and loyal readerships, these periodicals crucially enabled grassroots discourses to reach a wide audience and provided a platform for positive models of same-sex desire. Despite contemporary Ruth Margarete Roellig claiming dismissively in her city guidebook that the periodicals for queer women were '[not] to be taken seriously' in comparison to those available to men, these weekly and monthly periodicals supported their readers in the self-reflective understanding of themselves as 'homosexual women' and served an important *Bildungs* function for the 'uninitiated' on matters of queer female desire.[16]

As well as providing women with a space to articulate their desires, these magazines also helped facilitate networks in more rural areas across the country. Borrowing from Benedict Anderson's analysis of nationalism in her study on the masculine woman in Weimar Germany, Katie Sutton has already comprehensively described how the (inter)national distribution of Berlin's queer publications helped to develop a larger network of women and create 'imagined communities' across the country that fulfilled 'an important function in breaking down a sense of rural isolation'.[17] However, despite the knowledge of the existence of an 'imagined community' for women in rural areas, this often did little to eliminate the provincial fear that one might be discovered to be 'different from the others'. An existence in the city may have helped provide women with an increased sense of anonymity and a physical support network if one was desired. Unlike for rural readers, it was not necessary for city-dwellers to have the periodical delivered directly to their place of residence where it might be discovered by a relative or neighbour. Instead, Berliners could travel to districts in which they were unknown to purchase their favourite magazine. However, as one contemporary testimony suggests, the sense of anonymity afforded to women by the labyrinthine *Millionenstadt* did not entirely relieve one of the fear attached to purchasing such publications:

> The first time I bought [*The Girlfriend*] was in the place I first saw it. After that, I bought it where I was unknown. Well, at the kiosk where nobody knew me ... then you felt as though you had a bomb in your pocket. So, I

would read it elsewhere. On the toilet! Where nobody bothered you ... and then straight into the blouse, so that nobody saw.[18]

Anxieties about being caught reading queer publications do not appear to have prevented the medium from becoming a central mode of communication between like-minded queer women. By promoting weekly activities, evening events and day trips, no other publication or media outlet in the city could keep queer women up to date with the latest subcultural developments quite like their own 'little newspaper', and Berlin's queer magazines became a visible part of the city's media landscape until Hitler's seizure of power in 1933.[19]

Yet, despite the popularity of these periodicals, they did not altogether escape the purview of press censorship. The Lex Heinze obscenity law, which had been passed in 1900 following a high-profile murder case involving Gottfried Heinze, prohibited the display of so-called 'immoral' publications and artwork, and stimulated a broader discussion on sexual morality and the protection of minors. As mentioned briefly in Chapter 1, the introduction of the Law against Trash and Filth Publications in 1926 was deployed as a means to limit the dissemination of knowledge about queer female desires, which meant that periodicals for women-who-desired-women were effectively under constant threat of press censorship. In spite of these difficulties, which would no doubt have influenced editorial decisions and possibilities (as will be discussed in Chapter 3), it is possible to say that queer media flourished and thrived in Berlin in a way that was unknown in most other European cities during the interwar period.

Amsterdam

Across the Dutch border, the development of a queer press experienced a markedly different trajectory. While queer women of means in Germany could purchase relevant publications at reliable stockists across Berlin or subscribe to them in the provinces, no such publications existed for women in Amsterdam, or indeed any other major city in the Netherlands, until well after the Second World War. Before the emergence of the magazines *Amarant* and *Diva* in the 1970s (the latter renamed *Side by Side* during the mid-1990s), only two periodicals in Amsterdam dared to engage explicitly with the interests and concerns of queer people. Aimed at male readers, the publications *We* and *The Right to Live* offer only hints of the experiences of Dutch women-who-desired-women and the existence of both magazines was to be short-lived. Following a raid by the vice squad in 1932, *We* was forced to cease printing after its inaugural issue. Editors for *The Right to Live* were able to publish three issues of the magazine before the German invasion of 1940, following which the organization responsible for the magazine disbanded. Between 1946 and 1947 a further twelve issues of the magazine were published.[20]

The difficulties faced by queer Dutch individuals in establishing periodicals reflects, to some degree, a social context in which the Spenglerian fear of the power of the print press to influence the opinions and actions of the public had taken a firm hold. The introduction of the austere Morality Bill in the Netherlands in 1911, alongside the growing presence of vice squads in many major Dutch cities, was inextricably tied to the understanding of queer desire as an *act* rather than *identity*. Framed by what Anna Tijsseling has termed the 'Dracula thesis', queer desire in the Netherlands was associated with pederasty and contagion in the first half of the twentieth century.[21] Following the theories of Forel and others, there existed a fear that Dutch youths who had yet to 'form' their sexual preferences could easily be seduced into committing homosexual acts by older predatory men. While the surveillance of Sapphic publications in Berlin was enacted through intermittent censorship, the Dutch vice squad (*zedenpolitie*) ensured that any organization or publication that was perceived to be 'immoral' was banned with immediate effect. Despite a relatively relaxed attitude towards press censorship in the Netherlands more generally, any periodical that strove to strengthen the 'unity and … bonds of friendship' between queer men (and one might assume, by extension, queer women) was considered to be a publication too dangerous to remain in the public domain, where it might influence young minds or encourage 'predatory' behaviours.[22] Of course, targeted censorship and the presence of the vice squad are not the only reasons why a queer media did not develop in Amsterdam as it did in Berlin. Logistical matters concerning the production and distribution of magazines and newspapers also played a crucial role in the failure of queer organizations to establish a regular run of periodicals in the Dutch context.

During the early nineteenth century, newspapers in the Netherlands were restricted in their content and available only to privileged members of Dutch society due to the introduction of an expensive newspaper stamp (*dagbladzegel*) under the French occupation in 1812. This tax could be added either to the price of a reader's monthly subscription or to the cost of the individual newspaper itself. Once the levy had been paid by the reader/subscriber, the newspaper would be given a stamp to demonstrate proof of proper purchase. The 'taxes on knowledge' placed on these newspapers were by no means a meagre sum; often, the tax payable by any one publication amounted to at least half of the annual turnover of the periodical itself, which in turn meant a larger additional fee for the reader and made periodicals an unaffordable luxury for many. Furthermore, it was not only monthly newspapers that bore the brunt of the knowledge tax; pamphlets, placards and advertising posters were also subject to taxation.[23] With duties to pay on the periodical itself, as well as taxes being placed on advertising posters that might help sell magazines, the newspaper stamp essentially obstructed the growth of smaller journals in the Netherlands for much of the first half of the nineteenth century. However, after a prolonged campaign from 1850, the newspaper stamp was eventually overturned in 1869 and the prices of newspapers fell, which made them more accessible to a broader reading public.[24] With reduced costs, newspapers could publish more frequently and the press landscape soon began to diversify. Indeed, as Henri Beunders and Marcella van der Weg suggest, it did not matter to which denomination or political group one belonged: 'there was a newspaper for every citizen of every conviction at the turn of the twentieth century'.[25] With a system of district living well established in Amsterdam by the interwar era, and smaller neighbourhood papers now able to thrive, the city quickly became recognized as the 'newspaper capital' of the Dutch-speaking world.[26]

Although the development of a modern 'mass media' in Berlin was characterized by the distinctive emergence of newspaper kiosks and street vendors across the city, on-street newspaper sales remained a rarity in Amsterdam. With less than 10% of newspaper sales across the country being derived from on-street sales, 'for which one had to leave the house', Dutch dailies invariably made their profits through weekly or monthly subscriptions.[27] Indeed, as Maarten Schneider outlines, a curious culture of newspaper 'rental' existed in the Netherlands, which extended long into the twentieth century. In his study, Schneider describes the leagues of newspaper couriers (*courantenverhuurders*) that could be seen delivering daily newspapers to primary subscribers each morning, who would pay the highest rate for immediate access to daily news. Once the primary reader had finished with their morning paper, it would be re-collected by the courier and delivered to the next client, who would pay slightly less than the first. According to Schneider, this process would be repeated, occasionally even four or five times, at which point the final 'lessee' often had to wait until the following day for their news, when the rental process had already begun afresh.[28] This variation on the system of 'direct subscriptions' (*rechtstreekse abonnementen*) was largely shaped and reinforced by the political and social pillarization of Dutch society. Each pillar had a central news organ to which members subscribed, with more regional and specific pillarized publications emerging in the early twentieth century. The desire to create a sense of community met with a need for economic prudence, and the practice of direct subscriptions was taken up keenly across the Catholic, Protestant and Socialist pillars. Alongside this, the thrifty nature of the culture of subscription arguably enabled the growth of smaller 'niche' newspapers after the abolition of the newspaper tax and people could afford more than one subscription per household, so long as they were willing to wait to receive it. Indeed, as Plasse notes, by the mid-1930s 'every association, club or group in the pillarised Netherlands appeared to have had its own newspaper'.[29]

Mirroring developments in Germany, the emergence of smaller 'minority' journals concomitantly witnessed a growth in popularity for illustrated magazines and periodicals aimed at women readers. By the late 1930s, each pillar boasted a range of magazines that specifically targeted its female audience. Although Amsterdam did not experience the same upsurge in female white-collar work as Berlin during the interwar period, which would suggest that female readers had less dispensable income to spend on commercial reading materials, women were nonetheless taken seriously as potential readers. The periodical *The Young Woman* (*De jonge vrouw*, 1925–38), for example, emerged as a popular publication for Protestant readers during the interwar era, while *Beatrice* (*Beatrijs*, 1939–42 and 1946–67) was the weekly journal for women who belonged to the Roman Catholic Church. For female readers from 'better circles', *The Amsterdam Ladies Chronicle* (*De Amsterdamsche Dameskroniek*, 1915–42), edited in its early years by the author Carry van Bruggen (1881–1932), was the most fashionable choice, while *The Proletarian Woman* (*De proletarische vrouw*, 1905–40) was the preferred publication for Socialist women.[30] The significance of these daily and weekly newspapers as a tool for building and maintaining communities in a pillarized Dutch society cannot be overemphasized, especially as 'the stove, the coffee, and the newspaper' were considered the cornerstones of Dutch daily life for the first half of the twentieth century.[31]

Although the absence of queer media in Amsterdam could be traced back to a Spenglerian fear that the press had the power to legitimate unsavoury 'knowledges' and to influence young minds, the Dutch system of 'direct subscription' might also be considered an obstruction to the development of a queer press. Within a culture of newspaper rental, there was little need for kiosks, which may have fostered a sense of anonymity and attracted new readers that could help the magazines bear printing costs. Moreover, although direct subscriptions made access to newspapers cheaper, it would still have been exceptional for a woman to have her own subscription without the means to purchase it for herself. Thus, while many more magazines aimed at female readers emerged in the early twentieth century, the reading of newspapers remained primarily the preserve of the father of the family, who would '[put] on his glasses and [act] as a master of ceremonies at the solemn event'.[32]

As well as the newspaper being considered the domain of men, the fact that female homosexual desire in the Netherlands was not understood as part of a woman's *social* identity at this time also suggests that a periodical intending to attract readers from this subsection of society would have encountered difficulties in reaching its target audience. As was discussed in Part I, many Dutch women became engaged in romantic and erotic relationships with other women without ever defining themselves as homosexual, lesbian or bisexual. However, as a reader letter from a Dutch transvestite in a 1931 issue of the German magazine *The Girlfriend* suggests, for those individuals in the Netherlands who *did* have an appetite for queer media – and an understanding of German – Berlin could provide the community, both real and 'imagined', that was lacking in Amsterdam.[33]

In the next two chapters, I will first describe the structure and format of the periodicals *The Girlfriend* and *Love of Women*, and *We* and *The Right to Live* within the wider frameworks of the homosexual organizations and communities that existed in Berlin and Amsterdam. Departing in many ways from dominant social narratives about same-sex desire, the queer agendas that appear in these publications offer a unique insight into the position of feminine women within two nascent queer communities. Focusing on two of the largest emancipation movements for homosexual citizens in Germany – the BfM and the DFV – Chapter 3 will explore the ways in which Magnus Hirschfeld's work on 'intermediate sexual states' formed a fundamental ideological rift that divided Berlin's queer communities. Focusing on the triptych of social, scientific and literary discourses that forms the broader framework of this book, I examine the periodicals *The Girlfriend* and *Love of Women* to assess the attitudes of these periodicals towards their queer feminine readers (and contributors). Furthermore, as both magazines also included supplements for the transvestite community, 'femininity' will be considered in as inclusive a manner as possible, referring both to sartorial and somatic constructions of womanhood, a particularly important discussion point in light of the hostile debates taking place at present around transgender women, their femininities and their place within lesbian (and) feminist communities. Chapter 4 will focus initially on presenting a broad sketch of the types of femininities made accessible, and desirable, to women in the Netherlands across the chief pillars of Dutch society, as outlined in Chapter 1. Using *The Young Woman* and *Beatrice* to form my corpus, I will examine the various modes of femininity presented in the articles, stories and reader letters in these periodicals to engage critically with the 'cult of motherhood' that shaped the cultural imagination during this time. Considering how the politics of maternalism might have fed into the late onset of naming and labelling queer desires in the Netherlands, I will ultimately ask what the absence of discourses on female desire in the periodicals *We* and *The Right to Live* might be able to tell us about hierarchies of desire that existed in the Netherlands during the interbellum, as well as the place of queer women within them.

Notes

1. Trans.: 'Was ist Wahrheit? Für die Menge das, was man ständig liest und hört ... Die andre, die öffentliche des Augenblicks, auf die es in der Tatsachenwelt der Wirkungen und Erfolge allein ankommt, ist heute ein Produkt der Presse. Was sie will, ist wahr. Ihre Befehlshaber erzeugen, verwandeln, vertauschen Wahrheiten. Drei Wochen Pressearbeit, und alle Welt hat die Wahrheit erkannt.' Oswald Spengler, *Der Untergang des Abendlandes: Umrisse einer Morphologie der Weltgeschichte*, vol. II (Munich: C.H. Becksche Verlagsbuchhandlung, 1922), p. 579.
2. Trans.: 'die ... in alle Häuser dringt [und] die Geister vom frühen Morgen an in ihren Bann zieht'. Ibid., p. 578.
3. Here, I do not mean 'reverse discourses'. In other words, I do not suggest that German and Dutch groups were attempting to reappropriate the categories used to oppress them as a form of empowerment. Indeed, the terms 'homosexual' and 'lesbian' were used in opposing ways by the two German magazines in question. In the magazine *Frauenliebe*, for instance, the terms 'homosexual woman' and 'lesbian woman' were often employed to signify sexualities that ran counter to heterosexual practices, those involved in *Die Freundin*, however, were focused instead on creating a sense of 'homonormativity' within the movement, which revolved around a politics of respectability in the first instance and assimilation into existing heterosexual social and erotic structures – through the adoption of binary gendered patterns – in the second.
4. Trans.: 'bezeichnender Anonymität'. As I will discuss in Chapter 3, the content of many queer magazines comprised debates, letters, poems and short stories that were submitted by readers, which positioned them dually as contributors. However, the decision of which content was published in the magazine remained at the discretion of the editors. See Spengler, *Der Untergang*, p. 578.
5. Trans.: 'eine Armee mit sorgfältig organisierten Waffengattungen, mit Journalisten als Offizieren, Lesern als Soldaten'. Spengler, *Der Untergang*, p. 580.
6. Bernhard Fulda, *Press and Politics in the Weimar Republic* (New York: Oxford University Press, 2009), p. 3.
7. Howard Eiland, *Walter Benjamin: A Critical Life* (Cambridge, MA: Belknap Press, 2014), p. 235.
8. Ibid.
9. Fulda, *Press and Politics*, p. 13.
10. Other publishing companies of the time, such as Scherl and Mosse, soon followed suit. For more on this, see Gideon Reuveni, *Reading Germany: Literature and Consumer Culture in Germany before 1933* (Oxford: Berghahn Books, 2009), p. 142.
11. Ibid., p. 112.
12. The *Spandauer Zeitung* is an example of one of the most popular *Bezirksblätter*, which regularly sold over 27,000 copies a day. By comparison, one of the smallest was the *Karlshorster Lokal-Anzeiger*, which sold approximately 2,500 copies daily. See Fulda, *Press and Politics*, p. 14.
13. After an article written by feminist activist Luise Otto-Peters on the conditions of political prisoners appeared in the *Frauen-Zeitung* in 1850, Saxon press officers inserted a paragraph that prohibited women from carrying out editorial decisions. The paragraph read: 'The editorial responsibility of a newspaper can only be taken on and continued by men.' See Petra Boden 'Political Writing and Women's Journals: The 1848 Revolutions', in Jo Catling (ed.), *A History of Women's Writing in Germany, Austria and Switzerland* (Cambridge: Cambridge University Press, 2000), p. 107.

14. Adrian Bingham, *Gender, Modernity, and the Popular Press in Inter-War Britain* (Oxford: Oxford University Press, 2004), p. 19.
15. Florence Tamagne, *The History of Homosexuality: Berlin, London, Paris Volume I & II* (New York: Algora Publishing, 2006), p. 78.
16. Trans.: '[nicht] ernst zu nehmen'. Roellig was herself a regular contributor to *Die Freundin*. Of the magazines available to queer women in this period, *Die Freundin* was certainly the most closely associated with the male emancipation movement and was considered by contemporaries and historians alike to be more political than *Frauenliebe*. I will contest this position in Chapter 3. See Ruth Margarete Roellig, *Berlins lesbische Frauen* (Leipzig: Bruno Gebauer Verlag, 1928), reprinted in Adele Meyer, *Lila Nächte: Die Damenklubs der Zwanziger Jahre* (Köln: Zitronenpresse, 1981), p. 23. All footnotes that follow will cite the title of Roellig's original work.
17. Indeed, the magazines inspired subgroups in Weimar, Zwickau, Halle and Karlsruhe, as well as some in more international locations in America, Switzerland and Austria. See Katie Sutton, *The Masculine Woman in Weimar Germany* (New York: Berghahn Books: 2011), p. 154.
18. Trans.: 'Ich habe [*Die Freundin*] zum erstenmal gekauft, wo ich sie gelesen habe. Dann habe ich sie mir dort gekauft, wo ich unbekannt war. Na, am Kiosk, wo mich keiner kannte … dann kamst du dir vor, als hättest du eine Bombe in der Tasche. Und dann habe ich sie sonstwo gelesen. Auf dem Klo! Wo dich keiner gestört hat … Und in die Bluse gesteckt, damit sie keiner sah.' Ilse Kokula, *Jahre des Glücks, Jahre des Leids: Gespräche mit älteren lesbischen Frauen* (Kiel: Frühlings Erwachen, 1986), p. 78.
19. Here, the 'kleine Zeitung' the interviewee is referring to is *Die Freundin*. Ibid.
20. The banning of *We* must be considered a strong intervention, given that the liberal censorship laws that had been place in the Netherlands since 1848 made it extremely difficult for a magazine – or book – to be censored or banned once it was in the public domain. For more on censorship laws and literature in the Dutch contexts, see in particular Marita Mathijsen (ed.), *Boeken onder druk: censuur en pers-onvrijheiden in Nederland sinds de boekdrukkunst* (Amsterdam: University of Amsterdam Press, 2011).
21. Anna Tijsseling, 'Schuldige Seks: homoseksuele zedendelicten rondom de Duitse bezettingstijd', unpublished doctoral thesis (Utrecht: University of Utrecht, 2009), p. 52'.
22. Trans.: 'eenheid en … vriendschapsbanden', *Wij*, 1, 1932, p. 4.
23. See Robert Justin Goldstein, *The War for the Public Mind: Political Censorship in Nineteenth Century Europe* (Westport, CT: Praeger, 2000).
24. As an attempt to circumvent taxation, the so-called 'lilliputter press' was established, consisting of various oppositional pamphlets, which were printed in such a small format that they could not be made subject to taxation. In 1845, the government put an end to this opposition by taxing *all* printed journal formats. See 'Dagbladzegel: belasting betalen om het lezen van kranten'. Retrieved 19 April 2022 from http://kunst-en-cultuur.infonu.nl/geschiedenis/161258-dagbladzegel-belasting-betalen-om-het-lezen-van-kranten.html.
25. Trans.: 'progressieve, christelijke, neutrale, volkse, het maakte niet uit: voor elke burger van elke gezindte was er omstreeks 1900 wel een krant'. Henri Beunders and Marcella van der Weg, *Pers en politie in Amsterdam* (Amsterdam: Bas Lubberhuizen, 2010), p. 37.
26. 'Introduction' in ibid., p. 13.
27. Trans.: 'waarvoor men de deur uit moet'. Maarten Schneider and Joan Hemels, *De Nederlandse krant: 1618–1978: van 'nieuwstydinghe' tot dagblad* (Amsterdam: Wereldvenster, 1979), p. 308.
28. Ibid.

29. Trans.: 'elke vereniging, club of groepering leek in het verzuilde Nederland haar eigen tijdschrift te hebben'. Jan van de Plasse, *Kroniek van de Nederlandse dagblad- en opiniepers* (Amsterdam: Otto Cramwinckel Uitgever, 2005), p. 122.
30. For more information on the context of these periodicals, see Jane Fenhoulet, *Making the Personal Political: Dutch Women Writers 1919–1970* (New York: Legenda, 2007), p. 57.
31. Trans.: 'de kachel, de koffie én de krant'. Schneider and Hemels, *De Nederlandse krant*, p. 287.
32. Trans.: 'die courant is in de eerste plaats voor den vader des gezins, die er zijn bril voor opzet en als die ceremonie-meester fungeert bij die plechtige gebeurtenis', ibid., p. 282.
33. 'Briefe die wir gerne lesen!', *Die Freundin*, 2 September 1931.

Chapter 3

FASHIONING FEMININITIES IN *THE GIRLFRIEND* (1924–33) AND *WOMEN'S LOVE* (1926–32)

In her guidebook *Berlin's Lesbian Women,* author and sexual topographer Ruth Margarete Roellig claimed that feelings of isolation had become a 'lesbian lament' by the late 1920s, even for those women living within reach of Berlin's bar culture.[1] One of the primary reasons for this, Roellig suggests, alongside growing political discontent and a trend towards cultural conservatism, was the deteriorating economic climate of the Weimar Republic, which dramatically altered the subcultural landscape for homosexual women, restricting the amount of space available to them either for discreet liaisons or gatherings with others 'of their kind'. As a way of bringing together like-minded others, magazines thus played a vital role in queer community building during the Weimar era, creating textual space in which women could legitimately explore the possibilities of nonheterosexual lifestyles and connect with likeminded individuals with whom they could share their sentiments and experiences. This was important not only for those women living in more provincial areas without access to the queer organizations and bar culture for which Berlin was becoming known, but indeed also for those in the German metropolis, where rapid industrialization had resulted in the somewhat double-edged sword of urban anonymity. 'Imagined communities' appeared in the form of at least seven German periodicals for queer women over the course of the interwar period: *The Girlfriend: Journal for Ideal Friendship* (*Die Freundin: Das ideale Freundschaftsblatt*), *Single Women* (*Ledige Frauen*) and *Garçonne*

were affiliated with the BfM. *Women's Love: Friendship, Love and Sexual Enlightenment* (*Frauenliebe: Freundschaft, Liebe und sexuelle Aufklärung*), *Women's Love and Life* (*Frauen, Liebe und Leben*) and *Loving Women* (*Liebende Frauen*) were affiliated with the DFV. *The Pages of Ideal Female Friendships* (*BIF – Blätter Idealer Frauenfreundschaften*) was a maverick publication and had no known affiliation with the larger organizations campaigning for homosexual rights.[2]

While *The Girlfriend* and *Women's Love* can be considered the 'original' magazines for queer women, the increasing difficulties faced by publishers in terms of press censorship and financial difficulty during the interwar period, as outlined in the introduction to Part II, meant that both magazines were placed intermittently on the list for 'Trash and Filth' writing and, as such, were replaced by the other magazines named above, which presented themselves as 'sister' publications.[3] Functioning in a more commercial way than the sexological research discussed in the Part I, the newspapers and magazines intended for nonheterosexual women nonetheless aimed to enlighten the layperson about the nature of Germany's homosexual citizens, while dually facilitating the establishment of wider queer networks. Both *The Girlfriend* and *Women's Love* were themselves affiliated with the two largest homosexual rights organizations in Germany: the League for Human Rights (BfM) and the German Friendship League (DFV), respectively. Indeed, in spite of the appearance of a cohesive sexual subculture in Berlin, queer communities in the Capital of Pleasure had become increasingly divided by the wider discursive dichotomies that structured the agendas of these two movements by the late 1920s. While *The Girlfriend* and *Women's Love* were both highly successful in connecting a diverse spectrum of women who may otherwise have become further isolated, the support networks facilitated by these magazines were often structured by competing discourses of desire. As *The Girlfriend* appears to have been imbued with many of the homonormativizing impulses of the BfM, the writers of *Women's Love* appear to have subscribed significantly more to Magnus Hirschfeld's theory of sexual intermediaries, which were central to the ideologies of the DFV. Examining the overlaps and contradictions between these positions, this chapter will focus on the role of femininity in two key periodicals aimed at queer women in Germany. After contextualizing *The Girlfriend* and *Women's Love* in terms of the wider homosexual emancipation movements to which they belonged, I will discuss how these magazines have been presented in historiographical studies, considering how enduring associations between femininity and frivolity have shaped the legacies of these publications. Throughout this analysis, I hope to demonstrate the significance of femininity to the shaping of desires that were being given increased meaning as social identities, while engaging with these magazines as discursive spaces in which desires, preferences and identities were both being contested and given form.

The Girlfriend: 'A Journal for Ideal Friendship'

Launched on 8 August 1924 under the auspices of the BfM, *The Girlfriend* was the first magazine available for queer women in Germany and, of those available to homosexual women during the interwar era, it was by far the most established and widely distributed.[4] Initially intended as a supplement in the publication *The Pages for Human Rights* (*Blätter für Menschenrecht*), *The Girlfriend* was established as an independent monthly publication following the success of its first three issues. Published at first by the Orplid Verlag and later the Carl Bergmann Verlag, the magazine ultimately became the responsibility of the Radszuweit publishing house, owned by chairperson of the BfM, Friedrich Radszuweit (1876–1932). While *The Girlfriend* was at first conceived as a monthly magazine, it was soon printed in twice-monthly editions and varied between eight and sixteen pages in length. It also included several images, most of which were nudes taken either from historical art works or soft pornographic tableaus. Costing between 20 and 30 Pfennig, there was an attempt to begin to sell a more copiously illustrated edition of the periodical for 50 Pfennig from April 1925. After the magazine disappeared from print in 1926 – appearing only sporadically as part of the magazine *The Journal of Friendship* (*Das Freundschaftsblatt*) – it returned in 1927, sold at its original sale price of 20 Pfennig.[5] Further interruptions to *The Girlfriend*'s circulation took place in 1928, when it was placed on the blacklist for Trash and Filth Publications for a year, and 1929, when it was blacklisted again for several months.

In its infancy, the layout and structure of *The Girlfriend* changed little. Most early issues contained at least one key discussion article, a selection of reader letters, news items from the BfM, short and serial stories, reader poems, a page of classified advertisements, and information on upcoming events at the bars that were associated with the organization. While the content was no doubt diverse, the magazine appears to have been built upon three main pillars: articles about the struggle for emancipation and equal rights, reader letters relating to community concerns and literary contributions. Indeed, during the years of its publication, *The Girlfriend* printed over five hundred poems, three hundred short stories, more than thirty serial stories and more than two hundred social commentaries in its pages. Although the earlier years of the magazine focused more on the contributions of its female editors, writers and readers, when Martin Butzko assumed the position of lead editor for the magazine in 1929, the focus of the publication shifted; editorials on sexological and social developments were now written by male contributors, and there was also a more sustained engagement with transvestite issues.[6] In November 1929, when Martin Radszuweit – Friedrich Radszuweit's adopted son and lover – became lead editor of the publication, the content shifted once again. Between 1930 and 1932, forty-two of the seventy-four editorials available in the archive were written by Friedrich Radszuweit himself, although it has not been possible to ascertain how many of these were copied from the magazines he published for men. Although Radszuweit's editorials focused chiefly on the campaign against Paragraph 175, they also detailed other sociopolitical advances made by the BfM and commented on the political developments taking place in Berlin and Germany more broadly. After June 1930, the sections 'Letters that you write to the Girlfriend', 'What the Girlfriend is talking about' and 'Our Readers have the Floor' were also removed from the regular layout and appeared only sporadically until 1933. These features, as Heike Schader has described, had facilitated conversations between readers on several contentious topics within the queer community, and the changes implemented by the new male editorial team meant that an important point of contact and exchange between readers, contributors and editors was effectively lost.[7] Prior to the editorial changes, sustained reader debates on several important issues relating to femininity can be seen: the divisiveness of the bobbed hairstyle (*Bubikopf*), for example, but also the issue of monogamy, the role of femininity in the political struggle for acceptance, and the apparently ephemerally thorny subject of bisexual desires. Although reader letters did appear in the publication periodically after 1929, they were no longer a regular feature of the magazine and the focus was undoubtedly on the advancements of the BfM, the struggle again Paragraph 175 and the troubling rise of the Nazi Party. Furthermore, the magazine published more articles by men after Martin Radszuweit assumed his position as chief editor. In spite of such changes, *The Girlfriend* maintained its function as a tool for the education and emancipation of queer women, which had been made clear to its readers from the very first issue.[8] In an article outlining the intentions of the editorial board, chief editor Aenne Weber wrote emphatically of *The Girlfriend*'s decisive role in the future campaign 'for the equal rights of women in social life'.[9] Although the magazine had always presented itself as a political organ, specifically for queer people, it was not until 1926 that a broader educative function was incorporated into its key aims.[10] As this coincided with the introduction of the Law for the Protection of Youth against Trash and Filth Publications (which will be discussed in more detail below), it is likely that this was a tactical decision made by the editors to avoid clashes with Berlin's State Youth Welfare Office (Landesjugendamt).

Women's Love: 'Friendship, Love and Sexual Emancipation'

Two years after the first issue of *The Girlfriend* appeared, a rival publication for queer women was established by the DFV, an organization that ran in direct competition with Friedrich Radszuweit's BfM. Between 1926 and 1930, *Women's Love* (*Frauenliebe*) functioned as the central news and entertainment organ for women involved with the DFV and, like *The Girlfriend*, was also sold at 20 Pfennig per issue and published by the Carl Bergmann Verlag, with which it stayed for the duration of its print run. There are no exact dates on the cover of *Women's Love*, which makes establishing an exact timeline for the periodical far more difficult than for *The Girlfriend*. Yet, from the available information, the magazine appeared from 1926 as a weekly publication with pauses in circulation due to blacklisting in 1930, after which it continued under the following names: *Women's Love and Life* (1928), *Loving Women* (no exact dates) and, finally, *Garçonne* (1930–32).[11] At a similar length to its competitor, *Women's Love* ran between eight and twelve pages in length, and was copiously illustrated with (nude) images, and replete with literary supplements, discussion articles, advertorials and personal pages.

With groups for female members of the DFV and readers of *Women's Love* listed in Berlin, Leipzig, Chemnitz, Dresden and Vienna, it seems likely that the periodical would have been particularly popular in these locations. However, letters to the editors from across the country attest to the publication's widespread popularity and show that, like *The Girlfriend*, readers subscribed to the magazine in rural as well as urban areas, and from both within and outside of Germany. As far as it is possible to tell from the information provided about the editors in the magazine, the editor-in-chief of the first three issues was Margot Roma, who was then followed by 'Karen', who remained the editor for almost the entire existence of the publication. While male members of the DFV did contribute articles to the periodical, as Stefan Micheler observes, the chief editorial team of the magazine always appeared to consist of female members and there do not seem to have been any attempts at an editorial takeover by male members of the DFV, as was the case with *The Girlfriend*.[12] Although many of the articles were written by women, contributors to *Women's Love*, much like those to *The Girlfriend*, made ample use of creative pseudonyms – such as 'XYZ', 'Faust' and even 'Ano Nymus' – which means it is impossible to claim with any certainty that all writers in the magazine identified as female.

Unlike its rival, *Women's Love* has rarely been conceived of as a political periodical in recent historiographical studies. Florence Tamagne's *History of Homosexuality* suggests that contemporary readers of queer magazines would have turned to *The Girlfriend* instead of *Women's Love* for 'a serious analysis of the lesbian situation in Germany'.[13] Similarly, Petra Schlierkamp notes in her article on *Garçonne*, the successor to *Women's Love*, that the magazine was primarily considered a 'entertainment journal' (*Unterhaltungsblatt*), in which discussions of lesbian identity and political developments 'faded … into the background'.[14] Yet, although political editorials and articles do not appear as frequently or as explicitly in *Women's Love* as they did in *The Girlfriend*, I will suggest in this chapter that the political potential of the periodical has been largely overlooked in these recent studies.

Indeed, as I will argue, it appears that the political potential of *Women's Love* has been underestimated primarily due to the magazine's dedication to 'feminine' interests such as social commentaries, literary contributions, reader debates, poems and personal advertisements. However, dismissing *Women's Love* as a mere 'entertainment journal' denies the publication the political significance it had for many women and devalues the political potential of the aforementioned genres of 'entertainment' writing on account of their being considered 'feminine'. Furthermore, such conclusions do not account for the magazine's arguably 'woman-centred' ideology, which shaped many of its discussions about sexuality and gender. Certainly, contributors to *Women's Love* clearly recognized the importance of the periodical as a political organ for social emancipation, with editors describing their desire to create from the magazine a 'campaign of the girlfriends'.[15] Like its rival, *Women's Love* frequently presented itself as an educative medium through which writers could enlighten nonqueer individuals about their needs and their plight, something that the writers saw as a fundamental step in achieving emancipation. As 'Ikarus', a regular contributor to the magazine, claimed to readers in 1930:

> No one should forget, not even for a moment, that this journal is the voice that should offer a step for our fellow human beings, a step of understanding. For everything that one understands becomes knowledge. This knowledge brings to other people the consciousness of a new, that is, our sex.[16]

As well as promoting the idea that the magazine could serve a didactic purpose, educating 'fellow human beings' about a 'new sex', Ikarus' employment of terms such as 'knowledge' (*Erkenntnis*) and 'consciousness' (*Bewusstsein*) feeds back into the spirit of the Weimar Republic's culture of intellectualism. The significance of the magazine to the DFV's struggle for queer emancipation was a recurrent theme in the periodical, and contributors regularly encouraged their readers to strive to live more openly and to organize politically. 'Only the masses can guide us to the goal', Ikarus rallies at the end of the article: 'Freedom for love on all fronts!'[17]

As both *Women's Love* and *The Girlfriend* survived in print until the final years of the interwar era, it can be assumed that they enjoyed a loyal and faithful readership. As the official organ for female members of the BfM, *The Girlfriend* had the initial advantage over *Women's Love* of being the first, and most established, periodical for same-sex-desiring women. Yet, while it is no longer possible to trace circulation figures for *The Girlfriend*, or indeed for any of the magazines that were produced by the Radszuweit Verlag, the periodical's affiliation with the BfM suggest that one can assume readership figures for the periodical were reasonably high. Yet, even concerning the membership figures of the organization, conflicting reports emerge. While statements issued by Radszuweit in 1929 state that the organization had 48,000 members, a representative of the DFV claimed that the BfM had as few as 380 members at this time and that the BfM's chief publication, *The Journal of Friendship*, circulated approximately 2,900 copies.[18] Comparatively, the Carl Bergmann Verlag reported sales figures for *Women's Love* of 10,000 copies in 1928.[19] Although it is almost impossible to state either readership or membership figures with any degree of certainty, the fact that both magazines were able to survive a ruinous economic climate, with relatively little interference to the frequency of their circulation or price, indicates that the periodicals sold in reasonable numbers and had sufficient subscribers and readers. Even the recurrent interruptions to sales of both magazines after the implementation of the Law for the Protection of Youth against Trash and Filth Publications do not appear to have affected the survival of the magazines significantly.

As outlined in the Introduction to Part II, by virtue of the fundamental freedom of the press established in the Weimar Constitution of 1919, a diverse queer press circuit was able to develop during the interwar period, through which events and gatherings were advertised, and aided the beginnings of what would become a short-lived but vibrant queer subculture. However, the Law for the Protection of Youth against Trash and Filth Publications, which was introduced in a bid to protect the 'moral, intellectual [and] hygienic development' of the German youth on 18 December 1926, effectively established a form of press censorship, banning media that could be considered damaging or dangerous to young people.[20] The nebulousness of the terms 'Trash' and 'Filth' meant that these categories were employed generally, as Gideon Reuveni observes, as 'a label to mark writings of reputedly low aesthetic and ethical value in order to exclude them'.[21] Publications that had been placed on the blacklist were banned from advertising their periodicals and news kiosks were prohibited from displaying them publicly. If a periodical had been blacklisted twice in a single sales year, a further ban on the offending periodical was served that could last anywhere between three and twelve months. Yet, once the ban had been lifted, the magazine could be sold again at kiosks so long as its content did not contravene any of the restrictions set out by the law.

Although the Law for the Protection of Youth against Trash and Filth Publications stated that a publication could not be blacklisted 'because of its political, social, religious, ethical or ideological inclinations', the editing board of both *The Girlfriend* and *Women's Love* believed that their periodicals had been targeted specifically on account of the associations they had with queer organizations.[22] In an article printed originally in *The Journal of Friendship* and later *The Girlfriend*, Friedrich Radszuweit argued that the BfM's magazines had been targeted by the vice squad in order to impede the periodical's broader aims of social justice: 'It is always the same old story that offices for youth welfare "allegedly" campaign against trash and filth but in reality they campaign essentially against homosexuality. The little cloak of trash and filth is only ever employed when one wants to get one over on homosexual people.'[23] Although Radszuweit suggested that the law was brought to bear against homosexual magazines to 'get one over' on the (male) homosexual movement, Karen, the editor of *Women's Love*, argued that such laws were being used especially to target *women's* writing and experiences. Examining the aspects of the law that might be employed to attack literary and cultural pursuits that were classified as 'low' culture and gendered 'feminine', Karen reflected:

> If one considers in more detail what could possibly be effected by the new law, we conclude that it is, strikingly, mostly women's writings. That is, journals for beauty, nudism, and dance, personal hygiene, marriage, women's lives and loves ... So, it is about the woman, then! Not about the woman as a person, but as a sexual being.[24]

The divergences between the editorial perspectives outlined briefly above characterize the primary rift between the two publications. While the focus of *The Girlfriend* was on how the Law for the Protection of Youth against Trash and Filth Publications could affect the (male) homosexual community more generally, *Women's Love* concentrated specifically on how such laws could be used to restrict the representation of the experiences and voices of (feminine) women.

However, to put these two magazines at opposing ends of this ideological conflict would certainly be too reductive. In the struggle for visibility and acceptance, there were clearly common aims and mutual interests between the two organizations responsible for the publication of the magazines that no doubt went some way towards uniting the contributors and readers of both periodicals. Yet, when it comes to the primary aims and objectives of the BfM and the DFV, which were informed by many of the sexological discourses seen in Chapter 2, there appear to have been very few intersections of agreement on matters of identity and community. As will be discussed later on in this chapter, these rifts created ideological clefts between the publications that invariably shaped their depictions of queer femininity and desire. Nonetheless, as we shall discover, feminine desires were sites of conflicted and vested interest in both magazines. In *Women's Love* and *The Girlfriend*, feminine desires are presented, at times, as positively protean and transmutable, with authors transgressing strict binary stratifications. At others, such desires are seen to shore up gendered and sexual bifurcations, reinforcing the social structures that positioned femininity as that which is heterosexual and queer femininity as temporary and transient.

Discursive Divisions within Berlin's Queer Subculture

In 1919, Karl-Schultz-Verlag published its first issue of the magazine *Friendship* (*Die Freundschaft*, 1919–33) in Berlin, a weekly publication that was meant for the 'enlightenment and the spiritual elevation of ideal friendship'.[25] The emergence of this magazine coincided with an unprecedented rise in the number of 'friendship leagues' in the city, which served as a support network for homosexual people in the struggle against Paragraph 175. Soon becoming popular across Germany, the leaders of these leagues quickly realized that it would be beneficial to band together to form part of an umbrella organization that could enable regional groups to undertake combined actions for civil rights reforms.[26] Following this proposal, the DFV was formed in Berlin in August 1920 with Hans Janus at the helm. Working closely with Magnus Hirschfeld's Scientific Humanitarian Committee, as well as Adolf Brand's Community of the Special (Gemeinschaft der Eigenen, GdE), towards the abolition of Paragraph 175, the DFV disseminated educational materials about the nature of homosexuality to politicians, the police force and other notable figures with social and political influence.[27] By the time that Friedrich Radszuweit, chairperson of Berlin's friendship league the Association of Male Friends and Female Friends, changed the name of his branch to the League for Human Rights (BfM), cracks had already begun to appear within the wider organization of the DFV, with a series of disagreements leading to a leadership challenge in the early 1920s. While still a relative newcomer to the association, Radszuweit managed to assume control of the DFV in 1923, renaming the organization after his own Berlin faction. With Radszuweit leading the now-named League for Human Rights, the organization established several new periodicals, many of which were produced by Radszuweit's own private publishing company.[28] Yet, already by 1925, several central members of the newly formed BfM had become unhappy with the way that Radszuweit was running his 'personal empire' and decided to secede in order to resume the activities of the former DFV.[29] Max Danielsen and Hans Janus, editors of the journal *Friendship*, were elected as the group's leaders. Soon after the split, the DFV began to publish its own periodicals for queer readers under the auspices of Carl Bergmann Verlag, which ran in direct competition with Radszuweit's publishing house.

Although on the surface the rift between the DFV and the BfM appears to have been caused by a series of superficial power struggles, the frictions between the two organizations were founded upon much deeper ideological divisions concerning their approaches to homosexual emancipation, identity, and desire. While Radszuweit and his supporters forcefully rejected the 'elitist scientific attitudes' of Magnus Hirschfeld and his acolytes, the DFV was keen to employ Hirschfeld's theories in its publications to further its campaign for social emancipation and change.[30] In his publications, Radszuweit openly accused Hirschfeld of creating a 'display of abnormalities' through his research and suggested that the shadow of the sexologist's work had cast the homosexual movement in a 'bad light'.[31] Radszuweit even claimed in 1931 that the theory of sexual intermediaries, which had been propagated by Hirschfeld and the Scientific Humanitarian Committee (WhK), was to blame for the homophobic slander of the growing Nazi movement.[32] Distancing the BfM from what Radszuweit perceived as a damaging stereotype of 'effeminate' homosexual desires, the organization instead began to advocate for the rights of masculine and, more importantly, respectable (*anständig*) male homosexuals.

Although Radszuweit's glorification of the masculine homosexual male suggests that he may have been aligned with 'antifeminist, antimedical, antimodernist' masculinists, such as Adolf Brand and Benedict Friedlaender, the latter's celebration of a 'pederastic *Eros*' had very little to do with Radszuweit's desire to create a respectable homosexual orthodoxy that took shape in what might be classified as a form of 'homonormativity'.[33] Indeed, Radszuweit frequently discussed the protection of male youth against the blackmail of male sex workers and rejected the idea of an extramarital, pederastic bisexuality that was proposed by Brand and his followers. Furthermore, although women did not comprise a particularly significant role within the leadership positions of the BfM, female members were made welcome in the BfM, unlike in those circles of Brand and his followers, which had supported several misogynist campaigns. While the BfM was welcoming to women, Radszuweit and his organization nonetheless venerated bourgeois forms of masculine enterprise. Relying upon what Smith-Rosenberg has termed the 'ancient polarity of woman/body-man/mind', Radszuweit created a clear hierarchy of queer conduct, which positioned respectable forms of masculinity at its summit.[34] Throughout the existence of the BfM and its publications, Radszuweit appears to have paid little attention to the specific needs and desires of feminine people (male or female). Indeed, as we shall see, it was often only through the embodiment of the positive elements of bourgeois masculinity that queer women could find a legitimate place within the BfM community.

In contrast to the BfM, the leaders of the DFV strengthened the connection of their organization with Magnus Hirschfeld and the Institute for the Study of Sexual Science following the split from the BfM in 1925. Hirschfeld's theory of intermediary sexual forms shaped the ideological tenets of many of the DFV's publications and created space for more open conversations on topics such as bisexuality, polyamory and relationships

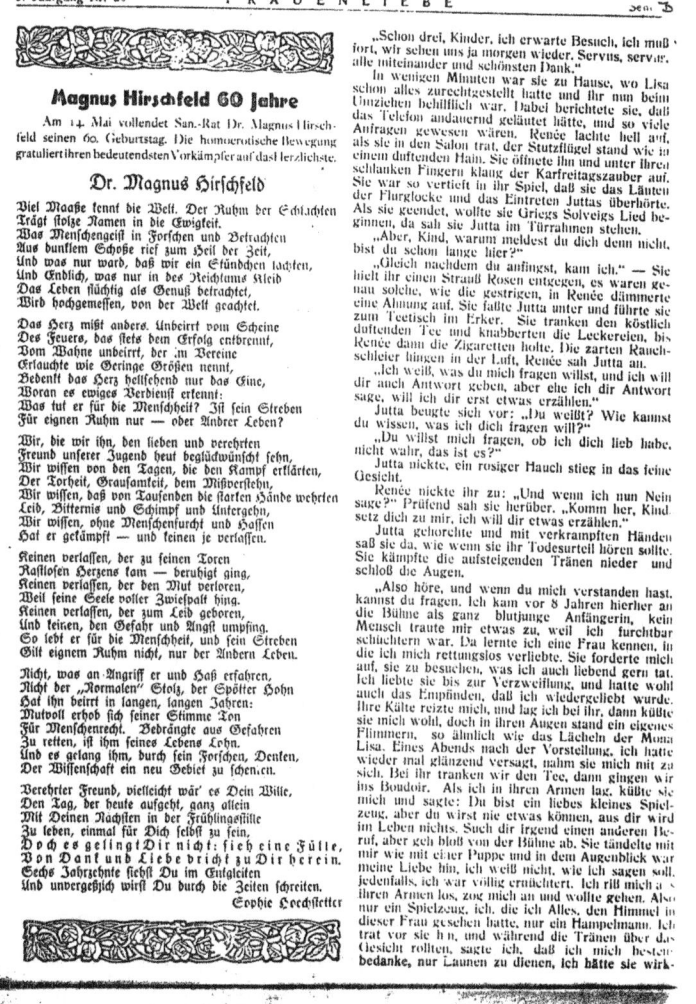

Figure 3.1. 'A Poem Dedicated to the Work of Magnus Hirschfeld', *Women's Love*, 1928. Spinnboden Archive, used with permission.

that were not configured around complementary gender roles. The growing influence of the life reform movement (Lebensreformbewegung) in Berlin, which promoted nudism, sexual freedom and a simpler 'back-to-nature' lifestyle, also inspired a more liberal approach to the conceptualization of gender and sexuality within the DFV's periodicals.

Women's Love also regularly recommended books such as Anton Putz zu Adlersthurn's serial novel *The Island of Nudes* (*Die Insel der Nackten*, 1927–32) and Rudolf Quanter's *Free Love* (*Die freie Liebe*, 1906), for example, and promoted lectures such as 'How Do I Keep Myself Young and Beautiful?' and 'Rejuvenation of the Appearance through Cosmetic Self-Treatment'. Hirschfeld's unwavering support for Austrian endocrinologist Eugen Steinach also appears to have influenced the faithful focus on rejuvenation (Verjüngung).[35]

The tensions between the theoretical underpinnings of the BfM and the DFV frequently led to their associated publications being utilized as instruments with which to undermine the actions of the rival group. In an article published by Max Danielsen in *Women's Love*, for example, Radszuweit is criticized for the alleged abuse of his position and for falsifying membership and sales figures. Danielsen denounced the BfM as the 'demagogue for "human rights"' and suggested that if Radszuweit did not step down from his position, the tension between the two organizations would lead to the 'most difficult internal struggle ... that the homosexual movement [had] ever undergone'.[36] Although the writers of *Women's Love* appear to have targeted Radszuweit as the key figure of their discontent, *The Girlfriend* was not above publishing defamatory articles about Danielsen, Bergmann or the DFV more generally. In a thought piece concerning the state of play of queer women's clubs in Berlin, Lotte Hahm, a prominent lesbian figure and leader of several women's clubs, criticized Carl Bergmann's role in the homosexual movement as a publisher and contributor, and claimed that it was 'grotesque ... that a heterosexual man should be the leader of homosexual woman'.[37] Relaying rumours of Bergmann's financial problems, Hahm concludes her article in a similarly threatening tone to Danielsen's earlier tirade: 'Should Bergmann have any desire to grind an axe with me, I will call forth further facts from the archives about which the ladies will be astonished and Karl [sic] Bergmann will be horrified.'[38] As will become clear in the following analysis of the sexological, literary and medicosocial discourses presented in the magazines, the conflicts that existed between the two organizations responsible for *The Girlfriend* and *Women's Love* can be said to have been of central importance to the decisions made about the content of the periodicals and, ultimately, the approaches taken to the construction of queer feminine identities and desires within them.

Defining the Parameters of the Feminine

In the inaugural issue of *The Girlfriend*, chief editor Aenne Weber described for her readers the gendered landscape that she believed characterized Berlin's queer scene. Entitled 'The Homosexual Woman', Weber's article drew on the more conservative somatic discourses seen in the previous chapter to highlight a sharp distinction between two seemingly discrete categories of women:

> There are two types of homosexual woman. The virile – that is, the masculine – and the feminine – that is, the womanly – woman. The virile woman is characterised above all by her independence ... The feminine woman is quite the opposite ... She is a woman through and through, of delicate nature and clingy character.[39]

Positioning the masculine partner in 'the role of the protector', Weber created an idealized image of a masculine homosexual woman who she believed to be distinct from the mannish 'woman without morals'. Much in agreement with August Forel, Weber claimed that the latter type of mannish woman was predisposed to 'unrestrained sensuality', 'alcoholism' and 'gambling'. Similarly, while the 'clingy behaviours' of the feminine homosexual woman in Weber's descriptions may appear undesirable, they were sharply distinguished from the degenerate desires of the 'pseudo-homosexual' *femme fatale*. Indeed, the descriptions of the feminine homosexual woman in Weber's article embodies the delicate, vulnerable and sexually passive nature epitomized in the ideals of Wilhelmine womanhood. Deviating little from the traditional active-masculine and passive-feminine dichotomy, *The Girlfriend*'s inaugural discussion of gender therefore frames its queer community in terms of already constituted cultural norms and standards. Readers are advised in Weber's article that homosexual relationships should not deviate from hegemonic norms, but, instead, should strive to fulfil them. Although this strict adherence to gender roles does not appear to be particularly radical, Weber's suggestion of 'two types' of queer women nonetheless presents conceptual space in which to imagine 'authentic' queer feminine desires, even if this character is submissive and 'clingy' in nature. Of course, Weber's binary coding only grants legitimacy to the figure of the queer feminine woman as a partner of a more visible and respected masculine partner.

While Weber's opening article presents the reader with two types of homosexual women, in the sociomedical articles, literary texts and reader debates that followed in *The Girlfriend* over the years, the idealized image of female queerness is constructed faithfully around the figure of the masculine woman, with femininity being considered its more troubling counterpart. Excerpts from Otto Weininger's conservative *Sex and Character* (1903), for instance, were printed in the magazine in 1931 devoid of any context or critical discussion.[40] While it is difficult to discern whether the editorial board and the magazine's readers shared Weininger's ideas, his suggestion that the homosexual woman's masculine nature facilitated her worldly achievements appears, in many respects, to correspond with *The Girlfriend*'s understanding of acceptable gendered roles. Indeed, the tone of Selli Engler's article 'To the Independent Homosexual Women!' printed in April 1931 suggests that Weininger's view of same-sex desires and gender performance was likely to have been received positively by the periodical's readers and contributors. Engler's open letter to those she claims are 'independent' begins by praising the achievements of masculine women and, like Weininger, suggests that it is only 'the man' in the homosexual woman that drives her to achieve 'visible success'. Engler draws on a wide range of historical examples in order to attribute the exceptionalism of women such as Catherine II of Russia, Queen Christina of Sweden and Sappho to their 'male' element.[41]

Perhaps unsurprisingly for a magazine that aligned social success with masculinity, Engler makes no reference to femininity in her article. Indeed,

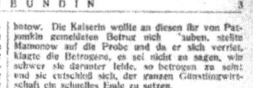

Figure 3.2. 'Katharina II of Russia', *The Girlfriend*, 1927. Spinnboden Archive, used with permission.

unlike Weber's article from 1924, which had suggested femininity did not preclude genuine homosexual desire, Engler's clear endorsement of Weininger's theories points to a more conservative gendered shift in *The Girlfriend* over the years, arguably associated with the change in editors and the growing male influence on the content of the magazine mentioned earlier in this chapter. Yet, already by 1928, when queer women were largely still responsible for the editorial decisions relating to the content of the magazine, queer feminine women were being openly maligned and were denounced in the magazine as a group of homosexual individuals 'about whom one does not speak, about whom no one can say anything special'.[42]

Unlike the masculine leanings of its rival, *Women's Love* was influenced far more strongly by the theoretical frameworks of Magnus Hirschfeld, whose work was frequently published in the magazine and whose publications were reprinted and referenced in numerous discussion pieces over the years.[43] Aside from reprints of Hirschfeld's sexological theories, the editors of *Women's Love* often favoured social commentaries on sexological developments produced by their female contributors over reprints of original sexological articles as seen in *The Girlfriend*. In comparison to its rival, the editors of *Women's Love* published fewer explicitly scientific articles on gender variance and same-sex desire, and instead preferred to respond to them, creating in many ways an interesting dialogue between queer women and the sexologists that wrote about their desires. Regular contributor Herta Laser's response to Weininger's work, 'What Weininger Says about Women', for example, stands in stark contrast to *The Girlfriend*'s uncritical reprint of the philosopher's misogynistic and anti-Semitic study. As an immediate rebuttal of Weininger's theory that only the masculine element is capable of greatness, Laser begins her article with a list of examples from history in which feminine women were acknowledged as 'the rulers in the home'.[44] Arguing that the 'bold spirit' and 'far-sighted gaze' associated with these historical women should be considered traits that are characteristic of 'the aspiring woman' more generally, Laser claims that bravery and gallantry are not the privilege only of masculine (wo)men.[45] Her approach of broadening the parameters of what could be considered feminine characteristics and behavioural traits would be taken up enthusiastically by other authors in later discussions of gender and identity in the magazine.

In an article entitled 'Amazons' from the same year, for example, it is argued that characteristics that are considered traditionally 'masculine' are also embodied by women perceived as nonmasculine. Focusing on the history of separatist female communities, Amazon women are described in the article as hunter-gatherers, who survive tough climates and wage successful wars against enemy men. However, despite the masculine implications of such behaviours, the author of the article does not at any point suggest that these women were 'manly' or 'masculine'. Instead, like Laser, the author proposes the reader develops a broader understanding of femininity, which would encompass the behaviours of these independent women – a subversive argument for this period.[46] Furthermore, in terms of the frameworks that positioned the queer feminine woman's desire for other women as a temporary deviation from her ultimate male-object choice, it is the Amazon's sexual encounters with *men* that are positioned in this article as temporal. These sexual activities have only the aim of producing female offspring and, in the eyes of the author, certainly do not preclude the strong, feminine Amazon woman from being considered authentically queer:

> Travellers of all times across each continent, America, Africa, Asia, Australia, and even in Europe, gave reports of women in certain areas who lived together in communities without men. They hunted and like to wage war against the men of neighbouring districts ... In order not to die out, they allowed men from neighbouring tribes to join them temporarily, but kept only the girls they bore with them, the boys were either separated to the paternal tribe or killed.[47]

The complexity of the Amazon woman's relationship with the maternal instinct is not avoided here but rather deployed to blur the boundaries of the traditionally feminine further: while nurture and care can be extended to a young daughter, a son must be rejected or killed. Although this most extreme form of separatist logic is found sparingly in the magazine, there is a clear desire in the periodical to promote a broader understanding of what feminine gender forms can comprise. The fierceness of Amazon women, according to this contributor, comes *not* from an innate feeling of masculinity but rather forms *part* of her femininity, complicating the cultural norms concerning maternalism and ideal womanhood. While there is no doubt that the masculine woman still had a clear role to play in the erotic imaginations of contributors to and readers of *Women's Love*, as will be discussed later, what has been hitherto overlooked is the far broader range of gendered characteristics assigned to the category 'feminine' in this magazine than in the pages of its rival, whose authors considered the feminine woman to be a principally 'dependent' and even 'smothering' figure. Underscoring the magazine's support of Hirschfeld's theory of intermediary sexual forms, *Women's Love* contributor Helga Karig concluded in her article against the supposed inferiority of the feminine woman that 'every thinking and unprejudiced person knows: the absolute man and the absolute woman are only abstractions, in reality there are only transitional stages'.[48] While the theoretical backbones of the organizations to which the magazines belonged shaped the social commentaries that were often published by the editors of the periodicals, these frameworks are also perceptible in the literary submissions, written both by readers and regular contributors.

Literary Discourses of Feminine Desire

Given the position of *The Girlfriend* as the periodical for women associated with Radszuweit's bourgeois and masculine League for Human Rights, it is no surprise that the masculine female invert and the tomboy lover feature as the primary protagonists in many of *The Girlfriend*'s original literary contributions. In such stories, the feminine woman often appears in the guise of the 'unattainable' love object or the deceiving lover. However, not all stories and poems in the magazine were narrated from a masculine perspective. In 'The Girlfriend of Olga Diers' by Nils Lermann, a serial that ran over seven issues in 1924, the 'most dear' stagehand Gudrun Garell is positioned as the protagonist of the story. Initially a shy and passive character, Gudrun develops a wild romantic longing for the masculine performer, Olga Diers, following their close encounters during Olga's time onstage – a romantic trajectory that is redolent, of course, of the earlier theories of Auguste Forel. Although Olga is categorized as a woman who 'feels like a man', even she is depicted as having a soft and gentle nature, as she delivers a passionate speech in which she confesses her love for the younger woman. In an inversion of the emotional-rational binary, as well as traditional thinking on active-passive desires, Olga's emotional revelation is shown to be followed by the feminine Gudrun actively controlling their first sexual encounter: 'That evening, Gudrun gave [Olga] that which she had been thirsting for since their first meeting.'[49] Gudrun is not shown to be seduced by Olga's aggressive masculine lusts, but rather it is she who pursues and charms the performer and she who decides when, where and how their romantic affair will begin. Despite calling into question the inherent passivity of feminine desire, the author positions Gudrun's femininity as the central site of the protagonist's inner conflict. In a dramatic turn of events, Gudrun is exposed as having engaged in affairs with both women and men – a 'failing' that is linked back to her mother's history of sex work – and she ultimately breaks Olga's heart. Thus, while the story spotlights a feminine protagonist – an unusual choice for the writers of the magazine – Gudrun is still defined as the 'Girlfriend of Olga Diers', with her desires being depicted as less authentic than those of the masculine actress and associated with degenerate forms of lust. As we shall see in the following section, the subject of the bisexual, feminine woman in *The Girlfriend* was one that provoked fierce feelings among its readers and contributors.

As well as imagining feminine protagonists, *The Girlfriend* also produced stories that strayed away from the binary configurations that structure many of its social commentaries. 'The Reunion' by Dusia, for example, tells the story of Helga, a twenty-five-year-old 'slim and willowy' woman, who travels around Europe to enjoy skiing, horseriding and driving motorcars. As Helga sits at the wheel of her 'dove blue convertible, just as certain as she would be on horseback', she fantasizes about a woman 'who has a personality like her own, someone she does not have to look down on, someone who is mature enough for her and who can be more than a lover'.[50] Meeting a similarly masculine woman during the narrative arc, Dusia's story concludes with a happy ending – one that precludes the feminine. While the romantic pairing of two masculine women is uncommon in literary contributions published in *The Girlfriend*, the implied denigration of the feminine as an 'immature' subject position, or the feminine woman as an oversexed or untrustworthy partner, ran through many of the magazine's literary works. Although both Dusia's and Nils Lermann's stories recycle negative tropes about pseudohomosexuality and hypersexuality, *The Girlfriend* also employed a more positive form of cultural resignification in its publication through which contemporary paradigms of femininity and sexuality were arguably subverted and challenged. On several occasions, the magazine reprinted popular poems by respected German authors, curating an image of the periodical as a publication that traded in high cultural artefacts. The reproduction of these icons of high culture served not only to bolster the publication's image as a promotor of bourgeois norms and values, but also allowed for new queer readings of canonical poems and literary works. By reprinting Heinrich Heine's 'Maiden with the Little Red Mouth' from his collection *Book of Songs* (*Buch der Lieder*, 1827), for example, the editors brought the assumed heterosexuality of Heine's subject into question. Traditional markers of womanhood, such as the protagonist's 'little red mouth' and 'white hand', can be thus resignified as queer, challenging the meaning of dominant cultural motifs of heterosexual femininity, while assigning classic German publications a subversive Sapphic subtext. Building on what Clare Rogan has noted of the nude images printed on the covers of queer magazines, it could be said that *The Girlfriend* was therefore engaging in a specific form of 'bricolage', removing Heine's poem from its original (heterosexual) context and placing it within a new queer setting.[51] Indeed, using Gayatri Spivak's definition of the term 'bricolage', poems such as those by Heine can thus be considered as part of 'a radical proto-deconstructive cultural practice' that revises and destabilizes traditional notions of femininity, putting them in a perpetual process of 'becoming' and 'undoing'.[52]

In contrast to *The Girlfriend*'s reprints of poems by canonical authors such as Heine, *Women's Love* rarely recycled or borrowed written material from other sources. Indeed, much of the fiction published in the periodical was written by its own regular contributors, writers on the queer circuit, or readers who submitted their amateur poems and prose. Although Roellig claimed in the introduction to her guidebook that the 'literary level' of lesbian magazines was 'below zero', the short stories in *Women's Love* often present sharp critiques of the gender binary, crafted as a way of conceptualizing new approaches to gender and desire.[53] In comparison to the short and serial stories presented in *The Girlfriend*, feminine women are much more frequently positioned as protagonists in the literary submissions in *Women's Love*. There are also stories about relationships between men and women, and even some stories narrated from an arguably queer male perspective. In general, the literary contributions to *Women's Love* appear to be far more playful in terms of their approach to gender roles and more open to exploring and experimenting with different gendered configurations. In the cover story 'The Sex of Tomorrow', for example, the reader follows a humorous conversation between Georgia and her boyfriend Werner, which inverts stereotypically gendered behaviours:

> Werner yawned languidly and reached into the box of confectionery with his well-manicured hand. Suddenly, he gave a forced cough. 'Georgia', he said, 'You are smoking a new tobacco again, aren't you? You know that the scratchy stuff, like it is today, causes me throat ailments.' [Georgia] laid down her pipe, shocked, and stroked his hair. 'Forgive me', she ventured to say. 'By the way', he continued, and swiftly swallowed one piece of candy after the other, 'You've hardly paid me any attention over the past week … You know how I suffer emotionally.'[54]

While Werner embodies the feminine male traits that came to be associated with the *Zwitter*, a figure that Friedrich Radszuweit sought to dispel from his rival movement, Georgia adopts the characteristics associated with the masculine female invert. While this sketch was no doubt meant in many respects to offer readers comic relief, Georgia's brief narrative arc also touches upon contemporary feminist themes, such as women's career prospects, financial independence and the social meaning of marriage proposals. While the effeminacy of Werner might be perceived in a negative light, the gender queering of the binary heterosexual paradigm, arguably suggests that contributors were also considering ways in which they could challenge conventional roles in their relationships with male partners. As well as presenting critical – and comedic – re-assessments of gender norms, contributors to *Women's Love* also engaged directly with the more negative stereotypes associated with feminine women within the queer community. The first-person narrator in the short story 'Those Who Live from Love', for example, tells the tale of her tragic encounter with a younger, feminine girl.

After experiencing what she believes to be 'an immediate connection' with a girl on a tram who has been unable to afford her fare, the protagonist offers to pay for the younger woman's ticket and to take her out for lunch. After some polite conversation, the protagonist buys the young shop assistant food and wine and, as they walk home, she kisses the girl, who promises to meet her the following day. Weeks after the protagonist has been stood up, she catches a glimpse of the girl with another older woman and realizes that she has been duped: 'So, she was one of those – with a whimsical recklessness in her blood she would sit here again tomorrow with someone else – would drink wine again with the same carefree joy – kiss the person sitting opposite her again with the same harmless infatuation.'[55] Drawing on the sexological depictions of temporal queer desire, and arguably the trope of queer feminine women as sex workers, the writer of the story uses the young girl's duplicitous behaviour to serve as a warning to her readers against undesirable forms of femininity. Yet, while 'Those Who Live from Love' draws on similar stereotypical images of femininity as the stories found in *The Girlfriend*, these generalizations of 'bad femininity' were rare in *Women's Love* before 1930, a period during which the magazine presented itself first and foremost as a periodical for the fashion-forward, feminine queer woman. Turning now more specifically to femininity and the associated culture of consumerism, I will analyse the role of cosmetics and clothing in the fashioning of queer femininities in *The Girlfriend* and *Women's Love*.

Fashioning Femininities

While Hirschfeld's theories shaped many of the discussions on homosexual desire that took place in the scientific articles and literary contributions published in *Women's Love*, it was arguably the periodical's promotion of beauty and body culture that drew most heavily on scientific theories. Through what I am terming 'medicoconsumerist' discourses, the writers of *Women's Love* deployed supposedly masculine forms of disquisition to give weight to interests and concerns associated with femininity. While in the late nineteenth century, the trading and exchanging of goods, as well as the marketing and advertising of merchandises was primarily a masculine endeavour, by the turn of the twentieth century, consumer culture, as Kathy Peiss notes, was inextricably 'bound up in notions of the feminine', which makes it a significant point of consideration for this current volume.[56] As women began to consume for pleasure rather than purely for domestic reasons, consumption became 'an entire way of life' for many female shoppers, which, one could argue, took on an erotic social function. This, especially as shopping was stimulated by 'the pleasures of looking and touching', as well as the 'merchants [who] encouraged women to desire goods and be seduced by them'.[57] Yet, in spite of the sensuous consumer experience, shopping nonetheless remained a respectable pursuit of pleasure for many bourgeois women: 'Like attending a matinee, eating in a restaurant, or going to the beauty parlor – all new activities for women – shopping took place in a semi-public, commercial and safe realm, an important consideration for women concerned about their respectability.'[58] Indeed, in the nineteenth century, cosmetic practices for bourgeois women had largely been frowned upon, with Wilhelmine women restricting themselves to cold creams and subtle scents. In an era concerned with the growth of sex work and syphilis, cosmetics were strongly associated with 'painted women' who supposedly employed cosmetic enhancement deceptively to appeal to customers.[59] However, as Madeleine Marsh notes, the rise of cosmetologists such as Elizabeth Arden and Max Factor in the early 1900s effectively 'transformed make-up from a guilty secret into an everyday handbag essential'.[60] As was discussed in Chapter 1, maintaining a well-presented appearance further became an essential endeavour for women by the 1930s, particularly for those women who wanted to secure office work or other forms of white-collar employment. Thus, the popular scientific tone of medicoconsumerist discourses would not only have been used to engage with the modern reader, but would have also lent weight to the idea that the readers' financial future might be secured with the aid of certain cosmetics. Indeed, in her recent monograph on German beauty politics, Annelie Ramsbrock carefully examined the extent to which 'social cosmetics' might be considered 'a form of social medicine' in Weimar Berlin.[61] Certainly, as Ramsbrock contends, while cosmetics and cosmetic surgery 'did not serve the health of the community', they no doubt elevated the social standing and, arguably, the economic position of many individuals.[62] Unlike the beauty regimens associated with the 'painted' woman, the notion of social cosmetics and rejuvenation practices presented consumers with new ways of conceptualizing feminine beauty routines 'that corresponded to … social-science paradigms'.[63]

Inspired by Hirschfeld and Steinach's studies on rejuvenation, as well as the models of healthy living and beauty promoted by the body culture (*Körperkultur*) movement, articles that adopt a medicoconsumerist tone in *Women's Love* consistently appear to construct gendered ideals around notions of youth and beauty. In discussions of beauty products and rejuvenation, contributors can be seen to merge modern scientific theories about wellbeing with their own promotion of femininity, while not forgetting their desire to turn over a profit.

A cover story entitled 'The Personal Perfume', for example, draws heavily on the scientific impulse to taxonomize, while promoting certain ideas around acceptable types of femininity, and hoping to sell several of the

160 • Different from the Others

Bekenntnis!

Geliebte, seit ich Dich gefunden,
Mein Dasein hat erst rechten Sinn;
Wie fliehen golden mir die Stunden
In Deiner holden Nähe hin!

Wie grüße ich mit Lust das Leben;
Durch Nacht bin ich zum Licht erwacht!
Ach, all Dein Nehmen — all Dein Geben,
Wie überglücklich es mich macht! …

Du bist verwachsen meinem Leben;
Restlos erfüllst Du ganz mein Sein!
Und so, wie Du Dich mir gegeben,
Wie ich Dein höchstes Glück im Leben,
So bin ich ewig — ewig Dein!

Kaete Lippert.

Das persönliche Parfüm
Etwas über den Duft, der eine schöne Frau umgeben soll!
Von Adele.

Der Volksmund behauptet, der Geruchssinn des Menschen sei eigentlich ein Luxussinn! Diese Ansicht ist durchaus gerechtfertigt, denn es gibt wohl keine Frau von Geschmack, die sich nicht parfümiert und die nicht auf der Suche nach einem eigenartigen Parfüm ist wie nach einer Näscherei. Ueber eine geglückte Entdeckung kann sie sich ebenso freuen, wie über den ungeahnten Geschmack eines besonderen Leckerbissens! Und die Parfümindustrie kommt ihr außerdem weitestgehend entgegen. Man ist bemüht, immer neue Parfüms ausfindig zu machen, Kombinationen zu schaffen und einen „lebendigen" Duft herzustellen. Ein gutes Parfüm ist immer ein solches, das ein anhaltendes, gesundes, nicht exzentrisches, unaufdringliches, gleich-

Figure 3.3. 'The Personal Perfume', *Women's Love*, 1931. Spinnboden Archive, used with permission.

magazine's own beauty products. Aimed at typically modern feminine women – the 'office clerk', 'stenographer', and 'housewife' – the article begins by positioning the feminine reader in the role of researcher and scientist. Before the sales pitch commences, the unnamed author empathizes with the reader on the difficult process of finding the right perfume. In the article that follows, the author curates the image of an inquisitive young woman who scientifically researches various scents and experimentally brings together various perfumed blends: 'one always endeavours to identify new perfumes, to create combinations, to produce a "living" fragrance'.[64] After explaining the development of their own scientific process to deduce the most suitable scent for a range of feminine temperaments, the author concludes that a 'delicate violet fragrance or discreet iris perfume corresponds to modesty, which is why those two are especially suited to the outwardly modest and restrained woman'.[65] More socially extroverted women aged between twenty and thirty were instead advised to choose between 'lilac, jasmine, ylang-ylang, heliotrope and Peau d'Espagne'.[66] As well as including a range of articles that borrowed from scientific frameworks, the supplement 'Femina: Pages for Somatic Refinement and Beauty Care' was another forum in which medicoconsumerist discourses were employed to facilitate serious discussions about femininity, as well as to appeal to women's supposedly increasing purchasing power. Appearing as a regular addition to the magazine after 1928, 'Femina' was a feature in which beauty supplies created in the publication's own 'cosmetic laboratory' were discussed and appraised by contributors and readers alike. In a reoccurring advertorial, readers were encouraged to buy a range of health and beauty products directly from the magazine, including 'Harlem Drops', which would help readers maintain 'clear eyes and an animated, fiery gaze', and 'Nerana-Crème', which, if used regularly, would preserve 'the soft skin of a beautiful woman'.[67] Playing into the contemporary social discourse that maintained 'physical attractiveness as one of women's most important assets', the articles and advertorials printed in *Women's Love* may appear initially to be restricted in their ability to break free from hegemonic norms of femininity and beauty.[68] Yet, when placed within the context of the magazine's political aims and its desire to establish a broader understanding of the category femininity, the discussion of beauty products may itself be considered an emancipatory – if capitalist – act. By producing and promoting products for women that helped to preserve their 'animated and fiery gaze', the editors of *Women's Love* arguably believed themselves to be helping women to keep their position in the workplace, even if they stopped short of challenging the frameworks that stipulated that female workers needed to comply with impossible beauty standards to earn a wage in the first place.

In spite of the magazine's promotion of beauty products, the feminine woman is rarely positioned as the object of visual pleasure in such advertisements and articles, but remains an active subject, who identifies the best products to suit her purpose. The periodical's beauty columns and adverts provide further evidence of the active engagement of its readers. The 'On Demand' section of the supplement, for example, demonstrates that readers regularly challenged the publication's suggestions and recommendations. On the subject of the highly marketed Nerana Crème, one reader complains curtly: 'all of the creams you mention are ineffective. Even if they do no harm, they do not help much either'.[69] Another reader snubs the elaborate equations and scientific assessments presented in 'The Personal Perfume' by offering her own modest choice of scent to her fellow readers with the simple suggestion: 'use Eau de Cologne'.[70] The discussions instigated by the readers of 'Femina', as well as their judgements on the products promoted by the supplement, indicate that they engaged critically with the creation of a modern feminine aesthetic in *Women's Love* and actively participated in the shaping of queer femininities within the magazine.

While the contributors to *Women's Love* attempted to engage with queer feminine women directly as independent consumers, the editorial board of *The Girlfriend* chose not to include these kinds of beauty supplements in their publication. Eager to emphasize the scientific nature of the magazine, editors stressed that sexuality and gender were not characteristics that should be profited from, but, rather, should be studied with scientific objectivity: 'Sexuality is not a market commodity … but rather a necessary requirement that is inherent in every living being … which can only be understood through the acquired knowledge of sexual psychology.'[71] While articles on beauty products and cosmetic enhancement did not feature strongly in the format of *The Girlfriend*, it would be unfair to suggest that the magazine ignored the concept entirely or, indeed, that beauty and wellbeing should be considered as only feminine matters. In October 1929, the clubhouse 'Violetta', which was strongly affiliated with the female subgroups of the BfM, advertised a beauty competition, for instance, in which both 'the most beautiful masculine woman' and 'the most beautiful feminine woman' would be crowned. Later that year, it was announced that an 'entirely unique' fashion show would be taking place in which masculine women would act as models: 'only rarely are we given the opportunity to see a fashion show in which masculine women are also taking part as "mannequins"'.[72]

The advert continues by stating that the apparent incongruity of these concepts – that is, female masculinity, beauty and fashion – would be disproved at the fashion show where there would be 'a rich programme' during an exhibition of the 'most elegant masculine women'.[73] Inclusive of transvestite models, the authors reassured their readers that during the

Figure 3.4. 'Fashionable Masculine Transvestites', *The Girlfriend*, 1929. Spinnboden Archive, used with permission.

show, there would be 'something to everybody's taste'.[74] That more frequent masculine fashion shows were not reported in the magazine is perhaps an indication of the success of the event and although fashion was discussed in *The Girlfriend*, the celebration of masculine beauty in the magazine should be considered an exception rather than the rule.

In terms of fashion and beauty culture in *The Girlfriend*, topics that were primarily associated with femininity, contemporary trends were most often assessed in terms of their functionality rather than aesthetic appeal. Editors of the magazine appear far more critical of modern beauty standards than those contributors to *Women's Love*, who considered cosmetics and fashion to be subjects of serious interest and, moreover, a means to maintaining their income streams, as well as those of their readers. In the social commentary 'Which Skirt Works Best?', for example, readers of *The Girlfriend* are presented with a broad range of suggestions for the most practical skirts to wear to work based on the results of a cited scientific study: 'Ladies were most tired in skirts made of linen, velvet, and other heavy fabrics, while in skirts made of silk and gabardine, they showed the least signs of fatigue.'[75] While some fashion topics caused great furore among the readers, such as the controversial *Bubikopf* hairstyle, most articles concerning fashion resulted in little reader engagement. After the contributor concludes that a skirt with a width of two metres and a hip measurement of 48 inches would afford women with most comfort in the workplace, for example, the conversation is closed and no further comment on the subject is made in subsequent issues.[76] Rarely marketed as commodities in the articles of *The Girlfriend*, the discourses of 'social cosmetics' and 'medicoconsumerism' that were employed by its rival are largely absent from its pages. Yet, as well as considering what is practical in terms of clothing, contributors and readers of *The Girlfriend* also resorted to biological discourses and scientific studies to engage with the so-called feminine subjects of fashion and style. During the reader debate 'For or against the Bubikopf', which ran over several issues in 1928, readers drew repeatedly on sexological models of female inversion and physiological studies to argue their case on the appropriateness of the bobbed *Bubikopf* haircut for queer women. While one reader claims that shorter hair 'belongs' to a homosexual woman, another reader deploys arguments rooted in physiognomic research to dispute her fellow reader's claim: 'the head shape of a woman [is] quite different from that of a man, consequently she requires quite a different haircut'.[77] Unlike the employment of medicoconsumerist discourses in *Women's Love* to make serious the discussion of femininity and to engage its readers in the creative – and yet capitalist – experimentation with their gendered presentation, it was through sexological and physiognomic discourses that *The Girlfriend* was most able to engage with popular fashion trends and to criticize the limitations placed on the woman's role in society. While making beauty an available position to masculine women through the promotion of 'masculine' fashion shows certainly broadens the scope of norms and expectations of masculine readers, the editors of *The Girlfriend* were little interested in engaging with, or supporting, a supposedly feminine consumer culture or taking beauty and fashion seriously as subjects of debate or even entertainment.

Trans Femininities

While *The Girlfriend* and *Women's Love* demonstrate varying levels of interest and investment in the trends in fashion and beauty that were associated with feminine women, these topics were discussed at great length in the regular transvestite supplements that existed for both magazines. Following the publication of Magnus Hirschfeld's *The Transvestites* in 1910, there was a swell in scientific studies on the nuances between sexual inversion and the expression of a gender that did not correspond to one's biological sex – phenomena that had previously been framed as the same 'condition'.[78] This increased social awareness of cross-dressing individuals, sparked the beginnings of several transvestite communities that became ever more closely linked to the clubs and organizations that were established for queer women through the auspices of the BfM and the DFV.[79] Acting as microcosms of their main publications, *The Girlfriend*'s transvestite supplement 'The World of Transvestites' and the supplement for *Women's Love* 'The Transvestite' included a diverse range of articles on scientific, cultural and social issues, as well as reader letters and serial stories. Focusing primarily on the experiences of male-to-female cross-dressers, the supplements that were provided for transvestites in *The Girlfriend* and *Women's Love* provide an invaluable source for the examination of the ways in which femininities were fashioned in magazines by a range of women, whose sex may not always have corresponded to their gender identity.

In a very similar manner to the contributors and readers of *The Girlfriend*, 'The World of Transvestites', as Katie Sutton notes, stresses an image of transvestites as 'respectable, upstanding citizens', whose femininities can be carefully distinguished from the 'degenerate effeminacy' of male homosexuals and male sex workers.[80] In an early letter from a male-to-female transvestite that was published in *The Girlfriend*'s supplement, for example, the suggestion that the feminine gendered performance of transvestites should be considered 'effeminate' is forcefully rejected. To this end, the reader argues that their feelings of womanliness could be said to surpass even those who are born and live as women: 'It is impossible for me to behave at all

Figure 3.5. 'The Queen: Memories of a Transvestite', 'The World of Transvestites', *The Girlfriend*, 1930. Spinnboden Archive, used with permission.

effeminately, as so many people unfortunately believe that I must do. In spite of this or, perhaps, because of it, I think, in many respects, I feel more feminine than some real women do.'[81]

While this statement may appear to shore up the idea of the existence of 'real women' and 'not-real women', this contributor's disavowal of effeminacy must be read in the context of the gender politics of the BfM, which wished to distance itself from Hirschfeld's panoply of sexual and gendered expressions and, in particular, from the effeminate homosexual male. Many transvestite contributors therefore saw the rejection of homosexual male effeminacy as a means to evidence their innate and natural femaleness. This was of particular importance given that gender confirmation surgeries were in their infancy during this period and would have been available only to very few of those who wished to undertake such risky and expensive procedures.[82] In its bid to challenge conflations of cross-dressing with queer effeminacy, 'The World of Transvestites' also strove further to promote the idea that many male-to-female transvestites could be considered 'normal' in their sexual preferences: 'In general they [transvestites] are counted as homosexuals. But this does not always apply to male transvestites.'[83] While historical trans experiences most often cannot – and should not – be reduced to conventional gendered categories, in the transvestite community associated with the BfM, it is broadly possible to identify two main groups of male-to-female transvestites that were represented in 'The World of Transvestites': on the one hand, there existed so-called 'temporary transvestites' who cross-dressed only occasionally; on the other hand, there were transvestites who felt that their gender did not correspond to their sex. In the articles written by self-identified transvestites who experienced a disconnect between their biological sex and gender, as highlighted above, it is often possible to see attempts to prove the respectability of their feminine nature through comparisons of their gender presentations with those who are assigned female at birth and continue to live as women. Yet, those transvestites who practised only discrete periods of cross-dressing more frequently differentiated themselves from 'effeminate' male homosexuals by asserting the normalcy of their heterosexual desires.

Indeed, one of the most common subjects of reader letters and personal advertisements written by so-called 'temporary transvestites' corresponds to the difficulty of finding sympathetic female partners. Interestingly, none of these letters suggests that the readers would have considered their romantic or erotic encounters with another woman to be anything other than heterosexual. In this way, gender presentation was made distinct from sexual preference and avoided conflation with 'unsavoury' queer desires. As well as first-hand accounts from 'temporary transvestites', 'The World of Transvestites' also published several articles written by the wives of such persons in a bid to encourage female readers to be more sensitive to the needs of heterosexual transvestite men. Such letters frequently suggested that the feminine characteristics of 'temporary transvestites' should make these men more attractive to women. One wife claimed, for example: 'Often a man is harsh and closed – much to the misery of the woman. Now, you take the transvestite … He is soft, affectionate, and tender – just as many "misunderstood" women want men to be.'[84] While this image of a 'soft' and 'tender' male partner effectively nuances the traditional masculine-feminine binary that was generally favoured by editors and contributors to *The Girlfriend*, there is little further discussion about the socio-political potential of such a radical form of heterosexuality. Instead, as Sutton has suggested, it was the cultivation of an image of respectable bourgeois heterosexuality that was of primary concern to the supplement. Only in this way was it possible for *The Girlfriend* to ensure that 'notions of hegemonic masculinity continued to define hierarchies of value' in the magazine, and even in its transvestite supplement.[85]

Much like the transvestite supplement of its rival, the column 'The Transvestite', published as part of *Women's Love*, strays very little from the content and ideological focus of its main publication. Favouring literary submissions over scientific articles, 'The Transvestite' also maintained the strong focus on fashion and beauty as did its chief publication. Articles such as 'The Essence of Transvestism' by Maria Weiß, as well as the multiauthored series 'Clothing and Transvestism', also suggest that medicoconsumerist discourses that structured *Women's Love* also shaped its transvestite column.

Indeed, the 'small ads' that targeted the transvestite community follow a strikingly similar approach to those promotions aimed at the readers of the main magazine. Announcing a miracle cure against beard growth, for example, one advert exclaims: 'Transvestites! After years of experimentation, I have finally found a radical remedy for stubble and other body hairs!'[86] While the issues of an advertisement that places the hairless body as the idealized image of transvestite femininity are many, the advert itself, which posits beauty as a process of scientific experimentation, closely replicates the overarching rhetoric of 'The Personal Perfume', mentioned earlier in this chapter, and forms part of the magazine's approach to 'social cosmetics'. The creation of beauty ideals through cosmetic enhancement in the supplement can also be seen in the advertisements from D'Eon, the DFV's suborganization for transvestites, which regularly publicized its courses on how to apply cosmetics, held at Hirschfeld's Institute for the Study of Sexual Science. Thus, while the early issues of *Women's Love* appear to attempt to reassess the meaning of femininity through its discussion of historically separatist communities and the queering of heterosexual models, many of the reader debates and articles that were printed in its transvestite supplement focus instead on achieving normative feminine beauty standards,

Fashioning Femininities • 169

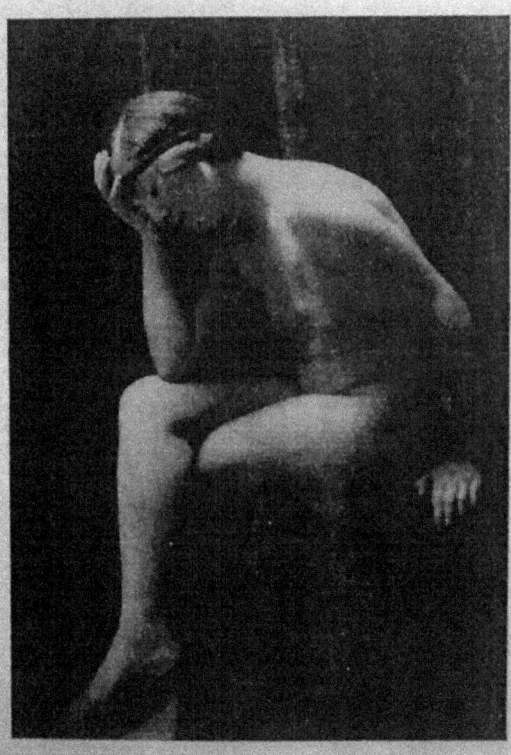

Figure 3.6. 'Clothing and Transvestism', *Women's Love*, 1927. Spinnboden Archive, used with permission.

which brings 'The Transvestite' more in alignment with the ideals promoted in the transvestite supplement for members of the BfM. Yet, the creation of these ideals in 'The Transvestite' relies primarily on a consumer culture that was largely absent in the magazines of the BfM. This can be seen in many of the literary contributions in 'The Transvestite', which feature detailed descriptions of clothing and cosmetics, as protagonists assess dresses made of extravagant silk, and wistfully admire delicate patent shoes in shop windows. With a primary focus on fashion and 'passing' in the transvestite supplement for *Women's Love*, femininity appears to have been constructed around an aspirational ideal of bourgeois beauty, which was bound to somatic and sartorial enactments of the idealized female forms. However, although there is a focus on physical appearances, many advertisements in the supplement further demonstrate an awareness of the specific and routine issues faced by transvestites, such as the sympathetic seamstress, who offered transvestites a space in which they could safely and discreetly complete their 'transformation'. Or, another salesperson who emphasized the wide range of female shoe and clothing sizes on offer to male-to-female transvestites who may have found it difficult to buy suitable garments in 'generic' female sizes.

Moreover, while Sutton has suggested that transvestite supplements were likely published in queer magazines for women as a 'concession to financial realities', it seems that many queer women were more closely allied with the transvestite community than this comment might initially imply.[87] Events such as *The Girlfriend*'s fashion show that included transvestite models, as well as the reviews of lectures on transvestite issues that were published regularly in *Women's Love*, demonstrate that many women-who-desired-women supported transvestite communities and attended events to learn more about their concerns. The same can be said too of the transvestite communities, who were seen to support their sisters in arms, both in the club house and in the lecture theatre.

Anti-feminine Discourses

The rejection of male homosexual 'effeminacy' in *The Girlfriend*'s transvestite supplement, and the literary supplements discussed earlier in this chapter, form only part of the thread of anti-feminine discourse that can be seen to run throughout the publication. In one of the most controversial and long-standing discussions to appear in the magazine, an intense debate on monogamy, femininity and bisexuality was sparked that ran over several issues. Initially published by Xela Eckats in 1928, the article on 'marriages of friendship' begins with a reflection on the supposed changes that had taken place in the attitudes towards monogamous relationships within Berlin's queer community. Providing readers with a summary of her early relationships with women, which she claims had been 'pure and beautiful', Eckats suggests that the increasing number of young feminine women attending Berlin's queer bars had meant that her recent relationships had ended in 'disappointment'.[88] After deliberating on the link between the gender presentation of her partners and the disappointment she encountered, she laments the untrustworthy nature of feminine lovers: 'For the masculine partner it is largely a matter of course to be particularly supportive of their girlfriends in times of need; because then we have the opportunity to prove our love! So why do feminine partners almost always fail in such cases?'[89] Drawing on traditional nineteenth-century notions of masculinity and friendship to position the masculine woman as a loyal figure who would honour a bond, Eckats suggests that the feminine woman, who is ruled by her body, is incapable of such devotion. Her implicit suggestion that a feminine woman would take a male partner in times of (financial) difficulty makes further recourse to the sexological stereotypes of the queer feminine woman as a fickle figure or a 'pseudo-homosexual'. The betrayal of the loyal masculine invert by the temporal desires of feminine and/or bisexual women posed a fundamental threat to the BfM's broader aim to present queer relationships as 'pure' and 'respectable'. Endangering the organization's aims to weave homosexuals subtly into the heterosocial social fabric, the 'problem' of the feminine woman was to be solved, as Eckats concludes, by educating these women on the importance of creating longstanding, and monogamous, marriages of friendship. Compounding the BfM's attempts to create a sense of 'homonormativity' within its movement, Eckats concluded that through the mimicking of heteronormative institutions, queer individuals could prove themselves worthy of the support of the heterosexual world: 'People, who stick together firmly and faithfully in all circumstances of life will also be respected by the normal world.'[90]

Five years later, anonymous contributor XYZ developed Eckats' discussion of 'marriages of friendship' in their article 'Girlfriend-Marriage'. In what can be considered a social update on Eckats' earlier commentary, XYZ states that longlasting marriages of friendship had become a reality for many homosexual couples in Berlin's queer community. Foregrounding the 'decent' and 'restrained' nature of these relationships, XYZ suggests that the ideal queer relationship is one that is imperceptible to the 'normal' world:

> I know many women, very many in fact, who live, operate, and work together with a girlfriend in a close bond, and for whom nothing but death will separate them. These friendships are often so inconspicuous, so subtle and restrained, that only those who are initiated in such matters will understand that there is an erotic friendship here, also.[91]

Believing that openly erotic relationships between women would only harm the wider aims of the movement, XYZ agrees with Eckats that loyalty and monogamy would help society understand the decent nature of queer relationships. Although this view was encouraged by many of the contributors to *The Girlfriend*, reader letters suggest that monogamous bonds and long-term partnerships between queer women were not always commonplace. While some readers claimed that the blame for the breakdown of romantic relationships between women lay at the feet of the virile lesbian Lothario, who sought the 'thrill of the chase', others asserted that the responsibility for the failure of these relationships was to be found with the feminine woman. Returning to the idea of Eckats' capricious *femme fatale*, one reader suggested that most feminine women were often 'not homosexual at all', but rather 'bisexual or perhaps only curious'. In an echo of the models promoted by Forel, the reader claimed that the feminine bisexual woman's 'uncontrolled passions' and irrepressible desire 'to "experience" something by any means' resulted in her casual sexual experimentations with other women.[92] The tensions that arose around this debate frequently became heated, as can be seen in another contributor's feverish warning to masculine readers: 'Stay away from married, bisexual women and those single women who also belong to the male! Steer clear of those who are double-natured, who enjoy both sexes out of the pleasure of salaciousness – they kick our love into the dirt!'[93] That bisexual women ultimately 'belonged to the male' was a common idea among readers of *The Girlfriend*, as was the notion that bisexuality and femininity were invariably linked. Although some masculine women claimed to make a 'sport' of seducing married feminine women, the warning above shows how contentious this issue remained in the BfM's queer community. Yet, as well as tirades against feminine and bisexual women, *The Girlfriend* also published letters that defended those bisexual and queer women who are assigned female at birth and continue to live as women. Indeed, as one reader responds to the argument above: 'I do not agree with your strict rejection of bisexual women. Are they not people on the inside, just like us? Perhaps because of the discord in which they live, they feel much unhappier than it appears.'[94] Such demonstrations of 'support' for bisexual – and feminine – women in *The Girlfriend* were nonetheless rare and advocacy for bisexual acceptance was often swiftly derailed by readers who held opposing views: 'I dispute your claim that bisexual women are equal to us, because you cannot serve two masters … such types of women do not belong with a homosexual girlfriend because the feelings that they arouse are not real, and this can be a disaster for the genuine girlfriend.'[95] Not only is the feminine and bisexual women shown here to be disingenuous for attempting to serve 'two masters', the author of the letter also makes recourse to theories of the oversexed feminine woman to situate the unidirectional desires of masculine women as being more authentically queer: 'The struggle for existence is difficult; but a homosexual women could never be made into a harlot or the object of man's pleasure, for that is not in her nature.'[96] Denying women in relationships with men any kind of sexual or erotic agency, the reader creates a space in which only the desires of the masculine woman can be considered authentic and decent.

Although the feminine – and bisexual – woman was at the heart of many debates during the print run of *The Girlfriend*, discussions on same-sex identities and desires rarely focused on feminine women in their own right. Yet, in an article in *Women's Love* from 1926, editor Herta Laser expounded at length on the specific difficulties faced by feminine women in the queer community. Unlike *The Girlfriend*'s general position that feminine homosexuals were simply 'inquisitive' and whimsical, Laser contends that 'ruling fashions' were of little relevance to a feminine woman's queer desires.[97] Asserting that most feminine women in the homosexual community were 'true homoerotes', Laser wrote, perhaps for the first time in a queer magazine, about the struggles that were specific to queer feminine experiences:

> Isn't it much more difficult for the feminine woman in our circles than a heterogenous woman? ... In most cases, a heterogenous woman will no longer pursue her job if she lives with a man ... But if two women live together, both must go about their careers ... The feminine partner must now conclude her working hours and make herself busy with housework, with creating a cosy apartment, showing a friendly smile, and being a spiritual companion for the girlfriend.[98]

While Laser's comparisons between the feminine homosexual woman and the heterosexual woman imply that some sort of queer hierarchy of femininity did indeed exist in the ideology of the DFV, there is doubtless a departure from *The Girlfriend*'s belief that queer feminine desire was a temporary curiosity. Here, the feminine partner is portrayed as a homemaker and a reliable 'spiritual companion' for her masculine partner. Although the framework Laser employs to discuss queer female experiences remains in many ways dyadic and deeply traditional, that she gives space to issues faced by queer feminine women in a (sub)culture that frequently dismissed or rejected their existence nevertheless remains a subversive move.

In a contribution to the section 'Exchange of Opinions' in 1928, Hirschfeld's theory of transitional forms highlights perhaps most clearly one of the major discursive rifts between the two magazines on the subjects of queer femininity, respectability and desire. Asking readers for their opinions on a particularly contentious issue, reader and contributor Cläre posits: 'What would you do, ladies, if you met a woman today, you know she is married, she lives with her husband in the closest companionship but does not want to miss her girlfriend?'[99] Suggesting that this kind of situation is one 'that is not an isolated occurrence today', Cläre opens a conversation on queer desire that points to the radical potential of nonmonogamous relationships and suggests that bisexual women do not automatically 'lose' their queer identity once they enter into a heterosexual relationship. While some readers declared that they would not want to be the 'play things of married women', Cläre appears to have taken little issue with engaging in a relationship with a married woman, suggesting self-assuredly that while the husband might be a 'kind hearted guy', love between women 'is quite different'.[100] Although this position does not resolve the issue of bisexual erasure – indeed, Cläre arguably undermines the significance of her partner's heterosexual relationship for her own purposes – it points nonetheless to the alternative relationship models that already existed successfully outside of respected bourgeois norms during this period, yet that were rarely being discussed. Yet, despite demonstrating more progressive views on gender presentation and relationship models in its early years, when *Women's Love* returned after being blacklisted as *Garçonne* in 1930, there appears to have been a shift in its ideological leanings. Increasingly, bisexual women were depicted as 'untrustworthy' in literary contributions and social commentaries, and nonmonogamous relationships were portrayed almost exclusively as damaging and unsustainable. While this tendency toward more antifeminine discourses after 1930 mirrors the developments seen in *The Girlfriend*, *Women's Love* advocated powerfully in its early years for the rights of feminine women to take up space within the queer community, making it one of the only periodicals of its time to have represented the desires and aspirations of these queer individuals.

Conclusions

The construction of feminine identities and desires in *The Girlfriend* and *Women's Love* was a complex process, and one that appears to have been mired in inconsistency and contradiction for both periodicals. As publications in which literary, sexological and social discourses converged, these magazines offer an unparalleled insight into the way in which queer women were engaging with the social and cultural discourses of their time. Informed by the theoretical underpinnings of the BfM and the DFV, the tensions that existed between the organizations responsible for the magazines meant that decidedly different images of queer femininity emerged in their respective publications. Seeking to establish a sense of bourgeois respectability across their periodical, the editors of *The Girlfriend* curated content that complied with a strict sense of middle-class morality and bourgeois masculine principles. Although the feminine woman was not entirely absent from this construction, she became a figure that was both denigrated and desired, and ultimately only visible as the 'complement' of her queer masculine partner. In the reader debates featured in *The Girlfriend*, the feminine woman was often maligned as a fickle *femme fatale* who would 'return' to men during times of economic difficulty. While bisexual women were almost invariably vilified for supposedly 'belonging to men', it appeared that any feminine-presenting woman was considered a threat to the principles of bourgeois respectability that *The Girlfriend* strove to embody. Given the theories of hypersexuality and degeneracy that coloured the cultural knowledge of queer feminine desires, it is perhaps not surprising that a magazine committed to the concept of 'ideal' women's friendships would distance itself from the 'damaging' image of queer feminine desire. Although *The Girlfriend*'s reappropriation of high cultural artefacts served to 'queer' heteronormative femininities, the feminine woman nonetheless remained the object of the (queer) masculine gaze, and typically feminine interests were sidelined in the studies of science and culture written by male contributors.

Rejecting the restrictive middle-class mandates adopted by its rival, *Women's Love* embraced a more progressive understanding of sex and sexuality, and engaged with a much wider range of desires in its articles. Certainly, in its early years, the periodical maintained its position as a woman-centred magazine. Broadening the parameters of acceptable feminine behaviour with articles concerning mythical Amazon warriors and separatist women's communities, the magazine embraced a nontraditional view of femininity. With a focus on social commentaries, literary contributions and reader debates, the periodical remained a point of contact for feminine women, and sympathetic friends, until it was ultimately banned in 1932. Not only were the difficulties that feminine women faced in the queer community given space in the magazine, but it also considered and represented the experiences of bisexual and married women. Although *Women's Love* has frequently been overlooked as a political periodical, feminine women were depicted as being active politicized subjects and not simply passive consumers. Arguably engaging with the much wider development of Berlin's social welfare system and the pressures on women to look youthful, *Women's Love* and its supplement 'Femina' considered beauty to be a way of securing an independent social existence. However, this approach, as well as the focus of the supplement 'The Transvestite' on 'passing', appears less to challenge hegemonic and patriarchal modes of established gender norms, than arguably to profit from them and, in this way, to support the very systems that oppressed their female readers.

As I hope the analysis of the literary, social and scientific features of *Women's Love* and *The Girlfriend* in this chapter has shown, contributors and readers did not broach the subject of queer femininity or desire in any uniform way. Indeed, as Amy Young has noted, the magazines frequently depicted desires 'that borrowed from and broke with mainstream images of sexuality and sexual identity' and, at times, called into question the ideologies upheld within the organizations responsible for their publication[101] While the moral and conceptual leanings of the DFV and the BfM often resulted in quite different depictions of feminine women and their desires, the mutual quest for the social emancipation for queer people that structures both periodicals also points to the existence of shared aims and ambitions that would no doubt have united readerships in many respects, which may account for the changes, and apparent conflicts, in ideological focus. Over the years and across multiple discursive forms, contributors to *The Girlfriend* and *Women's Love* outlined a complex and conflicting series of hierarchies and orthodoxies in their magazines. While these were certainly not always inclusive and supportive of queer feminine women, the articles and advertorials published in these magazines nonetheless took the existence of queer feminine women seriously and acknowledged their desires, making queer feminine women visible and accessible in ways that sexologists had failed to do.

Notes

1. Heike Schader, *Virile, Vamps und wilde Veilchen: Sexualität, Begehren und Erotik in den Zeitschriften homosexueller Frauen im Berlin der 1920er Jahre* (Königstein: Ulrike Helmer, 2004), p. 14.
2. Available between 1924 and 1927, *BIF* was produced and edited by contemporary queer icon Selma 'Selli' Engler (1899–1982), who stopped publishing the periodical due to financial difficulties and health problems. It is likely that this periodical was linked to Sengler's organization Bund idealer Frauenfreundschaft. As a maverick magazine, *BIF* enjoyed a limited readership in comparison to either *The Girlfriend* or *Women's Love* and, on a more practical level, Engler's *BIF* has not been as comprehensively catalogued as the other queer publications, meaning it is less readily available in the archives. *BIF* will therefore not be discussed in the following analysis, since the special circumstances of its production, publication and dissemination mean that it is not comparable to the other periodicals, although it certainly warrants a separate discussion. See Amy D. Young, '"Club of Friends": Lesbian Periodicals in the Weimar Republic', in Mary McAuliffe and Sonja Tiernan (eds), *Tribades, Tommies and Transgressives: Histories of Sexualities, Volume I* (Newcastle: Cambridge Scholars, 2008), p. 169.
3. Although the primary focus of this chapter will be on these two publications, the fact that *Single Women* replaced the original periodical *The Girlfriend* when it was banned for coming into conflict with the Law for the Protection of Youth against Trash and Filth Publications in 1927 means that it will also appear in the analysis. Similarly, when *Women's Love* intermittently ran into censorship difficulties, the magazines *Women's Love and Life*, *Loving Women* and *Garçonne* served as replacements for the original title and

will therefore also be examined. However, to avoid confusion, these periodicals will be referred to using their original titles only, unless the change of name is significant to the analysis.
4. Although actual circulation figures do not exist for *Die Freundin* or, in fact, any of Friedrich Radszuweit's publications geared towards homosexuals, its relationship with the League for Human Rights, the largest group for homosexual people in Germany, means that it can be assumed that circulation figures for this magazine were reasonably high. For further information on the popularity of *Die Freundin* in comparison to other Weimar lesbian periodicals, see, for example, Schader, *Virile, Vamps und wilde Veilchen*; Angeles Espinaco-Virseda, '"I Feel That I Belong to You": Subculture, *Die Freundin* and Weimar Lesbian Identities', *Spaces of Identity: Tradition, Cultural Boundaries and Identity Formation in Central Europe* 4 (2004), 83–100.
5. As far as can be told, only one bumper issue was published at the higher price. This is presumably due either to a slump in sales or unsustainable printing costs.
6. Given that experiments in gender confirmation surgery were not being practised until the early 1930s, the term 'transvestite' is used in the magazines to encompass a diverse range of experiences. The term was used to describe both individuals who engaged in discrete periods of cross-dressing and those whose gender identity did not align with their birth sex. However, as it is difficult to distinguish in the supplements between cross-dressers and historical subjects who would now be considered transgender, I will continue to deploy the term 'transvestite' throughout this chapter as the term that was most often used by the individuals themselves, unless they describe their identities in other terms, which I will duly recognize.
7. Stefan Micheler, 'Zeitschriften, Verbände und Lokale: gleichgeschlechtlich begehrender Menschen in der Weimarer Republik', *Invertito – Jahrbuch für die Geschichte der Homosexualitäten*, 10 (2008), 2–72 (at p. 31).
8. However, the magazine does not appear to have been party political and did not associate itself with any specific political agenda other than the emancipation of queer people.
9. Trans.: 'für die Gleichberechtigung der Frauen im gesellschaftlichen Leben'. Verlag und Redaktion, 'Zur Beachtung!', *Die Freundin*, 15 September 1924, p. 2.
10. Schader, *Virile, Vamps und wilde Veilchen*, p. 47.
11. It is likely that *Garçonne* was named after *La Garçonne* (1923), Victor Margueritte's popular French novel about queer female desires.
12. Micheler, 'Zeitschriften, Verbände und Lokale', p. 60.
13. Florence Tamagne, *A History of Homosexuality in Europe Vol 1: Berlin, London, Paris 1919–1939* (New York: Algora, 2004), p. 111.
14. Trans.: 'traten … in den Hintergrund'. Petra Schlierkamp, 'Die Garconne', in Michael Bollé et al.(eds), *Eldorado: Homosexuelle Frauen und Männer in Berlin 1850–1950 Geschichte, Alltag und Kultur* (Berlin: Fröhlich & Kaufmann, 1984), p. 171.
15. Trans.: 'Kampforgan der Freundinnen'. Ikarus, 'An meine Mitschwestern', *Frauenliebe*, 5 January 1928.
16. Trans.: 'Niemand darf auch nur einen Augenblick vergessen, dass diese Zeitschrift das Organ ist, welches unseren Mitmenschen eine Stufe sein soll, eine Stufe des Begreifens. Denn alles, was man begreift, wird Erkenntnis. Diese Erkenntnis bringt den anderen Menschen das Bewußtsein eines neuen, d.h. unseren Geschlechts.' Ibid.
17. Trans.: 'Nur die Masse führt zum Ziel: Freiheit für die Liebe auf der ganzen Front.' Ibid.
18. Max Danielsen, 'Die Wahrheit über den "Bund für Menschenrecht"', *Frauenliebe*, 14, 1928.
19. For further information on the divisions between the BfM and the DFV, and the popularity of Weimar lesbian periodicals, see, for example, Micheler, 'Zeitschriften,

Verbände und Lokale'; Schader, *Virile, Vamps und wilde Veilchen*; Espinaco-Virseda, '"I Feel That I Belong to You"'; Young, '"Club of Friends"'.

20. Gideon Reuveni, '"Productivist" and "Consumerist" Narratives of Jews in German History', in Neil Gregor et al. (eds), *German History from the Margins* (Bloomington: Indiana University Press, 2006), p. 164.

21. Ibid., p. 166.

22. Trans.: 'wegen ihrer politischen, sozialen, religiösen, ethischen oder weltanschaulichen Tendenz'. 'Gesetz zur Bewahrung der Jugend vor Schund- und Schmutzschriften', http://www.zaoerv.de/01_1929/1_1929_2_b_533_2_536_1.pdf (retrieved 19 April 2022).

23. Trans.: 'Es ist immer wieder das altes Lied, daß die Jugendämter angeblich gegen Schund und Schmutz kämpfen, in Wirklichkeit aber kämpfen sie gegen die Homosexualität als solche. Das Mäntelchen Schund und Schmutz wird immer nur dann gebraucht, wenn man den homosexuellen Menschen eins auswischen will.' Friedrich Radszuweit, 'Gefühlsumnebelung', *Die Freundin*, 16 November 1932.

24. Trans.: 'Ueberlegt man nun genauer, was wohl von dem neuen Gesetz betroffen werden könnte, so kommt man zu dem Ergebnis, daß es auffallenderweise – zumeist Frauenschriften sind. Also Blätter für Schönheit, Nacktkultur, auch Tanz, Körperpflege, Ehe, Frauenleben, und –lieben ... Also um die Frau dreht es sich! Nicht um die Frau als Mensch, sondern als Geschlechtswesen.' Karen, 'Das Schund- und Schmutz Gesetz und wir Frauen', *Frauenliebe*, 17, 1927.

25. Trans.: 'Aufklärung und geistige Hebung der idealen Freundschaft.'

26. Tamagne, *A History of Homosexuality*, p. 32.

27. After the magazine returned in 1929, Bruno Balz was positioned as editor. From 1930, Martin Butzkow-Radszuweit, the adopted son and lover of Friedrich Radszuweit, managed the editorial functions of *Die Freundin* as well as the BfM's magazines for men *Die Insel* and the *Blätter für Menschenrecht*. See Micheler, 'Zeitschriften, Verbände und Lokale'.

28. These included *Die Insel – Magazin der Einsamen* (1926–31) and *Das dritte Geschlecht* (1930–31).

29. Marti M. Lybeck, *Desiring Emancipation: New Women and Homosexuality in Germany 1890–1933* (Albany, NY: SUNY Press, 2014), p. 161.

30. Mark Blasius and Shane Phelan, 'Combining Political and Cultural Work: The League for Human Rights', in *We Are Everywhere: A Historical Sourcebook of Gay and Lesbian Politics* (New York: Routledge, 1997), p. 174.

31. Trans.: 'Schaustellungen von Abnormitäten'; 'schlechtes Licht'. Friedrich Radszuweit, 'Ihr Stammtisch wird lachen!', *Die Freundin*, 9 July 1930.

32. Tamagne, *A History of Homosexuality*, p. 155.

33. In *The Twilight of Equality*, Lisa Duggan defines homonormativity as 'a politics that does not contest dominant heteronormative assumptions and institutions, but upholds and sustains them, while promising the possibility of a demobilized gay constituency and a privatized, depoliticized gay culture anchored in domesticity and consumption'. While Laurie Marhoefer suggests in her most recent contribution to queer history that the BfM cannot be described as 'homonormative', I argue that in terms of Lisa Duggan's definition of 'homonormativity', *Die Freundin* does 'not contest dominant heteronormative assumptions and institutions but upholds and sustains them while promising the possibility of a demobilized gay constituency and a privatized, depoliticized gay culture' and might therefore still be considered 'homonormative'. See Lisa Duggan, 'The New Homonormativity: The Sexual Politics of Neoliberalism', in Russ Castronovo and Dana Nelson (eds), *Materializing Democracy: Toward a Revitalized*

Cultural Politics (Durham, NC: Duke University Press, 2002), pp. 175–94 (at p. 179); Laurie Marhoefer, *Sex and the Weimar Republic: German Homosexual Emancipation and the Rise of the Nazis* (Toronto: University of Toronto Press, 2015).
34. Under the terms 'bourgeois respectability' and 'bourgeois masculinity', I include the upholding of class norms, as well as the sense of loyalty, honour and friendship that was idealized by the middle classes. See Carroll Smith-Rosenberg, *Disorderly Conduct: Visions of Gender in Victorian America* (Oxford: Oxford University Press, 1985), p. 278.
35. The Viennese surgeon Eugen Steinach was a pioneer of experimental sex surgeries. He believed that the process of sterilization, which became known the Steinach Operation, had rejuvenating effects on the body. Steinach also proposed that replacing the testicles of a homosexual man with those of a heterosexual man would help 'redirect' the patient to a normal sex instinct. See P. Södersten et al., 'Eugen Steinach: The First Neuroendocrinologist', *Endocrinology*, 3 (2014), 688–95; Thomas Schlich, *The Origins of Organ Transplantation: Surgery and Laboratory Science, 1880–1930* (New York: Rochester University Press, 2014).
36. Trans.: 'Demagoge für 'Menschenrechte'; 'schwersten inneren Kämpfen ... die die homosexuelle Bewegung durchgemacht hat'. Danielsen, 'Die Wahrheit', p. 7.
37. Trans.: 'grotesk ... daß ein heterosexueller Mann der Führer der homosexuellen Frauen sein sollte'. Lotte Hahm, 'Klubnachrichten über Violetta', *Die Freundin*, 25 September 1929.
38. Trans.: 'Sollte Bergmann Gelüste haben, mit mir ein Hühnchen zu pflücken, so werde ich aus meinem Archiv weitere Tatsache hervorholen worüber die Damen staunen und Karl Bergmann entsetzt sein wird.' Ibid.
39. Trans.: 'Es gibt zwei Arten von homosexuellen Frauen. Die virile – d.i. männliche – und die feminine – d.i. weibliche – Frau. Die Virile zeichnet sich vor allen Dingen durch ihre Selbständigkeit ... Die feminine Frau ist ganz das Gegenteil ... Sie ist durch und durch Frau, von zartem Wesen und anschmiegendem Charakter.' Aenne Weber, 'Die homosexuelle Frau', *Die Freundin*, 8 August 1924.
40. Otto Weininger, 'Geschlecht und Charakter', *Die Freundin*, 14 January 1931.
41. Selli Engler, 'An die selbständigen homosexuellen Frauen!', *Die Freundin*, 25 February 1931.
42. Trans.: 'von denen man nicht spricht, über die kein Mensch etwas Besonderes sagen kann'. Marie-Luise von Bern, 'Der Klub der Freundinnen', *Die Freundin*, 30 April 1928.
43. Hirschfeld's sixtieth birthday was even celebrated in the magazine with a special article dedicated to his greatest achievements. D.J., 'Die Geburtstagsfeier', *Frauenliebe* 20, 1928, pp. 1–3.
44. Trans.: 'die Herrschende im Hause'. Herta Laser, 'Was sagt Weininger über die Frau', *Frauenliebe*, 2, 1928, p. 3.
45. Trans.: 'kühnen Geist'; 'weitschauenden Blick'; 'der vorwärts strebenden Frau'. Laser concludes that the suggestion of a 'Vermännlichung' of homosexual women could only harm (*nur schaden*) the goals and aims of the homosexual movement. Ibid.
46. 'Amazonen', *Frauenliebe*, 13, 1926, p. 2.
47. Trans.: 'Reisende aller Zeiten wußten von Weibern in gewissen Gegenden aller Erdteile, in Amerika, Afrika, Asien, Australien, selbst in Europa zu berichten, die ohne Männer in Gemeinschaften zusammenlebten. Sie trieben Jagd und führten gern Kriege mit den Männern benachbarter Bezirke ... Um aber nicht auszusterben, ließen sie zeitweilig Männer benachbarter Stämme zu, behielten jedoch nur die Mädchen bei sich; die Knaben wurden entweder an den väterlichen Stamm abgetrennt oder getötet.' The image of the mythical Amazon warrior also blurs gendered norms. The Amazon's

missing breast, for example, removed to make bearing arms in war an easier task, undercuts the idealized image of the feminine. However, maintaining a single breast for the nurturing of female offspring retains a level of traditional maternalism. Therefore, the Amazon could be seen as an archetypal bisexual woman in the original sense of the term. Ibid.
48. Trans.: 'Jeder denkende und vorurteilsfreie Mensch weiß: der absolute Mann und die absolute Frau sind nur Abstraktionen; in der Wirklichkeit gibt es Übergänge.' Helga Karig, 'Relativität der Minderwertigkeit', *Frauenliebe* 50, 1927.
49. Trans.: 'Den Abend gab Gudrun der Freundin, wonach diese seit Tagen, seit ihrem ersten Kennenlernen lechzte'. Nils Lermann, 'Die Freundin der Olga Diers', *Die Freundin*, 8 August 1924.
50. Trans.: 'taubenblauen Cabriolets, so sicher wie auf dem Pferderücken'; 'die gleich ihr eine Persönlichkeit ist, zu der sie nicht hinunterschauen muss, die ihr gewachsen ist und mehr als Geliebte sein kann'. Dusia, 'Das Wiedersehen', *Die Freundin*, 1 March 1933.
51. Clare Rogan, '"Good Nude Photographs": Images for Desire in Weimar Germany's Lesbian Diaries', in McAuliffe and Tiernan (eds), *Tribades, Tommies and Transgressives*, p. 146.
52. Gayatri Chakravorty Spivak, *Worlds: Essays in Cultural Politics* (New York: Methuen, 1987), p. 170.
53. Ruth Margarete Roellig, *Berlins lesbische Frauen* in Adele Meyer, *Lila Nächte: Die Damenklubs der Zwanziger Jahre* (Cologne: Zitronenpresse, 1981), p. 38.
54. Trans.: 'Werner gähnte gelangweilt und griff mit seiner gepflegten Hand in die Konfektschachtel. Plötzlich hüstelte er etwas gezwungen. "Georgia", sagte er, "ich glaube Du rauchst schon wieder einen anderen Tabak. Du weißt, daß ich bei solch kratzigem Zeug, wie es der heutige ist, stets Halsaffektionen become". Sie legte erschrocken die Pfeife aus der Hand und strich ihm übers Haar. "Verzeih", – wagte sie dann nur noch zu sagen. "Uebrigens", fuhr er fort, und ließ dabei wieder eine Süßigkeit den Weg der anderen gehen, "finde ich, daß Du Dich in der letzten Woche fast gar nicht um mich bekümmert hast … Du weißt, wie ich dann immer seelisch leide".' Hanna, 'Geschlecht von Morgen', *Frauenliebe* 13, 1930, pp. 1–2.
55. Trans.: 'So eine also war sie – mit dem lachenden Leichtsinn im Blut würde sie morgen mit einer Anderen wieder hier sitzen – würde wieder mit derselben sorglosen Freude Wein trinken – wieder mit derselben harmlosen Verliebtheit ihr Gegenüber küssen'. Inge, 'Die von der Liebe leben …', *Frauenliebe* 35, 1927, p. 3.
56. Kathy L. Peiss, 'American Women and the Making of Modern Consumer Culture', https://www.albany.edu/jmmh/vol1no1/peiss-text.html (retrieved 19 April 2022).
57. Ibid.
58. Ibid.
59. Madeleine Marsh, *Compacts and Cosmetics: Beauty from Victorian Times to the Present Day* (Barnsley: Remember When, 2009), p. 97.
60. Ibid.
61. Annelie Ramsbrock, *The Science of Beauty: Culture and Cosmetics in Modern Germany 1750–1930*, trans. by David Burnett (New York: Palgrave Macmillan, 2015), p. 162.
62. Annelie Ramsbrock, 'Social Cosmetics: Weimar Beauty Politics between Welfare and Empowerment', *German History*, 4 (2016), 555–78 (at p. 555).
63. Considered in this way, adverts for lectures such as 'How I Keep Myself Young and Beautiful' in the magazine *Women's Love* and its supplement 'Femina' fit into the much wider development of Berlin's growing social trends and consumer culture. Ibid., p. 557.

64. Trans.: 'Man ist bemüht immer neue Parfüms ausfindig zu machen, Kombinationen zu schaffen und ein "lebendigen" Duft herzustellen.' Adele, 'Das persönliche Parfüm', *Frauenliebe*, 1931, p. 1.
65. Trans.: 'Zarter Veilchenduft oder diskretes Irisparfüm entspricht der Bescheidenheit, und darum passen diese beiden vornehmlich zu der äußerlich bescheiden und zurückhaltenden Frau.' Ibid.
66. Trans.: 'Flieder, Jasmin, Ylang-Ylang, Heliotrop und Peau d'Espange.' Ibid.
67. Trans.: 'klarer Augen und eines belebten feurigen Blickes'; 'die zarte Haut einer schönen Frau'. Regular advertisement, 'Schönheit und Jugend der Freundin' found in *Frauenliebe* between 1928–1930.
68. Sabrina Brauneis, *The Relationship of Body Weight and Skepticism towards Advertising* (Wiesbaden: Springer Gabler, 2016), p. 43.
69. Trans.: 'alle von Ihnen [Femina C.S.] genannten Cremes sind wirkungslos. Wenn sie schon nicht schaden, so helfen sie doch wenigstens auch nichts'. 'Auf Anfrage', *Femina* 4, 1929.
70. Trans.: '"Benutzen Sie kölnisches Wasser.' Ibid.
71. Trans.: '"Sexualität ist keine Marktware ... sondern eine von Natur aus in jedes Lebenswesen gelegte Notwendigkeit der Bedürfnisse, die man mit Moral allein nicht verurteilen, sondern nur durch die erworbenen Kenntnisse der Sexualpsychologie verstehen kann.' H.M, 'Verurteilt sie nicht!', *Die Freundin*, 9 January 1933, p. 2.
72. Trans.: 'nur selten wird uns Gelegenheit gegeben, eine Modenschau, an der auch männliche Frauen als Mannequins teilnehmen, zu sehen'. 'Transvestiten-Modenschau – 6 November', *Die Freundin*, 15 October 1930.
73. Trans.: 'ein reichhaltiges Programm'; Trans.: 'elegantesten männlichen Frauen'. Ibid.
74. Trans.: 'jeder einzelne für seinen Geschmack etwas herausfindet'. Ibid.
75. Trans.: 'Am raschtesten ermüdeten die Damen in Röcken aus Leinen, Samt und anderen schweren Stoffen, während sie in Röcken aus Seide und Gabardine die geringsten Ermüdungserscheinungen aufwiesen.' 'In welchem Rock geht es sich am besten?', *Die Freundin*, 16 April 1928, p. 3.
76. Ibid.
77. Trans.: 'die Kopfform einer Frau [ist] ganz anders als die eines Mannes, folglich bedingt sie eine ganz andere Haartracht'. Paulowna, 'Für oder gegen den Bubikopf', *Die Freundin*, 16 April 1928, p. 7.
78. For more information specifically concerning the historiographical practices that have shaped transgender history, see Susan Stryker, *Transgender History: The Roots of Today's Revolution*, 2nd edn (Berkeley: Seal Press, 2012).
79. Katie Sutton, 'Sexological Cases and the Prehistory of Transgender Identity Politics in Interwar Germany', in Joy Damousi et al. (eds), *Case Studies and Dissemination of Knowledge* (Abingdon: Routledge, 2015), p. 86.
80. Katie Sutton, '"We Too Deserve a Place in the Sun": The Politics of Transvestite Identity in Weimar Germany', *German Studies Review*, 2 (2012), 335–54; Lybeck, *Desiring Emancipation*.
81. Trans.: 'Es ist mir unmöglich, mich irgendwie weibisch zu benehmen, wie es leider so viele glauben tun zu müssen. Aber trotzdem, oder gerade deshalb, glaube ich in vieler Hinsicht weiblicher zu empfinden wie manche wirkliche Frau.' 'Die Welt der Transvestiten', *Die Freundin*, 1924.
82. Of course, surgery may not have been a desirable option for many trans women even if it had been available to them. And many of the trans women featured in the supplement for *The Girlfriend* focus on how they express their femininities – and to a lesser degree

masculinities – in ways that did not require surgery, taking pains to argue that this fact did not make them any less of a woman.
83. In most cases, authors and article in these periodicals were concerned with 'male transvestites'. Trans.: 'Im Allgemeinen rechnet man sie [Transvestiten C.S] zu den Homosexuellen. Doch trifft dies bei den männlichen Transvestiten nicht immer zu.' Käthe Karl, 'Aus dem Leben der Transvestiten', 'Die Welt der Transvestiten', *Die Freundin*, 1925, p. 8.
84. Trans.: 'Ein Mann als solcher ist oft herb und verschlossen – sehr zum Kummer der Frau. Nun nehme man mal den Transvestiten ... Er ist weich, liebevoll und zärtlich – ganz so, wie sich wohl manche "unverstandene" Frau den Mann wünscht.' 'Frau und Transvestit', 'Der Welt der Transvestiten', *Die Freundin*, 1930.
85. Sutton, '"We Too Deserve a Place in the Sun"', p. 345.
86. Trans.: 'Transvestiten! Nach jahrelangen Experimenten fand ich endlich ein Radikalmittel gegen Bartstoppeln und andere Körperhaare [mit Wurzeln]!' 'Kleine Anzeigen', *Frauenliebe* 10, 1927.
87. Sutton, '"We Too Deserve a Place in the Sun"', p. 339.
88. Trans.: 'rein und schön'; 'Enttäuschung'. Xela Eckats, 'Freundschaftsehen', *Die Freundin*, 30 April 1928, p. 5.
89. Trans.: 'Es ist für den maskulinen Teil in überwiegendem Maße eine Selbstverständlichkeit, in Zeiten der Not der Freundin ganz besonders beizustehen; denn gerade dann haben wir ja Gelegenheit, unsere Liebe zu beweisen! Warum versagen in solchen Fällen fast immer die femininen Partnerinnen.' Ibid.
90. Trans.: 'Menschen, die in allen Lebenslagen fest und treu zusammenhalten, wird auch die normale Welt respektieren.' Ibid., p. 5.
91. Trans.: 'Ich kenne viele Frauen, sehr viele sogar, die mit einer Freundin in einer festen Bindung zusammenleben, wirken und arbeiten, und die nichts als der Tod trennen wird. Diese Freundschaften sind oft so unauffällig, so dezent und zurückhaltend, dass nur der Eingeweihte weiß, dass hier auch eine erotische Freundschaft vorliegt.' XYZ, 'Freundinnen-Ehe', *Die Freundin*, 1933.
92. 'Briefe die man der Freundin schreibt', *Die Freundin*, 20 February 1928, p. 7
93. Trans.: 'Hände weg von verheirateten, bisexuellen Frauen und solchen Ledigen, die auch noch dem Manne gehören! Hände weg von jenen Zweinaturen, die aus Lust an der Wollust beide Geschlechter genießen! – Sie treten unsere Liebe in den Schmutz!' Clara K., 'Soll eine homosexuelle Frau mit einer bisexuellen Freundschaft schließen?', *Die Freundin*, 20 February 1928.
94. Trans.: 'Ich finde Ihre strikte Ablehnung der bisexuellen Frauen nicht recht. Sind es im Innern nicht genau so Menschen wie wir? Vielleicht fühlen dieselben sich durch ihren Zwiespalt, in dem sie leben, viel unglücklicher als es scheint'. S.S., 'Duisburg zur Antwort', *Die Freundin*, 19 March 1928.
95. Trans.: 'Ihre Behauptung, bisexuelle Frauen seien uns gleich, bestreite ich, denn man kann nicht zwei Herren dienen ... solche Art Frauen gehören nicht zu einer homosexuellen Freundin, denn die Gefühle, die sie wecken sind nicht echt und können der echten Freundin zur Katastrophe werden.' Duisburg, 'Zur Beantwortung', *Die Freundin*, 5 March 1928.
96. Trans.: 'Der Kampf ums Dasein ist schwer; aber eine homosexuelle Frau würde sich deshalb niemals zur Dirne und zum Vergnügungsobjekt des Mannes machen lassen, denn das liegt ihrer Natur nicht.' Ibid.
97. Herta Laser, 'Aus der Bewegung', *Frauenliebe* 28, 1927, p. 3.
98. Trans.: 'Hat es nicht die weibliche Frau unserer Kreise viel schwerer als eine heterogene Frau? ... Eine heterogene Frau wird in den meisten Fällen, lebt sie mit einem Manne

zusammen, nicht mehr ihrem Beruf nachgehen ... Leben aber zwei Frauen zusammen, so gehen beide ihren Beruf nach ... Der weibliche Teil muß nun nach Schluß den Dienststunden sich mit Hausarbeiten beschäftigen, soll eine gemütliche Wohnung herrichten, ein freundliches Lächeln zeigen, und soll der Freundin eine geistige Gefährtin sein.' Ibid.
99. Trans.: 'Was würden Sie, meine Damen, tun, wenn Sie heute eine Frau kennen lernen, wüßten, sie ist verheiratet, lebt mit ihrem Manne in engster Gemeinschaft, möchte aber auch die Freundin nicht missen?' Cläre, 'Meinungsaustausch', *Frauenliebe* 4, 1928, p. 8.
100. Trans.: 'herzensguter Kerl'; 'ganz was anderes'. Ibid.
101. Amy Young, '"Das gesprengte Korsett": Gender in Lesbian Periodicals in Berlin 1924–1933', unpublished doctoral thesis (Lincoln, NE: University of Nebraska, 2004), p. 8.

Chapter 4

MARYS AND MOLLYS
Identifying Queer Feminine Desires on the Dutch Press Landscape

It's here! 'We' – A magazine for *us*. Finally!
—*We*, 10 September 1932[1]

This magazine is for the Marthas and the Marys, for the young woman and the experienced mother, for all ranks and statuses, for every age, because all women will find in it what keeps all Catholic women united: domesticity, steadfastness of character and a sense for what is good.[2]
—*Beatrice*, 5 January 1939

Penélopé or Monthly Magazine for the Female Sex (*Penélopé of maandwerk aan het vrouwelijk geslacht toegewijd*) was one of the first regular periodicals to be published in the Dutch language for women and was in circulation between 1821 and 1835. While magazines for women had existed in the Netherlands prior to this pioneering publication, these pages had been frequently translated from other languages, usually French, and relied entirely on the lifespan and content of the original native copy for their survival, lasting anywhere between a matter of months and a couple of years.[3] The arguably queer 'fits and starts' that characterized the emergence of a media devoted to (shaping) the social, political and commercial interests of women in the

Netherlands appear to have petered out following the entrance of *Penélopé*, which inspired a steady range of new popular – and political – reading materials for women. Many of these were closely based on the rubrics found in this original magazine – and those international papers upon which it had been based – which was edited by writer and boarding school proprietor Anna Barbara van Meerten-Schilperoort. For much of its print life, *Penélopé* centred its content on 'the description and illustration of all kinds of female handicrafts' as well as providing 'reading matter concerning subjects from female circles'.[4] In addition to setting the tone for the so-called 'hobby' magazines that followed in its wake, 'the tension' that existed in *Penélopé* 'between nationalism and internationalism and between theory and practice', as literary and cultural historian Lotte Jensen observes, continued to be a characteristic of women's periodicals in the Netherlands long into the twentieth century.[5] It is precisely in these tensions that the problematics of depicting femininity within the Dutch media landscape already began to come to the fore. Indeed, in its desire to construct more specifically Dutch forms of idealized womanhood, *Penélopé* appears largely to have been torn between the aspirational images of a more internationally oriented modern woman, who was encouraged to broaden her horizons intellectually and geographically, and the more domestically focused housewife, who would 'develop her intellectual capacities, but only to a certain degree' and who 'if not busy with household tasks … would busy herself with embroidery'.[6] It was in this latter function, as a commercial mouthpiece that prepared 'Dutch girls for their future roles as wives and mothers', where *Penélopé* set a precedent for popular women's magazines in the Netherlands that would endure for more than a century.[7]

Following *Penélopé*'s arrival on to the press circuit, several other women's magazines emerged in the Netherlands, which frequently combined their core religious or political content with a range of commercial interests and aims. As mentioned in the Introduction to Part II, women were being considered as a newly profitable category of readership by publishing houses from the mid-nineteenth century onwards – sources of revenue that had hitherto been untapped. And, by the turn of the twentieth century, housewives in the Netherlands were firmly regarded, as David Machin and Theo van Leeuwen observe, as 'the "purchase managers" of the household', figures who controlled the acquisition of all consumables found on domestic terrain.[8] Targeting women in their role as purchasers, many women's periodicals in the Netherlands at the fin-de-siècle attempt to combine a 'practical-informational mission' through articles on food, clothing and childrearing, for instance, with a highly conspicuous and conservative 'moral tone'.[9] Of course, the conservative moral discourses that can be found in many women's magazines at this time should not be considered to have been received by an uncritical reader. Moreover, as these periodicals began to incorporate more reader letters, debate articles and social commentaries into their pages, the productions themselves grew increasingly polysemic, which served to create from the producers and consumers of media content what literary scholar Stanley Fish has described as 'interpretive communities'.[10] Indeed, rather than being an arbiter of the various conservative moral discourses of their time, print media in the nineteenth century, as Margaret Beetham writes, must be considered as important textual spaces – especially for women – in which 'meanings are contested and made'.[11]

Yet, while the content that was created within these Dutch periodicals arguably resulted from a more multivocal process that involved editors, contributors and readers, several consistent themes nonetheless emerged that transcended the vectors of class, religion and political background that distinguished one magazine from another. The most significant of these in the Dutch context were the subjects of motherhood and domesticity. By the interwar era, the figure of the mother and housewife, as feminist historian Deirdre Beddoe maintains, was 'the one desirable image held up to women by all mainstream media'.[12] This was especially true in the Netherlands, where the 'breadwinner' and 'housewife' remained the cornerstones of what was still a highly gendered cultural landscape. Although a diverse range of magazines for women existed in each sociopolitical pillar in the Netherlands by the interwar era, women readers appear in such media to be consistently addressed by editors in their role 'as housewives and, especially, mothers'.[13] In periodicals for Catholic as well as Socialist women, for Jewish as for Liberal women, one invariably finds articles common to them all, which often pertain to 'doctor's advice, parental advice, patterns for sewing children's clothes [and] tips for removing stains'.[14] In those magazines targeting younger and unmarried female readers, the literary content, advice columns and reader letters focus almost exclusively on the subject of marriage or how to be a good daughter/sister/mother. The significance of the 'collective notions' pertaining to the categories of 'housewife' and 'mother' within magazines for women in the interwar era, as Fiona Seaton Hackney writes, often surpassed even those 'identities that had been understood in terms of class, education or religion'.[15] Yet, crucially, as Seaton Hackney further observes, the meanings of what it was to be 'a good mother, a desirable (and desiring) woman, smart, capable, a fulfilled and successful housewife, a respectable working wife, a lover or an efficient employee' were never entirely distinct from these previous categories either.[16] This should remind us that gender presentations have always existed in a complex enmeshment with dominant notions of class, race and religion.

Concerned thematically with 'how to balance the demands of the workplace and the home, of public and private lives', Dutch women's magazines of the interwar era provide present-day readers with an unparalleled window into the central dilemmas that faced female media consumers during this period. Yet, as Deborah Chambers rightly observes, women's pages that centralize themes of femininity and motherhood have often been 'celebrated and scorned' in the mainstream, as well as being 'dismissed as superficial and conservative [promotions of] gendered stereotyping that dominates much of popular culture' within historical research.[17] In order to avoid the 'dangerous tendency' of reproducing 'received views' about women's magazines of the interwar era – that is, that they acted as mirrors of conservative heterosexual cultural norms and values – I hope to draw on historical source material in this chapter to explore the potential variation in meanings assigned to femininity in two popular periodicals for Protestant and Catholic women from the interwar era. Examining the inescapability of maternal discourses that shaped much of the content within these magazines, I will further investigate the ways in which these images may have diverged from 'collective notions' of the bourgeois housewife and mother. While these periodicals were not aimed at queer women, print media such as these, as Anja van Kooten Niekerk and Sacha Wijmer remind us, would have comprised a large degree of the leisure reading material that was available to young (queer) women in a pillarized Dutch society. And, as central communicators of cultural norms, as well as spaces in which such norms could be contested and disrupted, (heterosexual) women's magazines 'posit a collective and yet multivalent female subjectivity, which they simultaneously address and construct'.[18] Indeed, as we shall see in Part III of this book, the discourses of maternalism and domesticity that are visible in these nonqueer periodicals were taken up in new ways in the queer textual productions produced by women writers during this time. In this way, I argue that magazines such as *The Young Woman* (*De jonge vrouw*, 1924–35) and *Beatrice* (*Beatrijs* 1939–67) can still be considered productive source material for the study of queer desire in the Netherlands, by providing us with insights into the ways in which queer Dutch women were configuring their desires during a time in which no magazines existed exclusively for women loving women.[19] Examining the various models of femininity that are presented through the articles, stories and reader letters in these magazines, I hope to present a flavour of the discourses of domesticity and femininity that would have been available to (queer) women during this period.[20] Suggesting that the politics of maternalism and femininity might have fed into the late onset of naming and labelling queer desires in the Netherlands through my discussion of the articles found in *The Young Woman* and *Beatrice*, I will take the conclusions of this analysis into my study of the queer periodicals *We* and *The Right to Live* in order to ask what the absence of femininity from these magazines might tell us further about the experiences of women within queer communities in the Netherlands during the interbellum.

The Cult of Domesticity

From at least the eighteenth century, domesticity existed as a foundational concept within the Dutch social imaginary. While cultures of homeliness certainly existed elsewhere on mainland Europe – and beyond – the unparalleled traction that they found within Dutch religious strongholds means that the so-called 'Cult of Domesticity' could endure in the Netherlands even while it began to wane in neighbouring countries. Dividing 'the nineteenth-century preoccupation with domesticity' broadly into two categories, spatial historian Anna P.H. Geurts suggests that notions of homeliness attended several significant social and private functions in the Netherlands in the nineteenth century. While home was a space that ruling powers hoped would '[shield] its inhabitant from the corrupting social struggle for wealth and power, and the allure of revolution', it equally provided a plot in which 'to be human, to be Christian, or to be oneself'.[21] Thoughts on what it was to be 'homely' were shaped most often by Dutch ideas of comfort and cleanliness. However, in order to make a space comfortable and clean, one also had to wrestle with judgements of taste and respectability. Identity, here, was thus linked strongly to ideas of ownership, which also allowed one to exercise a freedom of (tasteful) expression over an environment, with the home offering 'the possibility to arrange *one* place on earth completely according to [one's] wishes'.[22] For Dutch women in their 'emerging profession' as housewives, the home also played a vital function in cementing certain gendered values and mores. The ability to create a comfortable domestic sphere by the turn of the twentieth century therefore was considered to be 'the characteristic of a good woman' and, as such, integral to the values associated with the Cult of Domesticity.[23]

As we will see in the discussions that emerged from *Beatrice* and *The Young Woman*, the chief moral imperatives that determined what it was to be a good woman in the Netherlands were consistently infused with ideas of 'thrift, order, respect for authority, a strong work ethic, self-control and, especially regarding food preparation, frugality'.[24] Therefore, as a good housewife, one had to be able both to create a homely atmosphere through carefully chosen furnishings *and* to handle financial constraints smartly and effectively. Also termed the 'Cult of True Womanhood', the embodiment and practice of nineteenth and early twentieth-century ideals of domesticity was based, as Barbara Welter has suggested, on the virtues of piety, purity and submission, all of which served to keep women in their rightful place: the home.[25] The fact that these value systems were espoused by elite, white, religious circles in Dutch society also means of course that many women were effectively barred from the status of 'true' woman, even while all women were expected to uphold the values associated with this idealized gendered form. Indeed, the 'pedestal' upon which white women of means were placed within the Cult of Domesticity indicates, as Meredith Worthen observes, that the phenomenon 'had no room for poor women, immigrants, or women of colour', which ultimately served to mark 'broad swaths of women as deviant'.[26] Certainly, while *Beatrice* and *The Young Woman* both claim on occasions to serve the aims of *all* women, it is clear that this extends only to women of a certain religions or class backgrounds, and it is almost impossible for the present-day reader to ignore the assumption by editors that the readers of such magazines would have been white. Indeed, while the politics of sexuality, class and race undoubtedly belong to discussions concerning the domestic sphere, these subjects are rarely touched upon in either magazine. In spite of these pitfalls, I hope to use these materials to challenge the practice of considering historical documents with preordained conclusions, as well as pointing to the potential fruits of including ostensibly nonqueer resources in historical studies about the queer past. Offering only a snapshot of the vast amount of content produced by these under-researched magazines, I hope to begin a conversation about what discourses of domesticity and motherhood may have meant for a Dutch woman who loved and desired other women.

Beatrice (1939–67)

First released by the De Spaarnestad publishing house in Haarlem on 5 January 1939, *Beatrice* quickly found a popular following as the 'only weekly magazine for Catholic women'.[27] A highly successful publication in the Netherlands, as well as the colonies of Indonesia, the Dutch Antilles and Suriname, *Beatrice* enjoyed a print circulation of approximately 90,000 copies at its peak, which dropped to a little over 60,000 before 1967, when it was taken over by the women's publication *Libelle*. This takeover was largely linked to an increase in competition, as a growing number of magazines for Catholic women had been established by this time, as well as women having increased access to nondenominational print media as the stronghold of pillarization began to weaken heading into the 1970s. In terms of the management of the magazine, there are no names or identifying details for the editors before 1942 and within the remit of this volume, it has been impossible to trace who was responsible for the shape and structure of the content during the magazine's early years.[28] However, from 1946, C.P.M. Lautenslager and E.G.H. Bornewasser were named as chief editors, and when the magazine became subsumed by the larger magazine *Libelle* – also published by De Spaarnestad – D. Hendrikse followed as their successor, remaining the sole editor of the magazine for several years.

In terms of its circulation, *Beatrice* was a consistent and reliable publication, experiencing breaks in printing due only to paper shortages during the war efforts and after the magazine was banned following the Nazi invasion. Comprising between thirty-two and forty-eight pages per issue in the years under study here, *Beatrice* sold individual copies for 10 cents. Alternatively, a subscription cost seven and a half cents per week or 1 guilder each quarter.

Compared to the magazines created by and for queer women in Germany (see Chapter 3), *Beatrice* was far better placed to promote itself to its target audience and to attract a healthy readership. Printed by a popular Catholic publishing house, it was also able to offer readers substantial subscription gifts, such as foldable baskets for handicrafts, silver-plated cheese slicers and salt shakers, photo albums, portraits of Catholic ministers and even elaborate jigsaw puzzles. Like the publications discussed in the previous chapter, *Beatrice* also included a number of advertisements for novels published by De Spaarnestad, as well as other forms of educational and religious reading material. However, diverging from the commercial content of *The Girlfriend* and *Women's Love*, *Beatrice* initially did not include any advertisements for beauty products or clothing. From 1940, approximately 0.75 pages of the magazine per issue were newly dedicated to commercial advertisements.[29] The sudden inclusion of advertorials, as Marloes Hülsken writes, had as much to do with ensuring the continued existence of the magazine as it did with enabling the publication to make money. Indeed, *Beatrice*, just like its chief competitors *Libelle* and *Margriet*, was a commercial product, produced 'first and foremost to turn a profit'.[30] In terms of the type of advertorial content that was included in *Beatrice* from 1940, there are adverts for consumables, care and medicinal products such as soap, shampoo and food supplements, as well as cleaning products and general items for the maintenance of the home. However, these adverts formed only a small part of the magazine. The rest of the content consisted of articles on cooking, childcare and global and/or political issues, special features on religious holidays, weekly columns by the Catholic priest B.G. Henning and other social commentaries by prominent figures. In addition, editors included serial stories written by regular contributors and readers alike, shorter literary submissions and poems, as well as pages for reader letters and debate articles.

Having identified a gap in the market for a 'reliable/respectable [*degelijk*], Catholic, practical, universal women's weekly', the editors of *Beatrice* set out to produce a magazine to which Catholic women could turn for advice about childcare, how to be thrifty with their cooking and handicrafts, or even for tips on how best to care for the plants and animals found on the homestead.[31] In those articles and stories that included a discussion of more 'frivolous' topics, such as fashion and beauty trends, *Beatrice* appears to have been more modest than some of its competitors and attempted to steer its readers away from the beauty ideals that were being introduced into Dutch culture through glamorous cinematic glimpses of the American 'Girl'. While maintaining an image of respectability was of utmost importance to the editors of the magazine, the sleek evening gowns and fashionable dresses that were presented to readers through photo reports nonetheless suggest that an aspirational element to the publication did exist, which encouraged women to fantasize about an existence *outside* of the home, one in which they could selfishly indulge their commercial desires – or, at least, to a degree. While *Beatrice* frequently included sewing and knitting patterns for children's clothing, as well as simple day or weekend dresses for the readers themselves, there were also articles that dually attempted to indulge the desires of women to be *less* frugal while encouraging them simultaneously to think carefully about money. In a double-page spread depicting lavish images of the latest fashions for bold prints, for example, an unnamed author verbalizes the desire of the reader to purchase extravagant items, while wrestling with the need to be economically prudent: 'Is there anything more pleasant for us women to imagine than a fun afternoon shopping with just enough money in our pockets so as not to get desperate from all those "bargains" that we have to pass up, and just little enough with us not to buy crazy things that we cannot use after all, or maybe only need in a year's time?'[32] Writing of the dangers presented by imminent 'clearance sales', the author reminds women to be on their guard so as not to be 'deceived' by supposedly advantageous purchases and convincing sales pitches. Here, however, we see how the idealized image of the frugal women upheld by *Beatrice* remained in tension with the social requirement for the bourgeois woman to be always presentable – and fashionable. After discussing several prints that could be worn 'for more than one season', the writer admits that the *most* fashionable of clothing items will forever present Dutch women with an impossible dilemma: 'the enormous bouquets that we see printed on our supple summer fabrics this year, and which are very *en vogue* at present, are very likely not to be so highly favoured in Women's Fashion next year'.[33] The fickleness of fashion and growing popularity of off-the-rack and throwaway trends was increasingly at odds with the frugality that was considered a desirable characteristic for the 'True Woman'. In many instances, fashion writers for *Beatrice* attempted to circumvent this issue by encouraging women to indulge in their desires for extravagant and aspirational feminine styles, but *only* once all other necessary items for the family and home had been acquired.

In stark contrast to the fashion articles presented in *The Girlfriend*, as examined in the previous chapter, in which discussions that concerned clothing and accessories were limited largely to the practicality and comfort of an item, the need to maintain a respectable and fashionable image in *Beatrice* often went so far as attempting to frame even the most practical of items as fashionable. In a photo report entitled 'The Eternally Feminine and Air-Raid Protection', for instance, author Emmy Andriesse mourns the effects of the gas mask on the 'appealing faces', 'elegant hairstyles' and 'beautiful eyes' of previously presentable Dutch women: 'It is practical, easy to put on and nice and warm but that's about it for the good qualities [of the gas mask]. It is impossible to say that it is flattering. It is a dark woollen sack into which all feminine beauty vanishes.'[34] Lamenting the loss of beauty due to the need for more practical wartime accessories, Andriesse offers the readers of her article tips on how best to dress in such difficult times, remaining steadfast in her belief that true femininity could be maintained even when women are forced to literally and figuratively mask their beauty. Describing the 'new world' in which women did not wear dark glasses to protect against the sun's rays, but instead 'against the bright light of exploding bombs', Andriesse asks her readers to have 'courage and faith' and to believe that 'the eternal feminine will overcome even these hard times'.[35] While the image of the 'eternal feminine' was encouraged in *Beatrice* through photo stories such as those of Andriesse and the fashion spread mentioned previously, there are also a surprising number of articles around the time of the war in which women are celebrated in typically non-feminine roles.

Returning to the tensions of inter/nationalism mentioned earlier in this chapter, Beatrice wanted to be considered as *the* newspaper for the respectable Catholic Dutch woman, while also situating itself as a modern and forward-looking periodical with an eye on global events. To achieve this goal, *Beatrice* often featured stories that shone a light on some of the 'extraordinary exploits' that were being undertaken by women elsewhere in the world. These stories were presented not only in reports of missionary actions but also in general news items about women's organizations across the globe and articles on how women in other countries were faring during the war. In the article 'Five Thousand Female Chauffeurs for London's Ambulance Service', for example, the author writes in admiration of the 'high demands' that were being placed upon women drivers, who were expected not only to drive the ambulance but also to repair it when necessary. Indeed, the usually fashion-forward writers are even forced to acknowledge the need for and usages of practical uniforms when writing about women in the British police force in the article 'The Girls in Boulder Blue', even as they appear unable to leave the language of current trends behind them altogether: 'As inelegant as their uniform is, it is easy and comfortable to wear. The helmet is also as light as a feather because it is made of cork, which is covered with a dark blue fabric.'[36]

Figure 4.1. 'The Eternally Feminine and Air-Raid Protection', *Beatrice*, 1939. IISG, used with permission.

Figure 4.2. 'The Girls in Boulder Blue', *Beatrice*, 1939. IISG, used with permission.

In a separate article on women in the armed forces, there is a more cautious discussion of the Lotta Svärd group in Finland, a voluntary and part-time organization in which women were trained to support the (male) army. Although the author approvingly mentions the 'regular competitions in rowing, running and skiing' that were undertaken by members of the Finnish women's army, which included women of some seventy years of age, the author is equally at pains to emphasize that this work is particularly suited to *Finnish* women on account of their physiognomic differences to Dutch women, while also highlighting the essential feminine nature of the jobs being undertaken: 'As has already been understood from the above, these women do not wield guns or hand grenades, they only carry out specifically female activities such as nursing the sick, cooking food for the soldiers, and all kinds of work which, by nature, suits a woman better than a man.'[37] Surprisingly, perhaps, these careful – and heavily caveated – depictions of women in gender nonconforming roles were not the only deviations from typical gendered norms to appear in the magazine. Indeed, the editors of *Beatrice* also allowed space for the inclusion of (literary) portrayals of men who also transgressed traditional gendered boundaries.

The serial story *Deliverance: An Actor's Novel* by Molly Veness ran over multiple issues between 1939 and 1940. A coming-of-age narrative about British boy David Barnett, Veness' serial story invokes several tropes of queer femininity in its details of the struggles of a protagonist who is said to be 'different from the others'. As a child, David is described by the narrator as 'dreamy', 'sensitive' and 'misunderstood', which distinguishes him greatly from his older brother who is presented as a 'sporty, happy boy'.[38] During the scenes of his early childhood, the reader is told that David is someone who should 'never marry' (*moet nooit trouwen*) and he later develops a close friendship at boarding school with 'the handsome spoiled rascal' Roy Sutherland, who soon becomes his 'bosom buddy'.[39] Throughout his childhood, David is shown to take great pleasure in music and art, and the reader is told of his eye for beauty. Observing his mother one evening, child-David is shown to admire her elegance, appreciating her refined garments and glamour:

> David thought she was the most beautiful thing in the whole world. She had such big dark eyes and such nice short, wavy hair, and she was wearing such nice clothes. He was curious how her dress felt tonight. He crept a little closer, and reached out to touch the cream-coloured cloth. It was soft and cool.[40]

While both *The Girlfriend* and *Women's Love* included supplements for transvestite women in their pages, literary contributions such as these would likely have been the closest to a form of Dutch media representation for trans(vestite) women in the Netherlands.[41] Yet, while David greatly admires his mother, she is shown in the story to have little tolerance for her son's 'tiresome' sensitivities and, following her death, David is forced to leave the family home after expressing his wish to pursue a career as a writer. Soon finding himself in dire straits after he relocates to Fleet Street, the media hub of the great British metropolis, David is depicted as exhausted and near starvation when he is saved by childhood friend Roy, who returns into his life and draws him into the 'mysterious wondrous glory' of the theatre. Here, David takes part-time work as an actor to finance his attempts to write a novel. Although finding initial happiness among Roy's bohemian circles, David feels he is unable to produce any work of literary merit and falls into a depression. Following several tragic twists and turns, which include the protagonist marrying a fellow female actor he had met in childhood, and her subsequent death during childbirth, David turns away from the theatre and those men there who he believes to be 'too dolled up' and who create through their performances 'a false life … an unsavoury life'.[42] Culminating with David finally producing a novel that achieves critical acclaim, the protagonist finds solace in a Catholic monastery located in Scotland.[43] While such a moralistic ending may seem in many respects 'preordained', given the conservative culture in which it was written, the delicate authorial nods to the sexological discourses of their time nonetheless remain remarkable for a Catholic women's magazine published in the first half of the twentieth century. Indeed, it is in these subtle deviations from the 'collective notions' of 'True Womanhood' that *Beatrice* points to the richness of feminine discourses that were available to Dutch women during the interwar period. Be it in depicting women in nontraditional roles such as the army, the police force or the ambulance service, or in literary offerings pointing to little understood queer lives, the content in *Beatrice* presented women material from which they could conceive of alternative experiences of femininity and womanhood. While this conservative Catholic newspaper was certainly by no means a publication that represented the experiences of *all* Dutch women, it was nonetheless a space in which feminine desires could be constructed and contested, and in which queerness might well have existed for those who knew how to read for it.

The Young Woman (1924–38)

The first issue of *The Young Woman* was released on 1 July 1924 by the Christian publishing house Bosch & Keuning in Baarn. Coedited by J.M. Westerbrink-Wirtz, A.M. de Vries Robbé-Bergmans and P. Keuning, the magazine was published in monthly editions on the first Thursday of every month and became available at the end of each year as a bumper annual. Existing as a continuation of the journal *Girlhood* (*Meisjesleven*, 1918–24), *The Young Woman* served the function of educating Christian girls on their position in the home and within society. Costing 2 guilders and 25 cents per half-year subscription, the magazine later became available in a 'luxury edition' (*luxe-uitgave*) in response to the enthusiastic demands of its readership. The 'luxury' of this edition resulted from its being printed on more thickly printed art paper, an improvement that the editors suggested would mean 'the images would turn out much more prettily' and a pleasure for which the reader would pay an additional guilder.[44] With striking cover illustrations commissioned for the magazine from artists such as Corrie Formijne (1896–1977), this would no doubt have been a popular offer.[45]

Figure 4.3. An example of a popular cover style for *The Young Woman*, 1932. IISG, used with permission.

In terms of creating a base of regular readers, *The Young Woman* was not as extravagant as *Beatrice* in terms of the gifts it was able to present to subscribers. Indeed, editors are frequently seen to encourage their existing readers to help them reach new audiences, offering them a book for each new reader they could motivate to subscribe to the magazine. For the new readers themselves, subscription gifts were mostly limited to receiving a free range of magazines from the previous quarter. Since it ceased publication in 1938, *The Young Woman* has received scant attention in secondary material concerning women's periodicals in the Netherlands, even in spite of its supposed popularity among young Christian women during the interwar period. Offering likely more fantasy than fact, an early issue of the magazine sees editors boast of an 'army of thousands of young women' who had gathered around to support the development of 'the *cheapest* and the *best* magazine for the Christian woman in the Netherlands'.[46] Turning Oswald Spengler's militaristic imagery on its head, the editors claimed that this 'army' of readers was growing larger every day and concluded that the launch of the magazine had been a resounding success, positioning their periodical as an innovative mouthpiece for the modern Christian woman: '*The Young Woman* is a success. This monthly magazine, attractive in content and appearance, brings the message to the Christian woman who is ahead of her time, doing so in a form that captivates time and again.'[47]

Aside from inferences to readership and popularity that can be found within the magazine itself – details, of course, that may well have been embellished or exaggerated – there remains very little secondary information about the production of the magazine. There are no figures pertaining to the annual number of copies sold or the subscription figures that the magazine achieved, as the archives of the publishing house to which it belonged now exist only in fragments. However, from the magazine's editorial content, *The Young Woman* appears to have been aimed not only at adolescent readers but also adults – the mothers and older female relatives of the primary target reader – as well as young mothers themselves. Like *Beatrice*, *The Young Woman* contained a broad range of educational content that focused on training its readers to become good housewives and mothers. Outlining the aims of the magazine in its inaugural bumper edition, the editorial board described the publication as a 'respectable/proper' (*keurig*) magazine, which is 'tastefully decorated in all its parts'.[48] Offering the reader a comprehensive guide to the kind of content they would find, the editors also effectively give guardians an opportunity to decide whether the material presented was suitable for younger audiences: 'In the various issues, there are articles about English boarding schools, about well-known house plants, about weaving and other practical things, about kitchen secrets … short meditations, book reviews, correspondences from the editors, mutual correspondences, sections of verses, news items from our circle, riddles and illustrations.'[49] In contrast to *Beatrice*, which was aimed at an adult female audience, *The Young Woman* also features far fewer aspirational fashion images, stories and advertorials. Of those stories and literary contributions that were included, the narrative arc deviated little from the spiritual journey of a young female protagonist on her way to motherhood. However, this is not to say that the magazine avoided discussions of feminine fashions altogether or that advertising content only reproduced rigid descriptions of the practical purposes of their products. Most advertisements for healthcare products often referenced the additional beautifying functions of the product in question and consistently promoted what Annelie Ramsbrock terms 'social cosmetics'. In a regular advert for the toothpaste 'Pearls', for example, readers are asked to consider the importance of their teeth both for their health as well as for their appearance: 'if pearls are so precious, then even more so are your teeth. Think what they mean for your health, for your beauty'.[50] Concomitantly, contributors writing fashion reports argued in a similar way to the editors of the German supplement *Femina* that maintaining a youthful appearance was a goal that every woman should strive to achieve. In an article on the latest rejuvenating fashion trends, for example, one contributor suggests that desire to remain young points only to good common sense: 'Who really wants to be old? A gleam of satisfaction crosses over your face when you are told in earnest that you still look so young. This is not the place to search for the deeper causes of the phenomenon; we are merely pointing out the fact.'[51] Yet, while writers seem here to promote the ideals of a growing cosmetics industry, *The Young Woman* did not include the luxurious fashion prints seen in *Beatrice*, with the editors preferring instead to offer simpler sewing patterns for their readers to follow that would have been made from muslin or more durable fabrics such as poplin. That frugality wins out in the fashion articles found in *The Young Woman* largely speaks of how ideals of femininity and womanhood had to be adapted in media to suit the needs of each specific readership. If readers had less disposable income, for example, frugality appears to have been promoted as an essential and desirable female trait; however, if a woman found herself with funds to spare, then good taste and a keen sense for what was 'proper' instead became the indispensable characteristics of a 'True Woman'.

While keeping their fashion rubrics closely aligned with the ideals of piety and frugality, the editors of *The Young Woman* were not bound exclusively to the conservative discourses of 'True Womanhood'. Indeed, many of the stories included in the magazine navigated the complexities of maintaining Christian value systems while enjoying the pleasures of modern lifestyles. In the serial letter exchange 'From Both Sides' (*Van twee kanten*), for instance, the reader is made privy to a set of fictionalized communications between modern Christian woman Toos and her aunt and uncle. Throughout the exchange, both younger and older women discuss the merits of the modern-day approaches to marriage that were being encouraged by educators such Theodoor van de Velde, as was discussed in Chapter 2. According to Toos' aunt, young couples should make sure that they are well matched before marriage and she admits that one should not expect perfection from the marital union without hard work. Claiming that it is important for a couple to strive to understand one another's perspectives, she suggests that Toos should attempt to find a romantic partner who will take her opinions seriously. However, such a modern approach to heterosexual pairings is shown also to have its limits. When Toos sends a letter in which her aunt believes she appears rather *too* emancipated, the niece receives a response that begs her to have a more realistic expectation of a woman's role in a marriage:

> Your last letter shows that your sense of independence has developed greatly in recent times. Toos does not want this and Toos does not want that. This is not for Toos and Toos does not like that ... When your Aunt read your letter, she shook her head and thought ... Oh, oh, what a lot that Toos has left to learn ... Of *course* you have your principles, it would not be good if you did not have them. But do remember, Toos, that we cannot always achieve our ideals.[52]

Thus, while *The Young Woman* sought to make good on its promise to be the mouthpiece for the Christian woman 'ahead of her time', authors contributing to the publication were clearly still conflicted by what it meant to be a good woman, and a good wife and mother. In a brief segment about the lack of enthusiasm shown by children on the annual Mother's Day celebration, for instance, one unnamed contributor is shown to criticize the figure of the modern mother, whose work is taking her away from the home: 'Ah, we have so few *mothers* left. How can children love these mothers? Let mothers be *mothers* again and then the love of the children will return.'[53] The struggle of editors to maintain the magazine's position as a forward-looking periodical, while nonetheless critiquing modern forms of femininity and motherhood that were becoming increasingly popular among its younger readers, can also be seen in the responses of the readership itself to the magazine's stories and social commentaries.

In a serial from 1926 aptly titled 'Bobbed-Hair' by N. van Dijk-Has, for instance, the reader is made privy to the domestic concerns of Annie and her close friend Dora, as well as the worldly adventures of Lo van Delden, who is positioned as Annie's love interest. In the opening scenes of the story, the reader is told how Annie has recently 'acquired' a 'bobby-kop' (bobbed haircut), which is subsequently much admired by Dora, who is depicted throughout the serial as a frivolous and fanciful girl. However, as an upstanding Protestant man, Lo is shown to be demonstrably shocked to see his love interest's modern haircut upon returning from his studies abroad and he is unable to hide his disappointment.

Figure 4.4. 'Bobbed Hair', *The Young Woman*, 1926. IISG, used with permission.

Catching a glimpse of Annie in a train carriage sitting next to a smoking Dora, Lo fears that she has '*become* a girl with bobbed-hair' and, on greeting her at the station, responds coolly to Annie's gestures of affection. Discovering only later from a relative that the protagonist lost her hair following a 'terrible sickness', Lo is quickly overcome with regret for his actions and apologizes to Annie in the hope that he might win her back. Although responding 'proudly and bitterly' (*trotsch en bitter*) to Lo's apology, arguing that his remorse comes only from the realization that she 'could not help becoming so ugly', Annie ultimately forgives Lo, after which he swiftly proposes.[54]

While the story of 'Bobbed-Hair' does not offer much of interest in and of itself to the study of queer femininity, unless we read Dora's 'degenerate' modernity as code for equally degenerate queer desires, the reader responses to the story that were printed by the editorial board of the magazine suggest that there was a large degree of critical engagement with such content. In a summary of the 'countless' letters received by the editorial board, we can not only discern a conflict in the opinions of readers about the bobbed haircut, but can also gain an insight into the associations that such a style may have conjured in this period:

> Hans defends Lo, and furthermore she thinks that smoking for women is ghastly. Wildsang and Stormvogel agree wholeheartedly with the bluestockings [Annie and Dora]. Vera doesn't think it strange at all that Lo should consider Annie's appearance. After all, a girl's clothes and behaviour say a lot about her character. Vera does not think girls who sacrifice their hair for a whim of fashion are very wise.[55]

The debate between readers concerning the behaviours of Lo towards Annie continued over several issues with the conservative ideals of Annie's love interest remaining a divisive topic. One reader, for instance, argues that Lo is too much of a bigot (*dweper*) about Annie's bobbed haircut and questions the plausibility of such a narrative: 'I think it a bit exaggerated that Lo did not want to ask Annie [to marry him] at first because she has bobbed hair ... he would certainly not be my ideal [man].'[56] At the same time, however, another reader is seen to claim that the behaviour of Lo was 'entirely defensible' (*geheel te verdedigen*). While the editorial board peppered this debate with an occasional witty flourish or textual nod of approval, they appear for the most part to allow for – and even encourage – a degree of disagreement with the content they offered to their readers.

Beginning as a discussion springing from the content of Van Dijk-Has' serial story, the discussion on bobbed-hair continued for a number of years in the magazine and led to a surprising conversation about the need for women-only forums after a male reader offered his opinion on the matter in 1928. Caveating his comments with the acknowledgement that 'perhaps the editors will not want to give me, one of the "gentleman" a place in this section, which is only intended for women', reader 'Johan' decides that he 'wants to give it a shot, anyway'.[57] In an extensive commentary about the modern woman, Johan airs his concerns about the respectability of the modern woman and wonders where the phenomenon of the bobbed haircut might lead: 'I read about trips to the cinema and bobbed-hair … and, then, when I look around me I see all those girls in their modern clothes and I notice that they actually look down rather contemptuously on the work of the housewife, and then I don't know really whether this is the right track [for women].'[58] Although the editors decided they would make 'an exception to the rule' by including Johan's comment in their magazine, they humorously handed the task of issuing a response to their readers: 'We will remain quiet and gladly give our female readers the word. We sincerely hope that Johan will get what is coming to him, but do go easy on the young man.'[59] In the following issue, the editors warn Johan that he is only receiving 'the first droplets' of 'the thunderstorm that has been released over [his] head' and suggest that he should be ready to 'put up [his] umbrella when the next issue comes out'.[60] While evidence of this thunderstorm of responses unfortunately can no longer to be traced, given that the issue in question is missing from archival records, the initial replies to Johan's contribution offer a glimpse of what was to come. While one reader agrees with Johan and claims that he is 'in no way exaggerating' (*overdrijft helemaal niet*) the effects of modernity on the housewife, others were keen to emphasize that views of men such as Johan were not welcome in the pages of *The Young Woman*: 'I was amazed that a "gentleman" was admitted, even by way of exception. I think that a man does not belong in this corner, and especially not one that adopts an attitude like Johan's.'[61] The effects of Johan's entrance into the female sphere were even felt two years later, as a reader refers back to the hypocrisy that appeared to characterize his condescending explanations of the female experience. Describing more general social interactions with members of the male sex, one reader concludes: 'Most brothers act just like "our" Johan: they begin with "Dear Ladies!" and, at the end of the song and dance, they are sitting mercilessly on your head.'[62] Thus, while the story of Annie and Lo remains largely representative of the traditional gendered norms that clearly occupied many contributors to the magazine, the intervention of readers into the debate nonetheless led to interesting discussions concerning the need for women-only (textual) spaces. Appearing in the first instance to cater little to the needs of queer audiences in the commentaries, stories and exchanges that were featured in *The Young Woman*, such calls for a safe community space in which (white Christian) women could discuss issues concerning gender and desire would no doubt have resonated strongly with those women who were attempting to carve out existences without male partners. Having access to a critical and 'interpretive community' of women would have been of unparalleled value to those readers who loved members of their own sex, particularly as their interests do not appear to have been included in those community-based publications that claimed to represent them.

We (1932)

After meeting with a small group of acquaintances at the *Empire* café on the Amsterdam Nes in 1932, lawyer Johan Ellenberger and author Joannes Henri François prepared for the publication of the Netherlands' first magazine dedicated to the interests of the queer community: *We* (*Wij*). With the aim of encouraging interest in establishing a Dutch League for Human Rights, a Dutch branch of Friedrich Radszuweit's Berlin-based League for Human Rights (BfM), Ellenberger and François managed to print only one issue of the magazine before it was outlawed by the Amsterdam vice squad and the embryonic organization responsible for its dissemination was forced to disband. Looking back on the series of events that led to the magazine's banning in an autobiographical account that appeared in Benno Stokvis' *The Homosexuals* (which is discussed in Chapter 2), Ellenberger states:

> We believed that with our own organ, we would be in a better position to challenge the unfair opinions that still exist about homosexuality in so very many people. We also felt that we could establish closer contact with other homosexuals through it. Indeed, in September 1932 the first (and unfortunately also the last) issue of 'We' was established.[63]

Prior to the first issue of *We* and the attempts of Ellenberger and François to establish an affiliated organization, Jacob Schorer's NWHK had been the only Dutch organization to campaign against Article 248bis, the law that restricted homosexual acts between adults and minors. As there is no price on the periodical for the purchase of single copies, it might be assumed that this first issue was disseminated by hand to visitors of the *Empire* and passed on between friends, or otherwise collected in person from the editors. Aside from Ellenberger's statement above in Stokvis' anthology, little information about the intentions of the group behind the publication of *We* remains available in the archive, which means it is difficult to trace any kind of envisioned trajectory for the future of the magazine. Yet, from the subscription form that was printed in the first issue, it appears that the publication was planned as a monthly periodical at a cost of 1 guilder and 50 cents for a three-month subscription, and 5 guilders and 50 cents for an annual subscription. This makes it more expensive than either *Beatrice* or *The Young Woman,* even when taking inflation into account, whose larger and more established readerships would likely have enabled them to offer their publication at a lower cost. Furthermore, instead of offering their new subscribers luxurious gifts, the editors of *We* were instead at pains to reassure their readers that the magazine could be delivered 'in a closed envelope' to a home address or picked up from an alternative location. This need for discretion also distinguished *We* from other community-based publications such as *Beatrice* and *The Young Woman,* which enjoyed the freedom of being able to promote their periodicals broadly and with little fear of censorship. As there is no information about overseas subscription fees, it is unlikely that Ellenberger and François printed the publication with grand plans of acquiring an international readership, despite themselves being influenced by homosexual organizations and publications in Germany. As an entirely Dutch-language journal, *We* would have likely had limited appeal outside the Netherlands. However, the subscription form that was provided with the later emerging magazine *Right to Live* suggests that an overseas audience with an appetite for queer Dutch-language reading material *did* become more established with time.

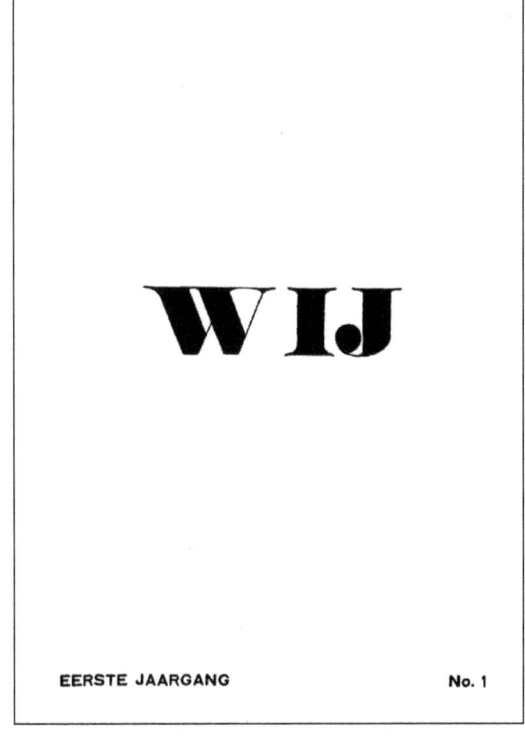

Figure 4.5. Title page of *We*, 1932. IHLIA, used with permission.

For a first-time 'minority' journal, *We* ran at an impressive twenty pages. Many of the articles in the inaugural issue can be read as 'calls to action' by the editorial team, who were attempting to arouse interest in the publication and, furthermore, the establishment of a social and political organization to accompany it. Alongside these letters to the reader, *We*, like the journals discussed in the previous chapter, also included poems, short stories and a translated excerpt from the novel *Death Watch* (*Dodenwacht*) by Ernst von Kleinenberg. For the issue that was envisioned to follow, the editors promised the beginning of a serial story by Adrian Trabak, the author of the novel *The Way Back* (*De Terugweg*, 1921). The pool of contributors to the first issue appears to have been rather small and some of the sobriquets listed, such as 'ko operator', appeared under several articles in the magazine. In a similar way to the magazines *The Girlfriend* and *Women's Love*, readers were encouraged in this first publication to become active participants in the content production by submitting their own literary contributions, social commentaries and reviews to the magazine's headquarters on the Nes in Amsterdam. However, what remains unclear about the production of *We* is quite how the periodical was financed or produced. As it is impossible to track down how many issues of the magazine may have been printed and distributed, it is difficult to estimate how costly an endeavour this might have been. Furthermore, with a reliance on subscriptions as opposed to on-street newspaper kiosks, the harsh press landscape in the Netherlands would have made the initial monetary outlay for a minority publication challenging without the backing of larger organizations such the League for Human Rights or the German Friendship Association.

Although Ellenberger and François strove to create an organization similar to Friedrich Radszuweit's BfM, there is no evidence that Radszuweit or his publishing house had any connection to the production of *We*. Furthermore, while the magazine was praised by the leader of the Community of the Special (Gemeinschaft der Eigenen) Adolf Brand, who congratulated Ellenberger and François on the periodical, financial support from Brand is unlikely, not least because his own periodicals were under financial strain during this time.[64] The monetary difficulties encountered by the publication in its teething period are noted in the opening editorial of the magazine and a grateful nod is given to the 'few friends who sympathised with this endeavour' and who supported the magazine through financial donations.[65]

That the magazine could survive financially was of paramount importance to the editors, who made it clear that the publication was critical to the creation of a network of same-sex desiring individuals in the Netherlands that could support one another through difficult times:

15

AAN DE REDACTIE VAN
HET MAANDBLAD „WIJ",
NES 17, AMSTERDAM (C.).

De ondergeteekende ....

wonende ....
wenscht zich te abonneeren op het Maandblad „WIJ" voor den tijd van:
  (3 maanden à ƒ 1.50 per 3 maanden.
* (6   ,,   ,, ,, 2.75   ,, 6   ,,
  (12   ,,   ,, ,, 5.50   ,, 12   ,,
    bij vooruitbetaling te voldoen.
*   Wenscht dat over het bedrag bij hem aan huis zal worden gedisponeerd.
*   Zal het bedrag per .... over maken.
    Het blad moet hem worden toegezonden onder gesloten couvert aan het bovenstaande adres *of aan: ....

....

....

(handteekening

....

* Doorhalen wat niet gewenscht wordt.

Figure 4.6. 'To the Editors', *We*, 1932. IHLIA, used with permission.

> Let us become aware that we belong together, that our lives are better and more beautiful if we are able to live them together ... And let us therefore ensure that this, OUR magazine, prospers! ... We must sincerely strive to make ourselves strong through solidarity. And if this monthly magazine can help us feel this sense of solidarity more and more, then perhaps it can be a great support to us in our not so always easy lives.[66]

The author, who published under the initial 'L.', was convinced that *We* could help to bring together individuals in a united struggle against persecution. Speaking at length about the isolation faced by queer people, the magazine appears in many respects as a rallying cry from one small group who wished to make itself known to a larger, undefined community. Placing considerable emphasis on the written word, and on the mouthpiece *We* specifically, L. claims that the periodical could help mobilize and create communities of people who felt they were 'different from the others'. With a successful magazine, the writer believed that a sociopolitical subculture would no doubt soon follow in its stead. Indeed, in a country where newspapers were considered the 'cornerstone' of daily life, a journal was a vital step in the building and bringing together of individuals to form a wider community based on common political, as well as romantic/erotic, interests. However, the fact that Ellenberger and François published *We* with the intention of amassing interest in creating an organization was not a method that had been tested in Germany. In Berlin, the magazine *The Friendship* had appeared as a conduit for community news from 'friendship leagues' that were already in existence and, similarly, *The Girlfriend* and *Women's Love* appeared for women who were already – or at least in part – organized. Yet, in L.'s article, the friendship leagues existing in Berlin and across Germany appear to be little more than a distant daydream for same-sex-desiring Dutch citizens, as L. suggests that the gap between the experiences of queer people in Germany and the Netherlands may rise from a 'difference in national character [*volksgeest*]'.[67] As was outlined earlier in this volume, the introduction of Article 248bis and the vice squad, as well as the established religious conservatism that had become an entrenched part of the Dutch political landscape by the 1930s, meant, as L. explains, that behaviours that were 'generally tolerated' in Berlin were still considered to be sinful in Amsterdam.[68]

Women and We

In his comparison of queer life in the two capital cities, L. presents Radszuweit's League for Human Rights as the most established embodiment of the German homosexual movement, describing the importance of the BfM's various periodicals as channels for community news. Given that

We was meant to mark the beginnings of a Dutch branch of the BfM, L.'s omission of the DFV and Hirschfeld's WhK is not surprising. In considering the BfM's reputation as a 'society of men' (*Männerbund*), the glorification of Radszuweit's organization indicates that the Dutch association also hoped to follow a similar course. Further endorsed by masculinist activist Adolf Brand, *We* offers nothing in its content or through its support network to suggest that the organization it looked to establish would engage with the interests of queer female readers.[69] Although the 'conditions of entry to the organization' that were proposed on the agenda for the group's first meeting placed a restriction only on the age of those attending, suggesting that women were welcome to join the organization, no attempts are made in the first issue to represent queer women's social or political needs. Indeed, female homosexual desire appears to have been entirely absent from the publication and was further excluded from the frameworks of queer desire that were employed within the magazine.

As well as a primary objective to stimulate the establishment of a support network, Ellenberger and François also hoped that the journal would serve a broader educative function. In an open letter to readers that fulfilled both of these objectives, contributor 'C.P' writes of the universal sense of isolation that existed among those who desired their own sex in Amsterdam, who had been ostracized because of the lack of understanding about queer desire among the general public: 'We all feel the lack of unity, as well as of strong, honest bonds of friendship among those of us who, through a dearth of understanding from society, are more or less regarded as outcasts.'[70] C.P's assertion is taken up in another article, 'Try to Understand! To All Those Who are Normal', by Ellenberger. Directing his plea to an unidentified 'you' – a figure who represents opposite-sex desiring citizens – Ellenberger describes the ways in which 'normal' people have historically oppressed queer individuals and emphasizes the role that heterosexual people could instead play in queer emancipation. Adopting a reproachful tone, Ellenberger rebukes the 'normal' reader:

> Do you know that the happiness of so many [people] is dependent on your judgement? ... It is a fact that you have never tried to understand! ... You have judged us because you did not understand [us] but you will never understand because you are not like us ... What is unnatural for you is normal [*gewoon*] for us: because we are born that way ... Try to learn a little about us and our lives, then perhaps you can allow us to live in freedom as you do. Try to understand!derzijds[71]

Although many of the articles that were included in the first issue of *We* were aimed at encouraging queer citizens to join the ranks of a nascent organization, this appeal also served an educative function. Unlike the periodicals that became popular in Berlin, which spoke almost exclusively to a queer readership – despite claims to have an educative function when threatened with blacklisting – *We* attempted very clearly to enlighten 'normal' people about the historical oppression of homosexuals. Indeed, published at a time when the sexual networks that *We* strove to emulate had been flourishing in Berlin for many years, the description of same-sex experiences and desires in the magazine remains strikingly caught between the categories of 'normalcy' and 'deviance'. The identitarian terms 'homo-sexueel' and 'Uranier' are rarely deployed in the magazine and, instead, the primary division is drawn between those who are 'normal' and those who are not. Although there was doubtless an attempt to create a sense of collective identity in Amsterdam's first queer periodical – indeed, one need look no further than the title of the magazine for such an insight – it remains initially unclear to whom the collective pronoun 'we' refers. Creating a clear distinction between the reader from outside of the 'circle' (*kring*) and those who were directly affected by the issues presented in *We*, the contributions create a shared sense of being 'pariahs among the people', as one contributor terms it, that trumps all other notions of difference.[72] Interestingly, neither political orientation nor religious faith strongly features in the periodical and, indeed, it appears that the desire to create a network that promotes 'honest and strong friendships' in the magazine transcended any other formation of (male) social identity. The importance of unity in achieving the goal of social acceptance was clearly more important to Ellenberger and François than any moral obligation or allegiance to their own socio-political pillars. Indeed, as contributor C.P reassures readers: 'Who I am, writing this, does not matter ... I am like you ... and that gives me the right and the duty to call myself your friend.'[73]

Mindful of the limitations of drawing conclusions based on such a restricted sample of material, the content of *We* nonetheless stresses some interesting points about the structure of queer groups and identities in Amsterdam during the interwar era. The periodical's attempt to emulate Friedrich Radszuweit's League for Human Rights and Adolf Brand's endorsement of the publication, for instance, indicates that the magazine was familiar with the masculinist discourses fostered by the two German organizations. However, in promoting only the masculinist ideals of 'friendship and freedom', it does not appear that the collective pronoun *We* ever intended to include (feminine) queer women. Indeed, the specific issues faced by queer women during this time are not mentioned anywhere in the magazine. Yet, when the *Empire* café was raided by the vice squad in 1932 and Ellenberger was detained and forced to cease the publication of *We*, what happened to the eighteen women who were also arrested that evening? Had they attended the *Empire* with the intention of joining Ellenberger and François' League for

Human Rights? Did they also consider *We* to be a mouthpiece for women-loving-women? Or did they, like the feminists who signed the petition for equal rights for queer people, attend in support of the emancipation of those men being persecuted? Little is known about the lives of these women or their reasons for being in the *Empire* that evening and such questions remain unanswerable from the scant archival material that exists. Following the raid, and increasingly disillusioned with the lack of support he was receiving from queer people in the Netherlands, Ellenberger attempted, instead, to forge a surprising connection with Jacob Schorer and the NWHK, who supported Hirschfeld's theories on congenital inversion. Despite subscribing to the magazine in advance, Schorer had already predicted the downfall of *We* before its publication. Referring to 'the mentality of "our" people', Schorer considered the Netherlands 'too small' for such a periodical. Nevertheless, he was happy to support new queer endeavours in conjunction with the NWHK committee, so long as the goals of the organizations did not 'overlap'.[74] Looking to the future of the collaboration between *We* and the NWHK, Schorer was clear to set out his desire for visibility over 'discretion', asserting that 'a battle fought under pseudonyms will never have any chance of success'.[75] For Schorer, it was clear that what was needed most to unite disparate groups of queer individuals was for more people to become visible in the campaign for human rights, just as he himself had done. Yet, the visibility of queer desires that Schorer considered fundamental to furthering the movement for emancipation was not a self-evident step for most individuals. The formation of an identity around a shared sense of difference in the magazine *We*, rather than an established practice of self-reflexive identitarian labelling – as can be seen in the magazines *The Girlfriend* and *Women's Love* as early as 1924 – suggests that same-sex desire remained a *crimen nefandum* (unmentionable vice) in the Netherlands even in the 1930s, and was discussed mostly in moral and religious terms.

Following the introduction of Article 248bis to the Dutch Penal Code in 1911 and the establishment of the Dutch Scientific Humanitarian Committee in 1912, a wave of educative articles appeared across the Netherlands, promoting both sides of the campaign to abolish Article 248bis. Even a cursory glance at these documents demonstrates that the development of an identitarian discourse around queerness was much slower to gain traction here than in Germany, which goes some way towards explaining the struggle of journals that were attempting to serve identitarian purposes. In its incipient years, Schorer's NWHK borrowed heavily from the earlier publications of Magnus Hirschfeld's WhK as it attempted to spread its message about the congenital nature of queer desire. The first pamphlet produced by the committee, *What Everybody Should Know about Uranism* (*Wat iedereen behoort te weten omtrent Uranisme*, 1912), was largely a copy of the earlier German publication *Was muss das Volk vom dritten Geschlecht wissen?* (1901). Aside from the obvious distinctions between the titles, the Dutch publication makes several departures from the original document to support the argument that sexual desires did not widely constitute a sexual identity in the Netherlands in this period. In the earlier pamphlet distributed by the WhK, the terms 'Uranism', which described a 'psychic' inversion of the soul, and 'drittes Geschlecht', a term implying a psychic and somatic inversion of gender traits, were considered recognizable enough as descriptors of homosexual desire to go unannotated in the text. However, in the later Dutch version, such terminology was not understood as self-evident for the average lay reader. Glossing their introduction – and title page – with a clarification of the categories upon which the publication was based, the authors state: 'Our goal is to inform the general public more accurately about the true nature of Uranism (= homosexuality = love for members of the same sex).'[76] With further elucidations of the term 'Uranism' dotted throughout the pamphlet, it is clear that such terms and labels remained unfamiliar to the average Dutch reading public for whom this first publication was intended.

Three years after the appearance of the NWHK's *What Everybody Should Know about Uranism*, queer activist and author Joannes Henri François (1884–1948), who later worked with Ellenberger on *We*, published the anonymous *Open Letter to Those Who Are Different, From One of Them* (*Open brief aan hen die anders zijn dan de anderen, door een hunner*, 1915). Under the auspices of the NWHK, over 40,000 copies of the pamphlet were sent to leading figures in the Dutch government, as well as to medical practitioners and editors of several major Dutch newspapers.[77] François' letter, which offered words of support to 'like-minded individuals' across the country, was preceded by an introduction from Felix Ortt (1866–1959), a prominent theorist of the Dutch Christian anarchist movement. In his introduction, Ortt warns the 'normal reader' that the content of the publication would be 'intimate' as 'the writer – homosexual – is speaking to his fellow-homosexuals'.[78] Although Ortt is quick to identify François as 'homosexual' in his introduction, in the following letter, François does not define his desires in such terms. Although he acknowledges a perceptible 'difference' between those who experienced homosexual feelings and those who did not, his letter does not indicate that he himself identified as 'homosexual'. Moreover, the letter is not directed at a 'homosexual' collective, but rather, with a striking lack of specificity, at those who are 'different from the others' (*anders dan de anderen*).[79] Writing primarily about the male 'non-normal', François directs his attention in the final pages of his letter to female 'comrades in feeling' (*gevoels-genoten*). Despite asserting that same-sex desire occurs in women just as frequently as it does in men, François concedes – in a manner that had become typical of the circular way in which male sexologists and writers dismissed the subject of female sexuality – that he knew little about the circumstances of 'women constituted that way' (*zoo-aangelegde vrouwen*) because their existence had been so poorly documented (see Chapter 2). The 'problem' at the root of this lack of evidence, François suggests, was that the 'woman like that' (*zoo-vrouw*) could express her feelings publicly with 'much less difficulty' than her male counterpart, given that 'intimate contact between two women is given far less attention than that between two men'.[80]

The intimacy between women that François alludes to in his letter evokes the image of homosocial networks that existed earlier in the nineteenth century, which have been most comprehensively outlined in Carroll Smith-Rosenberg's article 'The Female World of Love and Ritual' (1975) and Lillian Faderman's *Surpassing the Love of Men* (1981). Focusing on romantic female friendships, Smith-Rosenberg suggests that prior to the medicalization of same-sex desires, there existed a diverse range of social structures and norms that actively encouraged the development of exclusively homosocial environments. These passionate and loving female friendships existed at a time in which romanticism and desire were organized and structured in ways that were independent of the twentieth-century 'sex-pleasure ethic'.[81] Thus, François' assertion that public life was much easier for queer women suggests that similar homosocial structures existed in the Netherlands in the early twentieth century and presented many women with the freedom to articulate desires for the same sex without arousing societal suspicion.[82] In addition, although the category 'homosexual' had gained some traction among experts in the Netherlands by this time – as evidenced by the fact that there is no longer a glossing of terms in Ortt's introduction – there is no indication in François' writing that such a category was used by individuals who desired the same sex to refer to themselves or to a wider queer community.

Reflecting on this discussion of early queer female desires, many of the interviews in Anja van Kooten Niekerk's and Sacha Wijmer's sociological study *The Wrong Kind of Friendship* (*Verkeerde vriendschap*, 1985) confirm the idea that many women did not see their 'non-normative' desires as constituent parts of a social identity during the early twentieth century. Those women who had engaged in same-sex relationships during the first half of the twentieth century distance themselves in the interviews from the term 'lesbian' as it was deployed in the 1980s, when the study was undertaken. In the two interviews with women born between 1905 and 1915, for example, the subjects claim that they would not have described themselves as 'lesbian' in the past and did not describe themselves as 'lesbian' at the time of the interview. While some of the interviewees struggle to unite traditional markers of femininity (such as maternal desires) with the term 'lesbian', others appear uncertain about who had the authority to determine who *is* lesbian and who *is not*. Melanie Wansink, born in 1912, for example, believed her desire to have children precluded her from defining her sexual preferences under the label 'lesbian': 'I'm very much on the border, you know. I'm not really 100% lesbian ... I wanted children an awful lot, so I'm a very dubious case.'[83] Catherine Groenendaal, born in 1913, also avoided the label 'lesbian' because she had been married: 'I'm not lesbian, even though a real lesbian friend of mine says that I am. But I was married for seven years, so I don't know, you [van Kooten Niekerk and Wijmer] should decide.'[84] Summing up the differences between lesbian life in the 1980s and love between women in the 1920s, Maria Verhoeven, born in 1905, suggests more ambiguously: 'I found it more sociable, more intimate, in the old days ... I don't think that you have the same warm and pleasant life that we had. Our life was freer in a way.'[85] The fact that contemporary sexual categorizations were rejected by many of the interviewees to account for their sexual desires in the past (and also at the time of the study) highlights the need to pay closer attention to the discords and inconsistencies in the history of female same-sex desire rather than projecting backwards an image that one infers must have existed in the past. But, in terms of the examination of the materials for this study, the fact that women were not gathering around a name, and did not engage in self-reflexive processes of labelling desires to create broader communities, may go some way towards explaining the discrepancies between the established queer press that was able exist in Berlin and the lack of such pages for women in Amsterdam.

The Right to Live (1940–46)

In 1940, a second queer publication was printed in Amsterdam under the name *The Right to Live* (*Levensrecht*). The political and social significance of a queer magazine emerging during this historical moment is highly remarkable. In the eight years that had passed since *We* had ceased publication, tensions within Europe had escalated to the point of war. By the mid-1930s, fascist powers were firmly established in some of the most economically powerful countries in the continent. Even in the Netherlands, which had managed to maintain a neutral position during the First World War, fascism had become 'a well-organized political force that threatened the fabric of Dutch political pluralism'.[86] After Hitler took power in Germany in 1933, *The Girlfriend* and *Women's Love* were required to cease publication and the vibrant queer nightlife that had made Berlin so (in)famous during the Weimar era was forced underground. The overtly anti-homosexual rhetoric

„Levensrecht"

Maandblad
voor Vriendschap en Vrijheid, onder redactie van Bob Angelo
Redactie en Administratie: Noorderstraat 62, Amsterdam-C.
Postrekening No. 371115 t.n.v. J. H. Diekmann. Abonnementsprijs f 4.— per jaar, buitenland f 5.—. Per halfjaar f 2.50, bij vooruitbetaling. Losse nummers f 0.40.

Een woord vooraf
door BOB ANGELO.

Een nieuw maandblad! Nieuw in meer dan enig opzicht, want zowel de opzet als de strekking zijn een unicum in ons land. Daarin echter mag de verschijning van LEVENSRECHT niet uitsluitend zijn rechtvaardiging vinden. Het uitzonderlijke karakter van het maandblad dat voorjaar 1940 het licht ziet, laat geen twijfel bestaan, naar welke zijde het tribunaal der initiatiefnemers in de eerste plaats gekeerd is. En het is ook van die zijde, dat zij steevast gehoor en solidaire belangstelling verwachten. Het moge een bont legioen zijn van tienduizenden, wier religieuse en staatkundige belijdenis een onontwarbaar kluwen van schier onoverkomelijke verdeeldheid schijnt, even waar is het dat dit legioen boven die verdeeldheid uit een heimelijk teken heeft en overeenkomstige idealen ronddraagt. Is voor de subjectief belanghebbenden een eigen maandblad, dat „vlees van hun vlees en bloed van hun bloed" is, niet meer en minder dan het geestelijk verzamelpunt, van waaruit zij als legionairs in de strijd om levensgeluk levensrecht moeten vestigen?

Heeft anderzijds het leven dier anderen niet tal van facetten, die het bestaan van een eigen maandblad rechtvaardigen? En ligt tenslotte in de rijkdom der geestelijke nalatenschap van een Socrates, Plato, Shakespeare, Oscar Wilde, Platen Winckelmann, Verlaine, Rimbaud en andere reuzen uit het rijk van den geest, niet zoveel schoons dat het plicht blijft ook „deze liefde", mysterieus en onwezenlijk schijnend, recht te doen wedervaren?

En wie zullen zich het recht op het leven, zoals dat in hen ontstaan is, laten ontnemen?

Een farizeësche 20 eeuwse beschaving mag nog zo knap jongleren met de begrippen goed en kwaad, zedelijk en onzedelijk, haar strijd tegen een kleine minderheid eindigt altijd in een Pyrrhusoverwinning. En geen vervolging kan zo wreed zijn, geen uitsluiting zo afdoende of de Eros der „anderen" herrijst ongeschonden uit de solfer van vernietiging en verguizing.

Een niet begrijpende meerderheid, irrationeel voorgelicht en voortgedreven kan zich herhaaldelijk te buiten gaan aan Don Quichotterie, de wieken van 't eeuwig wentelende leven in al zijn variëteit,

1

Figure 4.7. Cover Image for *The Right to Live*, 1940. IHLIA, used with permission.

that had gained traction during Hitler's rise to power was legitimated further following the assassination of the leader of the Nazi Sturmabteilung (SA), Ernst Röhm, who was rumoured to have had affairs with men. When war broke out in 1939, the Netherlands declared itself, once again, to be neutral. Yet, on 10 May 1940, the Wehrmacht invaded and took control of the country. Only two months prior to this invasion, a second attempt had been made to bring together queer people under the banner of science and justice in order to fight for the 'right to live'.

In many respects, *The Right to Live* can be considered the successor of the earlier publication *We*. Both François, who now published under the pseudonym Charley van Heezen, and Jaap van Leeuwen (1892–1978), who published under the pseudonym Arent van Santhorst, had been involved with the production of the first publication. Dismissing Schorer's earlier warnings, François and van Leeuwen remained determined to demonstrate the potential of an educative medium that brought together a disparate community. Irrespective of the continued anonymity of many of its contributors; *The Right to Live*, they argued, was 'necessary enlightenment'.[87] Although the editors had clear didactic aims for the magazine, a new attempt to create a queer community was strategized through the combination of 'education and entertainment'.[88] This approach was pioneered by radical socialist and editor of *The Right to Live* Niek/Nico Engelschman (1913–88), who later launched the social and political group the Centre for Culture and Leisure (Cultuur en Ontspanningscentrum, COC) in 1946, which still plays an important function within the queer communities of Amsterdam in the present day. Engelschman (who wrote under the pseudonym Bob Angelo) was further supported by van Leeuwen – who, as Engelschman claimed, was 'the brain' of the organization – and Johan Diekman (1896–1986), who was financially responsible for the publication and print of the periodical.[89] Engelschman had worked closely with the Dutch vice squad to help identify pornographic material and, in this way, believed himself capable of ensuring that his publication did not meet the same premature end as *We*.[90] Although van Leeuwen had been a friend of Jacob Schorer and a member of the NWHK since 1920, *The Right to Live* was not affiliated with the organization. Following Hirschfeld's motto *per scientiam ad justitiam*, Schorer and the NWHK were resolute in the belief that only scientific study could bring about the emancipation of queer people, and Schorer rejected most endeavours to establish social groups. As reader letters were not printed in the magazine, it is not possible to track the level of engagement readers may have had with the content or to gauge an appraisal of its themes. However, by April 1940, there appear to have been 110 subscribers, which had risen to 190 by May. The diversity of this readership was alluded to in an editorial in the third issue of the publication, which declared that *The Right to Live* had received countless 'colourful and varied' letters from readers 'from different places and from many milieus'.[91]

The three copies of *The Right to Live* to appear in 1940 were each sixteen pages in length and could be purchased in 'single copies' (*losse nummers*) for 40 cents or as part of a subscription for 4 guilders per year. Production costs for *The Right to Live*, according to Engelschman, were covered by Diekman, about whom little is known. The annual subscription costs and voluntary donations made by financial supporters also helped the magazine to stay afloat. The initials of these benefactors appeared on the final page of each issue, alongside the total figure that they had donated. To make the magazine accessible to a broader readership, a quarterly price of 1 guilder and 25 cents was introduced, presumably to break up an expensive subscription. Unlike *We*, which had been focused on the activities of queer people within the Netherlands, *The Right to Live* was keen to emphasize its international outlook, by revealing a desire to reach readers with a knowledge of Dutch across national borders.[92] A report from the editorial board in the third issue of the magazine claims that international readership figures had risen after a promotional article about *The Right to Live* had appeared in the Swiss homosexual periodical, *Human Rights*.[93] In terms of its content, *The Right to Live* consisted primarily of literary contributions and serial stories, reprints and extracts from novels, political calls to action, and news from the editorial board. The magazine also discussed historical figures, such as Shakespeare, Michelangelo and Walt Whitman, in what can be considered an early attempt in Dutch queer activism to 'recover' figures from history, a method that had also been employed by queer magazines in Germany. With articles and literary items frequently 'borrowed' from other sources, the magazine can hardly be considered an original creative contribution, despite the calls for new content that were printed by the editorial board. Yet, while the magazine remained a form of 'bricolage' throughout its existence, the assortment of articles it reproduced nonetheless enable us to trace some of the theoretical frameworks that structured *The Right to Live* and the objectives of its editorial board.[94]

The article 'The Theory of Mutation and Its Significance for Our Society', for instance, was printed as an abridged form of a lecture presented by Professor Dr T.J. Stomps at the University of Amsterdam in 1935. In it, psychoanalytical theories of queer desire, such as those disseminated by Sigmund Freud and H.J. Groenewegen, are declared to be 'completely worthless'.[95] Stomps describes 'the problem of homosexuality' as a problem of 'intersexuality' (*intersexualiteit*), a phenomenon that was neither 'mysterious' (*geheimzinnig*) nor 'shameful' (*schandelijk*), but one for which society should have sympathy. Those who are affected by homosexual impulses,

Stomps argues, must forgo the highest of social experiences which gives life its purpose: 'the founding of a family'.[96] Referring to studies on the eye colour of banana flies to demonstrate that gene mutation can cause variations in plants, insects and humans, Stomps' proposal that homosexuality was 'not acquired ... but inborn' builds on the position that had already been adopted in the earlier periodical *We*, when Ellenberger defiantly claimed that 'normal' people could not understand the lives of queer individuals as they had not been 'born that way'.[97] The publication of an article that dismisses psychoanalytical theories of homosexuality also lends support to the idea of the shift towards sexological theories of somatic inversion that had been taking place in the Netherlands since the late 1930s, as was discussed in Chapter 2.

In the article 'An Open Response to a Secret Correspondence' in the second issue of the publication, the editorial staff take the anonymous 'N.N.' to task for a letter sent to the magazine claiming that queer people were a 'mistake of nature'.[98] The editors place their emphasis not only on the congenital nature of same-sex desires by claiming that 'nature does not act unnaturally', but also point to the natural existence of an 'infinite series of transitions'.[99] Although *We* did not engage with the theory of sex-gender inversion – further evidence, perhaps, that the magazine's agenda was more closely aligned with those of the League for Human Rights and the Community of the Special who had forcefully rejected the image of the 'Zwitter' – the editors of *The Right to Live* drew theories of intermediary states to promote a polymorphous image of sexual identity that was congenital rather than acquired: 'no two leaves from a tree, no two human thumbs are the same. It would be a supernatural wonder if sexuality revealed itself to be uniform in nature'.[100] The article further acknowledges the existence of queer male femininities, although the author chides such men for not standing up to heterosexuals who threaten them: 'homosexuals are all too inclined, on account of their timid feminine disposition, to nod rapidly "yes" even when the biggest lot of twaddle is being barked at them by some "bloke"'.[101] In general, *The Right to Live* appears to have had a much stronger focus on the 'unsolvable riddle' (*onoplosbaar raadsel*) of the nature and origins of homosexual behaviours than its predecessor, suggesting a departure from frameworks of normative/non-normative behaviours to an understanding of sexual preferences that considered 'heterosexuality' and 'homosexuality' as established social and sexual categories.

But it was not until van Leeuwen – writing under the pseudonym Arent van Santhorst – published a review of Benno Stokvis' anthology *The Homosexuals* for the readers of *The Right to Live*, that queer women became visible in a Dutch magazine meant for same-sex desiring readers for the first time. The popularity of Stokvis' text, as well as the growing numbers of

Boekbespreking

Serie „Menschenleed" (deel I) 35 Autobiographieën.
Verz. en ingel. door Mr. Dr. B e n n o J. S t o k v i s.
Uitgave „De Tijdstroom". Lochem 1939. — ƒ 5.90.

De Homosexueelen

„Nous traiterons chez vous, de vous, sans vous," beet de Abbé de Polignac den vertegenwoordigers van de verslagen Republiek der Vereenigde Nederlanden bewustbeleedigend toe bij de vredesonderhandelingen te Utrecht in 1712. De gemakkelijke houding van de brute overmacht tegenover den zwakke.
Zoo was tot nu toe vrijwel altijd en overal de houding van de meerderheid in alle rangen en standen tegenover onze kleine minderheid en ook de man van wetenschap bleef niet vrij van deze allure ondanks het feit dat wetenschap niet rekenen mag met vooroordeel wil deze niet in-boeten aan waarde.
Wetenschapbeoefenaars die op bevooroordeeld standpunt staan — pro of contra een bepaalde zienswijze dat doet er niet toe — verhinderen dikwijls de oplossing van de problemen of werken althans remmend.
Hoe vaak zien wij niet, vooral in de onderhavige kwestie, dat een man, overigens wellicht van hoogstaand karakter, aan zijn schrijfbureau plaats neemt en een omvangrijk werk entameert over het onderwerp zonder voorafgaand onderzoek. Hij schrijft dan vanuit een standpunt, dat bepaald wordt door eigen beperkt inzicht of maatschappelijk vooroordeel. De zaken moeten blijven zoals zij nu eenmaal gegroeid zijn en wat in den weg staat dient opgeruimd. Voor afwijkend gevoelen geen plaats!
Niet alzoo Mr. Dr. Benno J. Stokvis.
Als echt-wetenschappelijk man begon hij met onderzoek in te stellen aan de bron zelve. Objectief de feiten te laten spreken, te ordenen, te rangschikken. Niet de werkelijkheid geweld aan te doen doch deze onbevangen onder de oogen te zien. En ziehier als resultaat het hierboven geciteerde prachtwerk, dat wij met ontroering lazen en vanaf deze plaats een ieder raden, aan te schaffen. Voor onze menschen bevat het een schat van gegevens en in elk van de 35 autobiographieën zullen zij elementen aantreffen, die ook deel uitmaken van hun eigen leven.
De schrijver bepaalde zich ertoe op een werk van 200 blz. een inleiding te schrijven van 32 blz. gevolgd door 7 blz. aanhalingen

12

Figure 4.8. Book Review for Benno Stokvis' *The Homosexuals* in *The Right to Live*, 1940. IHLIA, used with permission.

novels published about queer desires, the press reports of the moral scandal in The Hague in 1936 and the Dutch East Indies in 1939, and the increasing number of anti-homosexual religious pamphlets, led to a heightened level of social visibility for male homosexual desire within Dutch society.[102] And Stokvis' text in particular (see Chapter 2) offered visibility to the issues of queer women unlike any Dutch publication had ever done before. Yet, in spite of this increased visibility, or perhaps as a direct result of it, there developed a growing sense of isolation for the 'zoo-vrouw', a paradox that van Leeuwen approaches with sympathetic consideration in his review of Stokvis' work:

> On the subject of women: nothing but praise. Without exception, we read her biographies with extreme interest. That it is for them, precisely as it is 'comme chez nous', was a revelation to us and increased our sympathy for this group of women, for whom it will frequently be even more difficult than it is for us, because there exist far fewer connections between them.[103]

Although he does not dwell on the matter further or consider how his own magazine might be used to create such connections, van Leeuwen alludes to the increasingly organized male homosexual subculture that had developed in Amsterdam by 1940, as well as the lack of women who were unable to, or did not want to, engage with such networks. As illustrated by the successful existence of *The Right to Live*, a growing scientific interest in the more 'visible' somatic invert in the Netherlands, as well as the rising number of cafés and meeting points that were being established for queer people, there was a growing social understanding of what it meant to 'be' a homosexual person by the 1940s. However, the rising acknowledgement of female homosexual desire within Dutch society meant that same-sex intimacies between women had suddenly been pushed outside of the 'natural' homosocial order into a more pathologized and suspect sphere, where intimacy between women – particularly when combined with gender deviance – could result in negative social consequences. The fact that the biographies about the experiences of queer women were a 'surprise' for van Leeuwen also suggests that women did not form part of the groups or organizations that existed for queer men, discussed earlier in this chapter.

In many respects, the ways in which 'the sexes and their pleasures' were organized in the Netherlands in the first half of the twentieth century was little removed from the world of 'love and ritual' that Smith-Rosenberg has described in her pioneering article on nineteenth-century female romantic friendships.[104] Homosocial networks continued to thrive in the early twentieth century in Dutch contexts, and the 'private' and 'public' spheres remained the traditional domains of women and men respectively, even after the Second World War. The notion that intimate networks of women who did not self-reflexively define their behaviours as 'lesbian' or 'homosexual' existed during the beginning of the interwar era suggests that sexological categories of homosexual desire did not – and cannot – accurately reflect the vicissitudes of Dutch women's same-sex experiences before 1940, exactly as van Leeuwen's comments on Stokvis' study implies. This changing of the tide is also reflected in the editors' understanding of the position of queer Dutch subjects within a new world order. While an admiration for German queer subcultures is visible across the articles published in *We*, the editors of *The Right to Live* are no longer envious of the German 'volksgeest'. Instead, they remark only on their good fortune to live in a land 'where this enlightenment is still possible'.[105]

Conclusions

In this chapter, I have attempted to bring to the fore some of the key press discourses that were available to Dutch women during the interwar period. While no magazine existed for queer women during this time, a fact that has encouraged the image of lesbian desire as a 'Silent Conspiracy' in the Netherlands for the first half of the twentieth century, I have argued that there is still much to learn about queer self-image forming through other types of community-based magazines such as *Beatrice* and *The Young Woman*. By bringing large communities of women together to form safe spaces to discuss issues pertaining to the female sex, these periodicals formed much of the reading material that would have been accessible to queer women and, as such, would likely have exerted more influence on formations of queer identity than has hitherto been appreciated. Frequently conflating femininity with ideals of domesticity and maternalism, these periodicals mirror many of the dominant social discourses that were shaping women's social imaginaries. However, as I have argued in the first half of this chapter, these women's magazines did not deal exclusively in the conservative moralizing value systems of their time. As I hope to have demonstrated, both *Beatrice* and *The Young Woman* offered their readers a vital space to challenge prevailing norms and consider alternative forms of femininity for themselves. Striving to find ways in which the ideals of 'True Womanhood' might be integrated into more modern gendered landscapes, the discourses made available to women in these magazines take up several of the concerns that were of interest to women authors who wrote about queer topics. As we shall see in the final part of this book, maternalism, class, and the struggle between desire and respectability were of great importance to queer women writers. Moreover, the fact that such weekly or monthly newspapers could provide women with a sense of community would no doubt have been especially appreciated by queer women, given that the organizations that did exist in the Netherlands for queer individuals were run almost exclusively by and for men.

As significant instruments in the processes of recognition, identification and desire, queer periodicals in Germany and the Netherlands drew on a wide range of social, literary and scientific discourses to create continually evolving community-based knowledges and 'truths' about same-sex experiences. These periodicals were used both to educate the public about the nature of queer people and to act as testing grounds for women to explore their desires, and to create identities that were meaningful and recognizable to like-minded individuals. The development of queer media in Berlin and Amsterdam highlights important differences in the processes of Sapphic self-fashioning in the two cities. The change in the circulation of newspapers in Berlin from subscription to on-street purchase, as well as the growth of district newspapers and a burgeoning homosexual club culture, facilitated the growth of minority publications that were supported by and disseminated among established homosexual groups. However, the content printed in these periodicals demonstrates that no single or universal opinion existed as to what it meant to be a woman-who-desired-women in this period. While the magazines produced by the BfM focused primarily on political engagement and the replication of bourgeois rituals to ensure the incorporation of homosexual people into heterosexual paradigms, those of the DFV were formed around Hirschfeld's theory of sexual intermediaries and influenced by a growing consumer culture that had emerged in the German metropolis. The finer points of the publications highlight subtle but important differences between the process of identity building in Berlin's lesbian subculture, and stress the disconnect that took place between the aims of the publication and the experiences and desires of the reader. Nonetheless, the establishment of queer magazines for women meant that female readers could share experiences, build communities (both real and imagined), and create truths and knowledges that the whole world might acknowledge.[106]

In the Netherlands, the legacy of the newspaper stamp, the process of direct subscription, the lack of newspaper kiosks in Amsterdam, and the growing presence of the vice squad meant that the establishment of a Dutch queer press was hindered from the start. Moreover, the NWHK – the only recognized Dutch organization campaigning for the emancipation of homosexual people – believed that emancipation could only be achieved through scientific enlightenment, which meant they rejected most forms of social community building. The lack of such a social group arguably hampered the development of a 'pink press' in the Netherlands further. However, setting matters of queer socialising aside, the invisibility of female homosexual experiences in the Netherlands resulted in the experiences of same-sex desiring women being overlooked in the publication of *We*, which focused instead on 'non-normative' and masculine men. The absence of women in the later publication *The Right to Live* suggests that, even at a time when male homosexual organizations were becoming more established in Amsterdam, queer women were still yet to organize socially or politically around a sexual label or name in the same way as queer male subjects. The suggestion that networks of same-sex desiring women, who did not self-reflexively define their behaviours as lesbian or homosexual, existed during the beginning of the interwar era points to the need for alternative approaches to understand the significance of female same-sex desire to women in the Netherlands during this period. These approaches, up to now, have remained unexplored. The sociopolitical and cultural shifts that resulted in the increased visibility of lesbian desire after the 1930s underlines, however, the fragility of earlier homosocial structures, particularly within the wider context of the increasingly conservative social and political debates on 'immoral behaviour' that took place in Dutch interwar society. By continuing to look more closely at what the silences and omissions in queer history might tell us, a more comprehensive understanding of the historic configurations and organizations of female same-sex desire in the Netherlands might be possible in the future.

Notes

1. Trans.: 'Het is er! "Wij – een blad voor óns. Eindelijk!"', *Wij*, 10 September 1932, p. 4.
2. Trans.: 'Dit blad is voor de Martha's en voor de Maria's, voor de jonge vrouw en voor de ervaren moeder, voor alle rang en stand, voor iederen leeftijd, want alle vrouwen zullen er in terugvinden, wat alle Katholieke vrouwen vereenigd houdt: huishoudelijkheid, karaktervastheid en zin voor het goede', *Beatrijs*, 5 January 1939, p. 1.
3. Lotte Jensen, *Bij uitsluiting voor de vrouwelijke sekse geschikt: Vrouwentijdschriften en journalistes in Nederland in de achttiende en negentiende eeuw* (Hilversum: Verloren, 2001), p. 288.
4. Trans.: 'De beschrijving en afbeelding van allerhande soorten van vrouwelijke handwerken'; 'eenige lektuur, over onderwerpen uit den vrouwelijken kring', https://www.kb.nl/themas/tijdschriften/penelope (retrieved 23 April 2022).
5. Jensen, *Bij uitsluiting voor de vrouwelijke sekse geschikt*, p. 289.
6. Ibid.
7. Ibid.
8. David Machin and Theo van Leeuwen, *Global Media Discourse: A Critical Introduction* (New York: Routledge, 2007), p. 31.
9. Ibid.

10. See Stanley Fish, *Is There a Text in This Class? The Authority of Interpretive Communities* (Cambridge, MA: Harvard University Press, 1980).
11. Margaret Beetham, *A Magazine of Her Own? Domesticity and Desire in the Woman's Magazine 1880–1914* (New York: Routledge, 1996), p. 5.
12. Deidre Beddoe, *Back to Home and Duty: Women between the Wars, 1918–1939* (London: Pandora, 1989), p. 8.
13. Machin and Leeuwen, *Global Media Discourse*, p. 31
14. Ibid.
15. Fiona Anne Seaton Hackney, '"They Opened up a Whole New World": Feminine Modernty and the Feminine Imagination in Women's Magazines 1919–1939', unpublished doctoral thesis (London: Goldsmith's College, 2010), p. 12.
16. Ibid.
17. Deborah Chambers, 'The Women's Pages: Women, Journalism, and Mid-20th-Century Mainstream Newspapers'in Karen Ross, Ingrid Bachmann, Valentina Cardo, Sujata Moorti and Cosmio Marco Scarcelli (eds), *The International Encyclopedia of Gender, Media, and Communication* (Chichester: Wiley-Blackwell, 2020).
18. Ros Ballaster, Margaret Beetham, Elizabeth Frazer and Sandra Hebron, *Women's Worlds: Ideology, Femininity and the Woman's Magazine* (London: Macmillan, 1991), p. 172.
19. The full titles of the magazines are as follows: *De jonge vrouw: geillustreerd christelijk tijdschrift voor de vrouwelijke jeugd ter voorbereiding van de taak der vrouw in huis en maatschappij* and *Beatrijs: katholiek weekblad voor de vrouw*. Subsequent references will use the abridged name found in the main text.
20. Given that this study focuses on texts written before 1940, I have had to limit my analysis of newspapers to the period before this time. This means that I examined each issue of *Beatrice* published between the years 1939 and 1940, while drawing on a selective number of issues – one per month for each year of its print run – from the catalogue of *The Young Woman*.
21. Trans.: 'om mens te zijn, om christen te zijn, of om jezelf te zijn'; 'schermde zijn bewoners af van de corrumperende maatschappelijke strijd om rijkdom en macht en de aantrekkingskracht van revolutie'. Anna P.H. Geurts, 'Elders thuis. Noord-Nederlandse reizigers in Europese steden, 1815–1914', in Inge Bertels et al. (eds), *Tussen beleving en verbeelding: de stad in de negentiende-eeuwse literatuur* (Leuven: Universitaire Pers Leuven, 2013), p. 267.
22. Trans.: 'de mogelijkheid één plek op aarde helemaal naar wens in te richten'. Ibid., p. 268.
23. Trans.: 'opkomende beroep'; 'het kenmerk van een goede vrouw'. Ibid.
24. Sylvia Holla and Antia Wiersma, 'Serving Morality on a Platter: Moral Imperatives and Cultural Repertoires in Writings on Food in the Dutch Women's Magazine *Margriet*', in Bettina Bock and Jessica Duncan (eds), *Gendered Food Practices from Seed to Waste: Yearbook of Women's History* (Hilversum: Verloren, 2017), p. 168.
25. See Barbara Welter, 'The Cult of True Womanhood: 1820–1860', *American Quarterly* 18(2), 154–74.
26. Meredith G.F. Worthen, *Sexual Deviance and Society: A Sociological Examination* (New York: Routledge, 2016), p. 101.
27. Trans.: 'Het eenige katholieke damesweekblad.' This was the subline that was placed on the cover of the magazine in 1939. It was then replaced with 'Katholiek weekblad voor de vrouw' between 1940 and 1946.
28. The publishing house did not distinguish between editors of different magazines, as writers produced content for the various magazines that were produced there.

29. Joan Hemels, *Het geïllustreerde tijdschrift in Nederland: Bron van kennis en vermaak, lust voor het oog: bibliografie* (Amsterdam: Otto Cramwinckel, 1997), p. 365.
30. Trans.: 'Libelle, Margriet en Beatrijs werden in eerste plaats uitgegeven en geproduceerd om winst te maken. Deze rol van commercie in het bestaan en voortbestaan van die drie vrouwenbladen is een gegeven.' Marloes Hülsken, *Kiezen voor kinderen. Vrouwentijdschriften en hun lezeressen over het katholieke huwelijksleven, 1950–1975* (Hilversum: Verloren, 2010), p. 49.
31. Trans.: 'degelijk, katholiek, prakties [sic], alzijdig vrouwenweekblad', *Beatrijs*, 5 January 1939, p. 1.
32. Trans.: 'Is er voor ons vrouwen een gezelliger pretje te bedenken dan een middag genoeglijk winkelen met net genoeg geld op zak om niet wanhopig te worden van al die "spotkoopjes", die we moeten laten liggen, en net weinig genoeg bij ons om geen gekke dingen te koopen, die we toch niet kunnen gebruiken of misschien over een jaar pas noodig hebben?' *Beatrijs*, 13 July 1939, p. 5.
33. Trans.: 'de reusachtige bouquetten, die we dit jaar op onze soepele zomerstoffen zien gedrukt en die op het oogenblik zeer en vogue zijn, loopen zeer veel kans een volgend jaar niet meer zoo hoog in de gunst van Vrouw Mode te staan'. Ibid., p. 6.
34. Trans.: 'de aardige gezichtjes'; 'de elegante kapseltjes'; 'mooie oogen'; 'Het is prachtisch, gemakkelijk aan te trekken en lekker warm, maar daar zijn de goede eigenschappen dan ook mee opgenoemd. Men kan onmogelijk beweren, dat het flatteus staat. Het is een donkere wollen zak, waarin het heele vrouwelijke schoon verdwijnt'. *Beatrijs*, 7 December 1939, p. 24.
35. Trans.: 'dus: moed en vertrouwen! Het eeuwig vrouwelijke zal ook deze zware tijden te boven komen'. Ibid., p. 25.
36. Trans.: 'Zoo onelegant hun uniform is, zoo gemakkelijk en comfortabel is het in het dragen. Ook de helm is als een veer zoo licht, want hij is gemaakt van kurk, die met donkerblauwe stof bekleed is'. *Beatrijs*, 14 September 1939, p. 25.
37. Trans.: 'zooals men uit het bovenstaande reeds heeft kunnen begrijpen, hanteeren deze vrouwen geen geweren of handgranaten, zij doen alleen specifiek vrouwelijke bezigheden als zieken verplegen, eten koken voor de soldaten en allen arbeid, die een vrouw van nature nu eenmaal beter ligt dan een man'. *Beatrijs*, 20 July 1939, p. 17.
38. Trans.: 'Lennard, de oudste, is een sportieve, vroolijke jongen. David is een droomerig, gevoelig kind, dat noch door zijn ouders noch door andere menscheen goed begrepen wordt.' *Beatrijs*, 3 August 1939, p. 13.
39. Trans.: 'Eén boezemvriend had hij gekregen: Roy Sunderland, den knappen, verwenden rakker.' *Beatrijs*, 17 August 1939, p. 18.
40. Trans.: 'David vond haar het mooiste van de heele wereld. Ze had zulke groote donkere oogen en van dat leuke korte golvende haar, en ze had zulke mooie kleeren aan. Hij was benieuwd, hoe haar japon vanavond voelde. Hij sloop éen beetje dichter bij, en stak zijn hand uit om de roomkleurige stof aan te raken, 't Was zacht en koel.' *Beatrijs*, 3 August 1939, p. 19.
41. For a compelling and comprehensive history of transgender lives from the 1950s to the present day in the Netherlands, see Alex Bakker, *Transgender: Een buitengewone geschiedenis in Nederland* (Amsterdam: Boom, 2018).
42. Trans.: 'een onécht leven … een onsmakelijke leven'. *Beatrijs*, 14 September 1939, p. 15.
43. Scotland is an interesting choice for the depiction of a Catholic haven, given the anti-Irish sentiment that was rising in certain areas. See Chris Bambery, *A People's History of Scotland* (London: Verso, 2014), p. 173.
44. Trans: 'de illustratie's nog veel mooier zullen uitkomen'. *De Jonge Vrouw*, October 1931, p. 36.

45. Marjan Groot, *Vrouwen in de vormgeving in Nederland 1880–1940* (Rotterdam: Uitgeverij 010, 2007), p. 310.
46. Trans.: 'het *goedkoopste* en *beste* tijdschrift voor de christenvrouw in Nederland'. *De Jonge Vrouw*, August 1924, p. 1.
47. Trans.: '*De Jonge Vrouw* is een succes. Dit maandschrift, aantrekkelijk naar inhoud en uiterlijk, brengt de christenvrouw de boodschap voor háár tijd en doet dat in een vorm, die steeds weer opnieuw bekoort.' Ibid.
48. Trans.: 'keurig uitgegeven en met smaak verzorgd'. *De Jonge Vrouw*, February 1925, p. 1.
49. Trans.: 'In de verschillende afleveringen vinden we artikelen over de Engelsche meisjeskostscholen, over bekende kamerplanten, over weven en andere practische dingen, over keukengeheimen … korte meditatie, boekenschouw, correspondentie van de Redactie, een onderlinge-correspondentie afdeeling verzen, mededeeling van nieuws uit eigen kring, raadsels, illustraties. Het tijdschrift is keurig uitgegeven en in al zijn onderdeelen met smaak verzorgd.' Ibid.
50. Trans.: 'Als paarlen zoo kostbaar, ja kostbaarder nog, zijn Uw tanden, Bedenk wat zij beteekenen voor Uw gezondheid, voor Uw schoonheid.' *De Jonge Vrouw*, December 1927, p. 8.
51. Trans.: 'Wie wil er nu graag oud zijn? Een glans van vergenoegen komt over uw gezicht, wanneer men u in vollen ernst zegt, dat ge er nog zoo jong uitziet. Het is hier de plaats niet, naar de diepere oorzaken van dit verschijnsel te zoeken; wij wijzen alleen op het feit.' *De Jonge Vrouw*, June 1926, p. 212.
52. Trans.: 'Je laatste brief geeft er wel blijk van, dat je zelfstandigheidsgevoel in den laatsten tijd zich zéér ontwikkeld heeft. Toos wil dit niet en Toos wil dat niet. Dit is niets voor Toos en dat vindt Toos niet leuk. En toen tante je brief las, schudde ze haar hoofd en zei: … Och, och, wat zal die Toos nog veel moeten leeren … Natuurlijk heb je je idealen, 't Zou niet goed zijn, als je ze niet had. Maar denk er aan, Toos, dat wij niet altijd onze idealen kunnen bereiken.' *De Jonge Vrouw*, August 1926, p. 280.
53. Trans.: 'Ach, we hebben zoo weinig *moeders* meer. Hoe willen de kinderen deze *moeders* liefhebben? Laten de moeders weer *moeders* zijn, dan is er de kinderliefde ook wel weer.' *De Jonge Vrouw*, November 1926, p. 260.
54. Trans.: 'niets aan doen kan zoo leelijk te zijn geworden'. *De Jonge Vrouw*, May 1926, p. 28.
55. Trans.: 'Hans geeft een verdediging van Lo, verder vindt ze 't rooken voor vrouwen afschuwelijk. Wildzang en Stormvogel zijn het met de blauwkousen reuze eens. Vera vindt het heelemaal niet vreemd, dat Lo naar het uiterlijk van Annie kijkt. Uit de kleeding van een meisje en uit wat ze doet spreekt immers haar karakter. Meisjes, die haar mooie haar offeren voor een modegril vindt Vera niet verstandig.' *De Jonge Vrouw*, September 1926, p. 287.
56. Trans.: 'ik vind het wel wat overdreven dat Lo eerst Annie niet wil vragen omdat zij bobbed hair heeft … mijn ideaal zou hij niet zijn'. *De Jonge Vrouw*, November 1926, p. 264.
57. Trans.: 'misschien zal de redactie mij, een der "heeren geen plaats willen geven in deze rubriek, die alleen voor de damens is bestemd'; 'maar ik wil het er toch op wagen'. *De Jonge Vrouw*, November 1928, p. 286.
58. Trans.: 'Ik lees van bioscoopsbezoek en bobbedhaar … En als ik dan eens om mij heen kijk, en ik zie al die meisjes in hun moderne kleeding en ik merk, dat ze eigenlijk zoo'n beetje minachtend op het werk van de huisvrouw neerzien, dan weet ik het niet of het zoo wel een goede weg is.' Ibid., 287.

59. Trans.: 'Wij doen er het zwijgen toe en wij laten gaarne onze lezeressen aan 't woord. Wij hopen van harte, dat Johan er van langs zal krijgen, maar handelt zachtkens met den jongeling.' Ibid.
60. Trans.: 'van de onweersbui die boven je hoofd is losgebarsten, krijg je nu pas de eerste dropjes'; 'Zet je paraplu maar op wanneer 't volgende nummer uitkomt'. *De Jonge Vrouw*, December 1928, p. 336.
61. Trans.: 'het heeft me verwonderd dat een "heer" ook zelfs "bij uitzondering" werd toegelaten. Ik vind, een heer past niet in dit hoekje en dan vooral niet een heer, met zoo'n houding als Johan aanneemt'. Ibid.
62. Trans.: 'De meeste broers doen net als "onze" Johan: ze beginnen met "hooggeachte dames!" en 't eind van 't lied is dat ze je ongenadig op je kop zitten!' *De Jonge Vrouw*, February 1930, p. 160.
63. Corroborating Ellenberger's memories of the event, there is a date of 10 September 1932 on the final page of the magazine. Trans.: 'Wij meenden dat wij met een eigen orgaan beter dan tot dusverre in staat zouden zijn, de verkeerde opvattingen, die omtrent homosexualiteit bij nog zoo heel veel menschen bestaan te bestrijden. Tevens meenden wij hierdoor een inniger contact met andere homosexueelen te zullen verkrijgen. In September 1932 kwam inderdaad het eerste (tevens helaas het laatste) nummer van "Wij" tot stand.' Benno Stokvis, *De homosexueelen* (Lochem: De Tijdstroom, 1939), p. 101.
64. Brand's published the first queer anarchist magazine, *Der Eigene*, in 1896. Brand was a proponent of Greek forms of eros, particularly pederastic ideals. *Der Eigene* was frequently censored on account of the nude images and its 'kitsch' literary contributions. Brand even served a short prison sentence for morality charges relating to the magazine. Benedict Friedlaender, another supporter of 'Greek love', was the main financial contributor to *Der Eigene*. See Robert Beachy, *Gay Berlin: Birthplace of a Modern Identity* (New York: Vintage Books, 2014), pp. 100–10.
65. Trans.: 'eenige vrienden, die met dezen opzet sympathiseerden'. *Wij*, 1932, p. 8.
66. Trans.: 'Laten wij er ons van bewust worden, dat wij bij elkaar hooren, dat ons leven beter en mooier is als wij het te zamen leven … En laten wij daarom ervoor zorgen dat dit ONS blad gedijt! … Wij moeten ernstig trachten ons krachtig te maken door saamhoorigheid. En als dit maandblad er toe kan bijdragen ons deze saamhoorigheid meer en meer te doen gevoelen, dan kan het ons in ons niet altijd gemakkelijk leven wellicht een goeden steun zijn.' L., 'Wij in den vreemde', *Wij*, pp. 7–8.
67. Ibid., p. 7.
68. Ibid.
69. Adolf Brand's endorsement stated: 'I congratulate you on this idea and I wholeheartedly wish your new association and your new magazine a resounding success, which, due to its social influence, will make the repeated persecution of homosexuals in Holland simply impossible!' Trans.: 'Ich beglückwünsche Sie zu dieser Idee und wünsche Ihrer neuen Vereinigung und Ihrer neuen Zeitschrift von ganze Herzen einen durchschlagenden Erfolg, der in Zukunft die Wiederholung von Homoerotenverfolgungen in Holland durch seinen gesellschaftlichen Einfluss einfach unmöglich machen muss!'. *Wij*, 1932, p. 5.
70. Trans.: 'Wij allen gevoelen het gemis aan eenheid en sterke eerlijke vriendschapsbanden onder ons die door gebrek aan inzicht der maatschappij min of meer als uitgestooten zijn te beschouwen'. C.P., 'Vrienden!', *Wij*, 1932, p. 5.
71. Trans.: 'Weet ge, dat het geluk van zoo velen van Uw meening afhankelijk is? … Een feit is het, dat ge nimmer hebt getracht, te begrijpen! … Ge hebt veroordeeld omdat ge niet begreept en ge zult het ook nimmer begrijpen, omdat gij niet zóó zijn als wij … Wat

voor U onnatuurlijk is, is voor ons gewoon; omdat wij zoo zijn geboren ... Tracht iets van ons en ons leven te weten te komen, misschien kunt gij ons dan toestaan in vrijheid te leven zooals gij. Tracht te begrijpen!' J.E., 'Tracht te begrijpen! Aan allen die normaal zijn', *Wij*, 1932, p. 6.

72. Trans.: 'Als paria's onder de menschen', *Wij*, 1932, p. 3.
73. Trans.: 'Wie ik ben, die dit schrijft doet niets ter zake ... Ik ben als Gij ... en dat geeft mij het recht en den plicht mij Uw Vriend te noemen.' C.P., 'Aan allen!', *Wij*, 1932, p. 12.
74. Rob Tielman, 'Schorer en het Nederlandsch Wetenschappelijk Humanitair Komitee (1911–1940)', in Michael Dallas et al. (eds), *Homojaarboek 1: Artikelen over emancipatie en homoseksualiteit* (Amsterdam: Van Gennep, 1981), pp. 128–29.
75. Trans.: 'Een strijd van anonymi heeft nooit kans op succes'. Ibid., p. 129.
76. Although the categories 'Uranism' and 'Uranier' appear in this initial pamphlet to describe both men and women, no specific distinction was made between the experiences of queer men and women in the text. None of the authors responsible for the publication was a woman and of the thirty-two signatories of the attached petition to abolish the laws restricting homosexuality, only one was female: the feminist Maria (Mietje) Rutgers-Hoitsma (1847–1934), wife of sex reformer Jan Rutgers (1850–1924). Trans.: 'Uranisme (= Homosexualiteit = Liefde voor personen van het eigen geslacht)'. NWHK, *Wat iedereen behoort te weten omtrent Uranisme* (The Hague: Gebr. Belinfante, 1912), p. 2.
77. Joannes Henri François often wrote under the pseudonym 'Charley van Heezen', under which he published the homosexual novels *Anders* (*Different*, 1918) and *Het Masker* (*The Mask*, 1922). He also published in both *We* and *The Right to Live*. 'Bewaar mij voor de waanzin van het recht – 100 jaar strafrecht en homoseksualiteit in Nederland', Exhibition in the IHLIA Archive, Amsterdam, between 18 November 2011 and 29 February 2012, http://www.ihlia.nl/wp-content/uploads/2015/03/Bewaar-mij_brochure-FINAL-small-min.pdf (retrieved 23 April 2022).
78. Trans.: 'de schrijver – homosexueel – spreekt tot zijn mede-homosexueelen'. Joannes Henri François, *Open brief aan hen die anders zijn dan de anderen. Door een hunner* (The Hague: H.J. Berkhout, 1915), p. 8.
79. This is not to say, of course, that such terms were not being used in Germany at this time. The film *Anders als die Andern* (1919) directed by Richard Oswald and financially supported by Magnus Hirschfeld and the Wissenschaftlich-Humanitäres Komitee, for example, highlights that such euphemisms were still widely employed in German society, alongside the practice of self-reflexive labelling.
80. Trans.: 'aan een intiemen omgang tusschen twee vrouwen [wordt] veel minder aandacht geschonken dan aan dien tusschen twee mannen'. François, *Open brief*, p. 40.
81. See Caroll Smith-Rosenberg, 'The Female World of Love and Ritual: Relations between Women in Nineteenth-Century America', *Signs* 1 (1975), 1–29.
82. This is a view that Lillian Faderman put forward in her article on the 'morbidification' of love between women, in which she claimed, like Smith-Rosenberg, that in the late nineteenth century, a much broader spectrum of socially acceptable loving and affectionate relationships existed between women that were ultimately rejected and 'morbidified' with the advent of sexological writings. See Lillian Faderman, 'The Morbidification of Love between Women by 19th-Century Sexologists', *Journal of Homosexuality* 4(1) (1978), 73-90.
83. Trans.: 'Ik zit zeer op de grens hoor. Ik been echt niet helemaal 100% lesbisch ... Ik wilde dolgraag kinderen, dus ik ben een zeer dubieus geval.' Anja van Kooten Niekerk and Sacha Wijmer, *Verkeerde vriendschap: Lesbisch leven in de jaren 1920–1960* (Amsterdam: Feministische uitgeverij Sara, 1985), p. 73.

84. Trans.: 'Ik ben niet lesbisch, al zei een echte lesbische vriendin van mij van wél. Maar ik ben toch zeven jaar getrouwd geweest, dus ik weet het niet, jullie moeten het maar zeggen.' Ibid., p. 71.
85. Trans.: 'vroeger vond ik het gezelliger, intiemer ... Ik geloof niet dat jullie zo'n gezellig leven hebben op de manier zoals wij dat hadden. Ons leven was eigenlijk vrijer.' Ibid., p. 178.
86. Dietrich Orlow, *The Lure of Fascism in Europe: German Nazis, Dutch and French Fascists 1933–1939* (New York: Palgrave Macmillan, 2009), p. 12.
87. Trans.: 'Noodzakelijke voorlichting.' John Bradley, 'Om de vrije mens der nieuwe gemeenschap', *Levensrecht*, 3, 1940, p. 4.
88. Trans.: 'ontwikkeling en ontspanning'. Bob Angelo, 'Een woord vooraf', *Levensrecht*, 1, 1940, p. 2.
89. Although Engelschman contends that Diekman financially supported the magazine, at the time of writing, I have been able to find out little about who Diekman was or with what means he was able to fund *Levensrecht*.
90. Dagmar Herzog, *Sexuality in Europe: A Twentieth-Century History* (Cambridge: Cambridge University Press, 2011), p. 122.
91. Trans.: ' bonte en gevarieerde'; 'uit verschillende plaatsen en uit vele milieus'. Editors, 'Een kaleidoscoop van enthousiasme en ingenomenheid', *Levensrecht*, 2, 1940, p. 15.
92. The cost for an international subscription was 5 guilders annually.
93. *Menschenrecht* was an international queer Swiss magazine that was originally published under the title *Schweizerisches Freundschaftsbanner* between 1932 and 1967. It changed its name to *Menschenrecht* in 1937 and later to *Der Kreis* in 1942. It was a magazine for both women and men, and was produced as a joint endeavour between the queer female group Amicitia and the queer men's organization Herrenclub Excentric. Editors, 'Mededelingen van de redactie', *Levensrecht*, 3, 1940, p. 16.
94. Professor Dr T.J. Stomps, 'De Mutatietheorie in hare beteekenis voor onze samenleving', *Levensrecht*, 2, 1940, pp. 1–2; John Bradley, 'Om de vrije mens der nieuwe gemeenschap', *Levensrecht*, 3, 1940, pp. 1–4.
95. Trans.: 'volstrekt waardeloos'. Stomps, 'De Mutatietheorie', p. 1.
96. Trans.: 'het stichten van een gezin'. Ibid., p. 2.
97. Ibid., p. 2.
98. Trans.: ' Natuurlijke vergissing'. Editors, 'Een openbaar antwoord op een geheim schrijven', *Levensrecht*, 2, 1940, p. 11.
99. Trans.: 'Een openbaar antwoord op een geheim schrijven'; 'eindelooze reeks van overgangen.' Ibid., p. 12.
100. Trans.: 'Geen twee boombladeren, geen twee menschenduimen zijn gelijk. Het zou wel een boven-natuurlijk wonder zijn wanneer de sexualiteit éénvormig zich openbaarde.' Ibid.
101. Trans.: 'homosexueelen zijn maar al te geneigd, ook door hun meer vrouwelijken timiden aanleg gauw 'ja' te knikken, zelfs wanneer hun de grootste nonsens door een 'kerel' wordt toegebulderd'. Ibid.
102. The moral scandals at The Hague (1936) and in the Dutch East Indies (1938) caused outrage in the Dutch media. In the earlier scandal at The Hague, chief treasurer L.A. Ries was arrested alongside other members of the government for homosexual offences. Ries was fired despite much of the evidence against him not holding up in court. The affair in the Dutch East Indies came to light under the banner of 'moral cleansing and hygiene'. Several high-ranking officials were charged with homosexual offences against local boys. For more on these events, see Pieter Koenders *Homoseksualiteit in bezet Nederland: Verzwegen hoofdstuk* ('s-Gravenhage: De Woelrat, 1983).

103. Trans.: 'Over de vrouwen niets dan lof. Haar biographieën lazen wij zonder uitzondering met interesse. Dat het aan den overkant al precies is "comme chez nous", was een openbaring en vergroot onze sympathie voor deze groep van vrouwen, die het dikwijls nog veel moeilijker zullen hebben dan wij, omdat er nog veel minder verband bestaat.' Arent van Santhorst, 'Boekbespreking: De homosexueelen', *Levensrecht*, 1, 1940, p. 15.
104. Smith-Rosenberg, 'The Female World of Love and Ritual'.
105. Trans.: 'waar deze voorlichting nog mogelijk is'. Angelo, 'Een woord vooraf', p. 2.
106. Oswald Spengler, *Der Untergang des Abendlandes: Umrisse einer Morphologie der Weltgeschichte*, vol. II (Munich: C.H. Becksche Verlagsbuchhandlung, 1922), p. 579.

Part III

Literary Discourses

> By chance I got my hands on a book about homosexuality. With it my eyes were forced wide open. My childhood, the mystified looks with which people sometimes stared at me, my restlessness, the feeling of abandonment, I saw it all now in its full significance.[1]
> —'XXIX', Benno Stokvis, *De homosexueelen* (1939)

From the early fragments of poetry composed by Sappho for female lovers to the gendered ambiguity of Virginia Woolf's novel *Orlando* (1928), representations of queer love in literature and verse offer the present-day reader a window into the innumerable ways in which same-sex desires have been configured and imagined across cultures and time. Although the literary text cannot be held up as a mirror of the society and culture in which it was written – or even as representative of the audience for whom it was intended – it nonetheless presents an interpretation of broader cultural sentiments, as well as a creative and critical response to specific historical moments. As demonstrated in the first two parts of this book, scientific developments taking place in German-speaking countries had sparked great social interest in sexual behaviours and taxonomical categorizations in the early twentieth century. This growing public curiosity in what the performance of sexual acts meant in terms of newly forming social identities encouraged many authors to take up 'non-normative' sex and its subjects in their literary works.[2] Although many of these novels focused on the experiences of nonheterosexual men, the first half of the twentieth century also saw the figure of the fricatrice form more fully in the literary imagination.

Aimée Duc's *Are These Women? Novel about the Third Sex* (*Sind es Frauen: Roman über das dritte Geschlecht*, 1901), Maria Eichhorn's *Miss Don Juan* (*Fräulein Don Juan*, 1903), Alfred Döblin's *The Two Girlfriends Commit Murder by Poison* (*Die beiden Freundinnen und ihr Giftmord*, 1924) and Erich Kästner's *Fabian: The Story of a Moralist* (*Fabian: Die Geschichte eines Moralisten*, 1931) present just a snapshot of the complex and conflicting images of female same-sex desire that were presented in German literature in the early decades of the twentieth century. In some of these texts, Sapphic love was deployed as a symbol of urban growth and development. In others, the desires of queer women were used to signal the dangers of a decadent modern era. And while Germany was undoubtedly one of the largest purveyors of literary and scientific texts about same-sex desires, more than forty-five fictional works exploring the idea of love and desire between women were published in the Netherlands in the period between 1880 and 1940, of which thirty-six were originally written in Dutch.[3] Much like authors across the German border, Dutch writers tended to set their narratives in homosocial environments – such as the boarding school and convent – or chose to explore the 'darker' side of homosexual desires, with novels centralizing the sexual decadence of the *bohème*, or lives of petty criminals and sex workers.

The appearance of sexological themes in fiction at the fin de siècle marked a critical moment in the growth of sexual knowledges among the lay public. Literary texts served not only to popularize contemporary medical discourses but also to make previously obscure sexual knowledges available to a wider audience. For many readers, fictional writing offered an unparalleled insight into a world of rapidly changing formations of sexual desire and identity, depicted within the heady setting of the modern metropolis. Moreover, within the context of this volume, the literary text presents a view into the various ways in which queer desires were conceptualized by women, whose voices and theories, as we have seen earlier in this book, were often ignored in favour of the opinions of the male 'expert'. Although women had rarely been the subjects of sexological study in their own right, queer female writers – in magazines and novels – often engaged actively with sexological writing, as Laura Doan observes, in order 'to create, out of the very texts that had marginalized and even excluded them, innovative reconceptualizations of the lesbian subject'.[4]

In the final two chapters of this book, I will explore the construction of queer feminine desires and identities through fictional writing published by four female authors between 1919 and 1939. Looking at what Anna Katherina Schaffner has termed the 'conceptual transfer' between 'imaginary and scientific narratives', these chapters will explore the fraught relationship between queer writing by women and the social and sexological discourses that had been produced *about* queer subjects.[5] Paying attention to the ways in which these chosen authors challenge dominant discourses about same-sex desires, this final part will describe how the synthesis of contemporary sexological research with the literary imagination presented both a model of identification and the promise of possibility, and of how literary writing more generally provided women with an essential platform upon which to explore the gendered specificity of the contemporary struggle with sexological categories and names. Bearing in mind the divergences between the discourses of queer female desire that existed in Germany and the Netherlands, this analysis further seeks to address the invisibilizing of queer female desires in Dutch contexts, which were largely overlooked in subcultural publications and sexological writings. The comparison of novels by Dutch and German writers from across the interwar era should be considered an attempt therefore to map affinities across territorial borders, while acknowledging the very real social and cultural differences that appear in women's cultural productions during a period fraught with tremendous social and political upheaval.

Sexology and the Literary Imagination

The 'conceptual exchange' that was taking place between sexological and literary texts at the turn of the twentieth century was not a new phenomenon. Indeed, the sexual sciences had a long-established tradition of borrowing from images found in the literary world. As was discussed in Chapter 2, the sophisticated schema of sexual subcategories created by Karl Heinrich Ulrichs had largely been shaped by Aristophanes' speech in Plato's *Symposium*. Richard von Krafft-Ebing also acknowledged his own debt to literature later in his work, particularly the novels of Marquis de Sade and Leopold von Sacher-Masoch, when he coined the terms 'sadism' and 'masochism'.[6] Although Krafft-Ebing famously published the more explicit sections of his work in Latin to prevent them from being accessed by those looking for salacious materials, improving the accessibility of an educated (male) public to sexual knowledge was of vital importance to many sexual scientists by the end of the nineteenth century. Given the increased popularity of – and accessibility to – pornographic material, as well as the growing concerns around venereal disease and sex work, it had become a social imperative for sexual scientists and social activists that male readers were better versed in the dangers of promiscuous sexual activity. To bridge the discursive gap between the expert and the reader, literature was often employed in sexological studies, as Heike Bauer notes, as 'a common language' that worked as a conduit for conceptual chasms, and made critical concepts in sexological theory 'available to readers without scientific training'.[7]

The complexity of the transfers between literature and sexology are perhaps demonstrated best by returning to Benno Stokvis' collection *The Homosexuals* (1939), which was discussed in Chapter 2 and Chapter 4. Compiled – and presumably edited – by Stokvis, who was a lawyer and author, and concluding with an excerpt from the work of French novelist Emile Zola (1840–1902), the first Dutch anthology of homosexual experience further included several 'autobiographical' contributions written in literary form. One of the nine female autobiographies to appear in the compilation, for example, has been identified by Myriam Everard as a text produced by Dutch author Anna Blaman (1905–60). Placed alongside other more 'traditional' autobiographical accounts, Blaman's autofictive narrative on the tragic love life of masculine protagonist 'Hansi' was analysed by sexologists of the time in much the same way as the other autobiographies in the collection, continuing the tradition of literature being deployed as a tool to further scientific understandings of queer desires. The importance of literature to women's recognition of their own queerness also becomes apparent in the nonfictional contributions to the collection. Participant 'XXXI', for example, recalls her first encounter with Radclyffe Hall's writing and the significance of Hall's novel to the recognition of her own sexual difference: 'When I was about twenty years old, I read *The Well of Loneliness* ... and with great joy, I would even go so far as to say: gratitude, I realised that love between two women is possible.'[8] For this participant, as well as two other female contributors to Stokvis' collection, Hall's writing was a key source of queer knowledge. Moreover, as well as presenting them with their first model of female same-sex desire, it provided them with the knowledge that there were indeed others who felt as they did.[9] As 'discourses of desire', then, sexology and literature have long existed as queer bedfellows. Following the examples of early nineteenth-century activists, physicians and psychologists, who had drawn on literary examples to develop and disseminate theories about same-sex desires, authors at the fin de siècle employed sexological tropes in their fictional work to position themselves, in many respects, as 'educators' of a growing reading public. The knowledges that these authors shared were often closely linked to the sexological traditions of their home countries.

In the Netherlands, where sexual object choice was not considered a defining characteristic of a woman's social identity until at least the late 1930s, the field of psychoanalysis informed much of the fictional writing about queer desires, where little emphasis was placed upon physical inversion of gendered traits. However, in German-speaking countries, the stress on somatic theories of sexological inversion had resulted in the image of the virile female invert dominating fictional works. Since the publication of Westphal's study on Fräulein N, masculinity had been considered a key marker of congenital – and therefore 'natural' – queer desire in women. The incorporation of a 'case study' into later sexological research marked a significant shift in the ways in which data about sex were collected, and particularly those that concerned queer female desire. Sexologists weaved the 'confessions' from their sources into contextualizing descriptions of physical aberrations and familial psychiatric histories, creating story-like narratives from the conversations that occurred between physician and patient. Through this mediated form of scientific 'confession', the voice of the patient was given an authority within sexological theories and studies in a way that it had not been before.[10] This is not to say that rigorous interventions into the narratives were not made by sexologists; indeed, the privileging of certain aspects of patient testimonies and the omission of others was often considered a necessary measure to create a cohesive and convincing theoretical framework. In this way, the sexological case study might be considered to belong 'to the very archetypes of narration', thus making it no surprise that when a surge of fictional texts on queer desires began to emerge in the early twentieth century, 'case-like narratives' were among the most popular types of genre.[11] Indeed, Radclyffe Hall's groundbreaking novel mentioned above merged a variety of existing genres, 'including the medical case study, the romance and the *Bildungsroman*', and was profoundly shaped by the case studies on female inversion recorded in Krafft-Ebing's *Psychopathia Sexualis*.[12] The growing significance of the field of psychoanalysis during the 1920s further signalled a change in narrative focus from what the patient said to an exploration of the unarticulated desires of an individual, which arguably stimulated the rise in psychological crime novels during this period. Thus, while some authors such as Hall were employing the model of the sexological case study in their writings to make visible certain elements of queer experience, there existed alongside her a growing number of writers who sought to profit from the cultural cachet of queer desire, while ultimately safeguarding the binary that positioned queerness as dangerous and detrimental to wider social interests.[13] Given that so many authors were tackling the subject of queer desires in their literary works, and sexologists were presenting semifictional narratives in their sexological writing, it becomes important to define what constitutes queer fiction within the remit of this volume and to assess the limitations of such writings in shaping the social realities of queer women during this period.

Literary Que(e)ries

The fictional texts that will be examined in this final part have long since been read as queer works of literature and have been subsumed within the lesbian literary canon – if such a thing can be said to exist or even to be desirable.[14] Yet, while half of the novels considered here were received as explorations of female same-sex desire at the time of their publication, the other half were classified as such only after their (re)discovery by feminist literary critics in the second half of the twentieth century. Moreover, although some of the fictional texts chosen for this analysis explicitly articulate same-sex desires through textual declarations of love and lust, others produce their queer elements through the complex coded transfer between writer and reader, which requires a knowledge of subcultural symbols and their emic significance. Although there will not be an explicit attempt to *queer* literary texts in this section – that is, I do not stray from texts previously identified as LBTQ to focus on actions that resist normative frameworks in otherwise 'straight' narratives – using 'queer' as a category of identification in any sense requires something of an explanation. Moving away from the ideas of early lesbian literary criticism, which define lesbian texts as those novels that place 'love between women, including sexual passion, at the centre of its story', as Lilian Faderman has suggested, this volume also includes those works that are characterized, in the words of Judith Roof, 'by the perpetual interplay of desire and lack'.[15] Acknowledging that desire between women, and especially the desires of feminine women, are most often felt in literary writing in their 'absences' and 'silences', this volume moves closer to the practice of what literary scholar and cultural historian Maaike Meijer describes as 'reading as a lesbian'. Such a practice, Meijer contends, 'consists of a knowledge of context and codes, of lesbian history and of other lesbian texts, from a willingness to allow for lesbian meanings, and from a sensibility for what has been silenced'.[16] Yet, while such intertextual processes certainly point to ways in which readers might stray away from early text-centric interpretations of same-sex desire, the lesbian-ness of 'reading as lesbian' presupposes a conclusion about the construction of such desires that may well close them off to other interpretations. As the novels that have been chosen for this study often resist the identity narratives that have inspired scholars in their quest to recover texts from lesbian pasts, a practice of reading as *queer* might be better suited as a method of accounting for the silences and absences alluded to above. Indeed, as Eve Kosofsky Sedgwick acknowledges, the very practice of reading queerly is one that must remain open to broad interpretation. While the *genius loci* for such queer readings is considered to be 'the child or adolescent whose sense of personal queerness may or may not (yet?) have resolved into a sexual specificity of proscribed object choice, aim, site, or identification', the readings themselves may 'begin from or move toward sites of same-sex, interpersonal eroticism – but not necessarily so'.[17] Unlike Meijer, then, Sedgwick suggests moving away from readings that are shaped by knowledges of predefined codes and constructs, and towards a reading 'for important news … without knowing what form that news will take; with only the patchiest familiarity with its codes; without, even, more than hungrily hypothesizing to what questions this news may proffer an answer'.[18]

More importantly even than creating a space for questions that do not have predefined answers, the practice of reading queerly enables readers to imagine a literary world in which the 'specificity of proscribed object choice … or identification' *remains* unclear, presenting an advantageous approach to texts by German and Dutch women writers, who were not necessarily describing desires in ways that conform to present-day understandings of 'lesbian' or 'queer'. Thus, by remaining open to the 'mesh of possibilities, gaps, overlaps, dissonances and resonances, lapses and excesses of meaning' in which textual expressions of same-sex desire may result, reading *as* queer allows for a comparison of two diverse literary, social and sexological landscapes, and all the possible meanings of same-sex desire within them.[19] Thus, the category 'queer' will be employed in these chapters as a practice that aims to discover what the 'lapses and excesses of meaning' in fictional writing might tell us about novels that reclaiming texts simply as 'lesbian' or 'homosexual' cannot. However, in a discussion of women writers in the early twentieth century, whose works were often dismissed as 'trivial' or 'popular', it is not only the descriptor queer that requires explanation; within the context of contemporary literary criticism and reception, terms such as 'literature' and 'fiction' were also considered equally contestable. And although increasing numbers of female authors entered the literary sphere in Germany and the Netherlands in the nineteenth and early twentieth centuries with commercial success, publications produced by women writers were frequently received as literature of a 'lower form' and dismissed by critics. The postwar hostility to women's growing social ambitions, as discussed in Chapter 1, fed further into an already-established sentiment that women were 'not capable of matching dominant masculine artistic production' or, as literary critic and historian Annie Romein-Verschoor concluded in her literary history of 1935, that women writers were simply 'not cut from the same cloth … from which Balzacs were made'.[20]

Indeed, as Elaine Showalter argues, the 'exclusion of women's writing from serious critical consideration' and the 'hostility towards female authorship and feminine values' essentially stigmatized women's writing at the turn of the twentieth century.[21] The feminine values that Showalter mentions refer to the thematization in novels of the late nineteenth and early twentieth centuries of topics such as the educational opportunities for (bourgeois) women and/or (the escape from) the domestic sphere. These types of 'novelettes for ladies', as they were disparagingly termed, were not considered to be either significant or relevant to the contemporary (male) reader, or, indeed, to the later (male) literary historian. Yet, here, as we have seen elsewhere, there exist marked cultural divergences in the way in which German and Dutch women's writing was received by contemporary authors and has since been appraised by literary scholars. In Germany, women writers had been publishing well-received novels since the mid-eighteenth century, and by the mid-1920s, many women writers were leading successful literary careers. However, this is not to say that German women's writing was appraised by contemporary critics in the same way as that of male authors. Certainly, what Andreas Huyssen terms as the concerns of 'high' and 'low' cultural forms at the turn of the twentieth century led to any successful work by female writers – that is, work that escaped the trappings of mass cultural forms – being considered as a mimicry of 'masculine thought or expression'.[22] Thus, women writers at the turn of the twentieth century, as Gianfranca Balestra suggests, 'found themselves between worlds', simultaneously trying to create new artistic forms while navigating the tension between 'the artistic tradition they aspired to enter and the fiction they wanted to create'.[23] Women's writing that did not meet the strict standards of the literary elite was consequently dismissed as 'Frauenliteratur', a category that contemporary critics suggested 'was pronounced with a mocking undertone, even in spite of the right to vote and equal rights'.[24]

In the Netherlands, women had not entered literary circles in quite in the same way by the early twentieth century. The emphasis on the domestic sphere in much Dutch women's writing before the 1920s had led to women's literary work being typified as 'hyperfeminine' and, consequently, of little interest to paying (male) audiences. Facing similar tensions that Balestra identifies in American women's writing of the same era, the novels of Dutch authors Eva Raedt-de Canter and Josine Reuling (which will be discussed in the following chapters) were judged harshly by fellow author and historian Annie Romein-Verschoor in her early literary history of the Netherlands. In an indictment of writings that could be considered 'too womanly', Romein-Verschoor summarizes: 'In the past decade, there have appeared several women's novels that ... characteristically give free rein to feminine, sometimes all too feminine, attributes. We can include in this the works of Eva Raedt-de Canter, Henriëtte Mooy, Josine Reuling, and the fresh, lone contribution of Jo Zwartendijk.'[25] Romein-Verschoor's reproach of these 'all too feminine' works belongs to her much wider study of Dutch women's writing between 1880 and 1935. Yet, the existence of this study itself marks an exception in Dutch literary histories. Indeed, as Jane Fenoulhet contends, the contention of literary critics that Dutch women writers were incapable of the imaginative innovation needed to create works of literary greatness effectively disqualified women and their works from entering the literary canon and, accordingly, into later literary histories.[26] A further indication of the ways in which women's writing has been appraised and appreciated differently in the German and Dutch contexts can be seen in the attempts to recover lesbian literary works in the 1970s and 1980s. Pioneered by a number of feminist publishing houses, many neglected women's novels were rediscovered during the second half of the twentieth century, which afforded these works a new following and, often, queer cult status.[27] The novels of both Christa Winsloe and Anna Elisabet Weirauch, for example, discussed in the final two chapters of this book, have already had celebrated reprints in recent years and have been translated into numerous languages. Fenoulhet's contention that female Dutch writers have been largely ignored in literary histories – and, indeed, more broadly from the recovery agenda of feminist organizations – appears to hold true as neither Raedt-de Canter's nor Reuling's novels have yet been reprinted or translated in recent decades for international audiences.

Queer Subjects, Feminine Objects

Exploring the interplay between psychomedical theory and literary writing, the final part of this book will look at the conceptualization of queer feminine desires in fictional form. In the first instance, I will examine Eva Raedt-de Canter's *The Boarding School* (*Internaat*, 1930) and Christa Winsloe's *The Girl Manuela* (*Das Mädchen Manuela*, 1933) in order to consider how texts that foreground the experiences of the queer 'tomboy' are ultimately shaped by the queer feminine women who are positioned as desirable 'objects'. Here, the extent to which the sexological theories outlined earlier in this book appear to have shaped narratives of adolescent queerness, and the constituent objects of their desires, will serve as the core focus of comparison. Looking at how Raedt-de Canter and Winsloe engage with the social and sexological discourses of their time, I will examine what this engagement might tell us broadly about the ways in which discourses about identity and sexuality were culturally contingent, and to what extent concepts were shared. Although early twentieth-century sexological research accorded the experiences of masculine women a certain status, a comparison between Winsloe's and Raedt-de Canter's novels highlights the limits of employing only a 'sexological lens' to read for same-sex desire in literary writing. While Winsloe's novel draws explicitly on the format of the sexological case study to explore the sexual development of her protagonist, Raedt-de Canter's work gives little more than a nod to the nascent sexological studies emerging in the Netherlands at the time of her writing. However, in both novels, the role of sexological and religious 'confessions' are key to explorations of sexual 'truths' and (lacking) identities as well as the wider questions of selfhood in relation to society. In each of these explorations, the role of the feminine 'object' will be foregrounded through an examination of the queer maternal encounters that take place in each of the novels.

In Chapter 6, Josine Reuling's *Back to the Island* (*Terug naar het eiland*, 1937) and Anna Elisabet Weirauch's trilogy *The Scorpion* (*Der Skorpion*, 1919–31) will offer a 'counterpoint' to the figure of the queer tomboy by comparing two novels that decentre the sexological invert and take as their respective protagonists two queer feminine women.[28] Juxtaposing established sexological signifiers with subtle subcultural cyphers, *Back to the Island* and *The Scorpion* offer departures from binary definitions of gendered and sexual preference, presenting, as I argue, alternative frameworks to contemporary sexological systems. Models of congenital inversion are rejected outright by the protagonists of these novels and queer feminine desires are encoded through maternal longings and tensions between rural and urban settings. By comparing the codification of sexual difference in these novels, I will argue, in agreement with Julian Carter, that it becomes possible to read queer feminine models as 'nonlesbian' alternatives to contemporary sexological categories.[29] Turning to the conclusion, these four texts will be examined together in order to consider the significance of the discursive construction of queer feminine desire more broadly for literary studies concerning a period 'where women began to work on their own subjectivity through the act of writing'.[30]

Notes

1. Trans.: 'ik kreeg toevallig een boek over homosexualiteit in handen. Toen gingen mij de oogen [*sic*] wagenwijd open. Mijn kindsheid, de verwonderde blikken waarmede de menschen mij soms aanstaarden, ik zag het alles nu in de volle betekenis'. 'XXIX' in Benno Stokvis, *De homosexueelen* (Lochem: De Tijdstroom, 1939), p. 157.
2. For more detailed surveys of the rise of LGB literature in the early twentieth century, see, for example, Rictor Norton, *The Homosexual Literary Tradition* (New York: Revisionist Press, 1974); Jeffrey Meyers, *Homosexuality and Literature: 1890–1930* (Montreal: McGill-Queen's University Press, 1977). For studies specific to LGB literature in German and Dutch contexts, see Christoph Lorey and John Plews (eds), *Queering the Canon: Defying Sights in German Literature and Culture* (Columbia, SC: Camden House, 1998); Myriam Everard, 'Galerij der vrouwenliefde: "Sex variant women" in Nederlandstalige literatuur 1880–1940', in *Homojaarboek 2: Artikelen over emancipatie en homoseksualiteit* (Amsterdam: Van Gennep, 1983), pp. 80–133.
3. Everard, 'Galerij der vrouwenliefde', p. 106.
4. Laura Doan, *Fashioning Sapphism: The Origins of a Modern English Lesbian Culture* (New York: Columbia University Press, 2001), p. 163.

5. Anna Katharina Schaffner, *Modernism and Perversion: Sexual Deviance in Sexology and Literature, 1850–1930* (New York: Palgrave Macmillan, 2012), p. 23.
6. On the importance of literary writings to the understanding of 'non-normative' sexual proclivities, Krafft-Ebing even suggested in the preface of his first edition of *Psychopathia Sexualis* that 'the poet is the better psychologist … for he is swayed by sentiment, rather than reason, and always treats his subject in a partial fashion' Trans: 'Vorläufig dürfen die Dichter bessere Psychologen sein, als die Psychologen und Philosophen von Fach … sie sind Gefühls und nicht Verstandesmenschen und mindestens einseitig in der Betrachtung des Gegenstands'. Krafft-Ebing, *Psychopathia Sexualis: Eine klinisch-forensische Studie* (Stuttgart: Ferdinand Enke, 1886), p. iv.
7. Heike Bauer, 'Literary Sexualities', in *The Cambridge Companion to the Body in Literature* (New York: Cambridge University Press, 2015), p. 106.
8. Trans.: 'Toen ik ongeveer 20 jaar was, las ik "De bron van eenzaamheid" … En met groote blijdschap, ik zou haast zeggen: dankbaarheid, ontdekte ik dat liefde tusschen twee vrouwen mogelijk is.' 'XXXI', in Stokvis, *De homosexueelen*, p. 163.
9. Completing the cyclical link between literature and sexology, Hall's novel was prefaced by a commentary from the British sexologist Havelock Ellis and, on the dustjacket, publisher Jonathan Cape emphasized the importance of 'a broader and more general treatment' of the subject of female same-sex desire, which, he suggests, had 'not been treated frankly outside the regions of scientific text-books'. For more on the opinions of Cape and Ellis in relation to Hall's work, see Alison Oram and Annmarie Turnbull, 'The Well of Loneliness', in *The Lesbian History Sourcebook: Love and Sex between Women in Britain from 1780–1970* (London: Routledge, 2001), pp. 181–201 (at p. 185).
10. As was discussed in Chapter 2, it was not until the fieldwork of Moll and Hirschfeld that Krafft-Ebing's pathologization of patient discourses was challenged by the appearance of case studies that engaged with the queer community on their terms.
11. 'Introduction', in Joy Damousi et al. (eds), *Case Studies and the Dissemination of Knowledge* (New York: Routledge, 2015), p. 2.
12. Esther Saxey, 'Introduction', in *The Well of Loneliness* (Ware: Wordsworth Editions, 2005), p. vii.
13. In her work *The Lesbian Menace: Ideology, Identity, and the Representation of Lesbian Life* (Amherst: University of Massachusetts Press, 1997), Sherrie Inness reminds us that not all queer people who read *The Well of Loneliness* identified with the experiences it represented. While some critics believed the novel's unhappy ending to form part of the 'anti-homosexual propaganda' it sought to dispel, others, like writer and socialite Violet Trefusis, believed Stephen Gordon to be a 'loathsome example' of lesbianism that confirmed rather than challenged the heterosexual 'norm' (at pp. 13–16).
14. While the idea of a queer literary canon must surely be considered as antithetical to the aims of queer writing, Liana Borghi defines the construction of a 'lesbian literary canon' as a strategy of 'resistance to the varied and complex heteropatriarchal practice of eradicating lesbian desire'. See Liana Borghi, 'Lesbian Literary Studies', in Theo Sandford et al. (eds), *Lesbian and Gay Studies: An Introductory, Interdisciplinary Approach* (London: SAGE, 2000), p. 156.
15. This is not to say that the term 'lesbian literature' has not been contested; indeed, as Bonnie Zimmerman acknowledges, the category has long since been 'plagued with the problem of definition'. See Bonnie Zimmerman, *The Safe Sea of Women: Lesbian Fiction, 1969–1989* (Boston: Beacon, 1990), p. 15; Lillian Faderman, *Surpassing the Love of Men: Romantic Friendship and Love between Women from Renaissance to Present* (New York: HarperCollins, 1981), p. 53; Judith Roof, *The Lure of Knowledge: Lesbian Sexuality and Theory* (New York: Columbia University Press, 1991), pp. 88–89.

16. Trans.: 'lezen als lesbo'; 'bestaat uit kennis van context en codes, van lesbische geschiedenis en van andere lesbische teksten, uit een bereidheid lesbische betekenissen toe te laten, uit een sensibiliteit voor het verzwegene'. Maaike Meijer, *De lust tot lezen: Nederlandse dichteressen en het literaire system* (Amsterdam: Sara/Van Gennep, 1988), p. 250.
17. 'Introduction', in Eve Kosofsky Sedgwick (ed.), *Novel Gazing: Queer Readings in Fiction* (Durham, NC: Duke University Press, 1997), p. 2.
18. Ibid., p. 3.
19. Eve Kosofsky Sedgwick, *Tendencies* (Durham, NC: Duke University Press, 1993), p. 8.
20. Trans.: 'niet van het hout gesneden ... waaruit men Balzacs maakt'. Annie Romein-Verschoor, *Vrouwenspiegel: een literair-sociologische studie over de Nederlandse romanschrijfster na 1800* (Leiden: Hoeijenbos & Co., 1935), p. 151.
21. Elaine Showalter, *Sister's Choice: Tradition and Change in American Women's Writing* (Oxford: Oxford University Press, 1994), p. 108.
22. Trans.: 'männlichen Denk- oder Ausdrucksweise'. Hedwig Lothringer, 'Frauenbücher. Die Romane von Anna Elisabeth [sic] Weirauch', *Neuer Berliner Zeitung*, 12 February 1920. This article forms one among dozens of a collection of newspapers clippings that can be found in Anna Elisabet Weirauch's scrapbook. The scrapbook is now in the possession of the Spinnboden Archiv in Berlin.
23. Gianfrance Balestra, 'Women Writers on the Verge of the Twentieth Century: Edith Wharton *et al*', *RSA*, 23 (2012), 10–24 (at p. 14).
24. Trans.: 'Frauenliteratur, trotz Stimmrecht und Gleichberechtigung, wird mit einem spöttischen Unterton ausgesprochen.' Lothringer, 'Frauenbücher'.
25. Interestingly, in the 1977 edition of the work, Romein-Verschoor includes an afterword entitled: 'A Lonely Adventure in Literary Sociology' ('Een eenzaam avontuur in de literaire sociologie'), which most likely refers to one of the most famous books in the Dutch lesbian canon – *Eenzaam avontuur* (1948), written by Anna Blaman. Trans.: 'Er zijn in het laatste decennium nog een aantal vrouwen-romans verschenen, die ... het kenmerk mee delen van het botvieren van vrouwelijk, soms al te vrouwelijk eigenschappen. Wij rekenen daartoe het werk van Eva Raedt-de Canter, van Henriëtte Mooy, van Josine Reuling en de frisse eenling van Jo Zwartendijk.' Annie Romein-Verschoor *Vrouwenspiegel: een literair-sociologische studie over de Nederlandse romanschrijfster na 1880* (Nijmegen: SUN, 1935), p. 158.
26. Jane Fenoulhet, *Making the Personal Political: Dutch Women Writers 1919–1970* (London: Legenda, 2007), p. 60.
27. In 1978, the feminist publishing house Virago established the 'Modern Classics' series, which, as Jane Potter notes, was 'instrumental in the rediscovery of a forgotten female literary tradition'. See Jane Potter, 'Women's Publishing', in Giles Noel Clark and Angus Phillips (eds), *Inside Book Publishing* (Abingdon: Routledge, 2008), p. 14.
28. Although this distinction between 'masculine' and 'feminine' protagonists seems to shore up the gendered binary that I have sought to contest in this volume, I refer here primarily to the ways in which the characters have been presented in secondary literature. In the following chapters, I will approach these protagonists as multivalent figures who offer dynamic rather than static representations of female same-sex desire.
29. Julian Carter, 'On Mother-Love: History, Queer Theory, and Nonlesbian Identity', *Journal of the History of Sexuality*, 14 (2005), 107–38.
30. Fenoulhet, *Making the Personal Political*, p. 2.

Chapter 5

A MOTHER'S LOVE
Eva Raedt-de Canter's *Boarding School* (1930) and
Christa Winsloe's *The Girl Manuela* (1933)

The behaviours and aspirations of the wild-spirited tomboy were the cause of fervent discussion in the early twentieth century. Long since established as a figure who inveighed against gender norms and expectations, the boyish girl divided social commentators and medical authorities alike. While some of these conceived of tomboyism as a 'positive and beneficial phenomenon' for young women, which promoted healthier and more active lifestyles, others detected in the tomboy's scraped knees, scowling face and sense of worldly adventure the early signs of sexual dissidence.[1] At a time when the aetiology of homosexual desire was one of the greatest preoccupations of the sexological world, it is perhaps easy to understand why the tomboy was a character of social suspicion and sexological interest. Wanting to experience the social mobilities accorded to her male counterparts, the tomboy in interwar literature was often presented as a wilful and headstrong individual, who rejected activities specific to her sex and transgressed the boundaries established by social convention. For those sexologists and physicians who subscribed to the theory of sexual inversion, the tomboy – and her male equivalent, the 'sissy' – crucially confirmed their central thesis, which remained contingent upon evidence of childhood gender nonconformity. In later editions of *Psychopathia Sexualis*, for example, Krafft-Ebing writes quite unceremoniously about the existence of 'Urning girls' and 'Urning boys', presenting tomboyism as a primary marker of latent homosexual desire in women:

> The favourite place of the female Urning is the playground of boys. She seeks to rival them in their games. She will hear nothing of dolls; her passion is for playing on the rocking horse, playing soldier and robber games … The consciousness of being born a woman brings about painful reflections … Great is the urge to wear her hair and clothing in the fashion of men and, when opportunity allows for it, to appear and to impress in men's attire.[2]

It is not only the rejection of traditional feminine pastimes in Krafft-Ebing's account that points to homosexuality, but also the compulsion (*Drang*) to cross-dress and adopt 'male' behaviours. In a later article, 'The Urning Child' ('Das urnische Kind', 1903), Magnus Hirschfeld endorses Krafft-Ebing's theory that it was possible to identify homosexuality in (pre-)pubescent children, claiming that he had regularly been able to make 'the diagnosis of Uranism' in children between the ages of ten and fourteen.[3] Armed with extensive collections of longitudinal data, Hirschfeld returned to one of his early subjects to provide evidence for the natural progression of the boy's inborn 'girlishness' to his later erotic desire for the male sex. Referring to his first encounter with the sensitive and emotional thirteen-year-old boy, Hirschfeld concluded: 'From the Urning child became a homosexual man, with the same natural necessity with which a normal child becomes a heterosexual person.'[4]

Although the descriptions outlined above appear to present the gender-nonconforming child as a homogeneous figure who defies the gender-specific standards of any given society, exactly how one defines a 'transgression into boys' territory' differs according to each sociocultural context one is describing.[5] Accounting for the significance of class, location and historical specificity in relation to how one defines a gender 'transgression', Michelle Abate writes:

> wearing bloomers may have been the epitome of tomboyish daring during the nineteenth century, but that is no longer the case today. Similarly, working outside the home is often seen as the apogee of tomboyish independence for wealthy women, but it is a basic fact of life for their working-class counterparts. Finally, plowing the fields, baling hay or herding livestock might seem acutely tomboyish for many urban girls, but it constitutes a common chore for those who live on a farm or ranch.[6]

Further to the rural/urban divide outlined above, racial and religious markers of identity play a crucial role in how gender nonconforming behaviours are socially constructed and policed. Exactly what constitutes gender dissidence within a specific cultural context, and what such gender deviant behaviours may – or may not – signify, will shape the following discussion of the presumed tomboy protagonists and their feminine love interests that feature in Eva Raedt-de Canter's *Boarding School* (*Internaat*, 1930) and Christa Winsloe's *The Girl Manuela* (*Das Mädchen Manuela*, 1933). As was discussed in Part I of this book, sexological writing on the subject of sexual inversion had fixed the figure of the masculine homosexual woman firmly in the German cultural imagination by the 1930s. However, prior to the publication of Benno Stokvis' *The Homosexuals* in 1939, such signifiers had been slow to gain traction in Dutch circles, and the relationship between gender deviance and homosexual desire was not considered self-evident. Indeed, while fiction that explores themes of sexual difference has often been analysed by literary scholars 'as having always contained the [protagonist's] "true self"', Raedt-de Canter's depictions of her protagonist, as we shall see, do not manifest themselves in identitarian politics of Sapphic self-fashioning.[7] In the first section of this chapter, I will examine how both novels take up gender nonconformity and sexual desire in ways that resist easy social/sexological categorization. Against the religious backdrop of early twentieth-century Dutch society, Raedt-de Canter presents an image of queer desire that is framed by a series of acts rather than identitarian declarations – or diagnosis from the outside – and comprises all the connotations of sexual fluidity and slipperiness that I have argued characterized Dutch female same-sex desire in the first half of the twentieth century. In Christa Winsloe's novel, a narrative that engages explicitly with the framework of the sexological case study, configurations of queer desire are also shown to resist more reductive readings of congenital inversion through moments of gender blending in the performative camp sensibility that one can read into the eponymous protagonist. In the second section of this chapter, I will spotlight the maternal femininities qualities of the protagonists' love interests. Here, I argue that maternal impulses are expressed in explicitly erotic terms that often defy contemporary sexological models of maternalism, upending the theory that directing women towards motherhood could 'cure' homosexual tendencies – and not least and affording new significance to the maternal aspects of love and desire between women. Finally, I will analyse the act of confession in the novels in order to explore the limits of employing the sexological lens of inversion across cultural borders, with specific attention being paid to the ways in which one understood – and valued – oneself as a sexual subject in Germany and the Netherlands during the interwar period. As Raedt-de Canter's novel *Boarding School* is virtually unknown outside queer Dutch circles and Winsloe's novel makes several important departures from the plot of the arguably more famous filmic adaptions *Girls in Uniform* (*Mädchen in Uniform*, 1931/1958), the analysis outlined above will be prefaced with a brief biographical sketch of the authors and a summary of their texts.

Eva Raedt-de Canter (1900–75)

Born in Breda in 1900, little is known about the personal life of Eva Raedt-de Canter, the pseudonym adopted by Dutch author Anna Elisabeth Johanna de Mooij. Secretary of the literary journal *Great Netherlands* (*Groot Nederland*), Raedt-de Canter published several successful psychological novels in the 1930s that centralized the experiences of women and children, most often in the context of the school or home. Working further as a translator, Raedt-de Canter was thoroughly proficient in at least German, Czech and English, and produced the Dutch translations for Heinrich Hauser's *The Last Sailing Ships* (*Het laatste zeilschip*, 1931), Karel Čapek's *The Gardener's Year* (*Het jaar van den tuinman*, 1932), and Humphrey Cobb's *Paths of Glory* (*Kogels en kruisen*, 1947). While themes of gender, social identity and sexuality emerge across several of her works, Raedt-de Canter is not known to have had any romantic/erotic connections with women inhabiting the queer circuits of Amsterdam or Berlin, as described in Part I of this book, although she remained a familiar face in artistic and bohemian circles throughout her literary career. Married initially to the Dutch sculptor Jacobus 'Jaap' Kaas, with whom she had one daughter, Raedt-de Canter later married ceramicist and sculptor Willem Hendrik de Vries.[8]

Described as an author of 'undeniable talent' in the social democratic *Utrecht People's Journal* in 1938, Raedt-de Canter was a popular writer in the Netherlands prior to the Nazi invasion.[9] Her most successful works during this time explored the effects of enforced homosocial environments on women, such as her debut *Boarding School* (*Internaat*, 1930) and her later novel *Women's Prison* (*Vrouwengevangenis*, 1935). The innovative style that she employed in her debut, a strategy that incorporates the reader into the diegesis through its nonlinear second-person perspective, resulted in the novel achieving critical acclaim, with comparisons drawn between her writings and those of pioneering feminist author Carry van Bruggen (1881–1932). Originally published in 1930 by Querido and again in 1934 as part of the publishing house's new Salamander collection – a compendium of the 'best original Dutch and translated novels' – *Boarding School* was celebrated by respected Dutch critics as a novel that was as 'fresh as the spring wind'.[10] Poet and author Roel Houwink (1899–1987) even concluded in the literary journal *The Golden Shop* (*Den Gulden Winckel*) that in order to enjoy Raedt-de Canter's novel, 'one simply had to open it'.[11] Further reviews of the novel *Boarding School* from Socialist and Liberal newspapers praised the text for its depiction of 'the narrow-minded bigotry of the unworldly nuns' and critics caroused in its criticism of 'the foolish, rotten, heartlessness of the petty pedagogues'.[12] Perhaps on account of the general hostility towards women writers by most Dutch literary critics, as was discussed in the Introduction to Part III, attitudes towards Raedt-de Canter's work soured after the initial success of her first novels. Thus, while she published 'book after book' before 1940, she – and her contributions to Dutch literature – faded into relative obscurity following the end of the Second World War and she published little before her death in Edam in 1975.[13]

Christa Winsloe (1888–1944)

Born twelve years before Raedt-de Canter in the provincial town of Darmstadt in 1888, Christa Winsloe was sent to a boarding school in Potsdam following the death of her mother and brother. Leaving the Kaiserin-Augusta-Stift in 1905, Winsloe studied in Munich and travelled widely around Germany and Italy as an established animal sculptor. After marrying the Hungarian Baron Lajos Hatvany (1880–1961), she moved to live in the Hatvan Castle in Hungary in 1913 and travelled between Budapest, Berlin and Vienna to complete her artistic work. Following her divorce from Hatvany in 1922, an event that 'hurt her very much', she relocated to Berlin, where she began publishing articles in the *Berlin Daily* (*Berliner Tageblatt*), *Cross Section* (*Querschnitt*) and *Tempo*, before she made her creative breakthrough with *Knight Nérestan* (*Ritter Nérestan*) in 1930, a play about a schoolgirl named Manuela.[14] Critics at the debut performance of the play in Leipzig were collectively surprised by the strength of a piece that consisted solely of female characters and were impressed with the skill with which Winsloe's script had been brought to the stage. In the following year, the play was performed in Berlin under the direction of Leontine Sagan (1889–1974) and bore the new title: *Then and Now* (*Gestern und Heute*).[15] The success of both productions saw Friedrich Dammann (1901–1969) engaged alongside Winsloe as a screenwriter for the filmic adaptation of the play under the name *Girls in Uniform*. Directed again by Sagan, the movie made cinematic history as the first feature film to consist of an almost entirely female ensemble. Yet, while the casting and crew remained virtually unchanged, there were notable departures from the original plot. While Sagan supposedly directed the play performed in Berlin as a piece that was 'purely lesbian', the queerness of the original was considerably muted in the later film. Furthermore, the play's tragic ending is bypassed in its cinematic adaptation, in which Manuela survives her experiences at the austere Prussian boarding school. Despite the alterations that were made to the plot and dénouement of the original play, the film was deemed 'a great success' by critics and, as Doris Hermanns observes, Winsloe became 'world famous – if only for a short time'.[16]

Shortly following the release of the film, Winsloe re-encountered the influential American journalist Dorothy Thompson (1893–1961), with whom she had been in contact during her marriage with Hatvany, and the two began a passionate affair. When Hitler seized power in Germany in 1933, Winsloe and Thompson relocated to the United States, where the former took up work once again as a journalist. In the same year as her relocation, Winsloe published the novel *The Girl Manuela* in Amsterdam with the Allert de Lange publishing house, which offered publishing opportunities to German émigré authors.[17] Winsloe moved back to Europe in 1938 to travel around the French Riviera, leaving Thompson in America. Here, she met the French-Swiss pianist and novelist Simone Gentet (1898–1944) and the pair embarked on what was to be a short-lived but turbulent romantic relationship. Travelling together through France after the outbreak of the Second World War, Winsloe and Gentet arrived in Burgundy in 1944. It was here that they were shot dead by a criminal who claimed to be working for the French Resistance, who later contended that he had believed the couple to be German spies.[18] Yet, even after her death, Winsloe's work was able to continue reaching new audiences when a second cinematic adaptation of *Girls in Uniform* was released in 1958, with child actor Romy Schneider cast in the leading role of Manuela von Meinhardis.

Boarding School (1930)

A subscript on the original cover of Eva Raedt-de Canter's debut novel recommends that *Boarding School* be read as 'a complaint … that pictures the perilous, anxious, joyless, and cruelly damaged life of a child'.[19] Written in the second-person form, the novel tells the story of a young student, Eva, who finds herself trapped in the 'world of horror' of a religious boarding school.[20] The intersubjectivity generated by the reader–protagonist–author relationship encourages a heightened sense of empathy with the central character from the outset of the novel, which only grows as the reader partakes in the protagonist's joys and pains and becomes complicit in the 'sins' that she commits. Commencing with the statement 'At five o'clock the bell rings like a distant horror in your dreams', the scene is set for an exploration of the 'suffocating shadow' of Catholicism, embodied by the cruel Sister Alphonse.[21]

Divided into five chapters that span the academic year, the narrator/protagonist describes the physical and mental punishments she endures for her perceived rebellion against the religious and moral value systems. During the first half of the text, which is restricted to the confines of the school, the protagonist is made, for example, to copy the Nicene Creed forty times from memory for refusing to bow to Sister Alphonse, she is forced to sit outside in winter without a jacket for speaking out of turn and, later, she is banished to a room filled with disturbing stuffed animals for smearing shoe polish on a classmate. After her punishments, which are depicted at a feverish pace within the nonlinear narrative, the protagonist is sent to confess to her sins – an instrumental and formalized performance that involves the protagonist's engagement in a self-regulatory and reflective process of examination. However, despite the drudgery of school life, the story is also peppered with compassionate characters, for whom the protagonist develops short-lived romantic attachments. Most notable are the motherly nurse Veronica, the older student Fenna and a mysterious girl who kisses the protagonist each evening before bed. In the second half of the text, the reader is introduced to life outside of the school grounds, where, following an adventurous escape from the school with a friend, we see the protagonist return home for the summer. Here, she resentfully notes the change in the way in which her male friends treat her. No longer is she invited to wrestle and play with them as an equal, and she reflects on her initial dislike of their romantic advances. Later, she begins a relationship with her friend's brother, Pierre, who presents her with his portrait photo to take back with her to school. When the protagonist returns for a new semester, another student is expelled for being in possession of a similar image. Returning to the photo of Pierre, the protagonist holds her thumb over the boy's face, distorting the image into an unidentifiable blur, which she keeps in her catechism as a silent symbol of rebellion.

The Girl Manuela (1933)

The oppressive environment that features in *Boarding School* also provides the setting for Christa Winsloe's text *The Girl Manuela*, which was published three years after Raedt-de Canter's debut. While the tools of oppression employed in the French convent school in Raedt-de Canter's writing and the school for daughters of military families documented in Winsloe's novel are operated by different loci of power, the protagonists' struggles against authority, their social isolation and the development of their nascent queer desires are nonetheless strikingly similar. As mentioned earlier, the story of *The Girl Manuela* has a complex history. First conceived as the play *Knight*

Nérestan, which was also performed as *Then and Now*, the story was later twice adapted into a film named *Girls in Uniform*. Two years after the first film's release, Winsloe published the novel *The Girl Manuela* while she was living with Dorothy Thompson in the United States. Making no secret of the novel's connection to its cinematic predecessor, Winsloe returned to the original plot of her play and re-emphasized the erotic aspects of the story that had been softened onscreen. Further refusing to retain the 'Happy Ending' of the first filmic release, Winsloe produced what Christa Reinig has termed 'a book against the film'.[22]

While both the play and the film focus exclusively on the boarding school environment, Winsloe begins her novel with the birth of Manuela von Meinhardis and narrates in detail the tragic events of the protagonist's childhood. Following the death of her brother and mother, Manuela's governess fears that the child's behaviour is growing 'wild' and urges the widowed Major von Meinhardis to send his daughter to boarding school, which he reluctantly agrees is for the best. Upon her arrival at the school, Manuela is presented with a secondhand uniform and an initialled red cockade. Identifying the letters 'E.v.B' on the rosette, Manuela is told that the previous owner of the uniform must have felt 'something extra' for the teacher Elisabeth von Bernburg.[23] While initially confused, Manuela soon begins to understand the feelings of the previous owner of the uniform. Following a series of ceremonial goodnight kisses from Fräulein von Bernburg as she puts her students to bed, Manuela grows increasingly enamoured with her teacher. Later, when Manuela is given a lead role in the school production of Voltaire's *Zaïre*, she acts out her growing affection for Fräulein von Bernburg onstage under the guise of the 'trouser role' and is praised by both staff and students for her authentic portrayal of the young knight.[24] After her triumphant thespian debut and emboldened by too much punch, she confesses her feelings for Fräulein von Bernburg to her classmates. Overheard by the fearsome Frau Oberin, this confession has dramatic consequences for Manuela, who is isolated from her classmates and, most painfully, her beloved teacher. Seeing no way to live without Fräulein von Bernburg, she jumps from the clock tower and ends her life.

The themes of punishment, rebellion and confession that shape the novels of Raedt-de Canter and Winsloe position both texts at a cross-section of literary genres. Although the authors drew heavily from elements in their own experiences at boarding schools, neither text can be considered strictly autobiographical.[25] Indeed, as Winsloe explained in the programme to the debut performance of *Knight* Nérestan in Leipzig:

> Many years of my childhood were spent in the same environment as described in 'Knight Nérestan'. The Manuela Case is authentic, even if the form it is

presented in here cannot be considered a direct documentation. Individual persons from my childhood experiences have, of course, been reworked and reshaped, although everything that concerns the details of the school environment can be considered a faithful depiction of the conditions.[26]

Secondary literature on Winsloe's writing suggests that the novel could be interpreted as a form of 'diagnosis narrative', a genre defined by Mara Taylor as 'a specifically German narrative of sexual identity that can be located in multiple discourses from 1900 onward'.[27] Much like the case study that was discussed in Chapter 2, the 'diagnosis narrative' was often framed by descriptive fragments about the mental and physical state of the protagonist's parents, the protagonist's childhood experiences and, most importantly, details of the protagonist's first erotic encounter. Like the case study, the diagnosis narrative acts as a form of mediated discourse, facilitated and reformulated by the author. The fact that the author is positioned as a mediator and not narrator or protagonist is fundamental to the genre because, as Taylor asserts, 'the primary mode of coming to awareness of one's sexuality in turn-of-the-century and early twentieth-century Germany was experienced as a diagnosis from outside'.[28]

Although diagnosis does not form part of Raedt-de Canter's novel, some scholars have claimed that the work belongs to the genre of 'confessional literature'.[29] However, the author blurs the lines between herself and the protagonist by juxtaposing her insertion of what Paul de Man terms an authorial 'surrogate'– a young female protagonist named Eva de Canter – with her use of the second-person narrative form.[30] Like Winsloe's *The Girl Manuela*, Raedt-de Canter's novel includes the possibility of self-revelation – although one must accept that the author's narrative does indeed include some lived experiences – the second-person narrative employed fundamentally tests the traditional parameters of this genre: the narrator, author and protagonist are *not* the same figure. In this way, Raedt-de Canter's 'you-form' renders the reader culpable for the textual transgressions that take place in the novel, positioning them in the role of the transgressor/confessor. When the protagonist, Eva, is punished for speaking out of turn, for instance, it is the reader who feels reprimanded: 'think about the burden you are for us', Sister Alfonse addresses the reader, 'your soul stinks of corruption'.[31] Therefore, in this blending of historical contextualization, autobiographical moments and the text's later lesbian symbolism, it could be suggested that Raedt-de Canter's work belongs instead to what Audre Lorde has termed a genre of 'biomythography': a combination of 'dreams/myths/histories that give [the] book shape'.[32] Looking now at the dreams, myths and histories that shape the protagonists' experiences both in *Boarding School* and *The Girl Manuela*, I will consider how the novels nuance sexological discourses of their time and present alternatives to the medicalizing narratives of congenital inversion.

'Alone in the World': Dynamic Desires in *Boarding School*

For the most part, the subject of same-sex desire in Raedt-de Canter's novel *Boarding School* is alluded to symbolically, being presented to the reader through subtle images of wild gardens, homosocial institutions and fixations on mother-like figures.[33] Nonetheless, this erotic symbolism culminates in physical manifestations of queer pleasure in the novel, during which the protagonist is kissed night after night by a mysterious girl, who is disguised by the darkness of the dormitory. As a novel written in the early twentieth century that circles around themes of queer longing and desire, and features a transgressive and socially nonconformist protagonist, it is certainly tempting to approach *Boarding School* through the lens of sexological inversion. However, in this section, I will demonstrate how Raedt-de Canter's passages about queer desires remain largely unconcerned with the search for origins and make no attempt to diagnose or label such feelings as deviant or even sinful. Indeed, while homage is paid to established queer literary tropes of the time, and sexological signifiers are scattered throughout the text, the multivalence of Raedt-de Canter's protagonist refuses any single rendering of her gendered performance or sexual preferences, which creates an alternative model of desire that remains unknowable and unfixed.

Positioned as an outsider from the opening scenes, the protagonist (who shares the position of the reader and the name of the author) is presented as a lonely child who speaks of her envy of what she considers to be the other students' sense of 'togetherness/solidarity' (*saamhorigheid*). During the Sunday reading hour, the protagonist's feelings are further laid bare as she is consumed by the exploits of the central male character René in Hector Malot's *Alone in the World* (*Sans Famille*, 1878 – translated into Dutch as *Alleen op de Wereld*, 1880).[34] Although the degree to which the protagonist actively seeks out her own company remains ambiguous in the novel, her rebellious nature and refusal to conform to gendered expectations often result in her being spurned by her classmates or forcibly separated from her fellow pupils as punishment. Published two years after Radclyffe Hall's *The Well of Loneliness*, the religious homosocial setting of the novel, the descriptions of the school as an 'abyss of loneliness' and the protagonist's early identification with the male character 'René' all appear to engage consciously with existing queer literary tropes present in Western European writing of this time.[35] Yet, while the stage seems set for an exploration of the aetiology of her protagonist's queer desires, Raedt-de Canter's writing deviates quickly and markedly from sexological models of sexual and gendered fixity. From the outset of the novel, her deployment of the second-person narrative challenges the framework of the sexological case study and interrupts the reader's search for origins. As mentioned above, the reader and the protagonist are, for all intents and purposes, supposed to comprise the *same figure*, which makes the reading experience anything but an objective analysis. Arguably to allow the reader to insert themselves more easily into the narrative, Raedt-de Canter offers very few physical descriptions of the protagonist and gives no lengthy accounts of her familial or social background. Indeed, it is only through judgements of other characters in the novel that an image of the protagonist is constituted in the mind of the reader. When the protagonist claims to be 'fiercely envious' of other students who have 'beautiful, gifted faces ... prompt manners, [and] fine clothes', for example, it is the image of a protagonist without such physical, behavioural and material markers that is woven into the mind of the reader.[36] When the protagonist later prays for long golden ringlets like her friend Mariette, the reader is again able to infer a protagonist with shorter, straighter and darker hair. However, such physiological clues remain few and far between in the novel. In this way, Raedt-de Canter avoids creating any singular image of the tomboyish 'child invert'. The physical appearance of the protagonist can only be constructed in relation to that which she is *not*, rather than conforming to pre-existing images based on medicosocial categories. In fact, the only direct description of the protagonist's physical appearance by another character comes in the final chapter, when a male friend voices the opinion that the protagonist 'has become beautiful'.

While scant information is provided about the appearance of the protagonist, her behavioural misdemeanours encourage the reader to view her as a nonconformist within the context of the conservative religious boarding school that she attends. The protagonist's wish to rebel against the social expectations she is confronted with is explored most explicitly after she returns to the domestic setting during her summer holiday. After dismissing the compliment mentioned above that she has 'become beautiful' – the traditional marker of female worth – the protagonist desires to demonstrate her social value instead by fighting and wrestling with her male friends and cousins. Yet, the protagonist is soon left frustrated, as she realizes that she is being treated differently by her male peers, especially her childhood friend Harry, who no longer wishes to wrestle with her, but to kiss her instead:

> Broer and Trump are fighting. You watch with fierce interest. 'Should we join in, Harry?' ... 'Us, fight? Of course not. But I know what I'd rather do ...'

> You become impatient and reply petulantly: 'Not me. We have always fought together, why not now?' 'Because I don't want to fight with a nice girl.' There it was. You look at him but he meant it … You feel yourself in uncharted territory with this strange new Harry, who definitely does not want to fight with you, and you begin to doubt any of the arguments you might use to persuade him otherwise.[37]

Finding herself in 'uncharted territory' with her male friends, the protagonist reluctantly resolves that she and Harry 'will no longer fight together, no longer play [Cowboys and] Indians … Not this summer and not the following summer, either'.[38] Concluding that the protagonist has achieved a sense of closure on the matter, Harry confesses his love for her and suggests that they marry when they are older. When the protagonist responds affirmatively – albeit indifferently – to his 'proposal', Harry succumbs to the protagonist's desire to wrestle with him. Yet, in spite of the initial pleasure the protagonist takes in their game and the joyful memories that are stirred in her mind of previous 'battles', the gendered dynamic that newly structures her relationship with her friend leaves her feeling bitter:

> Harry wins. Straddling you he roars a victory cry across the room and you are definitively defeated. But then he bends over and kisses you three, four times in a row, quickly and firmly. 'There, there, and there. You can have it your way but I can also have it mine. You are such a sweet girl.' As you head back to your bed, tired and sore, there is for the first time a feeling of resentment in you against the male sense of superiority.[39]

Having been put in her place during her tussle – that is, both physically and symbolically beneath Harry – the protagonist resents the unexpected (social) position in which she finds herself, calling to mind the 'painful reflections' of Krafft-Ebing's 'child invert'. Particularly when read in the context of the erotic encounters that the protagonist experiences with fellow female students, which will be discussed in the second section of this chapter, the protagonist's resistance to gender expectations and the advances of her male friends baits the modern reader to make recourse to more reductive sexological frameworks. However, almost immediately, Raedt-de Canter steers the reader towards a more nuanced and complicated gendered and sexual narrative.

As is typical of the novel's nonlinear structure, the encounter with Harry ends abruptly and shifts to a passage that appears to take place towards the end of the summer holiday. Here, the protagonist is found relaxing with her new love interest, Pierre, on a 'bright Limburgian summer afternoon'.[40] Relishing the feeling of the sun on her skin as she lies in the meadow, the protagonist allows her surroundings to wash over her: 'The air is balmy and warm and light ... The coolness of the grass against your back and the depth of the blue sky into which your eyes can gaze endlessly.'[41] Having been humiliated by Harry in the previous scene and insulted by the label of 'sweet girl', the protagonist is paradoxically pictured here as being 'endlessly' fulfilled by nature – an image that appears to shore up the very gendered tropes she had so recently – in the text – sought to resist. However, the permanence of this picture is again destabilized as the protagonist begins to question 'the meaning of fate', as her gaze lands on the swing set beside her drifting 'slowly in and out, wavering, indecisive'.[42] Thus, while the protagonist is placed in a traditionally gendered setting and is seemingly fulfilled by the nature that surrounds her, the very indecisiveness of this landscape renders the gendered norms it calls to mind themselves unstable. The frenetic temporal jumps between scenes during the episode with Pierre further upsets the idea of a teleological gendered narrative, or a story of the search for the genealogical 'origins' of the protagonist's erotic desire. Indeed, throughout the novel, the protagonist's desires refuse, just like Eve Kosofsky Sedgwick's 'reading child', to resolve themselves 'into a sexual specificity of proscribed object choice, aim site or identification'. The kisses she experiences with the 'new' Harry and the blonde, cherub-faced Pierre are said to be 'strange and exciting', just as those with the girl in the dormitory are described as 'wonderful' and 'mysterious'. Thus, while Raedt-de Canter depicts a protagonist who is isolated from the world around her, resistant to gendered norms, and desirous of the feminine and maternal, little recourse made to the somatic signifiers or fixidity that formed the foundations of Krafft-Ebing's and Hirschfeld's theories on congenital homosexual desires or inversion. Indeed, the protagonist's resistance to social categories of gender and desire holds true even in the final sentences of the novel. As she smudges a portrait of Pierre with her thumb to keep the image safe from prying eyes, the reader is told that Pierre 'disappears into the darkness', just like the girl in the dormitory: 'it is funny to see. Just as if he is melting, flowing away ... no one shall ever know'.[43] In this way, the image is emblematic of the protagonist's romantic experiences more broadly; her gendered performance and sexual desires remain indeterminate and unspecified throughout the novel and cannot – or refuse to be – fixed.

'I Want to Be a Boy': Queering Sexological Tropes in *The Girl Manuela*

Christa Winsloe's *The Girl Manuela* sits structurally much closer to the genre of 'diagnosis narrative' than Raedt-de Canter's nonlinear novel. Unlike Raedt-de Canter's work, *The Girl Manuela* does not focus solely on the school environment, but also includes a detailed history of Manuela's childhood, giving the reader ample chance to analyse the 'elementary data' that sexologists such as Havelock Ellis conceived as being central to the construction of a case study.[44] The fact that 'The Manuela Case', as Winsloe herself termed it, existed in two visual forms – the stage play and the film – prior to the publication of the novel further suggests that readers would have had a mental imprint of the protagonist before reading the text, encouraging them in their search for further pieces of the sexological puzzle. Here, the text does not disappoint. Opening with the birth of Manuela von Meinhardis, the novel chronicles the events of the protagonist's childhood, which is preceded by some portentous prophesying by the novel's omniscient narrator. Declaring that 'Manuela was [destined] to be a girl', the narrator describes a host of other divinations relating to the protagonist's birth. Arriving like 'a Christmas present', Manuela is initially depicted as a treasured member of the Family von Meinhardis. However, despite such fairytale beginnings, foreshadowings of the protagonist's tragic future are already intimated on the first page. Indeed, while the reader has been told that Manuela is '[destined] to be a girl', the visits from close family that follow her birth show the protagonist falling at the first hurdle of gender conformity: 'Although everybody said that the child was beautiful, it was not true. For above the dark eyes, whose whites were blue, there were no eyebrows. A bonnet was pulled over the infant's head to hide the baldness of the skull.'[45] Here, the visitors are invested in the claim that Manuela is a beautiful child *because* she has been assigned the status of 'girl'. Yet, in telling the reader that Manuela is in fact *not* beautiful, the narrator points to the artifice of social constructions of gender on the one hand, while contributing to the frameworks that uphold them on the other. In other words, the reader is presented with the idea that there exists an objective 'truth' about the nature of beauty and femininity (and femaleness) – one that is tied up in physiognomic markers such hair and eye colour, for example – *and* that the narrator is qualified to parse this truth on their behalf. Consequently, Manuela is stigmatized from the very outset of the novel: that she does not meet the standards of femininity, even as she takes her first breaths, effectively bars her from entry into the female world.[46] Yet, to read this text as the story of the 'child invert' would be to ignore the nuances in Manuela's embodiments of masculinity. Rather, in her figurative – and later literal – reprisals of queer camp, I argue it is possible to read productions of masculine *femininities*, which serve to challenge readings in which gendered inversion is reduced to the notion of 'girl-wanting-to-be-boy'.

Just as in the case studies discussed in Part I of this book, the first half of Winsloe's novel is dedicated to descriptions of the troubling and traumatic events that precede Manuela's arrival at the boarding school. Ample evidence of Manuela's gender nonconformity is presented to the reader during scenes depicting her desires to engage in 'boyish' pastimes. During a game of Cowboys and Indians, for example, she is seen to be frustrated by her lot after she is relegated to the role of the 'squaw'. She imagines instead what life would be like if she were able to enjoy the freedoms of her male siblings:

> Manuela is the squaw and must stay home and cook while the men embark on the warpath ... She is sad that she is just a squaw. Once again, she ponders about the misfortune that she is a girl and not allowed to wear Indian trousers ... It must be wonderful, to be able to brawl and wrangle just like a man, with a gun in one's belt.[47]

Like Hirschfeld's subjects 'Helene N.', who 'was very wild [and] took a lively interest in games of Indians and soldiers', and 'Fräulein Katharina T.', who 'never felt she was a girl ... she preferred to play the pirate, at the helm with a sabre and a whip', Manuela frequently conceives of herself as the male hero in her childhood games.[48] Thus, as the very picture of Krafft-Ebing's 'Urning girl', Manuela is shown to engage in 'painful reflections' about the inescapability of her biological sex and consequently to embody the male role in her fantasies and games. Yet, while Manuela dreams of brawling and wrangling 'just like a man', this hypermasculine imagery is destabilized by the detachable phallic gun that she imagines carrying in her belt, as well as the associated homoeroticism of the world of cowboy men. Indeed, in a community devoid of women and with 'props – like guns and horses' carrying an undeniably 'erotic charge', the ranch cultures that were depicted in British and American literary writing during the nineteenth century often focused on a central male-male friendship, which led to a social interest in the 'homoerotic cowboy romance'. This interest, as Robert Martin observes, 'lingered on in popular culture well into the twentieth century'.[49] During one of Manuela's first scenes of gendered transgression, then, it is certainly suggestive that the type of masculinity that she wishes to embody may have already brought to mind queerness in the imaginations of some of Winsloe's readers.

Yet, it is not only with queer heroic masculinities, in the form of the cowboy, that Manuela identifies; more overtly feminine male figures, such as the acrobat, also feature strongly in the protagonist's fantasies. While the acrobat was doubtlessly associated with the traditional masculine characteristics of strength and courage, by the 1930s such performers were also affiliated strongly with queer desire and effeminacy. The homoerotic paintings of American artist Paul Cadmus (1904–1999), for example, as well as the musings of French poet Jean Cocteau (1899–1963) on cross-dressing striptease and trapeze artist 'Barbette' and the photographs of performers such as German dancer and poet Sebastian Droste, all contributed to the establishment of a queerly coded male circus performer, who was dressed in flamboyant costumes and exaggerated stage make-up. Merging the masculine strength of the strongman with the elegance of the dancer, the acrobat was depicted as a highly androgynous character. At once neither/nor and both, the figure of the 'androgyne', as Susan Sontag suggests, has become 'one of the great images of Camp sensibility'.[50] Yet, while women have historically been positioned as the 'objects of camp and subject to it' rather than as 'camp subjects' in their own right, as Pamela Robertson has noted, in a scene that precedes an interaction with a female student for whom Manuela has developed intense romantic feelings, the reader is presented with an interesting framing of tomboy masculinity:[51]

> there was a huge audience and [Manuela] was poised in the circus dome. The spotlights hit her and the music stopped when she did the 'Great Wave' and then whirled with a flourish as she jumped in a high arc through the air, sank into a squat and, following one final jump, stood up. The applause rang out and Manuela, who was of course a man, in a tight, white, silk jersey, took a bow, smiling, as if to say: Oh please, that's nothing …[52]

In Manuela's imaginary game, she is presented at once 'of course' as a man, but *also* as a girl, as suggested by the continued use of the pronouns 'she' and 'her'. Moreover, her fantasy act is situated very explicitly as an exaggerated *performance* of gender, complete with spotlights, music and applause. The protagonist's description of the 'tight, white, silk jersey' of her trapeze artist, the whirling flourishes she undertakes and her ironic dismissal of the applause that she critically seeks out further manifests a 'love of the unnatural: of artifice and exaggeration', which codifies Sontag's notion of 'Camp'.[53] Certainly, in a very similar way to Jean Cocteau's descriptions of trapeze artist Barbette, as s/he flies through the air, the image of Manuela's whirling flourishes might be considered to '[function] as a metaphor for the leap "across the boundaries" separating male and female gender into a space that is neither male nor female, but androgynous'.[54] In this way, Manuela's embodiments of queer masculinity are able to produce both the flamboyance of camp and the neither/nor of the androgyne, which, I argue, results in an intricate performance of queer femininity *through* masculinity. However, Manuela's enjoyment of her camp performances of femininity are often belied in the book by the realities of her biological sex, which bring about a more forceful rejection of her womanhood – as well as her 'male femininity' – and, consequently, a more determined desire to cast off the feminine as something that is 'bad'.

Following Manuela's arrival at the boarding school, the protagonist experiences a milestone moment that demands a self-reflexive engagement with her own body. Discovering that she has begun her monthly bleeding, Manuela approaches Fräulein von Bernburg for guidance. As 'a culturally scripted physiological event', Janet Lee suggests that the menarche 'has important implications for a girl's sense of herself and her world'.[55] Indeed, it is telling that only shortly after the scene of Manuela's menarche, she is reprimanded by the head teacher, Frau Oberin, for acting like a 'boy'. When Fräulein von Bernburg questions Manuela about this misconduct, the protagonist attempts to explain her feelings of dissatisfaction with her femaleness, admitting a desire to *be* male: 'It is because I want to be a boy. I do not like my hair or my skirt, at home I always wore trousers when I played with my brothers, I would prefer to wear them always. I do not want to be a woman – I want to be a man and always be there for you, Fräulein von Bernburg.'[56] It is only here, when Manuela's tomboyism is combined with her growing desire for her teacher, that her gender transgressions are considered dangerous. Unlike the tomboy's counterpart, the sissy – for whom gender nonconformity is always a dangerous occupation – female masculinity, as Jack Halberstam notes, becomes a social problem only when it appears as 'the sign of extreme male identification'.[57] Halberstam concludes that if gender dissonance is not refocused during adolescence, when sexual feelings are expected to develop, 'the full force of gender conformity descends on the girl'.[58] Fittingly, then, it is following Manuela's menarche, a time during which her desire to deny her womanhood and her desire for maternal care are combined with queer longings, that her 'extreme identification' with the male role is forcefully punished.

While Manuela's acrobatic flights of camp fantasy present her with an outlet for her early exploration with gendered norms and expectations, it is in the character of the knight Nérestan at the end of the novel that the protagonist begins to identify more fully with the masculine male hero. Dressed 'entirely in silver', Manuela is described in the rehearsals as 'slowly, more and more, becoming the knight Nérestan'.[59] And, during the final performance of the play, Manuela leaves her classmates awestruck by her authentic portrayal of protagonist: 'your voice was … quite dark and then, all of a sudden, the way that you moved, so genuine … anyone would have believed tonight that you are actually half boy'.[60] While the knight is presented as a masculine figure, if we return to the image of the camp androgyne, Manuela is described as *almost* becoming Nérestan on stage in her position as 'half boy'. Indeed, the abovementioned appraisals of Manuela's classmates show striking parallels to Cocteau's assessment of the performances of cross-dressing circus artist Barbette, which he described as: 'a real masterpiece of pantomime, summing up in parody all the women [Barbette] has ever studied, *becoming himself the woman*' (emphasis added).[61] However, there remains at least one key distinction between the two. Cocteau reminds his readers of the artifice of Barbette's androgynous display: 'we are in the magic light of the theatre, in this trick-factory where truth has no currency, where anything natural has no value ... where the only things that convince us are card tricks and sleights of hand'.[62] Manuela's gendered performance on the other hand, in spite of the literal stage she performs upon, is considered by others to be 'authentic' and 'genuine'. Here, again, Winsloe queers the framework of the literary case study, which found the truth of same-sex desire in accounts of immutable, binary gendered inversion. Indeed, by creating space in her writing for performative moments of camp sensibility, Winsloe suggests that these unsettled evocations of masculine femininity are equally 'true' to her protagonist's nature and desires. While I have to this point argued that Manuela's gendered performances might be read as an expression of queer male femininity, it is in her romantic interactions with Fräulein von Bernburg that the significance of queer *female* femininity to the construction and experience of desire between women most pertinently comes to the fore.

A Mother's Love

The homosocial setting of the boarding school has been considered 'the preferred locus for most fictions about women loving women' since the resurgence of interest in Sappho's poems during the nineteenth century.[63] Although there is no evidence that Sappho's followers formed any kind of 'gynaecium' or followed the male erastes/eromenos tradition, the image of the school 'ruled by the seductive or seducing teacher' is a trope that has long since stirred the Sapphic imagination in Western Europe.[64] In sexological literature, the nurturing and guiding teacher was thought to play a pivotal role in the life of the 'Urning child', serving to shape their educational interests and support them in their social development. This connection was of specific significance, as Magnus Hirschfeld observes, for 'Urning girls' whose 'interest for the subject often stands in close connection with the personhood of the teacher. The worship ... of these Urning girls for certain teachers and governesses often bears the character of an idolatrous infatuation'.[65] Within the conventions of what Elaine Marks terms the 'lesbian fairy tale based on the model of Sappho', the 'idolatrous infatuation' of the younger girl for the older woman in literary texts has historically been presented through the essence of an erotic mother–daughter bond:

> The younger woman, whose point of view usually dominates, is always passionate and innocent ... The older woman as object of the younger woman's desire is restrained and admirable, beautiful and cultivated ... The exchanges between the older and younger woman are reminiscent of a mother-daughter relationship. The mother of the younger woman is either dead or in some explicit way inadequate. Her absence is implied by the young woman's insistent

need for a good-night kiss. The dénouement in these lesbian fairy tales is often brought about by a public event during which private passions explode.[66]

As Richard Dyer notes, Marks' framework effectively chronicles the events of Winsloe's play, film and novel. Indeed, when Manuela arrives at the boarding school, it is 'the restrained and admirable, beautiful and cultivated' Fräulein von Bernburg with her ritualistic goodnight kiss who causes Manuela's 'private passions' to explode during a 'public event'.[67] In Raedt-de Canter's novel, too, the mother-figure shapes the formation of the protagonist's same-sex desires, along with the protagonist's secret longing for a motherly goodnight kiss, even as the 'public' confession of these desires is not articulated in the text. Yet, while the mother–child model has served as a literary framework through which to make female same-sex desires visible, its very eroticism has often been rendered taboo in Western cultures. As Susan Weisskopf has rightly observed, there exists in Western Europe a 'cultural belief that mothers are not, and should not be, sexual persons'.[68] Geetha Ramanathan acknowledges this fact, too, as she analyses the role of the maternal in Sagan's cinematic adaptation *Girls in Uniform*, suggesting that the 'discomfiture' of the viewer regarding the relationship between Fräulein von Bernburg and Manuela comes from a 'deeply buried cultural beliefs about the maternal, the maternal body, and the maternal erotic'.[69] The social denial of existing forms of eroticism that draw on maternal models, and are shaped dually by eroticized power differences and authority, has often served to desexualize depictions of love between women and to obfuscate the connection between the maternal and the erotic. However, in the following section, I will argue that Winsloe and Raedt-de Canter's deployment of what Bethany Jacobs terms the 'Erotic Mother "essence"' does not serve only to make queer desires *visible*, but also offers new ways in which to interpret the relationship between the queer and the feminine/maternal more generally.

In Raedt-de Canter's novel, the figure of the biological mother – or caregiver – is present, in a Derridean sense, only through her absence. Yet, while the protagonist's mother does not appear in the novel, maternalism and the femininity are shown to be central to the textual construction of queer longing and the protagonist's experience of erotic desire. Already in the opening scenes of the novel, the protagonist's desire for maternal care is shown to be something that stirs deep sensual feelings. After smearing shoe polish on another student, she is sent to sit in a room filled with disturbing taxidermy figures by the cruel Sister Alphonse. Scared and alone, the protagonist swallows a 'frightened "mother" cry' before the scene shifts abruptly to the school sanatorium.[70] In this sanctuary, a place that inspires both a 'feeling of home' and 'a nagging homesickness', the protagonist experiences her first emotional, and arguably romantic, attachment to the motherly school nurse,

Sister Veronica.⁷¹ Following the silenced cry for her mother, the scene with Sister Veronica is described with allusions to violets and wild gardens, both historic symbols of love between women: 'Sister Veronica … Veronica. You see a flowerbed of dark violets when, gently, on the tip of your tongue, you say: Veronica … A flower bed full, in a dim old yard with swaying trees and mossy paths.'⁷² As well as the natural setting of this fantasy offering a queer counterpoint to the later scene in the meadow with Pierre, the references to tongue tips, fecund flowerbeds and mossy paths are suffused with a sense of maternal eroticism, urging a queer reading of the potential romantic/sexual feelings of the protagonist towards the school nurse. However, when the protagonist attempts to bypass the boundaries of propriety that distance her from the nurse with an informality, she is gently rebuffed: '"Veronica …" you said and paused. "Sister Veronica…" "Oh, Veronica…" you said, embarrassed, and rubbed your head along her warm, rough, cotton sleeve.'⁷³ The suggestion of the sheepish protagonist rubbing her head against the nurse's 'warm, rough, cotton sleeve' positions the caregiver, who had answered the protagonist's 'mother cry', in an erotic – and explicitly maternal – light. Furthermore, Sister Veronica's rejection of the protagonist's intimate form of address only appears to serve to strengthen the erotic tension experienced by the protagonist. Indeed, the fact that Sister Veronica's nurturing remains firmly within the traditional role of 'woman as maternal caregiver' is vital to maintaining the eroticism of the scene. As Ramanathan notes of Manuela's attraction to Fräulein von Bernburg in the film *Girls in Uniform*, the erotic power of the maternal appears to be entirely dependent on the paradoxical 'promise of authority being jarred', while only ever being further confirmed and preserved.⁷⁴ The desire felt for the maternal authority figure Sister Veronica lays the foundations for a pattern that becomes paradigmatic of the protagonist's romantic and erotic encounters with female characters in the novel. Although the desires of the protagonist remain ambiguous at this point, she undeniably experiences pleasure through the maternal care of the nurse, who offers her a sense of 'home'. Thus, desire in this scene is also able to break away from limited notions of (sexual) bodily pleasure, and the reader/protagonist is able to identify erotic elements in everything from 'mossy paths' to 'cotton sleeves', arguably anticipating Lorde's vision of an eroticism that 'places the erotic on the spectrum of the sexual but includes more than sex'.⁷⁵

When the protagonist is later sent to sit outside in the cold as a punishment, it is an older student who takes on the role of the 'Erotic Mother'. Initially described by the protagonist as 'ugly', 'fat', 'broad' and 'weak', Fenna van Beers brings the protagonist food and carries her inside to the warmth of a radiator. These simple acts of maternal care appear to transform the protagonist's opinions of the older student. Her eager but embarrassed response to Fenna's suggestion that she tuck the protagonist into her bed harks back to the earlier scene with Sister Veronica: '"Just like old times?" Strange that you are so embarrassed by this question.'[76] As Fenna carries her to the dormitory, the protagonist draws direct comparisons between the older student and her (missing) mother: '[Fenna] smells like mother smelled, she walks like mother walked.'[77] Inhaling what she calls Fenna's 'mother smell' (*moedergeur*), the protagonist allows herself to be 'cradled like a small, helpless child'.[78] Concluding this motherly collage, Fenna tucks the protagonist into bed with a gently admonishing goodnight wish, to which the protagonist responds affectionately 'sleep well, mother Fenna'.[79] Just as with Sister Veronica, Fenna's motherly reprimand critically maintains a power imbalance between the protagonist and herself, although this time, the motherly rebuke is shown to be pretence, as Fenna asks the protagonist to promise to tell Sister Alphonse that the older student had been 'very strict' (*heel streng*) with her. This 'strictness', alongside Fenna's 'mother smell', expresses what Adrienne Rich has described as the 'primal sensation' associated with the feelings of 'continuity and stability – but also the rejections and refusals' that are experienced in childhood 'through a woman's hands, eyes, body [and] voice'.[80] And, moreover, the 'mother smell' further evokes Helene Deutsch's suggestion of a 'desire for the mother [that] acquires characteristics of a fantasy about the mother's body'.[81] However, the protagonist's early fantasies of the maternal body emerge in their fullest sense in what is arguably the most explicitly erotic scene of the novel.

In a culmination of these earlier maternal encounters, the protagonist is found searching in her dormitory for her mother's rosary, an object that she must keep hidden from the prying eyes of Sister Alphonse. As she locates the beads and holds them to her cheek, a 'burly' girl steals up behind her in the darkness, turns her around and kisses her firmly on the mouth:

> The kiss! How simultaneously sinful and glorious! ... She had thrown two arms, soft, warmly-clad arms, around your neck and, calmly and firmly, two cool, moist lips had kissed your mouth. Your heart was pounding when she let you go. Why? ... A strange, unknown hunger was stilled by her kiss. A strange, uncontainable hunger was left behind. For, what did that blazingly fierce, thrilling desire mean, that made you blush so painfully, made you feel sinful and abandoned but, at the same time, weighed in your heart like a heavy treasure?[82]

Raedt-de Canter's deployment of the second-person narrative form ensures that the reader is equally as consumed by the kiss as the protagonist and, moreover, is made complicit in this erotic act. The author's use of metonymic personification again recalls Deutsch's 'fantasy about the mother's body': it is the mysterious girl's warmly clad arms (*warm-bemouwde armen* – lit.

warmly sleeved arms) and lips that consume the protagonist in the darkness, just as it was Fenna's 'mother smell' that soothed the protagonist in the earlier scene. Broken down into bodily pieces of erotic significance, the 'strong' maternal body with its 'round, firm breasts' is seen to tower over the protagonist as the unknown girl bestows upon her the longed-for goodnight kiss. The imagery of the 'warmly clad' arms and the 'blazingly fierce, thrilling desire' that the protagonist experiences during the kiss remind the reader of the pattern that links the maternal to sensual and erotic pleasure, all the while building on an intensity that is only ever implied in earlier scenes. Here, the maternal is situated as something that is undeniably erotic and connected to an unknown – and unknowable – 'hunger'. The fact that the kiss is preceded by the protagonist's search for her mother's missing rosary might suggest that the unknown girl is the Freudian replacement for the mother – an idea that might promote the pervading myth of the 'sexless mother' and serve to de-eroticize the kiss. Rather, cast in the light of earlier scenes in the novel, the pleasure experienced by the protagonist during the kiss suggests that maternalism itself creates space for experiences of the erotic. In this way, as Richard Dyer and Julianne Pidduck have written, 'the mother/daughter quality of the relationship only makes it more lesbian, not less'.[83] However, as is typical of Raedt-de Canter's approach to desire in this novel, no further reference is made to the series of goodnight kisses following this scene, neither when the protagonist is angry at Harry for forcing a kiss upon her nor when her later love interest Pierre asks her if she has ever been kissed before. The kiss disappears from the text without further trace, an erotic maternal moment of 'mysterious glory'.[84]

In a similar way to Raedt-de Canter, Winsloe adopts the erotic mother-figure as the original site for her protagonist's queer desires. Already by the second page of the novel, the reader is informed that Manuela's mother is the centre of her childhood universe: 'Mother was she, who was always there. She who came when Lela shrieked, she who calmed when Lela cried.'[85] When Manuela's mother leaves the family home to care for her sick son in the countryside, the protagonist is shown to be devastated by the disappearance of her mother and consumed by the desire for 'mother's kiss'.[86] Following the deaths of her mother and her brother early on in the novel, Manuela befriends a young boy named Fritz Lennartz, who invites her to his musical performance at the Christmas bazaar. As Fritz plays onstage, Manuela catches a glimpse of the boy's mother in a moment that marks the protagonist's first romantic/erotic attachment to an older female figure: 'When Lela saw this new face, something froze inside her. Involuntarily she moved forward a little in her chair to look closer. What was it? This woman, who had Fritzy's face – only nicer, softer, lovelier …'[87] Manuela is captivated by the maternal figure and her body responds immediately to the woman's presence: '[Manuela's] ears had turned red, her face had become pale with exertion. Her mouth dried up, her palms became sweaty. What was it? What? It hurt so painfully and, at the same time, it did not.'[88] Echoing the 'unknown hunger' that is both 'sinful and wonderful' in Raedt-de Canter's *Boarding School*, Manuela's desires initially appear indecipherable to her and fill her with a curious inner conflict. After the performance, the protagonist is introduced to the older woman in a moment she describes as 'dusk with mother'.[89] Here, the image of Fritz's mother is conflated with her own missing mother, but, as she is invited to sit on the older woman's lap, Manuela is shown to take pleasure in the maternal more generally, as she closes her eyes and breathes in 'the scent that came from the strange woman, lavender and mother'.[90] Much like Fenna's 'mother-smell' in Raedt-de Canter's novel, the scent of Fritz's mother alludes to the importance of the primal mother–child bond. Yet, in both novels, these sensual maternal attributes are associated with an erotic longing that has a profound effect on their respective protagonists. After Manuela's connection with Fritz's mother is cut short when she is sent to boarding school, the figure of the 'Ersatz-Mother' and the moment of the goodnight kiss are united in their full queer significance.

When Fräulein von Bernburg arrives in the dormitory to tuck her students into bed, the students are shown to grow giddy in delight as they wait for their special moment with their favourite teacher. As she approaches Manuela, the teacher is quickly reduced by the narrator, just as in Raedt-de Canter's novel, to a series of body parts that carry out the maternal act Manuela has been longing for since her mother's death:

> 'We have not properly greeted one another yet, little Manuela!' … and before Manuela can answer … the hands bend down, the voice bends down, a warm bosom bends down, a person bends down to her, and Fräulein von Bernburg kisses Manuela's forehead, as if she saw nothing of the tears that were now running freely down both sides of her face.[91]

The hands, voice and warm bosom of Fräulein von Bernburg are detached from the teacher until the very moment of the goodnight kiss, during which they are merged in the full form of the maternal figure. Yet, while Fräulein von Bernburg is described as kissing the foreheads of each of her students before bed in a routine and ritualistic manner – calling to mind the restrained maternalism of Sister Veronica in Raedt-de Canter's text – the teacher crosses a seemingly unspoken maternal boundary after witnessing a more extreme emotional outburst from the protagonist later in the novel. Left humiliated after forgetting a religious passage during her recital for Fräulein von Bernburg's class, Manuela breaks down when the teacher makes her round of the dormitory:

[Manuela] spread her arms and threw herself, losing all her strength, around Fräulein von Bernburg's neck, who almost lost balance and, shocked, held the shivering child tightly ... Gently, she tried to pull the arms from her neck. Lela grabbed greedily after the hands ... The hands did not resist. They let it happen. They took up the tear stained face of the child and Fräulein von Bernburg leaned down and kissed her trembling mouth.[92]

While Fräulein von Bernburg initially attempts to free herself from Manuela's emotional embrace, the narrator suggests that the teacher's hands ultimately resign themselves to Manuela's affection – they 'let it happen'. Yet, as Fräulein von Bernburg leans down to kiss Manuela's 'trembling mouth', the maternal figure is shown to initiate further contact consciously, actively participating in the eroticization of the mother–child model.[93] Although the kiss is the first – and only – explicitly erotic moment to occur in the novel, the maternal qualities of Fräulein von Bernburg are shown to ring consistently with an awareness for the romantic and the erotic even in scenes that are presented as more familial in nature.

When Manuela notices that she has begun her monthly bleeding, for instance, Fräulein von Bernburg adopts the function of the maternal educator, as she declares: 'I will have to take on the mother-role for you ... and tell you what to do when they come.'[94] In the scene that follows, Manuela and Fräulein von Bernburg experience a pivotal moment of mother–daughter interconnectedness that Lee suggests happens during a child's 'menstrual education'.[95] The image of Fräulein von Bernburg sitting bent over Manuela as the protagonist lies 'beautifully' in bed listening 'more to the sound of the voice that was teaching her than to the words themselves' seems to presage the 'fantasy of the mother' depicted in Audre Lorde's biomythography *Zami: A New Spelling of My Name* (1982).[96] In Lorde's *Zami*, the protagonist Audre recounts her own moment of erotic mother–daughter menstrual instruction that she recalls consists of 'our touching and caressing each other's most secret places'.[97] Yet, while the interaction between student and teacher is itself not so explicitly erotic, the description of Fräulein von Bernburg's feelings following the encounter nonetheless casts the passage in a decidedly romantic light. Musing to herself about Manuela's question as to whether she was happy, the teacher concludes: 'She experienced the love of this child like an unknown and undeserved happiness, which was so very much more real than the touching affection and idolatry of the other children around her ... she was made happy by this child and ... she loved it back, endlessly, with all the strength of her heart.'[98] Thus, unlike Raedt-de Canter's *Boarding School*, where the reader *is* the protagonist and therefore is party only to a narrow perspective on the events told, in Winsloe's novel the reader is made privy to the inner thoughts and feelings of Fräulein von Bernburg through an inwardly focalized narrative form. The shift in focalization that takes place in this scene – that is, from Manuela's enjoyment of the sound of Fräulein von Bernburg's voice to Fräulein von Bernburg's pleasure in Manuela's presence – gives the reader a vital insight into how the 'object' of Manuela's affections conceives of their growing attachment. Yet, while Fräulein von Bernburg is said to experience an 'unknown … happiness' on account of her bond with Manuela, she is also demonstrably troubled by her feelings. Realizing that her exclusive focus on Manuela has breached the established boundaries of teacher–student relationships, Fräulein von Bernburg concludes her thoughts on the encounter by convincing herself that 'there was nothing else for it, other than self-discipline and sacrifice'.[99] In this moment of regret following Manuela's menstrual education, it becomes clear that Fräulein von Bernburg's maternal behaviours have not only been eroticized by the protagonist, but that the teacher herself is aware of the erotic potential of her maternal feelings. In this way, and in an extension of what Ramanathan notes of the film, the mother–child model in Winsloe's novel is able to successfully '[articulate] female desire without foreclosing maternal desire'.[100]

Indeed, the significance of the maternal to the enactment of queer desire is stressed again in the final scenes of the novel. Having been confined to the sanatorium following her dramatic confession, Manuela escapes the infirmary to apologize to Fräulein von Bernburg. When the two characters meet following Manuela's confession, the reader is made aware that a shift has taken place in the erotic dynamic between the pair as the narrator describes the silence that 'fell between the two women'.[101] With the erotic bond effectively broken from the outside, Fräulein von Bernburg and her student face each other as two women, forcibly removed from the dyad of mother–child and its concomitant erotic imbalance of power. However, as Manuela falls to the ground, beseeching forgiveness, the balance of power shifts once again, and Fräulein von Bernburg rushes to the protagonist's side accordingly, comforting her with the 'hasty, warm, good, little words': 'child' and 'darling'.[102] As Fräulein von Bernburg clasps Manuela's hand, the reader witnesses the teacher's maternal instincts reawaken, even as she declares: 'You must not love me so much Manuela, it is not good. One has to fight that, overcome it, kill it.'[103] While engaged in an act of motherly care, Fräulein von Bernburg manages to reassert herself as a figure of authority, deploying the Eros that exists between Manuela and herself in an attempt to control the chaos that has been wrought as a result. In this painful parting statement, Fräulein von Bernburg both acknowledges Manuela's erotic attachment to her motherly presence and, with the use of the impersonal pronoun 'one', suggests that this mother–daughter model holds erotic meaning for her too. Although this does not go unnoticed by the protagonist, Manuela sees 'no home, no family, no world' without the presence of her beloved motherly teacher and, as a consequence, throws herself from the clock tower in the final scene of the novel.

While such a tragic demise might suggest, in the first instance, that queer relationships have no place in the homosocial community presented in Winsloe's novel, the mother–child model that shapes Manuela's relationship with Fräulein von Bernburg is experienced by the two characters as a configuration that brings pleasure to them both. Through depictions of erotic acts of maternal care, Winsloe manages in both her film and novel 'to discuss maternal desire and subjectivity without articulating distaste for either' and to draw on the tabooed eroticism inherent in familial bonds to explore the significance of the queer maternal to love between women.[104] Indeed, the fact that both Winsloe and Raedt-de Canter centralize the maternal in their navigations of the relationship between caregiving practices and the erotic suggests that the mother–child paradigm held a significance within queer communities that was able to transcend cultural borders. However, in both novels the precise meaning of this significance remains mysterious, unknowable and glorious in equal measure. Having discussed the ways in which the feminine, maternal body is ascribed erotic meaning in the novels, I will now turn in the final section of this chapter to the act of confession and the subject of queer identity formation. Here, I will suggest that scenes that include confession as an 'incitement to discourse' can present us with with vital insights into the manifold ways in which queer desires between women may have been culturally conceptualized in Germany and the Netherlands during the first half of the twentieth century.

'Confessions' and 'Comings-out': Queer Desires as Queer Identities?

Engaging critically with the social and cultural values of their time, Raedt-de Canter's and Winsloe's novels point to some key conceptual differences in the framing of same-sex desires between Germany and the Netherlands during the interwar era. By focusing on the act of confession in the novels, this final section explores the limits of Foucault's contention that the homosexual had become 'a species' by the end of the nineteenth century and will consider more generally how this statement aligns with the wider arguments of this book. As 'one of the main rituals we rely on for the production of truth' in Western societies, confession, according to Foucault, sits 'at the heart of the procedures of individualization by power'.[105] Arguing that religious authority has historically been utilized as 'a form of power which makes individuals subjects', Foucault suggests that acts of confession can be considered performative processes of 'becoming' that '[categorise] the individual, marks him [*sic*] by his own identity, imposes a law of truth upon him which he must recognise and which others have to recognise in him'.[106] Therefore, by undergoing a rigorous process of self-examination – such as that demanded, for example, by the normalizing and disciplinary practices of religious confession – it becomes possible to produce a 'truth' about who/what one *is*. Or, rather, through a process of telling 'the truth about oneself', one can constitute oneself – or, indeed, be constituted – as a social/sexual subject.[107] The question of what 'truth' comprises, of course, has a complex history of its own. If one considers, for example, confession to be process of 'power at the centre inducing people at the margins to internalise what is said about them', to quote Jeremy Tambling, there appears to be little room for the agency of the subject, who is forced 'to accept that discourse and to live it, and thereby to live their oppression'.[108] According to this interpretation, the confession of 'truth' has not constituted an individual as a subject insomuch as a social discourse that is used to police and discipline that individual has been internalized and 'lived' by them. But if we consider the existence of creative forms of counterdiscourse that challenge the hegemonic powers that seek to regulate and normalize, such as those discussed in Part II, it becomes possible to conceive of practices of self-fashioning through which new discourses make available alternative positions to which subjects might 'confess'. While both Raedt-de Canter's and Winsloe's novels may be conceived more broadly as pieces of confessional literature in and of themselves, in this section I will focus specifically on moments of literal confession within the texts to analyse which discourses appear to have been made 'available' to the protagonists and how this shapes the depiction of their desires.

In Raedt-de Canter's *Boarding School*, the existence of a coercive system of control that seeks to forbid pleasure, even as it defines it, is already established in the opening scenes of the novel. Joining the protagonist as she gets out of bed and washes her hands and face, the reader is told that she leaves the rest of her body untouched and unwashed because 'to be further uncovered is immoral'.[109] Provided with a note from the doctor after her family claim that such practices are 'dirty' (*vies*), the protagonist is subsequently entitled to a monthly bath. Made to wash while wearing a bathrobe in order to protect her modesty, she is supervised in this act by Sister Willibrord. The cold water, clinging bathrobe and careful surveillance cumulatively turn a potentially pleasurable experience into something that is almost unbearable for the protagonist: 'You imagine how much you would love God … if you did not have to wear the long, wet bathrobe until your own undershirt was pulled over your head and gradually down your body, as the bathrobe, wet and heavy and cold, slipped onto the ground. Leaving you wet and cold in your damp, clinging clothes.'[110] Biting temperatures leave the protagonist's 'skin open' for the rest of the day following the bath and serve as a constant reminder of the consequences of exposing one's flesh. During these moments, the protagonist ponders the relationship between bodily pleasure and sin: 'God gave you a body and you were not allowed to look at it. You were not allowed to wash it, you were not allowed to touch it. You sinned against God's commands if you displayed yourself as he created you. God gave you a free will and, if you used it freely, you sinned.'[111] That this denial of bodily pleasure and physical indulgence forms part of a larger system of cultural practices is evidenced in the protagonist's later joy at receiving 'witbrood' (white bread) for supper, an item that she describes as 'particularly delicious because of its paucity'.[112] The regulation of the body and its pleasures, a form of what Foucault terms 'biopower', has been considered instrumental to the act of confession – a ritual that demands a self-reflective assessment of one's daily actions and the disclosure of one's misdemeanours to a privileged listener who will consequently 'judge, punish, forgive, console, and reconcile'.[113] The effects of such corrective systems on the individual quickly become manifest in the novel when the protagonist takes up the pathologizing discourses that are used to punish her, internalizes them and replicates them as part of her own identity formation. In an early scene in the novel, for example, the cruel Sister Alphonse condemns the protagonist as a 'little serpent' whose soul 'stinks of depravity'.[114] While the protagonist is initially shown to dismiss the nun's rebuke, the power that Sister Alphonse's punitive words exert over her sense of self becomes evident as she enters the dining hall later that evening. As her fellow students turn to stare at her, the disgraced protagonist concedes: 'You know immediately how bad you are. How bewilderingly and mysteriously characterised [you are] by sin and corruption.'[115]

While the power of confession to create subjects that collude in their own surveillance and oppression is a theme that runs throughout the novel, the significance of confession as a transformative act – that is, one that constitutes the individual as a subject – is illustrated most powerfully in the novel during a scene in which the protagonist confesses to something that she has *not* done. When Sister Padua hears a voice speaking out of turn as she accompanies the students to their dormitory after evening prayer, she seeks to identify the culprit. In the scene that follows, the protagonist – a known transgressor – ostensibly tests the boundaries of confession as a subject-forming practice:

> Sister Padua asked: 'Qui a parlé?' It pulled you out of your dreams and you wondered whether she would believe you if you raised your hand. If you spoke and did not raise your hand, they never believed you. Whether she would also not believe you *now* when you had been silent and dreamy and

had not spoken? Your curiosity filled you with questions, questions that insisted upon an answer and, with a small cry, you raised your hand, fiercely. She pulled you out of the line. 'Attendez là.' 'But I did not even speak, I just wanted to …'[116]

Ultimately, the protagonist's experiment highlights how little bearing 'truth' has on the formation of a subject following a confession. The protagonist's admission of guilt effectively *makes* her guilty, even though she is not. Following this fabricated confession, the protagonist is forced by the authority figure to live the reality of the ostracized Other, as she is called out of line and punished. Already identified as a transgressor by Sister Alphonse in the earlier scene, the protagonist's 'economy of credibility' is in debit, meaning that her plea of innocence is dismissed by Sister Padua.[117] The power of confession in the novel to constitute one as a certain type of individual – one who is 'bad' or 'guilty', for example – suggests that the protagonist's queer desires might have the potential to result in an equally subject-forming experience *if* confessed. Certainly, the central scenes of erotic desire in the novel appear to be framed so clearly by the religious regulatory practices used to control the body and its pleasures to make this seem almost inevitable.

Before the central scene of confession takes place in the novel, the protagonist and her friend Mariette are depicted hiding in the school canteen to escape the cold. It is here that they find a bushel of dried apples. Hungry, and unable to resist temptation, they gorge on the fruit. Like Eve who ate of the Tree of Knowledge, the protagonist Eva swiftly incurs a 'punishment from God' for her wrongdoing, when the two friends fall sick. While Mariette is acquitted of her crime after a prompt confession, the protagonist's economy of credibility has already been damaged and she is sent to a dark attic to contemplate her misdemeanor. It is here, after she has symbolically eaten the 'fruit of knowledge', that she begins to daydream about the goodnight kiss that takes place in her dormitory each evening. Describing the event as something 'inexplicable, for which there was no name', the protagonist recounts the first occurrence of the event, which, like the eating of the fruit, is 'simultaneously sinful and delicious'.[118] By anticipating her experiences of queer desire with a passage that mirrors the act of 'original sin', Raedt-de Canter presents the reader with a character at the precipice of new sexual knowledge, yet wracked, at the same time, by associated feelings of shame and guilt. Thinking about the kiss, the protagonist attempts to categorize it according to the value systems that surround her, as she wonders glibly: 'Was it a sin, perhaps? Kissing *was* a sin; even sisters were not allowed to kiss each other. Was this, then, not a sin?'[119] Indeed, by the time that *Boarding School* was published, the Catholic Church had long begun to make a distinction between 'homosexuality as *inclination* (predisposition) and homosexuality as *deed*.[120] Thus, in the eyes of the Church, the protagonist – who not only 'hungers after the kiss' but also engages in the homoerotic act itself – would undoubtedly have been judged as committing a sinful act. Yet, in spite of the regime of bodily regulations the protagonist endures in the novel, she concludes that the kiss – and the pleasure that she experiences because of it – is not sinful, but had instead been 'sent from God to save you from your loneliness'.[121]

Shortly after her existential musings on the kiss, the protagonist is required to undertake the Sacrament of Confession. As she prepares herself for the task, a clear sense of excitement – and fear – rises within her: 'how wonderfully your heart would beat as, after careful examination and with the list of misdemeanours already on your lips, you kneeled behind the closed lattice window in the confessional box'.[122] In spite of the careful process of excavation that takes place before her confession and the moments of reverie she experiences in the attic, she does not mention the kiss to the rector and instead rattles off a list of 'ever identical offences in a habitual drone': '[I have] spoken three times in church, was naughty fifteen times, insolent seven times, disrespectful during prayer thirty-eight times [I displayed] insensitivity, slovenliness, laziness, impoliteness at the dinner table, lickerishness … All of those very often but I don't know precisely in figures.'[123] So, while the Foucauldian notion of confession as a 'technology of the self' is indeed shown to have transformative power in Raedt-de Canter's *Boarding School*, the practice of confession seemingly has little to do with acts of sexual self-fashioning. Even as the protagonist briefly considers whether the act might be considered sinful, she does not attempt to seek redemption for her desires. In this way, the unknown remains unknowable in the text and the protagonist's pleasure remains pleasurable. While she is shown to internalize the idea of 'sin' throughout the novel, the desires of the protagonist persistently refuse categorization, remaining at the discursive periphery, which means that the kiss does not ever become 'subject to discourse'.

Confession also plays a pivotal role in Christa Winsloe's novel *The Girl Manuela*. However, the public declaration of Manuela's love for Fräulein von Bernburg, which ultimately leads to the protagonist's suicide, is not the only performative act to take place in the text; rather, mimicking the perpetual cycle of 'coming out', Manuela makes several earlier attempts to articulate her desires before her final – and fatal – declaration.[124] In early moments of confession, the intersubjectivity of the confessional act points to the limitations of 'truth' to function as a subject-making discourse, particularly when penitent and confessor do not share conceptual frameworks. For example, when Manuela's father wishes to send her to boarding school after misguidedly assuming Fritz to be the object of her childhood affection, she attempts to convince her father to allow her to stay by presenting the reason for her so-called lovesickness: 'No Papa, it is not because of Fritz – it is because of his mother ...'[125] Yet, Manuela's confession of truth is dismissed as a ruse. Indeed, the fact that Manuela does not desire Fritz, but the older, motherly Frau Lennartz is unfathomable to Major von Meinhardis, who appears not to have access to a discourse that would account for Manuela's longings: 'Oh, you are splendid! You are just like me, girl. Always an excuse at hand ... But, you know what, there is still one thing you must learn. If you want to talk yourself out of something, you must do it better. No one would have fallen for that.'[126] In an inversion of the 'false confession' made by the protagonist in *Boarding School*, Manuela tells her father the truth, but is not believed. Thus, while Manuela's father has the power to 'identify' and 'punish' his daughter desires, he lacks a shared knowledge of the significance of such desires, which means they cannot be spoken into existence, even as Manuela acknowledges them openly. In a very similar way to *Boarding School*, the protagonist's initial confession is not able to constitute her as a sexual subject, only as a dishonest one. Indeed, it is only when Manuela's desires are articulated within a system that seeks to punish and control them that her confessions are shown to have transformative potential.

Shortly after Manuela arrives at the boarding school, her second significant confession takes place. After being admonished by Frau Oberin for acting 'like a boy', she attempts to explain the cause of her misconduct to Fräulein von Bernburg: 'I don't want to be a woman – I would like to be a man and always to be there for you, Fräulein von Bernburg.'[127] Unlike Manuela's father, for whom queer desire is a discursive impossibility, Fräulein von Bernburg recognizes the social implications of Manuela's admission and therefore is placed in the position to 'judge, punish, [and] forgive'. Acknowledging the power of discourse to make transgressive desires knowable, and punishable, Fräulein von Bernburg cautions her student with the stern decree: 'Such words must not pass between us.'[128] In punishment for her transgression, Manuela is asked to apologize to Frau Oberin, who consequently presses the protagonist on whether she belongs to the students who are 'too keen' on Fräulein von Bernburg. With her beloved teacher's caution fresh in her mind, Manuela is forced to deny the feelings that she had recently declared so openly. Referring back to this discussion with Manuela, Frau Oberin later warns Fräulein von Bernburg that such 'elements' can be 'poisonous if one does not put them back in their place'.[129] Seen in Manuela's various attempts to articulate her desires, then, the practice of 'closeting', as Eve Kosofsky Sedgwick has observed, is 'initiated ... by the speech act of a silence – not a particular silence, but a silence that accrues particularity by fits and starts, in relation to the discourse that surrounds and differentially constitutes it'.[130] Frau Oberin's regulatory response following the 'fits and starts' of Manuela's gender deviance 'differentially constitutes' it within a corrective system of established norms and forces the protagonist to internalize the discourse that is being used to control her body and pleasures.

However, the self-regulation of her desires becomes an increasingly difficult task as her feelings for her teacher grow more intense. When Fräulein von Bernburg gives Manuela one of her own undershirts after noticing that the student's is beyond repair, the protagonist breaks down at the generous gesture. Questioned about her outburst, Manuela explains that it is 'difficult to say'; however, after further encouragement from her teacher, she attempts to articulate the cause of her grief: 'When I go to bed in the evening and you [Fräulein von Bernburg] close the door, I experience such a longing for you that I simply cannot stop staring at the door, and then I tell myself that I am not allowed do that, and I grip tightly to the bed.'[131] Shown to have internalized the normativizing discourses that recently constituted her desires as 'poisonous', Manuela is aware that her longings are 'not allowed'. Yet, as the emotional dam breaks, it becomes clear that the protagonist's feelings will not be so easily returned to their 'place':

> For too long, [Manuela] had pushed this all back. Both arms around the hips of the woman standing in front of her, she lets the words stream out of her. 'I cannot help it. I love you, dear Fräulein von Bernburg. I love you so much, as much as my mother and, yes, much, much more. When I see your hands, I feel drawn to touch them. Your voice, when you call, grabs me, pulls at me – I cannot do anything for it, I love, love you.'[132]

With these words, Manuela speaks her desires into discursive existence. Moreover, the fact that Manuela and Fräulein von Bernburg both share a framework for the possibilities of love and desire between women means that the confession carries a subject-forming significance. Yet, at the very moment Manuela's desires become 'knowable' through discourse, they equally become available to the pathologizing powers that seek to control and punish them. Indeed, the extent to which Fräulein von Bernburg is already familiar with the self-regulatory practices demanded by these punitive systems becomes evident in her response to Manuela's confession: 'You have to pull yourself together. One must be able to control oneself. Do you understand? Everyone must be able to control themselves, Manuela. I control myself, too.'[133] In what is described as Fräulein von Bernburg's own 'grave confession', the teacher is seen both to reject Manuela's love and to acknowledge it, making herself complicit in its broader social significance. The social meanings that are prescribed such queer desires become all too apparent during Manuela's final public declaration.

In a state of inebriation following her performance as knight Nérestan in Voltaire's *Zaïre*, Manuela theatrically reveals her teacher's undershirt to her curious audience backstage: 'Fräulein von Bernburg's chemise ... given to me. She went to her wardrobe and took [it] out and gave it to me. I should wear it, wear it and think of her ... No, she did not say that but I know now ... I know ... that she loves me.'[134] Articulated in literal 'fits and starts', Manuela's final confession holds significance for what it does not reveal as much as for what it does. Effectively 'outing' her teacher, Manuela's statement exposes the desires of both women to the punitive powers they had sought to evade through their rigorous practices of self-regulation and denial. Indeed, no sooner does the knowledge of Manuela's transgression reach Frau Oberin than the desires of the protagonist are categorized against normative social strictures and consequently punished. Described as 'scandalous' and 'unhealthy', Manuela's confession is used by her confessor/oppressor to constitute her as a social deviant. Through what Taylor calls a 'diagnosis from the outside', Frau Oberin draws on the authority of medicosocial taxonomies of the time to classify Manuela as a subject with an 'abnormal disposition', stirring the moral panic that facilitates Manuela's social exile. In this way, Manuela is forced to live her oppression and give up the object of her desire.

Conclusions

As a popular work of fiction, Raedt-de Canter's *Boarding School* communicated the erotic potential of the maternal to a mass audience. However, whether the protagonist's tomboyishness, her desire for the maternal and feminine, and her 'uncontainable hunger' for the secret midnight kiss were read as queer signifiers by a contemporary audience cannot be known. The very structure of the nonlinear narrative, with its chaotic temporal shifts back and forth, resists the teleological narrative of search for sexual origins and reflects much about the experiences of contemporary Dutch women who did not consider queer desire to be an identitarian marker. Considering the state of sexual discourse in Dutch interwar society, *Boarding School* can thus be considered as a novel situated on the brink of a new language with which to discuss sexual desires and preferences. Although there are traces of sexological theory in Raedt-de Canter's novel, the conceptualization of queer desire as a constitutive element of one's identity does not manifest itself in her writing. The protagonist's queer encounters leave her hungering for a maternal touch, yet the inarticulability of these 'strange', 'mysterious' and 'exciting' desires means that they remain outside of the remit of the discursive powers that seek to control and punish them. In this way, the novel appears to reject labels of 'abnormality' and 'sin' as received categories, while nonetheless presenting the journey of the protagonist who is exploring the meanings of her pleasures and desires.[135] The maternal imagery that colours the protagonist's queer encounters further suggests alternative models through which love between women has been conceptualized and configured in the interwar period, which had clear significance that crossed cultural borders. As well as eroticizing caregiving practices outside of familial paradigms, the image of the 'strong' and 'burly' maternal body, and the sensual descriptions of comforting mother smells also point to the erotic potential of concepts such as security and sanctuary in relationships between women.

Unlike Raedt-de Canter's novel, Winsloe's text engages expressly with the genre of the case study from its opening pages. Detailing the origins of her protagonist's queer desires and gender nonconforming behaviours, the author makes use of a lexicon of signs and signifiers that had become easily recognizable to readers following the explosion of sociosexological (literary) texts within the German-speaking market. As well as encouraging the reader to remain vigilant for markers of nonconformity, the novel itself bears witness to a diagnosis from the outside, as Frau Oberin deploys theories of somatic inversion to constitute Manuela as a perverse sexual subject. Yet, while this framework encourages a reading of the text as a journey towards sexual selfhood, Manuela's gender nonconformity remains layered and complex. In the process of 'becoming' a man, the protagonist paradoxically grants herself permission to access and enjoy her femininity, which, in turn, creates performative moments of camp sensibility or accents of femininity *through* masculinity. Winsloe's engagement with the vicissitudes of gender rejects the idea that there was any one model through which a queer subject could be fully described and nuances the image of the child invert, even as she draws on sexological ideas. While sexological theories of queer masculinity are deployed to constitute Manuela as a sexual subject, the essence of the 'Erotic Mother' figure also points to alternative models of loving between women, in which feminine and maternal desires can be conceived of as authentic, erotic and powerful. Significantly, the mother–child model is not only eroticized from Manuela's perspective, but Fräulein von Bernburg also acknowledges the eroticism of her maternal instincts, which are suppressed only through a constant practice of self-surveillance and sacrifice – arguably the most maternal act of the text.

Considering that the subject of sexual desire in these texts was shaped by distinctive discursive traditions in Germany and the Netherlands during the interwar era, it is not surprising that the act of confession results in two quite different experiences for the protagonists. While confession is depicted in Raedt-de Canter's work as a religious condition for punishment and redemption for certain acts and thoughts, confession functions in *The Girl Manuela* as a mechanism through which the 'truth' of one's identity is revealed through a series of subject-forming declarations. These moments of confession demonstrate most clearly how the internalization of a discourse about the 'Self', and the later confession of this 'truth', could only take place if a specific discourse had been made available to the subject in the first instance. In other words, utterances of queer selfhood may have held meaning in one social milieu, but not in others, or, indeed, in one cultural context but not another. Moreover, a supposed truth of the self may have contained elements that were used to oppress rather than liberate the subject and, although dynamic, the process of self-fashioning through 'confession' remains always intersubjective and reliant upon shared forms of cultural/sexual knowledge. Quite how such forms of shared cultural knowledge about topics such as class and desire influenced the depictions of queer feminine protagonists will be discussed in the final chapter of this volume.

Notes

1. Michelle Ann Abate, *Tomboys: A Literary and Cultural History* (Philadelphia: Temple University Press, 2008), p. xxiii.
2. Trans.: 'Der Lieblingsaufenthalt des weiblichen Urnings ist der Tummelplatz der Knaben. In deren Spielen sucht er mit ihnen zu rivalisieren. Von Puppen will das Urningsmädchen nichts wissen, seine Passion ist das Steckenpferd, das Soldaten- und Räuberspiel ... Schmerzliche Reflexionen ruft das Bewusstsein hervor, als Weib geboren zu sein ... Gross ist der Drang, auch Haar und Zuschnitt der Kleidung männlich zu tragen, unter günstigen Umständen sogar in der Kleidung des Mannes aufzutreten und als solcher zu imponieren.' Von Krafft-Ebing, Richard, *Psychopathia Sexualis: Eine klinisch-forensische Studie* (Stuttgart: Ferdinand Enke, 1886), p. 297.
3. Magnus Hirschfeld, 'Das urnische Kind', *Zeitschrift für Kinderforschung* 8 (1903), 241–57 (at p. 255).
4. Trans.: 'Aus dem urnischen Kinde war ein homosexueller Mann geworden mit derselben Naturnotwendigkeit mit der sich aus dem Normalkinde ein heterosexueller Mensch entwickelt.' Hirschfeld, 'Das urnische Kind', p. 256. Hirschfeld often kept contact with the subjects of his case studies for ten years or longer. See Magnus Hirschfeld, *Die Transvestiten: eine Untersuchung über den erotischen Verkleidungstrieb mit umfangreichem casuistischen und historischen Material* (Berlin: A. Pulvermacher, 1910).
5. See, for example, Lynne Yamaguchi and Karen Barber (eds), *Tomboys! Tales of Dyke Derring-do* (Los Angeles: Alyson, 1995).
6. Abate, *Tomboys*, p. xvi. Already in Hirschfeld's study *Die Transvestiten* (1910), the sexologist explores the meaning of gender variance across cultural borders, noting the existence of the Sakalaven tribe in Madagascar where it was culturally acceptable to raise boys 'as girls' if they appeared to their parents 'gentle and weak' (see Hirschfeld, *Die Transvestiten*, p. 331).

7. 'Introduction', in Karen E. Lovaas et al. (eds), *LGBT Studies and Queer Theory: New Conflicts, Collaborations, and Contested Terrain* (New York: Harrington Park Press, 2006), p. 5.
8. 'Eva Raedt-de Canter', in Gerrit Jan van Bork and Pieter Jozias Verkruijsse (eds), *De Nederlandse en Vlaamse Auteurs: Van middeleeuwen tot heden met inbegrip van de Friese auteurs* (Weesp: De Haan, 1985), p. 467.
9. 'De geschiedenis van een succes', *Utrechts volksblad*, 4 May 1938, p. 8.
10. Trans.: 'beste oorspronkelijke en vertaalde romans'. Eva Raedt-de Canter, *Internaat*, (Amsterdam: Querido, 1933). Trans.: 'frisch als de voorjaarswind'. Adrianus Michiel de Jong, 'Letterkundige Kroniek', *Het Volk*, 9 April 1931, p. 8.
11. Trans.: 'hebben wij het maar open te slaan'. Roel Houwink, 'Kroniek van het proza', *Den Gulden Winckel* 30 (1931), p. 148.
12. Trans.: 'de bekrompen bigotterie van de wereldvreemde nonnen'. De Jong, 'Letterkundige Kroniek'. Trans.: 'de domme, grove, liefdeloosheid der benepen pedagogen'. Maurits Uyldert, 'Letterkundige kroniek', *Nieuwe Amsterdamsche Courant*, 15 August 1931, p. 9.
13. Adrianus Michiel de Jong, 'Een stap terug', 'Letterkundige Kroniek', *Het Volk*, 3 October 1933, p. 8.
14. Doris Hermanns, *Meerkatzen, Meißel und das Mädchen Manuela: Die Schriftstellerin und Tierbildhauerin Christa Winsloe* (Berlin, AvivA, 2012), p. 83.
15. Winsloe decided to change the name to *Gestern und Heute* after receiving complaints from theatregoers who expected the original Voltaire play *Zaïre* (1733). See ibid., pp. 111–13.
16. Trans.: 'ein großer Erfolg'; 'weltberühmt – wenn auch nur für kurze Zeit'. Doris Hermanns, 'Nachwort', in *Das Mädchen Manuela: Der Roman zum Film Mädchen in Uniform* (Berlin: Krug & Schadenberg, 2012), p. 283.
17. Although *Das Mädchen Manuela* was published after Winsloe had relocated to the United States, the fact that the novel was based on an earlier play that had been reworked into a film means that the novel cannot strictly be considered a piece of exile literature. Indeed, Winsloe's novel was also published in Leipzig and Vienna in 1934, but was quickly banned by the Nazi regime. Although the novel may well have been influenced by Winsloe's self-imposed exile, I will not be examining the text as a piece of 'exile' literature in this chapter, although I acknowledge the insights that such an approach might bring to future studies. See Hermanns, 'Nachwort', pp. 287–88.
18. The circumstances of Winsloe's death have been subject to much speculation. While some scholars contend that Winsloe was shot by French officers who believed the couple were spies, yet more have suggested that the women were murdered by petty criminals who presented themselves to the women as officers. See Hermanns, *Meerkatzen*, pp. 255–72.
19. Annelies van Heijst, 'The Disputed Charity of Catholic Nuns: Dualistic Spiritual Heritage as a Source of Affliction', *Feminist Theology* 21(2) (2013) 155–72 (at p. 165).
20. De Jong, 'Letterkundige Kroniek', p. 8.
21. Trans.: 'Om vijf uur gaat de bel als een verre verschrikking door je dromen'. Raedt-de Canter, *Internaat*, p. 7.
22. Trans.: 'ein Buch gegen den Film'. Christa Reinig, 'Nachwort', in Christa Winsloe, *Mädchen in Uniform* (Munich: Frauenoffensive, 1983), pp. 241–48.
23. Trans.: 'was übrig'. Christa Winsloe, *Das Mädchen Manuela: Das Roman zum Film Mädchen in Uniform* (Berlin: Krug & Schadenberg, 2012), p. 155.
24. In the first cinematic adaptation of *Mädchen in Uniform* (1931), Manuela makes her thespian debut as Don Carlos in Friedrich Schiller's eponymous play. In the second

adaptation (1958), Manuela is seen to take on the character of Romeo in Shakespeare's *Romeo and Juliet*.
25. As well as being considered 'autofictive accounts', both novels could also be situated within the genre of girls' boarding school novels, which gained in popularity after the turn of the twentieth century with the entrance of (middle-class) girls into secondary education. For more on the *Mädchenpensionat* genre, see Gisela Wilkending, *Mädchen der Kaiserzeit: zwischen weiblicher Identifizierung und Grenzüberschreitung* (Stuttgart: Metzler, 2003).
26. Trans.: 'Viele Jahre meiner Kindheit brachte ich in dem Milieu zu, das in "Ritter Nérestan" geschildert ist. Der Fall Manuela ist authentisch, wenn auch nicht dokumentarisch in der hier gegebenen Form. Die einzelnen Personen meines Kindheitserlebnisses sind natürlich verarbeitet und umgeformt, während alles, was Milieu und Details anbelangt, treue Schilderung der Zustände ist.' Hermanns, *Meerkatzen*, p. 111.
27. Mara Taylor, 'Diagnosing Deviants: The Figure of the Lesbian in Sexological and Literary Discourses 1860–1931', unpublished dissertation (Philadelphia: University of Pennsylvania, 2010), p. 12.
28. Ibid.
29. As Lisa Bernstein outlines, confessional literature is a hybrid genre created from a fusion of autobiographical forms such as the memoir and the epistle. In terms of the Western canon, confessional literature has primarily been associated with male authors such as Augustine, Rousseau and Gide. Yet, the 'autobiographical or confessional impulse' that is central to the genre also has a strong history of female voices, which, as Bernstein observes, can be traced back to the thirteenth-century visionary writings of medieval nuns. See Lisa Bernstein 'Confessional and Testimonial Literature', in Friederike Ursula Eigler and Susanne Kord (eds), *The Feminist Encyclopedia of German Literature* (Westport, CT: Greenwood Publishing Group, 1997), pp. 76–77.
30. The author surrogate, de Man suggests, is 'an alignment between ... two subjects' – author and protagonist, for example – which involves a 'process of reading in which [these subjects] determine each other by mutual reflexive substitution'. See Paul de Man, 'Autobiography as De-facement', *Modern Language Notes* 94(5) (1979), 919–30 (at p. 921).
31. Trans.: 'denk eens na, over de last die je bent voor ons ... Je ziel stinkt van verdorvenheid'. Raedt-de Canter, *Internaat*, pp. 14–15.
32. Audre Lorde, *Zami: A New Spelling of My Name; A Biomythography* (London: Penguin/Random House, 2018), p. 305.
33. For a more detailed discussion of the various tropes and symbolic language used in queer literature between 1900 and 1940, see, for example, Bonnie Zimmerman (ed.), *Encyclopedia of Lesbian Histories and Cultures* (New York: Routledge, 2012), specifically pp. 747–48.
34. In Hector Malot's original novel *Sans Famille* (1878), the protagonist is called Rémi. Although, of course, this may have been an oversight by Raedt-de Canter, the androgyny of the name René is certainly suggestive of Freudian ideas of bisexuality. Indeed, it may be of more than cursory interest that Raedt-de Canter did not choose to reference Malot's novel *En Famille* (*Nobody's Girl*), published in 1893, which focuses on the adventures of the female protagonist, Perrine.
35. Trans.: 'de afgrond van eenzaamheid'. Raedt-de Canter, *Internaat*, p. 15.
36. Trans.: 'fel jaloers ben je op hun mooie gave gezichtjes, hun vlotte manieren, hun goede kleren'. Ibid., p. 57.
37. Trans.: 'Broer en Trump zijn aan 't vechten. Je kijkt hevig geïnteresseerd toe. "Zullen we ook Harry?" ... "Wij vechten? Welnee. Ik weet wel wat ik liever doe ..." Je wordt

er ongeduldig van en zegt kribbig: "Ik niet. We hebben toch altijd samen gevochten, waarom nu dan niet?" "Omdat ik met een lief meisje niet wil vechten" … Je voelt je nu op onbekend terrein met deze nieuwe, vreemde Harry, die absoluut niet wil vechten en je twijfelt aan alle argumenten die je zoudt kunnen aanvoeren.' Ibid., pp. 134–35.
38. Trans.: 'we zullen niet meer samen vechten, niet meer samen indiaantje spelen … ook niet de volgende vacantie'. Ibid., p. 144.
39. Trans.: 'Harry wint. Schrijlings over je heen gezeten, brult hij zijn overwinnarsroep door de kamer en je bent definitief verslagen. Maar dan buigt hij zich voorover en kust je, drie, vier keer achter elkaar, vlug en stevig. "Daar, daar, daar. Jij je zin, maar ik ook m'n zin. Je bent een lieve schat." Als je, moe en pijnlijk, naar je bed terug gaat, is er voor het eerst rancune in je, tegenover het mannelijk superioriteitsgevoel'. Ibid., p. 146.
40. Trans.: 'een lichte, Limburgse zomermiddag'. Ibid.
41. Trans.: 'Het is zoel en warm en licht in de lucht … De koelte van het gras in je rug en de diepte van de blauwe lucht, waarin je ogen kijken kunnen, eindeloos.' Ibid.
42. Trans.: '[de schommel] drijft langzaam uit, zwaaiend, besluiteloos'. Ibid.
43. Trans.: 'Het is grappig om te zien. Net alsof hij smelt, uitvloeit … Niemand zal het ooit weten.' Ibid., pp. 158–59.
44. Heike Bauer, 'Literary Sexualities', in *The Cambridge Companion to the Body in Literature* (New York: Cambridge University Press, 2015), p. 108.
45. Trans.: 'Obwohl jeder sagte, das Kind sei schön, entsprach das nicht der Wahrheit. Denn die dunklen Augen, deren Weißes Blau war, entbehrten der Augenbrauen. Man stülpte dem Säugling ein Häubchen auf, um die Kahlheit des Schädels zu decken.' Winsloe, *Das Mädchen Manuela*, pp. 7–8.
46. However, as Efrat Tseëlon rightly observes, *all* women can be considered 'stigmatised by the very expectation to be beautiful, and they are always potentially deviant if they are not careful'. See Efrat Tseëlon, *The Masque of Femininity: The Presentation of Woman in Everyday Life* (London: SAGE Publications, 1995), p. 88.
47. Trans.: 'Manuela ist die Squaw und hat zu Hause zu bleiben und zu kochen, während die Männer, sich auf den Kriegspfad begeben … Sie ist traurig, daß sie bloß eine Squaw ist. Wieder einmal grübelt sie über das Unglück nach, daß sie ein Mädchen ist und keine Indianerhosen tragen darf … es muß doch wunderbar sein, so wie ein Mann daherstreiten zu können, eine Waffe im Gürtel.' Ibid., p. 32.
48. Of the seventeen cases presented in Hirschfeld's almost 600-page treatise, *Die Transvestiten* (1914), Helene N. (Fall XV pp. 116–27) is the only female-to-male transvestite case study. The story of Fräulein Katharina T. was discussed as part of the work's 'Kritische Teil: Differentialdiagnose' and in the section dedicated to the nuances of cross-dressing and homosexual desire.
49. Michael S. Kimmel, *The History of Men: Essays on the History of American and British Masculinities* (Albany: State University of New York Press, 2005), p. 233.
50. Susan Sontag, 'Notes on Camp', in *Against Interpretation* (New York: Dell Publishing, 1966), p. 279.
51. Pamela Robertson, *Guilty Pleasures: Feminist Camp from Mae West to Madonna* (Durham, NC: Duke University Press, 1996), p. 5.
52. Trans.: 'Dann war da ein riesiges Publikum, und sie schwebte in der Zirkuskuppel, und alle Scheinwerfer beleuchteten sie, und die Musik hielt an, wenn sie die "Große Welle" machte, und wirbelte einen Tusch, wenn sie in hohem Bogen durch die Luft absprang, in die Kniebeuge versank und mit einem weiteren Sprung stand. Dann raste Applaus, und Manuela, die natürlich ein Mann war, in engem, weißem Seidentrikot, verneigte sich lächelnd, als wollte sie sagen: Oh bitte sehr, das ist noch gar nichts …' Winsloe, *Das Mädchen Manuela*, p. 55.

53. Ibid., p. 275.
54. Jennifer Forrest, 'Cocteau au cirque: The Poetics of Parade and "Le Numéro Barbette"', *Studies in 20th & 21st Century Literature* 27(1) (2003), 9–46 (at p. 15).
55. Janet Lee, '"A Kotex and a Smile": Mothers and Daughters at Menarche', *Journal of Family Issues* 29(10) (2008), 1325–47 (at p. 1325).
56. Trans.: 'weil ich ja ein Junge sein will. Ich mag meine Haare nicht und meinen Rock, zu Hause habe ich immer Hosen getragen, wenn ich mit meinem Bruder geturnt habe, und am liebsten trüge ich sie immer … Ich mag keine Frau werden – ich möchte ein Mann sein und immer für Sie da sein, Fräulein von Bernburg'. Winsloe, *Das Mädchen Manuela*, pp. 181–82.
57. Jack Halberstam, *Female Masculinity* (Durham, NC: Duke University Press, 1998, p. 6.
58. Ibid.
59. Trans.: 'Sie fühlte, wie sie langsam mehr und mehr zum Ritter Nérestan wurde.' Winsloe, *Das Mädchen Manuela*, p. 223.
60. Trans.: 'Deine Stimme war … ganz dunkel, und dann hattest du auf einmal Bewegungen, so echt … dir hat man heute Abend geglaubt daß du – daß du eigentlich ein halber Junge bist.' Ibid., p. 234.
61. Cited in F. Michael Moore, *Drag! Male and Female Impersonators on Stage, Screen, and Television: An Illustrated World History* (Jefferson, NC: McFarland, 1994), p. 119
62. Ibid.
63. Elaine Marks, 'Lesbian Intertextuality', in George Stambolian and Elaine Marks (eds), *Homosexualities and French Literature: Cultural Context/Critical Texts* (Ithaca, NY: Cornell University Press, 1979), pp. 357–58.
64. The erastes/eromenos tradition was a socially acknowledged and idealized erotic relationship between an adult male (the *erastes*) and a younger boy (the *eromenos*) in ancient Greek culture. The younger would be in adolescence and the relationship would end once the boy had reached adulthood. While the relationship was certainly erotic, it was important that such pederastic relationships should serve the pursuit of knowledge. See Kenneth James Dover, *Greek Homosexuality* (Cambridge MA: Harvard University Press, 1978).
65. Trans.: 'das Interesse für den Unterrichtsgegenstand steht bei vielen im engsten Zusammenhang mit der Person des Lehrers. Die Verehrung … diejenige urnischer Mädchen für bestimmte Lehrerinnen und Erzieherinnen trägt oft den Charakter abgöttischer Schwärmerei'. Hirschfeld, 'Das urnische Kind', p. 246.
66. Marks, 'Lesbian Intertextuality', p. 358.
67. Richard Dyer and Julianne Pidduck, *Now You See It: Studies on Lesbian and Gay Film* (London: Routledge, 1990), p. 55.
68. Susan (Contratto) Weisskopf, 'Maternal Sexuality and Asexual Motherhood', *Signs* 5(4) (1980), 766–67.
69. Geetha Ramanathan, *Feminist Auteurs: Reading Women's Films* (London: Wallflower, 2006), p. 201.
70. Trans.: 'angstige 'moeder' roep'. Ibid.
71. Trans.: 'een gevoel van thuis'; 'een zuigend heimwee'. Ibid., p. 17
72. Trans.: 'Soeur Veronica … Veronica. Een perkje vol donkere violen zie je, als je zachtjes, voor op je tong, Veronica zegt … Een perk vol, in een schemerige, oude hof met wuivende bomen en bemoste paden.' Ibid.
73. Trans.: '"Veronica …" Zei je en zweeg. 'Soeur Veronica …" "Och, Veronica …" Zei je verlegen en wreef je hoofd langs haar ruw katoenen, warme mouw.' Ibid., p. 18.
74. Ramanathan, *Feminist Auteurs*, p. 201.

75. See Audre Lorde, 'Uses of the Erotic: The Erotic as Power', in *Sister Outsider* (Berkeley: Ten Speed Press, 2007), pp. 53–59; Bethany Jacobs, 'Mothering Herself: Manifesto of the Erotic Mother in Audree Lorde's *Zami: A New Spelling of My Name*', *MELUS* 40(4) (2015), 110–28 (at p. 114).
76. Trans.: '"Net als vroeger?" Vreemd, dat je zo verlegen wordt van deze vraag.' Ibid., p. 59.
77. Trans.: '[Fenna] ruikt zoals moeder rook, zij loopt zoals moeder liep.' Ibid., p. 61.
78. Trans: 'je … snuift haar moedergeur [en] laat je stil wiegen, als een hulpeloos, klein kindje'. Ibid.
79. Trans.: 'wel te rusten, moeder Fenna'. Ibid., p. 62.
80. Adrienne Rich, *Of Woman Born: Motherhood as Experience and Institution* (New York: Bantam Books, 1977), p. 12.
81. Helene Deutsch, 'Über die weibliche Homosexualität', *Internationale Zeitschrift für Psychoanalyse* 18(2) (1932), 219–41 (at p. 239).
82. Trans.: 'De kus! Hoe zondig en heerlijk tegelijk … twee armen, zachte, warm-bemouwde armen had ze om je hals geslagen en twee koele, vochtige lippen hadden even, rustig en ferm, jouw mond gekust. Je hart bonsde toen ze je losliet. Waarom? … Wat toch dat brandendfelle, zinderende verlangen beduidde, dat je pijnlijk deed blozen, je zondig en verworpen maakte en tegelijk als een zware schat in je hart woog?' Raedt-de Canter, *Internaat*, pp. 73–74.
83. Dyer and Pidduck, *Now You See It*, p. 56.
84. Trans.: 'een wondere heerlijkheid'. Raedt-de Canter, *Internaat*, p. 75.
85. Trans.: 'Mutter war sie, die immer da war. Sie, die kam, wenn Lela schrie, sie, die beruhigte, wenn Lela weinte.' Winsloe, *Das Mädchen Manuela*, p. 8.
86. Trans.: 'Muttis Kuß.' Ibid., p. 92.
87. Trans.: 'Als Lela dieses neue Gesicht sah, erstarrte etwas in ihr. Unwillkürlich rückte sie auf ihrem Stuhl etwas vor, um näher hinsehen zu können. Was war das? Diese Frau hatte Fritzens Gesicht – nur schöner, weicher, liebreizender …' Ibid., pp. 122–23.
88. Trans.: '[Manuelas] Ohren färbten sich rot, ihr Gesicht erblaßte vor Anstrengung. Ihr Mund trocknete aus, ihre Handflächen wurden feucht. Was war es nur, was? Es tat weh furchtbar weh, und auch wieder nicht.' Ibid.
89. Trans.: 'Dämmerstunde mit Mutter.' Ibid., p. 130.
90. Trans.: 'atmete den Duft, der von der fremden Frau kam: Lavendel und Mutter'. Ibid.
91. Trans.: '"Wir haben uns noch nicht richtig begrüßt, kleine Manuela!" … und ehe Manuela antworten kann … beugen sich die Hände, beugt sich die Stimme, beugt eine warme Brust, beugt ein Mensch zu sich nieder, und Fräulein von Bernburg küßt Manuelas Stirn, ganz als ob sie von den Tränen nichts sähe, die jetzt zu beiden Seiten befriedend niederinnen.' Ibid., p. 169.
92. Trans.: '[Manuela] breitete die Arme aus und warf sich, alle Kraft verlierend, Fräulein von Bernburg um den Hals, die fast das Gleichgewicht verlor und erschrocken das zitternde Kind festhielt … Zart versucht sie, die Arme um ihren Hals zu lösen. Lela griff gierig nach den Händen … Die Hände wehrten sich nicht. Sie ließen geschehen. Sie nahmen das tränennasse Gesicht des Kindes auf, und Fräulein von Bernburg beugte sich herab und küßte den bebenden Mund.' Ibid., p. 202.
93. The kiss as a romantic act has long been conceived to have much broader symbolic potential. Freud had already suggested two decades earlier in his *Introductory Lectures on Psychoanalysis* (*Vorlesungen zur Einführung in die Psychoanalyse*, 1916/1917) that a kiss could be described as the 'softened hint of the sexual act'. Trans.: 'gemilderte Andeutung des Sexualaktes'. Sigmund Freud, *Vorlesungen zur Einführung in die Psychoanalyse* (Frankfurt: S. Fischer Verlag, 1916), p. 262.

94. Trans.: 'nun muß ich wohl schon ein wenig Mutterstelle an dir vertreten und dir sagen, was du zu tun hast, wenn sie kommen'. Ibid., pp. 174–75.
95. Lee, '"A Kotex and a Smile"', p. 1325.
96. Trans.: 'Sie lag bleich und schön auf ihren Kissen und lauschte mehr dem Klang der Stimme, die sie unterwies, als den Worten selber.' Winsloe, *Das Mädchen Manuela*, p. 175.
97. Lorde, *Zami*, p. 88.
98. Trans.: 'Wie eine Wohltat, wie ein ganz unverdientes niemals gekanntes Glück empfand sie die Liebe dieses Kindes, die um so vieles echter war als die rührende Zuneigung und Vergötterung der anderen Kinder rings um sie … sie [war] glücklich durch dieses Kind und daß sie es wiederliebte, grundlos, mit aller Kraft ihres Herzens.' Winsloe, *Das Mädchen Manuela*, p. 176.
99. Trans.: 'durfte es nichts anderes für sie geben als Selbstzucht und Verzicht'. Ibid.
100. Ramanathan, *Feminist Auteurs*, p. 199.
101. Trans.: 'Stille liegt zwischen den beiden Frauen.' Winsloe, *Das Mädchen Manuela*, p. 264.
102. Trans.: 'hastige, warme, gute kleine, Worte'; 'Kind, Liebling', ibid. p. 265.
103. Trans.: 'Du darfst mich nicht so lieb haben Manuela, das ist nicht gut. Das muß man bekämpfen, das muß man überwinden, abtöten'. Ibid., p. 268.
104. Ramanathan, *Feminist Auteurs*, p. 202.
105. Michel Foucault, *The History of Sexuality: Volume I* trans. by Robert Hurley (London: Penguin, 1984), p. 58.
106. Michel Foucault, 'The Subject and the Power', *Critical Inquiry* 8(4) (1982), 777–95 (at p. 781).
107. Michel Foucault, *Technologies of the Self*, ed. by Luther H. Martin et al. (Amherst: University of Massachusetts Press, 1988), p. 16.
108. Jeremy Tambling, *Confession: Sexuality, Sin, the Subject* (Manchester: Manchester University Press, 1990), p. 6.
109. Trans.: 'verder bloot te staan is onzedelijk'. Raedt-de Canter, *Internaat*, p. 8.
110. Trans.: 'Je stelt je voor, hoe je God zou liefhebben … als je niet het lange natte hemd moest aanhouden tot je eigen hemd over je hoofd zat en geleidelijke volgde, wanneer de badjas, nat en zwaar en koud, op de grond gleed. Om je nat en koud en klevend in je kille kleren achter te laten.' Ibid., p. 9.
111. Trans.: 'God gaf je een lichaam en je mocht er niet naar kijken. Je mocht het niet wassen, je mocht het niet betasten. Je zondigde tegen Gods geboden als je je vertoonde, zoals hij je schiep. God gaf je een vrije wil en als je hem vrij gebruikte, zondigde je.' Ibid., p. 9.
112. Trans.: 'witbrood is door zijn zeldzaamheid iets bijzonder kostelijks'. Ibid., p. 10.
113. Foucault, *The History of Sexuality*, p. 61.
114. Trans.: 'hier klein serpent … je ziel stinkt van verdorvenheid'. Ibid., pp. 14–15.
115. Trans.: 'Je weet ineens weer, hoe slecht je bent. Hoe verwarrend en raadselachtig getekend door zondigheid en verderf.' Ibid., p. 11.
116. Trans.: 'Soeur Padua vroeg: Qui a parlé? Het haalde je uit je dromen en je vroeg je af, of ze je geloven zou, wanneer je een vinger opstak. Als je sprak en je stak geen vinger op, geloofden ze je nooit. Of ze je nu óók niet geloven zou, nu je stil was en dromerig en niet gesproken hadt? Je nieuwsgierigheid vulde je met vragen, vragen die aandrongen op een antwoord en je stak fel, met een kreetje, je vinger op. Ze had je uit de rij gehaald. "Attendez là." "Maar ik sprak niet eens, ik wou …"' Ibid., p. 31.
117. See Miranda Fricker, *Epistemic Injustice: Power and the Ethics of Knowing* (Oxford: Oxford University Press, 2007), p. 3.

284 • Different from the Others

118. Trans.: 'zondig en heerlijk tegelijk'. Raedt-de Canter, *Internaat*, p. 73.
119. Trans.: 'Was het wellicht zonde? Kussen wàs zonde; zelfs zusjes mochten elkaar niet kussen. Was dit dan geen zonde?' Ibid., p. 75.
120. Emphasis in original. Trans.: 'homosexualiteit als *neiging* (aanleg) en homosexualiteit als *daad*'. Dr. L Bender, *Verderfelijke Propaganda* (Heemstede: Comité van Katholieke Actie 'Voor God', 1937), p. 3.
121. Trans.: 'Stuurde God je iemand, die je … in je eenzaamheid een nachtzoen bracht?' Raedt-de Canter, *Internaat*, p. 75.
122. Trans.: 'hoe wonderlijk klopte je hart, als je na zorgvuldig onderzoek, met de lijst van overtreding volledig op je lippen, neerknielde achter het nog gesloten tralieraampje in de biechtstoel'. Ibid., p. 76.
123. Trans.: 'De altijd eendere vergrijpen in gewoontedreun: driemaal gesproken in de kerk, vijftienmaal ongehoorzaam geweest, zevenmaal brutaal, acht en dertig maal oneerbiedig onder het gebed … liefdeloosheid, slordigheid, luiheid, onbeleefdheid aan tafel, snoepzucht. Allemaal heel vaak, maar ik weet het niet precies in cijfers.' Ibid., pp. 76–77.
124. As Julia Creet writes: 'homosexual, gay, lesbian "identities", formulated as identities rather than strictly as behavior, have been predicated on a speech act: "coming out". This act often describes a process of signification, of naming or categorizing feelings that had previously existed. A single utterance will not suffice, for new situations demanding the revelation of identity are encountered constantly.' See Julia Creet, 'Anxieties of Identity: Coming out and Coming Undone', in Monica Dorenkamp and Richard Henke (eds), *Negotiating Lesbian and Gay Subjects* (New York: Routledge, 1995), p. 182.
125. Trans.: 'Nein Papa, es ist nicht wegen Fritz – es ist wegen seiner Mama …' Ibid., p. 137.
126. Trans.: 'Ach, du bist ja großartig! Mädel, bist du mir ähnlich! Eine Ausrede hat sie gleich bei der Hand … Aber weißt du, eins mußt du noch lernen. Wenn du dich rausreden willst, mußt du das besser machen. So fällt keiner drauf rein.' Ibid.
127. Trans.: 'Ich mag keine Frau werden – ich möchte ein Mann sein und immer für Sie da sein, Fräulein von Bernburg.' Ibid., p. 182.
128. Trans.: 'Solche Worte dürfen zwischen uns nicht fallen.' Ibid., p. 182.
129. Trans.: 'solche Elemente [können] vergiftend wirken, wenn man sie nicht in ihre Schranken zurückweist'. Ibid., p. 183.
130. Eve Kosofsky Sedgwick, *Epistemology of the Closet* (Berkeley: University of California Press, 1990), p. 3.
131. Trans.: 'Wenn ich abends zu Bett gehe und Sie machen die Tür zu, dann habe ich … solche Sehnsucht, weil Sie nicht mehr da sind, und ich muss immer auf die Tür starren, und dann denke ich, das darf ich nicht, und halt mich fest am Bett.' Winsloe, *Das Mädchen Manuela*, p. 210.
132. Trans.: 'Zu lang hat sie dies alles zurückgedrängt. Beide Arme um die Hüften der vor ihr stehenden Frau, läßt sie die Worte aus sich hervorstürzen. "Ich kann ich kann nicht anders. Ich liebe Sie, liebes Fräulein von Bernburg. Ich liebe Sie, so, so sehr wie meine Mutter, ja, und auch viel viel mehr. Wenn ich Ihre Hände sehe, zieht es mich hin, sie zu fühlen. Ihre Stimme, wenn Sie rufen, packt mich, reißt mich – ich kann nichts dafür, ich liebe, liebe Sie".' Ibid., p. 210.
133. Trans.: 'Du mußt dich zusammennehmen. Man muß sich beherrschen können. Verstehst du? Jeder Mensch muß sich beherrschen können, Manuela. Ich beherrsche mich auch.' Ibid., p. 211.

134. Trans.: 'Fräulein von Bernburgs Hemd ... mir geschenkt ... An ihren Schrank ist sie gegangen und hat ein Hemd herausgenommen und es mir gegeben, ich soll es tragen, tragen und an sie denken ... Nein, das hat sie nicht gesagt aber ich weiß es doch nun ... daß sie mich lieb hat ... das weiß ich.' Ibid, p. 237.
135. Although for those readers who recognized themselves in the text, the novel may well have played a formative role of some kind, enabling them to recognize that desires between women exist, having a similar function to Radclyffe Hall's *The Well of Loneliness*, which several Dutch women mentioned as being their 'gateway' into the queer world. See Benno Stokvis, *De homosexueelen* (Lochem: De Tijdstroom, 1939).

Chapter 6

WHEN OBJECT BECOMES SUBJECT

Feminine Protagonists in Anna Elisabet Weirauch's *The Scorpion* Trilogy (1919–31) and Josine Reuling's *Back to the Island* (1937)

The final chapter of this book will be used to rethink relationships between femininity, agency and queer desire in fictional writing. Taking Anna Elisabet Weirauch's trilogy *The Scorpion* (*Der Skorpion*, 1919–31) and Josine Reuling's novel *Back to the Island* (*Terug naar het eiland*, 1937) as 'counter-discourses' of queer desire and experience, I will explore the extent to which these novels might be considered to be challenges to the contemporary medicosocial discourses that positioned the queer feminine woman as either 'innocent' desired object or as deviant hyper-sexed subject. As the protagonists of these novels reject the virile female invert as a model of identification and have feminine love interests themselves, alternative paradigms and configurations of queer desire are created between the characters, arguably enabling space for the protagonists to speak from what Julian Carter calls 'nonlesbian subject positions'.[1] With a handful of notable exceptions, the experiences of queer feminine women in literature remain a neglected site of investigation. Yet, as Hannah O'Connor notes, the exclusive focus on female masculinities is particularly problematic when looking at novels about queer desire in the early twentieth century, 'which are still deeply preoccupied with questions of femininity and the place of the Sapphic subject in the feminine roles traditionally ascribed to them'.[2] To build further on what Shane Phelan describes as the 'irreducible plurality' of depictions of female same-sex desire in literature, this chapter will foreground the complex interactions between class, gender and desire experienced by queer, bourgeois feminine figures in fictional writing in the interwar era.[3] Although both *The Scorpion* and *Back to the Island* have been the focus of several important scholarly studies in German and Dutch literary fields, the significance of the protagonist's gender expressions within these studies has largely been disregarded. However, as I will argue, it is precisely the potential of queer femininities to destabilize the dyad that posits homosexual desire as 'non-normative' and 'immoral' that enables authors to challenge the image of the queer woman as sexual 'Other', as well as making an alternatve discourse of desire available to those women who did not identify with the figure of the sexological invert.

As has already been discussed in Chapter 3, the feminine woman was a figure both revered and reviled within German queer communities. While feminine women were frequently exalted in the magazine *The Girlfriend* as desirable objects, the image of the modern 'coquette' was one that was largely rejected by women belonging to the League for Human Rights (BfM) as a figure who threatened the politics of respectability that were fundamental to the broader aims of the homosexual emancipation movement. For the most part, feminine women were considered to be less politically invested in their lesbianism than masculine women, to be fickle romantic partners, and to be dangerous as erotic spectacles. This view was also upheld in sexological writing in which the queer feminine woman was primarily viewed as a 'pseudo-homosexual'. However, in the magazine *Women's Love*, the feminine woman was shown frequently to be a strong and female-focused figure, who enveloped gender nonconforming elements into her peformance of femininity. In their submissions, several contributors to *Woman's Love* pointed to the plurality of queer feminine experience and refused to dismiss the validity of bisexual desires. Some writers even explored the polyamorous experiences of married women who took a female girlfriend 'on the side'. Magnus Hirschfeld's later more progressive approach to gender presentation also suggested that while the most visible group of female homosexuals consisted of virile and mannish women, there existed 'a no less large group' of women who were respectably feminine in their behaviours and appearance.[4] Anna Elisabet Weirauch's and Josine Reuling's novels present the experiences of exactly these types of protagonists, as well as those feminine women whose gender presentations were considered dangerous and undesirable by contemporary queer activists and sexologists. Examining the authors' engagements with – and departures from – contemporary discourses of queer female desire in the novels, I will demonstrate the multiple and conflicting ways in which queer femininities were portrayed in two novels across cultural borders. Furthermore, I will argue that the protagonist's explicit critical engagement with psychosexual discourses of queer desire within their specific cultural contexts – as well as with traditional markers of femininity such as maternalism, modesty and morality – challenge what it meant to represent as a (queer) woman by re-signifying culturally rooted codes of femininity. Finally, this chapter will be used to comment more broadly on some of the overarching themes that appear to have emerged in literary constructions of queer desire in the German and Dutch contexts. Here, I will focus specifically on what this literature might tell us about the role of femininity in discourses about 'non-normative' desires and how they may have been conceptualized in different cultural contexts and across a turbulent sociopolitical period.

Anna Elisabet Weirauch (1887–1970)

Born in Galați in 1887, Anna Elisabet Weirauch was the youngest of four children. After her father passed away in 1891 and her two brothers died in early childhood, Weirauch's mother relocated with her daughters to Germany, where they eventually settled in Berlin. In the German capital, Weirauch received acting lessons from a young age, making her stage debut in an reprisal of Shakespeare's *The Winter's Tale* in 1903. Discovered by the director of the German Theatre (Deutsches Theater) in Berlin, Max Reinhardt, when she was eighteen, Weirauch quickly developed a good reputation and appeared no less than eighty times as part of Reinhardt's ensemble.[5] In 1908, she wrote and directed her first stage play, *Treulieb and Wunderhold: A Christmas Fairytale in Eight Tableaux*, which was a resounding critical success. Followed by *In a Zeppelin to Mars* (1909) and *The Bad Girl* (1911), Weirauch continued to write and produce plays while pursuing her own stage career, winning the 'Golden Medal for Art and Science' in 1916 for her contributions to theatre. In 1918, she published her first novel *The Little Dagmar*, which some critics suggested showed 'a strong literary talent'.[6] She published her first work that included explicit homosexual themes, *The Day of Artemis*, in 1919. In the same year, she also released the first novel in a trilogy that would make her name as a queer writer: *The Scorpion*. Described in *The Girlfriend* as a 'new and exciting addition' to a growing number of queer literary works emerging at this time, this first novel focuses on the experiences of a bourgeois girl who falls in love with an older woman. Written over a period of twelve years, the three instalments of *The Scorpion* proved to be immensely popular in queer communities and were advertised in both *Woman's Love* and *The Girlfriend*.[7] Indeed, Weirauch's contribution to the 'sensitive topic of same-sex love' was considered by critics both from queer and national newspapers to be well-informed and 'decent'.[8] However, following the Nazi assumption of power in 1933, Weirauch's trilogy was soon blacklisted as unwanted literature, and she moved to Gastag in Bavaria with her Dutch partner Helena Geisenhainer, who was ten years her junior. It was only after Weirauch joined the Reich Literature Chamber (Reichsschrifttumskammer) in the 1930s that she was able to continue publishing novels. Neither she nor Geisenhainer became members of the Nazi Party.[9] After the end of the Second World War, the couple moved to Munich, where Weirauch continued writing, before returning to Berlin in 1961, where they lived together in a boarding house for former actresses until Weirauch's death in 1970.

Josine Reuling (1899–1961)

Born in Amsterdam in 1899, Gerardina Anna Reuling spent much of her youth travelling through Russia with her parents. Returning to the Netherlands with her family at the age of fifteen, Reuling settled after many years of travel in Amsterdam, a city she came to see as 'a paradise'.[10] Working initially as a secretary for the paper wholesalers G.H. Bührmann, she published her debut novel *Siempie* in 1927, which was praised in national newspapers as a candid snapshot of humanity. Several of Reuling's early publications, which appeared under her childhood nickname 'Josine', were inspired by her upbringing in Eastern Europe, which was coloured by the bohemian lifestyle of her opera-singing parents, and the later task of caring for her dying mother. When Reuling began work on her second novel *Sara Vierhout*, she resigned from her position at G.H. Bührmann due to her own poor health, before moving to Switzerland to recover. Printed initially as a serial story in *Elsevier's Illustrated Monthly Magazine* (*Elsevier's Geïllustreerd Maandschrift*, 1891–1940) and later as a novel, *Sara Vierhout* received praise by critics such as Emmy Lockhurst for its authentic depictions of family life. However, many male critics appear to have been left 'cold' by the novel, which they believed to be too 'feminine'. With the release of *Interlude with Ernst* (*Intermezzo met Ernst*, 1934), the first in a series of more psychological publications, Reuling was granted a place in the Dutch-speaking literary world of her time. While her writing continued to receive critical acclaim in liberal journals, there appears to have been a shift in the critical reception of her work in religious publications. Her later novels frequently challenged the increasingly conservative societal attitudes towards sexuality and gender, and offered detailed depictions of figures on the margins of society. As such, they were often received negatively by conservative critics, who saw the novels as portrayals of individuals with 'abnormal' lifestyles.[11] Religious newspaper *The Times* (*De Tijd*), for example, believed that there was 'no place in Catholic libraries' for Reuling's independent female characters, in particular *Interlude*'s modern protagonist Bep, whose lifestyle and behaviours, according to one critic, showed 'unforgivable weaknesses'.[12]

Like her protagonist, Reuling was an independent and modern woman who belonged to the only known queer literary circle in the Netherlands, which included the authors Anna Blaman (1905–60) and Marie-Louise Doudart de la Grée (1909–81).[13] Moving from Switzerland to France, a country she called her 'second homeland' (*tweede vaderland*), Reuling finished her fourth novel *Back to the Island* (*Terug naar het eiland*) in 1937, which came to be known as the first Dutch literary text to centralize erotic love between women.[14] Despite her early success, this novel also met with strong criticism in literary journals in the Netherlands, as well as newspapers in its colonies, on account of its portrayal of 'the abnormal affection for one's own sex'.[15] Following the Second World War, Reuling returned to Amsterdam, where she took up work as the secretary for the director of a public library. She left her position a short while later to travel and to write, and she began to give lessons in Dutch literature at the open library and organized popular reading groups. Despite having battled with poor health for much of her life, she continued to publish smaller projects while working in Amsterdam and remained dedicated to the idea of bringing literature to a broader audience until she moved into a retirement home, where she died in 1961.

The Scorpion (1919–31)

Printed between 1919 and 1931, Weirauch's trilogy is the most extensive and enduring depiction of love between women by a female author to exist from the Weimar era. Set across Berlin, Munich and Hamburg, Melitta Rudloff – known throughout the text as Mette – grows up in a privileged but conservative household under the care of her father, Franz Rudloff, and her aunt following the death of her mother shortly after her birth. In a moment that Mette recalls as 'the prelude to [her] life', a young governess, Friedel Eggebrecht, arrives at the family home to take care of her.[16] Mette becomes infatuated with Friedel, who teaches her how to pawn the family silver and rewards her with confectionery and embraces. After Mette's 'crime' is discovered, a psychologist is called to the house and Friedel is dismissed. The rest of Mette's youth passes in a relatively uneventful manner, until she encounters Olga Radó. Ten years older than Mette, Olga attracts the protagonist's romantic attention with her intelligence and beauty. Introducing her to the pleasure of knowledge by schooling her in literary history and French, Olga becomes Mette's teacher and friend. Soon after Olga gives in to the protagonist's desires, Mette receives news that her father is dying following a stroke. After having sent someone to spy on the couple, Mette's aunt calls the police to Olga's flat and, upon being confronted, Olga denies her relationship with Mette. Devastated by this betrayal, Mette retreats from social life and becomes engaged to a man in a bid to live a 'normal' life. Soon thereafter, she is informed that Olga has committed suicide and she calls off her wedding. In the final pages of the first novel, the reader sees Mette with Olga's revolver and her lover's most treasured possession: a cigarette case emblazoned with the sigil of a scorpion.

In the second novel, the reader joins Mette in a small boarding house in Munich. Alone and depressed after Olga's death, Mette finds herself caught between two distinct groups of lodgers: the moral and respectable circle of Luise Peters and the 'loose' friends of cabaret artist Mara Luigi. Although Mette feels instinctively that she belongs to the 'class' of Luise Peters, upon hearing that a woman in Mara's circle, Gisela Werkenthin, has been driven to morphine because a woman has broken her heart, Mette approaches Mara and befriends her.[17] Through the cabaret artist, Mette is introduced to Sophie Degebrodt and her disabled partner Nora von Hersfeld, whose home serves as a gateway to Munich's queer subculture. At a party thrown by Sophie and Nora, she encounters the enchanting Corona von Gjellerström, the woman responsible for Gisela Werkenthin's heartache. However, when Sophie later confesses her love for Mette, she asks Mette to leave Munich so that she can save her relationship with Nora. After a final night of drinking and gambling, Mette resolves to kill herself with Olga's pistol. Luise Peters, whose conventional 'circle' Mette had initially snubbed, saves her and suggests to her that she should spend some time recovering with her well-to-do family in Hamburg. Mette agrees and is soon surrounded by the bourgeois elite that she had sought to escape. Here, Mette is approached by the young Gwendolen and her love interest, Fred Wietinghoff, who draw Mette into their friendship. After the three take a short weekend break together, Gwen confronts Metta in their shared bedroom about her past affairs with women and seduces her. As Mette gives in to Gwen's advances, Fred appears in the room to join the erotic scene playing out before him. Disgusted by the pair and hurt by yet another betrayal, Mette packs her bags.

In the final instalment of Weirauch's trilogy, Mette has taken a room in a boarding house in the countryside. Frustrated by her lot, she decides to buy some land upon which she can build a house. In order to do this, she enlists the help of her old friend Otto Petermann and she returns briefly to Berlin. In Petermann's house, Mette is reunited with Corona von Gjellerström, the woman who had broken Gisela Werkenthin's heart in the second novel. Here, she discovers that it was Corona who had originally given Olga the symbolic cigarette case. Mette and Corona embark on a turbulent affair that is subject to Corona's frequently changing moods and Mette's jealousy. After Mette's house has been built, she returns to the countryside to work the land and live a solitary life. When Corona finally arrives to join her lover, it becomes clear that she does not approve of Mette's isolated existence and the pair decide that they must part ways. As the trilogy comes to an end, Mette is seen to be happy in her country home, arriving at the conclusion that she must learn to live alone before she can share her life with another.

Back to the Island (1937)

In another story about a young woman from a wealthy family, Josine Reuling explores the early childhood experiences and young adult life of her protagonist Brita Salin. Moving between Stockholm, Paris and the fictional Swedish island of Semmarö, the novel depicts Brita's relationships with her family and her various female partners. In a similar manner to Weirauch, Reuling begins her novel with detailed descriptions of Brita's childhood and her close relationship with her Swiss governess, Mademoiselle Henriëtte Chabert, who is referred to throughout the text as 'Zelle'. Following an outline of Brita's youth that foregrounds the frequent absences of her father, the text describes Brita as a much-desired debutante who, to the bewilderment of her mother, states that she is 'unsuitable for marriage' and refuses to find a (male) partner. Uninterested in the lessons she is taught at school and unwilling to commit herself to the hobbies of a woman of her standing, Brita instead publishes a collection of poetry entitled *Dark Dreams* (*Donkere dromen*) on her twenty-first birthday, establishing her name on the literary scene as an upcoming and experimental writer. Disowned by her grandmother, who believes that such an occupation is unsuitable for a young woman, and with increasing pressure from her mother to marry, Brita begins to spend longer periods between Paris and Semmarö.

During one of her summer holidays in Paris, Brita has an affair with Marja Wastouwska, a seemingly fickle Hungarian socialite. When Marja lies to Brita about dining with the Swedish consul in a bid to draw an invitation to Brita's familial home, Brita forces her lover to leave the flat they share and cuts off all further contact with her. When Marja realizes that her chance to join Swedish high society is lost to her, she enacts her revenge. Travelling to Sweden with a bundle of letters that had been sent to her by Brita, Marja visits Brita's father to blackmail him with details of her relationship with his daughter in return for 10,000 kronor. Brita's father pays Marja the money, but leaves the letters unopened. Furious that 'perfect Brita' has not seen received her comeuppance, Marja sends a poison pen letter to Brita's mother, revealing the nature of Brita's 'perverse' sexual inclinations.

When Brita's parents realize the implications of their daughter's affair, she is disinherited and is forced to move to Paris, helped initially by her governess Zelle, who supports her financially. During Brita's time in the capital, the reader is informed of her attempts to find community on the Parisian bar scene and the social prejudice that she faces as a queer woman. Brita's friend, the psychologist Hans Thorstad, makes repeated attempts during this time to 'heal' her so that he can marry her and 'cure her with the power of his love'. However, Brita remains adamant that she cannot be cured. Amid Hans' attempts to persuade her to undergo psychoanalytic treatments, she meets the boyish artist Renée and falls deeply in love with her. When Brita and Hans go on a holiday together, Renée promises to meet them in Nice. However, as the pair are driving to meet Renée, a drunk Hans loses control of the car and crashes into a tree. While Hans survives the incident, Brita's body is shipped in the final scenes back to Sweden, where it is buried on the island of Semmarö.

Challenging Sexological Frameworks

Prefaced with an observational prologue from an almost entirely heterodiegetic narrator, *The Scorpion* is positioned unambiguously within the contemporary sociomedical discourses of its time. Unlike Eva Raedt-de Canter and Christa Winsloe, in whose work the reader identifies nods and gestures to the narrative structures of the sexological case study, Weirauch engages consciously and critically with the 'diagnosis narrative' from the opening pages of her trilogy. Adopting a markedly different approach from Raedt-de Canter, whose second-person narrative form conflates the position of protagonist, narrator and reader, Weirauch adopts a clear authorial distance from the narrator and plays ironically with the rhetoric employed by contemporary sex researchers. Writing 'with the clear and cold joy of the researcher', Weirauch's narrator suggests that their study of Mette Rudloff is stimulated by an interest in 'the sick, the lost [and] the outcasts'.[18] In a manner similar to Felix Ortt's statement in Joannes Henri François' *Open Letter*, which was examined in Chapter 4, the narrator attempts to present a level of professional detachment from their subject matter, claiming only to have sought out the protagonist in order 'to vivisect, to analyse, to box [her desires] into systems'.[19] Yet, the narrator goes much further than Ortt, suggesting that they are not even *capable* of subjective thought: 'I am not created to defend or indict. I follow no purpose in describing the things I do. I have no goals or intentions, not even an opinion or a judgment, and hardly even a feeling.'[20] Through the increasingly desperate attempts of the narrator to convince the reader of the scientific objectivity of the novel, Weirauch creates a satirical sexological performance that mocks the idea of scientific impartiality, while drawing on the genre of the diagnosis narrative to attest to the novel's authority on its subject. Indeed, while Weirauch's deployment of the diagnosis narrative no doubt reflects the fashions in literary writing of the time – while also subverting them – it further acts, as Nancy Nenno suggests of the genre more generally, 'as a revelation of, and an attempt to fill, the lacunae that the scientific discourse had created in its narratives of female homosexuality'.[21] While literature was being deployed in sexological studies to bridge conceptual gaps, authors were drawing on sexological frameworks to fill the voids in medical writing and knowledge about female homosexual desire. As we will see, Weirauch's novels challenge several of the most trenchantly held scientific views concerning queer feminine desires, and create conceptual space for new and difficult discussions about femininity, class, respectability politics and desire.

After setting the scene for their study, the narrator embarks with a truncated case history of the protagonist, which includes a veritable tick list of sexological signifiers. Shaped by the hypothesis that Mette's homosexual tendencies are the result of a pathological criminal urge and the lack of a mother figure, the inchoate image of Mette and her love interests are shaped quite clearly by the dominant sexological theories of the time. Fitting each noteworthy episode of the protagonist's life into crude medical categories, the narrator draws on the active (masculine) and passive (feminine) framework of desire in order to be able to 'make sense' of the feminine protagonist's queer longings. Mette's primary love interest, Olga Radó, is thus introduced to the reader by the narrator as a 'strange woman ... a trickster with pronounced masculine behaviours'.[22] Suggesting that the older woman may have 'seduced' Mette, the narrator draws on several recognized tropes of female same-sex desire, portraying Olga as both the active and masculine counterpart to the feminine protagonist, and the decadent criminal seductress who takes advantage of her sexually innocent and 'underage' (*unmündig*) partner. Notwithstanding the narrator's efforts to pin the protagonist down to a series of sexological signifiers – that is, rendering the feminine woman as seducible and naïve – the theory that feminine women can be cured of their homosexual desires comes largely undone in the course of the prologue. Indeed, even before the protagonist appears on the page proper, the narrator admits to their shame at having sought out the protagonist 'in the arrogant delusion of being able to help, to make better – to lead her, with pure and kind hands, to brighter paths'.[23] While Weirauch's ironic reworking of the sexological voice serves more subtly to subvert the genre of the diagnosis narrative, this statement throws down the gauntlet to those sexologists who argued that queer feminine desires were temporal and curable. Indeed, as Mara Taylor observes, this 'textual moment' demonstrates how 'the sexologist narrator doubts – goes beyond doubting – specifically rejects the possibility of curing the lesbian. It cannot be done and it is a delusion of the sexologist [to imagine] that it could be'.[24] As the novel progresses, the narrator's pseudoscientific observations slowly begin to fade from the narrative voice, making far fewer interventions in the text. By the end of the first novel, in fact, the narrative voice is focalized almost entirely through the protagonist and has lost nearly all semblance of its previous proposed 'objectivity'. In light of Weirauch's conscious attempts to subvert the diagnosis narrative, it would appear that the narrator is forced to break with the scientific framework because, as Nenno suggests, they have '[attempted] to delve into precisely those aspects of Mette's life which elude scientific categories'.[25] Yet, while Nenno accurately identifies the discursive slipperiness of the protagonist's experiences and desires, I would suggest more strongly that this stems precisely from the gendered forms that structure and shape them. For it is not desire between women more broadly that the narrator is unable to categorize, but, rather, as I will outline later in this chapter, the active desires of *feminine* women for their own sex that appear to confuse and confound them.

The case study framework and the 'scientific' observations of the narrator are not the only shadows of the sexological world to appear in Weirauch's trilogy. Introducing several figures of medical authority into the text, Weirauch thematizes and challenges the discourses that dismissed the desires of queer feminine women, especially those pertaining to the active/passive binary and the supposed curability of the 'hysterical' woman. For example, having been presented with the narrator's assessment of the 'masculine charlatan' Olga Radó in the first scenes of the novel, the reader is quickly offered a counterweight depiction of this view during the protagonist's first meeting with her. In only a few sentences, Olga can be seen to complicate the strict masculine-feminine binary imposed by the narrator. Focalized almost entirely through the protagonist, this scene presents Olga as a far more complex figure, whose appearance and demeanour are characterized by 'a strange contrast'.[26] Her tone, described by Mette as 'sharp and hard', stands in stark juxtaposition with the timbre and cadence of her voice, which instead evokes a 'soft cello sound'. Olga's 'almost threatening expression' is further said to be contrasted by her striking features and 'beautiful hands'.[27] Indeed, while Olga is described as having behaviours that were considered typically more masculine, such as her fondness for cigarettes, her thirst for knowledge and her desire for independent travel, her gender expression is in fact more nuanced than the narrator's initial physiognomic evaluation would suggest. Mette's description creates, like Winsloe's protagonist Manuela von Meinhardis, the image of a figure that can be read as neither/nor, and/or, both/none. As Mette comes to know Olga better, this image is complicated further with references to the mother–child paradigm and Olga's maternal desires, which will be discussed later in this chapter. The subtle nuancing of the narrator's initial gendered appraisal is built upon further through the introduction of other characters of medical authority into the text, through which Weirauch tackles the fallibility of the process of diagnosis from the outside, while engaging further in her own 'vivisection' and 'analysis' of the theories that related to the queer desires of feminine women.

Aside from the narrator, the reader's first introduction to the exacting interventions of medical authorities comes after Mette's governess, Friedel Eggebrecht, convinces the child-protagonist to help her 'loan out' the family silver in exchange for embraces. Upon being caught pawning the silver, Mette is examined for signs of more serious pathological conditions by a doctor who bears the 'terrifying and sinister title "psychiatrist"'.[28] While sexologists such as Krafft-Ebing and Hirschfeld suggested that inversion could already be identified in adolescence, little is learned from this initial examination, as Mette refuses to speak. However, what does become clear is the reflection of the social anxiety that any deviant action could be a sign of sexual abnormality, as well as the contention that if caught early enough, the desires of (feminine) women could be contained and cured. In a later mirroring of this experience, Mette is forced to endure further medical scrutiny after she pawns the family silverware to save Olga from debt. During what can only be described as a confrontation with the psychiatrist, Mette is shown to be mindful of the threat that medicalization poses to her. Telling the doctor that she refuses to trust him, she makes clear that she is keenly aware that any 'silly response' could lead to her being 'locked in a madhouse'.[29] True to form, the psychiatrist seeks to identify hints and traces that will help him unravel the riddle of Mette's queer desires – everything from her penchant for cigarettes to her passion for reading is suspect. Yet, reminding the reader of the dearth of research on the figure of the queer feminine woman, the psychiatrist finds himself unable to make diagnosis of deviance, as Mette does not conform to his predefined images of the congenital invert. Instead, he reverts to stereotypes of bourgeois feminine *naïveté*, concluding that Mette is 'a child who does not know what danger it is in'.[30] Positioning Olga as the 'pernicious' (*verderbliches*) influence, on account of what he perceives to be her masculine nature, and Mette the 'innocent' woman who has been seduced, the psychiatrist suggests that Mette might make a 'full recovery' if she is removed from the damaging influences of the virile element. Denying Mette any form of sexual agency as a feminine woman, the psychiatrist draws on class associations that conflated femininity with respectability and propriety, to offer Mette 'refuge' within the class-bound gender formations that sought to shore up the heterosexual matrix.[31] While the focus of the examination remains fixed on the protagonist's behavioural transgressions and criminal actions, the spectre of the more invasive physical interventions of medical experts looms large in the background.

After becoming aware that her aunt rifled through her private possessions and sent investigators to spy on her and Olga, Mette claims that she feels as though 'merciless hands [had torn] the clothes from her body piece by piece'.[32] Highlighting further that this physical threat was never far away, Mette's aunt corners the psychiatrist following his talk with her niece and demands that he carry out an examination of Mette's body in order to identify any signs of 'physical anomalies'.[33] As the psychiatrist is unable to make a diagnosis based on what he has heard, Mette's aunt seeks to draw on the complex system of corporeal codes to identify and categorize the protagonist's homosexual tendencies. As was seen in Chapter 2, these physical anomalies could have comprised anything from a slightly larger cerebellum to the supposed atrophy or hypertrophy of body parts such as the breasts and clitoris. While Mette escapes the examination, she nevertheless feels cornered, 'like a hunted ... animal. Nowhere a way out, nowhere a possibility for escape', and her body is continued to be perceived as a threat to those around her.[34] When Mette is sent to the countryside home of her uncle and aunt to separate her from Olga, for instance, her young cousin Hermann is forbidden from visiting her bedroom because of the 'danger of contagion' (*Ansteckungsgefahr*).[35] Asked later by her cousin if she has recovered from her 'illness', Mette euphemistically explains: 'I was stung by a scorpion. And you know: Scorpion venom is the only thing that helps against scorpion poison ... I think it may be deadly – but it is not contagious.'[36] Showing how sexological theories had reached even the most provincial of places, the scenes with Mette's relatives are further used to challenge reductive theories same-sex desire. While the stinging scorpion with which Olga is associated may evoke the image of the seductive phallic woman, Mette suggests that her feminine body also contains 'the venom', which helps her to combat 'the poison'.

As well as challenging the more conservative views of same-sex desires through Mette's encounters with her extended family, Mette's introduction to sexological literature to points to the dearth of literature on sexual subjectivities that sit outside the paradigm of the congenital invert. Following the death of her father and Olga's public denial of their relationship, Mette resolves to isolate herself in her father's study. Here, she finds a range of 'books, booklets, brochures ... novels, medical works [and] annotated newspapers', which have been planted assiduously on her desk by her aunt.[37] When Mette finally ventures to make a closer examination of the material, it soon becomes clear that it pertains to one principal theme:

> There were strange, odd stories of countesses hanging around in hedge taverns in men's clothing ... reports of disgusting orgies in big clubs where hundreds of women dressed and behaved as men ... portrayals of the psychological life of 'contrary-sexuals', which suggested that these thousands of people formed a large community with one another, a community that was fraternised by nothing ... nothing but the impulse for the same debauchery.[38]

Redolent of the descriptions of the virile 'Lothario' presented in Auguste Forel's study *The Sexual Question*, the images in the books left behind by her aunt leave Mette disgusted.[39] While the protagonist's rejection of the idea of a community based on 'debauchery', as well as the image of the queer woman who dressed as a man, might be considered, as Taylor suggests, as the protagonist's attempt to 'sever herself from all possibilities of being "read" as lesbian', I would argue that there is no possibility of Mette being able to 'read' herself into this image in the first instance.[40] Indeed, just as her femininity precluded a diagnosis from the psychiatrist, her gender presentation prevents her from recognizing herself in the studies that she reads. The more Mette reveals to the reader of her discoveries, the more apparent becomes the case that only the masculine female invert is depicted in this 'research':

> When there was talk of male-minded women, much was made of their superior intellect, their thirst for knowledge and their urge to be educated. Also of a morbid wastefulness, of a passionate propensity for extravagance, of an unnatural predilection for beautiful boots. Or of sinister Don Juan figures, who sped from adventure to adventure with an insatiable greed for pleasure.[41]

Although the 'thirst for knowledge and urge to be educated' and the 'passionate propensity for extravagance' are recognizable character traits in her lover Olga, who the reader is told has 'almost a morbid aversion of everything that was cheap', Mette is unable to recognize her own experiences in the theories she is being presented with.[42] Falling into 'agonising confusion', she imagines herself confronting Olga: 'Explain this to me. Are there people like this? Are you like that? Am I like that?'[43] While Mette's conventional, bourgeois background may have made her sensitive to the 'orgiastic scenes' depicted in the documents, the fact that there is no representation of feminine desire in the texts that is at the heart of her rejection of them. Furthermore, in spite of her erotic encounters with Olga, Mette does not appear to conceive of their love as such, a term that offends her sense of bourgeois respectability: 'Mette shuddered, when she thought of the word love in this context. Sometimes she felt as if she would suffocate in excrement and filth.'[44] While there are doubtless deeply problematic properties to Mette's classist construction of what constitutes 'good' and 'bad' desires, as will be discussed later in the chapter, Mette's encounter with sexological literature highlights first and foremost the lacuna in sexological research on queer feminine desires and the complex class negotiations that shaped bourgeois experiences of erotic pleasure.

Having scorned the idea of a community based on 'debauchery' in the final scenes of the first novel, Mette is shown to be drawn to those who 'share her fate' following Olga's suicide. In the second instalment of the trilogy, Mette rejects the bourgeois circle to which she 'instinctively' belongs and instead joins the notorious group associated with bisexual cabaret artist Mara Luigi. That the community to which Mette is drawn is depicted as diversely gendered and inclusive of feminine women breaks the reader away from the image of the monolithic masculine woman. When Mette spends a night at a bar in Munich, for example, the reader is introduced to a veritable parade of queer types:

> There was a whole range of appearances there. Those who wore a stiff collar with their dark dress coat, fitted with lapel and breast pocket, who wore a small man's hat with their short-cropped hair – others, who betrayed themselves only through the faintest hint – some whose sharp features and character spoke for themselves, others who were of the coquettish type.[45]

Presenting a gamut of visual aesthetics and tastes in the bar, Weirauch stresses the plurality of the queer scene in her novel; while there are masculine types with stiff collars and cropped hair, there also exist those people who are less 'visibly' queer, expressing their proclivities through only 'the faintest hint'. However, the fact that Mette's own expression of femininity is informed so strongly by prevailing bourgeois attitudes means that the erotic community she encounters in Munich is one with which she is unable to identify. After consuming copious amounts of cocaine, allowing herself to be complemented on the allures of her body, and kissing a tomboyish figure, Mette feels a sudden 'horror and disgust' at her behaviour and her surroundings and returns home with the intention of committing suicide.[46] This dramatic response explores the tension that existed for many women during this period between the need to maintain an appearance of respectability and achieving erotic fulfilment. Indeed, the existence of a classist 'realm of respectability and power', as Marti Lybeck terms it, meant that for most bourgeois women, maintaining a respectable reputation was contingent on embodying certain types of femininity that centred the values of modesty, virtue and restraint.[47] Thus, it is no surprise that after Mette experiences her 'fall from grace' and enters a community brought together by desire, it is the dignified and bourgeois Luise Peters who saves her moments before she can pull the trigger. Thus, while Weirauch attempts to challenge sexological frameworks in her writing, by offering insights into the polymorphous nature of queer experience and calling into question some of the most pervasive myths about queer women, her protagonist remains bound by the confines of bourgeois femininity and the politics of respectability. Mette's struggle with these limits ultimately leads her to reject of the bohemian queer community she finds in Munich, as well as the masculine invert she encounters within sexological literature.

Femininity in the Foreground

The complex negotiations of sexual desire and class, as well as the growing social awareness of psychosomatic discourses of desire, are themes that also figure prominently in Josine Reuling's novel *Back to the Island*. However, structured more explicitly by the psychoanalytic writings of Freud than by the sexological discourses of Krafft-Ebing and others, Reuling's novel refuses to render queerness visible to her readers through the lens of anatomical inversion. With a much more radical departure from bourgeois conceptions of eroticism than is seen in Weirauch's trilogy, Reuling's novel challenges the sexological models that coded same-sex impulses as a masculine drive, as well as the binary that equated femininity with passivity. While the novel offers the reader some of the hallmarks of the case study genre – complete with a potted life history of its protagonist in the first few pages – Reuling's narrator offers no semblance of the scientific objectivity that Weirauch's narrator purports to embody. With liberal use of free indirect speech, Reuling's narrative is instead peppered with insights into the thoughts and emotions of her central characters, a form that is stylistically much closer to Christa Winsloe's *The Girl Manuela*. Following a brief introduction to the protagonist's parents – a rich timber trader and the daughter of one of Sweden's wealthiest families – the reader is made privy to a rapid chronicling of some key events in the protagonist's youth. However, reading for signs of physical or behavioural deviance or pathological drive in these flashbacks appears to be a futile exercise. Instead of stories of gender transgressions and feelings of otherness, the memories that are relayed to the reader about Brita's childhood detail her poor performance in the sciences, her talent for creative writing, and the tearful farewells that take place each time her father leaves the island of Semmarö to return to work during the holidays. Unlike the authors discussed in the previous chapter, Reuling does not portray her protagonist as an unhappy or lonely child, positioning her instead as an independent and liberated young woman. Even more utopic, Brita suffers few social setbacks in her desire to achieve independence as a woman; her parents allow her 'complete freedom' as she grows up, interfering little in her life or her decisions and even promise her a trip round the world if she achieves a position to study at university.

Described as 'sweet' and 'amiable' in these early chapters, Brita is associated little with masculine markers of identity and not at all with the criminal pathological tendencies that are read into Weirauch's protagonist, Mette. Highlighting the social imperative to codify bourgeois women as feminine, in the few instances that nontraditional gender traits *are* associated with the protagonist, they appear to be couched between hyperbolic assertions of her gender conformity, such as the moment her father thinks about his daughter as an 'exceptionally pretty girl, extremely sporty, yet so feminine, so charming', or when her mother prefaces a comment about her daughter's athleticism with a claim that Brita is 'the sweetest, most charming girl there was'.[48] Indeed, in Reuling's lengthy descriptions of the protagonist's beauty, charm and good manners, a stark contrast is presented to the depictions of the masculine invert and the queer feminine woman in contemporary sexological writing. Contesting Havelock Ellis' suggestion that queer feminine women belonged 'to the pick ... of women the average man would pass by', Brita's femininity is never depicted as 'lesser' than that of 'normal' women.[49] With her seemingly endless line of male suitors and admirers, Brita is presented as the very picture of the heterosexual ideal, complete with blonde hair, blue eyes and a captivating smile. Moreover, when Brita's behaviour flouts the conventions of propriety in the novel, the reader is invited to view this as primarily a contravention of class rather than a transgression of gender roles. After Brita publishes the bundle of poems entitled *Dark Dreams*, for instance, her grandmother threatens to disinherit her after claiming that Brita had broached subjects in her collection that 'one did not speak of'.[50] Underlining the tension inherent in the relationship between bourgeois femininity and desire, the statement suggests that while women do experience desire, it was the making manifest of such desires through discourse that was indecent. Interestingly, Brita's grandmother states that she is not against the pursuit of publishing altogether – something that was still frequently considered a masculine endeavour at this time – but rather that her granddaughter's choice of subject should be reformulated into something more 'appropriate' and 'respectable'.[51] Similarly, when Brita announces her intention to paint the summer house on the island of Semmarö, her mother responds that it 'is no job for a girl'.[52] While there is clearly a gendered element to this observation, her mother's suggestion that they 'get someone' to paint the summer house for the protagonist implies more distinctly that such a job is not appropriate for a girl of Brita's *standing*. Yet, while Brita is shown to deviate from the mandates of the elite class to which she belongs, especially in relation to the candid discussion of eroticism in her poetry, her moral code is nonetheless strongly informed by the values of respectability and honour. When Brita leaves her girlfriend Marja Woustouska alone over the summer holiday to visit the island of Semmarö with her governess Zella, for example, Marja wonders whether the protagonist is deceiving her with another lover. However, very quickly, she concludes bitterly that Brita 'did not tell lies. Oh, goodness no, she was far too sincere for that, too by-the-book, too this and too that, nothing but respectable qualities'.[53]

Shaped by the same sense of moral honour as Weirauch's protagonist, Brita's class affiliations cut her off equally from the queer bohemian community she finds on the Parisian circuit. Yet, while Brita embodies the same commitment to bourgeois moral codes as Mette, she embraces the sensuality and decadence of these communities that cause Weirauch's protagonist to turn away from them in 'horror'. Spending her fortune on providing funding for struggling artists and financially assisting her queer friends in Paris, Brita uses her economic independence to gain access to the queer world around her, as well as to continue to refuse heterosexual marriage. Yet, in spite of the access to queer space that is afforded by her privilege, Brita's class ultimately precludes her from being truly part of the circles she wishes to join: 'Brita longed to return to Paris, although she knew that they would never see her as one of their own. She was and remained: the rich Swede, la bourgeoisie …'.[54] Thus, while Weirauch's protagonist rejects a community that makes no distinction between 'love' and 'erotic desire', Brita longs for a fellowship of like-minded individuals who understand that 'love without eroticism is not possible', yet is barred from achieving a true sense of belonging by her bourgeois background.[55] That the erotic impulse is of great significance to Brita's conception of love is shown in the publication of her poetry anthology *Dark Dreams*. Brita's collection of love poems is said to be largely 'undecipherable' to the older generation around her, encouraging them into a 'muddle of admiration and fear'.[56] The theme of a generational rift in thinking about eroticism is picked up again after Brita's second publication, which is definitively entitled *Desires* (*Verlangen*). Following the publication, Brita claims to find her mother's embarrassment about the themes of her poetry 'almost charming' and she cannot help but laugh at the latter's unease when talking about such supposedly 'delicate issues'.[57] While Brita's mother attempts to render the subject of desire euphemistically benign in the text, I suggest that these euphemisms present a microcosm of the larger conceptual changes that were taking place in Dutch society more broadly during this time. Indeed, in the scene of dialogue between the two women about marriage, not only does there appear to be an ostensible gap in sexual knowledge between mother and daughter, but the 'conceptual chasms' that made queer Dutch desires inarticulable in an identitarian sense also mean that Brita finds it impossible to make her desires understood by the world around her.

While Brita is granted freedoms by her parents in terms of travel and access to education, they remain resolute in their desire for their daughter to find a suitable partner in marriage. After turning away several (seemingly) suitable suitors, Brita is forced to explain to her parents that she will 'likely never marry'.[58] When pressed on the issue by her mother, she explains that she is 'not suitable for marriage' because she 'does not love men'.[59] In a comic miscommunication – or, indeed, a wilful misunderstanding – Brita's mother is shown to be perplexed by her daughter's suggestion that in order to love one man, she would have to be able to love *all* men: 'All men? repeated mama. You have such strange ideas. I understand you less and less. *One* seems more than enough to me.'[60] Believing that her daughter is worried that intimate encounters with a man might undermine her feminine 'modesty', Brita's mother seeks to reassure her daughter: 'oh my girl, we must all go through that. ... you must be able to keep a man at a distance, especially in a marriage, you must make sure that you do not lose your self-esteem as a woman'.[61] Here, however, Brita is shocked by the fact that her mother believes her incapable of erotic thought more generally, rather than realizing that it is the idea of heterosexual eroticism that is unthinkable for her daughter:

> Brita burst out laughing. She laughed heartily, almost exuberantly, her big mouth wide open, her small, firm teeth glittering, almost a little too whitely against the lips painted light red. Mama's eyes filled with tears of anger and indignation. Without saying a word, she got up and left the room. In the afternoon, she did not come to the table.[62]

The confusion continues after this scene, when Brita's mother presumes that her daughter's laughter was caused by the embarrassment that her mother had broached the subject of 'things about which most mothers used to leave their daughters entirely in the dark'.[63] Returning to the conflict between class and respectability politics, this generational rupture could be said to be indicative of the changing conceptions of femininity and sexuality in Dutch society taking place at the end of the 1930s. While Brita does not see erotic desire as a negation of her feminine essence, but rather as a marker of it, her mother considers sexual modesty to be a key element to maintaining one's 'self-esteem as a woman'. After this conversation at cross purposes, Brita realizes that she has only ever been able to communicate with her parents in 'incomplete phrases' and resolves to tell her parents 'the truth' (*de waarheid*). However, in the textual gaps and euphemistic phrasing that appear in the conversation that follows, the reader is made aware of the complexity of the politics of the unsaid. As Foucault contends, silence – or that which is 'not-articulated' or cannot be articulated – has a significant social function *alongside* discourse, which suggests that it might not always be possible in historical documents to distinguish between what could not be articulated in the past and the things 'one declines to say, or is forbidden to name'.[64] In spite of such difficulties, I suggest that the tensions between Brita's nonarticulations – as she urges herself 'just to say something!' – and her parents' euphemistic allusions to 'things' that were 'left in the dark' point to the ways in which Dutch society appeared to be on the brink of a new discourse of desire during this period. Indeed, to draw on the words of Foucault, it was moreover a society that was trying 'to determine the different ways of not saying such things, how those who can and those who cannot speak of them are distributed, which type of discourse is authorized, or which form of discretion is required in either case'.[65] Highly suggestive of the discursive distinctions that existed between German and Dutch conceptions of queer desire more generally during the interwar period, the gaps that appear in Reuling's narrative, marked by ellipses within the text, as well as the use of indefinite nominal phrases such as 'now she *had* to say it', occupy a space that is taken up explicitly in Weirauch's novel by identitarian referents such as 'contrary-sexual' and 'male-minded woman'.[66] Although Brita tries hard to express in words her romantic and erotic love for women, she does not – or is unable to – use existing frameworks to make these desires understood. Neither Brita nor any of the other character in the novel refer to her desires for women with any sense of an identitarian framework or lexicon. Instead, intentional textual omissions and suggestive phrases such as 'non-normative inclinations' point to the persistently complex negotiation of articulating same-sex desire as a subject-forming practice within the Dutch context. While the novel moves towards a recognition of sexual desire 'as identity', which is most apparent in the sought-after community Brita finds in Paris, it also points to the discursive divide between sexological approaches that categorize sexual desires based on somatic signifiers and a psychoanalytical conceptualization of queer feminine desire that were shaped by that which was unconscious and, arguably, imperceptible.

Brita's closest friend in the novel, the 'doctor of psychology' Hans Thorstadt, is shown to make several attempts to persuade her to undergo psychoanalytic therapy to 'heal' her, so that she might focus on her true destiny: marriage and motherhood.[67] Considering homosexual desire to be a psychological problem and himself to be an authority on the matter, Hans positions the field of psychoanalysis in direct opposition to the medicoscientific frameworks that shape Weirauch's *Scorpion* trilogy. Well-versed in the works of Adler, Jung and 'the master himself' Freud, Hans concludes that discourses of somatic inversion are 'dead'.[68] Arguing that medical doctors are fixated on determining pathological deviance through somatic signifiers, Hans presents psychoanalysis as a more refined and progressive study of the inner workings of the mind, suggesting that psychiatrists are keenly aware that 'healing the soul required other methods than those used to heal the body, to operate it you needed finer tools than the surgeon used'.[69] Yet, while Hans hopes definitively to distinguish the approaches and results of psychoanalytic study from those of sexological research, presenting the former as a more liberated way of viewing human sexuality, Brita sees little difference between the processes of psychoanalysis and other more conservative cultural discourses:

> [Hans] also thought in dogmas, he also presented theories; this label must fit that statement, this conclusion must be drawn from that deed. It must. It was logical, inevitable ... 'We psychoanalysts can help, heal.' – 'We, the Catholic Church, can help, heal.' – 'We, the Calvinists, pure in our teachings, can help, heal.'[70]

Exposing the inconsistencies in Hans' argument, Brita's statement further highlights the connection between psychoanalytic truth seeking and the practices of religious institutions, as has already been discussed in Chapter 2 and Chapter 5. While Freud did not hide his disdain for religious doctrine, terming it the 'universal obsessional neurosis of humanity', his enduring interest in spirituality nevertheless informed his portrayal of psychoanalysis as a science of the soul.[71] Indeed, speaking of the relationship between religious confession and the practice of psychoanalysis, Freud suggested that 'the cathartic method was the immediate precursor of Psycho-analysis; and, in spite of every extension of experience and of every modification of theory, it is still contained within it as its nucleus'.[72] Bearing in mind the conclusions reached in Chapter 5 – that is, that the parameters of desire in the Netherlands in the early twentieth century were strongly informed by religious principles – it is not surprising that Reuling's novel takes the so-called 'talking cure' as its scientific basis over frameworks of biological inversion. Written and published in a deeply religious and morally conservative society, the novel's drawing on a 'science of the soul' that built on the confessional technologies already established through religious practices appears to have been the most logical way to begin a conversation about queer female desires in literary form.[73] Ultimately rejecting the genre of the case study, as well as the model of the masculine invert, Reuling's novel seeks to align the queer erotic impulse of her protagonist with an embodiment of femininity that is still considered honourable and 'by the book'. However, the primary struggle of the protagonist throughout the novel is shown to have little to do with the gender of her object-choice of desire. Instead, Brita's central battle appears to be against the societal understanding that conceived of female respectability as incompatible with the erotic drive.

Hierarchies of Gender and Desire

Rendered invisible by contemporary sexological and psychoanalytical studies that analysed female same-sex desire, Weirauch's and Reuling's feminine protagonists unsurprisingly find little comfort in the medicosocial discourses of desire that sought to intervene and to 'cure'. Yet, rather than attempting to fit the desires of their protagonists into pre-existing frameworks, both Weirauch and Reuling choose to challenge the discourses that deny their protagonists the legitimation of their queer experiences. By creating new hierarchies of desire, the authors call into question the contemporary masculinist coding of female same-sex eroticism, as well as challenging the assumption that nonheterosexual is non-normative. While Weirauch appears to want to do away with binary thinking by nuancing binaries of 'good' and 'bad' desire, Reuling's creation of an alternative queer orthodoxy inverts the binary of normativity and positions same-sex desire as normative and natural. After looking more closely at these attempts to subvert existing sexological paradigms, I will finally return to the essence of the 'Erotic Mother' in the texts, as the authors attempt to make visible the queer feminine desires of their protagonists through the portrayal of arguably 'nonlesbian' subject positions.

Throughout the course of *The Scorpion* trilogy, Mette is depicted as being perpetually occupied with the question of whether 'she was a good or a bad person'.[74] In her attempts to position herself as 'good', Mette is shown to deploy the moralizing bourgeois dictates of her class background to create a queer hierarchy in which her own same-sex preferences are deemed honourable, and others deviant. In this way, as Michael Warner observes: 'the image of the Good Gay is never invoked without its shadow in mind – the Bad Queer, the kind who has sex, who talks about it, and who builds with other queers a way of life that ordinary folk do not understand or control'.[75] Indeed, as we shall see, in order to get 'rid' of her sexual shame, Mette consistently attempts to 'pin it on someone else'.[76] While the binary of 'good' and 'bad' initially appears in Weirauch's novel as a rather crude dualism, the oppositional pairing that is drawn up by the protagonist becomes more complicated through the series, as characters who are initially dismissed by Mette as 'objectionable' are embedded within more rounded storylines. When Mette first meets Mara Luigi's circle in Munich, for example, she is overwhelmed by a group that visibly rankles her bourgeois sensibilities. On first encountering the 'nauseatingly' Ephebic Johannes, a young man who dresses in kimonos and lipstick and who is caught up in a conspicuous financial relationship with the disreputable Drencker, the reader is told of Mette's disgust at his 'impersonation' of coquettish femininity. She also judges the 'excessive' gendered embodiments of the 'too voluptuous'

Nora von Hersfeld and 'the pageboy' Sophie Degebrodt, the older couple who form the heart of Munich's queer scene, and finally the 'shockingly deformed' Eccarius, who acts as Mette's guide and chaperone as she tours the city. After being drawn to this group in a state of depression because they 'share her fate', Mette's first assessment of each of the characters grows increasingly more sympathetic and nuanced as she comes to know more about their backgrounds.

Nora nuances Mette's view of the effeminate Johannes, for example, when she tells the protagonist that the former is in a 'kept' relationship with the unsavoury Drencker only so that he can help finance the studies of failing heterosexual artist Willi Kraft, with whom he is in love. Yet, while Nora depicts the love Johannes feels for Willi as 'selfless' and 'pure', this story is complicated further still when Sophie speaks of the mutual benefits that each reaps from the sexual situation. Explaining that Willi is now financially able to produce his art, even if it means he must succumb to Johannes' attentions, and that Drencker will no longer worry that young boys might blackmail him, Sophie concludes:

> But the happiest of all is little Johannes … He is sought after, spoiled, worshipped. He sees his beauty, which he knows well to appreciate, in its rightful place. He spends half his days sitting in front of his three-piece bathroom mirror, admiring himself, taking care of himself with ointments and powders and hair lotions. And he does all this for the sake of Willi Krafft? Do not try to kid yourselves. He would do just the same without Willi Krafft![77]

Contradicting Nora's contention that Johannes' love for Willi is selfless, Sophie nonetheless agrees that the romantic situation between the three defies a simplistic verdict of 'good' or 'bad'. Against the backdrop of the complex interaction between the three men, Johannes' queer desire to be desired is considered acceptable and understandable by his friends, and neither good nor bad. As the novel continues, Mette's often rash and reductive moral judgements are frequently revisited and re-evaluated upon reflection. Just as the 'shockingly deformed' Eccarius is shown to be a 'kind guardian' through his persistent care for the protagonist, so too is the 'too voluptuous' Nora revealed as a character of more motherly and moral value than Mette had originally believed possible: 'in the next moment, when Mette held her warm, womanly hand and as [Nora] radiated a smile of indescribable cordiality and goodness, she forgot the question of beauty and ugliness, and unconditionally surrendered to the mild magic of this figure'.[78] Thus, while Mette initially deploys the binary of 'good' and 'bad' to preserve her own moral sense of normality and to position her own desires as 'respectable', the characters that she meets in Munich reveal to her that 'everything, good and bad, is so intertwined that it is not possible to separate it in order to weigh one against the other'.[79] Nowhere in the novel does this statement hold more truth than in Weirauch's engagement with the desires of the (heterosexual) bourgeois elite that Mette is shown instinctively to believe to be good, honourable and respectable on account of an assumed shared moral value system.

Following Mette's retreat from the queer community in Munich, Luise Peters places the protagonist in contact with Gwendolen and Fred Wietinghoff, two young friends who are considered to be 'more suitable company' for the protagonist than Mara Luigi's circle. The pair, who enjoy a casual but clandestine relationship, are presented as the picture of physical perfection:

> Mette was delighted ... as Gwendolen, beautifully and confidently, set down her slender feet, with their springy joints, and as the slim, firm forms showed themselves from under the white dress, and as the curly hair glistened and shimmered in the sun ... Her heart was made equally happy when she saw Fred Wietinghoff, who was walking beside Gwendolen, much taller than she, broad in the shoulders, narrow in the hips, showing all the contours of his muscles under the silk shirt.[80]

Soon considering her friendship with Gwendolen and Fred to be a relationship of immeasurably more worth than those she left behind in Munich, Mette believes that their shared economic roots and bourgeois conventions create an affinity between them that surpasses that of a community based on shared sexual desires. The fact that the appearance and behaviours of the bourgeois couple serve what Butler terms the 'heterosexual matrix' means that Mette trusts them unreservedly to be morally upstanding individuals, who can offer her 'good and honest friendship'.[81] Feeling as though she has been given 'a key to [her] inner being' in her role as an 'honest comrade', she believes that she has finally found her place in the world. However, the unresolved conflict between her erotic desires and her sense of bourgeois honour forces its way to the surface as Gwendolen attempts to seduce Mette during a weekend trip away. After drinking several bottles of wine and toasting to the importance of being a 'good comrade' with Fred and Gwendolen, Mette retires to the bedroom that she is sharing with her female friend:

> Gwen threw herself on [Mette] and kissed her mouth and eyelids, neck and cheeks. 'I don't want to', thought Mette, 'she is entrusted to me and I am not going to touch her. I am [Fred's] comrade ... I am his comrade ...' Rose-red waves grew inside her. They went up to her neck, all the way to her eyes. The room seemed to be swaying, as if in trembling breath, as in uneven heartbeats. Suddenly ... there was something in the room, which had not been

there before. A purple stain. And above that, Fred Wietinghoff's face. Fred Wietinghoff's eyes. Burning. Greedy ... 'A set up. A complete set up.' [Mette] straightened herself up and grabbed her clothes.[82]

During this scene, Mette attempts to resist her re-emerging desires, believing that an erotic encounter with Gwendolen would hurt her 'honest comrade' Fred. However, when it becomes apparent that Gwendolen and Fred seek to include her in their existing sexual relationship, Mette's belief in the couple's honour is shaken and she leaves Luise Peters' circle. Blurring the boundaries between 'good' and 'bad', as well as 'normative' and 'non-normative', then, Weirauch is frequently shown to prescribe the negative behaviours and characteristics associated in sexological work with queer individuals to supposedly 'normal' characters, revealing the fragility of the cultural norms of gender and normativity that shape Mette's social and sexual experiences.

In another example, Mette is introduced to Sophie and Nora at one of their celebrated soirées in Munich, when she becomes aware that Nora is partially paralysed. Through Eccarius, Mette learns that, prior to her relationship with Sophie, Nora was tricked into marriage with the 'healed' syphilitic Majorat von Hersfeld. Entirely unaware of the cause of her firstborn child's untreatable sickness, Nora is later enlightened by the doctor about her husband's condition after she 'irresponsibly' becomes pregnant for the second time. Soon after she hears this news, Nora experiences a fall from a hayloft. She loses her child and suffers internal injuries from which she never recovers. With Nora left crippled, the Majorat procures a divorce and embarks on a new relationship with a 'beautiful, innocent young girl from the best of families'.[83] Although sexual illness was not explicitly associated with queer desires until later in the twentieth century, the 'uncontrollable urges' of the Majorat, and his later death from a 'softening of the brain', were certainly tropes that had long since cast a shadow over the lives of same-sex-desiring subjects. Thus, while Nora is depicted as 'sick', her paralysis is presented as the result of the excessive lusts of her *heterosexual* partner, from whom she is eventually 'saved' by her queer lover Sophie. Attempting to complicate the binary of good and evil throughout her series, Weirauch engages critically with the assumption that non-normative desires are deviant, while heterosexual love is inherently good. So, even while the protagonist rejects the 'bad queers' she encounters on the Munich scene, and the image of the masculine invert that she is confronted with in the sexological literature, her inner conflict does not appear to lie with the stigmatization of her sexual object choice. Rather, much like Reuling's protagonist, Mette's struggle is with the internalization of a societal expectation that considers feminine respectability to be achievable only at the cost of the erotic. As she attempts to 'learn to live alone' in a house she has commissioned in the countryside, she turns to her friends Eccarius and Peterchen in the final scenes of the trilogy: '"But how does one find the way?" Mette asked desperately. "How does one know which door is the right one?"'[84] As Eccarius consoles Mette by suggesting she will 'just know', and Peterchen cryptically responds '"door twenty-two!"', Weirauch appears to concede to the reader that Mette's struggle to make her way to 'brighter paths' will perhaps never truly be resolved.[85]

Unlike Mette, who is conflicted by her desire for decency and her erotic desires more generally, Reuling's protagonist Brita exhibits an unwavering sense of the normalcy of her sexual longings in spite of her class background. Describing the common, and deep-seated, antipathy towards same-sex-desiring subjects after Hans attempts to 'cure' her, Brita is shown not to be naïve of the prejudice of wider society: 'According to the teachings of Freud – and therefore of Hans – she was sick. According to the teachings of Christianity, she was sinful. According to science, she was a physical abnormality. In the opinion of the public, she was strange, sinister, immoral, unhappy, pathetic; and the latter was exceedingly merciful.'[86] Even when Hans attempts to harness the shifting sociopolitical tide to convince Brita to lead a 'normal' lifestyle, Brita chooses to ignore his 'friendly' advice: 'Living together with a woman is not accepted. Socially speaking, you are an outsider ... It is only acceptable in world-cities like Paris and, even then, only in certain circles; in Germany currently, you would be locked up in a concentration camp as "socially abhorrent". I know such cases, I am not telling you stories.'[87] Indeed, in spite of Hans' desperate attempts to cure the protagonist of her 'abnormal sympathies', Brita forcefully rejects the idea that her desires deviate from what *she* considers to be normal. In arguably the most explicit line taken on sexual preference in the novel, Brita contends that it is she who is normal and women who desire men who are *not*: 'She, Brita Salin, declared that she believed herself to be normal, and all the others, who were not like her: abnormal. For her, every woman who desired to hold a man – who was capable of giving her love, her passion, to a man – was a wonder, an entirely incomprehensible figure, whom she observed with astonishment and masked aversion.'[88] Inverting the contemporary dyad that positioned heterosexual desires as the natural alternative to 'non-normative' perversions, Brita adopts the discourses of her oppressors in order to liberate herself from them: 'she did precisely the same to them as they did to her. With the only difference being that they had the right to express their disgust openly ... Well, the disgust she could understand. She felt it rise within her, too, when she saw a man and a woman dancing intimately together, or even just walking closely together arm in arm.'[89] Instead of internalizing the oppressive discourses of 'sin' and 'sickness', like the protagonist in Raedt-de Canter's *Boarding School*, Brita chooses to appropriate the discourse of disgust as a means to position the normative as *ab*normal. Yet, while she claims not to understand the feelings of women who love men, she appears equally resistant to those women who she believes want 'to *be* men'. For example, during one of the novel's flashbacks to Brita's experiences in Paris, the reader is told that the protagonist finds the idea of love between women in terms of gendered inversion to be unsavoury and, throughout the novel, she rejects the medical models that coded desire for women as a masculine drive: 'She no longer visited special bars, the professionals were too *dégoutant*. Why did those women imitate a sex to which they had an aversion? Why did they dress as men, with shirts and ties, closely cropped hair, and brusque masculine movements? ... She had never understood it.'[90] The 'professionals' of the Parisian queer scene, as Brita terms them, are incomprehensible to her and she finds their gender nonconforming styles and behaviours objectionable. Indeed, while femininity is not anchored to heterosexuality in Reuling's writing, Brita uses her conforming gender presentation to instil in herself a sense of normalcy. To this end, while her desires may deviate from hegemonic norms, Brita is fully committed to the idea of being a woman and presenting this womanhood through typically feminine behaviours. In a proud declaration of her femininity, Brita asserts firmly that: 'She was happy that she was a woman, she wanted nothing other than to be a woman.'[91] In this way, her contempt for women who desire the opposite sex functions as part of a broader attempt in the novel to establish an alternative hierarchy of desire in which heterosexual and binary instincts are perceived to be objectionable and base, in much a similar way to Elberskirchen's theorizing discussed in Chapter 2. However, in this subversion of heteronormative frameworks, Brita's positioning of homosexual desire as normal can *only* come at the cost of heterosexuality's hegemonic position as such. In this way, in contrast to Weirauch's trilogy, the binary of 'normative/non-normative' in Reuling's writing is not so much nuanced as it is inverted.

Brita's subversive notion of what ought to be considered 'normal' (*gewoon*) is further reinforced by evidence of what she considers to be the 'naturalness' of her sexual instincts and aversions. When Hans suggests that the power of his love could cure Brita, for example, the reader is told that she is overwhelmed by a 'sick feeling of disgust' as he embraces her, 'the kind that knots your stomach and rises into your nose'.[92] While her physical reaction to Hans' embrace is used to suggest that her aversion to the opposite sex originates from an inherently instinctive impulse, it is not a masculine but a feminine one. The protagonist's distaste for the masculine and virile element is also visible in the choice of her female partners, who are all feminine-presenting. Even Brita's lover Renée, who is given an androgynous name and described by Hans as 'mischievous' and 'boy-like', is ultimately prescribed traditionally feminine qualities. Taking on the role of a nurse for her sick neighbour, Renée is shown to have a caring and nurturing nature, which is continually foregrounded by Brita over her tomboyish qualities. Brita's championing of the figure of the queer feminine woman and her intention to challenge the contemporary frameworks of normativity therefore only become possible through the creation of her own rigid gendered and sexual orthodoxies, through which she also determines the limits and boundaries of acceptable and appropriate queer femininity. In her relationship with the Hungarian socialite Marja Woustowskja, who blackmails her father with the knowledge of his daughter's 'deviant' desires, the reader is presented with an example of what Brita perceives to be an unacceptable form of feminine desire. After she refuses to take her lover home with her to meet her rich parents and elite friends, Marja commits what the protagonist perceives to be an unforgivable act. Fearing that her opportunity to be introduced to Scandinavian aristocracy is slipping away, Marja resorts to positioning herself as a *femme fatale* in a flirtatious encounter with a Swedish consul. During this encounter, Brita is disgusted by Marja's excessive and exaggerated performance of femininity, while the consul considers Marja's incessant winking and open flirting 'not nice and a little vulgar'.[93] After Marja arranges a secret meeting with the consul, telling Brita that she is going to a Hungarian lecture, the protagonist denounces Marja as a 'mistake' (*vergissing*) upon discovering her deception. The fact that Marja is prepared, through a display of excessive femininity, to engage in heterosexual flirtations to achieve her social aims leads Brita to a harsh realization: 'she was not like me, I was mistaken'.[94] Yet, it is not only the queer *femme fatale* whose gender performance Brita dismisses as excessive and undesirable. Thinking back to her first romantic encounter as a schoolgirl, she compares her own 'respectable' inclinations with the unrestrained passions of her friend and classmate Vera. When Brita departs for her summer holiday on the island of Semmarö, the reader is told that Vera 'did not eat, did not sleep ... cried for days and did not want to get out of bed in the morning'.[95] Describing the moment she and her friend finally parted ways, the narrator's ideas reflect much of the societal attitudes towards schoolgirl *Schwärmerei*: 'Vera became sick and did nothing but weep and call out for Brita – well, at fourteen years of age girls can behave so excessively! Fortunately, she was soon better.'[96] Here, Vera's 'hysteric' passions are associated with sickness and a temporal deviation from the norm – she is said to recover from her 'illness' after she moves to Switzerland and breaks off contact with Brita – while Brita's own controlled and enduring passions are positioned in this encounter to be fixed, healthy and normal.

While Brita distances herself from excessive queer desires and bisexuality more generally, the most dangerous form of desire presented in the novel is without question the obsessive love of heterosexual Hans, which ultimately leads to Brita's untimely death. Although Hans repeatedly asserts that he has 'healthy sexual desires', his relentless efforts to convince Brita to undergo therapy so that he can heal her by marrying her provide the reader with myriad evidence to the contrary. From the fetishistic desire to carry with him a piece of cloth from Brita's evening gown to his desperate suggestion that he marry Brita and allow her to continue her relationship with Renée, Hans remains blind to the selfish nature of his own love for the protagonist. During the road trip to Nice that takes place at the end of the novel, throughout which Brita is depicted as eagerly awaiting her reunion with her lover and increasingly frustrated with Hans' romantic advances, Hans prolongs the car journey to spend more time alone with the protagonist. Interspersing the trip with needless pit stops, Hans uses the excursion to make his final attempt to convince Brita of the integrity of his romantic intentions. Stopping short of their ultimate destination because of inclement weather, Hans invites Brita to a meal at a bar, during which he drinks heavily and convinces the protagonist to dance with him – an act she had previously admitted to being disgusted by. Employing much the same discourse as Fred Wietinghoff in Weirauch's *The Scorpion*, Hans reveals his true erotic intentions only *after* couching them in the rhetoric of camaraderie: 'Do you know what I think? No, what I am imagining, now that we are together like this and going out dancing? … I imagine that it is normal [*gewoon*] and I can tell you this because we are such good friends, such good comrades: I imagine that we are married and soon on our way home together.'[97] Reiterating to Brita that she is a 'true comrade', Hans deploys a term of equality to make palatable his attempt to enforce his will on the protagonist. After a final drink, Hans persuades Brita to take a trip to the next town so that they can continue their evening together at a dance hall: 'At a rapid pace, they drove along the abandoned shiny wet roads; trees shot past like ghosts, the tires bit and squeaked over the gravel as Hans took the corners at high speed … Then the car spun in a semicircle. Brita saw Hans tugging convulsively at the steering wheel. It was over. They drove into a tree. Against that – there …'[98] In light of the discussion earlier in this chapter concerning the discursive and conceptual gaps that characterized the Dutch discussion of queer desire during this period, Brita's death is highly symbolic of the unspeakability of queerness in the Netherlands in the first half of the twentieth century. Nonetheless, it remains suggestive that Reuling posits the interpretive and smothering attentions of those who want to 'heal' Brita as the ultimate cause of her death.

Mother-Love and 'Nonlesbian' Subjects

As was described in Chapter 5, the mother–child paradigm has been a popular literary model for exploring expressions of love between women already for centuries. An exciting interpretation of this paradigm has been put forward by Julian Carter, who identifies that queer femininities in history and literature have long since been understood 'to *obscure* lesbianism'.[99] Taking this tenet to its logical conclusion, Carter suggests that it could be argued that 'feminine gender has often shaped same-sex love and desire *into nonlesbian forms*'.[100] One of the most frequently recurring forms of 'nonlesbian' sexual expression between women, Carter contends, is the concept of 'mother-love', which they loosely define as both the 'love mothers feel' and the 'love felt for mothers'.[101] Arguing, as this book has done of Dutch women living in the Netherlands during the interwar era, that queer feminine women in America in the early twentieth century did not identify with lesbian subject positions, Carter observes that 'feminine women understood their sexual intimacies with other women in terms of the love between mothers and daughters', which they classify in their work as a 'nonlesbian' expression of desire.[102] As has already been discussed in Chapter 5, this maternal love – and the love for the maternal – has appeared frequently in literary work as a romantic 'essence' in relationships between women that include an eroticized imbalance of power. Understanding Carter's concept of mother-love as an alternative 'mode' of desire between women, I will seek to analyse how the maternal shapes the erotic desires of the feminine protagonists within *The Scorpion* and *Back to the Island*.

Strongly influenced by the sexological frameworks of the diagnosis narrative, the introduction to Weirauch's *The Scorpion* informs the reader that Mette's mother died shortly after the protagonist's birth. Following the incident with the silverware, and her first psychiatric examination, the protagonist begins to connect the loss of her mother with the tragic earlier events that shape her life: '[Mette] had a fantastic idea of the nature of a mother and always believed that the early death of her own had caused all the misery in her life.'[103] As with Raedt-de Canter's protagonist in *Boarding School*, Mette is seen frequently to cry out in times of anguish for her mother and she often considers this absence in her life. When Mette initially meets Olga Radó, their relationship is formed around the basis of the didactic Sapphic model discussed in Chapter 5, with Olga in the role of stern teacher and Mette acting as the enamoured student. During her school years, Mette is shown to be an uninterested and untalented student who learns only 'the bare minimum' in order to avoid lengthy reproaches. Yet, with the arrival of the educated and worldly Olga, Mette experiences a sudden urge to broaden her academic horizons. After hearing of Olga's interest in French literature, for example, she is spurred into action: 'It really was a scandal to know so little French. Tomorrow she wanted to go to father and ask him for French conversation lessons. He would be happy if she were to come to him with those types of requests for once.'[104] Just as Magnus Hirschfeld suggested of the 'idolatrous infatuation' that female teachers can inspire in their students, Olga creates a 'burning passion' in Mette for everything in which the former is interested. Asking the protagonist to visit her at her boarding house for lessons in history and literature, Olga establishes a relationship with Mette that is built on an intimate imparting of knowledge: '"Would you [*Sie*] like to learn with me? ... If you [*du*] haven't anything else to do, you [*du*] can read a good one hundred pages a day – oh, more – and when you're finished – every three, four days – depending – you [*Sie*] can come here and exchange the volume for another and we can drink some tea and chat for a while." ... That is how it began.'[105] Olga's employment of the terms 'child', 'girl' and 'little lamb' during their classes, as well as the code switching between the formal you (*Sie*) and the informal (*du*), as Hannah O'Connor observes, 'not only emphasises her superior knowledge and age, but also situates Olga as a maternal figure'.[106] Unlike the pederastic images of the erastes/eromenos relationship, Olga is shown to take unselfish joy in the nurturing of her student's education. As an older female figure of authority, her very presence creates an erotic tension that leaves Mette, much like Winsloe's Manuela, struggling to navigate her fears and desires: 'Mette had a dry throat and a racing heart when she was supposed to read. She had never been so scared at school ... Each word appeared to have a trap hidden within it. She would mispronounce everything and embarrass herself beyond recovery.'[107]

Although these initial interactions are not depicted explicitly as erotic, it is important to remember, as Carter reminds us, that 'the mother–child relationship in [such] affairs is not only about tenderness or responsibility, it is also about sexual desire and activity'.[108] Thus, it is not insignificant that the relationship being cultivated between Mette and Olga begins to develop increasingly erotic undertones as their pedagogic journey develops also. On reading the letters of Bettina von Arnim and Karoline von Günderrode, two eighteenth-century Romantic poets, during one of her meetings with Olga, Mette is presented with a passionate friendship that appears to be the very picture of the idealized forms of love and companionship that she is seeking. Indeed, the relationship between the two poets, as presented in the novel, has been read convincingly by Anjeana Kaur Hans as the original script for the romantic relationship between Olga and Mette, which 'not only denies pseudo-medical definitions, but also discards these generalized models (constructed by men) for one written by a woman'.[109] Certainly, von Arnim and Günderrode's friendship can be read as part of Weirauch's creation of alternative nonlesbian paradigms for love between women in the novel; one that rejects sexological suggestions of excessive desire in favour of a model of spiritual connection, an impulse that can be considered honourable, bourgeois and feminine. Yet, Olga's own declaration of love for Günderrode ultimately imbues this spiritual passionate friendship with something of the erotic, which is developed in Mette's subsequent jealous outburst. As Olga tells Mette of her first encounters with Günderrode's writings, she describes the love that she felt as 'almost like a sickness' and 'torturous'. Recalling the feeling of her 'wildly beating heart' and her face 'turning red then pale when someone mentioned [Günderrode's] name', Olga's spiritual longing for the writer clearly comprises a very physical element of erotic desire. Thus, while Weirauch draws on the image of romantic friendship to present alternative ways of loving between women, through the teacher/student/mother/child paradigm, she further creates a space in which the spiritual connection can be complemented by sensual desires. Likewise, the spiritual essence of 'mother-love' is also complemented by explicitly sexual longings, which are depicted in the most intimate scenes of the novel.

When Mette is forcibly separated from Olga and sent to live with her uncle and aunt, Olga is conflated for the first time with the protagonist's own missing mother, as Mette considers her feelings of 'unbearable loneliness': '"Mother!" [Mette] thought, and something of a convulsive sob welled up in her throat. "Dear, good mother, why did you leave me alone, all alone in the world?" "Alone!?" It was as if she heard this word coming strongly and clearly from Olga's voice … A hot wave flooded over her heart.'[110] Throughout their relationship, Olga is consistently positioned in the role of an eroticized teacher or mother – a figure who is knowledgeable and worldly, but equally caring and nurturing. Yet, when Mette steals from her uncle in order to be reunited with Olga, the passions 'that explode' between the protagonist and her lover are presented to the reader in far more egalitarian terms, first through the imagery of two wild animals and, ultimately, two tired children:

> Their bodies reared up against each other, just as wild animals rattle against the bars of their cages. They dug their nails into the smoothness of the other's flesh and bit their teeth into the other's swollen muscles. And they lay nestled together like children tired from playing, and their lips touched the other's eyelids and cheeks, so softly, so gently, like a butterfly wing touches swaying blossoms. 'Little one', said Olga, and all the bells chimed in her voice. 'My beauty, my dear! … Are you not proud, little girl, that you can perform such miracles?'[111]

In this highly charged and erotic scene, the desire to conform to norms of bourgeois respectability has been entirely displaced by the 'wild' urges of two desirous beings. Moreover, blurring the previously strictly demarcated roles of the mother–child paradigm, Mette and Olga are instead depicted here as equals vying for erotic power. Both characters use nails and teeth to penetrate the other's flesh and, following this climactic exchange, both are described as 'children tired from playing'. This theme of sexual parity continues with a Freudian fantasy of the return to the womb, as the couple cling to one another 'as if each wanted to flow over into the other, to merge, to become one'.[112] In this image, both characters could be read as mother and both also as child. Yet, Olga's use of the terms 'little one' and 'little girl', as well as her concluding words of praise after their sexual encounter, arguably anticpate a return to the mother-child model. This is further supported by Mette's final declaration of the scene, in which she claims she felt as though she '[had been] born' through her erotic experience with Olga.[113] That the maternal dynamic is shown to shift back and forth between Mette and Olga in this scene implies that the mother–child paradigm might be viewed more as a vacillating 'mode' of desire than as a static sexual model. In this way, the novel's depictions of desire appear able to escape the binaries that structured the images of the 'active masculine invert' and the 'passive feminine woman', instead offering a mode of loving that is expressed in arguably 'nonlesbian' forms.

Demonstrating the flexibility of mother-love as a mode of desire, Reuling's novel *Back to the Island* is the only text in Part III not to be structured in some way by the trope of the 'absent mother'. On the contrary, Brita's mother is shown to be a constant and smothering presence in the protagonist's life, while it is Brita's father who is absent for most of her childhood. During the brief case history presented in the first pages of the novel, the reader is informed that Brita's father, a timber trader, is rarely able to visit the island of Semmarö, where his daughter spends her summers: 'His business did not allow him any time. "The Timber", said the family. He immersed himself a little too much in it.'[114] The protagonist is described as enjoying an exceptionally strong bond with her father who, until the protagonist meets Renée, is described as 'the only person [Brita] had ever truly loved'. Indeed, although Brita is left unhappy by her lover Marja's betrayal, it is only when she is rejected by her father after he receives the latter's poison pen letter that she is shown to reach an emotional breaking point: 'No one, nothing, could give her back her father … Brita cried. It was a shaking, shocking cry, which might last for days. She knew it. It was like a sudden fever, which rose high and suddenly dropped and left you empty and exhausted. You could not do anything about it, you had to let it rage.'[115] Much like the 'mother cry' depicted in the other novels in this section, the tears Brita sheds for her father are couched in erotically suggestive terms, with the references to rising and dropping fevers, that 'leave you empty and exhausted'.[116] Yet, in spite of the protagonist's unconditional love for her father, a large and impressively built man who appears himself 'to be carved from wood', and the Freudian theories that are present throughout the narrative, Reuling does not depict Brita as envious or desirous of the masculine element; she does not seek out a father figure in her partners and nor does she want to *be* her father. Indeed, as was discussed earlier in this chapter, Brita's lovers are decidedly feminine and even the tomboyish Renée is characterized primarily by her traditionally feminine behaviours and characteristics.

Presented in the role of the caregiver and homemaker, Renée acts as a nurse for her sick neighbour each evening and Brita watches in awe as her lover nurtures a stray cat back to health. Renée also cares for a pet tortoise she adopted from a friend and it is for this reason that she stays behind while Hans and Brita depart on their holiday. Interestingly, it is also the boyish Renée who speaks at most length about the concept of mother-love, positioning it – much like Weirauch's depiction of von Arnim and Günderrode – as a variation on the 'ideal' model of passionate love:

> 'The people who love us the most are the least demanding. I am thinking now especially of motherly love, which comes closest to ideal love ... It has nothing to do with *being* a mother. Most women who have children think that they possess mother-love, but they are mistaken. Every woman can have a child, almost every woman can nurture it but, even if they have a child and mother's milk, that does not mean that they possess a mother's love ... I even know a father who possesses the ideal mother's love for his children.' 'Then you must say father-love, otherwise you do him a disservice.' Renée was having none of it. The sentiment was intrinsically feminine, father-love was something totally different.[117]

Here, Renée conceives of mother-love as a fundamentally feminine experience, but equally as a concept that is fluid, something that can be mapped across genders and onto various types of relationships. Renée's interpretation of mother-love as an essence that has 'nothing to do with mothers' underscores most strongly the malleability of the mother–daughter paradigm as a workable concept through which to conceive of erotic desire, irrespective of whether the relationship is typified by a substantial age gap or even power difference. Furthermore, while Renée is shown to embody strongly maternal instincts, nursing her neighbour back to health and adopting stray animals, she is also described by Brita as 'child-like', which points again to the dynamism of a mode of loving that shifts depending on the needs of those within its erotic structures. In a similar way to Weirauch, then, Reuling positions mother-love as an alternative model to sexological and psychoanalytic discourses of desire. In a scene that shows Renée both offering maternal care to Brita while conveying a 'child-like expression', for example, Brita confesses her love for her friend, who is taken aback by the simplicity with which Brita states her feelings: 'Oh, if you want it less simply, ask Hans. He would be happy to give you a straightforward explanation of what he believes to be our "abnormal sympathies" for each other; he can explain to you exactly which complexes, childhood impressions, repressed feelings and unconscious tendencies have stimulated us.'[118] Here the medicalizing view of psychoanalysts is set in direct opposition to the model of mother-love that Brita perceives to be 'natural' and 'intrinsically feminine'.

While the concept of mother-love in the text primarily concerns the protagonist's desires for maternal women, the second half of the novel explores more explicitly the 'love mothers feel'. For example, when Hans tries to convince Brita that she ought to undergo psychoanalytic therapy so that she might fulfil her role 'as a mother', the reader is told that Brita desperately wants a child, but is unsure whether this will ever be possible on account of the 'struggles' she is experiencing in her life:

> If she were more mature she would want to have a child, it would certainly be the best training for her … But she had to postpone this wish for the time being, to ignore it, although sometimes it could be desperately tormenting: 'Your daughter is knocking and wants to be born', [Brita] would sigh and smile shyly. 'You will have to wait a little while, lamb, your Ma is at a crossroads, her life is taking a different turn and she doesn't know how she will emerge from this new struggle. And she doesn't know whether she has the right to raise you without a father, whether the masculine element is not indispensable for a child.'[119]

Although Brita's longing for a child is framed by the psychoanalytic questions of sociosexual maturity, her desire to become a mother does not appear in any way to negate her desire for other women; in fact, her desire for a child forms an integral part of the femininity that she considers to be key to the expression of her love for other women. Moreover, she does not conceive of bringing a child into the world with a male partner and she persistently rejects any male advances, even the supposedly platonic suggestion of Hans' marriage proposal so that he might offer the protagonist and her lover Renée 'social protection'. Curiously, Brita – a figure who finds even the act of walking arm in arm with a man 'nauseating' – does not dwell on how such a child might be brought into existence. Her only concern appears to be that the child might 'miss' the masculine element in its life, something that she excludes from her own romantic and sexual partnerships. Yet, Brita concludes that her longing to be a mother is ultimately self-seeking: 'Is it selfishness, this desire [*verlangen*] for you, my child? According to Hans, and all the intelligent and intellectual people who unravel our emotions, who explain them and put them neatly into boxes, everything we do, everything that we desire, is selfish. "Desire and aversion", says Freud, "is at the core of all our actions, of our being, and all our motives."[120] Arguably, Brita's desires for a child shape the erotic attraction that she feels towards both maternal and child-like women. In this way, these romantic encounters enable her to live out her fantasy of being a mother and, crucially, do not preclude the erotic from the concept of 'mother-love'.

Conclusions

In the novels written by Weirauch and Reuling, we witness challenges being made to the medicoscientific and social discourses that classified queer feminine women as a 'pseudohomosexuals' and queer feminine desires as temporary and curable. Presenting models of feminine desire that destabilize the relationship between gender inversion and sexual preference, the authors call into question the broader concept of what constituted 'normative' and 'non-normative' behaviours through their subversive representations of same-sex-loving women. While sexological and psychoanalytic theories provide the authors with an entry point into the discussion of same-sex desire, Weirauch and Reuling in no way attempt to reproduce the sexual paradigms created by contemporary sex researchers in their writing. Through a destabilization of the dyad that posits homosexual desire as 'non-normative' and 'immoral' in the novels, the authors counter the image of the queer woman as sexual 'Other' and foreground the complex identitarian interactions that take place between class, gender and desire. Furthermore, while the supposed passivity and temporal nature of the feminine woman's queer desires suggested a distinct possibility of a 'return' to 'normal' heterosexual tendencies, both Mette and Brita are depicted as being resolute in their queerness – and in their gender identities. Indeed, in neither narrative can there be a 'return' to men because there is never shown to be a beginning. Mette's disastrous attempt to marry a (class-) suitable man after the breakdown of her relationship with Olga functions only to extend the theory that marriage would harm masculine inverts to the queer feminine woman also. Furthermore, the desires of the protagonists are not made visible through the masculine since – much like Johanna Elberskirchen's theories of the feminine homosexual woman – both protagonists are presented as feminine subjects who desire feminine objects. In this way, we might conceive of the novels as disruptions to the models of complementarity, placing queer feminine desire outside the dominant active–passive dichotomy and giving sexual agency to women who have historically been denied it.

However, the search for alternative paradigms of feminine desire in the novels takes the authors in decidedly different directions. While Mette's longings in *The Scorpion* trilogy are shaped by the dominant norms and practices of her class and limited by her desire to conform to the regimes of respectable bourgeois behaviour, Brita aggressively rails against societal expectations of female desire, attempting to denaturalize the assumptions of heteronormativity by positioning her queerness as the only way of 'being' normal. Yet, Brita's subversion of the binary that positions the queer woman as non-normative inscribes only another regime of gender norms and boundaries onto her, leaving little room for 'excessive' passions, the bisexual inclinations of her lover Marja or the masculine behaviours of the virile women seen on the Parisian bar circuit. Veering away from the inversion of the binary of 'good' and 'bad', Weirauch's novels instead focus on the nuancing of binary thinking through Mette's encounters with a diverse range of queer and heterosexual characters. Not shying away from the sexological stereotypes of femininity as excessive, degenerate and temporary with her depictions of the Munich scene, Weirauch's characters are nonetheless rounded and complex, and often challenge the rigid gendered and sexual orthodoxies of sexological study.

Written in Dutch about a Swedish protagonist who lives in Paris and who is ultimately killed in a car crash, Reuling's novel illustrates the complex layers of 'Othering' that were still taking place in discussions about queer female desire in the Netherlands at the end of the interwar period. Indeed, like Raedt-de Canter's novel *Boarding School*, the fact that Brita can only express her desires to her parents and Hans 'in phrases' highlights the continued difficulty of articulating queer desires in the Dutch context. Yet, in spite of the lack of specific identitarian terminology in Reuling's discussion of female queerness, the imperative Brita experiences to articulate a 'truth' (*waarheid*) about herself already marks a strong departure from Raedt-de Canter's novel in the ways in which queer female desires were being conceived and expressed. Importantly, however, Reuling's protagonist is *not* lesbian: Brita forcefully rejects the image of the third sex and theories of somatic inversion that had come to be associated with this label. Brita's femininity and the traditional behaviours associated with this gendered marker – such as her desire for a child – enable her to take up a *nonlesbian* subject position. One that ultimately upends the contemporary frameworks that conceived of same-sex desire as an 'abnormal tendency'.

In a similar way, Weirauch's protagonist distances herself from the labels and categories she finds in sexological studies. Unable to recognize herself in the images she encounters in medical writing, Mette ultimately rejects the queer community that she initially embraced as a group of people who 'shared her fate'. Her 'return to nature' in the final instalment of the trilogy, as well as her distancing from the erotic love that she experiences with Olga Radó and Corona von Gjellerström, underscores her desire to be conceived, above all, as a bourgeois feminine woman. While she does not ever resolve her struggle with the bourgeois politics of respectability, the deployment of the mother–daughter model offers readers a new mode through which to conceive of erotic love that sit outside sexological theories of active masculine and passive feminine drives. While neither author acts as a champion for the freedom of queer desire in all its complexity, both Reuling and Weirauch complicate the dialogue that existed between contemporary sexological discourses on (homo)sexuality and literary writing in this period. By positioning the feminine woman as subject *and* object within their novels, these authors push the masculine invert to the margins of their narratives, while challenging culturally rooted codes of respectability, femininity and desire.

Notes

1. Julian Carter, 'On Mother-Love: History, Queer Theory, and Nonlesbian Identity', *Journal of the History of Sexuality*, 14 (2005), 107–38.
2. Hannah O'Connor, 'Sapphic Spectres: Lesbian Gothic in Interwar German Narratives', unpublished doctoral thesis (Cardiff: Cardiff University, 2014), p. 17.
3. Shane Phelan, *Getting Specific: Postmodern Lesbian Politics* (Minneapolis: Minnesota University Press, 1994), p. 96.
4. Trans.: 'in ihren Gefühls-, Geschmacks- und Gedankenäußerungen so durchaus weiblich, daß sie niemand für homosexuell halten würde'. Although this appears to bolster the image of the 'true' virile homosexual woman, Hirschfeld's studies also challenged the assumption that the desires of feminine women were temporal and 'curable'. Magnus Hirschfeld, *Die Homosexualität des Mannes und des Weibes* (Berlin: Louis Marcus, 1914), p. 292.
5. Claudia Schoppman, *Der Skorpion: Frauenliebe in der Weimarer Republik* (Kiel: Frühlings Erwachen, 1985), p. 14.
6. Trans.: 'ein starkes schriftstellerisches Talent'. In 1921, the novel was adapted into a film directed by Alfred Halm (1861–1951) and starred Grete Reinwald (1902–83) in the leading role.
7. One contributor to *The Girlfriend* claimed that the first two novels '[were] almost completely out of print immediately after publication'. Trans.: 'fast sofort nach Erscheinen vollkommen vergriffen [gewesen seien]'. The author of the article also claimed that, in 1931, the first two novels of Weirauch's trilogy were 'no longer available in book shops' as they were sold out. Trans.: 'im Buchhandel nicht mehr erhältlich'. 'Was Sie interessieren dürfte …', *Die Freundin*, 9 November 1932.

8. Trans.: 'heikles Thema von der gleichgeschlechtlichen Liebe'. Manfred Georg, 'Der Skorpion' *Berliner Zeitung*, 28 August 1919. Although I have been unable to locate reviews for the final novel, it can be assumed that, at least among the queer community, the third instalment was equally as popular. All three novels remained in *Die Freundin*'s 'book charts' and were available for purchase through the *Friedrich Radszuweit Verlag* until the magazine ceased printing in 1933. In 1921, there was a suggestion in the *Berliner Zeitung am Mittag* that Weirauch was working with the director Käthe Wienskowitz (1887–1943) on a cinematic adaptation of *Der Skorpion*. However, this endeavour did not come to fruition. See *Berliner Zeitung am Mittag*, 12 October 1921.
9. Schoppman, *Der Skorpion*, p. 15.
10. Trans.: 'leek het … haar een paradijs'. G.A. van Riemsdijk, 'Josine Reuling', *Jaarboek van de Maatschappij der Nederlandse Letterkunde* (1972) (252–258), p. 253.
11. 'Boek en Blad: Intermezzo met Ernst', *De Tijd*, 11 October 1934, p. 2.
12. Ibid.
13. See Judith Schuyf, 'Lesbian Emancipation in the Netherlands', in Alex van Naerssen (ed.), *Gay Life in Dutch Society* (New York: Harrington Park Press, 1987).
14. As Myriam Everard has noted, forty-seven literary works containing references to female same-sex desire were published in the Dutch language between 1880 and 1940, of which thirty-six were written originally in Dutch. Over half of the total number were written by female authors. Yet, it was not until Reuling's publication that love between women became visible as a central theme in Dutch literary writing. See Myriam Everard, 'Galerij der vrouwenliefde: Sex variant women" in Nederlandstalige literatuur 1880-1940', in *Homojaarboek 2: Artikelen over emancipatie en homoseksualiteit* (Amsterdam: Van Gennep, 1983).
15. It should be noted that there was a difference in the receptions of the novel between the colonial and national Dutch press. In the Netherlands, *Terug naar het eiland* received relatively mixed reviews; while the Liberal and Socialist newspapers remained generally indifferent to the release of the novel, religious newspapers were more negative in their descriptions of the text. However, the nationalist and religious press in the Dutch colonies was united in its dismissal of the novel and openly attacked the literary merit of the author as well as her subject matter – a form of attack against queer female writers that would resurface following the publication of Anna Blaman's *Lonely Adventure* (*Eenzaam avontuur*, 1948). See, for example, 'Het nieuwe boek: Terug naar het eiland, door Josine Reuling', *De Sumatra Post*, 16 October 1937, p. 12.
16. Trans.: 'der Auftakt zu [ihrem] Leben'. Anna Elisabet Weirauch, *Der Skorpion* (Frankfurt: Ullstein, 1993), p. 29.
17. The themes of queerness and the desires of the bourgeois protagonist to become an outsider relative to 'respectable' society had already been taken up earlier by male queer writers; see, for example, Thomas Mann's *Tonio Kröger* in *Tristan: Sechs Novellen* (Berlin: S. Fischer, 1903).
18. There has been no scholarly consensus concerning the gender of the narrator. While Cathrin Winkelmann suggests that the narrator is female, essentially conflating Weirauch with her narrator, Mara Taylor considers that it would be in line with the contemporary gender norms of the time to conclude that the narrator is male. Nancy P. Nenno's work on the novel avoids the question of the gender of the narrator altogether. As Weirauch intentionally does not gender her narrator, the pronouns used in this chapter adhere to the author's original neutral narrative perspective. Trans.: 'mit der klaren und kalten Freude des Forschers'. Anna E. Weirauch, *Der Skorpion: Band I* (Berlin: Feministischer Buchverlag, 1997), p. 7. Trans.: 'die Kranken, die Verlorenen [und] die Ausgestoßenen'. Ibid.

19. Trans.: 'um sie zu vivisezieren, zu analysieren, sie in Systeme einzuschachteln'. Weirauch, *Der Skorpion: Band I*, p. 7.
20. Trans.: 'Ich bin nicht dazu geschaffen, zu verteidigen oder anzuklagen. Ich verfolge keinen Zweck, wenn ich etwas erzähle. Ich habe keine Ziele und keine Absichten, nicht einmal eine Meinung oder ein Urteil, und kaum ein Gefühl.' Ibid., p. 9.
21. Nancy P. Nenno, '*Bildung* and Desire: Anna Elisabet Weirauch's *Der Skorpion*', in Christoph Lorey and John L. Plews (eds), *Queering the Canon: Defying Sights in German Literature and Culture* (Columbia, SC: Camden House, 1998), p. 213.
22. Trans.: 'merkwürdigen Frau … einer Hochstaplerin mit ausgesprochen männlichem Gebaren'. Weirauch, *Der Skorpion: Band I*, p. 8.
23. Trans.: 'in dem überheblichen Wahn, helfen zu können, bessern zu können – sie mit reinen und gütigen Händen hellere Wege zu führen'. Ibid., pp. 7–8.
24. Mara Taylor, 'Diagnosing Deviants: The Figure of the Lesbian in Sexological and Literary Discourses 1860–1931', unpublished doctoral thesis (Philadelphia: University of Pennsylvania, 2010), p. 409.
25. Nenno, '*Bildung* and Desire', p. 213.
26. Trans.: 'einen sonderbaren Kontrast'. Weirauch, *Der Skorpion: Band I*, p. 32.
27. Trans.: 'scharf und hart'; 'weichen Celloklang'. Ibid., p. 31; Trans.: 'fast drohenden Ausdruck'; 'wunderschöne Hände'. Ibid., p. 32.
28. Trans.: 'der den grauenerregenden und unheimlichen Titel "Psychiater" führte'. Ibid., p. 40.
29. Trans.: 'Und da ich doch den Verdacht nicht ganz los bin, daß Sie mir aus irgendeiner dummen Antwort einen Schwachsinn konstruieren.' Ibid., p. 238.
30. Trans.: 'ein Kind, das gar nicht weiß, in welcher Gefahr es schwebt'. Ibid., p. 135. The concept of the bourgeois 'child-woman', who was innocent in sexual matters and is typified in the novel by the 'boring' Möbius daughters, ultimately creates a space in which Mette's desires can be considered temporary and 'curable'. Interestingly, it was German neurologist Paul Julius Möbius who wrote perhaps one of the most damning indictments of the infantilized bourgeois woman in Über *den physiologischen Schwachsinn des Weibes* (Halle: Carl Marhold, 1906), in which he claimed that the female subject was 'a middle thing between child and man'. Trans.: 'ein Mittelding zwischen Kind und Mann' (at p. 28).
31. As well as portraying through medical authorities embedded in the text the various theories that pertained to the 'curing' of homosexual desires, Weirauch also depicts how these ideas were taken up in wider society. In the second instalment of her trilogy, for example, morphine addict Gisela Werkendam is approached by her friend Giesbert, who suggests that because Gisela is 'not a man-woman' (kein Mannweib) she can be cured: 'Just try it once with a real man and you will be forever healed and saved. I would be happy to make myself available to you, free of charge and postage paid. You have no idea of the kind of fun you would have.' Trans.: 'Versuch es nur einmal mit einem reellen Mann, und du bist für immer geheilt und gerettet. Ich stelle mich dir gern zur Verfügung, gratis und franko. Du ahnst ja nicht, was für einen Spaß du haben wirst.' Anna E. Weirauch, *Der Skorpion: Band II* (Berlin, Feministischer Buchverlag, 1993), pp. 129–30.
32. Trans.: 'als ob erbarmungslose Hände ihr Stück für Stück der Kleidung vom Leibe rissen'. Weirauch, *Der Skorpion: Band I*, p. 136.
33. Trans.: 'körperlichen Anomalien'. Ibid., p. 139.
34. Trans.: 'Sie warf einen Blick um sich wie ein gehetztes, in die Enge getriebenes Tier. Nirgends ein Ausweg, nirgends eine Möglichkeit zur Flucht.' Ibid., p. 140.
35. Weirauch, *Der Skorpion: Band I*, p. 142.

36. Trans.: 'Weißt du, Männe ... mich hat ein Skorpion gestochen. Nun ist mein ganzes Blut vergiftet. Und du weißt doch: Gegen Skorpionengift hilft nur Skorpionengift ... Ich glaube wohl, dass es *tödlich* sein kann – aber ansteckend ist es nicht.' Ibid., p. 143. The image of Mette's blood being 'poisonous' calls to mind the earlier ideas of Karl Heinrich Ulrichs, who suggested in *Formatrix: Anthropologische Studien* über *urnische Liebe* (1864) that a blood transfusion might have the effect of turning an 'Urning' into a 'normal man' and vice versa. See Hubert Kennedy, *Ulrichs: The Life and Works of Karl Heinrich Ulrichs: Pioneer of the Modern Gay Movement* (Boston, MA: Alyson Publications Inc., 1988).
37. Trans.: 'Bücher, Hefte, Broschüren ... Romane, medizinische Werke [und] angestrichene Tageszeitungen.' Weirauch, *Der Skorpion Band I*, p. 373.
38. Trans.: 'Da waren seltsame und unheimliche Geschichten von Gräfinnen, die sich in Männerkleidung in Kaschemmen herumtrieben ... Berichte von widerlichen Orgien in großen Clubs, wo Hunderte von Weibern sich als Männer anzogen und gebärdeten ... Schilderungen aus dem Seelenleben Konträr-Sexualer, die vermuten ließen, daß diese Tausende von Menschen alle miteinander eine große Gemeinde bildeten, eine Gemeinde, die durch nichts verbrüdert wurde, ... nichts als den Trieb zur gleichen Ausschweifung.' Ibid.
39. Forel described the congenital female invert as a figure who 'dresses like a man and feels like a man towards other women' ('kleidet sich gerne als Mann, fühlt sich auch als Mann anderen Frauen gegenüber') and who is frequently 'colossally sexually excited' ('sexuell kolossal aufgeregt') and can seduce even the most heterosexual of women. Writing of the 'the purest Don Juans' ('den reinsten Don Juans'), Forel claimed that alcoholism often fuelled the excesses of these women, whose voracious sexual appetites supposedly led not infrequently to orgies where 'in most cases one orgasm follows the other, day and night, almost without interruption' ('ein Orgasmus folgt in manchen Fällen dem anderen, Tag und Nacht, fast ohne Unterbruch'). See Forel, *Die sexuelle Frage: Eine naturwissenschaftliche, psychologische, hygienische und soziologische Studie* für *Gebildete* 9th edn. (Munich: E. Reinhardt, 1909), p. 287.
40. Taylor, 'Diagnosing Deviants', p. 422.
41. Trans.: 'Wenn von männlich veranlagten Frauen gesprochen wurde, war viel von ihrem überlegenen Geist, von ihrem Wissensdurst und Bildungsdrang die Rede. Auch von einer krankhaften Verschwendungssucht mitunter, von einem leidenschaftlichen Hang zum Luxus, von einer unnatürlichen Vorliebe für schöne Stiefel. Oder auch von unheimlichen Don-Juan-Naturen, die mit unersättlicher Genußgier von Abenteuer zu Abenteuer rasten.' Weirauch, *Der Skorpion: Band I*, p. 375.
42. Trans.: 'eine fast krankhafte Abneigung gegen alles, was billig war'. Ibid., p. 52.
43. Trans.: 'erklär mir das. Gibt es solche Menschen? Bist du so? Bin ich so?' Ibid., p. 376.
44. Trans.: 'Mette schauderte, wenn sie das Wort Liebe in diesem Zusammenhang nur dachte. Manchmal war ihr, als müsse sie ersticken in Kot und Unflat.' Ibid. p. 375.
45. Trans.: 'Es war eine ganze Stufenleiter von Erscheinungen da. Solche, die zum dunklen Jackenkleid mit Aufschlag und Brusttasche den steifen Kragen, zum kurzgeschnittenen Haar den kleinen Herrenhut trugen – andere, die sich nur durch eine leise Schattierung verrieten – einige, aus deren scharfen Zügen Geist und Charakter sprachen, andere, die ganz den Typ der Kokotte vertraten.' Ibid., pp. 313–14.
46. Trans.: 'Grauen und Ekel vor sich selber.' Weirauch, *Der Skorpion: Band I*, p. 326.
47. Marti M. Lybeck, *Desiring Emancipation: New Women and Homosexuality in Germany 1890–1933* (Albany, NY: SUNY Press, 2014), p. 154.
48. Trans.: 'Daarbij is zij een bizonder [*sic*] knap meisje, zeer sportief en toch zo vrouwelijk, zo charmant.' Josine Reuling, *Terug naar het eiland* (Amsterdam: Querido, 1937), p. 32.

49. Havelock Ellis, 'Sexual Inversion in Women', in *Studies in the Psychology of Sex: Volume II* (New York: Random House, 1936 [1897]), p. 222.
50. Trans.: 'dingen die je niet zèi'. Reuling, *Terug*, p. 18.
51. Brita's grandmother holds up the Swedish author Selma Lagerlöf, whose novels about rural Swedish life won her the Nobel Prize in Literature, as an example. She further claims that if her granddaughter's writing thematized the Swedish landscape and morals (*zeden*), she would have nothing against the practice. Of note, Lagerlöf was known to have had several passionate relationships with women during her lifetime and fell deeply in love with the Jewish-Swedish author Sophie Elkan. See Rose Collis, *Portraits to the Wall: Historic Lesbian Lives Unveiled* (London: Bloomsbury, 1994), pp. 87–103.
52. Trans.: 'ik vind het geen werk voor een meisje'. Reuling, *Terug*, p. 53.
53. Trans.: 'Brita vertelde geen leugens. Got-o-got, daar was zij te oprecht voor, te rechtdoor-zee, te dit en te dat, niets dan verheven eigenschappen.' Ibid., p. 85.
54. Trans.: 'dan verlangde Brita naar Parijs, al wist zij dat zij haar nooit als een der hunnen zouden beschouwen. Zij was en bleef: de rijke Zweedse, la bourgeoisie ...'. Ibid., p. 56.
55. Trans.: 'liefde zonder erotiek niet mogelijk is'. Ibid., p. 156.
56. Brita's publication may have been inspired by the cultural revival of the analysis of unconscious desires after Carl Jung's lectures on *Dreams and Dream Analysis* (1931), Trans.: 'mengelmoes van bewondering en vrees'. Ibid., p. 17.
57. Trans.: '"delicate kwesties"'. Ibid., p. 38.
58. Trans.: 'Ik trouw waarschijnlijk nooit'. Ibid., p. 36.
59. Trans.: 'niet geschikt voor het huwelijk'; 'houd niet van mannen'. Ibid., p. 37.
60. Trans.: 'Alle mannen? Je hebt zonderlinge ideeën. Ik begrijp je steeds minder. Mij lijkt één meer dan voldoende.' Ibid.
61. Trans.: 'Ach meisje, daar moeten wij allen doorheen, ik geef toe, dat ... je moet een man op een afstand weten te houden, juist in een huwelijk, je moet zorgen, dat je je eigenwaarde als vrouw niet verliest.' Ibid.
62. Trans.: 'Brita [barstte] in lachen uit. Zij lachte hartelijk, bijna uitbundig, haar grote mond breed open, haar kleine stevige tanden glinsterden, staken iets te wit af tegen de lichtrood geverfde lippen. Mama schoten van drift en verontwaardiging de tranen in de ogen. Zonder een woord te zeggen, stond zij op en ging de kamer uit. 's Middags kwam zij niet aan tafel.' Ibid., pp. 37–38.
63. Trans.: 'dingen, waaromtrent menige moeder haar dochter volkomen in het duister liet'. Ibid., p. 39.
64. Michel Foucault, *The History of Sexuality: Volume I*, trans. by Robert Hurley (London: Penguin, 1984), p. 27.
65. Ibid.
66. Furthermore, by creating omissions in the text, the author invites the reader to take part in the creative process of interpreting the meanings created by the gaps in the dialogue for themselves. Trans.: 'nu *moest* zij het zeggen'. Ibid., p. 42.
67. Although Brita forcefully rejects the notion of gender inversion, she appears more willing to accept the theories of psychoanalysis, claiming at one point that if she were 'rijper' (more mature) she would have been able to have a child (this will be discussed later on in this chapter). Ibid., p. 137.
68. Trans.: 'De wetenschap als zodanig is dood.' Ibid., p. 167.
69. Trans.: 'de ziel te genezen eiste andere methoden dan het lichaam, om haar te opereren had je fijnere instrumenten nodig dan de chirurg gebruikte'. Ibid., p. 166.
70. Trans.: 'En toch dacht ook [Hans] in dogma's, toch hing ook hij theorieën op; dit etiket moest passen op die stelling, deze conclusie moest getrokken worden uit die handeling. Het moest. Het was logisch, onvermijdelijk ... "Wij psycho-analytici, kunnen helpen,

genezen." – "Wij, katholieke kerk, kunnen helpen, genezen." – "Wij, gereformeerden, zuiveren in de leer, kunnen helpen, genezen."' Ibid., pp. 166–67.
71. Jean-Michel Quinodoz, *Reading Freud: A Chronological Exploration of Freud's Writings*, trans. by David Alcorn (New York: Routledge, 2005), p. 231.
72. Sigmund Freud, 'Psychoanalysis: Exploring the Hidden Recesses of the Mind', in *These Eventful Years: The Twentieth Century in the Making as Told By Many of Its Makers*, trans. A.A. Brill (London: Encyclopedia Britannica Company, 1924), pp. 520–1.
73. However, it should be noted that the model of confession does not appear to fit in with the norms of the Protestant Swedish society in which Reuling's novel is set. Indeed, the author's references to Calvinists and Catholics in the text show it to be a novel influenced much more by the Dutch context in which she was writing.
74. Trans.: 'ob sie ein guter oder schlechter Mensch war'. Weirauch, *Der Skorpion: Band II*, p. 35.
75. Michael Warner, *The Trouble with Normal: Sex, Politics, and the Ethics of Queer Life* (Cambridge, MA: Harvard University Press, 1999), p. 114.
76. Ibid., p. 3.
77. Trans.: 'Am Glücklichsten aber ist der kleine Johannes. Er führt das Leben, wozu seine eigentliche Natur ihn treibt … Jetzt hat er alles, was er sich im Grunde immer ersehnt hat. Er ist begehrt, verwöhnt, angebetet. Er sieht seine Schönheit, die er nebenbei sehr zu schätzen weiß, im richtigen Rahmen. Er bringt halbe Tage damit zu, vor seinem dreiteiligen Toilettenspiegel zu sitzen, sich zu bewundern, sich mit Salben und Pudern und Haarwassern zu pflegen. Das tut er alles Willi Krafft zuliebe? Redet euch doch so etwas nicht ein. Er täte es ohne Willi Krafft genauso.' Ibid., pp. 153–54.
78. Trans.: 'im nächsten Augenblick, als Mette ihr warme, frauliche Hand hielt, als ein Lächeln von unbeschreiblich wärmender Herzlichkeit und Güte sie ausstrahlte, vergaß sie, nach Schönheit und Häßlichkeit zu fragen und gab sich bedingungslos dem milden Zauber dieser Persönlichkeit hin'. Ibid., p. 72.
79. Trans.: 'Alles, Gute und Böse, ist so ineinander verquickt, daß wir es gar nicht auseinander lösen können, um eins gegen das andere abzuwägen.' Ibid., p. 149.
80. Trans.: 'Mette war von neuem entzückt, wie Gwendolen die schmalen Füße mit den federnden Gelenken schön und sicher setzte, wie die schlanken, festen Formen sich unter dem weißen Kleid zeichneten, wie das lockige Haar in der Sonne gleißte und flirrte … Ihr Herz war ebenso froh, wenn sie Fred Wietinghoff sah, der neben Gwedolen ging, viel größer als sie, breit in den Schultern, schmal in den Hüften, alle Konturen der Muskeln zeigend unter dem seidenen Hemd.' Ibid., p. 351–52.
81. Trans.: 'gute und ehrliche Kameradschaft'. Ibid., p. 449.
82. Trans.: 'ein Schlüssel zu meinen Innern'. Ibid., p. 453. 'Gwen warf sich über [Mette] und küßte ihr Mund und Augenlider, Hals und Wangen. "Ich will nicht", dachte Mette, "sie ist mir anvertraut, und ich rühre sie nicht an. Ich bin [Freds] Kamerad … ich bin sein Kamerad …" Rosenrote Wellen hoben sich. Sie stiegen ihr bis zum Hals, bis über die Augen. Das Zimmer schien zu schwanken, wie in zitternden Atemzügen, wie in ruckweisen Herzstößen. Plötzlich war alles still, hell, es war wie ein blendendes Licht, und wie ein schmetternder Hornstoß … Irgend etwas war im Zimmer, was vorher nicht da gewesen war. Ein violetter Fleck. Und darüber Fred Wietinghoffs Gesicht. Fred Wietinghoffs Augen. Brennend. Gierig. Ganz unverhüllt, wie die Augen brünstiger Tiere – ganz nackte Augen … Abgekartet. Alles abgekartet. [Mette] richtete sich auf und griff nach ihren Kleidern.' Ibid., pp. 457–59.
83. Trans.: 'schönes, unschuldiges junges Mädchen aus bester Familie'. Ibid., p. 234.
84. Trans.: '"Aber, wie soll man den Weg wissen?" fragte Mette verzweifelt. "Wie soll man wissen, welche Tür die richtige ist?"' Anna E. Weirauch, *Der Skorpion: Band III* (Berlin: Feministischer Buchverlag, 1993), p. 334.

328 • Different from the Others

85. In this mirroring of the opening scene of the first novel, where the medical narrator attempts to lead the protagonist to 'brighter paths', the protagonist is shown to be still searching for the way.
86. Trans.: 'Volgens de leer van Freud – en dus van Hans – was zij ziek. Volgens de leer van het Christendom was zij zondig. Volgens de wetenschap was zij een physieke afwijking. Volgens de opvattingen van de massa was zij raar, griezelig, onzedelijk, ongelukkig, zielig; dit laatste was uiterst clement.' Reuling, *Terug,* p. 138.
87. Trans.: 'Samenleven met een vrouw wordt niet erkend. Je bent sociaal gesproken – een outsider ... Enkel in wereldsteden zoals Parijs en dan nog in zekere kringen, wordt het geaccepteerd; in Duitsland zou je op het ogenblik als "staatswidrig" in een concentratiekamp worden opgesloten. Ik ken zulke gevallen, ik vertel geen verhaaltjes.' Ibid., p. 180.
88. Trans.: 'zij, Brita Salin, verklaarde, dat zij zichzelf normaal vond en alle anderen, die niet waren zoals zij: abnormaal. Voor haar was elke vrouw, die ernaar verlangde, een man te omhelzen, die in staat was haar liefde, haar hartstocht te geven aan een man, een wonder, een haar volkomen onbegrijpelijk wezen, dat zij met verbazing en heimelijke afkeer bekeek'. Ibid., p. 138.
89. Trans.: 'zij deed precies hetzelfde tegenover hen als de anderen tegenover haar. Met dit verschil, dat zij het recht hadden om hun afschuw openlijk te uiten ... Goed, de afschuw kon zij begrijpen. Ook zij voelde die in zich opkomen, als zij een man en een vrouw innig samen zag dansen, zelfs innig gearmd zag lopen'. Ibid.
90. Trans.: 'Speciale bars had zij niet meer gefrequenteerd, de professionals waren te dégoutant. Waarom imiteerden die vrouwen een sexe, waar zij een afkeer van hadden? Waarom kleedden zij zich als mannen, met overhemden en dassen en kortgeknipte haren en hadden bruuske mannelijke bewegingen? ... Zij had het nooit begrepen.' Ibid., p. 140.
91. Trans.: 'zij was blij dat zijn een vrouw was, zij wilde niets anders zijn dan vrouw'. Ibid.
92. Trans.: 'wee gevoel van walging'; 'dat je maag samenkneep en in je neus omhoogsteeg'. Ibid., p. 143.
93. Trans.: 'niet aardig en een weinig vulgair'. Ibid., p. 30.
94. Trans.: 'zij was niet zoals ik – ik heb mij in haar vergist'. Ibid., p. 49.
95. Trans.: 'dat zij niet at, niet sliep ... en 's ochtends niet wilde opstaan als Brita met de grote vacantie naar Semmarö ging vond de ouders iets tè overdreven'. Ibid., p. 165.
96. The use of free indirect speech here makes it difficult to distinguish between the voice of the narrator, the views of the protagonist and the ironic rendering of the opinions of 'wider society'. Trans.: 'Toen was Vera ziek geworden en had niets anders gedaan dan huilen en roepen om Brita – ach, met veertien jaar konden meisjes zo overdreven doen! Gelukkig, dat zij spoedig beter werd'. Ibid., pp. 164–65.
97. Trans.: 'weet je, wat ik denk? Nee, wat ik me verbeeld, nu wij zo samenzijn en uitgaan en dansen? ... ik stel me voor, dat het gewoon is en omdat wij zulke goede vrienden zijn, echte kameraden, kan ik 't je zeggen: ik verbeeld mij, dat wij getrouwd zijn en straks naar huis rijden'. Ibid., p. 266.
98. Trans.: 'In razend tempo reden zij over de verlaten, natglimmende weg; bomen schoten voorbij als schimmen, de banden snerpten en knersten over het grint, als Hans die bochten nam in nauwelijks verminderde vaart ... Bayonne, Brita, riep Hans. Nu zijn wij er bijna. O juist, riep zij terug. Nog acht kilometer. Zij reden over grote, hobbelige keien langs de buitenkant van de stad. Vaal licht van booglampen verhelderde nu de straatweg ... Het begon opnieuw te regenen, in fijne stralen, maar het was de moeite niet waard om de kap op te zetten, zij wàren er. Toen slipte de wagen, tolde in een halve cirkel. Brita zag Hans één ondeelbaar onderdeel van een seconde voorovergebogen

krampachtig aan het stuur rukken. Het was uit! Zij reden tegen een boom op. Tegen die – daar ...' Ibid., pp. 272–73.
99. Carter, 'Mother-Love', p. 111.
100. Ibid.
101. Ibid., p. 134.
102. Ibid., p. 108.
103. Trans.: '[Mette] hat eine phantastische Vorstellung von der Wesenheit einer Mutter und glaubte immer, daß der frühe Tod der ihren alles Unheil ihres Lebens verursacht hätte.' Weirauch, *Der Skorpion: Band I*, p. 8.
104. Trans.: 'Es war wirklich ein Skandal, so wenig Französisch zu können. Morgen wollte sie zu Vater gehen und ihn bitten um französische Konversationsstunden bitten. Er würde sich freuen, wenn sie ihm einmal mit solchen Anliegen kam.' Ibid., p. 55.
105. Trans.: '"Wollen Sie lesen lernen bei mir? ... Kommen Sie zu mir herauf, sooft Sie wollen, bis es Ihnen langweilig wird ... Wenn du weiter nix tust, kannst du gut hundert Seiten am Tag lesen – ach mehr – und wenn du fertig bist – alle drei, vier Tage – je nachdem – kommen Sie her und tauschen sich den Band ein und trinken hier Tee, und wir plaudern ein bissel ... Wollen wir's so halten?" So fing es an.' Ibid., pp. 58–59.
106. O'Connor, 'Sapphic Spectres', p. 70.
107. Trans.: 'Mette verspürte Trockenheit im Hals und rasendes Herzklopfen, als sie lesen sollte. Nie hatte sie sich in der Schule so geängstigt ... In jedem Wort schien ihr eine Fußangel versteckt. Sie würde alles falsch aussprechen und sich unrettbar blamieren.' Weirauch, *Der Skorpion: Band I*, p. 53–54.
108. Carter, 'Mother-Love', p. 129.
109. Anjeana Kaur Hans, 'Defining Desires: Homosexual Identity and German Discourses 1900–1933', unpublished doctoral thesis (Cambridge, MA: Harvard University, 2005), p. 185.
110. '"Mutter!" dachte sie, und etwas wie ein krampfhaftes Schluchzen quoll in ihrem Halse auf. "Liebe, gute Mutter, warum hast du mich allein gelassen, ganz allein auf der Welt?" "Allein!?" Ihr war, als hörte sie stark und deutlich dies Wort von Olgas Stimme ... Eine heiße Welle flutete über ihr Herz.' Weirauch, *Der Skorpion*, p. 235.
111. Trans.: 'Ihre Leiber bäumten sich gegeneinander wie wilde Tiere, wenn sie an Käfiggittern rütteln. Sie gruben einander die Nägel in die Glätte der Haut und schlugen einander die Zähne in die geschwellten Muskeln. Und sie lagen aneinandergeschmiegt wie müde gespielte Kinder, und ihre Lippen berührten des anderen Lider und Wangen so sanft, so leise, wie Schmetterlingsflügel schwankende Blüten. "Kleines", sagte Olga, und alle Glocken schwangen in ihrer Stimme. "Mein Schönes, mein Gutes! ... Bist du nicht stolz, kleines Mädchen, daß du solche Wunder tun kannst?"' Weirauch, *Der Skorpion: Band I*, pp. 296–98.
112. Ibid., p. 296.
113. Trans.: 'Heut' bin ich geboren worden und nicht vor zwanzig Jahren. Jetzt kann ich zum erstenmal mit Bewußtsein sagen: Ich lebe!' Ibid., p. 300.
114. Trans.: 'Zijn zaken gunden hem geen tijd. "Het Hout", zei de familie. Hij ging er wel wat te veel in op.' Reuling, *Terug*, p. 5.
115. Trans.: 'de enige mens waar zij werkelijk van hield'. Ibid., p. 111; 'Niemand, niets kon haar haar vader teruggeven ... Brita huilde. Het was een schuddend, schokkend huilen, dat misschien dagen zou duren. Zij wist het. Het was als een plotselinge koorts, die hoog opliep en even plotseling weer afzakte en je uitgeput en leeg achterliet. Je kon er niets aan doen, je moest het laten razen'. Ibid., p. 112–14.
116. Trans.: 'Deze machteloosheid was erger dan de dood.' Ibid., p. 111.

117. Trans.: 'De mensen, die het meest van ons houden, zijn het minst veeleisend. Ik denk nu speciaal aan de moederlijke liefde, die toch de ideale liefde het meest nabij komt ... Met moeder-zijn heeft het niets te maken. De meeste vrouwen, die kinderen hebben, denken, dat zij dáárom ook de moederliefde bezitten, maar zij vergissen zich. Elke vrouw kan een kind krijgen, bijna elke vrouw kan het voeden, maar al hebben zij nog niet de moederliefde ... Ik ken zelfs een vader, die de ideale moederliefde bezit voor zijn kinderen. – Dan moet je zeggen: vader-liefde, anders doe je hem onrecht. Daar wilde Renée niets van weten. Het sentiment was als zodanig oer-vrouwelijk, vaderliefde was iets totaal anders.' Ibid., pp. 225–26.

118. Trans.: 'O, als je het minder eenvoudig wilt hebben, vraagt het aan Hans. Hij geeft je graag een heldere uiteenzetting omtrent onze volgens hem "abnormale sympathieën" voor elkaar; hij kan je precies uitleggen welke complexen, jeugdindrukken, verdrongen gevoelens en onbewuste neigingen onze drijfveren zijn.' Ibid., p. 198.

119. Trans.: 'Als zij rijper was zou zij een kind willen hebben, het zou zeker de beste leerschool zijn ... Nu moest zij deze wens voorlopig opschuiven, er geen gehoor aan schenken, al kon hij soms dringend, kwellend worden. "Je dochter klopt aan en wil geboren worden", zuchtte zij dan en glimlachte verlegen. Je moet nog even wachten schaap, je Ma staat aan een kruispunt, haar leven neemt een andere wending en zij weet niet hoe zij uit deze nieuwe strijd te voorschijn zal komen. Zij weet ook niet of zij het recht heeft om je zonder vader groot te brengen, of niet het mannelijk element onmisbaar is voor een kind.' Ibid., p. 140–41.

120. Trans.: 'Is het egoïsme, dit verlangen naar jou, mijn kind? Volgens Hans en alle intelligente en intellectuele mensen, die onze emoties uiteenrafelen, ze verklaren en ze keurig registreren, is alles wat wij doen, waarnaar wij verlangen, egoïsme. "Lust en unlust", zegt Freud, "is de kern van al ons handelen, van ons wezen en al zijn drijfveren."' Ibid. pp. 141–42.

Conclusion

Throughout this book, I have sought to examine and compare historical constructions of queer femininity and desire across a range of textual discourses published between 1860 and 1939 in German and Dutch contexts with a focus on the interwar period. Considering how the gendered and sexual experiences of feminine women were depicted in sexological, literary and periodical writing, this study has sought to redress the conspicuous absence of female-bodied femininities within queer histories and to shed new light on experiences that have traditionally been elided from discussions about the queer past. In foregrounding texts that concern queer feminine women and their desires, this analysis has highlighted several significant aspects of women's love for their own sex that have previously been denied their historical meaning, which has left little room for an appreciation of how gender conformity might shape experiences of so-called sexual deviance. In adjusting the gendered lens of enquiry across multiple discursive sites, it has been possible to demonstrate the varied and often conflicting ways in which queer femininity has been conceptualized in both in medicosocial and 'community' discourses in Germany and the Netherlands in the late nineteenth and early twentieth centuries. Moreover, by examining the vested sociopolitical and sexological interests in conflating femininity with heterosexual desire, it has been possible to consider the discursive destabilization of the relationship between gender inversion and sexual preference in women's literary writing during the interbellum, as a subversive act that ultimately challenged broader contemporary conceptions of what constituted 'normative' and 'non-normative' sexual behaviours. Through a closer analysis of these wider divergences, this volume has shown how women engaged – or did not engage – in the self-reflexive process of labelling their sexual desires as sexual identities during the first half of the twentieth century and how this may have influenced their understandings of themselves and their desires. Highlighting the productive potential of a revaluation of the supposedly 'normative', I also hope to have shown through this volume the necessity of paying closer attention to the cultural specificities of feminine experiences in order to resist 'the desire for the recognition of the present in the past'.[1]

Considered the 'birthplace of a modern identity', Berlin's short-lived but successful consumer and leisure culture after 1923 enabled the development of an unprecedented number of bars, organizations and periodicals aimed at queer individuals. The city's vice squad exercised a surprising degree of tolerance for the development of such establishments, which meant that sexual subcultures could flourish with a degree of visibility in the German capital that was unseen almost anywhere else in Europe during this period. With more women working in paid roles such as those of sales assistants, office clerks and stenographers than prior to the First World War, the gendered make up of the 'public sphere' in the German capital was also experiencing extraordinary change at this time. This, in conjunction with the vice squad allowing queer establishments to exist within 'certain limits' presented the newly emerging white collar class with opportunities that had not existed for them previously. Moreover, that same-sex acts between women had been omitted from the purview of Paragraph 175 meant that women faced less severe legal punishments for so-called sexual transgressions, although the fear of social stigma – and its economic consequences – invariably remained present in queer women's lives. Across the western border in postwar Amsterdam, society remained structured primarily by a fin-de-siècle religious morality that had embedded itself culturally in the gendered roles of 'breadwinners' and 'caregivers'. Moreover, the lives of most Dutch citizens were organized by the social segmentation of Dutch society – a phenomenon that impacted women's lives and social experiences in particular. This resulted in women's social experiences being more inward-looking and directed towards domesticity, which was an ideology that cut across almost every pillar. In addition, with the introduction of Article 248bis in 1911, same-sex desires were regulated by law for both men *and* women in the Netherlands. And, unlike the relative tolerance that vice squads were almost forced to exercise in the bar scene found in labyrinthine Berlin, the relatively small size of Amsterdam meant that it was easier to regulate 'immoral' activities and to shut down with speed those organizations or bars that were considered to have contravened laws against morality. These morality laws effectively hindered the development of an established and visible urban sexual subculture in the Dutch capital until the early 1960s. However, in both countries, it seems that femininity worked both to provide women with access to certain spaces – such as the workplace – as well as precluding their entry to others. For many young modern women, compliance with stringent aesthetic standards enabled them to secure paid work, which led to the possibility of certain economic freedoms. Yet, this access was contingent upon the ability of these women to be able (financially) to live up to ever-changing cosmetic expectations and to accept the transience of such precarious positions. Moreover, women's embodiment of such ideals arguably fed back into the trappings of the 'imperialist white-supremacist capitalist patriarchy' that supressed them and, particularly, the most socially marginalized among them – such as (queer) women of colour.[2] Additionally, for women navigating queer urban spaces in Berlin, expressing femininity frequently denied them access to certain bars and clubs, such as the *Tavern*, in which the doors were closed to those women who were not masculine presenting. And both within and without queer communities in the German capital – as evidenced in sexological literature, city guides and periodicals written by queer women – feminine women who frequented 'mixed' spaces were most often dismissed as sexual tourists, and who should be avoided by 'true' homosexuals searching for serious romantic partners.

In terms of the social visibility of queer feminine women, the widespread rejection of 'the somatic style of medicine' and the anatomical-physiological school of sexological thought in the Netherlands, as discussed in Chapter 2, meant that the figure of the sexological 'invert' was far less established in the Dutch context than in it was in Germany.[3] Terms such as 'Uranisme' and 'homosexualiteit' were also broadly considered to represent only male same-sex practices, which meant that queer love between women remained virtually unconceptualizable within sociomedical discourses in the Netherlands until after the interwar period. In Germany, which must be considered 'the intellectual homeland of the burgeoning scientia sexualis', theories depicting the virile female invert had served to give queer female desire 'a name and an image' already since the mid-nineteenth century.[4] Moreover, through the writings of more progressive sexologists such as Magnus Hirschfeld and Albert Moll, and especially the endeavours to map more nuanced theories about homosexual desires by feminist activists such as Johanna Elberskirchen, also offered a name and image to queer feminine women in German-language research during this period. For Hirschfeld and Moll, the combination of female femininity and the desire for the female sex was only logical within a schema of millions of intermediary gendered and sexual forms, while for Elberskirchen, this expression of love presented the most feminine of impulses, as it excluded the masculine element at every social and sexual turn. While femininity moved from the margins of sexological research to the heart of feminist sexual theorizing during the early twentieth century, much sexological writing concerning the desires of queer feminine women at this time remained moored to a discourse that relied upon ideas of situational and curable 'pseudo-homosexuality', which fuelled debates relating not only to sexual 'contagion' and the fear of a growing moral 'evil', but also the legitimacy of feminine women within queer communities and spaces.

The engagement with community-based periodicals in Chapters 3 and 4 has demonstrated how queer women engaged with, reflected upon and sometimes outright rejected the medicosocial discourses of their time. Contributing to existing studies of queer print media, the examination of the ways in which femininity is configured in the social, sexological and literary discourses published in the German magazines *The Girlfriend* and *Women's Love* has shown how queer women 'borrowed from and broke with mainstream images of sexuality and sexual identity' to establish their own gendered hierarchies and orthodoxies that shaped their subcultural experiences. Furthermore, in studying the aims of the organizations to which these magazines were affiliated, it has become clear that *Women's Love* has been unfairly dismissed in previous scholarly research as solely an 'entertainment newspaper', due to its favouring of typically 'feminine' content. The political calls to action, the blurring of gendered binaries and the discussion of topics such as bisexuality and polyamory found within its pages make this periodical an exciting source for the exploration of historical queer femininities. The at times problematic commercialization of idealized forms of femininity notwithstanding, *Women's Love* offered space to a wide range of queer voices, which were underrepresented even within the queer communities in which they ought to have been heard. In comparison, *The Girlfriend* appears to have been characterized more acutely by an appropriation of bourgeois forms of masculinity and morality, which served to help promote the periodical as a respectable cultural resource – and thereby evade the Law for the Protection of Youth against Trash and Filth Publications – as well as presenting itself as serious reading material for campaigners of sexual freedom, given that many of the magazine's sexological and political articles, particularly in its later years, were written by the chief campaigners within the BfM against Paragraph 175. While the writers and contributors often engaged with feminine women positively as desirable objects in their stories and commentaries, it was rare to hear from feminine or bisexual women themselves and there appears to have been little engagement in the magazine more broadly with 'feminine' topics, such as fashion or rejuvenating practices.

In light of the lack of newspapers for queer women in the Netherlands, Chapter 4 has engaged with two magazines for women printed in the interwar period: *Beatrice* and *The Young Woman*, as well as two queer periodicals aimed at men: *We* and *The Right to Live*. As popular publications for young women in Catholic and Protestant communities, *Beatrice* and *The Young Woman* offer a novel insights into the image-making and identity-forming of women from these communities. Steeped in the social discourses of their time, the content published in these magazines demonstrates how important the concepts of maternalism and domesticity remained to understandings of Dutch womanhood in the interwar era. Yet, while engaging with these culturally embedded norms, these magazines also presented women with space – in their sections for reader letters and literary contributions – to challenge prevailing value systems if they so desired. Furthermore, the publication of stories like *Deliverance* suggest that queer themes may well have been visible in these periodicals for those with a sensitive eye for certain tropes. As the potential significance of (heterosexual) women's weekly magazines to the formation of queer female identities during the interwar period has been a largely under-researched area, my preliminary findings in this chapter suggest that this could be a productive avenue for further study. As well as looking to mainstream magazines to locate traces of queer femininity, I have also argued in Chapter 4 that the silences and omissions surrounding the subject of female same-sex desire in the queer Dutch periodicals *We* and *The Right to Live* can tell us much about the masculinist leanings of Dutch queer organizations during this time. While the membership of the organizations responsible for these publications was nominally open to women, the primary male actors and drivers in these organizations appear rarely to have considered the needs of a female readership. Although many more community-based periodicals were beginning to emerge for (heterosexual) women across the pillars, women's frequent lack of access to independent finances would have made subscribing to such a newspaper difficult. In terms of promoting itself to purchasers, then, it made less sense for the editors of *We* and *The Right to Live* to cater to the interests of women, who would have made little commercial and financial contribution to the success of their publications. However, turning to the ideological shifts that appear to have taken place in the time between the emergence of the two magazines, there appears to have been a turning point in Dutch history, a point during which female same-sex desire became more visible and 'knowable' in society. The female contributions presented in Benno Stokvis' collection *The Homosexuals* (1939) highlight this shift particularly well.

The final analysis of queer femininity in fictional writing, presented in Chapters 5 and 6, further contribute to existing literary studies of same-sex desire in order to shed light on the dialogues that existed between medicosocial discourses and queer literary writing about femininity during the interwar era. Looking first at Eva Raedt-de Canter's *Boarding School* and Christa Winsloe's *The Girl Manuela*, the analysis showed the significance of the erotic maternal imagery to the shaping of the protagonists' queer desires in the interwar period, pointing to alternative models through which female same-sex desire may have been conceived (across borders) in the first half of the twentieth century. As this chapter suggested, such familial paradigms should not be conceived as models that contribute to the desexualization of same-sex desire, but rather as frameworks in which the complexity of maternal longings is extended to include the erotic, and arguably to *enable* it. Furthermore, the comparison of two boarding school novels from different cultural contexts has highlighted the distinction in the ways that the desires and identities of tomboy protagonists were conceived conceptually during the first half of the twentieth century. While Raedt-de Canter does not depict a protagonist with a self-reflective understanding of themselves as sexual 'Other', Winsloe actively engages with the discourses of the child 'invert' through the diagnosis narrative. Although the lack of a formal articulation of queer desire in subject terms in Raedt-de Canter's novel may disappoint those seeking strictly lesbian themes, it reflects quite remarkably the situation for queer women in Dutch society between the two World Wars, women who did not consider their experiences to be represented by fixed labels and categories. In the final chapter of this volume, Anna Elisabet Weirauch's *The Scorpion* and Josine Reuling's *Back to the Island* are analysed as texts in which the experiences of queer feminine characters are consciously centralized. Here, the various meanings of the erotic maternal and the delicate subject of desire and class is foregrounded in their textual explorations of love between feminine women. The forcible rejection of the figure of the female invert in both texts suggests that the authors were seeking to create space for other, 'nonlesbian' configurations of desire, in which they could describe the experiences of their protagonists, an interpretation that has hitherto received little scholarly attention in the secondary literature relating to these novels. Indeed, by positioning feminine women in their writing as both desiring subjects *and* desired objects, Reuling and Weirauch force the masculine invert to the margins of their narratives, and offer new perspectives on queer feminine desires that complicate the contemporary scientific and social discourses of their time.

By bringing a queer feminist practice of resistant reading to bear upon a range of 'discourses of desire', this volume has pointed to several gaps in queer history writing, which I argue have resulted largely from the marginalization of the feminine woman both historically and presently. Although I maintain that discourses of female masculinity are of vital importance to our understandings of sexual and gendered experiences in the past, it is of equal importance to pay attention to the discords and inconsistencies that do not fit with the aforementioned narrative. It is only in this way that we can depict more convincingly the 'irreducible plurality' of the historical circumstances of women-loving-women. Of course, there remains much to be examined about the ways in which queer feminine women organized and experienced their desires for one another both in the past and the present. Beyond the scope of this volume, for instance, was a closer analysis of the cultural transfers and exchanges that took place between queer individuals and groups in Germany and the Netherlands during the interwar era. Winsloe's play *Now and Then*, for example, was also performed in the Netherlands in 1932, translated and directed by Pierre Mols (1885–1961). The title of the play was changed from *Girls in Uniform* (*Meisjes in uniform*) to *Young Ladies in Uniform* (*Jongedames in uniform*), ironically so as to de-emphasize the play's (sexual) content. In order to further safeguard minors newspaper adverts for the performances furthermore highlighted that it was 'only suitable for adults'.[5] An analysis of the play, its directorship, and its reception in Germany and the Netherlands would no doubt point to further divergences of interest in the cultural conception of queerness, a discussion that I hope already to have contributed to through this book. Building on these notions of dialogue and exchange, it would also be productive to analyse more recent narratives of German and Dutch queer feminine identities and experiences in light of those under examination in this volume. By doing so, it might be possible to examine the productivity and limits of Valerie Traub's 'cycles of salience' more fully and to identify more explicitly those 'recurring patterns of identification, social statuses, behaviour, and meanings of women who erotically desired other women across large spans of time'.[6]

As new and exciting directions for the historical study of same-sex desires open and emerge with recent research, scholars of Dutch contexts might take the impulses of this volume to reflect on the omissions and gaps in their own histories of female same-sex desire. Those considering further research in German contexts must continue to question the inherent privileging of masculinity within the field. Moreover, we must persist with conversations about what the privileging of masculinity means more broadly for historical examinations of female same-sex desire and how this shapes our understanding of the histories of urban spaces, and those desires that existed within them. In terms of the current state of play across Anglo-American queer politics, I hope that this volume can be considered a contribution to (inevitably uncomfortable) conversations about why embodiments of femininity by queer and trans women continue to be devalued and maligned within queer communities, and what kind of politics are being striven for through repeated enactments of anti-feminine and anti-trans discourses. This discussion must also be nuanced further through continued reflections on the importance of class, race, ethnicity, religion and ability to the experience of sexual subjectivity and desire – or, indeed, the absence of (sexual) desire. Certainly, it will only be through these kinds of exchanges that our approaches to the queer past – in concurrence with present-day political actions to secure better queer futures – might be able to account more fully for the nuances of those experiences and desires of women who were 'different from the others'.

Notes

1. Julian Carter, 'On Mother-Love: History, Queer Theory, and Nonlesbian Identity', *Journal of the History of Sexuality* 14 (2005), 107–38 (at p. 108).
2. bell hooks, *The Will to Change: Men, Masculinity, and Love* (New York: Washington Square Press, 2004), p. 17.
3. Ilse Bulhof, 'Psychoanalysis in the Netherlands', *Comparative Studies in Society and History* 24(4) (1982), 572–88 (at p. 575).
4. Kirsten Leng, 'Permutations of the Third Sex: Sexology, Subjectivity, and Antimaternalist Feminism at the Turn of the Twentieth Century', *Signs* 40(1) (2014), 227–54 (at p. 227); Jeffrey Weeks, *Sex, Politics and Society: The Regulations of Sexuality since 1800* (Abingdon: Routledge, 2014), p. 146.
5. Trans.: 'alleen geschikt voor volwassenen'. 'Jongedames in uniform', *Algemeen handelsblad*, 5 August 1932, p. 9.
6. Valerie Traub, 'The Present Future of Lesbian Historiography', in George E. Haggerty and Molly McGarry (eds), *A Companion to Lesbian, Gay, Bisexual and Transgender, and Queer Studies* (Oxford: Wiley Blackwell, 2007), p. 125.

Bibliography

Newspapers and Periodicals

Beatrijs
Berliner Zeitung
Berliner Zeitung am Mittag
Frauenliebe
Frauenliebe und Leben
Die Freundin
Garçonne
Den Gulden Winckel
Jaarboek van de Maatschappij der Nederlandse Letterkunde
De Jonge Vrouw
Liebende Frauen
Nieuwe Amsterdamsche Courant
Nieuwsblad van het Noorden
De Sumatra Post
De Tijd
Het Volk
Wij

Primary Sources

Bender, L. *Verderfelijke propaganda* (Heemstede: Comité van Katholieke Actie 'Voor God', 1937).
Bloch, Iwan, *Das Sexualleben unserer Zeit in seinen Beziehungen zur modernen Kultur* (Berlin: Louis Marcus, 1907).
Boudier-Bakker, Ina, *De moderne vrouw en haar tekort* (Amsterdam: P.N. van Kampen en zoon, 1921).

Deutsch, Helene, 'Über die weibliche Homosexualität', *Internationale Zeitschrift für Psychoanalyse* 18(2) (1932), 219–41.
Elberskirchen, Johanna, *Die Liebe des dritten Geschlechts: Homosexualität, eine bisexuelle Varietät keine Entartung – keine Schuld* (Leipzig: Max Spohr, 1904).
———. 'Offener Brief an Fräulein Dr. phil. Ella Mensch', *Frauen Rundschau*, 5(12) (1904) 376–82.
———. *Was hat der Mann aus Weib, Kind und sich gemacht? Revolution und Erlösung des Weibes; eine Abrechnung mit dem Mann – ein Wegweiser in die Zukunft!* (Berlin: Magazin, 1904).
———. *Geschlechtsleben und Geschlechtsenthaltsamkeit des Weibes* (Munich: Seitz & Schauer, 1905).
Ellis, Havelock, 'Sexual Inversion in Women', in *Studies in the Psychology of Sex: Volume II* (New York: Random House, 1936 [1897]).
———. *Studies in the Psychology of Sex: Sexual Inversion*, 2nd edn (Philadelphia, F.A. Davis, 1908).
Ellis, Havelock, and John Addington Symonds, *Das Konträre Geschlechtsgefühl*, trans. Hans Kurella (Leipzig: Georg H. Wigand's, 1896).
Forel, Auguste, *Die sexuelle Frage. Eine naturwissenschaftliche, psychologische, hygienische und soziologische Studie für Gebildete*, 9th edn (Munich: E. Reinhardt, 1909).
François, Joannes Henri, *Open brief aan hen die anders zijn dan de anderen. Door een hunner* (The Hague: H.J. Berkhout, 1915).
Freud, Sigmund, *Vorlesungen zur Einführung in die Psychoanalyse* (Frankfurt am Main: S. Fischer Verlag, 1916).
———. 'Über die Psychogenese eines Falles von weiblicher Homosexualität', *Internationale Zeitschrift für Psychoanalyse* 6 (1920), 1–24.
———. 'Psychoanalysis: Exploring the Hidden Recesses of the Mind', in *These Eventful Years: The Twentieth Century in the Making as Told by Many of Its Makers*, trans. by A.A. Brill (London: Encyclopaedia Britannica Company, 1924).
———. *Sexuality and the Psychology of Love* (New York: Touchstone, 1997).
———. *Drei Abhandlungen zur Sexualtheorie* (Göttingen: Vienna University Press, 2015).
Hirschfeld, Magnus, 'Das urnische Kind', *Zeitschrift für Kinderforschung* 8 (1903), 241–57.
———. *Der urnische Mensch* (Leipzig: Max Spohr, 1903).
———. 'Ursachen und Wesen des Uranismus', *Jahrbuch für sexuelle Zwischenstufen* 5 (1903), 1–159.
———. *Berlins drittes Geschlecht* (Berlin: H. Seemann, 1904).
———. 'Besprechung des Jahrbuchs', *Jahrbuch für sexuelle Zwischenstufen* 10 (1909), 3–30.
———. *Die Homosexualität des Mannes und des Weibes* (Berlin: Louis Marcus, 1914).
———. *Die Transvestiten: eine Untersuchung über den erotischen Verkleidungstrieb*, 2nd edn (Leipzig: Ferdinand Spohr, 1925).
Hodann, Max, *Geschlecht und Liebe in biologischer und gesellschaftlicher Beziehung* (Berlin: Universitas, 1932).
Kracauer, Siegfried, *The Mass Ornament: Weimar Essays*, trans. by Thomas Y. Levin (Cambridge, MA: Harvard University Press, 1995).
Krukenberg, Elsbeth '§175', in Ilse Kokula (ed.), *Weibliche Homosexualität um 1900 in zeitgenössischen Dokumenten*, (Munich: Frauenoffensive, 1981).
———. *The Salaried Masses: Duty and Distraction in Weimar Germany*, trans. by Quintin Hoare (New York: Verso, 1998).
Möbius, Paul Julius, *Über den physiologischen Schwachsinn des Weibes* (Halle: Carl Marhold, 1906).

Moll, Albert, *Die konträre Sexualempfindung*, 3rd edn (Berlin: Fischer's Medicinische Buchhandlung, 1899).
———. 'Die Behandlung der Homosexualität', *Jahrbuch für sexuelle Zwischenstufen* 2 (1900), 1–29.
Moreck, Curt, *Führer durch das 'lasterhafte' Berlin* (Leipzig: Verlag moderner Stadtführer, 1931).
Numantius, Numa, *Inclusa: Forschungen über das Räthsel der mannmännlichen Liebe* (Leipzig: Heinrich Matthes, 1864).
NWHK, *Wat iedereen behoort te weten omtrent Uranisme* (The Hague, Gebr. Belinfante, 1912).
Pappritz, Anna, 'Zum §175', in Ilse Kokula (ed.), *Weibliche Homosexualität um 1900 in zeitgenössischen Dokumenten* (Munich: Frauenoffensive, 1981).
Plato, *Symposium and Phaedrus* (New York: Cosimo, 2010).
Raedt-de Canter, Eva, *Internaat* (Amsterdam: Querido, 1948).
Reuling, Josine, *Terug naar het eiland* (Amsterdam: Querido, 1937).
Roellig, Ruth Margarete, *Berlins lesbische Frauen* in Adele Meyer, *Lila Nächte: Die Damenklubs der Zwanziger Jahre* (Cologne: Zitronenpresse, 1981).
Romein-Verschoor, Annie, *Vrouwenspiegel: een literair-sociologische studie over de Nederlandse romanschrijfster na 1800* (Leiden: Hoeijenbos & Co., 1935).
Rüling, Anna, 'Welches Interesse hat die Frauenbewegung an der Lösung der homosexuellen Problems?', *Jahrbuch für sexuelle Zwischenstufen* 7 (1905), 131–51.
Schirmacher, Käthe, '§175 des deutschen Strafgesetzes', in Ilse Kokula (ed.), *Weibliche Homosexualität um 1900 in zeitgenössischen Dokumenten* (Munich: Frauenoffensive, 1981).
Spengler, Oswald, *Der Untergang des Abendlandes: Umrisse einer Morphologie der Weltgeschichte*, vol. II (Munich: C.H. Beckische Verlagsbuchhandlung, 1922).
Stirner, Max, *Der Einzige und sein Eigentum* (Leipzig: Otto Wigand, 1844).
Stöcker, Helene 'Die beabsichtigte Ausdehnung des §175 auf die Frau', in Ilse Kokula (ed.), *Weibliche Homosexualität um 1900 in zeitgenössische Dokumenten* (Munich: Frauenoffensive, 1981).
Stokvis, Benno, *De homosexueelen* (Lochem: De Tijdstroom, 1939)
Stopes, Marie, *Married Love: A New Contribution to the Solution of Sex Difficulties* (London: A.C. Fifield, 1918).
Ulrichs, Carl Heinrich, *Formatrix: Anthropologische Studien über urnische Liebe* (Leipzig: Heinrich Matthes, 1864).
———. *Vindex: Social-juristische Studien über mannmännliche Liebe* (Leipzig: Max Spohr, 1898).
Van de Velde, Theodoor, *Ideal Marriage: Its Physiology and Technique*, 20th edn (London: William Heinemann Medical Books, 1947).
Von Krafft-Ebing, Richard, *Psychopathia Sexualis: Eine klinisch-forensische Studie* (Stuttgart: Ferdinand Enke, 1886).
———. *Psychopathia sexualis mit besonderer Berücksichtigung der konträren Sexualempfindung: eine medizinisch-gerichtliche Studie für Ärtze und Juristen*, 13th edn (Stuttgart: Ferdinand Enke, 1907).
———. 'Neue Studien auf dem Gebiete der Homosexualität', *Jahrbuch für sexuelle Zwischenstufen* 3 (1901), 1–36.
Weininger, Otto, *Geschlecht und Charakter: Eine prinzipielle Untersuchung*, 10th edn (Vienna: Wilhelm Braumüller, 1910).
Weirauch, Anna Elisabet, *Der Skorpion Band I–III* (Berlin: Lesbenselbstverlag, 1977).

Westphal, Carl, 'Die conträre Sexualempfindung, Symptom eines neuropathischen (psychopathischen) Zustandes', *Archiv für Psychiatrie und Nervenkrankheiten* 2(1) (1869), 73–108.
Winsloe, Christa, *Das Mädchen Manuela: Das Roman zum Film Mädchen in Uniform* (Berlin: Krug & Schadenberg, 2012).

Secondary Sources

Abate, Michelle Ann, *Tomboys: A Literary and Cultural History* (Philadelphia: Temple University Press, 2008).
Abbenhuis, Maartje M., *The Art of Staying Neutral: The Netherlands in the First World War, 1914–1918* (Amsterdam: Amsterdam University Press, 2006).
Akass, Kim, and Janet McCabe, *Reading 'The L Word': Outing Contemporary Television* (New York: I.B. Taurus, 2006).
Altena, Peter, and Myriam Everard (eds), *Onbreekbare burgerharten. De historie van Betje Wolff en Aagje Deken* (Nijmegen: Vantilt, 2004).
Andeweg, Rudy B., and Galen A. Irwin, *Governance and Politics of the Netherlands*, 4th edn (Basingstoke: Palgrave Macmillan, 2014).
Angelides, Steven, *A History of Bisexuality* (Chicago: University of Chicago Press, 2001).
Bakker, Alex, *Transgender: Een buitengewone geschiedenis in Nederland* (Amsterdam: Boom, 2018).
Balestra, Gianfrance, 'Women Writers on the Verge of the Twentieth Century: Edith Wharton et al', *RSA* 23 (2012), 10–24.
Ballaster Ros, Margaret Beetham, Elizabeth Frazer and Sandra Hebron, *Women's Worlds: Ideology, Femininity and the Woman's Magazine* (London: Macmillan, 1991).
Bambery, Chris, *A People's History of Scotland* (London: Verso, 2014).
Bauer, Heike, 'Literary Sexualities', in *The Cambridge Companion to the Body in Literature* (New York: Cambridge University Press, 2015).
———. *The Hirschfeld Archives: Violence, Death and Modern Queer Culture* (Philadelphia: Temple University Press, 2017).
Beachy, Robert, *Gay Berlin: Birthplace of a Modern Identity* (New York: Vintage Books, 2014).
Beddoe, Deidre, *Back to Home and Duty: Women between the Wars, 1918–1939* (London: Pandora Press, 1989).
Beetham, Margaret, *A Magazine of Her Own? Domesticity and Desire in the Woman's Magazine 1880–1914* (New York: Routledge, 1996).
Bell, Anne Oliver, and Andrew McNeillie (eds), *The Diary of Virginia Woolf Vol. IV* (New York: Harcourt Brace, 1983).
Bengry, Justin, 'Courting the Pink Pound: *Men Only* and the Queer Consumer, 1935–1939', *History Workshop Journal* 68 (2009), 122–48.
Bessel, Richard, *Germany after the First World War* (Oxford: Clarendon Press, 1993).
Bernauer, James, 'Michel Foucault's Ecstatic Thinking', in James Bernauer and David Rasmussen (eds), *The Final Foucault* (Cambridge, MA: MIT Press, 1987).
Bernstein, Lisa, 'Confessional and Testimonial Literature', in Friederike Ursula Eigler and Susanne Kord (eds), *The Feminist Encyclopedia of German Literature* (Westport, CT: Greenwood Publishing Group, 1997).
Beunders, Henri et al. (eds), *Pers en politie in Amsterdam* (Amsterdam: Bas Lubberhuizen, 2010).

Bingham, Adrian, *Gender, Modernity, and the Popular Press in Inter-War Britain* (Oxford: Oxford University Press, 2004).
Bland, Lucy, and Laura Doan (eds), *Sexology in Culture: Labelling Bodies and Desires* (Cambridge: Polity Press, 1998).
Blasius, Mark, and Shane Phelan, 'Combining Political and Cultural Work: The League for Human Rights', in *We Are Everywhere: A Historical Sourcebook of Gay and Lesbian Politics* (New York: Routledge, 1997).
Bleijenbergh, Inge, and Jet Bussemaker, 'The Women's Vote in the Netherlands: From the 'Houseman's Vote', in Blanca Rodríguez-Ruiz and Ruth Rubio-Marín (eds), *The Struggle for Female Suffrage in Europe: Voting to Become Citizens* (Leiden: Brill, 2012).
Boak, Helen, *Women in the Weimar Republic* (Manchester: Manchester University Press, 2013).
Boden, Petra, 'Political Writing and Women's Journals: The 1848 Revolutions', in Jo Catling (ed.), *A History of Women's Writing in Germany, Austria and Switzerland* (Cambridge, Cambridge University Press, 2000).
Bolle, Michael (ed.), *Eldorado: Homosexuelle Frauen und Männer in Berlin 1850–1950. Geschichte, Alltag und Kultur* (Berlin: Fröhlich und Kaufman, 1984).
Borghi, Liana, 'Lesbian Literary Studies', in Theo Sandford et al. (eds), *Lesbian and Gay Studies: An Introductory, Interdisciplinary Approach* (London: SAGE, 2000).
Bosch, Mineke, 'History and Historiography of First-Wave Feminism in the Netherlands 1860–1922', in Sylvia Paletschek and Bianka Pietrow-Ennker (eds), *Women's Emancipation Movements in the Nineteenth Century: A European Perspective* (Stanford: Stanford University Press, 2004).
———. 'Domesticity, Pillarization and Gender: Historical Explanations for the Divergent Pattern of Dutch Women's Economic Citizenship', *BMGN – The Low Countries Historical Review*, 125 (2010), 269–300.
Boswell, John, 'Revolutions, Universals, and Sexual Categories', in Martin Duberman et al. (eds), *Hidden from History: Reclaiming the Gay and Lesbian Past* (New York: Meridian, 1989).
Brauneis, Sabrina, *The Relationship of Body Weight and Skepticism towards Advertising* (Wiesbaden: Springer Gabler, 2016).
Bridenthal, Renate, and Claudia Koonz, 'Beyond Kinder, Küche, Kirche: Weimar Women in Politics and Work', in Renate Bridenthal et al. (eds), *When Biology Became Destiny Women in Weimar and Nazi Germany* (New York: Monthly Review Press, 1984).
Bruns, Claudia, 'Masculinity, Sexuality, and the German Nation: The Eulenburg Scandals and Kaiser Wilhelm II in Political Cartoons', in Udo K. Hebel and Christoph Wagner (eds), *Pictorial Cultures and Political Iconographies: Approaches, Perspectives, Case Studies from Europe and America* (Berlin: Walter de Gruyter, 2011).
Bulhof, Ilse, 'Psychoanalysis in the Netherlands', *Comparative Studies in Society and History* 24(4) (1982), 572–88.
———. *Freud en Nederland: de interpretatie en invloed van zijn ideeën* (Baarn: Ambo, 1983).
Burke, Jennifer (ed.), *Visible: A Femmethology* (Michigan: Homofactus Press, 2009).
Bussemaker, Jet, 'Gender and the Separation of Spheres in Twentieth Century Dutch Society: Pillarisation, Welfare State Formation and Individualisation', in Jet Bussemaker and Rian Voet (eds), *Gender, Participation and Citizenship in the Netherlands* (Aldershot: Ashgate, 1998).
Bussemaker, Jet, and Rian Voet (eds), *Gender Participation and Citizenship in the Netherlands* (Aldershot: Ashgate, 1998).
Butler, Judith, *Gender Trouble* (New York: Routledge, 1990)
———. *Bodies That Matter: On the Discursive Limits of 'Sex'* (New York: Routledge, 1993).

Canning, Kathleen, Kerstin Barndt and Kristin McGuire, *Weimar Publics/Weimar Subjects: Rethinking the Political Culture of Germany in the 1920s* (New York: Berghahn Books, 2010).

Carter, Julian, 'On Mother-Love: History, Queer Theory, and Nonlesbian Identity', *Journal of the History of Sexuality* 14 (2005), 107–38.

Cefai, Sarah, 'Navigating Silences, Disavowing Femininity and the Construction of Lesbian Identities', *Geography and Gender Reconsidered: Women and Geography Study Group* (2004), 108–17.

Clark, Danae, 'Commodity Lesbianism', in Corey K. Creekmur and Alexander Doty (eds), *Out in Culture: Gay, Lesbian and Queer Essays on Popular Culture* (Durham, NC: Duke University Press, 1995).

Clark, Giles Noel, and Angus Phillips (eds), *Inside Book Publishing* (Abingdon: Routledge, 2008).

Chambers, Deborah, 'The Women's Pages: Women, Journalism, and Mid-20th-Century Mainstream Newspapers', in Karen Ross, Ingrid Bachmann, Valentina Cardo, Sujata Moorti and Cosimo Marco Scarcelli (eds), *The International Encyclopedia of Gender, Media, and Communication* (Chichester: Wiley-Blackwell, 2020).

Chauncey, George, 'From Sexual Inversion to Homosexuality: Medicine and the Changing Conceptualization of Female Deviance', *Salmagundi* 59 (1983), 114–46.

Ciasullo, Ann M., 'Making Her (In)Visible: Cultural Representations of Lesbianism and the Lesbian Body in the 1990s', *Feminist Studies* 27(3) (2001), 577–608.

Collis, Rose, *Portraits to the Wall: Historic Lesbian Lives Unveiled* (London: Bloomsbury, 1994).

Colvin, Sarah, and Peter Davies (eds), *Masculinities in German Culture* (Rochester, NY: Camden House, 2008).

Creet, Julia, 'Anxieties of Identity: Coming out and Coming Undone', in Monica Dorenkamp and Richard Henke (eds), *Negotiating Lesbian and Gay Subjects* (New York: Routledge, 1995).

Crozier, Ivan, 'Introduction: Havelock Ellis, John Addington Symonds and the Construction of *Sexual Inversion*', in *Sexual Inversion: A Critical Edition* (London: Palgrave Macmillan, 2008).

Damousi, Joy et al. (eds), *Case Studies and the Dissemination of Knowledge* (New York: Routledge, 2015).

Davis Madeline, 'Epilogue, Nine Years Later', in Joan Nestle (ed.), *The Persistent Desire* (Boston, MA: Alyson Publications, 1992).

D'Emilio, John, 'Capitalism and Gay Identity', in Henry Abelove et al. (eds), *The Gay and Lesbian Studies Reader* (London: Routledge, 1993).

De Haan, Francisca, *Gender and Politics of Office Work: The Netherlands 1860–1940* (Amsterdam: Amsterdam University Press, 1998).

De Lauretis, Teresa (1991) 'Queer Theory: Lesbian and Gay Sexualities', *Differences: A Journal of Feminist Cultural Studies* 3(2), iii–xviii.

De Man, Paul, 'Autobiography as De-facement', *Modern Language Notes* 94(5) (1979), 919–30.

Deckwitz, Sjuul, 'Bet van Beeren', in Gert Hekma et al. (eds), *Goed verkeerd: een geschiedenis van homoseksuele mannen en lesbische vrouwen in Nederland* (Amsterdam: Meulenhoff, 1989).

Dekker, Rudolf, and Lotte van de Pol, *Vrouwen in mannenkleren: de geschiedenis van een tegendraadse traditie Europa 1500–1800* (Amsterdam: Wereldbibliotheek, 1989).

Dickinson, Edward Ross, *Sex, Freedom, and Power in Imperial Germany 1880–1914* (New York: Cambridge University Press, 2014).

Dinshaw, Carolyn, *Getting Medieval: Sexualities and Communities, Pre- and Postmodern* (Durham, NC: Duke University Press, 1999).
Doan, Laura, *Fashioning Sapphism: The Origins of a Modern English Lesbian Culture* (New York: Columbia University Press, 2001).
———. *Disturbing Practices: History, Sexuality, and Women's Experience of Modern War* (Chicago: University of Chicago Press, 2013).
Doan, Laura, and Jane Garrity (eds), *Sapphic Modernities: Sexuality, Women and National Culture* (New York: Palgrave Macmillan, 2006).
Dover, Kenneth James, *Greek Homosexuality* (Cambridge, MA: Harvard University Press, 1978).
Drescher, Barbara, 'The Social Enforcement of Heterosexuality and Lesbian Resistance in the 1920s', in Amy Swerdlow and Hanna Lessinger (eds), *Class, Race, and Sex: The Dynamics of Control* (Boston, MA: Barnard College Women's Center, 1983).
———. 'Die "Neue Frau"', in Walter Fähnders and Helga Karrenbrock (eds), *Autorinnen der Weimarer Republik* (Bielefeld: Aisthesis Verlag, 2004).
Duggan, Lisa, 'The Social Enforcement of Heterosexuality and Lesbian Resistance in the 1920s', in Amy Swerdlow and Hanna Lessinger (eds), *Class, Race, and Sex: The Dynamics of Control* (Boston, MA: Barnard College Women's Center, 1983).
———. 'The Discipline Problem: Queer Theory Meets Gay and Lesbian History', *GLQ: A Journal of Lesbian and Gay Studies* 2(3) (1995), 179–91.
———. 'The New Homonormativity: The Sexual Politics of Neoliberalism', in Russ Castronovo and Dana Nelson (eds), *Materializing Democracy: Toward a Revitalized Cultural Politics* (Durham, NC: Duke University Press, 2002), 175–94.
———. *The Twilight of Equality? Neoliberalism, Cultural Politics, and the Attack on Democracy* (Boston, MA: Beacon, 2003).
Dyer, Richard and Julianne Pidduck, *Now You See It: Studies on Lesbian and Gay Film* (London: Routledge, 1990).
Eigler, Friederike Ursula, and Susanne Kord (eds), *The Feminist Encyclopedia of German Literature* (Westport, CT: Greenwood Publishing Group, 1997).
Eiland, Howard, *Walter Benjamin: A Critical Life* (Cambridge: Belknap Press, 2014).
Edelman, Lee, 'Queer Theory: Unstating Desire', *GLQ: A Journal of Lesbian and Gay Studies* 2(4) (1995), 343–46.
Eriksson, Brigitte, 'A Lesbian Execution in Germany, 1721: The Trial Records', *Journal of Homosexuality* 6 (1980/81), 27–40.
Eriksson, Brigitte, and Lillian Faderman (eds), *Lesbian-Feminism in Turn-of-the-Century Germany* (Tallahassee, FL: Naiad Press, 1980).
Espinaco-Virseda, Angeles, '"I Feel That I Belong to You"; Subculture, *Die Freundin* and Weimar Lesbian Identities', *Spaces of Identity: Tradition, Cultural Boundaries and Identity Formation in Central Europe* 4 (2004), 83–100.
Evans, Jennifer, and Matt Cook (eds), *Queer Cities, Queer Cultures: Europe since 1945* (London: Bloomsbury, 2014).
Everard, Myriam, 'Galerij der vrouwenliefde: "Sex Variant Women" in Nederlandstalige literatuur 1880–1940', in *Homojaarboek 2: Artikelen over emancipatie en homoseksualiteit* (Amsterdam: Van Gennep, 1983).
———. 'Vier feministen en het Nederlandsch Wetenschappelijk Humanitair Komitee: De historische verhouding tussen de Nederlandsche vrouwenbeweging en het lesbische', in Selma Sevenhuijsen et al. (eds), *Socialisties-Feministiese Teksten VIII* (Amsterdam, Sara, 1984).
Faderman, Lillian, 'The Morbidification of Love between Women by 19th-Century Sexologists', *Journal of Homosexuality* 4(1) (1978), 73–90.

———. *Surpassing the Love of Men: Romantic Friendship and Love between Women from the Renaissance to the Present* (New York: William Morrow, 1981).

———. *Odd Girls and Twilight Lovers: A History of Lesbian Life in Twentieth-Century America* (New York: Columbia University Press, 1991).

Farwell, Marilyn, *Heterosexual Plots and Lesbian Narratives* (New York: New York University Press, 1996).

Fenoulhet, Jane, 'Love, Marriage and Disappointment: Women's Lives in the Work of Ina Boudier-Bakker', *Dutch Crossing* 21(1) (1997), 52–68.

———. *Making the Personal Political: Dutch Women Writers 1919–1970* (London: Legenda, 2007).

Fish, Stanley, *Is There a Text in This Class? The Authority of Interpretive Communities* (Cambridge, MA: Harvard University Press, 1980).

Forrest, Jennifer, 'Cocteau au cirque: The Poetics of Parade and "Le Numéro Barbette"', *Studies in 20th & 21st Century Literature* 27(1) (2003), 9–46.

Foucault, Michel, *Discipline and Punish: The Birth of the Prison* (London: Allen Lane, 1975).

———. 'The Subject and the Power', *Critical Inquiry* 8(4) (1982), 777–95.

———. *The History of Sexuality: Volume I*, trans. by Robert Hurley (London: Penguin, 1984).

———. *Technologies of the Self*, ed. by Luther H. Martin et al. (Amherst: University of Massachusetts Press, 1988).

Freccero, Carla, 'The Queer Time of the Lesbian Premodern', in Noreen Giffney et al. (eds), *The Lesbian Premodern* (New York: Palgrave Macmillan, 2011).

Fricker, Miranda, *Epistemic Injustice: Power and the Ethics of Knowing* (Oxford: Oxford University Press, 2007).

Friedan, Betty, *The Feminine Mystique* (New York: W.W. Norton & Co., 1963).

Frevert, Ute, *Women in German History: From Bourgeois Emancipation to Sexual Liberation*, trans. by Stuart McKinnon-Evans (New York: Berg, 1993).

Frijhoff, Willem (ed.), *Geschiedenis van Amsterdam: Hoofdstad in Aanbouw 1813–1900* (Amsterdam, SUN, 2006).

Fulda, Bernhard, *Press and Politics in the Weimar Republic* (New York: Oxford University Press, 2009).

Ganeva, Mila, *Women in Weimar Fashion: Discourses and Displays in German Culture 1918–1933* (Rochester, NY: Camden House, 2008).

Geurts, Anna P.H., 'Elders thuis. Noord-Nederlandse reizigers in Europese steden, 1815–1914', in Inge Bertels et al. (eds), *Tussen beleving en verbeelding: de stad in de negentiende-eeuwse literatuur* (Leuven: Universitaire Pers Leuven, 2013).

Gieseking, Jen Jack, *A Queer New York: Geographies of Lesbians, Dykes, and Queers* (New York: New York University Press, 2020).

Giffney, Noreen, et al. (eds), *The Lesbian Premodern* (New York: Palgrave Macmillan, 2011).

Gilbert, Arthur, 'Conceptions of Homosexuality and Sodomy in Western History', *Journal of Homosexuality* 6(1/2) (1981), 57–68.

Gluckman, Amy and Betsy Reed, *Homo Economics: Capitalism, Community, and Lesbian and Gay Life* (New York: Routledge, 1999).

Goldberg, Jonathan and Madhavi Menon, 'Queering History', *PMLA* 120(5) (2005), 1608–17.

Goldstein, Robert Justin (ed.), *The War for the Public Mind: Political Censorship in Nineteenth Century Europe* (Westport, CT: Praeger, 2000).

Grever, Maria and Berteke Waaldijk, *Transforming the Public Sphere: The Dutch National Exhibition of Women's Labour in 1898*, trans by Mischa F.C. Hoyinck and Robert E. Chesal (Durham, NC: Duke University Press, 2004).

Groot, Marjan, *Vrouwen in de vormgeving in Nederland 1880–1940* (Rotterdam: Uitgeverij 010, 2007).
Haeberle, Erwin, *Anfänge der Sexualwissenschaft: Historische Dokumente* (Berlin: Walter de Gruyter, 1983).
Halberstam, Jack, *Female Masculinity* (Durham, NC: Duke University Press, 1998).
Halperin, David, *Saint Foucault: Towards a Gay Hagiography* (New York: Oxford University Press, 1995)
———. *How to Do the History of Homosexuality* (Chicago: University of Chicago Press, 2002).
Hammers, Corie, 'The Queer Logics of Sex/Desire and the "Missing" Discourse of Gender', *Sexualities* 18(7) (2015), 838–58.
Hans, Anjeana Kaur, 'Defining Desires: Homosexual Identity and German Discourses 1900–1933', unpublished doctoral thesis (Cambridge, MA: Harvard University, 2005).
Harris, Laura and Elizabeth Crocker (eds), *Femme: Feminists, Lesbians, and Bad Girls* (New York: Routledge, 1997).
Haunhorst Kerstin, *Das Bild der Neuen Frau im Frühwerk Irmgard Keuns: Entwürfe von Weiblichkeit am Ende der Weimarer Republik* (Hamburg: Diplomica, 2008).
Hausen, Karin, 'The German Nation's Obligation to the Heroes' Widows of World War One', in Margaret Randolph Higonnet et al. (eds), *Behind the Lines: Gender and the Two World Wars* (New Haven: Yale University Press, 1987).
Hekma, Gert, *Homoseksualiteit, een medische reputatie: de uitdoktering van de homoseksueel in negentiende-eeuws Nederland* (Amsterdam: SUA, 1987).
———. 'A History of Sexology: Social and Historical Aspects of Sexuality', in Jan Bremmer (ed.), *From Sappho to De Sade: Moments in the History of Sexuality* (New York: Routledge, 1991).
———. *De roze rand van donker Amsterdam* (Amsterdam: Van Gennep, 1992).
———. *Amsterdam: The Last Vestiges of the Sixties?* (Amsterdam: University of Amsterdam Press, 2000).
Hekma, Gert, and Jan Willem Duyvendak, 'Gay Men and Lesbians in the Netherlands', in Nancy L. Fischer and Steven Seidman (eds), *Introducing the New Sexuality Studies*, 3rd edn (New York: Routledge, 2016).
Hekma, Gert et al. (eds), *Goed verkeerd: een geschiedenis van homoseksuele mannen en lesbische vrouwen in Nederland* (Amsterdam: Meulenhoff, 1989).
Hemels, Joan, *Het geïllustreerde tijdschrift in Nederland: Bron van kennis en vermaak, lust voor het oog: bibliografie* (Amsterdam: Otto Cramwinckel, 1997).
Hemmings, Clare, 'Out of Sight, out of Mind? Theorizing Femme Narrative', *Sexualities* 2 (1999), 451–64.
———. *Bisexual Spaces: A Geography of Sexuality and Gender* (New York: Routledge, 2007).
Hermanns, Doris, *Meerkatzen, Meißel und das Mädchen Manuela: Die Schriftstellerin und Tierbildhauerin Christa Winsloe* (Berlin: AvivA, 2012).
———. 'Nachwort', in *Das Mädchen Manuela: Der Roman zum Film Mädchen in Uniform* (Berlin: Krug & Schadenberg, 2012).
Herzog, Dagmar, *Sexuality in Europe: A Twentieth-Century History* (Cambridge: Cambridge University Press, 2011).
Hessler, Martina, '"Damned Always to Alter, But Never to Be": Berlin's Culture of Change around 1900', in Miriam Levin et al. (eds), *Urban Modernity: Cultural Innovation in the Second Industrial Revolution* (Cambridge, MA: MIT Press, 2010).
Higgs, David (ed.), *Queer Sites: Gay Urban Histories since 1600* (New York: Routledge, 1999).

Hillege, Karen, 'Eén van de acht: Marie de Boer. Over Helmondse ondertekenaars van de Schorer-petitie', in Michael Dallas et al. (eds), *Homojaarboek 3: Artikelen over emancipatie en homoseksualiteit* (Amsterdam: Van Gennep, 1985).

Hohmann, Joachim S., *Sexualforschung und -aufklärung in der Weimarer Republik: Eine Übersicht in Materialien und Dokumenten* (Berlin: Foerster Verlag, 1985).

Holla, Sylvia, and Antia Wiersma, 'Serving Morality on a Platter: Moral Imperatives and Cultural Repetoires in Writings on Food in the Dutch Women's Magazine *Margriet*', in Bettina Bock and Jessica Duncan (eds), *Gendered Food Practices from Seed to Waste: Yearbook of Women's History* (Hilversum: Verloren, 2017).

Hollows, Joanne, *Feminism, Femininity and Popular Culture* (Manchester: Manchester University Press, 2000).

Hollway, Wendy, 'Gender Difference and the Production of Subjectivity', in *Changing the Subject: Psychology, Social Regulation and Subjectivity* (London: Routledge, 1984).

Honegger, Claudia, *Die Ordnung der Geschlechter. Die Wissenschaft vom Menschen und das Weib* (Frankfurt: Campus, 1991).

hooks, bell, *The Will to Change: Men, Masculinity, and Love* (New York: Washington Square Press, 2004).

Hoskin, Rhea Ashley and Katerina Hirschfeld, 'Beyond Aesthetics: A Femme Manifesto', *Atlantis: Critical Studies in Gender Culture, and Social Justice* 39(1) (2018), 85–87.

Huussen, Arend H., 'Sodomy in the Dutch Republic during the 18th Century', *Eighteenth Century Life* 9 (1985), 169–78.

Inness, Sherrie, *The Lesbian Menace: Ideology, Identity, and the Representation of Lesbian Life* (Amherst: University of Massachusetts Press, 1997).

Jacobs, Bethany, 'Mothering Herself: Manifesto of the Erotic Mother in Audree Lorde's *Zami: A New Spelling of My Name*', *MELUS* 40(4) (2015), 110–28.

Jensen, Lotte, *Bij uitsluiting voor de vrouwelijke sekse geschikt: Vrouwentijdschriften en journalistes in Nederland in de achttiende en negentiende eeuw* (Hilversum: Verloren, 2001).

Johnson, Mykel, 'Butchy Femme', in Joan Nestle (ed.), *The Persistent Desire* (Boston, MA: Alyson Publications, 1992).

Kaes, Anton, et al. (eds), *The Weimar Republic Sourcebook* (Berkeley: University of California Press, 1994).

Katz, Jonathan Ned, *The Invention of Heterosexuality* (Chicago: University of Chicago Press, 2007).

Kennedy, Elizabeth, and Madeline Davis, *Boots of Leather, Slippers of Gold: The History of a Lesbian Community* (New York: Routledge, 1993).

Kennedy, Hubert, *Ulrichs: The Life and Works of Karl Heinrich Ulrichs, Pioneer of the Modern Gay Movement* (Boston, MA: Alyson Publications, 1988).

Kennedy, Hubert, and Harry Oosterhuis (eds), *Homosexuality and Male Bonding in Pre-Nazi Germany: The Youth Movement, the Gay Movement and Male Bonding before Hitler's Rise* (New York: Routledge, 2011).

Kennedy, Rosanne, 'The Gorgeous Lesbian in *LA Law*: The Present Absence?', in Diane Hamer and Belinda Budge (eds), *The Good, the Bad, and the Gorgeous* (London: Pandora Press, 1994).

Kimmel, Michael S., *The History of Men: Essays on the History of American and British Masculinities* (Albany: State University of New York Press, 2005).

Kissling, Elizabeth, *Capitalizing on the Curse: The Business of Menstruation* (Boulder, CO: Lynne Rienner, 2006).

Koenders, Pieter, *Homoseksualiteit in bezet Nederland: Verzwegen hoofdstuk* ('s-Gravenhage: De Woelrat, 1983).

Kokula, Ilse, *Weibliche Homosexualität um 1900 in zeitgenössischen Dokumenten* (Munich: Frauenoffensive, 1981).

———. *Jahre des Glücks, Jahre des Leids: Gespräche mit älteren lesbischen Frauen* (Kiel: Frühlings Erwachen, 1986).

Kolb, Eberhard, *The Weimar Republic*, trans. by P.S. Falla and R.J. Park (London: Routledge, 2001).

Kuzniar, Alice A., *The Queer German Cinema* (Stanford: Stanford University Press, 2000).

Ladd, Brian, *The Ghosts of Berlin: Confronting German History in the Urban Landscape* (Chicago: University of Chicago Press, 1997).

Lang, Birgit, and Katie Sutton, 'The Queer Cases of Psychoanalysis: Rethinking the Scientific Study of Homosexuality, 1890s–1920s', *German History* 34(3) (2016), 419–44.

Langkau-Alex, Ursula, '"Naturally, Many Things Were Strange But I Could Adapt": Women Emigrés in the Netherlands', in Sibylle Quack (ed.), *Between Sorrow and Strength: Women Refugees of the Nazi Period* (Cambridge: Cambridge University Press, 2002).

Lanser, Susan, *The Sexuality of History: Modernity and the Sapphic 1565–1830* (Chicago: University of Chicago Press, 2014).

Lee, Janet, '"A Kotex and a Smile": Mothers and Daughters at Menarche', *Journal of Family Issues* 29(10) (2008), 1325–47.

Lee, Stephen J., *The Weimar Republic* (New York: Routledge, 1998).

Leidinger, Christiane, '"Anna Rüling": A Problematic Foremother of Lesbian History', *Journal of the History of Sexuality* 13 (2004), 477–99.

———. *Keine Tochter aus gutem Hause: Johanna Elberskirchen (1864–1943)* (Konstanz: UvK, 2008).

Leng, Kirsten, 'Contesting the Laws of Life: Feminism, Sexual Science, and Sexual Governance in Germany and Britain c. 1880–1914', unpublished doctoral thesis (Ann Arbor, University of Michigan, 2011).

———. 'Permutations of the Third Sex: Sexology, Subjectivity, and Antimaternalist Feminism at the Turn of the Twentieth Century', *Signs* 40(1) (2014), 227–54.

———. 'Culture, Difference, and Sexual Progress in Turn-of-the-Century Europe: Cultural Othering and the German League for the Protection of Mothers and Sexual Reform, 1905–1914', *Journal of the History of Sexuality* 25(1) (2016), 62–82.

———. *Sexual Politics and Feminist Science: Women Sexologists in Germany 1900–1933* (Ithaca, NY: Cornell University Press, 2018).

Lijphart, Arend, *The Politics of Accommodation: Pluralism and Democracy in the Netherlands* (Berkeley: University of California Press, 1975).

Lorde Audre, 'The Master's Tools will Never Dismantle the Master's House', in Reina Lewis and Sara Mills (eds), *Feminist Postcolonial Theory: A Reader* (Edinburgh: Edinburgh University Press, 2003).

———. 'Uses of the Erotic: The Erotic as Power', in *Sister Outsider* (Berkeley: Ten Speed Press, 2007).

———. *Zami: A New Spelling of My Name; A Biomythography* (London: Penguin/Random House, 2018).

Lorey, Christoph and John Plews (eds), *Queering the Canon: Defying Sights in German Literature and Culture* (New York: Camden House, 1998).

Lovaas, Karen E. et al., *LGBT Studies and Queer Theory: New Conflicts, Collaborations, and Contested Terrain* (New York: Harrington Park Press, 2006).

Lucassen, Leo, 'Sekse en nationaliteit als ordenend principe: De uitsluiting van vrouwen en vreemdelingen op de Nederlandse arbeidsmarkt (1900–1995)', in Corrie van de Eijl et al. (eds), *Sociaal Nederland* (Amsterdam: Askant, 2001).

Lybeck, Marti M., *Desiring Emancipation: New Women and Homosexuality in Germany 1890–1933* (Albany, NY: SUNY Press, 2014).
Machin, David, and Theo van Leeuwen, *Global Media Discourse: A Critical Introduction* (New York: Routledge, 2007).
MacLean, Rory, *Berlin: Imagine a City* (Berlin, Weidenfeld & Nicolson, 2014).
Mak, Geert, *Amsterdam: A Brief Life of the City*, trans. by Philipp Blom (London: Harvill Press, 1994).
Mak, Geertje, *Mannelijke vrouwen: Over de grenzen van sekse in de negentiende eeuw* (Amsterdam: Boom, 1997).
Marhoefer, Laurie, *Sex and the Weimar Republic: German Homosexual Emancipation and the Rise of the Nazis* (Toronto: University of Toronto Press, 2015).
Marks, Elaine, 'Lesbian Intertextuality', in George Stambolian and Elaine Marks (eds), *Homosexualities and French Literature: Cultural Context/Critical Texts* (Ithaca, NY: Cornell University Press, 1979).
Marsh, Madeleine, *Compacts and Cosmetics: Beauty from Victorian Times to the Present Day* (Barnsley: Remember When, 2009).
Martin, Biddy, *Femininity Played Straight: The Significance of Being a Lesbian* (New York: Routledge, 1996).
Mathijsen, Marita (ed.), *Boeken onder druk: censuur en pers-onvrijheiden in Nederland sinds de boekdrukkunst* (Amsterdam: University of Amsterdam Press, 2011).
Matysik, Tracie, *Reforming the Moral Subject: Ethics and Sexuality in Central Europe, 1890–1930* (Ithaca, NY: Cornell University Press, 2008).
McCann, Hannah, *Queering Femininity: Sexuality, Feminism and the Politics of Presentation* (New York: Routledge, 2017).
McCarron, Carmen, '"Sans famille" et "En famille": Le discours sexiste d'Hector Malot', unpublished Master's dissertation (Alberta: University of Calgary, 2000).
McCormick, Richard, *Gender and Sexuality in Weimar Modernity: Film, Literature, and 'New Objectivity'* (New York: Palgrave, 2001).
McElligott, Anthony, *The German Urban Experience: Modernity and Crisis 1900–1945* (New York: Routledge, 2001).
Meijer, Maaike, *De lust tot lezen: Nederlandse dichteressen en het literaire systeem* (Amsterdam: Sara/Van Gennep, 1988).
Melching, Willem, '"Het volkomen huwelijk" Opvattingen omtrent huwelijk en seksualiteit in het werk van Th. H. van de Velde', in Gert Hekma et al. (eds), *Grensgeschillen in de seks: Bijdragen tot een culturele geschiedenis van de seksualiteit* (Amsterdam: Atlanta, 1990).
Menon, Madhavi, *Unhistorical Shakespeare: Queer Theory in Shakespearean Literature and Film* (New York: Palgrave Macmillan, 2008).
Meyer, Adele, *Lila Nächte: Die Damenklubs der Zwanziger Jahre* (Cologne: Zitronenpresse, 1981).
Meyers, Jeffery, *Homosexuality and Literature: 1890–1930* (Montreal: McGill-Queen's University Press, 1977).
Micheler, Stefan, 'Zeitschriften, Verbände und Lokale: gleichgeschlechtlich begehrender Menschen in der Weimarer Republik', *Invertito – Jahrbuch für die Geschichte der Homosexualitäten* 10 (2008), 10–56.
Miller, D.A., *The Novel and the Police* (Berkeley: University of California Press, 1988).
Millet, Kate, *Sexual Politics* (New York: Avon Books, 1969).
Moore, F. Michael, *Drag! Male and Female Impersonators on Stage, Screen, and Television: An Illustrated World History* (Jefferson, NC: McFarland, 1994).
Mossop, Frances, *Mapping Berlin: Representations of Space in the Weimar Feuilleton* (Oxford: Peter Lang, 2015).

Musser, Amber Jamilla, *Sensual Excess: Queer Femininity and Brown Jouissance* (New York: New York University Press, 2018).
Nenno, Nancy P., 'Bildung and Desire: Anna Elisabet Weirauch's *Der Skorpion*', in Christoph Lorey and John L. Plews (eds), *Queering the Canon: Defying Sights in German Literature and Culture* (Columbia, SC: Camden House, 1998).
Nestle, Joan (ed.), *The Persistent Desire: A Femme-Butch Reader* (Boston, MA: Alyson Publications, 1992).
Newton, Esther, 'The Mythic Mannish Lesbian: Radclyffe Hall and the New Woman', in Martin Duberman et al. (eds), *Hidden from History* (New York: Meridian, 1989).
Noordam, Dirk Jaap, *Riskante relaties: Vijf eeuwen homoseksualiteit in Nederland 1233–1733* (Hilversum: Verloren, 1995).
Norton, Rictor, *Myth of the Modern Homosexual: Queer History and the Search for Cultural Unity* (London: Bloomsbury Academic, 2016).
——. *The Homosexual Literary Tradition* (New York: Revisionist Press, 1974).
O'Connor, Hannah, 'Sapphic Spectres: Lesbian Gothic in Interwar German Narratives', unpublished doctoral thesis (Cardiff: Cardiff University, 2014).
Oosterhuis, Harry, *Stepchildren of Nature: Krafft-Ebing, Psychiatry, and the Making of Sexual Identity* (Chicago: University of Chicago Press, 2000).
——. 'Insanity and Other Discomforts: A Century of Outpatient Psychiatry and Mental Health Care in the Netherlands 1900-2000', in Marijke Gijswijt-Hofstra et al. (eds), *Psychiatric Cultures Compared: Psychiatry and Mental Health Care in the Twentieth Century: Comparisons and Approaches* (Amsterdam: Amsterdam University Press, 2005).
——. 'Sexual Modernity in the Works of Richard von Krafft-Ebing and Albert Moll', *Medical History* 56(2) (2012), 133–55.
Oram, Alison, and Annmarie Turnbull, 'The Well of Loneliness', in Alison Oram and Annmarie Turnbull (eds), *The Lesbian History Sourcebook: Love and Sex between Women in Britain from 1780–1970* (London: Routledge, 2001).
Orlow, Dietrich, *The Lure of Fascism in Europe: German Nazis, Dutch and French Fascists 1933–1939* (New York: Palgrave Macmillan, 2009).
Peukert, Detlev, *The Weimar Republic: A Crisis of Classical Modernity*, trans. by Richard Deveson (London: Penguin, 1993).
Phelan, Shane, *Getting Specific: Postmodern Lesbian Politics* (Minneapolis: Minnesota University Press, 1994).
Piontek, Thomas, *Queering Gay and Lesbian Studies* (Champaign: University of Illinois Press, 2006).
Ponse, Barbara, *Identities in the Lesbian World: The Social Construction of Self* (Westport, CT: Greenwood Press, 1978).
Potter, Jane, 'Women's Publishing', in Giles Noel Clark and Angus Phillips (eds), *Inside Book Publishing* (London: Routledge, 2008).
Prak, Maarten, 'The Dutch Republic as a Bourgeois Society', *BMGN: Low Countries Historical Review* (125) 2.3, 107–39.
Puff, Helmut, 'After the History of (Male) Homosexuality', in Scott Spector et al. (eds), *After the History of Sexuality: German Genealogies with and Beyond Foucault* (New York: Berghahn Books, 2012).
Quinodoz, Jean-Michel, *Reading Freud: A Chronological Exploration of Freud's Writings*, trans. by David Alcorn (New York: Routledge, 2005).
Ramanathan, Geetha, *Feminist Auteurs: Reading Women's Films* (London: Wallflower, 2006).
Ramsbrock, Annelie, *The Science of Beauty: Culture and Cosmetics in Modern Germany 1750–1930*, trans. by David Burnett (New York: Palgrave Macmillan, 2015).

———. 'Social Cosmetics: Weimar Beauty Politics between Welfare and Empowerment', *German History*, 4 (2016), 555–78.

Reed, Christopher, *Art and Homosexuality: A History of Ideas* (Oxford: Oxford University Press, 2011).

Reinig, Christa, 'Nachwort', in *Mädchen in Uniform* (Munich: Frauenoffensive, 1983).

Reuveni, Gideon, '"Productivist" and "Consumerist" Narratives of Jews in German History', in Neil Gregor et al. (eds), *German History from the Margins* (Bloomington: Indiana University Press, 2006).

———. *Reading Germany: Literature and Consumer Culture in Germany before 1933* (Oxford: Berghahn Books, 2009).

Rich, Adrienne, *Of Woman Born: Motherhood as Experience and Institution* (New York: Bantam Books, 1977).

Rieder, Ines, and Diana Voigt, *Sidonie Csillag: La 'joven homosexual' de Freud* (Buenos Aires: El Cuenco de Plata, 2004).

Robertson, Pamela, *Guilty Pleasures: Feminist Camp from Mae West to Madonna* (Durham, NC: Duke University Press, 1996).

Roebroek, Joop M., 'The Arrival of the Welfare State in Twentieth Century Mass Society: The Dutch Case', in Bob Moore and Henk van Nierop (eds), *Twentieth Century mass society in Britain and the Netherlands* (Oxford: Berg, 2006).

Roegholt, Richter, *Amsterdam na 1900* (Amsterdam: Meppel, 1993).

Rogan, Clare, '"Good Nude Photographs": Images for Desire in Weimar Germany's Lesbian Diaries', in Mary McAuliffe and Sonja Tiernan (eds), *Tribades, Tommies and Transgressives Histories of Sexualities: Volume I* (Newcastle: Cambridge Scholars, 2008).

Roof, Judith, *The Lure of Knowledge: Lesbian Sexuality and Theory* (New York: Columbia University Press, 1991).

Rosario, Vernon A. (ed.), *Science and Homosexualities* (New York: Routledge, 1997).

Rowold, Katharina, *The Educated Woman: Minds, Bodies, and Women's Higher Education in Britain, Germany, and Spain 1865–1914* (New York: Routledge, 2010).

Rubin, Gayle, 'Of Catamites and Kings: Reflections on Butch, Gender and Boundaries', in Joan Nestle (ed.), *The Persistent Desire: A Femme-Butch Reader* (Boston, MA: Alyson Books, 1992).

Rupp, Leila J, *Sapphistries: A Global History of Love between Women* (New York: New York University Press, 2009).

Rützou Petersen, Vibeke, *Women and Modernity in Weimar Germany: Reality and Its Representation in Popular Fiction* (New York: Berghahn Books, 2001).

Salden, Maarten, 'Artikel 248 bis wetboek van Strafrecht de geschiedenis van een strafbaarstelling', *Groniek Historisch Tijdschrift* 66 (1980), 38–48.

Saxey, Esther, 'Introduction', in *The Well of Loneliness* (Bungay: Clays Ltd, 2005).

Schader, Heike, *Virile, Vamps und wilde Veilchen: Sexualität, Begehren und Erotik in den Zeitschriften homosexueller Frauen im Berlin der 1920er Jahre* (Königstein: Ulrike Helmer, 2004).

Schaffner, Anna Katharina, *Modernism and Perversion: Sexual Deviance in Sexology and Literature, 1850–1930* (New York: Palgrave Macmillan, 2012).

Scheub, Ute, *Verrückt nach Leben: Berliner Szenen in den zwanziger Jahren* (Reinbek: Rowohlt, *2000*).

Schlich, Thomas, *The Origins of Organ Transplantation: Surgery and Laboratory Science, 1880–1930* (New York: Rochester University Press, 2014).

Schlierkamp, Petra, 'Die Garconne', in Michael Bollé et al. (eds), *Eldorado: Homosexuelle Frauen und Männer in Berlin 1850–1950 Geschichte, Alltag und Kultur* (Berlin: Fröhlich & Kaufmann, 1984).

Schneider, Maarten, and Joan Hemels, *De Nederlandse krant: 1618–1978: van 'nieuwstydinghe' tot dagblad* (Amsterdam: Wereldvenster, 1979).

Schöffer, Ivo, *Veelvormig verleden: zeventien studies in de vaderlandse geschiedenis* (Amsterdam: Bataafsche Leeuw, 1987).

Schoppman, Claudia, *Der Skorpion: Frauenliebe in der Weimarer Republik* (Kiel: Frühlings Erwachen, 1985).

Schuster, David, *Neurasthenic Nation: America's Search for Health, Happiness, and Comfort 1869–1920* (New Brunswick, NJ: Rutgers University Press, 2011).

Schuyf, Judith, 'Lollepotterij. Geschiedenis van het "sapphisch vermaak", in Nederland tot 1940', in *Homojaarboek 1* (Amsterdam: Van Gennep, 1981).

——. 'Lesbian Emancipation in the Netherlands', in Axel van Naerssen (ed.), *Gay Life in Dutch Society* (New York: Harrington Park Press, 1987)

——. *Een stilzwijgende samenzwering: Lesbische vrouwen in Nederland 1920–1970* (The Hague: IISG, 1994).

——. Marloes Schoonheim 'Geschiedenis', in Mirjam Hemker and Linda Huijsmans (eds), *De lesbo- encyclopedie* (Amsterdam: Ambo-Anthos, 2009).

Seaton Hackney, Fiona Anne, '"They Opened up a Whole New World": Feminine Modernity and the Feminine Imagination in Women's Magazines 1919–1939', unpublished doctoral thesis (London: Goldsmith's College, 2010).

Sedgwick, Eve Kosofsky, *Tendencies* (Durham, NC: Duke University Press, 1993).

——. (ed.), *Novel Gazing: Queer Readings in Fiction* (Durham, NC: Duke University Press, 1997).

——. *Epistemology of the Closet* (Berkeley: University of California Press, 2008).

Showalter, Elaine, *A Literature of Their Own: British Women Novelists from Brontë to Lessing* (Princeton: Princeton University Press, 1977).

——. *Sexual Anarchy: Gender and Culture at the Fin de Siècle* (London: Virago, 1992).

——. *Sister's Choice: Tradition and Change in American Women's Writing* (Oxford: Oxford University Press, 1994).

Sieg, Katrin, *Exiles, Eccentrics, Activists: Women in Contemporary German Theater* (Ann Arbor: University of Michigan Press, 1994).

Sigusch, Volkmar, *Geschichte der Sexualwissenschaft* (Frankfurt: Campus, 2008).

Simonton, Deborah, *A History of European Women's Work: 1700 to the Present* (New York: Routledge, 1998).

Smith-Rosenberg, Carroll, 'The Female World of Love and Ritual: Relations between Women in Nineteenth Century America', *Signs* 1 (1975), 1–29.

——. *Disorderly Conduct: Visions of Gender in Victorian America* (Oxford: Oxford University Press, 1985).

Södersten, P. et al., 'Eugen Steinach: The First Neuroendocrinologist', *Endocrinology* 3 (2014), 688–95.

Sontag, Susan, 'Notes on Camp', in *Against Interpretation* (New York: Dell Publishing, 1966).

Spector, Scott, Helmut Puff and Dagmar Herzog (eds), *After the History of Sexuality: German Genealogies with and beyond Foucault* (New York: Berghahn Books, 2012).

Spivak, Gayatri Chakravorty, *Worlds: Essays in Cultural Politics* (New York: Methuen, 1987).

Steakley, James P., *The Homosexual Emancipation Movement in Germany* (New York: Arno Press, 1975).

Strega, Linda, 'The Big Sell-out: Lesbian Femininity', *Lesbian Ethics* 1(3) (1985), 73–84.

Stryker, Susan, *Transgender History: The Roots of Today's Revolution*, 2nd edn (Berkeley: Seal Press, 2012).

Stryker, Susan, and Stephen Whittle (eds), *The Transgender Studies Reader* (New York: Routledge, 2006).

Summers, Claude (ed.), *The Queer Encyclopedia of the Visual Arts* (San Francisco: Cleis Press, 2004).
Sutton, Katie, *The Masculine Woman in Weimar Germany* (Oxford: Berghahn Books, 2013).
———. 'Sexological Cases and the Prehistory of Transgender Identity Politics in Interwar Germany', in Joy Damousi et al. (eds0, *Case Studies and Dissemination of Knowledge* (Abingdon: Routledge, 2015).
———. '"We Too Deserve a Place in the Sun": The Politics of Transvestite Identity in Weimar Germany', *German Studies Review* 2 (2012), 335–54.
Tamagne, Florence, *The History of Homosexuality: Berlin, London, Paris Volume I & II* (New York: Algora Publishing, 2006).
Tambling, Jeremy, *Confession: Sexuality, Sin, the Subject* (Manchester: Manchester University Press, 1990).
Tatar, Maria, *Lustmord: Sexual Murder in Weimar Germany* (Princeton: Princeton University Press, 1995).
Taussig, Karen-Sue, *Ordinary Genomes: Science, Citizenship, and Genetic Identities* (Durham, NC: Duke University Press, 2009).
Taylor, Mara, 'Diagnosing Deviants: The Figure of the Lesbian in Sexological and Literary Discourses 1860–1931', unpublished doctoral thesis (Philadelphia: University of Pennsylvania, 2010).
Tielman, Rob, 'Schorer en het Nederlandsch Wetenschappelijk Humanitair Komitee (1911–1940)', in Michael Dallas et al. (eds), *Homojaarboek 1: Artikelen over emancipatie en homoseksualiteit* (Amsterdam: Van Gennep, 1981).
———. *Homoseksualiteit in Nederland* (Amsterdam: Boom Meppel, 1982).
Tijsseling, Anna, 'Schuldige Seks: homoseksuele zedendelicten rondom de Duitse bezettingstijd', unpublished doctoral thesis (Utrecht: University of Utrecht, 2009).
Tobin, Robert Deam, *Peripheral Desires: The German Discovery of Sex* (Philadelphia: University of Pennsylvania Press, 2015).
Trask, Michael, *Cruising Modernism: Class and Sexuality in American Literature and Social Thought* (Ithaca, NY: Cornell University Press, 2003).
Traub, Valerie, *Thinking Sex with the Early Moderns* (Philadelphia: University of Pennsylvania Press, 2016).
———. 'The Present Future of Lesbian Historiography', in Noreen Giffney et al. (eds), *The Lesbian Premodern: The New Middle Ages* (New York: Palgrave Macmillan, 2011).
Tseëlon, Efrat, *The Masque of Femininity: The Presentation of Woman in Everyday Life* (London: SAGE Publications, 1995).
Van Bork, G.J., and P.J. Verkruijsse (eds), *De Nederlandse en Vlaamse Auteurs: Van middeleeuwen tot heden met inbegrip van de Friese auteurs* (Weesp: De Haan, 1985).
Van de Plasse, Jan, *Kroniek van de Nederlandse dagblad- en opiniepers* (Amsterdam: Otto Cramwinckel Uitgever, 2005).
Van der Meer, Theo, *De wesentlijke sonde van sodomie en andere vuyligheeden. Sodomietenvervolgingen in Amsterdam 1730–1811* (Amsterdam: Tabula, 1984).
Van Eijl, Corrie, et al. 'Introduction', in *Sociaal Nederland: Contouren van de twintigste eeuw* (Amsterdam: Aksant, 2001).
Van Heek, H.J., '"Het Koekoeksei van Regout" De parlementaire geschiedenis van artikel 248 bis', in Maurice van Lieshout (ed.), *Een groeiend zedelijk kwaad: documenten over de criminalisering en emancipatie van homoseksuelen 1910–1916* (Amsterdam: Het Spinhuis, 1992).
Van Heijst, Annelies, 'The Disputed Charity of Catholic Nuns: Dualistic Spiritual Heritage as a Source of Affliction', *Feminist Theology* 21(2) (2013), 155–72.

Van Kooten Niekerk, Anja, and Sacha Wijmer, *Verkeerde vriendschap: Lesbisch leven in de jaren 1920–1960* (Amsterdam: Feministische uitgeverij Sara, 1985).
Van Lieshout, Maurice, 'Lustvijandig, wetenschappelijk voorzichtig en volhardend; de Nederlandse homobeweging in het begin van de 2e eeuw', *Groniek Historisch Tijdschrift* 66 (1980), 55–62.
——. 'De homosexueelen 1939: Mijnheer is zeker óók zoo?', *Seks* 11 (1981), 12–16.
Van Rooden, Peter, 'Long-Term Religious Developments in the Netherlands 1750–2000', in Hugh McLeod and Werner Ustorf (eds), *The Decline of Christendom in Western Europe, 1750–2000* (Cambridge: Cambridge University Press, 2002).
Van Vree, Frank, 'Media, Morality and Popular Culture: The Case of the Netherlands, 1870–1965', in Bob Moore and Henk van Nierop (eds), *Twentieth Century Mass Society in Britain and the Netherlands* (Oxford: Berg, 2006).
Von Ankum, Katharina, 'Gendered Urban Spaces in Irmgard Keun's *Das kunstseidene Mädchen*', in Katharina von Ankum (ed.), *Women in the Metropolis: Gender and Modernity in Weimar Culture* (Berkeley: University of California Press, 1997).
Walker, Lisa M., 'How to Recognize a Lesbian: The Cultural Politics of Looking like What You Are', *Signs* 18(4) (1993), 866–90.
——. *Looking Like What You Are: Sexual Style, Race, and Lesbian Identity* (New York: New York University Press, 2001).
Warner, Michael, *The Trouble with Normal: Sex, Politics, and the Ethics of Queer Life* (Cambridge, MA: Harvard University Press, 1999).
Weeks, Jeffrey, 'Capitalism and the Organization of Sex', in Gay Left Collective (ed.), *Homosexuality: Power and Politics* (London: Allison and Busby, 1980).
——. *Sexuality*, 4th edn (New York: Routledge, 2017).
Welter, Barbara, 'The Cult of True Womanhood: 1820–1860', *American Quarterly* 18(2) (1966), 154–74.
Weisskopf, Susan Contratto, 'Maternal Sexuality and Asexual Motherhood', *Signs* 5(4) (1980), 766–67.
Weitz, Eric, *Weimar Germany: Promise and Tragedy* (Princeton: Princeton University Press, 2007).
Whisnant, Clayton J., *Queer Identities and Politics in Germany: A History 1880–1945* (New York: Harrington Park Press, 2016).
Wilkending, Gisela, *Mädchen der Kaiserzeit: zwischen weiblicher Identifizierung und Grenzüberschreitung* (Stuttgart: Metzler, 2003).
Winkelmann, Cathrin, 'The Limits of Representation? The Expression and Repression of Desire in 20th-Century German Lesbian Narratives', unpublished doctoral thesis (Montreal: McGill University, 2001).
Wolfe, Susan J., and Lee Ann Roripaugh, 'Feminine Beauty and the Male Gaze in *The L-Word*', *MP: An Online Feminist Journal* 1(4) (2006), 1–7.
Worthen, Meredith, *Sexual Deviance and Society: A Sociological Examination* (New York: Routledge, 2016).
Yamaguchi, Lynne, and Karen Barber (eds), *Tomboys! Tales of Dyke Derring-do* (Los Angeles: Alyson, 1995).
Young, Amy D., '"Das gesprengte Korsett": Gender in Lesbian Periodicals in Berlin 1924–1933', unpublished doctoral thesis (Lincoln, NE: University of Nebraska, 2004).
——. '"Club of Friends": Lesbian Periodicals in the Weimar Republic', in Mary McAuliffe and Sonja Tiernan (eds), *Tribades, Tommies and Transgressives Histories of Sexualities: Volume I* (Newcastle: Cambridge Scholars, 2008).

Ziemann, Benjamin, 'Germany after the First World War: A Violent Society? Results and Implications of Recent Research on Weimar Germany', *Journal of Modern European History* 1(1) (2003), 80–95.
Zimmerman, Bonnie, 'What Has Never Been: An Overview of Lesbian Feminist Literary Criticism', *Feminist Studies* 7(3) (1981), 451–75.
———. *The Safe Sea of Women: Lesbian Fiction, 1969–1989* (Boston, MA: Beacon, 1990).
———. (ed.), *Encyclopedia of Lesbian Histories and Cultures* (New York: Routledge, 2012).

Online Sources

Berman, Judy, '*The L Word*: Generation Q Is a Valiant Effort. But the Show Is a Time Capsule That Should Have Stayed Buried' (2019). Retrieved 30 April 2022 from https://time.com/5744710/the-l-word-generation-q-review.
'Dagbladzegel: belasting betalen om het lezen van kranten'. Retrieved 30 April 2022 from http://kunst-en-cultuur.infonu.nl/geschiedenis/161258-dagbladzegel-belasting-betalen-om-het-lezen-van-kranten.html.
'Gesetz zur Bewahrung der Jugend vor Schund- und Schmutzschriften'. Retrieved 30 April 2022 from http://www.zaoerv.de/01_1929/1_1929_2_b_533_2_536_1.pdf.
Global Network of Sex Work Projects, 'Policy Brief: Sex Work as Work'. Retrieved 30 April 2022 from https://www.nswp.org/sites/nswp.org/files/policy_brief_sex_work_as_work_nswp_-_2017.pdf.
Goodloe, Amy, 'Queer Theory: Another "Battle of the Sexes?"' Retrieved 30 April 2022 from http://amygoodloe.com/papers/lesbian-feminism-and-queer-theory-another-battle-of-the-sexes.
Hofstee, Evert Willem, and Gerrit Andries Kooy, 'Class Structure in the Netherlands', transcript of a lecture given at the 50th Anniversary Meeting of the American Sociological Society, Washington DC, 2 September 1955. Retrieved 30 April 2022 from https://edepot.wur.nl/38393.
IHLIA, 'Bewaar mij voor de waanzin van het recht – 100 jaar strafrecht en homoseksualiteit in Nederland'. Exhibition in the IHLIA Archive, Amsterdam, 18 November 2011–29 February 2012. Retrieved 30 April 2022 from http://www.ihlia.nl/wp-content/uploads/2015/03/Bewaar-mij_brochure-FINAL-small-min.pdf.
Peiss, Kathy L., 'American Women and the Making of Modern Consumer Culture'. Retrieved 30 April 2022 from https://www.albany.edu/jmmh/vol1no1/peiss-text.html.
'Preußisches Strafgesetzbuch von 1851'. Retrieved 30 April 2022 from http://www.koeblergerhard.de/Fontes/StrafgesetzbuchPreussen1851.
Radicalesbians, 'The Woman-Identified Woman' (1970). Retrieved 30 April 2022 from https://repository.duke.edu/dc/wlmpc/wlmms01011.
Rapp, Linda, 'Radicalesbians'. Retrieved 30 April 2022 from http://www.glbtqarchive.com/ssh/radicalesbians_S.pdf.
Strega, Linda, 'The Big Sell-out'. Retrieved 30 April 2022 from https://bevjoradicallesbian.wordpress.com/2017/07/27/the-big-sell-out-lesbian-femininity-by-linda-strega.
Van den Heuij, Yvonne, and Diana van Laar 'Café 't Mandje'. Retrieved 30 April 2022 from http://www.cafetmandje.amsterdam/geschiedenis.

INDEX

A
Abate, Michelle, 244
(anti-) abortion, 56, 61, 65, 67, 68
Actie voor God (Action for God), 67
adolescence, 259, 281n64, 296
advertisements
    book, 150, 190, 288
    and commercial aims, 161, 190
    for cosmetics, 161–162, 167–168, 170, 199
    for events, 49, 145, 162
    as gendered space, 158
    personal, 141, 144
advice columns, 186, 190
age of consent, 65
Aletrino, Arnold, 57, 88, 116n18
Allert de Lange (publishing house), 248
Amarant. *See* queer periodicals
Amazon myth, 153–54, 180–81n47
ambulance service, 14, 192, 196
Amor Lesbicus, 102, 110
Amsterdam
    as conservative modern city, 39–44
    district living in …, 42, 133
    industrialization in …, 39–40
    queer subcultures in …, 52–55, 204, 208–216
    Socialist uprisings in …, 40
Amsterdamsche Dames Kroniek (Amsterdam Ladies Chronicle). *See* women's periodicals
Anders als die Andern (film), 228n79
Anderson, Benedict, 130. *See also* imagined communities
Andriesse, Emmy, 192
androgyny, 7, 10 97, 119n63, 258, 259, 312, 279n34
anonymity, 130, 134, 139, 216
Angelo, Bob, (pseud.). *See* Niek/Nico Engelschman
Ankum, Katharina von, 46
anti-feminism, 77n89, 90, 91
anti-Semitism, 86, 153
Arden, Elizabeth, 159
Arduin, P., 58
Arnim, Bettina von, 315, 316, 318
Article 248 bis, 57–59, 63–68, 332. *See also* crimen nefandum, Paragraph 175
asexuality, 93, 96, 113
autobiography, 104–106, 113, 204, 234, 250, 251, 279n29

B
Bab, Edwin, 58
Balestra, Gianfranca, 238
Balzac, Honoré de, 91, 100, 237
Barbette (acrobat), 257–259
Bauer, Heike, 95, 234
Baum, Vicki, 46
BDSM, 7
Beachy, Robert, 23, 49, 59, 78n101
Beatrijs (*Beatrice*). *See* women's periodicals
beauty
    and body culture, 158
    and consumerism, 159, 164, 190 (*see also* fashion)
    and femininity, 165, 192
    and heterosexuality, 8, 301

as marker of female worth, 45, 253, 256, 280n46
masculine ..., 162, 164
products, 161, 162as 'social cosmetics', 159, 164, 168, 199
standards, 71, 164, 168, 170, 191
and work, 45, 46, 175
Beddoe, Deirdre, 186
Beeren, Bet van, 54, 76n78, 81n152
Bennett, Judith M., 22
Beetham, Margaret, 186
Berlage, Hendrik Petrus, 41
Berlin
living conditions in ..., 38–39
industrialization in ..., 128, 139
as the metropolis of pleasure, 2, 35, 36
political uprisings in ..., 40
sexual violence in ..., 39, 72n11
Berlin's lesbische Frauen (*Berlin's Lesbian Women*, Ruth Margarete Roellig), 36, 50–51, 76n66, 130, 139, 157
Bergmann, Carl/Karl, 141, 143, 145, 148, 150
Bessel, Richard, 44
Beunders, Henri, 133
Bornewasser, E.G.H., 189
Bildungsbürgertum, 17
blackmail, 148, 292, 307, 312
Blaman, Anna, 234, 242n25, 290
Bleijenbergh, Inge, 41
Bloch, Iwan, 63, 86
Bluestocking, 202. *See also* feminism, women's movement
Blüher, Hans, 86
Blätter idealer Frauenfreundschaften (Pages of Ideal Women's Friendship). *See* queer periodicals
biomythography, 251, 266. *See also* Lorde, Audre
biopower, 87, 270
Bingham, Adrian, 129
bisexuality
and community prejudice, 172, 174, 175
and femininity, 155, 172–173
and maternalism, 112, 114
original ..., 102, 107, 112
and perceived promiscuity, 171, 172, 174
and perceived link with prostitution, 155

subcultural debates concerning ..., 142, 171–173
support for ..., 172, 174, 287
Boak, Helen, 17, 74n40, 74n46
boarding school
literature, 279n25
as site for homosexual desires, 232, 260–261
body culture, 158–159
Boer, Marie de, 68, 81n152
bobby-kop/Bubikopf (bobbed-hair), 142, 164, 200–204
body hair, 10, 168
Bond voor Grote Gezinnen (League for Large Families), 67
Bosch, Mineke, 41, 42
Bosch & Keuning (publishing house), 196–197
Boudier-Bakker, Ina, 87, 90–93
boulevard press, 128
bourgeois
femininity, 47, 84, 98, 159, 170, 187, 191, 287, 299, 300, 301, 316, 322, 324n30
masculinity, 148, 149, 155, 179n34, 334
morals and norms, 70, 71, 156, 174, 222, 237, 291, 299, 302, 306, 309, 334
respectability, 168, 174, 175, 179n34, 237, 296, 298, 299, 306, 317, 321, 322 (*see also* respectability, politics of)
shared ... values, 299, 302, 308
Brand, Adolf, 77n89, 86, 147, 206, 209, 210, 227n64, 227n69
'breadwinner' and 'caregiver' roles, 47, 48, 70, 186, 332
bricolage, 156, 217. *See also* Spivak, Gayatri,
Bridenthal, Renate, 39, 45
brothels, 62, 65
Bruggen, Carry van, 134, 246
'Bubis' and 'Mädis', 49–52. *See also* 'mothers' and 'fathers'
Bund für Menschenrecht (BfM, League for Human Rights), 50, 70, 127, 135, 140–150, 162, 165, 167, 170, 171, 172, 174, 176, 178n33, 204, 206, 208, 209, 222, 287, 334

Bund für Mutterschutz und Sexualreform (League for the Protection of Mothers), 62
Bussemaker, Jet, 36, 41, 42
butch-femme, 7, 8, 14, 28n40
butch, figure of the, 4, 7, 8, 10, 11, 27n26
Butler, Judith, 8, 19, 90, 102, 117n25, 120n88, 308
Butzko-Radszuweit, Martin, 142, 178n27

C
Cadmus, Paul, 257
cafés
 Empire, 53, 54, 204, 211
 Hirschgebouw (*Hirsch Building*), 53
 Rode Leeuw (*Red Lion*), 53
 Suisse, 53
 't Mandje (*The Little Basket*), 53–54
camp, 10, 245, 256, 258–260, 276. *See also* Susan Sontag
camaraderie, 212, 308, 309, 313
Čapek, Karel, 246
Carter, Julian, 3, 240, 286, 314, 315
Catherine the Great, 152
case study
 as genre, 251, 276, 293, 295, 300, 305
 literary ..., 251, 260 (*see also* diagnosis narrative)
 sexological ..., 96, 98, 111, 235, 239, 253, 256, 280n48, 295
Casper, Johann Ludwig, 94, 118n47
Catholicism
 and attitudes towards homosexuality, 64, 66–67, 272
 and censorship, 289
 and pillarization, 41–44, 73n30, 133
Cefai, Sarah, 4, 11
censorship
 of queer media, 61, 126, 131–132, 137n20, 140, 145, 176n3
 relaxation of ... laws, 49, 130, 205
 See also Schmutz- und Schundgesetz
Chambers, Deborah, 187
Ciasullo, Ann, 9
cinema, 2, 39, 191, 203, 247–248
Cixous, Hélène, 13
Cläre (pseud.), 173–174. *See also Frauenliebe*

Clark, Danae, 9
class
 and belonging, 299, 302, 308
 and race, 9, 16, 20, 188–189, 204, 337
 and religion, 16, 18, 20, 41–43, 73n30, 186, 189, 222, 337
 See also white-collar workers, working-class women
clubs
 Dorian Gray, 50
 Eldorado, 51, 52
 Klub Monbijou des Westens (*Club Monbijou of the West*), 50
 Taverne (*Tavern*), 51, 52, 71, 76n66, 333
 Violetta, 50
 Zauberflöte, Die (*The Magic Flute*), 50, 76n68
 See also cafés
Cobb, Humphrey, 246
Cocteau, Jean, 257–259
Colonialism, 40, 67, 81n143, 220, 229n102, 323n15
commodity lesbianism, 9
community
 building, 16, 19, 21, 42, 130, 133, 134, 139, 222–223, 334–335
 imagined, 130, 135, 139, 222 (*see also* Anderson, Benedict)
 queer, 4, 8–11, 15, 25, 58, 99, 102, 105, 115, 126, 130, 135, 140, 142, 151, 157, 171, 172, 173, 174, 187, 204, 208, 213, 214, 216, 268, 287, 288, 293, 298–299, 300, 302, 304, 308, 322, 323n8, 333, 334, 337
 separatist, 154, 168, 175, 203, 221–222 (*see also* separatism)
coming out, 272, 284n124
confession
 false, 270–271, 273
 as subject forming discourse, 123n120, 235, 240, 261, 268–269, 270–272, 273, 274, 275, 277, 304
 religious, 240, 269–273, 276–277, 305, 327n73
consumer
 culture, 38, 40, 45–46, 69, 129, 158, 165, 170, 180n63, 222, 332
 trends, 129

contagion theory, 111, 132, 297, 334. *See also* seduction theory
cosmetic
  enhancement, 159, 162, 168
  industry, 199
  practices, 159, 161, 170
  treatment, 150
  uniform, 46, 71
counterdiscourse, 126, 269, 287
Couperus, Louis, 64
Cowboys, 254, 257
criminalization of homosexuality. *See* crimen nefandum, Paragraph 175, Article 248bis
crimen nefandum, 211. *See also* Paragraph 175, Article 248bis
cross-dressing, 60, 65, 70, 165, 167, 177n6, 259, 280n48. *See also* transvestite law, transvestite pass
cruising, 52
Csonka, Margarethe, 111–113
Cultuur en Ontspanningscentrum (COC, Centre for Culture and Leisure), 216

D
Dame, Die (The Lady). *See* women's periodicals
Dammann, Friedrich, 247
  dagbladzegel. See newspaper stamp
Danielsen, Max, 147, 150
Dauthendy, Elisabeth, 58
Davis, Madeline, 7–8
Dawes Plan, 38, 49
(de)mobilization, and women's work, 45, 70
D'Eon (transvestite organization), 168
Derrida, Jacques, 261
desire
  aetiology of queer, 89, 95, 105, 112, 118n52, 218, 244, 252, 253, 255, 275, 276
  definitions of, 16–17
  erotic, 109, 114, 244, 255, 261, 262, 268, 271, 276, 300, 301, 302, 303, 306, 316, 318
  hierarchies of, 148, 306–314
  for (economic) independence, 17, 44, 157, 200, 300

labelling, 9, 15–16, 135, 187, 211, 212, 214, 223, 228n79, 252, 255, 276, 321, 332, 336
  modes of, 11, 14, 314, 317, 318
Deutsch, Helene, 263
Deutscher Freundschaftsverband (DFV, German Friendship Association), 50, 70, 127, 135, 140, 143, 144, 145, 146, 147, 148, 149, 150, 165, 168, 173, 174, 176, 177n19, 209, 222, 334
Different from the Others (film), 228n79
diagnosis, 244, 296, 297, 298
  'from the outside', 105, 245, 275, 276, 296
  narrative, 251, 255, 293, 294, 295, 314, 336 (*see also* case study, literary)
Dijk-Has, N. van, 200, 202
dildos, 60
Dinshaw, Carolyn, 21
disgust, 62, 93, 100, 298–299, 310–313
district living, 42, 129, 133
Diva. See queer periodicals
Dix, Otto, 39, 72n11
Doan, Laura, 3, 12, 15, 19, 21–22, 232
Döblin, Alfred, 232
domesticity
  Cult of ..., 184, 188–189, 332
  postwar, 5, 43, 91, 335
  queer ..., 173, 178n33
  trappings of ..., 6
domestic labour, 8, 42, 46
Doudart de la Grée, Marie-Louise, 290
Dracula thesis, 65, 132. *See also* seduction thesis
drittes Geschlecht, 212. *See also* Third Sex
Droste, Sebastian, 257
Drucker, Wilhelmina, 68
Duc, Aimée, 232
Duggan, Lisa, 21, 92, 178n33
Dusia (pseud.), 156. *See also Die Freundin*
Duursma, Ien, 66
Dyer, Richard, 261, 264

E
economic
  growth, 2, 38, 40, 49, 69
  inequalities, 52, 175

instability, 36, 38, 70, 76n75, 139, 145, 159 (*see also* Great Depression)
prudence, 133, 191 (*see also* thriftiness)
women's ... independence, 44, 45, 49, 53, 129, 302, 333
Eckats, Xela, 170–172
Edelman, Lee, 16
effeminacy, 79n111, 81n143, 97, 148, 157, 165, 167, 170, 257, 307
Eichhorn, Maria, 232
Eigene, Der (The Self-Owning). *See* queer periodicals
Elberskirchen, Johanna, 56, 58, 63, 79n118, 87, 107–110, 114, 122n109, 320, 333
Eldorado. *See* clubs
Elegante Welt (*Elegant World*). *See* women's periodicals
Ellenberger, Johan, 204, 205, 206, 208–212, 218
Ellis, Havelock, 1, 241n9, 256, 301
emancipation
  erotic, 7
  homosexual, 16, 19, 57, 59, 63, 67, 70, 94, 102, 104, 106, 127, 135, 140–143, 144, 148, 176, 209, 211, 212, 216, 222, 223, 287
  lesbian, 8
  women's, 41, 55, 56, 61, 62, 63, 66, 68, 70, 108
Empire. *See* cafés
Engelschman, Niek/Nico, 216, 217, 229n89
Engler, Selli, 152, 153, 176n2
Eriksson, Brigitte, 19
eugenics, 62, 8, 86, 109, 115n9
Everard, Myriam, 68, 234, 323n14
Exler, Marie Jacobus Johannes, 52, 53, 57, 64

F
Factor, Max, 159
Faderman, Lillian, 19, 22, 213, 228n82, 236
false consciousness, 7
family
  economic freedom from ..., 46, 75n59
  finances, 46, 192

arriving at/leaving the ... home, 44, 196, 264, 290
  political significance of ..., 36, 47
  roles within the ..., 48
  founding a ..., 93, 218
  values, 67
  work within the ..., 44, 74n40
Fascism, 24, 214
fashion
  fickleness of, 190–191
  functional, 164–165
  See also beauty
fate, 66, 255, 299, 307, 322
fem(me), 7, 8, 9, 11, 14
femme-ininity, 9
femininity
  and agency, 173, 286, 296, 321
  devaluation of ... in historical research, 6, 7, 15, 22, 144, 337
  'good' and 'bad', 5–11
  hyper-, 10, 28n34, 51, 238
  and innocence, 61, 110, 115, 286, 294, 296, 309, 310, 324n30
  and (queer) invisibility, 4, 10, 84, 85, 223, 233, 306as masquerade, 101
  'new', 47, 75n52
  trivialisation of, 25, 87
  and women's fulfilment, 5, 6, 91, 92, 111, 117n29, 186, 255, 319
femme fatale, 151, 172, 175, 312
feminine mystique, 5–7. *See also* Friedan, Betty
feminism
  and queer emancipation, 60–68 (*see also* women's movement)
  and sexology, 56–57, 58
Fenoulhet, Jane, 238, 239
film, 9, 39, 45, 51, 72n11, 228n79
  adaptations, 245, 248, 250, 256, 261, 262, 267–268, 278n17, 322n6
First World War. *See* war
Fish, Stanley, 186
flapper, 36, 44–49, 71
Forel, Auguste, 93–94, 98, 100, 110–11, 118n39, 124n130, 132, 151, 155, 172, 298, 325n39
Formijne, Corrie, 197

362 • Index

Foucault, Michel, 2, 19, 23, 85, 87, 268, 270, 303, 304
François, Joannes Henri, 204–210, 212–213, 216, 228n77, 293
Frau, Die (*The Woman*). *See* women's periodicals
Frau ohne Mann, Die (*The Woman without a Man*). *See* women's periodicals
Frauenliebe. *See* queer periodicals
Frauen, Liebe und Leben (*Women, Love and Life*). *See* queer periodicals
Frauenliteratur. *See* literature
Freccero, Carla, 22
free love, 107, 150
Freud, Sigmund, 86, 87, 89, 111–113, 116n22, 124n130, 217, 282n93, 300, 304, 305, 310, 320
Freundin, Die. *See* queer periodicals
Freundschaft, Die (*The Friendship*). *See* queer periodicals
Freundschaftsehen (marriage of friendship), 170, 171 *See also* marriage
Frevert, Ute, 44, 45
Friedan, Betty, 5–7, 27n16
Friedlaender, Benedict, 148, 227n64
friendship
  female, 213, 140
  leagues, 140, 147, 208
  male, 257
frugality, 188, 191, 199. *See also* economic prudence, thriftiness
Fulda, Bernhard, 128

G
Garçonne. *See* queer periodicals
Gemeinschaft der Eigenen (Community of the Special), 77n89, 147, 206, 218. *See also* Adolf Brand
generational rifts, 199, 200, 302, 303
genital examinations, 83, 115n5, 337
Gentet, Simone, 248
Geurts, Anna. P.H., 73n22, 188
'Girl' culture, 47, 191
Goodloe, Amy, 19
Great Depression, 48, 70. *See also* economic turbulence
Groenendaal, Catherine, 214
Groenewegen, H.J., 217

Gulden Winckel, Den (The Golden Shop). *See* periodicals
Günderrode, Karoline von, 315, 316, 318
guilt, 159, 271
gynaecium, 100, 260

H
Haan, Francisca de, 48
Haan, Jacob Israël de, 64
Hahm, Lotte, 150
Haemmerling, Konrad, 35, 36, 38, 46, 50, 51, 52, 71
Halberstam, Jack, 20, 21, 259
Hall, Radclyffe, 234, 235, 252, 285n135
Halperin, David, 16, 22
Hammers, Corie, 16
Hans, Anjeana Kaur, 315
Hartshalt-Zeehandelaar, Estella, 68
Hatvany, Lajos, 247, 248
Hauser, Heinrich, 246
Heezen, Charley van (pseud.). *See* François, Joannes Henri
Heine, Heinrich, 156
Hemmings, Clare, 10, 28n40
Hendrikse, D., 189
Henning, B.G., 190
Hermanns, Doris, 248
hermaphroditism, 94, 97, 98, 111
heteronormative
  assumptions, 320
  femininities, 175
  frameworks, 6, 311
  institutions, 16, 171, 178n33
heterosexuality
  and camaraderie, 308, 309, 312, 313
  compulsory, 117n25 (*see also* marriage)
heterosexual matrix, 90, 117n25, 298, 308. *See also* Butler, Judith
Hillege, Karen, 68
Hirschfeld, Magnus, 3, 52, 55–57, 62, 64, 77n89, 78n98. 78n99, 80n134, 86–88, 102–104, 106, 107, 114, 121n90, 121n94, 121n98, 135, 140, 147–150, 153, 154, 159, 165, 167, 168, 173, 179n43, 209, 211, 216, 222, 228n79, 241n10l, 244, 255, 257, 260, 277n4, 277n6, 280n48, 287, 296, 322n4,

333. *See also* Wissenschaftlich-Humanitäres Komitee (WhK)
Hirschgebouw (*Hirsch Building*). *See* cafés
Hitler, Adolf, 128, 131, 214, 216, 248
Hodann, Max, 90
Hofstee, Evert, 17, 18
Hollibaugh, Amber, 8
Hollows, Joanne, 25
homonormativity, 136n3, 148, 171, 178n33
homosociality, 54, 55, 63, 99, 103, 213, 220, 221, 223, 232, 246, 252, 260, 268
homemaker, 43, 48, 91, 173, 318
Honegger, Claudia, 94
Houwink, Roel, 246
Hülsken, Marloes, 190
hyperinflation, 49
hypersexuality, 96, 156, 175
hysteria, 295

I
ideological conflicts (between BfM and DFV), 135, 146, 147–150, 173, 176
Ikarus (pseud.), 144. *See also Die Freundin*
illustrated press, 129, 134, 141, 289
industrialization, 39, 40, 128, 129, 139. *See also* Amsterdam, Berlin
Institut für Sexualwissenschaft (Institute for the Study of Sexual Science), 56, 57, 88, 149, 168
internationalism, 36, 56, 58, 137n17, 185, 205, 217
interpretive community, 186, 204
invisible menace, the, 84, 85

J
Jacobs, Aletta, 68
Jacobs, Bethany, 261
Janus, Hans, 147
Jelgersma, Gerbrandus, 88
Jensen, Lotte, 185
Jewish communities, 41, 42, 43, 186, 326n51
Johnson, Mykel, 8, 10
Jonge Vrouw, De (*The Young Woman*). *See* women's periodicals

K
Kaas, Jacobus 'Jaap', 246
Karen (editor), 143, 146
Kästner, Erich, 232
Kennedy, Rosanne, 9
Keun, Irmgard, 46
Kleinenberg, Ernst von, 206
Klub Monbijou des Westens (*Club Monbijou of the West*). *See* clubs
kiosks, newspaper, 128, 129, 130, 133, 134, 206, 222. *See also* newspaper
Koenders, Pieter, 67
Koonz, Claudia, 45
Ko operator (pseud.) 206. *See also Wij*
Kooten Niekerk, Anja van, 12, 13, 14, 19, 43, 55, 65, 66, 68, 187, 214
Kracauer, Siegfried, 44, 45, 46
Krafft-Ebing, Richard von, 88, 89, 96–99, 101, 102, 111, 113, 114, 119n60–62, 120n69, 120n71–72, 233, 235, 241n6, 214n10, 244, 254, 255, 257, 296, 300
Krukenberg, Elsbeth, 63, 79n122

L
L Word, The, 9–11, 28n38
Lampl-de Groot, Jeanne, 88
Landesjugendamt (State Youth Welfare Office, Berlin), 142
lang, k.d., 28n34
Lang, Birgit, 111, 121n90
Lang, Fritz, 39
Lanser, Susan, 23
Laser, Herta, 153–154, 173, 179n45
Lauffer, Mie (Hermine Sophia Lauffer-van Exter), 53–54, 81n152
Lautenslager, C.P.M., 189
lavender menace, the, 6, 27n18
Lebensreformbewegung (life reform movement), 78n98, 150
Ledige Frauen (*Single Women*). *See* queer periodicals
Lee, Janet, 259, 266
Leeuwen, Jaap van, 216, 218, 220
Leeuwen, Theo van, 185
leisure culture, 38, 46, 69, 71, 129, 187, 332. *See also* consumer culture
Leng, Kirsten, 87, 109

Lermann, Nils, 155
lesbian
  codes, 70, 240
  continuum, 16, 29n58
  lipstick ..., 9
  non-..., 26, 240, 286, 306, 314, 316, 317, 321, 336
  politics, 5–11
  premodern, 21, 22, 23
  proto-..., 20
  reading as ..., 236
  self-image, 15, 221, 222
  symbolism, 4, 232, 236, 252, 262, 279n33
  telos, 15, 20
Levensrecht (The Right to Live). *See* queer periodicals
Lex Heinze law, 131
Libelle (Dragonfly). *See* women's periodicals
Liébault Institute, 89
Liebende Frauen (Loving Women). *See* queer periodicals
Lieshout, Maurice van, 88, 89
Lijphart, Arend, 42
Linck, Catharina Margaretha, 60, 78n105
Linden, Cort van der, 64, 65
literature
  confessional, 251, 269, 279n29
  high vs low, 146, 238–239
  lesbian, 236, 239, 241n14–15
  trivialisation of women writing in histories of ..., 237–239
loneliness, 241n13, 252, 272, 300, 316
Lorde, Audre, 27n21, 251, 262, 266
Lotta Svärd group, 195
love
  and erotic desire, 102, 109, 290, 304, 316, 322
  spiritual, 109, 114, 115, 147, 173, 316
Lustmord. *See* sexual murder
Lybeck, Marti, 13, 300

M
Mädchen in Uniform (film), 245, 247–248, 250, 261, 262, 337
  Machin, David, 185
Malot, Hector, 252, 279n34

Man, Paul de, 251, 279n30
Mandje, 't (*The Little Basket*). *See* cafés
Männerbund (society of men), 209
Margriet. *See* women's periodicals
Marhoefer, Laurie, 60, 115n9, 178n33
Marks, Elaine, 260–261
marriage
  companionate, 92
  as cure for sexual deviance, 85, 102, 110, 112, 319, 320
  guides, 90, 92–94
  and heteronormativity, 16, 90, 91, 100
  ideals, 90–93, 302
  modern ..., 90, 92, 199, 200
  of friendship, 171 (*see also Freundschaftsehen*)
  threats to institution of ..., 84, 90
  and women's employment, 48, 49, 70, 157
  as a woman's destiny, 92, 304
Marsh, Madeleine, 159
Martin, Biddy, 7, 9, 10
Martin, Robert, 257
Marxism, 17
mass media
  as communicator of hegemonic norms and values, 156, 187–188, 221, 335
  and 'imagined' communities, 130, 135, 139–141, 222
  influence of ... on public opinion, 125–127, 133, 134
masculinity
  privileging of, 4, 9–10, 337
  rejection of, 153–154, 319–320
masturbation. *See* onanism
maternal(ism)
  and femininity, 10, 91, 109, 154, 179n47, 187, 200, 221, 241, 245, 261, 276
  and same-sex desire, 26, 110, 112, 121n98, 240, 255, 261, 262, 264–268, 275, 276, 296, 314, 315, 317, 318, 319, 335
  and heterosexuality, 9, 114, 115, 245, 300
  (lack of) ... instincts, 93, 101, 102, 103, 104, 112, 115, 320, 336

as a mode of being, 14, 276, 317, 318, 319
social significance of …, 48, 49, 91, 127, 135, 154, 186, 187, 335
Matysik, Tracie, 60
medicoconsumerism, 158, 159, 161, 164, 168
Meisjesleven (Girlhood). *See* women's periodicals
menarche, 259, 267
menstruation, 266
Menon, Madhavi, 20–21
Meerten-Schilperoort, Anna Barbara van, 185
Meijer, Maaike, 236, 237
Michel, Ernest, 67
Micheler, Stefan, 43
misogyny, 148, 153
Möbius, Karl, 94, 324n30
modernity, 22, 23, 37, 38, 39, 41, 43, 202, 203
modesty, 47, 48, 68, 84, 92, 98, 109, 161, 162, 269, 288, 299, 303
Moll, Albert, 89, 99–102, 107, 111, 114, 120n75, 241n10, 333
monogamy, 16, 142, 170, 172
Mooy, Henriëtte, 238
Mooy, Anna Elisabeth Johanna de. *See* Raedt-de Canter, Eva
motherhood, cult of, 127, 135
mother
absent …, 260–261, 263, 265, 316, 317
-child model, 261, 265, 266, 267, 268, 276, 296, 314, 315, 316, 317
-love, 314, 316, 317, 318, 319
… replacement, 112, 264
'mothers' and 'fathers'. *See also* 'Bubis' and 'Mädis', 107
Morality Bill, 132–133
moral(s)
code, 59, 108, 301, 302
scandal, 220, 229n102
sexual …, 2, 36, 131
Moreck, Curt (pseud.). *See* Haemmerling, Konrad

N
National Socialism, 2, 13, 24, 78n99, 142, 148, 190, 216, 278n17, 288, 289
Nederlandsch Wetenschappelijk Humanitair Komitee (NWHK, Dutch Scientific Humanitarian Committee), 57, 58, 70, 78n99, 104, 106, 204, 211, 212, 222
Nelissen, Anton, 64–65
Nenno, Nancy, 294, 295
Nestle, Joan, 7, 8, 11, 13
neurasthenia, 84, 98
newspaper
couriers, 133
daily…, 125–127, 133, 134, 208
district…, 129, 222
rental, 133–134
stamp, 132–133, 222
street vendors, 128, 133
tax, 132–133, 137n24
Newton, Esther, 7
New Woman, 45
Nieuwsblad van het Noorden (*Newspaper of the North*). *See* periodicals
Norton, Rictor, 22, 63, 64
nudism, 146, 150

O
objectivity, scientific, 162, 293, 295, 300
O'Connor, Hannah, 286, 315
office work, 46, 91, 159. *See also* white-collar work
onanism, 82, 95, 118n52
Oosterhout, Ton, 66, 67
Oosterhuis, Harry, 111, 112
Ortt, Felix, 212, 213, 293

P
Pacification, of 1917, 42, 73n24
'painted' woman, the, 159
Pappritz, Anna, 62
paragraph
Paragraph 175, 50, 56, 59, 60–63, 69, 78n101, 142, 147, 332, 334
Paragraph 250, 61, 63, 68
Paragraph 297, 63

passing
  (male-to-female), 170, 175
  as straight, 8, 10
pathology, 83, 87, 96
pederasty, 132, 148, 227n64, 260, 281n64, 315
Peiss, Kathy, 158
piety, 188, 199
Pénélopé. See women's periodicals
periodicals
  Gulden Winckel, Den (the Golden Shop), 246
  Nieuwsblad van het Noorden (Newspaper of the North), 54
  Querschnitt (Cross Section), 247
  Sumatra Post, De (The Sumatra Post), 323n15
  Tijd, De (The Times), 289
perversion, 16, 98–99, 113
perversity, 89, 98–99, 113
Phelan, Shane, 286
Pidduck, Julianne, 264
pillarization, 18, 41–44, 133, 134, 187, 189
Plasse, Jan van de, 134
Plato, 94, 233
police force, 59, 66, 147, 192, 196, 291
polyamory, 150, 334
pornography, 7, 64, 65, 141, 216, 233
power
  eroticised ... differences, 8, 261, 262, 263, 267, 314, 317, 318, 322
  and knowledge, 18, 19, 23, 86–87, 126, 132, 268, 269, 271, 272, 273, 274, 275
Proletarische Vrouw, De (*The Protestant Woman*). See women's periodicals
promiscuity, 9, 233
Protestantism
  attitudes towards desire, 199–200
  communities, 25, 42, 335
  newspapers, 134, 187
  views on homosexuality, 66
pseudo-homosexuality, 110, 115, 151, 171, 287, 334
psychoanalysis, 88, 89, 110–113, 234, 304, 305, 326n67
psychology, 5, 89, 162, 304
public/private sphere, 38, 43, 91, 126, 186, 221, 332

public toilets, 60
punishment, 60, 61, 62, 64, 249, 250, 252, 262, 271, 273, 274, 276
purity, 188
Puttkamer, Leonie, 111–112

Q
queer
  activism, 55–58, 217
  historical practices, 11–15, 17, 19–221, 21, 223, 331, 336
  reading as ..., 236–237
queer periodicals
  Amarant, 131
  Diva, 131
  Blätter idealer Frauenfreundschaft (*Pages of Ideal Women's Friendship*) 140, 176n2
  Eigene, Der (The Self-Owning) (*see* queer periodicals, 77n89, 227n64)
  Frauenliebe (*Women's Love*) 13, 25, 136n3, 137n16, 140, 143–147, 149, 150, 153, 154, 156–162, 164, 165, 166, 168, 169, 170, 173, 174, 175, 176, 176n3, 180n63, 190, 195, 206, 208, 211, 214, 287, 334
  Frauen, Liebe und Leben (*Women, Love and Life*), 140
  Freundin, Die (*The Girlfriend*), 1, 13, 136n3, 137n16, 139, 140, 141–142, 143, 144, 145, 146, 147, 150, 151–153, 155–157, 158, 162, 163, 164, 165–166, 168, 170, 172, 173, 174–176, 177n4, 178n33, 190, 191, 195, 206, 208, 211, 214, 287, 288, 322n7, 334
  Freundschaft, Die (*The Friendship*), 147
  Garçonne, 140, 143, 144, 174, 176n3, 177n11
  Ledige Frauen (*Single Women*), 139
  Liebende Frauen (*Loving Women*), 140
  Levensrecht (*The Right to Live,*) 25, 127, 131, 135, 187, 214–221, 223, 228n77, 334, 335
  Wij (*We*), 25, 127, 131, 135, 187, 204–214, 228n77, 334
Querido (publishing house), 246
Querschnitt (Cross Section). See periodicals

R

race, 7, 16, 20, 86, 116n10, 186, 189, 244, 337
Radicalesbians, 7, 27n18. *See also* woman-identified-woman
radio, 41, 43
Radszuweit, Friedrich, 141, 142, 143, 145, 146, 147, 148, 149, 155, 157, 177n4, 204, 206, 208, 209, 210, 323n8
Raedt-de Canter, Eva, 25, 238, 239, 245, 246–247, 279n34, 293, 321, 335, 336
Ramanathan, Geetha, 261, 262, 267
Ramsbrock, Annelie, 159, 199
readership figures, 145, 177n4, 189, 190, 217
reader letters, 135, 141, 165, 167, 172, 186, 187, 190, 216, 335
'recovery' history, 12, 19, 20, 21, 22, 239
Regout, Edmond Hubert, 65
Reich, Wilhelm, 86
Reinhardt, Max, 288
rejuvenation practices, 150, 159, 179n35, 199, 334
religion
  and desire, 208, 211, 220, 249, 271–272
  and psychoanalysis, 89, 112, 113, 116n22, 305
Renterghem, Albert van, 88
reproduction, problematic of, 102, 114, 120n88
Reuveni, Gideon, 128, 145
Reuling, Josine, 8, 47, 238, 239, 240, 289–290, 320, 321, 322, 323n14, 336
respectability
  politics of ... 168, 174, 175, 179n34, 237, 294, 296, 298, 299, 303, 306, 317, 321, 322
Rich, Adrienne, 7, 16, 263
Riviere, Joan, 101
Robertson, Pamela, 258
rode week, de (The Red Week) 40
Rode Leeuw (Red Lion). *See* cafés
Roellig, Ruth Margarete, 36, 50, 51, 76n66, 130, 137n16, 139, 157
Röhm, Ernst, 216
Roma, Margot, 143
Romein-Verschoor, Annie, 237, 242n25
Romme, Carl, 48

Römer, Lucien von, 57, 88
Rooden, Peter van, 18
Roof, Judith, 236
Rose, Damaris, 11
Rubin, Gayle, 19
Rutgers, Jan, 88
Rutgers-Hoitsema, Maria, 68
Rüling, Anna, 61

S

Sacher-Masoch, Leopold von, 233
sacrifice, 267, 276
Sade, Marquis de, 233
sadomasochism (S&M), 96, 233
Sagan, Leontine, 247, 261
Santhorst, Arendt van (pseud.). *See* Leeuwen, Jaap van
Sappho, 100, 152, 231, 260
scientia sexualis, 25, 85, 333
Schader, Heike, 12, 13, 50, 142
Schaffner, Anna Katharina, 232
Schirmacher, Käthe, 62
Schlierkamp, Petra, 143
Schneider, Maarten, 133
Schneider, Romy, 248
Schöffer, Ivo, 42
Schoolstrijd, de (the School Struggle), 41–42
Schoondermark, Jacobus, 88
Schorer, Jacob Anton, 57, 58, 64, 67, 68, 70, 78n99, 204, 211, 216
Showalter, Elaine, 37, 237
Schuyf, Judith, 3, 12, 15, 65, 104
Schwabe, Toni, 56
Schwärmerei, 260, 312
Schwegman, Marjan, 47
Seaton Hackney, Fiona, 186
Second World War. *See* war
Sedgwick, Eve Kosofsky, 20, 21, 22, 30n79, 236, 237, 255, 275
seduction theory, 64–65, 111, 115, 297. *See also* Dracula thesis, contagion theory
separatism, lesbian/feminist, 7, 154, 155, 168, 175
sexual
  desire as identity, 3, 7, 13, 15, 16, 22, 23, 51, 105, 115, 126, 127, 141, 150, 174, 210, 211, 222, 231, 240, 245,

268, 275, 284n124, 302, 304, 320, 322, 332, 335
disease, 233, 39–310
intermediaries, 58, 98, 102, 103, 107, 140, 148, 222
knowledge, 2, 86, 126, 232, 233, 271, 277, 302
morality, 2, 36, 59, 64, 65, 70, 71, 131, 132, 174, 227n64, 332
murder, 39, 72n10, 72n11
objectification, 16, 28n40, 52
panic, 28n34, 36
revolution, 26n1, 37, 58, 84, 332
self-fashioning, 115, 127, 222, 245, 269, 272, 277
subjectivity, 12, 21, 23, 245, 273, 276, 297, 337
subordination, 7
(threat of) violence, 38, 39, 43, 46, 72n10, 72n11, 83
sexology
and literary writing, 233–236 (*see also* case study, literary)
politics and …, 71, 86, 87
race and …, 86, 87, 115n9 (*see also* eugenics)
women and, 25, 87, 107–110
sex reform movement, 56, 68, 91
sex work, 52, 53, 54, 55, 59, 62, 64, 70, 93, 99, 100, 111, 148, 155, 158, 159, 165, 232, 233
Showalter, Elaine, 37, 237
sickness, 195, 202, 264, 271, 293, 309, 310, 311, 312, 316
sissy, 67, 243, 259
Smith-Rosenberg, Carroll, 22, 148, 213, 220
Socialism, 40, 41, 43, 67, 75n53, 107, 133, 134, 186, 216, 247
Sontag, Susan, 258
Spaarnestad, de (publishing house), 189, 190
space
economic difficulties of maintaining queer …, 52, 76n75
lesbian and Sapphic subcultural …, 36, 49–55, 59, 71, 139, 302, 304, 333
safe …, 58, 203–204, 221, 237, 335

Spengler, Oswald, 125–126, 132, 134, 198
Spivak, Gayatri, 156. *See also* bricolage
Stärcke, August, 89
Steinach, Eugen, 150, 159, 179n35
stereotypes, 148, 157, 171, 296, 321
Stöcker, Helene, 56, 57, 61, 62
Stokvis, Benno, 88, 104, 105, 106, 113, 204, 218, 219, 220, 221, 232, 234, 245, 335
Stomps, T.J., 217, 218
Strega, Linda, 1, 8, 27n28
subscription fees, 128, 130, 132, 133, 134, 190, 197, 198, 204, 205, 206, 217, 222, 229n92
suicide, 272, 291, 299, 55, 103, 112, 123n125
Suisse. See cafés
Sumatra Post, De (*The Sumatra Post*). *See* periodicals
Sutton, Katie, 12, 45, 111, 121n100, 130, 165, 168, 170

T
talking cure, 111, 305
Tamagne, Florence, 130, 143
Tambling, Jeremy, 269
Tatar, Maria, 39, 72n11
Taverne (Tavern). *See* clubs
Taylor, Mara, 95, 251, 275, 294, 298, 323n18
Tempo. See periodicals
Third Sex, 3, 58, 77n89, 94, 95, 102, 107, 109, 232, 321. *See also* drittes Geschlecht
Thompson, Dorothy, 248, 250
thriftiness, 133, 188, 190. *See also* frugality
Tielman, Rob, 57, 67
Tijd, de (*The Times*). *See* periodicals
Tijsseling, Anna, 65, 132
Tobin, Robert Deam, 23, 116n15
tomboyism
and cultural context, 244, 277n6
as sign of homosexuality, 243, 244, 259
Topf, Gertrud, 56
tourism, 35, 36, 38, 49, 52, 59, 69, 71, 333
Transvestitenschein (transvestite pass) 80n134
transvestite(s)

communities, 135, 165, 167, 168, 170
law, 65, 70, 80n134
partners of, 167–168
surgeries, 167, 177n6, 181n82
terminology, 167, 177n6
Trabak, Adrian, 206
Traub, Valerie, 20, 21, 337
trouser role, 250
'True Womanhood', 188, 196, 199, 221
Trumbach, Randolph, 22
Tuuk, Titia van der, 68

U
Ulrichs, Karl Heinrich, 68, 82, 83, 88, 89, 94–97, 102, 113, 118n48, 233, 324n36
Uranisme, 67, 68, 97, 98, 211, 333
Urning, 94, 95, 96, 97, 110, 243, 244, 257, 260
urban/rural divide, 130, 244

V
Velde, Theodoor van de, 90–93, 117n31, 117n35, 200
Veness, Molly, 195
Verhoeven, Maria, 214
Versluys-Poelman, Annette, 68
vice squad (*zedenpolitie*; *Sittenpolizei*), 53, 54, 59, 64, 66, 69, 78n103, 131, 132, 146, 204, 208, 210, 216, 222, 332
Violetta. *See* clubs
visibility, 2, 11, 36, 90, 127, 146, 211, 220, 223, 332, 333
Volk, Het (*The People*). *See* periodicals
Voltaire, 250, 275, 278n15
Vries, Willem Hendrik de, 246
voyeurism, 51, 52
Vries Robbé-Bergmans, A.M. de, 196

W
waged work, 18, 44, 49, 70, 161. *See also* salaried work, white-collar work
Walker, Lisa, 9, 10, 84
Wansink, Melanie, 214
war
 economic effects of …, 5, 36

changing gender roles as a result of …, 5, 17, 24, 44, 47, 49, 69, 90, 92, 129, 221, 332
 loss of life during …, 36, 44
Warner, Michael, 306
Weber, Aenne, 142, 151, 153
Weeks, Jeffrey, 23, 24
Weg, Marcella van der, 133
Weisskopf, Susan, 261
Well of Loneliness (Radclyffe Hall), 234, 241n9, 252, 285n135
Welter, Barbara, 188
Weltliga für Sexualreform (World League for Sexual Reform), 56
Weininger, Otto, 62, 152, 153
Weirauch, Anna Elisabet, 8, 50, 239, 242n22, 288–289, 320, 322, 323n8, 336
Weiß, Maria, 168
Westerbrink-Wirtz, J.M., 196
Westphal, Carl Friedrich Otto, 82–84, 96, 97, 99, 103, 111, 113, 115n5, 121n94, 235
Whitman, Walt, 217
whiteness, 9, 11, 188, 189, 204, 333
white-collar work, 13, 17, 41, 45, 46, 47, 69, 71, 74n40, 129, 134
Wij. *See* queer periodicals
Wijmer, Sacha, 12, 13, 14, 19, 43, 55, 65, 66, 68, 187, 213, 214
Winsloe, Christa, 26, 239, 245, 247–248, 250–251, 276, 278n15, 278n17, 278n18, 293, 295, 300, 315, 335, 336, 337
Wissenschaftlich-Humanitäres Komitee (WhK, Scientific Humanitarian Committee), 3, 55, 56, 57, 58, 70, 77n89, 78n98, 106, 148, 209, 211, 212. *See also* Magnus Hirschfeld
Wolff, Charlotte, 56
woman-identified woman, 7
women's movement. *See also* feminism
 and homosexual emancipation, 60–68
 opposition to … 77n89, 90, 91
women's periodicals
 Amsterdamsche Dames Kroniek (Amsterdam Ladies Chronicle), 134

Beatrijs (*Beatrice*), 25, 134, 135, 184, 187, 188, 189–196, 198, 199, 205, 221, 224n20, 334, 335
Dame, Die (The Lady), 129
Elegante Welt (*Elegant World*), 129
Frau, Die (*The Woman*), 129
Frau ohne Mann, Die (*The Woman without a Man*), 129
jonge vrouw, de (The Young Woman), 25, 134, 187, 188, 189, 198–204, 205, 221, 224n19, 224n20, 334, 335
Libelle, 189, 190
Margriet, 190
Meisjesleven (Girlhood), 197
Penélopé, 184–185
Proletarische Vrouw, de (*The Protestant Woman*), 134
Woolf, Virginia, 35, 231
workplace
  and homosexuality, 44, 54–55, 71
  and sexual harassment, 46, 47, 70
Worthen, Meredith, 189

X
XYZ (pseud.), 143, 171, 172. *See also Die Freundin*

Y
youth, protection of, 65, 142, 145, 146, 176n3, 334. *See also Schund- und Schmutzgesetz*

Z
Zauberflöte, Die (*The Magic Flute*). *See* clubs
Zola, Emile, 100, 234
Zwartendijk, Jo, 238
Zwitter, 102, 148, 157, 218

Milton Keynes UK
Ingram Content Group UK Ltd.
UKHW021847300723
426044UK00004B/77